MW00955462

So It Was Written
A Time of Terror, Part Two

By AJ Berry

So It Was Written

So It Was Written

Cover Painting:
Entitled
Raonhanonhne` (He Watches Over)
A Study of Glenn Bentz (c)
Artist
Jamie Bentz

The Oneida Nation chose to support the American colonists cause for various in depth reasons and were the only Nation of the Iroquois to do so. In that decision they were faced with fighting not only British Loyalists but also the other Nations of their own people, known to most as the Iroquois Confederacy. This Confederacy consisted of 5 Nations originally the Seneca, Cayuga, Onondaga, Oneida and the Mohawk in its entirity.

Previously Published Works By The Author
A Time of Terror 2005- Trafford
Times Past 2005- Trafford

So It Was Written

Table of Contents

Life In The Valley After The War

Loyalists, After The War

Appendix

Index to: A Time of Terror and So It Was Written

Foreword

The story really belongs to the men who fought in the Revolution, as in any war the soldiers are on the front lines jeopardizing their lives for their country. Those familiar with <u>A Time of Terror, The Story of Colonel Jacob Klock's Regiment and The People They Protected, 1774-1783</u> said they would like to see more of the Pension Applications for the soldiers in the next book. So this book has more of the pension applications.

In telling the Palatine story, others compiled the lists in the past but I thought it would be worthwhile to get a view of the times by presenting the names from the various lists. Hopefully it will prove helpful in locating the family member you are seeking.

In the transcription of the pension applications, it was an uncertain process to decipher words and I am sure some were done incorrectly. Then things are confusing! When I first read about Landman's Battle, I read it as Lamphere's Battle, then I found it was called both! In some cases, the ink from the backside of a document bled through to the front and the handwriting on the first side dimmed with age. The information is not always correct either, the men did their pension applications from memory and incorrect dates for battles and names were commonly given, and sometimes the incoreect rank of an officer. This confuses genealogists. The pension applications are given as I read them, I did my best.

Within the pension applications an interesting story sometimes appears. One tells about a sergeant disobeying an order and the captain hitting him with his musket. The sergeant died a few days later. Nowhere else was this story found in any of the history books. Another pension application tells about the veteran just being released from debtor's prison and his daughter dying of consumption. It is sad that the veterans of the Revolutionary War had to wait so long for a pension and in many cases were denied because the men they served with were dead and they couldn't get someone to verify their service times. Records were poorly kept or not kept in that war, the earlier in the war, the worse the records. Almost all the pension applications plead because of time and infirmity, they cannot recall the exact details or dates of service. No wonder why, these men had to wait a very long time for their pension, by the time they could apply, they were very elderly, being in their late seventies and eighties.

During the time Fort Paris was being attacked, I read about the screams of the people inside the fort. They realized they didn't have enough firepower to defend the fort. It truly was a time of terror for all the people in the Mohawk Valley.

In this book, the Palatine story is told, who they were, where they came from, why they came to America, the tar camps, why the tar production failed, and the resettlement of the Palatines. To them deserves much of the credit for the war turning out the way it did, they dug in their heels and did what they had to do. As a nation, we owe them our heartfelt thanks. The Revolutionary War period was truly a time of terror for the inhabitants of the valley.

Here is a bit more to add to the first book. "Old" George Klock's son was the one who lived in Fort Haus after Christian House. Apparently "Old" George was quite a problem in his old age because Judge Jacob G. Klock made it known that someone in the family needed to take the old man in and take care of him. Then too, things happen! The Raid on Ephratah has the correct date in the Timeline, April 20, 1778 and an incorrect date in the story about the raid. Please note the correct date!

Please remember the veterans were very old when they applied for their pensions, they may have given incorrect ranks, dates, places, in their applications and I may have read the handwriting wrong!

Thanks is due to several people for this book. James F. Morrison who generously shared his pension applications with me, my son Pieter Decker who did the tedious job of proof reading for both books and let me stay at their house when I did research at the National Archives in Washington DC, and my ever patient mother who regularly put food in front of me.

Part Three of this series titled Brothers has been started and will be available sometime in 2006. It will cover the New York Line, more pension applications and probably some parts of Governor Clinton's public papers.

So It Was Written

Mohawk Valley Timeline
This is presented as a reference
for those who do not have part one, <u>A Time of Terror</u>

So It Was Written

Mohawk Valley Timeline

(For the full Timeline, please consult A Time of Terror)
1774 - 1775

by Gerald Horton

Aug 27, 1774

First Committee of Correspondence organized in Tryon County.

May 10, 1775

Meeting of Committee of Safety held in a Cherry Valley church. Article of Association was drafted.

May 15, 1775

A Liberty Pole was raised eight miles west of Fort Johnson (near present day Fonda, NY). Tryon County Sheriff Alexander White led a posse to disperse the Rebel gathering.

May 21, 1775

Palatine Committee of Safety adopted their Declaration of Independence

Aug 25, 1775

Council of the Six Nations and Northern Indian Department of the Continental Congress was held at Albany NY. Indian Department.

Nov 7, 1775

William Johnson, Jr. son of Sir William by Mary Brant, burst into Col. Jacob Klock's house. Armed with two pistols, a rifle, and a broadsword, he shouted he was a King's man and promised to bring a force of 500 to burn the valley.

Dec 1, 1775

By December 1775, the jail at Albany was so crowded (with Tories) that the Albany Committee of Safety was obliged to provide additional quarters and hire an extra jailer.

Mohawk Valley Timeline

1776

Jan 20, 1776

Sir John Johnson and his tenants surrender their arms to Rebel General Philip Schuyler at Johnstown.

Apr 29, 1776

Council with Rebels called by Iroquois at Albany.

May 21, 1776

Colonel Elias Dayton with 300 men arrive at Johnson Hall to arrest Sir John Johnson.

So It Was Written

Jul 1, 1776

Residents of Cherry Valley, Newtown-Martin, and Springfield petitioned the Provincial Congress of New York to keep a Militia Ranger company at Cherry Valley.

Aug 19, 1776

Some Rebels attempt to plunder Johnson Hall but were caught and sent to Albany for court-martial. Loyalist homes and furnishings were sold to American Patriots as a means of raising money for the war effort.

Oct 11, 1776

Battle of Valcour Island.

Mohawk Valley Timeline

1777

Mar 6, 1777

Loyalist property subject to confiscation

Apr 1777

Joseph Brant recruits volunteers. Joseph Brant, the Mohawk Sachem, was actively recruiting men to fight for the British.

Apr 20, 1777

Constitution of New York State approved. The Constitution of New York State was approved by the New York convention at Kingston, NY.

George Clinton was elected the first Governor of New York State under the new constitution.

May 1777

Revolutionary Colonel Peter Gansevoort succeeds Col. Elmore as commandant at Fort Stanwix.

May 27, 1777

Northern Department of the Bureau of War formed by Congress The Continental Congress voted a resolution declaring that "Albany, Ticonderoga, Fort Stanwix, and their dependencies, be henceforth considered as forming the Northern Department." General Schuyler was placed in command of the Northern Department.

Jun 2, 1777

Joseph Brant enters Unadilla. Joseph Brant and a party of Indians entered the settlement of Unadilla which was located a few miles from his headquarters at Onaquaga. He held a conference with the minister, William Johnston, and his son, Militia Captain Johnston. Brant requested provisions for his party. He told the Johnston's that Colonel John Butler would pay them when he came through Unadilla. The residents felt they had no alternative but to furnish cattle and food to Brant's men.

Following Brant's departure, many inhabitants feared the return of the Indians and fled to other more secure locations. Many returned to Cherry Valley from where they had originally moved.

Jun 6, 1777

Loyalist Col. John Butler, stationed at Fort Niagara, received letters from General Guy Carleton, Governor of Canada, informing him of Col. St. Leger's expedition down the Mohawk Valley. Carleton instructed Butler to assemble the Iroquois to participate in the expedition.

Jun 16, 1777

British General John Burgoyne's army sets out for Albany, NY from Fort St. Johns on the Richelieu River.

A British plan to split New England from the rest of the American Colonies was developed during the Winter of 1776 -- 1777. The plan called for General Burgoyne to attack from Canada down the Champlain Valley to Albany, NY. He would capture Fort Ticonderoga on the way. Lt. Col. Barry St. Leger was to sail from Canada to Oswego, NY via Lake Ontario. He would then move from Oswego down the Mohawk River to Albany and meet Burgoyne. St Leger was to capture Fort Stanwix (current Rome, NY) along the way. General Howe, who had wintered in New York City, was to move north and also link up with Burgoyne at Albany. The plan has come to be known as the three-pronged attack.

Burgoyne left Fort St. John with approximately 7,500 to 8,000 rank and file men. Half were British, half German. Historian Gregory Edgar includes in his number 100 Loyalists and 150 Canadian Militia. There was also a sizeable contingent of Indians (some reports said as many as one thousand) included in the total number of combatants. A total of about three hundred women and an unknown number of children accompanied the army.

Jun 21, 1777

General Burgoyne's army enters Lake Champlain. Historian John Pancake pulled together information from various journals and paints a colorful word picture: ""They were formed into a spectacular column, the Indians leading in their big war canoes. Then came two ship-rigged schooners, the Royal George and the Inflexible. They were followed by a line of hundreds ofbatteauscrowded with colors; red-coated British infantry, the green of the Jagers, the blue coats of the Brunswickers with their glittering cap plates (see NOTE below); in such perfect regularity as to form the most complete and splendid regatta you can possibly conceive.""

Pancake seems to indicate Burgoyne's army sailed down Lake Champlain. However, Historian Gregory Edgar cites several journals indicating that while the artillery and heavier baggage was floated down the lake, most of the army marched along the west shore.

An enormous baggage train accompanied the army. Over 500 two-wheel carts were used to transport equipment and provisions. Just the champagne and clothes for Burgoyne and his mistress required more than thirty carts.

Edgar also cites a journal kept by a German officer named Du Roi. Du Roi complained of the excessive amount of baggage being hauled through the wilderness. The army averaged eighteen miles per day, stopping long before dark to take elaborate precautions, even to the point of building breastworks for protection against surprise attacks by the Revolutionaries.

NOTE: Historian Richard Ketcham states that the great majority of German soldiers who came from Canada were not Hessians. Over two thousand of the Germans were from Braunschweig (Brunswick, as anglicized) and were Generally called Brunswickers. Landgrave Friedrich II of Hesse -- Cassel was the first German sovereign to provide troops to the British, and during the Revolution he furnished twenty thousand of them -- far more than any other ruler -- so it was natural for the Americans to apply the generic term "Hessian" to all German soldiers.

Jul 6, 1777

Revolutionary General St. Clair abandons Ft. Ticonderoga.

General St. Clair held several conferences with his officers once valid information was received concerning the numbers of Burgoyne's army. St. Clair had some two thousand effective fighting men. This should have been a sufficient defensive force for the fort. However, the British placed an artillery battery on Sugarloaf (renamed Mount Defiance) mountain. From this position, the British could fire on any point within the fort. St. Clair saw further defense of the fort as a useless waste of men and ordered the evacuation.

St. Clair was accused of cowardice and treason in the newspapers of the day. He appealed to General Washington for a court-martial. He was eventually granted one and was exonerated.

General Schuyler also came under criticism for allowing this "disaster" to occur under his command. Some historians believe this incident caused Schuyler to be replaced by General Horatio Gates prior to the Battles of Saratoga.

Jul 1777

Militia General Nicholas Herkimer confronts Joseph Brant at Unadilla. In early July, General Nicholas Herkimer came to Unadilla with 380 men. Herkimer and Joseph Brant had known each other in earlier days and Herkimer hoped to persuade Brant to curtail any violent activities in the area.

Brant agreed to a council if all were unarmed and Herkimer agreed. Brant bragged he had five hundRed Men in the woods but only had about 130 in his band at the time.

Herkimer asked Brant what his grievances were and Brant enumerated them. At one point, Colonel Ebenezer Cox made some insulting remarks to Brant whereupon Brant signaled his men and they ran to their camp and fired off weapons. Herkimer smoothed over the incident and the council continued.

Herkimer agreed to Brant's demands and the council ended amicably. Most people, including General Schuyler, were not happy with Herkimer's concessions.

Historians Stone and Simms related a story told by Sgt. Joseph Waggoner. The story has two versions depending on which historian's book you read. The first version (Stone) is that General Herkimer told Waggoner to get three good men and upon a signal from Herkimer they were to shoot Brant and his three Lieutenants. The second version (Simms) is that Herkimer told Waggoner to get three good men and should the council turn violent to shoot Brant and his three Lieutenants.

Most historians reject Stone's version of the incident. They believe Herkimer's character would not permit him to order such an act of cold-blooded murder.

Jul 11, 1777

George Clinton accepts office as first Governor of New York State.

Jul 13, 1777

Colonel John Butler holds Indian Council at Irondequoit.

Loyalist Col. John Butler ordered a grand council with the Iroquois at Oswego, but directed the greater number of Iroquois to Irondequoit (near present day Rochester, NY) to preserve provisions. Butler spoke to the assembled Sachems and reminded them of their alliance with the King. He also distributed a large number of presents, including rum, to remind them of the King's generosity to his subjects.

However, a number of Seneca Sachems reminded their brothers of the treaty with the Americans to remain neutral and keep the war out of their lands. Old Smoke and Cornplanter were the two most vigorous opponents of joining the British.

During the council, another ship of presents arrived. Butler pointed out that the Revolutionaries could not supply these goods. The Iroquois were well aware of that in their past dealings with the Rebels. Therefore, the decision to support the British was becoming closer to reality.

Jul 25, 1777

St. Leger's force reaches Fort Oswego.
British Lt. Col. Barry St. Leger's main column traveled up the St. Lawrence River from Montreal and then across Lake Ontario to Oswego.
St. Leger found the Indians still trying to decide if they should side with the British and break their treaty with the Revolutionaries. A large amount of presents and gifts were given to the Indians to try and convince them to join the British forces. Finally, the Indians were told they really didn't have to fight, just come with St. Leger (to Fort Stanwix) "and watch us whip the Rebels".

Jul 27, 1777

Girls killed outside Fort Stanwix.

Three girls picking raspberries not 200 yards from the fort were attacked by Indians. Two of the girls were killed and scalped and the third had two musket balls pass through her shoulder while fleeing her attackers.

Col. Gansevoort, the fort commander, was horrified by the incident and wrote to Col. Van Schaik, "By the best discoveries we have made, there were four Indians who perpetrated these murders. I had four men with arms just passed that place, but these mercenaries of Britain came not to fight, but to lie in wait to murder; and it is equally the same to them if they can get a scalp, whether it is from a soldier or an innocent babe."

Aug 3, 1777

Siege of Fort Stanwix begun. Lt. Col. Barry St. Leger sent Captain Gilbert Tice to the fort with a proclamation demanding that the Revolutionaries surrender. Tice was ushered out of the fort and Col. Gansevoort issued a formal written reply to St. Leger the following day. In the reply, Gansevoort stated, "It is my determined resolution to defend this fort and garrison to the last extremity, in behalf of the United American States, who have placed me here to defend it against all their enemies."

Aug 3, 1777

General Nicholas Herkimer issues orders for Tryon County Militia to assemble at German Flats.

Aug 4, 1777

General Herkimer's Militia (approximately 800 men) begins its march from Fort Dayton to Fort Stanwix.

Aug 4, 1777

Loyalist uprising in Schohary Valley.
McDonell and Chrysler secured the southern end of the valley while Mann used his tavern at the northern part of the valley as a Loyalist rallying point. Only 28 men stood in defense of the valley against the Loyalists. These men took position in Johannes Becker's stone house just north of Weyserstown (present day Middleburgh). The house became enclosed by the Middle fort which was at times called Fort Defyance (Defiance).

Militia Colonel John Harper was in the valley and visited Fort Defiance. He agreed to ride for help against the Loyalists.

Aug 6, 1777

Battle of Oriskany. The Tryon County Militia led by General Herkimer was ambushed near the Oneida Indian village of Oriska. The Militia was on the way to relieve the siege of Fort Stanwix.

General Herkimer had approximately 800 Militia and about 60 to 100 Oneida Warriors. He had sent several messengers to Fort Stanwix and asked Commander Gansevoort to send out a sortie from the fort. Herkimer hoped this would distract St. Leger's forces and allow the Militia to push through the enemy lines to the fort. Three successive cannon shots from the fort were to be the signal that Gansevoort had received the message and would proceed with the sortie.

A number of Herkimer's officers did not want to delay and wait for the signal. Herkimer was adamant that they wait. The argument over the delay became very heated and several of the Militia Colonels accused Herkimer of cowardice and worse yet -- of Tory sympathies.

Angered and goaded by these accusations, Herkimer ordered the Militia forward into the ambush that became the Battle of Oriskany.

Historians have estimated 750 to 800 Revolutionaries and Oneida Indians were engaged in the battle. Approximately 450 or 460 were killed, wounded or captured. Many families in the Mohawk Valley lost all or most of their male members. The Loyalists and Iroquois lost approximately 160 to 200 killed, wounded, or missing. The battle was particularly devastating to the Seneca Indians who lost 35 warriors including five Sachems. By Iroquois standards, these were terrible losses.

One significant result of the battle was that it marked the beginning of a civil war within the Six Nations (Iroquois). With the Oneidas and some other Iroquois siding with the Revolutionaries, the Great Peace that had held the Six Nations together for ages was now shattered. In one of his reports after the battle, Daniel Claus wrote, "they (the Six Nations) would become a divided people -- nation against nation, clan against clan, lodge against lodge."

Aug 13, 1777

Battle of the Flockey.

Militia Colonel Harper had ridden to Kingston, NY seeking reinforcements to quell the Loyalist uprising in the Schoharie Valley that began on August 4th. He arrived at Kingston on Aug 12th and was given the 41-man Second Troop of Second Continental Dragoons under Captain Jean-Louis de Vernejoux and the 29-man troop of Ulster County Light Horse under Captain Sylvester Salisbury.

The cavalry rode all night and arrived in the valley on the 13th at Mann's Tavern. They rounded up all the Loyalists there and moved on to the southern part of the valley.

The Loyalist force led by McDonell and Chrysler were holding the southern end of the valley. They decided to make a stand at Chrysler's farm. The cavalry forded the Schoharie River and reached some flat lands the early German settlers called Die Flache or 'the flats' (from which the corrupt word "Flockey" derived). In this area, the Loyalists established their position. The cavalry charged and the Loyalists retreated in disorder into the woods. The cavalry lost one officer killed and on man mortally wounded. No record of Loyalist casualties has been found.

Some Loyalists, including Chrysler, eventually went to Fort Niagara. John McDonell led 40 to 50 Loyalists to Oswego where they joined with Sir John Johnson on the British retreat from Fort Stanwix. The skirmish known as the Battle of the Flockey is believed to be the first cavalry charge of the United States Army.

Aug 13, 1777

General Schuyler orders Major-General Benedict Arnold to relieve the siege at Fort Stanwix.

Colonel Willett, having eluded the enemy surrounding For Stanwix, joins Arnold at Albany, NY and gives Arnold valuable intelligence concerning the siege.

Aug 13, 1777

Walter Butler ordered to recruit Loyalists. Concerned about limited manpower and flush with the victory over at Oriskany, Lt. Col. Barry St. Leger sent a recruiting party under the command of Walter Butler into the German Flats region of the Mohawk Valley. He was hoping to influence a number of Loyalist families to join their army and support King George.

Aug 15, 1777

Walter Butler arrested. During a Loyalist recruiting speech at Shoemaker's Tavern in German Flats, Walter Butler was arrested by Lt. Col. Brooks. Brooks was a Continental Officer stationed at Fort Dayton.

Aug 16, 1777

General Nicholas Herkimer dies. As a result of a wound suffered at the Battle of Oriskany, a surgeon under Benedict Arnold's command amputated Herkimer's leg. The surgeon could not stop the bleeding and Herkimer died.

Aug 17, 1777

Walter Butler court martialed. General Benedict Arnold orders that Walter Butler and several other Loyalists captured at Shoemaker's Tavern be court martialed for treason. Col. Marinus Willett is appointed Judge Advocate.

Aug 20, 1777

Walter Butler given death sentence. At his court martial, Walter Butler was found guilty of being a spy and was given the death sentence for treason.

Several Rebel officers knew Butler and pleaded for a reduced sentence. The reduced sentence was granted and Butler was sent to jail in Albany, NY.

Aug 22, 1777

Hanjost Schuyler delivers message to Lt. Col. St. Leger.

Revolutionary Lt. Col. Brooks suggests to General Benedict Arnold a ruse that may help lift the siege at Fort Stanwix. They would tell Hanjost (who was captured with Walter Butler) that they will execute his brother unless Hanjost delivers a message to St. Leger. The message was an embellished report of the number of soldiers Benedict Arnold was leading to attack St. Leger and lift the siege. A number of Oneida Indians were to arrive one after another to confirm and embellish Hanjost's account.

Aug 22, 1777

Lt. Col. St. Leger retreats. Upon hearing of the Revolutionary army moving to relieve Fort Stanwix, St. Leger called a council with his officers and Indian Sachems. The Indian Sachems all agreed that the British force should retreat to Fort Oswego. St. Leger gave the order to retreat.

There are many accounts that state the retreat was more like a rout. Stories also abound of the Indian allies attacking stragglers and carrying off supplies and booty acquired in the attacks.

Sep 1777

Molly Brant's home ransacked.

Revolutionaries pillaged Molly Brant's home in Canajoharie. Molly (Joseph Brant's sister) fled with her children to a Cayuga Indian village.

Sep 8, 1777

Mohawk village attacked.

Revolutionaries pillaged the Mohawk Indian settlement at Fort Hunter. Approximately one hundred Mohawks fled to Burgoyne's army and then to Montreal.

Sep 1777

John Stuart arrested. John Stuart, Anglican pastor to the Mohawks, was arrested as a Loyalist. Stuart's Anglican chapel at Fort Hunter was turned into a tavern by the Rebels, then a stable, and finally into a fort. Stuart's possessions and farm were confiscated. He was paroled within the limits of Schenectady. In 1781, he was permitted to go to Canada as part of a prisoner exchange.

Sep 19, 1777

First Battle of Saratoga (Freeman's Farm). This day-long battle left six hundred British and German soldiers killed, wounded, or captured. Revolutionary losses were about three hundred.

Oct 6, 1777

Forts Clinton and Montgomery taken by British. British General Vaughan directed an assault on Forts Clinton and Montgomery on the Hudson River. The Revolutionaries were forced to retreat leaving valuable stores and over sixty cannon behind.

The chain across the Hudson from Fort Montgomery to Anthony's Nose was destroyed.

Oct 7, 1777

Second Battle of Saratoga (Bemis Heights). This battle was clearly a Rebel victory. The British lost about 600 killed, wounded, or taken prisoner. Rebel losses were about 150. Burgoyne then retreated toward Saratoga.

Oct 12, 1777

Burgoyne surrounded. Revolutionary forces surround Burgoyne's army at Saratoga. He was cut off from a retreat to Fort Ticonderoga.

Oct 16. 1777

Kingston, NY burned. British General John Vaughan ordered the burning of Kingston. Some five hundred buildings were destroyed in the fire.

Oct 17, 1777

Burgoyne surrenders. Surrounded and with Winter coming, General Burgoyne surrendered to General Horatio Gates at Schuylerville, NY. Over 5,000 British and German soldiers became prisoners of war. The Continental Congress decided not to allow them to return to England on parole. The prisoners became known as the Convention Army and were moved from place to place throughout the states until their release in 1783.

Nov 2, 1777

New York State produces lead.

The Secretary of the Board of War authorizes New York Governor Clinton to use prisoners of war to mine lead in New York State.

New York was the leading producer of lead for musket balls in the initial years of the war. Lead mines were found in old Albany, Duchess, and Ulster counties. The principal mine was the Livingston Mine.

Mohawk Valley Timeline

1778

Mar 11, 1778

Schuyler letter concerning pillaging of Loyalist homes. The Tryon County Committee of Safety controlled the political and judicial aspects of the county. It remained the highest court of law even after the New York Constitution of 1777 provided for county judges. The committee was able to continue judicial activities because its members were often judges, but there was no trial by jury.

The committee imprisoned any suspected Loyalist and encouraged Oneida Indians to attack and burn Loyalist farms. The few Mohawks who remained in the county were robbed by whites with the tacit approval of the Committee.

General Philip Schuyler finally wrote to the committee on March 11, 1778, and warned them to take steps to prevent these abuses. Schuyler's letter, however, did not dampen the zeal of the Committee which continued to advocate strict suppression of suspected Loyalists.

In the spring of 1778, the state legislature abolished all Committees of Safety in New York in favor of "Commissioners of Conspiracy" to be appointed by the governor.
Even after all the other Committees in New York dissolved themselves, the Tryon County Committee would not relinquish their power to the state. They feared that Commissioners of Conspiracy, as government appointees, would be men of wealth, of influence, and therefore moderates.

The Committee's demise came in May 1778 when it decided to free a certain debtor who was being held in the county jail. The Committee organized an armed posse, forcibly removed the man from jail, and proceeded to charge the creditor with all costs of the case. When the state legislature learned of the case it demanded that the Committee disband. With its activities condemned by the state, the Committee had no choice but to dissolve.

Mar 15, 1778

Fairfield attacked. The small settlement of Fairfield was located eight miles north of present-day Herkimer, NY and three miles east of the West Canada Creek. The settlement had been divided in its politics, having a number of families devoted to the Johnsons. As feelings became bitter, these families left their homes and joined the Johnsons in Canada.

In mid-March 1778, a party of Indians and Tories, led by one of the former residents named Caselman, appeared on snowshoes, killed and scalped one boy, took twelve men prisoners, and burned the houses. No women were killed or taken prisoner.

Mar 29, 1778

Manheim attacked. The settlement of Snyder's Bush (four miles north of present-day Little Falls, NY) was attacked by the same raiding party that destroyed Fairfield. The party was again led by Mr. Caselman.

Eight men were taken prisoner, but the women were left unmolested. One mill was burned but no Private residences were put to the torch. No one was killed in the raid.

Apr 20, 1778

Ephratah attacked. The afternoon of April 20, 1778, while a small company of twenty Militia were drilling, a band of Indians and Tories appeared and began destroying homes and barns. Most of the

Militia went to defend their homes, but a small number pursued the attackers. In a skirmish, several Militiamen were killed including a boy of four.

Stragglers from the Loyalist band also took a boy captive at Kringsbush and killed a young woman in sight of Fort Klock.

These and the other raids north of the Mohawk River so frightened the inhabitants that most of those whom the Indians and Tories had missed moved down into the Mohawk Valley to gain protection in the forts. As far as the northern slope of the valley was concerned, the British effort to frighten the people away from their farms was a great success.

Apr 21, 1778

Walter Butler escapes. Walter Butler escaped from a house in Albany where he was being incarcerated for treason. He had been in the Albany jail, but complained of illness and through the influence of some friends in the area, was allowed on parole to a Private home in Albany.

He made his escape down Lake Champlain to the St. Lawrence River. He went to Quebec and then on to Fort Niagara to join his father, John Butler and Butler's Rangers.

May 30, 1778

Cobus Kill (Cobleskill) attacked. Cobus Kill was a settlement of about twenty families spread over three miles in the Cobus Kill Valley. A scout sent out from the settlement on May 30th discovered a party of Indians and reported this to Captain Patrick, the senior Continental officer in the area.

Capt. Patrick went in pursuit of the Indians and was led into an ambush. Capt. Patrick, his Lieutenant, and corporal were killed. Militia Capt. Christian Brown assumed command and ordered a retreat. As the troops passed the house of George Warner, five men took up position inside and returned fire at the attackers. The Indians set fire to the house. Three men burned to death inside, one was killed while trying to escape, and one (Jonathan Young, a Continental soldier) was said to have been captured and then tortured to death.

On hearing the firing, the families in the settlement fled into the woods or to Schoharie ten miles away. Several people stayed in the woods for three days. Ten houses and barns were burned in the raid. Livestock was either driven off or destroyed.

Most historians agree that twenty-two men (Continental and Militia) were killed in the raid. Six were wounded, and two taken prisoner. Simms notes that a "mulatto" who was with the enemy at the time of the raid and returned after the war, stated that twenty-five of the Indians and Loyalists were killed and that seven who were wounded died on the trek to Canada.

Jun 1778

Loyalists collect their families. The terror from the Spring raids was so pervasive that in June of 1778, a body of some one hundred Loyalists were allowed to enter the Mohawk Valley, collect members of their families, who, by prearrangement, had gathered at Fort Hunter, and depart with them unmolested by way of Johnstown and the Sacandaga River to the Hudson, Lake Champlain, and St. Johns. On their return trip they captured several prisoners and destroyed considerable property. They came and went without a hand being lifted against them.

Jul 18, 1778

Springfield and Andrews Town destroyed. Joseph Brant led his raiders against Springfield at the head of Otsego Lake and then Andrews Town (north of present-day Warren, NY). Both were small settlements with Andrews Town having seven families. Brant's force killed eight men and took fourteen prisoners between the two locations. Women and children were forced into one house and not molested. The surviving women and children fled to Cherry Valley or Schoharie.

Aug 10, 1778

Rebels raid Butternut Creek. Captain Ballard with sixty Militiamen raided Butternut Creek near the town of Morris, a settlement of several Loyalist families. The Loyalists were taken prisoner and their homes destroyed.

Sep 16, 1778

Adam Helmer's run. Adam Helmer was one of nine scouts sent out by Colonel Bellinger from German Flats to look for any Loyalist or Indian forces in the area. The scouts ran into an advance party of Indians. Three of the scouts were killed and Adam managed to hide until the large party had passed.

He then jumped up and ran for German Flats to warn the people and the forts of the large enemy force approaching. Helmer out ran all his pursuers and arrived in time for the people of German Flats to seek shelter in the forts. The number of miles covered by Helmer's run varies, but most people agree it was more than nine miles.

Sep 17, 1778

Attack on German Flats. At 6:00am on September 17th, a raiding party of some 300 Loyalists and 150 Indians attacked the German Flats area. Captain William Caldwell was the leader along with Joseph Brant and his volunteers and Indians.

Thanks to Adam Helmer's warning, the residents made it safely inside either Fort Herkimer or Fort Dayton. Three local men were caught outside the forts and killed. By noon, Caldwell and Brant's force had put both sides of the river to the torch. Some 63 houses, 57 barns, 3 gristmills and 1 sawmill were burned. Over seven hundred head of livestock (cattle, horses, sheep) were driven off.

The attack left 719 people (including 387 children) homeless –– but alive.

Sep 17, 1778

Oneidas raid Unadilla. A party of Oneidas and Tuscaroras plundered he Loyalist settlements of Unadilla and Butternuts. They took ten prisoners and freed William Dygert who was a prisoner of the Loyalists at Unadilla.

Oct 2, 1778

Col. William Butler marches on Unadilla and Onaquaga. Several high-ranking Militia officers had long seen the villages of Unadilla and Onaquaga (near present-day Windsor, NY) as bases for Joseph Brant's operations. Col. William Butler presented a plan to destroy these bases to General Stark, then Commander of the Northern Department of the Continental Army.

Stark accepted the plan and Col. Butler left Fort Defiance (Middle Fort in the Schoharie Valley) with 267 Continentals.

Oct 6, 1778

Col. William Butler arrives at Unadilla. Col. Butler's force arrives at Unadilla and learns from a prisoner that none of Brant's men are in the area. The prisoner told Col. Butler that Brant had left for Onaquaga several days ago.

Oct 8, 1778

Brant raids Ulster County. Joseph Brant, with about 80 Loyalists and a few Indians, was raiding in Ulster County. He was unaware of the Continental force destroying his base.

Oct 8, 1778

Col. Butler burns Onaquaga. Col. William Butler led his Continentals in a night attack on Onaquaga. As Joseph Brant was raiding in Ulster County, the settlement was deserted.

The next day Butler had his men burn 40 houses and 2,000 bushels of corn. He stated in his report to Governor Clinton that "It was the finest Indian Town I ever saw; on both sides of the River; there was about 40 good houses, Square logs, shingles & stone chimneys, good Floors, glass windows, etc."

Oct 10, 1778

Unadilla burned. Col. William Butler and his Continentals burned Unadilla on their return from Onaquaga. All residences except one (the man who acted as guide to Onaquaga) were put to the torch as well as a saw and gristmill.

Oct 24, 1778

Carleton Raid in Champlain Valley. On October 24th, Major Christopher Carleton left the Isle Aux Noix in the Richelieu River with a fleet of several large vessels, gunboats, b, and canoes. He commanded a party of 354 white officers and men and some 100 Indians.

Carleton's orders from General Frederick Haldimand, Governor-General of Quebec Province (Canada), were "to destroy all the supplies, provisions, and animals which the Rebels may have assembled on the shores of Lake Champlain, to take prisoner all the inhabitants who have settled there and have sworn allegiance to the Congress, sending their wives and children into the Colonies with orders not to return to the region." Also," to destroy all the boats which he could discover, as well as all the sawmills, and gristmills which could have been built in the area."

Haldimand's reason for the attack as explained in a letter to the British Colonial Secretary, George Germain, was that "there are some settlements upon the borders of Lake Champlain, Otter Creek, and about Ticonderoga and Crown Point that may furnish many conveniences and necessaries which would facilitate the approach of an Enemy."

Three weeks later the expedition returned to Canada with 39 prisoners. Carleton reported burning one sawmill, one gristmill, forty-seven houses and twenty- seven barns. A considerable amount of livestock were brought off or killed.

Nov 11, 1778

Attack on Cherry Valley. On November 11th, a raiding party led by Loyalist Captain Walter Butler attacked the settlement of Cherry Valley. Butler's force consisted of three hundred twenty-one Indians, one hundred fifty Rangers, and fifty men from the 8th Regiment. Joseph Brant was also with the raiders.

The commander in charge of the Continental detachment at Cherry Valley (Col. Ichabod Alden) had received notice from Fort Stanwix that scouts had reported a large Loyalist force headed in his direction. Col. Alden refused to believe the information. He assured the people in the settlement that his scouts would report any enemy activity.

Alden's scouts were captured so they never gave an alarm. Butler learned from a Loyalist in one of the scouts that all the officers were sleeping at the Wells' family home. Before the attack started, Butler had the house surrounded and as others began the main attack on the fort, the officers, including Col. Alden were killed trying to get to the fort.

The attack did not proceed as Butler planned. He lost control of the Indians. They began killing and scalping anyone they could find in the village. Several Mohawk and Seneca Chiefs, including Joseph Brant, attempted to stop the carnage. By the end of the day, sixteen soldiers and thirty-two civilians lay dead -- most of the latter being women and children. Seventy settlers, mostly women and children, were taken away as prisoners.

Before Butler's force left the area, forty of the seventy prisoners were released.

Reports of the carnage were shocking even in that time of brutal warfare. Many reports cited atrocities perpetrated by Loyalists as well as Indians in the party. This attack was particularly embarrassing to the British when the news reached the General public in England. There was an outcry among the British citizenry to stop using Indians in helping suppress the Revolutionaries.

Nov 22, 1778

Provisions for German Flats. Colonel Peter Bellinger, Rebel Militia commander at German Flats, wrote a letter to General Hand, Commander of the Northern Department of the Continental Army at Albany. He informed General Hand that the people of German Flats had been without provisions for fourteen days. There were over seven hundred homeless people in German Flats.

Provisions at the time allowed one pound of bread and one pound of beef per day for each person sixteen years and older. Half that ration was to be given to those under sixteen.

Mohawk Valley Timeline

1779

Jan 1779

Refugees of raids. Families who had been burned out of their homes and farms in the raids of 1778 sought refuge at Schenectady as well as Forts Herkimer and Dayton. Returns in the Clinton Papers showed 164 persons from Cherry Valley and 80 from Springfield were located in Schenectady while 700 were at Fort Herkimer or Fort Dayton. The refugees had no food and only the clothes on their backs. The situation prompted Abraham Yates, the local Militia commander, to write Governor Clinton stating, "God Knows where it will End; must it not very Soon Create a Famine?"

Apr 14, 1779

Refugee fund. New York State established a fund of 2,250 pounds for sufferers of "Cobus Kill, Cherry Valley, German Flats, Andrews Town, and Springfield who were incapable of gaining a livelihood."

Apr 21, 1779

Onondaga villages destroyed. An army of some 558 men led by Rebel Colonel Goose Van Schaick attacked and destroyed three Onondaga Indian villages just south and west of present day Onondaga Lake. The army killed 12 to 15 Onondagas and took thirty some prisoners (mostly women). This was the opening clash in the Rebel campaign against the Iroquois in 1779.

Jul 20, 1779

Attack on Minisink. The settlement of Minisink, that was ten miles west of Goshen, NY, was attacked by Joseph Brant. Brant's force consisted of sixty Indians and twenty-seven Loyalists. The primary aim of the attack was to obtain provisions.

During the attack, the schoolmaster, Jeremiah Van Auken was killed along with three others. Van Auken had told the children in the school to run, but Brant came upon them. He placed his paint mark on the girls' dresses to keep them from harm. The girls sat and spread their dresses over their male schoolmates protecting them as well. Most of the other members of the settlement made it to the protection of the fort.

Brant's force laid waste to the settlement except for the fort. Ten houses, eleven barns, a church, a gristmill, as well as stores of hay and grain were destroyed. They took three prisoners including two young boys.

On July 21st, Militia from Goshen caught up with Brant's force as they were driving cattle across a ford on the Delaware River. A battle raged for four hours until Brant counter attacked. The Militia retreated but Brant's men showed no quarter. All wounded and other prisoners taken were killed and scalped. About forty Militia were killed while Brant suffered three men killed and ten wounded.

One story that came out of this battle was that of John Wood. He was about to be killed when he gave the Master Mason's sign of distress. Brant, being a Mason, saw this and saved Wood's life.

Aug 22, 1779

Sullivan Expedition consolidates at Tioga, NY. In a move to punish the Iroquois for their part in the raids of 1778, General George Washington initiated a campaign into the Iroquois Territory. General John Sullivan led the campaign with General James Clinton, the brother of New York Governor George Clinton, as second in command.

Sullivan started out in Easton Pennsylvania and marched into the Wyoming Valley and up the Susquehanna River. Clinton started in Canajoharie and then dammed Lake Otsego. This allowed his more than 220 batteaux to easily float down the Susquehanna once the dam was removed. The two divisions of the expedition destroyed any Indian settlements they encountered along their routes of march.

The expedition became one force when they linked up at Tioga. From Tioga, the army of approximately 5,000 men, moved northwest into Iroquois lands.

British General Frederick Haldimand, Governor General of Quebec, did not see this move coming. He held back any troops believing the Rebels intended to attack Quebec. General Washington had sent Major Hazard to Connecticut with several companies of men to make it appear Hazard was ordered to start constructing a military road leading to Quebec. Haldimand believed the ruse and held back his troops in anticipation of an attack up the Champlain Valley. The Iroquois thus had to bear the full burden of their alliance with the king.

Aug 29, 1779

Battle of Newtown. Loyalist Major John Butler was dispatched from Fort Niagara to aid the Indians in trying to stop the Sullivan Expedition. Joseph Brant and his volunteers also joined the Indians opposing the threat to their lands. After seeing the size of the force they faced, both Butler and Brant counseled for harassing tactics against the Rebels. The Indians took a firm stance that they wanted to stand and fight the Rebels.

The Indians picked a spot approximately six miles southeast of present day Elmira, NY to set up an ambush. The Rebel scouts spotted the ambush and General Sullivan moved to flank the position. The combination of artillery fire and overwhelming force broke up the ambush and the Indians retreated.

Sep 15, 1779

Sullivan Expedition returns to Pennsylvania. After destroying a large Iroquois village near present day Geneseo, NY, General Sullivan turned his force around and returned to Pennsylvania. He considered his task accomplished. In his report to General Washington and the Continental Congress, Sullivan stated there was "not a single village left in the country of the five nations." He claimed to have destroyed forty villages, 160,000 bushels of corn, as well as numerous other crops and orchards. The campaign was judged a great success by Congress.

Not all, however, were so sure the campaign was a success. Rebel Major Fogg wrote in his journal a very prophetic observation: "The nests are destroyed, but the birds are still on the wing."

Sep 21, 1779

Iroquois refugees at Fort Niagara. Over five thousand Indians descended on Fort Niagara. The Indians blamed the British for their misfortunes and the loss of their villages to the Sullivan Expedition. They expected the British to provide food, shelter, and clothing. Corn and other supplies were procured from Quebec and Detroit.

Oct 22, 1779

Bill of Attainder. The New York State legislature passed the Bill of Attainder. To be attainted meant the person named was declared outlaw with loss of civil rights and forfeiture of any property. Fifty-nine prominent Loyalists were named in the bill. Among them were Sir John and Guy Johnson, Daniel Claus, as well as John and Walter Butler.

New York State realized $3.6 Million from the sale of the confiscated property.

Mohawk Valley Timeline

1780

Mar 1780

Indian raiding parties. During the Spring of 1780, Indian war parties were constantly leaving Fort Niagara for the frontiers of New York, Pennsylvania, and as far south as Virginia. The raiding parties ranged in size from six to seventy-five men. Returning to Fort Niagara, the parties brought in prisoners, livestock, and reports of settlers killed and barns burned.

April 7, 1780

Harpersfield attacked. A detachment of Rebel Militia under the command of Captain Alexander Harper traveled from Schoharie to Harpersfield (some thirty miles). Their purpose was to gather sap and produce maple syrup/sugar to supplement the meager food supplies at the Schoharie forts. While gathering the sap, the men were surprised by a war party led by the Mohawk Chief Joseph Brant. Three of the Rebels were killed and eleven taken prisoner including Capt. Harper.

One of the prisoners, Freegift Patchin, later related the story of their capture and travails as prisoners. He mentioned one Loyalist, a Mr. Beacraft, who threatened to kill them right after their capture. Patchin also remembered a confrontation between Capt. Harper and Joseph Brant. Brant was about to tomahawk Harper when, instead, he decided to question Harper about the Schoharie forts. Harper assumed Brant was on his way to attack the settlements and forts on the Schoharie Kill (Creek). When Brant asked him if there were Continental soldiers around, Harper replied that three hundred Continentals had just arrived to defend the forts. It was a lie, but Brant believed Harper and the war party with their prisoners departed for Fort Niagara.

Had Harper not been able to convince Brant to not attack Schoharie, the number of prisoners heading for Fort Niagara would have been much greater than eleven.

May 21, 1780

Sir John Johnson's first raid on Mohawk River area. In mid-March, a Loyalist scout returned to Quebec from the Mohawk Valley. He informed Governor-General Haldimand and Sir John Johnson that the Rebels were forcing men of military age to serve in units for home defense. Any who refused such service would be considered Tories, sent to prison, and their property confiscated.

Haldimand was upset by the persecution and suggested Sir John put together a small force to lead these Loyalists up the Champlain Valley to Quebec. Sir John agreed with Haldimand, but suggested they also use this opportunity to strike a blow at the Rebels. Final plans called for Johnson to lead a force of 528 whites and Indians into the Mohawk Valley. Rebel spies heard of the plan, but couldn't determine when this raid would take place or the route the invaders planned to use.

Using Lake Champlain and then marching southwest from Crown Point, Johnson's force entered the Scottish Settlement just north of Johnstown on May 21st. His force killed a number of prominent Rebels in the area and burnt their homes. Caughnawaga (near present day Fonda) was burned. In total, some 120 barns, mills, and houses were destroyed on the north side of the Mohawk River. Johnson gathered 143 Loyalists, including some women and children and thirty African slaves for the trek back to Quebec.

The Rebels mustered Continentals and Militia to pursue Johnson's force. However, a rumor was spread that the Mohawk Chief Joseph Brant was going to strike the south side of the river. This drew a good number of the Rebels away from the pursuit of Johnson. Johnson and the Loyalists he had collected made it to Lake Champlain and then to Quebec.

Jul 2, 1780

Indians join British. About 300 Indians who had been supporting the Rebels, entered Fort Niagara. These were some 80 Tuscaroras, 180 Onondagas (who had fled to Oneida villages after their own had been destroyed by the Rebel raids in previous year) and 2 Oneida families. They said they were seeking shelter from the Rebels. However, the Indians were not allowed to sit at the fort for long. They were told they had to immediately go to war as penance for the error of their ways and not deciding for the British cause sooner.

Jul 24, 1780

Brant raids Oneida village. Joseph Brant burned the Oneida Indian village of Canowaraghere. The Oneidas living in the village heard of the raiding party and fled to Fort Stanwix for protection. Brant burned all the homes, Rev. Kirkland's church, and a small fort.

Jul 26, 1780

Brant attacks Oneidas who had fled to Fort Stanwix.
Oneida Indians who fled from Brant's raid on Canowaraghere were camped outside Fort Stanwix. Joseph Brant and his war party attacked their camp. Most of the Oneidas escaped into the fort. Those caught outside were threatened until they promised to go to Fort Niagara and support the British. Before they left, Brant's party killed any horses and cattle they found outside the fort.

Aug 2, 1780

Brant attacks Canajoharie. Most of the Rebel Militia was heading for Fort Stanwix to try and trap Joseph Brant. However, Brant had moved on and was preparing to attack the settlement of Canajoharie. He had hoped to attack the settlement and nearby Fort Plank simultaneously.

As it turned out, some of Brant's Indians showed themselves and alarmed the settlement. This allowed most of the inhabitants to escape to Fort Plank. Brant's party had to content itself with burning about 100 houses and barns, two mills, the church, and destroying what grain and cattle they could find. Approximately thirty people were killed. According to Rebel Colonel Abraham Wemple, some were children. A swath of land some six miles long and four miles wide was devastated by the attack.

Aug 9, 1780

Vroomans land attacked. Joseph Brant and a small party of Indians and Tories attacked a portion of the Schoharie settlements near Middle Fort. Eleven members of the Vrooman family were made prisoner and three were killed, including the father, mother, and eight-year-old Peter. According to several reports, the Tory Benjamin Beacraft seized Peter, slit his throat, and then scalped him.

Oct 10, 1780

British Major Carleton captures Fort Ann and Fort George.
During the planning of Sir John Johnson's October raid on the Mohawk Valley, Sir Frederick Haldimand, Governor-General or Quebec Province, felt a diversion was needed to draw off a major portion of the Rebel Militia. To that end, Haldimand ordered Major Christopher Carleton to lead a force down the Champlain Valley into the upper Hudson River area. Carleton's force numbered close to one thousand men, half of which were British Regulars.

The Rebel Commandant of Fort Ann on Wood Creek, surrendered the fort upon seeing the force arrayed against him. Carleton continued south along the upper Hudson destroying farms, mills, and livestock on the way. He turned his force to return to Lake Champlain when they reached Saratoga. While returning to Lake Champlain, he captured Fort George on October 11th. Both Fort Ann and Fort George were burned.

Oct 12, 1780

Ballstown, NY attacked. On Oct 6th, Captain John Munro, in command of about 200 Loyalists and Indians, left Major Carleton's force and marched south along the Schroon River. He hoped to link up with Sir John Johnson's force and then attack Schenectady. On Oct 11th, Munro learned that Carleton had taken Fort Ann and Fort George and was returning to Fort Ticonderoga.

Carleton's return north left Munro with a decision to make. Should he keep trying to contact Sir John Johnson (Munro had sent two messengers who never returned) or should he do what damage he could and return to Ticonderoga as well? He decided on the latter and on October 12th attacked and destroyed Ballstown, NY. A number of Loyalist wives and children were being held at Ballstown. Munro collected them and returned north.

Oct 17, 1780

Sir John Johnson's second raid on the Mohawk Valley. Sir John Johnson began his raid down Schoharie Creek. His army of close to 900 Loyalists, Indians and British Regulars had camped the night of the 16th where Kennanagara Creek flowed into the Schoharie Kill (Creek).

Johnson's main force started out from Carleton Island and sailed across Lake Ontario to Oswego. From there, they used batteaux down the Oswego River to Onondaga Lake. They stored their boats and supplies by the lake and marched southeast to reach Schoharie Kill on October 16th.

Johnson bypassed the Upper Fort, just north of Bouck Farms Island, and marched up the east shore of the Schoharie Kill. They burned houses, barns, and crops as they went. When they reached the Middle Fort (Fort Defiance) just north of Middleburgh, NY Johnson attempted to gain the surrender of the fort's defenders. The fort did not surrender and they continued their destructive march north. After firing several cannon shots into it, Johnson bypassed the Lower Fort, just north of the village of Schoharie, and camped the night of the 17th where Fly Creek empties into the Schoharie.

On October 18th, Johnson ordered Joseph Brant and a small party to burn the settlement around Fort Hunter while the main force continued up the west side of the Schoharie to the confluence with the Mohawk River. Arriving at the Mohawk River, Sir John split his force and marched west on both sides of the Mohawk, looting and burning as they went.

Following the Battles of Stone Arabia and Klock's Field, Sir John and his force returned by several routes to Onondaga Lake and arrived back in Oswego on October 26th. In his report to Sir Frederick Haldimand, Sir John claimed to have destroyed six hundred thousand bushels of grain. Governor George Clinton put the destruction at one hundred fifty thousand bushels and 200 dwellings burned. So devastating was the raid, that Clinton stated Schenectady should now be considered the western frontier of New York State.

Oct 19, 1780

Battles of Stone Arabia and Klock's Field. As Sir John Johnson's army marched up the Mohawk Valley, he split his force sending about one hundred Loyalists and Indians across the river to the north shore. Rebel Colonel John Brown, in command of Fort Paris near Stone Arabia, heard of this smaller force and decided to attack it with about four hundred Men. Brown did not know that Sir John had just started to cross more of his army onto the north shore. At the time of the battle, Brown's force of 400 was facing about 170 of Sir John's army. Sir John's forces turned Brown's flanks and some forty Rebels were killed including Colonel Brown. The Rebels retreated back to Fort Paris.

Later that day, a Militia force of about nine hundred Men from Albany, led by General Van Rensselaer, attacked Sir John's army. The engagement began in early evening and continued into the night. Under cover of darkness, Sir John directed his force to move across the Mohawk to the south shore and return to Onondaga Lake. General Van Rensselaer did not press the night attack through the woods. On the morning of the 20th, Sir John's force was well ahead of Rebel pursuit.

Nov 1780

Oneida Indians at Schenectady. The remnants of the Oneida and Tuscarora Nations who supported the Rebels, congregated outside Schenectady, NY. Their village and food had been destroyed during Brant's raid in the Summer. Rebel General Philip Schuyler was appalled at their condition and appealed to Congress to aid these people who had fought "readily and loyally" for the Rebels. He felt the United States was "bound by every principal of honor" to come to the aid of a people who had been reduced to their desperate condition solely through their attachment to the cause of American liberty.

Some of the Indians moved north hoping to hunt and survive in small huts. However, their clothing was minimal and according to Schuyler, was not adequate to cover one eighth of their number.

On March 8, 1781, the New York State Legislature ordered 185 blankets to be purchased for the Indians. With Winter nearly over, they received some minimal clothing.

Mohawk Valley Timeline

1781

Feb 5, 1781

Gov. Clinton's letter to Congress. Historian Barbara Graymont described the damage inflicted on the New York frontier in 1780: "It included three hundred thirty killed or prisoners – fourteen of whom were officers – six forts and several mills destroyed, over seven hundred houses and barns burned, and nearly seven hundred head of cattle driven off. The grain destroyed was immense. Also to be considered was the terror instilled into the frontier inhabitants and their enforced flight from once flourishing settlements."

Governor George Clinton wrote to Congress: "We are now arrived at the year 1781, deprived of a great Portion of our most valuable and well inhabited Territory, numbers of our Citizens have been barbarously butchered by ruthless Hand of the Savages, many are carried away into Captivity, vast numbers entirely ruined, and these with their Families become a heavy Burthen to the distressed remainder … we shall soon approach to the Verge of Ruin."

Mar 1781

Indian war parties. During the 1781 campaign a large number of Iroquois war parties descended on the Mohawk and Schoharie Valleys. Many of them attacked settlements previously devastated and destroyed whatever had been rebuilt. Most of the parties were small, traveled swiftly, and did much damage.

Apr 28, 1781

Marinus Willett assumes command. New York Governor George Clinton appoints Col. Marinus Willett commander of the New York Militia on the frontier.

May 22, 1781

Fort Stanwix abandoned. In May 1781, Fort Stanwix was in extremely poor condition. The barracks had been mostly destroyed by fire and heavy Spring rains had nearly demolished the fort.

The fort had been of little service in recent months in keeping the enemy from the frontier. To repair it and keep it in a state of readiness would now require an enormous expense. Rebel

General James Clinton ordered the abandonment of the fort. The garrison was to take up quarters at Fort Herkimer where they could be more readily available for a defense of the Mohawk Valley.

Jul 9, 1781

Currytown attacked. Currytown settlement was attacked on the morning of July 9th. The raiders were led by Loyalist Lieutenant John Doxstader and consisted of about 300 (some sources say 500) Indians and a small number of Loyalists. They killed or captured the settlers and burned the settlement.

Jul 10, 1781

Battle of New Dorlach. Following the attack on Currystown, Rebel Col. Marrinus Willett, who was in headquarters at Fort Plain, saw the smoke from the settlement. Assuming this was the work of Loyalist raiders, he sent out a scouting party to try and find the enemy. The scouts found the raiders encamped in a cedar swamp in New Dorlach (present day Sharon Springs). Runners were sent to inform Col Willett. Upon learning of the enemy's location, Willett sent out a call for more Militia and immediately set out to engage the Loyalist force.

Willett used a favorite tactic of the Indians and led them into an ambush. The battle lasted an hour and a half. Thinking they were being attacked by a force larger than theirs, the Indians retreated leaving their booty from Currytown behind.

Fifty of the raiders were killed or wounded while Willett's force suffered five men killed and nine wounded. This was the first large raiding party the frontier Militia had defeated.

Sep 1, 1781

Cobus Kill raid. About twenty to thirty Indians and Loyalists attacked the settlement of Cobus Kill. They plundered and burned "dwellings and buildings which had escaped the enemy's visitation four years previous". One settler (George Fremire) was killed, and seven other men taken prisoner.

Sep 7, 1781

Scouting party attacked. Rebel Lieutenant Solomon Woodworth led a scout of forty-six Militia and six Oneida Indians from Fort Dayton up the West Canada Creek to look for signs of the enemy. The scout found tracks of a party of Indians and followed. Those tracks were made by a war party of seventy-four Onondagas and Cayugas led by Loyalist Lieutenant John Clement. Clement learned his party was being followed and set an ambush for the Rebels.

One of the Indian raiders showed himself and Woodworth's men pursued him. The entire Rebel scouting party was well into the trap as they chased the fleeing Indian. The enemy's first volley left ten of Woodworth's men dead or dying.

At the end of the skirmish, twenty-two Militia were dead including Lt. Woodworth. Nine were captured and taken to Canada. The rest of the Militia and the Oneidas escaped and returned to Fort Dayton. Only two of the raiders were wounded.

The site of the ambush was in a deep ravine three miles north of present day Herkimer on the east side of the West Canada Creek.

Oct 25, 1781

Warrensbush attacked. British Major John Ross and Loyalist Captain Walter Butler left Oswego on October 11th to attack the Mohawk Valley. Their force consisted of some 470 British and Loyalist troops as well as 130 Indians. On October 24th they attacked and plundered Currytown and then marched to Warrensbush (current Town of Florida).

At dawn on October 25th, Ross's force attacked and burned Warrensbush. In his report to General Haldimand, Ross estimated that they had destroyed nearly one hundred fine farms. Rebel witnesses stated the loss was less than thirty. Ross also stated the settlement had been a "nest of Rebels", but Rebel Colonel Willett said that most of the farms burned had belonged to "disaffected persons" or Loyalists.

Oct 25, 1781

Battle of Johnstown. After burning Warrensbush, Major Ross moved his force across the Mohawk River. This was not an easy task as the river was swollen from recent rains. The raiders moved within sight of Fort Johnstown. Some shots were exchanged, but no attempt was made to actually attack the fort. Ross moved his force through Johnstown to the west.

Rebel Colonel Willett received word of Ross's presence on October 24th. He moved from his headquarters at Fort Plain to intercept the raiders. On the morning of October 25th, he learned Ross had burned Warrensbush and then crossed the river and headed for Johnstown. Willett and his Militia force of about four hundred Men crossed the river at Caughnawaga (present Fonda, NY). He also had difficulty crossing and lost an ammunition cart in the process.

About 4:00 in the afternoon, Willett caught up with the raiders where they had encamped outside Johnstown. Willett split his force and attempted to surround Ross. The battle lasted until darkness fell and Ross retreated from the battlefield. The raiders had eleven men killed and thirty-two taken prisoner. Willett's force suffered twelve men killed, twenty-four wounded, and five taken prisoner.

Oct 30, 1781

Death of Loyalist Captain Walter Butler. Even before the Battle of Johnstown, Major Ross had decided not to return to Oswego, but to strike out across the lower Adirondack region to reach Carleton Island at the head of the St. Lawrence River. Following the battle, Ross traveled northwest. Col. Willett thought that was what Ross would do and marched to intercept him. Ross's force was moving swiftly and Willett could not intercept him, but did pursue the raiders for several days.

Ross was unaware of his pursuers until October 30th when his rear party was fired on by the Rebels. The British then pushed themselves even harder and crossed the West Canada Creek. Loyalist Captain Walter Butler was in charge of the rear guard. Once across the creek, Butler thought he was out of musket range and taunted the Rebels across the creek. One account had an Oneida Indian wounding Butler in the thigh and he fell from his horse. The Indian rushed across and was about to tomahawk Butler when Butler cried "Quarter!" The Indian cried he would give him "Cherry Valley Quarter" (Butler led the raid at Cherry Valley in 1778 that left some 32 civilians dead). He then proceeded to tomahawk and scalp Butler.

Years later, the son of one of the Rangers on the Ross expedition claimed that his father was with Butler at the time he was shot and that Butler was shot in the head. Butler would not have been able to call for quarter – or anything else. Several of Willett's men corroborated the story of Butler being shot in the head. Col. Willett, in his report to Governor Clinton, stated, "he (Butler) was not dead when found by one of our Indians, who finished his business for him and got a Considerable Booty".

Nov 13, 1781

Schoharie attacked. A raiding party of some twenty-eight Indians attacked the settlement of Schoharie. The party was led by Loyalist Lieutenant Adam Crysler. The raiders killed one man, burned several houses, and drove off about fifty head of cattle and horses. After several skirmishes with pursuing Militia, the raiders lost the livestock and retreated to Fort Niagara.

Mohawk Valley Timeline

1782-3

Spring 1782

Dietz family massacred. A small Indian war party killed nine people in the Dietz family near Beaver Dam in the Schoharie Valley. The victims were scalped and all their buildings were destroyed.

May 1782

Oswego rebuilt. Governor General Frederick Haldimand of Canada orders Major Ross to Oswego to rebuild the fort at that location.

Jul 1782

Farms in Schoharie attacked. Adam Crysler led a small war party and attacked the Zimmer farm along Foxes Creek in the Schoharie Valley

Feb 9, 1783

Willett sets out to attack Ft. Oswego. Rebel Col. Marinus Willett set out from Fort Herkimer to attack Fort Oswego and dislodge the British who were holding the fort. Willett's Indian guides became lost and the mission was compromised. He was forced to return to Ft. Herkimer.

The People They Protected
The Palatine Story

The Palatine Story

Who were those people, the Palatines? Why did they leave their homeland?

Many of the Palatine names still appear in the valley, but too few of the people realize or even care what their ancestors did for them many years ago. Those stubborn Palatines were determined to stay on their land, they had been forced to move too many times. The war was theirs to win or lose and the fate of the nation depended on them.   Before it was over, they lost almost everything, their buildings were burned, many were dead, families were torn apart, but the survivors endured once more and won their freedom. And they started over one more time.

The Palatine story is a complicated one, which will be simplified for the purpose of this book.

People from many countries settled in the Mohawk Valley, among the early people were the Dutch, French and the Palatines. Commonly, the Palatines were referred to as "those Dutchmen" here in America. Germany as a country did not exist in the eighteenth century but the area where Germany would come to be, was ruled by many princes. Here is a brief overview of the country we now know as Germany.

The Germanic tribes are believed to have come from Scandinavia to Germany about 100 B.C. Those Germanic tribes living to the west of the Rhine River and south of the Main River were soon subdued by the Romans and incorporated into the Roman Empire. Tribes living to the east and north of these rivers remained free but had more or less friendly relations with the Romans for several centuries. Beginning in the fourth century A.D., new westward migrations of eastern peoples caused the Germanic tribes to move into the Roman Empire, which by the late fifth century ceased to exist.

One of the largest tribes, the Franks, controlled the area that was to become France and much of what is now western Germany and part of Italy. In A.D. 800, Charlemagne, was crowned in Rome by the pope as emperor of all of this territory. Because it was so large, after Charlemagne's death the empire split into three kingdoms within the next two generations, the people of the West Frankish Kingdom spoke an early form of French and those in the East Frankish Kingdom spoke an early form of German. The tribes of the eastern kingdom; Franconians, Saxons, Bavarians, Swabians, and several others were ruled by descendants of Charlemagne until 911, when they elected a Franconian, Conrad I, to be their king.

German kings enlarged their realm and added the Middle Kingdom to become rulers of what would later be called the Holy Roman Empire. In 962 Otto I became the first of the Germanic kings crowned Holy Roman Emperor in Rome. By the middle of the next century, the German lands ruled by the emperors were the richest and most politically powerful part of Europe. German princes stopped the westward advances of the Magyar tribe, and Germans began moving eastward to begin a long process of colonization. But the Germans did not continue to increase their power. During the next few centuries, wars to maintain the empire against its enemies, and the power struggle with other German princes and the wealthy and powerful papacy and its allies, depleted the area's wealth and slowed its development. France and England had a central royal power over small regional princes. Germany remained divided into smaller little states that were often warring with one another.

The existence of many small states with different types of governing bodies, such as principalities, electorates, ecclesiastical territories, and free cities, remained from the early middle ages until 1871, when the country was finally united. The turmoil was increased by the Protestant Reformation of the sixteenth century, which ended Germany's Catholic unity by converting many Catholics to Lutheranism and Calvinism. Followers of these two varieties of Protestantism viewed each other with as much hostility and suspicion as they did Roman Catholics. As a result, Germans were divided not only by territory but also by religion.

The terrible destruction of the Thirty Years' War of 1618-48, reduced German independent regionalism, and so did the reforms enacted during the age of enlightened absolutism (1648-1789) where all the power rested with the head of state and later the growth of nationalism and industrialism in the nineteenth century.

In 1815 the Congress of Vienna stipulated that the several HUNDRED states existing in Germany before the French Revolution be replaced with thirty-eight states. In the following decades, the two largest of these states, Austria and Prussia, jockeyed for first place in a Germany that was gradually unified under a variety of social and economic pressures. The politician responsible for German unification was Otto von Bismarck, whose ruthless practices formed a united Germany in 1871. The new Germany did not include Austria and many non-German territories and peoples.

Our story about the Palatines begins in the early 1700s when shiploads of German peoples, estimated from two thousand upwards, arrived in London between May and November of 1709. Most of the group came from the Lower Palatinate, the name "Palatine" was applied to the rest of the immigrants, although they came from the neighboring territories as well.

How did this happen and most importantly, the question which precipitated the arrival of the Palatines is WHY did so many people suddenly pack up and leave their homeland?

The reasons they came were many. That reason most frequently mentioned was devastation by war. The end of the Thirty Years' War left the people of the Palatinate depleted. A recovery was underway, but prosperity was short-lived; in the latter part of the seventeenth century the Palatinate was repeatedly used as the battleground of Louis XIV's armies. The French king did not intervene to rescue the Palatines as some historical writers have claimed; rather he was simply using the Palatinate as a convenient battleground.

Following Louis XIV's armies, during the War of the Spanish Succession, Marshal Villars crossed the Rhine in May 1707, and terrorized southwestern Germany by plundering freely on the Palatinate, Wurtemberg, Baden and the Swabian Circle. In September of the same year, the French invaded across the Rhine. These invasions wiped out the start of a new and promising recovery. Living conditions were very poor and the people discouraged, rightly so. They were understandably weary of war.

To the devastation from endless wars was added the rage of nature, when the winter 1708-1709 set in. How cold was it? As early as the beginning of October the cold was intense, and by November firewood would not burn in the open air. In January of 1709 alcohol froze into solid blocks of ice; birds on the wing fell dead to the ground; and it is said saliva congealed in its fall from the mouth to the ground. Most of Western Europe was frozen tight. The Seine and all the other rivers were icebound and on the 8th of January, the Rhone, one of the most rapid rivers in Europe, was covered with ice. But what had never been seen before, the sea froze sufficiently all along the coasts to bear carts, even heavily laden carts. The Arctic weather lasted well into April. Perhaps the period of the most intense cold was from the 6th to the 25th of January. The fruit trees were killed and the vines were destroyed. Nature's timing was superb, just when things couldn't get any worse, they did.

The French Court at Versailles dazzled many European rulers and they tried to copy the opulent French Court at the expense of their people. Almost constant warfare added another burden to the people, the expenses had to be met by heavy taxes; often so heavy it left the peasants starving. Money, lots of money was needed to carry on war. The rulers seemed to see their own wants and not the needs of the starving peasants. This was the time of divine rule, the kings were absolute rulers, and their wishes and their dictates were law.

Another reason for dissatisfaction was possible religious persecution. To gain favor from softhearted people on their way to America, emigrants found it convenient to plead religious persecution. Friends of the immigration in England justified their help on religious grounds, while others fiercely attacked the authenticity of these claims.

What was the religious condition of the various little principalities in 1709? *Cuius regio, eius religio*, established at the Peace of Augsburg (1555) and modified by the Treaty of Westphalia (1648), this was still functioning. It recognized three churches: Catholic, Lutheran and Calvinist. The belief that religious persecution was a cause looked credible at first glance except that the Elector of the Palatinate in 1709 was John William who was a Catholic. To further discredit the idea of persecution from the Catholic Elector, he had issued on November 21, 1705, a declaration promising liberty of conscience.

The definition of elector according to Wikipedia: In the "Holy Roman Empire of German Nation", the collegiate of seven Electors (eight since 1648) *(Kurfürsten)* consisted of those lay or clerical princes who had the right to vote in the election of the king or Holy Roman Emperor.

In the 1708 immigration, of the first forty-one Germans, fifteen were Lutherans and twenty-six were vReformed or Calvinistic. Fourteen others who joined the group in London were also Protestants. This group, in their petition to the Queen made no mention of religious persecution. They spoke of the French destruction in 1708. The later families were of the following religious persuasion: Lutherans, 550; Reformed, 693; Catholics, 512; Baptists, 12; Mennonites, 3. Almost one-third of the Palatines in London on June 16, 1709, were of the Catholic faith. Religious persecution by the Catholic Elector might drive out Protestants, but it does not explain why the Catholics immigrated.

The Palatines were described as not a particularly religious lot of people. Only a few of these people, when they came to England, brought a prayer book or Bible. On the 27th of June 1709, the Council of the Protestant Consistory in the Palatinate issued a statement *denying the pretenses of the emigrants that they were persecuted*.

The Evangelical Lutheran Congregation in Pennsylvania made this statement, "*Some may think that it is unreasonable to care for these people, as the most of them went into this distant part of the globe from their own irregular impulse, and without necessity or calling, because it no longer suited them to comply with good order in their native lands.*"

A dispatch from The Netherlands in June, 1709, reported that the Palatines, Protestants and Catholics, "*seem to agree all very well, being several of them mixed together husbands and wives of different religion or united by parentage.*"

MAP OF RHINELAND, Germany, showing the sources of the Palatine emigration.

Religious persecution was not an important cause for the 1708-9 Palatine emigrations, but religious disputes and squabbles may have contributed in a minor way. It suited the Palatines to have the world think they were persecuted religiously. Due to the special conditions existing along the Rhine and in England, it was to their advantage to pose as *"poor German Protestants"* persecuted for their faith.

To devastation by war, oppression by petty princes imitating the life style of the French Court, the destructive winter of 1708-9, and religious bickering, maybe added another reason, a desire for adventure so common in the youth of any time. What about the adults in the groups? One stronger motivation for the adults was present, the thing that was always of utmost importance to the Palatines, LAND, LAND, lots of LAND. There was so little land available in Europe and almost none of it was for sale, but in America there were vast lands available, all ripe for the taking. A number of Palatines in New York were overheard to remark, *"We came to America to establish our families--to secure lands for our children on which they will be able to support themselves after we die."* Here now, is the real reason whey so many Palatines left their homes to come across the ocean to a new life. They called it Carolina. This word represented their hopes and dreams. It was a skillful marketing tool.

In a time without good communications, how did the people hear about the Promised Land over in America? To those Germans dissatisfied with their lot, came the answer to their prayers in the form of advertising. English proprietors for the colonies in America were advertising for people to come and settle their land. Pamphlets about the climate and life in the New World were distributed throughout the Palatinate. Agents for the proprietors entered into negotiations with interested parties. All these activities centered on a place they called Carolina or another place called Pennsylvania. New York was not promoted as a place to settle for the people who lived in the Rhine Valley.

A British parliamentary committee investigating the causes of the immigration reported: *"And upon the examination of several of them [the Palatines] what were the motives which induced them to leave their native country, it appears to the committee that there were books and papers dispersed in the Palatinate with the Queen's picture and the title pages in letters of gold to encourage them to come to England in order to be sent to Carolina or another of her Majesty's Plantations to be settled there."*

So there you have a variety of reasons for the emigration: war, oppression, religious freedom, lots of land in American and good advertising. The people were hungry for more information about America, about the Promised Land. The stage was set for a book published by Reverend Joshua Kocherthal who was described as a German evangelical minister, who had not been to America at the time he published his book, but he had been in England to make inquiries about the colonies. No definite promises are made in his book but several passages, coupled with the Queen's picture and the beautiful gold letters on the title page, gave the impression to the poor, mostly illiterate people that they might expect help from her, both in crossing the channel to England and after their arrival in England, in going to the colonies. One passage read, *"Whereupon finally the proposal was made that the queen be presented with a supplication to whether she herself would not grant the ships."* Pipe dreams were what the books were promoting and the people were ready to accept those dreams; they had a miserable life and longed for a better one.

Similar advertising concerning Pennsylvania was also producing its air castles for disgruntled Germanic people. William Penn, who later founded Pennsylvania, made several visits to the Rhine country where he discussed religious matters with many Lutherans and Calvinists of the Rhine Valley. The royal charter for Pennsylvania had been granted in 1681.

Penn offered to sell one hundred acres of land for two English pounds and a low rental. He advertised popular government, universal suffrage, and equal rights to all regardless of race or religious belief. Murder and treason were the only capital crimes; and reformation, not retaliation, was the object of punishment for their offenses. The fate of a person did not depend on a person of wealth or title, it truly sounded like an opportunity for a better life. This book appeared in translation in Amsterdam and its distribution in the upper Rhine country probably influenced the movement of Germans to Pennsylvania. English agents were sent throughout the Palatinate to promote immigration. The word Carolina was heard on many lips, the word was a representation of a dream for the poor, oppressed people. It sounded like an answer to many a prayer.

The decision to leave the homeland could not have been without some heart wrenching moments; the people were leaving their homeland, family, culture, social mores, language, and all that was familiar to go across an ocean to a new land. They must have been desperate for a new life, for the hope of a new existence.

This was a good time to approach Queen Anne about Protestant appeals because her consort/husband, Prince George of Denmark, died on October 28, 1708. Prince George was of

Germanic stock, a Lutheran, and had brought many of his countrymen and co-religionists to London. The funeral sermon that the Reverend John Tribbeko preached in the Royal Chapel on November 21st emphasized the Prince's interest in the Protestant cause. It probably softened the Queen's grief to help those of similar background and faith as her husband.

The first wave of the emigration was already well on its way down the Rhine. British authorities do not seem to have prepared for such a large immigration, or for a small immigration. They were caught by surprise. There appeared to be no advance planning and the authorities had no idea what to do if the appeal for immigrants succeeded. Considerable sums of money had to be spent to assist Protestant refugees in making their way to England and the English colonies. Still another reason was added to cause the tide of emigration, the tacit cooperation of the British Government.

The reasons for the large German emigration of the second decade of the eighteenth century was due to the following:
  (1) war devastation,
  (2) heavy taxation,
  (3) an extraordinarily severe winter,
  (4) religious quarrels, but not persecutions,
  (5) land hunger on the part of the elderly and desire for adventure on the part of the young,
  (6) liberal advertising by colonial proprietors, and finally
  (7) the benevolence and cooperation of the British government.

The stage was set; there was nothing to lose by seeking a new life in America and everything to gain. The idea spoke to the heart of an oppressed people; the Promised Land was just ahead, in their minds all they had to do was get to England.

The terrible winter of 1708-09 was barely over before people of the Rhine Valley for one reason or the other, with hope in their hearts, began preparations to go to England. These preparations were simple and consisted mainly of gathering up their few possessions and getting a recommendation that the person was of good character from the local authorities. Little did they know there would be severe hardships ahead for them and many of them would die along the way.

One of these documents has survived during these two centuries. Gerhart Schaeffer, preparing to emigrate in 1709, secured the following certificate of good character from the Mayor and the clerk of court of Hilgert Dorf, in Hesse-Nassau: *"He has lived with us in Hilgert Dorf with his housewife for 24 years and has conducted himself well and honestly, so that all his neighbors regarded him as a faithful neighbor and were entirely satisfied with him, and the neighbors would have been much pleased if it had been God's will that he should remain longer here."* It was signed by the Mayor, duly sealed and witnessed.

Passage down the Rhine to The Netherlands was not a short trip but took from four to six weeks. This journey was laden with many delays and inconveniences. Fees and tolls were frequently demanded. Along the Rhine River the Palatines were presented with money and food by pious countrymen, many of them considered the pilgrims with envious eyes, wishing they too were going to the land called America. Bread, meat, butter and cheese and even an occasional gift of clothing brightened the slow journey. Ever present was the fear that the authorities would stop them temporarily, as often occurred or worse yet, turn them back.

While the pioneer groups were preparing for the trip along the Rhine and its tributaries, individuals approached the British authorities in their behalf late in December 1708. The Netherlands certainly did not want the financial burden of taking care of the Palatines, and were eager to assist them on their way to England.

To refer to the country as Holland is to refer to a single province of Holland. The country properly is called The Kingdom of The Netherlands and the people are simply called the Dutch. For simplification, the country will be referred to as The Netherlands in this story.

Late in April four ships carried 852 Palatines to London, their food on the voyage was supplied by a private charity in the Low Countries. In fact, many contributions had to be made to keep the refugees alive. The Palatines were unprepared for a long delay in The Netherlands, they thought they would be promptly sent to England and then just as promptly shipped to their new home somewhere in America. Even if they had been aware of the length of the journey, they didn't have the resources to prepare to live such a long time without earning money.

Each name was carefully written down on a ship's log, the spelling of the name depended on how the name sounded to the writer and how well he could spell. In the process, the German spelling for the names was changed to the Dutch spelling. Many of the Palatines were illiterate and could not correct the spelling of their names. Then when they left from England, the spelling was again changed on the ships' logs and this is why so many of the names are not spelled as they were in their native land and why their descendants can't find their family name.

When the second convoy arrived to pick up some of the Palatines on May 10th, it was learned that only one ship had been ordered to receive Palatines. This presented a monumental problem since a thousand or more people were waiting for a ship to take them to England.

The Palatines continued to arrive in Rotterdam in increasing numbers. Early in June, the new arrivals numbered about a thousand a week. This rate of arrivals was maintained until late in July, when strenuous efforts to curtail the emigration were beginning to take effect. Most of the Palatines were poor and they were camped in shacks covered with reeds outside Rotterdam in miserable, unhealthy conditions.

In the meantime the shipping of the Palatines to England was being pushed ahead with all possible speed. By June 8th, the Commissioners, van Toren and van Gent in Rotterdam had shipped over 6,000 Palatines to England at the expense of the British government. Alarm at the exorbitant cost was sounded in England. The warnings to the Dutch authorities seem to have had little effect because the immigration was not stopped. The warnings became louder and louder. There seemed to be no way to stop the tide of people.

England requested the Dutch not allow any more Palatines to be transported, they replied that they could not prevent those already in The Netherlands from crossing to England, but that they would order their ministers at Cologne and Frankfort to warn the people not to come for that purpose.

The Netherlands was concerned about being saddled with the care of the stranded emigrants. The problem was not of their doing, and they did not want to have the expense and care of all the people now sitting on their shores. They were simply a way station for the Palatines.

The British government felt they had to be firm about not letting any more Palatines come into their country because if they waffled on their decision, there would be no end to the immigration. A Royal Proclamation was drawn up, printed in German and distributed widely in the Rhine Valley. It declared that no more people would be received in England, much less supported. All those Germans, who arrived since the first of October were sent back to Germany. All who intended to emigrate were warned that such attempts would surely fail, unless they had means of their own for support while on the way and fare for the voyages.

Here are the numbers for the Palatine immigration of 1709 to England:

852 sailed late in April and arrived early in May.
1,283 sailed May 12th and arrived about May 19th
2,926 sailed May 31st and arrived June 6th
1,794 sailed June 10th and arrived June 16th
2,776 sailed July 4th and arrived July 11th
1,433 sailed July 17th and arrived July 24th
1,000 sailed August 6th and arrived August 13th
1,082 sailed October 11th and arrived October 18th

This adds up to 13,146 who are mentioned in the official correspondence. 2,257 Roman Catholics were sent back late in September. Late in March of 1711, 618 Palatines, all Roman Catholics, were returned to The Netherlands. More than 3,000 Roman Catholics were sent back in all. With more than 3,500 returned, there were about 10,000 Palatines remaining, quite a problem for the government to deal with. What did the British authorities do with them? This presented an overwhelming problem for both countries to deal with and a huge financial burden.

In London, the local citizens were amazed at the constant arrival of the Palatines. In three months more than 11,000 people had landed on their shores and were camped in one way or another. London was not that large of a city that thousands could be suddenly plunked into it without discomfort to the natives. The squares, the taverns, all the spare and open places of London were crowded with Palatines. In addition, the Board of Ordnance issued 1,600 tents and encampments were formed on any open square in London. The crowded condition of these places of shelter made them unhealthy and miserable with absolutely no privacy and no provisions for sanitation. The Board of Trade was informed of this and tried to remedy the problem. Doctors were sent among the Palatines and efforts were made to lessen their discomfort. A huge problem was in the making, a recipe for disaster and widespread disease. The authorities realized this but didn't know what to do about the problem of the Palatines.

The Palatines expected that immediately after arriving in England they would be welcomed and then put on a ship to America, but this didn't happen. It wasn't planned when they left home that they would have to fend for themselves for any period of time and their meager resources were depleted before they even reached England. The Palatines were almost entirely dependent upon the government handouts to keep them from starvation. By June 14th, the subsistence of the Palatines was costing the government 80 pounds a day and the cost was going up daily as more of them landed on the shores of England.

Shortly after June 1st, the ministry hit upon the idea of raising money by public appeals. Letters were sent to the leading financial organizations, requesting voluntary contributions. A proclamation for the collection of alms and a board of commissioners was appointed to handle the funds and *"to perform every matter and thing . . . necessary and convenient for the better Employment and Settlement of the said poor Palatines."* The commissioners named were nearly a hundred in number and included the great dignitaries of the kingdom."' The collection was carried out largely through the organization of the churches.

To the London population, the Palatines and their camps were a novelty and something they all had to see. Every Sunday crowds would gather and the Palatines became the focus of curiosity seekers. The Palatines capitalized on this by making toys of small value and selling them to the crowds of people who came to gape at them. One account of the Palatines states, *"They are contented with very ordinary food, their bread being brown and their meat of the coarsest and cheapest sort, which, with a few herbs, they eat with much cheerfulness and thankfulness. On the whole, they appear to be an innocent, laborious, peaceable, healthy and ingenuous people, and may be rather reckoned a blessing than a burden to any nation where they shall be settled."*

The conditions among the Palatines were very bad and worsening daily. The government allowance was insufficient to sustain them properly. They resorted to begging on the streets of London; the married women did most of the begging.

←-Contemporary Woodcut, showing the Palatines encamped on Blackheath outside London. Courtesy of the Widener Library, Harvard University.

The novelty of the Palatines soon wore off for the people of London and a change of attitude set in, due to the tight economic conditions in England. The poorer classes of the English people began whispering the Palatines came to eat the bread of Englishmen, reduce the scale of wages, and take the few jobs that were available for them. Soon the people began to say openly that they were taking money and jobs away from the Englishmen; the whispers became a loud rumble. The Palatine encampments were occasionally attacked by London mobs. On one occasion about 2,000 frustrated Englishmen, armed with axes, scythes, and smith hammers, were said to have made an attack upon the Palatine camp and struck down all who did not flee before them.

Meanwhile the Palatines had little employment, and still the pressing problem was what to do with them; where to relocate them, how to transport them, house them, and feed them.

Over half of the Palatines were farmers and vinedressers, the rest were distributed in some 35 other trades. The next highest number of occupations represented were carpenters and about 75 textile workers. The lists included about 12 schoolmasters and three surgeons (doctors).

One of the schemes brought up was to settle 10,000 Palatines on the Rio de la Plata, in South America. A regiment would have been necessary to protect them and the calculated expense of over 200,000 pounds was prohibitive to relocate them. Another project called for a settlement in the Canary Islands.

It seemed everyone had a plan for the Palatines. Here are just a few of the proposals that were offered. The Board of Trade received a proposal from the Society of London for Royal Mines to employ the strongest of the Palatines in the silver and copper mines of Penlyn and Merionethshire, Wales.

The merchants of Bedford and Barnstable, concerned in the Newfoundland fishery, offered to employ 500 Palatines in their industry.

A project for settling some of them in Herefordshire and Gloucestershire, proposed by the Marquis of Kent, Lord Chamberlain, was also considered by the Board of Trade. The last project, it was found, would cost 150,000 pounds, if all were settled at the proposed rate; so it was abandoned.

An attempt was made to settle the Palatines throughout England by offering three pounds per head to the parishes, which would be willing to receive them, the government to pay the expense of sending them to the respective places. The bounty was taken in some instances and the immigrants, finding themselves uncared for, returned to London again.

Some of their experiences were interesting. One Palatine, who had been a hunter, was to his great disgust, required to take care of swine. Sixteen families were sent to the town of Sunderland, near Newcastle in Yorkshire. They expected grants of land, but were made day laborers.

Many of the Palatines, too poor to return or for other reasons, probably stayed where they were settled in spite of the conditions they found themselves in. The plan to locate the Palatines in England was given an honest attempt, but England was at a loss to place so many new people. The value of such sturdy workers did not pass unnoticed, and England tried everything to make use of these people. Many of the Palatines settled in Ireland, Pennsylvania and some in North Carolina.

322 entered the military service and 141 children were "purchased by the English," which means most probably that they were apprenticed perhaps for a price. At least 56 of the young people became domestic servants.

The Catholic Palatines in London and in Rotterdam who were waiting for transportation, were given their choice of becoming *"poor Protestants"* to be saved by the Queen, or of returning to their homes along the Rhine. Many of the Germans were devout people, yet some found it convenient to change their religion rather than be shipped back to the Palatinate.

In crowded quarters and with meager food supplies, the Palatines were sick from fevers and plagues. Death visited often in spite of their hardiness. It is not known how many died in their encampment at Blackheath and elsewhere in London, but the number has been estimated at nearly a thousand.

William Penn's advertising campaign was finally reaping the desired benefits, but where was Penn's proposal to take the Palatines off the hands of the government? Why didn't Penn carry out his promises? At this time, poor Mr. Penn was in no financial position to send the Palatines to his colony in 1709 or for that matter to anywhere else. He had suffered a nine months' imprisonment in 1708 for a 10,500 pound debt dishonestly claimed by former friends. When he was finally released from his debt, his expenses were heavy and his province was under mortgage to friends, who had assisted him.

The British government did not plan for this Palatine immigration in 1709. It prayed for some immigration as a general vague sort of blessing, but this avalanche of people was like a torrential overwhelming flood instead of a gentle blessing of rain.

About 1702, England began to have serious trouble with a foreign monopoly. This monopoly, established by the crown of Sweden, controlled the supply of naval stores, tar and pitch. Naval stores included ship's masts, and ship timber of all kinds as well as tar, pitch, rosin and hemp.

England was on her way to being the ruler of the seas, and she was in need of a reliable supply of naval stores. Sweden realized the opportunity to make a profit since she had an almost exclusive corner on the market and consequently, Swedish tar rose to profiteering prices. Agreement with Sweden was impossible, there was to be no compromise. The British envoy at Stockholm, in 1703, suggested the development of the resources of the colonies, even though it might cost a third more to bring supplies across the ocean. Here was a possible way to make use of the Palatines!

The Treasury Board and others began to seek comparisons between the cost of the continental supply and the probable cost of producing naval stores in the colonies. Colonel Benjamin Fletcher, Governor of New York, reported in August 1693, that tar was produced there for 12 pounds per 12 barrels. The Navy Board considered that too high, since they usually contracted for it at the rate of 11 pounds, 12 shillings and 6 pence. They admitted later that due to the *"loss of three of the Years Tarr Ships and the scarcity of it in Towne,"* they had to pay 13 pounds. A report in the Naval Office for January 30, 1694, showed that in 1693, pitch was 50%, tar 100%, and hemp about 30% higher than before the war (1689).

In that year, the Navy Board sent John Bridger and two others (William Partridge and Benjamin Jackson) to explore the possibility of producing ship timber and to instruct the American colonists in the making of tar and pitch. But the commissioners were not very well qualified themselves.

The commissioners inspected the woods of New England and experimented with the Finnish method of making tar. Bridger was hopeful that he could supply the demands of England for these commodities from the colonies, but his colleague, William Partridge, reminded Bridger about the lack of available labor in America and the fact the area was undeveloped without roads and the difficulty of bringing the tar out of the forests.

The samples of tar and pitch sent to England by the commissioners were pronounced inferior, but the Governor of New York, and the Board of Trade thought that the dockyard officials were prejudiced against products from the colonies. Late in 1702 another quantity of hemp and tar was sent to England that had been produced in New England with proper instruction and these were found acceptable for use.

In 1705 Bridger was appointed Surveyor of Woods in the colonies. His commission stated that, *"we are desirous that our Dominions be furnished with pitch, tar and hemp and other naval stores from the Plantations, and applications [have] been made to us by divers merchants and traders to the Plantations that a person expert in the producing and fabricating such stores should be sent to those parts. . . . ."*

Bridger wrote on March 9, 1708, *"I, last summer got the government to print directions and have been in most parts that make tarr in this Province, and have instructed and encouraged them to making of Tarr . . . But they want an example, saying let us see you do what you have directed, and if we see that answers, then we will proceed."*

On the 13th Bridger wrote, *"New York I know and upon Hudson River there is pitch pine enough to supply England with tar."*

On July 6th Bridger was *"well assured that at New Yorke there would be great quantitys of tar made there, if I was there to instruct them."*

In 1708, 55 Palatines, led by Reverend Kocherthal, were sent to New York to manufacture naval stores and to expand and to protect the frontier. The venture was not well thought out, neither preparations nor plans for the manufacture of naval stores were made for this group. They first settled at Newburgh on the Hudson River.

Then the next shiploads of Palatines, about 3,000 were to be sent to New York. Commissioners for managing the affairs of the Palatines November 4th notified the Commissioners of Transport to prepare two men-of-war ships for 3,000 Palatines to be sent to New York. The warships were to be ready by December 15th and orders were issued to Sir John Norris in command of the convoy to *"take care of the ships with the Palatines as far as his and their way shall be together."* Instead of going to Pennsylvania or Carolina as they expected, the Palatines were sent to New York. This particular wave of Palatines suffered severely with the conditions on ship and afterwards and many died. Many of the ships' lists are included in this book.

Four persons sufficiently instructed in the methods of making naval stores were to be sent along to teach the trade and supervise the work. Commissaries, clerks of stores, and other officers with sufficient funds would be needed. A number of cauldrons and other tar-making necessaries would have to be supplied in England.

Since some time would elapse before the Palatines could build huts for themselves, it was suggested that at least 600 tents be sent for temporary shelter. Since the people were *"to be planted on the Frontiers it will be absolutely necessary they be armed with 600 Firelocks & Bayonetts at least, from Her Majesty's Stores here, and a proportional quantity of powder and shott...."* A quantity of hemp seed was also to be taken along to provide immediate work by sowing it.

Newly appointed Governor Robert Hunter appeared before the Board with several problems on the proposed settlement, which he felt, should be resolved before he set sail with the Palatines

(1) On what lands were the Palatines to be planted?

(2) In what manner were the lands to be granted to them, and in what proportions and under what reservations?

(3) Would it not be advisable that the Palatines *"be servants to the Crown for a certain Term, or at least 'till they have repaid the Expenses the Crown is it in setting them to work, and subsisting them?"*

The governor estimated that twelve iron kettles twelve ladles and tunnels to each kettle, would be sufficient for the tar-making. As for instructors in the trade, he remarked, *"There being no great mystery in these manufactures, I believe Mr. Bridger with such as he can bring along with him, I ordered will be sufficient to instruct them."*

No great mystery indeed! This error in judgment presented a huge problem with disastrous consequences for both the governor and the Palatines!

The plan adopted was that the government was to transport and settle the Palatines in New York at its own expense. The Palatines were to make naval stores for the government in return for the money spent in their behalf. This sounds simple enough but carefully laid plans often go awry especially when the "expert" does not know what he is speaking about, and these plans certainly developed problems. The planners did not have a grasp on the conditions in New York or the resources.

The Board gave no definite answers to the Governor Hunter's questions about the settlement of the Palatines. They thought that the Palatines might be planted in a body or in different settlements wherever the governor found it most proper. The governor was to grant without fee or reward forty acres per person to each family, after they had *"repaid by the produce of their labour"* the expenses of their settlement. Then the usual quit-rents were to start seven years after the said grants. The Board advised that the Palatines be *"Encouraged to settle and work in partnership, that is 5 or more families to unite and Work in Common."*

As far the questions as where to settle the Palatines, the Board of Trade suggested the large tracts of land recently returned to the Crown, being the *"extravagant grants"* vacated by an Order in Council on June 2-6, 1708. Governor Fletcher had granted these lands in the Mohawk and Hudson Valleys of New York ten years earlier, just before he had been replaced. The excessive grants of land were to a number of colonial gentlemen, including Nicholas Bayard, Godfrey Dellius, Captain Evans and Caleb Heathcote, whose brother was governor of the Bank of England.

Several of the Palatines petitioned the Society for the Propagation of the Gospel in Foreign Parts to retain John Frederick Haeger as a clergyman in this capacity. Reverend Haeger agreed to Anglican ordination by the Bishop of London, then he was appointed by the Society at an annual salary of fifty pounds, with fifteen pounds extra for books.

←Governor Robert Hunter.

Meanwhile, Mr. Henry Bendysh, who acted as secretary to the Commissioners for Collecting and Settling of the Palatines, made the arrangements for transportation to New York. He contracted to carry about 3,300 Palatines to New York at five pounds, ten shillings per head. This was a low rate, since transportation to Carolina was above ten pounds, and seven pounds was the going rate for passage to Pennsylvania or Carolina.

The captains and their owners agreed to have their ships ready to take the Palatines and their goods on board between the 25th and 29th of December. They agreed to be at the buoy of the Nore about fifty miles from London on or before the 2nd of January, wind and weather permitting.

The Palatines boarded their ships in December 1709, but did not start across the ocean until April 10, 1710. They were on board ship for six long months and the sufferings of the Palatines were terrible.

The people were closely packed in the ships. Many of them suffered from the foul odor and vermin; some below deck could neither get fresh air nor see the light of day. Under such conditions the younger children died in great numbers and were buried at sea.

The journey across the sea to America was not for the faint of heart nor the weak in body. The first ship to arrive was the *Lyon*, which touched New York on June 13, 1710, Governor Hunter's ship and several others followed the next day. One, the *Herbert*, was wrecked on the east end of Long Island on July 7th, and the last did not arrive until August 2nd. The poor people on board the latter were eight months making the passage to New York.

2,500 diseased and ill Palatines landing on their shore was a cause for panic for New York City. The Palatines were on Nutten Island, now known as Governor's Island. Three doctors were sent to get a report on the condition of their health.

In their tents on Governor's Island, the Palatines were in a miserable condition. Typhus was still ravaging them. Two doctors, John Christopher Kurtz and John Philips Ruger, were in constant attendance. Governor Hunter reported to London on July 24th that about 470 Palatines had died on the voyage and during the first month in New York. They were slow in recovering their health after their wretched passage from England, from effects of the typhus and from the miserable living conditions on Nutten Island. Little or poor food did not help their desperate circumstances either.

With the high death rate, many children became orphans, this was solved by apprenticing them. According to the records 74 children were apprenticed by Governor Hunter from 1710-1714. Hunter did not stop with just the orphans; he also apprenticed children whose parents were still living and separated some of the families. A number of children were taken from their parents by the governor and bound out to the inhabitants of the colony, and among these were two sons of John Conrad Weiser, who afterwards became a leader among the Schoharie settlers; and also John Peter Zenger, the son of a poor widow, who was bound to William Bradford, a printer in New York. Later, this was one of the biggest complaints of the injustices the Palatines had about the treatment by Governor Hunter. It was another bitter pill for the Palatines to have to swallow.

The other empty spot brought about because of the death rate was death of a spouse. It didn't take any of the people long to find a person from the opposite sex to marry. Survival for the most part depended on a husband and wife working together to support and raise a family. One spouse could not do the whole task alone.

Four tracts in New York, part of the returned *"extravagant grants"*, were considered as possibilities for settlement while the Palatines were still in England. One was on the Mohawk River above Little Falls, 50 miles long by 4 miles wide (around Herkimer and German Flats); another, between 24 and 30 miles in length on the Schoharie River; a third, on the east side of the Hudson River, 12 miles long by 70 miles wide. A fourth was also considered, on the west side of the Hudson, 20 miles by 40 miles long. The Board of Trade recommended the settlement of Kocherthal's party in New York in 1708 on one of these vacated grants.

The Indians gave the gift of the Schoharie lands at Fort Albany, August 22, 1710, to the Queen for Christian settlements, possibly for the Palatines. Hunter had no obligation to settle the Palatines there and he had no orders from the Queen to do so.

A tract of land of 6,300 acres on the west side of the Hudson River was in the possession of the Crown. It had been granted to Captain Evans by Governor Fletcher, and had been returned as one of the *"extravagant grants"*. This land was used for the settlement of the Palatines and the experiment in making naval supplies. In addition, Hunter on Bridger's recommendation entered into an agreement with Robert Livingston, Commissioner of Indian Affairs, for another tract on the east side of the Hudson River. On September 29th, 6,000 acres were purchased with the liberty of using the pitch pine on the neighboring tract on Livingston's land.

Where did Robert Livingston get 6,000 acres? His deed said he only owned 2,600 acres! On October 20, 1714, the Deputy Surveyor found that Livingston Manor contained 160,240 acres, for which Livingston paid annually 28 shillings current money quit-rent! It looks like the government had selective blindness for certain patents and certain privileged people.

Hunter also purchased a tract of neighboring land from Thomas Fullerton, who was in the Custom Service of Scotland for the use of the Palatines. He paid more for this tract of 800 acres, saying that Fullerton could expect no profit from the Palatines' presence as was the case with Livingston.

Early in October the land was surveyed and five towns were marked out, three on the east side of the river and two on the west side of the river. First the Palatines cleared the trees and built themselves huts, each built according to his own abilities and own ideas. Later, In June, 1711 there were seven villages inhabited as follows: (on the east side) Hunterstown, 105 families; Queensbury, 102 families; Annsbury, 76 families; Haysbury, 59 families; (on the west side) Elizabeth Town, 42 families; George Town, 40 families; and New Town, 103 families. The total number of Palatines on the Hudson was 1,874.

As the Palatines arrived in Livingston Manor, Robert Livingston provided food, tools, tent-poles and other necessities. The Palatines were allotted small plots of land to build their huts. The lots for houses and small gardens were about forty feet by fifty feet. The huts were made of rough logs, and the cracks were plastered with mud. The Palatines were not to receive the forty acres promised to each of them, until they had fulfilled their contracts. They misunderstood and thought they would be granted the 40 acres immediately.

The agreement read to the Palatines about the arrangements is included later in this book on page 59.

In 1711 things necessary for the settlement of the Palatines were still wanting in so many areas. Among the items listed as needed immediately were steel for mending edged tools, three sets of smithy tools, three pairs of millstones, sixteen whipsaws, warehouses, and a church on each side of the river. Other essentials needed were plowshares, pitch and dung forks, and iron for horseshoes, nails, and harnesses for horses.

The Palatines were required to use the food provided for them, they received substandard food, and the meat for instance, was heavily salted and full of maggots. In addition, it galled them that they could not even bake their own bread but had to use stale bread provided.

In a letter written in March, 1711, by a member of the British government to one of his colleagues, the writer says: "I think it unhappy that Col. Hunter at his first arrival in his government fell into ill hands, for this Livingston has been known many years in that province for a very ill man, he formerly victualled the forces at Albany, in which he was guilty of most notorious frauds by which he greatly improved his estate; he has a mill and a brew-house upon his land, and if he can get the victualling of those Palatines who are conveniently posted for his purpose, he will make a very good addition to his estate, and I am persuaded the hopes he has of such a subsistance to be allowed, were the chief, if not the only inducements that prevailed with him to propose to Colo. Hunter to settle them upon his land."

Governor Hunter was no doubt the willing dupe of Livingston, and his imbecility had come to the knowledge of his superiors. His bills were protested and the adjustment of his accounts suspended for further examination and vouchers.

In May of 1711 a rebellion of some 300 or 400 Palatines gave excuse for a strong military rule and gave Governor Hunter the reason to impose his will on the Palatines. Some Palatines did not intend to remain on Livingston Manor and started to make it known they were leaving. Hunter met them and tried to reason with them, but they stubbornly demanded that they should receive "the lands appointed them by the Queen" in the Schoharie Valley.

Some of the Palatines, more violent, cried that "they would rather lose their lives immediately than remain where they were. To be forced by another, contract to remain no these lands all their lives, and work for her Majesty for the ships use, that they will never doe." **The Palatines charged that they were cheated by the contract. They did not believe that it was the same contract that was read to them in their own language in England.** They said that it had provided, that seven years after they had forty acres per person given them they were to repay the Queen with hemp, masts, tar, and pitch, not the other way around.

Hunter put them off until he could get a military detachment of 70 men from Albany, then he disarmed the Palatines in each village. He was slow in forgiving the affront. They were to be treated "as the Queen's hired Servants", which they were. Determined to prevent the recurrence of such disorders in the future, Hunter established a court over the Palatines and closer control over them.

Hunter cooked up a scheme with the threat of punishment as the incentive to keep the people at work. What a scheme it was, the plan was to keep the Palatines in debt to the government forever. We would say today that they belonged to the company store. The Palatines ended up paying the salaries of Livingston, and Sackett, a farmer who came to direct the tar work. Plus the subsistence accounts were kept in a "ledger", and the accounts were not accurate. Hunter himself admitted that all other miscellaneous expenses, besides the salaries of the officers, came out of the Palatines' meager subsistence allowances. Saddest of all, not all the sustenance the Palatines were charged for was received by them. They were cheated all the way around in every way possible. They didn't totally understand how it happened but they knew they were being cheated, and cheated badly. There seemed to be no way out, and they were unhappy.

In the first year in New York, Governor Hunter had spent 21,700 pounds sterling on the Palatines. Of this sum, Hunter said 19,200 pounds went for subsistence at the rate of 1,600 per month.

The tar instructor, Bridger received Hunter's permission to return to New England until spring, when he would be needed again for the tar preparation. Apparently he had no intention of returning to New York because in the spring of 1711, he refused to return to New York.

Why did Bridger leave Hunter and his project and refuse to return from New England to instruct the Palatines? Bridger wrote, *"I have apply'd to Col. Hunter, who refuses me travailing charges."* This he followed with other insinuations in 1711. He seemed to have been bitten with an ambition of his own: He made a proposal to manufacture naval stores in New England with soldier labor, providing he was made Lieutenant-Governor of New Hampshire. He certainly had ambitions of his own and a good plan for taking care of his comfortable retirement.

The manufacturing of tar in 1711 was held up by the second Canadian Expedition (1711). Preparations for the expedition took a great deal of Hunter's time and effort as well and 300 of the most able-bodied Palatines volunteered and went to fight in the Canadian Expedition. The Palatines readily accompanied Col. Nicholson in the expedition into Canada, and among these volunteers were: Henry Hoffman, Warner Dirchest, Fred. Bellinger, Hen. Wederwachs (Weatherwax), Frantz Finck, Martin Dillenback, Jacob Webber, William Nellis, George Dachstader (Dockstader), Christian Baucb, Mich. Ittick (Edick), Melch. Folts, Niclaus Loux, Hartman Windecker, Hans Hen. Zeller, Jno. Wm. Finck, Jno. Hen. Arendorff, Johan Schneider, Henry Feling (Failing), Job. Jost Petry and Lud. W. Schmit (Smith). They wanted to make the new country safe for their families. Of course, the tar business on the Hudson River suffered.

Hunter hired a new man to direct the tar business, Richard Sackett. Mr. Sackett was a local farmer who claimed to have lived three years in the *"Eastern countries"* among the manufacturers of tar. Hunter reported that he gave a very convincing account of the method of preparing the trees. Mr. Sackett took charge at once and the activity was stepped up. About 100,000 trees were barked, a special preparation necessary before the tar burning could take place. Carpenters were put to work building storehouses and barrels under a plan whereby they received two shillings a day, half in cash from Livingston, and the other half in credit on their accounts.

In plain sight while the Palatines worked, a detachment of soldiers stood by to enforce the decrees of the commissioners on Governor Hunter's orders and of course that did not create better feeling on the part of the Palatines towards their slave masters. The quality of food they were given was inferior, too little and distasteful. They were husbandmen and vine-dressers, not tar makers and they deeply resented their work and having to live on small plots of land they did not own. They disliked work in gangs and under rigid supervision. No matter how hard they worked, there was no incentive to work hard to pay back the funds spent on them; they wanted to receive the forty acres for their settlement right away. Instead of getting ahead, they went further into debt for their hard labor. They complained loudly that they came to America "*to secure lands for our children on which they will be able to support themselves after we die, and that we cannot do here.*" The Palatines worked, but with distaste and a churlish attitude. They did not come to America to be slaves but it sure looked like they were slaves.

The tar production reports were promising. On June 6, 1711, Hunter wrote from Albany, *"Our Tarr work goes on as we could wish God continue it. . . . We shall be at a losse for Casks in a little while for we go to work with the Knots. I have however sett all hands to work. . . ."* *"That no hands may be idle we employed the boys and girls in gathering knotts whilst their fathers were a barking, out of which hee [Sackett] had made about three score barrells of good tarr, and hath kills ready to sett on fire for about as much more soe soone as he getts casks ready to receive it."*

The appointment of Sackett as tar instructor caused concern in England, and the Board of Trade asked about his method of making naval stores, mostly tar. The Board decided to ask the British representative in Russia as to the method of making tar there. The representative, Mr. C. Whiteworth, described the *"Method of Preparing Tar in Muscovy."*

"The fir trees were barked in the month of October (not in the spring) from the bottom eight feet high, except for a strip three or four fingers broad, which was left up north side. In this condition the trees were to stand at least for a year, and better still, for two or three years. The turpentine settled in the barked parts during this period."

"When ready for use, the tree was cut down, the part which was barked was cut off, carried to the place where it was to be heated, and split full lengths into billets about the thickness of an arm. Then the billets were laid in piles six feet high, the slow heating or sweating was done in a kiln much like the process of making charcoal, except that more care had to be taken to prevent leakage. A trench had to be provided to drain the tar from the kiln."

The Board noticed that the Muscovy method was quite different from that of Mr. Sackett, and they forwarded the description of the process to Hunter with that concern.

Sackett used a different method to prepare the trees, he barked the north quarter of the tree's circumference about two feet in the spring; in the fall, the south quarter about two feet, four inches; the second spring, the east quarter about two feet, eight inches; and the second fall, the remaining quarter, approximately three feet. The cutting down of the trees, the splitting and the sweating process were the same as in the Muscovy method.

But Sackett's method brought poor results. Not more than 200 barrels of tar, if that, were produced from all the trees prepared, about 100,000. It would appear that Sackett had not barked the trees properly when the sap was flowing toward the roots and probably the inner bark had not been removed or not removed correctly. The results were disappointing.

Hunter was *"at a loss for the true cause of the disappointment from the trees prepared for tar, knowing nothing of the art. . . what I chiefly guess to be the cause of the miscarriage is this, that the trees being barked by an unruly multitude were for the most part pierced in the inward rind contrary to strict directions by which means they become exhausted by the sun's heat in the succeeding summer during which they stood, after the time appointed and proper for felling of them, many of them are good but not in the quantity that will answer the expence and labour. . ."*

It was suggested that the failure occurred because the pine trees of the Hudson could not produce tar and pitch in profitable quantities. When Bridger was asked about this accusation, he wrote to the Board of Trade and Secretary of State in London that he had *"view'd several great tracts of pitch pine proper for making tar and pitch,"* and he had selected the Livingston Manor site.

Was Bridger trustworthy in choosing the tract on Livingston Manor?

Did he deliberately establish the government industry in country barren of the pitch pine and ensure its failure?

In March, 1927 the State Botanist H. D. House wrote that, *"the pitch pine (pinus rigida) undoubtedly formed at that time a major portion of the forest upon the sandy and gravelly areas, and in general upon the areas of poor, sterile, or rocky soil throughout the Hudson Valley and north to Lake George. It is still one of the commonest and most conspicuous trees on this type of soil throughout the region, withstanding better than white pine, ground fires, etc."*

While the tar manufacture still promised so much another problem was becoming apparent to Governor Hunter. By March 1, 1712, Hunter was becoming very nervous with a problem that was growing more difficult every day. Hunter's bills of exchange continued to return to him with legal protests and no payment. The bills were simply not being paid for political reasons.

The governor continued to provide subsistence for the Palatines until September 12, 1712. A few widows and orphans were taken care of until the 23rd. The total expenditure was 32,144 pounds, 17 shillings and 2 pence sterling. Of this sum, he received 11,375 pounds: 10,000 pounds, the parliamentary appropriation made in 1709 for the encouragement of the production of colonial naval stores, intended for the payment of the bounty on tar and pitch; and 1,375 pounds, secured by the sale in 1715 of various supplies left from the unsuccessful venture. From the Palatine accounts there was due to the governor about 20,769 pounds sterling, a huge sum of money.

By 1715 Hunter's finances were in very bad shape, his credit was exhausted because of the debt he had made with the Palatine subsistence, and he had not received his salary as governor, which was then five years in arrears.

The colonial naval stores industry was developed very successfully, especially in the Carolinas. In 1718 the Carolina plantations sent England 82,084 barrels, which were seven times the amount secured from the European continent.

Why did the New York opportunity fail? The New York settlement failed because of:
(1) The lack of continued financial support by the English government.
(2) Because of an unwilling labor supply under frontier conditions
(3) And perhaps, because of poor management and incapable instruction in the methods of manufacturing naval stores.

Hunter could not believe that the project would be allowed to fail for lack of financial support from England. The Palatines, who had never received the full subsistence for which they were charged, petitioned the governor for more supplies.

Eight days later the blow fell. The pine trees received their last preparation, staves were prepared for barrels, the magazine was almost finished, and a road was nearly completed to the pine forest. The project was stopped dead in its tracks.

September 6, 1712, Hunter gave orders that the Palatines would have to fend for themselves until he gave further orders because his credit was exhausted. The Palatines were to hire themselves out if they could. They could go anywhere in New York or New Jersey, which were both under the jurisdiction of Hunter, but they had to get a ticket of leave and register their destination with the governor so he would know where they were. Hunter hoped in the future to resume production and wanted to keep the Palatines ready for future work.

The Palatines were taken by surprise and worried as to their ability to survive the winter and rightly so. It was to be the worst winter the Palatines ever faced.

Many of the Palatines scattered about the area seeking employment to provide themselves and their families with food during winter. Some remained in the settlements where they had been placed by Hunter, hoping for the best. During that winter without government aid their suffering was particularly hard. Their minister, the Reverend Haeger wrote to the Society for the Propagation of the Gospel on July 6, 1713 that *"they boil grass and the children eat the leaves of the trees. I have seen old men and women cry that it should almost have moved a stone. [Several] have for a whole week together had nothing but Welsh turnips which they did only scrape and eat without an salt or fat and bread."*

In the next five years many of the Palatines moved away from the camps. Several went to Pennsylvania, others to New Jersey, settling at Hackensack, still others pushed a few miles south to Rhinebeck, New York, and some returned to New York City, while quite a few remained on Livingston Manor itself. The last group had to accept Robert Livingston's terms and they were soon more heavily in his debt.

Some of the Palatines thought of the Schoharie lands the Indians gave when they were thrown on their own resources. On October 31, 1712, Hunter wrote to the Board of Trade relating that *"some hundreds of them took a resolution of possessing the land of Schoharee and are accordingly march'd thither have[ing] been busy in cutting a road from Schenectady to that place. . . .*

The Indians were easily persuaded to sell the land in the Schoharie Valley to the Palatines. In fact, they parted with their claims to the same lands three times, once when Nicholas Bayard purchased it about 1695, again when they gave the valley as a gift to Governor Hunter for the government, and then to the deputies for the Palatines.

The lands in the Schoharie came back to trouble the Palatines and once more force them to move.

The land title difficulties, which the Germans encountered, were partly due to the sporatic working memory of the Indians, who would sell their claims as often as they could get an offer. They really did not understand the white man's ownership of the land and why he wanted absolute control over it. The Indians all used the land, and they thought the white man strange to fence it in and put buildings on the land. The Indians simply moved to a place and when the trees were used for fires and the land was tired with little game to hunt, they moved on.

The path to secure title to land was well established by that time. There were many hands to grease along the way before one could get a secure title to land. First, one had to apply to the Governor in Council for a license to purchase a tract of a certain number of acres in a particular locality from the Indians. There were many fees involved with the process. Fees of 20 shillings to the Governor, 6 shillings to the Clerk of the Council, in addition to 1 shilling, 6 pence for reading the petition in Council and 6 pence for filing it (all in colonial currency) were necessary. Then the purchaser made his deal with the Indians for a deed in English, always with the aid of "fire-water." After securing the Indian deed, the prospective patentee applied to the Governor and Council for a survey of the grant, and received a warrant of survey for a fee of 6 shillings.

In the period of the early eighteenth century, these surveys were quite carelessly made and the land taken was usually many times larger than specified. One particular grant along the Mohawk River was said to have been done by moonlight from a canoe, but then, no one really kept track of such things. There was so much land, one hardly knew where to start. This is why the Palatines could not understand the governor's stingy use of the land and why with so much available, they could not have some.

When all the proper procedures were completed, then a patent was granted by the Governor and Council for the following fees in colonial currency:

(1) Clerk of Council, 3 shillings for drawing up a warrant or order for the patent;

(2) Attorney-General, 10 shillings for drafting the patent;

(4) Secretary of the Province,

(5) 30 shillings more or less for engrossing, sealing and recording;

(6) and the Governor, various amounts depending upon the size of the grant.

The Palatines were ignorant of this procedure and because they were, trouble with the patent was bound to happen in the future. Worse yet, it was necessary to have the Governor's blessing success in securing title to the land, and this they did not have and would never have. Hunter was greatly opposed to their moving to Schoharie.

When the Palatine representatives returned from Schoharie, about 150 families moved the same autumn (1712) to Albany and Schenectady. Conrad Weiser said his father stayed during the winter with Johannes Meynderton. He also related that bread was extraordinarily high but that the inhabitants were very liberal to the German visitors. In Schenectady, the Indian Quaynant visited his father and as a result Conrad was sent to live with the Indians about the end of November. It also appears that fifty more families could not wait for spring but cut a rough road from Schenectady to Schoharie in two weeks, where they put up rude log shelters or lived in caves. The caves were dug in the side of a hill and there the people lived until enough trees could be cut down for log houses. Animal skins were stretched across the opening of the caves to help keep out the cold as much as possible. With the help of the Indians they weathered the cold winter but survived with great suffering.

Governor Hunter sent orders to the Palatines, forbidding their settlement in Schoharie. Of course they paid no attention to the governor, the Palatines did not put much faith in him anyhow, for anything. March 1713, the remainder of the 150 families joined their friends at Schoharie, traveling with roughly made sledges through the snow.

They settled in seven villages, named for the deputies who made the arrangements with the Indians. The most northern village, Kniskerndorf, Gerlachsdorf, Fuchsendorf, Schmidsdorf, later called Smith's Town, Brunnendorf, later known as Fountaindorf or Waterstown, was around the site now occupied by St. Paul's Lutheran Church in Schoharie. The last three villages mentioned were in what is now the incorporated village of Schoharie and were all three within a radius of one mile. Two and a half miles southwest of Brunnendorf was Hartmansdorf. Two miles further south was Weiserdorf on the edge of the present town of Middleburgh. Oberweiserdorf, a split off from Weiserdorf some years later, was the most southern settlement about three miles away.

The first year in Schoharie (1713) was one of bitter and unbelievable struggles for the Palatines. Conrad Weiser wrote in his journal about how one person borrowed a horse and another a cow. Someone else borrowed a harness and a plow. Hitching the horse and cow together they broke up so much land that in 1714 they had almost enough corn for their needs. They often went hungry or ate wild potatoes and strawberries, which the Indians had shown to them and recommended them for eating.

For flour, Weiser said they had to go 35 or 40 miles, to and from Schenectady, where on credit they might come back with a skipple or two. (A skipple is less than a bushel. In colonial New York, *17th century*, an anglicized form of the Dutch schepel, a unit of dry capacity, about 27.8 liters 3.16 U. S. pecks.) The journey was started early in the morning, took all day, and then after their business was completed, they make the return trip which lasted throughout the night. Women as well as men took the trip. Weiser wrote of the pain and tears of the hungry ones awaiting their return. If they went to Albany, the journey took three or four days. The charity of the good people of Schenectady helped a lot. In 1713 the Dutch Church of New York sent supplies for the Palatines in Schoharie. Hunting and fishing supplemented their meager food supply. They were all very hard workers and did what they had to do to survive.

The Palatines did not bring the tools they used in the tar camps, they were afraid they might be charged with theft if they took them and so they left without anything to show for their labors. They fashioned workable substitutes with which to start building their settlement. For example: One settler fashioned a shovel from a log end, painstakingly hollowing it out. Another used the branches of a tree for a fork to be used in hay-making. A maul was made from a heavy knot of wood, the protruding branch being used as a handle. A mortar for grinding corn was made by taking a log two feet high, and cutting a hole 12 inches in diameter about 18 inches to 20 inches deep into one end. The sides at the top remained about an inch thick.

Their furniture, if one can call it that, was very crude. The people were busy trying to survive by clearing the land and raising food and didn't have time to use to make much furniture. In addition the family had cooking and farm work to do. In that day, ordinary chores were difficult under the best of conditions. Food was commonly served in a wooden trencher that was set in the center of the table and all ate from a common dish side by side to show unity. Sometimes each person had a trencher and they used simple wooden spoons or at first, or ate with their hands. These trenchers were made of a block of wood about ten or twelve inches square and three or four deep, hollowed down into a sort of bowl in the middle. Round trenchers for each person were considered extravagant.

A split log with four heavy sticks set in for legs was their table. Crude stools made the same way. The first huts lacked fireplaces; cooking was done in stone ovens out of doors and was built for the use of several neighboring families. As soon as more permanent dwellings could be built of log and stones, the fireplaces, which were necessary for heat in the winter, were made by attaching a stone chimney to the outside wall and preparing a small stone floor and stone sides for fire protection. A bar across the fireplace and chains for hanging the pots finished the fireplace for the *hausfrau*. This was different than the set up in the old country, most kitchens didn't have chimneys, but just had openings for the smoke to escape. As the years passed, bit by bit more furniture was added, rocking chairs were considered luxurious items to own, benches were added, solid tables and well made furniture replaced the homemade crude furniture. Some liked to decorate the furniture with bright colors and Bible verses. Being a superstitious people, hex signs were put around the property to ward off evil.

The earliest artificial lights used by the Palatines were pitch pine knots. Tallow dips were scarce, but they rose at dawn and retired at dusk. After a hard day of work, no one wanted to stay up very late anyway. The people were exhausted, but determined to survive. Their sturdy bodies and minds were needed for the difficult struggle to tame the wilderness.

The clothing provided for the Palatines by the British government soon wore out and the people turned to the Indian type of dress by using skins. The Palatines had large families as a rule, the children often numbered close to twenty or more, but the mortality rate was also exceptionally high. They had to have large families to ensure continuation of the line and to have someone to take care of them in their old age. Sometimes in the records you will see a name entered, for instance, John. And the next year, the same name, John, and the next year. Eventually a son named John would survive. The Palatine women were generally robust and strong and took childbearing in stride. Since the circuit preacher came, but not very often, couples sometimes neglected the marriage ceremony.

Conrad Weiser's Journal tells us that "*Here the people lived for a few years without preacher, without government, generally in peace. Each one did what he thought was right.*" Part of this orderly conduct was due to the respect held by the people for their listmasters, who were placed over them in the tar camps and who retained their authority in Schoharie too. Elderly John Conrad Weiser, a magistrate in old Wurtemberg in Germany, was perhaps the most prominent leader.

Governor Hunter was against the Palatines settling in Schoharie, probably because he was afraid they would never return to the tar camps along the Hudson; he had no leverage to force them to come back to the camps. He was correct in that assumption, they had no intention of returning to work in the tar industry ever again.

He comforted himself somewhat as he told the Board of Trade that the Palatines at least strengthened and expanded the border, and that the Palatines "*at Schoharee may be imploy'd in working in the vast pinewoods near to Albany, which they must be obliged to doe they having no pretense to possession of any land but by performing their part of the contract relating to that manufacture.*"

Slowly things were improving in the Schoharie Valley during the summer of 1714 when a gentleman by the name of Nicholas Bayard, visited the Palatines. He told them that if they would describe the boundaries of the land they held, he would issue a deed in the name of Queen Anne for their property. Remember Nicholas Bayard purchased the Schoharie lands about 1695 from the Indians before the Palatines purchased the same land? The Bayard who appeared in 1714 was his grandson. There is more to the story, the Bayard Patent had been disallowed by the Colonial and British authorities as an *"extravagant grant"* in 1708, and Bayard was trying to save something of his relative's investment. Had the Palatines accepted his deeds and claimed the land from him, his case would have been greatly strengthened because he could point to improvements and settlement, the lack of which was a strong argument against the original grant and one of the reasons it was considered an extravagant grant. It was simply another land speculation by a wealthy and titled gentleman with the Palatines used as a possible tool.

Bayard was seen as a representative of Hunter by the wary Palatines, and barely escaped with his life under the cover of darkness. The Palatines had been cheated enough and they weren't going to fall for this new scheme. Bayard was besieged in John George Smith's house by an angry mob and shots were exchanged. After nightfall, Mr. Bayard escaped to Schenectady and from there he sent word that if any would appear before him there, acknowledge him and name their boundaries, they would still receive a free deed and a lasting title. He was rewarded with silence from the Palatines.

The Palatine tradition says that Bayard went on to sell the Schoharie title to five citizens of Albany. This may refer to his grandfather's Indian land title, and this was strengthened when the partners received their patent from Hunter on November 3, 1714. It seems Hunter saw another opportunity to persecute the Palatines. In this grant was included 10,000 acres of Bayard's vacated grant upon which the Palatines were settled. The patentees were Myndert Schuyler, Peter van Brugh, Robert Livingston, Jr., John Schuyler and Peter Wileman. When Lewis Morris, Jr., and Andrus Coeman surveyed these lands for the Five Partners, they found that the flats of Fox Creek and a large part of Kniskerndorf had been omitted. These lands they secured for themselves and joined forces with the Albany group. The Five Partners became the Seven Partners. They meant still more trouble for the Palatines.

The Palatines were told in 1715 to purchase, lease, or vacate the land they had settled and built homes on in the Schoharie Valley. They refused to do so, and became violent. After all, they had purchased the land from the Indians but they did not go though the patent process with the colonial government.

When Adam Vrooman, a resident from Schenectady tried to settle on what he considered his land in Schoharie that he bought from the Indians in 1711 and then it was reinforced by a government patent in 1714, they tore up his fences and pulled down the stone walls of his home. The Palatines were sure the land was theirs, they after all, bought it. When warnings failed to drive out Vrooman's son, he was pulled from a wagon and beaten. When Vrooman reported these incidents to Governor Hunter, he also told him that John Conrad Weiser and several others spoke of going to Boston, intending to sail for England.

Hunter was furious and he issued a warrant for the arrest of John Conrad Weiser. With this in mind, a sheriff from Albany, named Adams, came into the Schoharie Valley. Adams, passed up through the valley and made a halt at Weiserdorf. No sooner had he explained his business and attempted the arrest of Weiser when a mob appeared. The Palatine women seemed to possess great strength. Under the direction of Magdalena Zeh, they took the sheriff and dealt with him. He was knocked down, and pushed into various places where the pigs delighted to wallow. Then Adams was put on a rail and ridden through several settlements. Afterwards he was left on a small bridge across a stream along the old Albany Road, a distance from the starting point of between six and seven miles, a painful trip to make on a rail. By then he must have been pretty well split open. The final indignity and injury was that he was beaten with a stick until two of his ribs were broken. He was rescued a little later by some compassionate people. Adams eventually recovered.

Things were quiet for two more years, but things didn't ever go easy for the Palatines for very long at a time. 1717 Hunter ordered that John Conrad Weiser, together with three men from each village appear before him. He told them he expected orders from England to move them to another region, unless they came to an agreement with the real owners of the land. They protested that they had built their homes and had made improvements on the land they had purchased. Hunter agreed with them and said he would send twelve men to estimate the value of their improvements and reimburse them, but he never followed through with this promise. They were told they were not to plow the land to plant their crops. Since they needed food, they sent deputies requesting permission to plow, and being refused, they disregarded the order and did the needed plowing.

In 1718 the Palatines sent John Conrad Weiser, William Scheff and Gerhart Walrath to London to plead their case and to ask for justice. They sailed from Philadelphia, but were robbed by pirates before they got very far. The ship stopped at Boston for new supplies, and when they reached London, the Palatine deputies were imprisoned for debt. Worse yet, their enemy Hunter himself had returned to London to try to recover his fortune. He claimed that the Palatines had taken possession of lands in Schoharie already granted to others. Then he said the true owners offered them easy terms; no rent for ten years and after this period of time, they needed only to pay a moderate rent. His suggestion that they be removed to other lands on the frontier was adopted.

From the Palatine end of the situation, they could not agree among themselves on what should be done to the land in the Schoharie Valley and argued. At last, Gerhart Walrath who was said to be homesick, sailed for New York but died before reaching his destination. Toward the close of 1721 William Scheff returned to American but he too died soon; in his case within six weeks of reaching his home. At last in November of 1723 John Conrad Weiser came back to New York but he was still unreconciled to the government's proposals.

Finally, Hunter was no longer governor. The new governor, William Burnet was ordered to settle the Palatines on some more suitable lands. In 1721 Burnet gave a number of the Palatines permission to purchase land from the Mohawks, provided that it was at least forty miles above Fort Hunter and at least eighty miles from Albany. He explained to the Board of Trade that he had made this condition in order to have the frontier extended. He also stated as evidence of the good will now prevailing that some Palatines had actually taken leases from the seven partners.

In 1722 Burnet purchased land in the Mohawk Valley (Burnetsfield) for the Palatines but they were slow in responding to the offer. About sixty families wanted to settle apart from the others. On October 19, 1723, the Stone Arabia Patent was issued to 27 persons. It contained 12,700 acres about two or three miles back from the Mohawk River on a high plateau. The annual quit-rent of 2 shillings, 6 pence per hundred acres and customary conditions were made. This settlement developed into the present day Village of Palatine Bridge and the Town of Palatine. (Quit-Rent: This was similar to our method of land taxes.)

Some of the Palatines moved to the Tulpehocken district just east of the Swatara Creek in Pennsylvania. They migrated there at the invitation of Sir William Keith, Governor of Pennsylvania.

Taking advantage of the offer made by Governor Burnet to settle the rest of the Palatines on the twenty-four mile tract above Little Falls, the family of Johan Jurgh Kast obtained in June 1724, a patent for 1,100 acres. The patent included the usual reservations and required 27 shilling, 6 pence for annual rent. Another group of Palatines settled west of the same falls on lands offered by the Governor. This land was purchased from the Indians by John Conrad Weiser and other Palatines on July 9, 1722.

The Burnetsfield Patent, granted April 13, 1725, provided one-hundred-acre lots to ninety persons. Some received their land all in one place, while others had thirty acres in the river bottom between the Mohawk River and the West Canada Creek, and seventy acres in woodlands back of the river. As was customary in the other patents they were required to pay the customary quit-rent. The meadow lands south of the river were later known as the German Flats while the village opposite was called Palatine Village and later Herkimer after General Nicholas Herkimer, who lost his life from the Battle of Oriskany in the Revolutionary War. The map of this patent is in the back of this book.

At last the Palatines occupied land to which they had undisputed possession. The Burnetsfield community prospered until the French and Indian War threatened the New York frontier.

In 1731, 8,000 acres on the south side of the river were granted to certain members of the colonial aristocracy. These lands as well as certain others granted a little earlier were located in the present towns of Minden and Canajoharie. Palatines had early settled on these lands and rented them from the Indians. There was considerable dispute between the Indians and the several colonial patentees in which the London authorities eventually intervened because of charges of fraud. A compromise was finally reached in 1768 and the Palatines eventually purchased the lands they were occupying.

The Francis Harrison Patent was purchased from the Mohawk Indians in 1722 for 700 Beaver skins, by Harrison and others *"in the name and behoof of our sovereign lord, George III, by the Grace of God, of Great Britain, France and Ireland, King, defender of the faith, etc."* and sold by the crown to the original patent holders. The patent included the land north of the

Mohawk from below the Palatine line on the east to the East Canada Creek on the west. The tract to the west was a patent of 7423 acres granted in the year 1786 to John Van Driessen the grandson of Dominie Petrus Honorias Van Driessen. The Harrison Patent is where part of the present Town of Palatine and the Town and Village of St. Johnsville is located. The Harrison Patent map is in the back of this book.

In time, groups of Germans purchased more land and the frontier was pushed west and south. About 1710 another group of Palatines, Mennonites, settled toward the Susquehanna in Pennsylvania. In 1717 one *hundred "sold themselves for servants to Pennsylvania for five years."* About 400 more were in London, awaiting disposition when in 1717, the registration of immigrants was required by the Pennsylvania colonial authorities.

On September 14, 1727, a ship from The Netherlands arrived in Philadelphia with 400 Palatines. This commanded the attention of the governor and council of Pennsylvania, who demanded a declaration of allegiance to the King and fidelity to the proprietary government. In fact in the following year, John Penn, one of the heirs of William Penn, considered the advisability of prohibiting or restricting the German Immigration.

The constant stream of *Deutches Volk* ran rather steadily to Pennsylvania. Writers touching on this subject have concluded the obvious preference for Pennsylvania rather than New York to the harsh treatment of the Palatines in the tar camps and to the Schoharie settlers.

The Germans who lived in New York, wrote to their relatives and friends and advised them, if ever they intended to come to America, NOT to settle in New York. This advice had such influence, that the Germans, who afterwards went in great numbers to North America, constantly avoided New York and went to Pennsylvania. Even those who booked passage to America and could not sail to Pennsylvania made short work of leaving New York and heading for Pennsylvania as fast as they could do so.

As far as the Schoharie problems went, Hunter sided with the speculators and powerful landowners. The Schoharie grant was given to the Seven Partners, young gentlemen, who were sons of the landed aristocracy, as a speculative venture. He also granted a large tract in Ulster County to his friend, Lewis Morris and others, in 1715, for speculative purposes. Of all the New York governors, Hunter, who was thought to be one of best, probably did the most to perpetuate the early land problems.

Hunter, was a party to a unique naturalization act, one which naturalized the dead! The purpose of the New York Act of 1715 was to confirm the possession of large tracts of land to certain land holders, whose titles might have been challenged as illegal. When the New Netherlands colony had been taken over finally by the English in 1674, the articles of surrender stipulated that all the people in the colony at the time should continue free denizens and enjoy their lands and houses and dispose of them as they pleased. An act of the Assembly of New York in 1683 naturalized all those of foreign nations then in the colony and professing Christianity. To further encourage the immigration of foreigners, it was also provided that any foreigners professing Christianity might any time after their arrival be naturalized by an act of the assembly, if they took the oaths of allegiance required.

The Articles of Surrender might not be fully carried out, and those who held lands based on patents issued before the surrender might have acquired land from persons of foreign birth who had neglected to be naturalized by act of the assembly as required by the law of 1683. Such persons of foreign birth could not sell or devise land legally and consequently such titles might be contested. The adoption of a new land policy by the Crown of restricting New York grants to 2,000 acres to any one person for a quit-rent of 2 shillings, 6 pence for every hundred acres and requiring the cultivation of at least three acres for every fifty acres held, within three years of receiving the grant, also hinted at trouble.

When Hunter arrived in the colony with the Palatines years before with instructions to have them naturalized immediately by act of the assembly "without fee or reward," the assembly did not act and the matter was set aside.

Years passed and nothing was done; the governor's salary was not paid and even the day to day expenses of the government were not paid. The English Parliament was considering a way to establish revenue for the New York government because they couldn't seem to do this for themselves. Governor Hunter grew tired of waiting for England to act, and finding his credit ruined by the attitude of the assembly and the lack of financial support from London for the Palatine project, he realized he needed to be

more open to the suggestions of the New York Assembly and their wishes and then he gave the Naturalization Act real attention.

In light of this thinking by Governor Hunter to be more open to suggestions, the Naturalization Act was passed July 5, 1715 as part of a working agreement arranged between the governor and the assembly. The governor was to approve the Naturalization Act and was to receive in reward *"an honourable support of the Government and not a scanty one"* for five years, and the payment of the debt owed to the governor by the province.

The Naturalization Act was seized by the anxious landed gentry in the assembly as a protection of their ill-gotten possessions, it provided that: all persons of foreign birth alive in New York in 1683, possessing land, were naturalized by the act and their grants made good; all persons of foreign birth who had come and inhabited New York since 1689 and secured lands, or died in possession of them, were deemed to be naturalized; and all persons of foreign birth inhabitants of New York in 1715 and Protestants were naturalized, provided they took the oath of Allegiance and Supremacy and subscribed to the Test and Abjuration Oath. But if the latter class died without taking the oaths within the nine months grace allowed, they were deemed to have been naturalized.

The act had the effect of making all weak land titles, which were in place before the English took possession of New York or acquired from persons of foreign birth since then, strengthened and made the titles to the lands secure. The Attorney-General of England, recommended the disallowance of this act, suggested that instead of encouraging foreigners to settle in the colonies without naturalization, it would be better to confirm the titles of the subjects of New York even though they were claimed by persons who were not naturalized. His suggestion does not appear to have been accepted.

A large number of Palatines took the opportunity for naturalization under the act.

The Palatine immigrations of 1708 and 1709 were diverted to New York by the British government for its own purposes. New York was a royal province and it was thought that the manufacture of naval stores could be promoted there. The other part of the reason the Palatines were settled in New York by England was that it was also considered quite important to strengthen the New York frontier. We should look at how the Palatines fared in their relations with the French and Indians.

The relations between the Indians and the Palatines of the Schoharie Valley were friendly. Perhaps the chief reason was the influence with the natives held by Conrad Weiser, who was taken when a young man by the Indian Chief named Quaynant to live with him. Weiser lived with the Indians for several years, often hiding in fear of his life from the drunken braves, but he learned their language and later served as interpreter and peacemaker between the settlers and the Indians.

The danger from drunken Indians was no small matter, as Reverend Frederick Haeger found on one occasion in October, 1717, while driving down from Schenectady to the Livingston Manor settlement. A party of Indians on a spree gave chase after the wagon. The driver whipped up the horses to such a speed that the pastor feared they would be dashed to pieces instead of being scalped. The Indians had no way to resist alcohol and craved the white man's fire water.

When settling of Palatines in New York was first considered by the Board of Trade on August 30, 1709, the Board had hopes they would not only serve as a frontier barrier to the French but that *"in process of time by marrying with the neighboring Indians (as the French did) they may be capable of rendering great service to Her Majesty's subjects there."*

The frontier was pushed west and south into the Schoharie, Mohawk, and Susquehanna Valleys by these Palatine pioneers, it does not appear that they intermarried with Indians very often.

The participation of 300 Palatines in the joint English and colonial expedition against Canada in 1711 was done willingly enough by the Palatines. They thought the expedition would make the frontier safe for their settlement and the failure of the expedition was a disappointment to them. The French and Indian Wars went on for a long span of time, (1689-1763) there would be a time of relative peace and then the war would break out all over again.   The earlier wars were tied into part of the larger wars in Europe and on the high seas. The most serious of the French and Indians Wars was from 1754-1763.   By the wars end, all were war weary and a lasting peace was formed. In the Treaty of Paris, Britain gained all of North America east of the Mississippi River, including Canada and Florida.

When the French and Indian Wars broke out once more in 1754, the Palatines in the Mohawk Valley were concerned for their safety, although they had five blockhouses, and a fort that was located several miles away. They made overtures to the French Indians, complaining of the treatment by the English, and proposed an alliance for joint defense against the English. The Indians reported the proposal to the Marquis de Vaudreuil, the Governor of Canada, in a conference on December 24, 1756. De Vaudreuil advised the Indians to inform the Palatines that if they were sincere, he would sustain them as soon as they joined the Indians, and *"If it [the Palatine nation] will retire close to me, I shall receive it and furnish it with lands."* But he warned that in case the proposal of the Palatines was offered only to guarantee the safety of their settlements against the French and their Indians, the trick would not help them.

The French Governor's threat to the Palatines was not a idle threat.

In 1756, the English fort at Oswego was captured, and the small fortifications on Wood Creek and the upper Mohawk were taken and demolished by the French; and on the 12th of November, 1757, an expedition under the command of M. de Belletre, composed of about three hundred Marines, Canadians and Indians, which had traveled the wilderness by the way of Black River, attacked and destroyed the Palatine settlements on the north side of the Mohawk River at or near the present Village of Herkimer.

Complacency on the settlers part was because of a long lapse in hostile visits, and proved in this case most unfortunate. It is said that these people were told the day before by friendly Indians, of the contemplated attack of the French and Indians, but they were not believed and the settlers gave no heed to these warnings. After all, their settlement was in sight of a fort on the south side of the river, garrisoned by three hundred and fifty men. But as it was, these people felt that if they were attacked, that they would be aided by an armed force so near at hand in stopping the assault. Militia forces from Albany had been ordered the year before to be stationed at the German Flats; and the fort mentioned in the French account and by Gov. De Lancy is described as a *"stockaded work around the church and blockhouse, with a ditch and a parapet palisaded, thrown up by Sir William Johnson a year ago [in 1756] upon an alarm then given."* The results of the raid were devastating. The following spring, April 30th, 1758, another raid came and once more with devastating results.

In November of 1757 a strong force of 300 Marine troops, Canadians and Indian braves descended on the Mohawk Valley Palatines. On November 12th, they attacked with such vigor and blood-curdling war-whoops that the Mayor of the Village of Palatine, Johan Jost Petrie, threw open one blockhouse and asked for quarter. After plundering forty-eight houses and standing off an English attack from the neighboring fort, the French and Indians left with nearly 150 men, women, and children as prisoners. They had taken a great booty and lost not a single man, or so they reported with glee. The Germans remained in Canada until they were exchanged in September of 1758, for other prisoners that were taken and held by the Americans.

At this period of the history of the Mohawk Valley, there were nearly five hundred houses between the East Canada Creek and Sir William Johnson's residence near Amsterdam, on both sides of the river, and the road or path usually traveled from Utica as far down as the East Canada Creek was on the south side of the river. There was no wagon or carriage track between the two creeks at that early day.

From 1689 to 1760, a period of seventy-one years, the colonies had been involved in four wars, which lasted in all, twenty-seven years, but their population had increased from two hundred thousand to nearly three million. Agriculture had steadily advanced, and trade and commerce had greatly increased but in arts and manufacturing little progress was made, the introduction of them was opposed by the mother country. The commercial enterprise of the colonists had encountered a few checks from the home government, and a direct trade with several of the Spanish and French colonies had been permitted, although contrary to the letter of the British navigation law. This trade was highly beneficial to the colonists, as it enabled them to exchange their products for gold and silver and other valuable commodities, then they were able to make payment for British manufactured items.

The continued experience the Palatines had with the British, first in the tar camps and then during the French and Indian Wars did not improve relations between the two, the mutual repugnance became more apparent. At the same time, Britain's expensive struggle with France depleted the British treasury, and Parliament was seeking additional revenue by taxing the American Colonies. The French and Indian Wars, helped set the wheels in motion for the Revolutionary War.

The difficulties caused by the short sighted opposition of colonial authorities and the selfish exploitation by colonial land speculators were courageously, one might even say obstinately, fought by the Palatine settlers. With many others from the other provinces, they were strongly opposed to taxation without representation. They wanted the right to trial by their own peer groups in court too. It did not seem to be a monumental request, but Britain did not hear her colonies. The clamor for attention from Great Britain grew louder and louder.

These, the Palatines were the sturdy people who settled the Mohawk Valley. They intended to stay, they had been forced out of their homes too many times and they remembered their treatment at the hands of the English. They were home at last, they built their houses and barns, cut down the trees and tilled the land. At last they had a place of their own, the opportunity they had been seeking. So many died in the quest, and never saw their Promised Land.

Some of the second and third generations of the original settlers fought in the Revolutionary War. Colonel Klock was born around 1700, if the record is correct. He was not the only elderly Palatine to take his musket and fight though he could have been exempt and not fought in the war. Experience was gained by the Palatines when they fought in the many French and Indian Wars. Nicholas Herkimer fought under Colonel Klock's command during this time. The students learned their skills from their teachers and used it against them in the Revolution.

Source Material:

Early Eighteenth Century Palatine Emigration
by Walter Allen Knittle, Ph.D.
Department of History, College of the City of New York, Published Philadelphia, 1937

Frontiersmen of New York
by Jeptha R. Simms, Albany, NY 1883

A History of Herkimer County
By Nathaniel S. Benton, 1856

The Story of Old Fort Plain and the Middle Mohawk Valley
by Nelson Greene, O'Connor Brothers Publishers, Fort Plain, NY 1915

Documents Relative to the Colonial History of the State of New York; procured in Holland, England and France by John Romeyn Broadhead, Esq., Agent, UNDER AND BY VIRTUE OF AN ACT OF THE LEGISLATURE ENTITLED "AN ACT TO APPOINT AN AGENT TO PROCURE AND TRANSCRIBE DOCUMENT IN EUROPE RELATIVE TO THE COLONIAL HISTORY OF THE STATE," PASSED MAY 2, 1839. VOLUME V., ALBANY; Weed, Pasons and Company, Printers, 1855.

The Book of Names
Especially Relating to The Early Palatines and the First Settlers in the Mohawk Valley
Compiled and Arranged by Lou D. MacWethy
Published by The Enterprise and News
St. Johnsville, NY. , 1933. Used with permission

Letters and Documents Regarding the Palatines.

To support the Palatine story, the following are of interest and of value. Punctuation is spotty and spelling varies because it is eighteenth century spelling, but the documents are certainly understandable.

The letters and documents are from: Documents Relative to the Colonial History of the State of New York; procured in Holland, England and France by John Romeyn Broadhead, Esq., Agent, UNDER AND BY VIRTUE OF AN ACT OF THE LEGISLATURE ENTITLED "AN ACT TO APPOINT AN AGENT TO PROCURE AND TRANSCRIBE DOCUMENT IN EUROPE RELATIVE TO THE COLONIAL HISTORY OF THE STATE," PASSED MAY 2, 1839. VOLUME V., ALBANY; Weed, Pasons and Company, Printers, 1855.

1708 Letters regarding the Palatines.

To the Right Hon. The Lords Commissioners of Trade & Plantations.

My Lords, Having laid before the Queen the Inclosed Petition of Joshua Kocherthal, Minister concerning several other Distressed Protestants newly arrived from the Palatinat & Holsteyn who are likewise desirous to be transported to Her Majesty's Plantations in American, in the same manner and with the same advandages as have been already granted to those who came before out of the Palatinate.

Her Majesty has thereupon commanded me to transmit the said Petition to Your Lord that you may examine whether the fourteen persons therein mentioned are proper objects of Her Majesty's Royal Compassions, as the others were. And in such case Her Majesty's pleasure is, that these which are the last arrived shou'd be taken care of, in the same manner as the former.

I am My Lords, Your Lords' most humble Servant H. Boyle
Whitehall
June 22d 1708.

Petition of the Reverend Joshua Kocherthal to the Queen.

[New York Entries, G. 271.]

The humble Petition of Joshua de Kocherthal Minister, on behalf of himself and other Distressed Persons, lately arrived from Palatinate and Holstein.

Most humbly Sheweth

That your sacred Majesty being pleased to receive the Petitioners late humble Petition with such great clemency and Royal favous, he is thereby incouraged to prostrate himself once more before Your Majesty, and to inform Your Majesty with the utmost submission, that fourteen Persons more three whereof are natives of Holstein, are Arrived here unexpetedly from the Palatinate who having suffer'd under the Calamity which happened last year in the Palatinate by the Invasion of the French, in this their Deplorable Condition are desireous to settle themselves in some of Your Majesty's Plantations in America, but by reason of their extream Poverty, they cannot Defray their charges for passage thither.

They humbly Implore Your Royal Majesty, That they may be permitted to go thither in company with the forty one persons, to whom Your Majesty has most graciously allowed a free passage thither; and that they may also enjoy the same Royal Mercy and Priviledges. And whereas your petitioner cannot hop; for competent subsistence in America, after his Arrival there, he most humbly Entreats Your Majesty to grant him such Sallary, for the Support of himself and family, as Your Majesty in Your Great Clemency shall think fit.

The data given in the list below was compiled from the following sources: P. R. O., C. O. 5, 67 iij N. Y. Col. Docs., V, 52, Doc. Hist., III, 543; C. C. 1706-1708, 722. "w." indicates wife in the family notations.

And Your Petit(rs) (as in Duty Bound) shall ever Pray, &c.

The Names, Trades, &c. of the German Protestants to be settled at New York
28th June 1708.

Names, Trades, Condition of Life, Sex, Age (year- months).

(1) Lorenz Schwisser, Husbandman & Vinyard, Married, M, 25
Anna Catharina Schwisserin, Wife, F., 26
Johanna Schwisserin, Child, F., 8 mo.

(2) Henry Rennau, Stockingmaker Husbandman & Vinyard, Married, M., 24
Johanna Renauin, Wife, F., 26
Susana Liboscha, Sister, Unmarried, F., 15
Maria Johana Liboscha, Sister, Unmarried, F., 10.
Lorenz Rennau, Child, M., 2.
Heinrich Rennau, Child, M., 5 mo.

(3) Andreas Volck, Husbandman and Vinyard, Married, M., 30
Ana Catharina Volckin, Wife, F., 27
Maria Barbara Volckin, Child, F,. 5
Ann Gertruda Volckin, Child, F., 1

(4) Michael Weigand, Husbandman, Married, M., 52
Ana Catharine Weigandin, Wife, F., 54.
Ana Maria Weigandin, Child, F., 13
Tobias Weigand, Child, M., 7
Georg Weigand, Child, M., 5

(5) Jacob Weber, Husbandman and Vinyard, Married, M., 30
Anna Elisebetha Weberin, Wife, F., 25
Eva Maria Weberin, Child, F., 5
Eva Elizabetha Webering, Child, F., 1

(6) Jacob Pletal, Husbandman and Vinyard, Married, M., 40
Ana Elisabetha Pletelin, Wife, F., 29
Margaretha Pletelin, Child, F., 10
Anna Sara Pletelin, Child, F., 8
Catharina Pletelin, Child, F., 3

(7) Johannes Fischer, Smith and Husbandman, Married, M., 27
Maria Barbara Fischerin, Wife, F., 26
Andreas Fischer, Child, M., 1/2 mo.

(8) Melchoir Gulch, Carpenter or Joiner, Married, M., 39
Ana Catharina Gulchin, Wife, F., 43
Magdalena Gulchin, Child, F., 12
Henrich Gulchin, Child, M., 10

(9) Isaac Turck, Husbandman, Unmarried, M., 23

(10 Josua Kocherthal, Minister, Married, M., 39
Sibylla Charlotta Kocherthal, Wife, F., 39
Benigna Sibylla Kocherthal, Child, F., 10
Christian Joshua Kocherthal, Child, M., 7
Susana Sibylla Kocherthal, Child, F., 3.

(11) Peter Rose, Cloth Weaver, Married, M., 34
Johanna Rosin, Wife, F., 45

(12) Maria Wemarin, Husbandwoman, Widuwe (Widow?) F, 37
Catharina Wemarin, Child, F. 2

(13) Isaac Feber, Husbandman and Vineyard, Married, M., 33
Chatarina Feberin, Wife, F., 30
Abraham Feber, Child, M., 2

(14) Daniel Fiere, Husbandman, Married, M., 32
Anna Maria Fiere, Wife, F., 30
Andreas Fiere, Child, M., 7
Johannes Fiere, Child, M., 6
Ex Holsatia
Herman Schuneman, Clerck, Unmarried, M., 28

Board of Trade to Mr. Secretary Boyle [New York Entries, G. 291]

To the Right Honourable Mr. Secretary Boyle.

SIR
      In Obedience to Her Majesty's Commands signified to us by Your letter of the 22d Instant upon a second petition of Joshua de Kocherthal, to Her Majesty, in behalf of himself and 14 other distressed Protestants lately arrived from the Palatinate and Holsteyn, Praying that they

may in Company of the 41 Lutherans already provided for, be transported to Her Majesty's Province of New York, and partake of the like allowance and Advantages the said Lutherans are to receive, as well during their stay here as at their Arrival in the said Provinc.

We have considered the same and find that the Testimonials which they have produced under this hands and Seals of the Ministers Baylifs or Principal Magistrates in the Villages where they dwelt, do give a good character of the said Poor Protestants, and certify that they are reduced to the utmost want, having lost all they had by the frequent Incursions of the French and Germans near Landau; find further that two of them have Entred themselves into the Service of the Lord Lovelace, so that there are but 12 to be provided for.

Whereupon We humbly Offer that the said 12 Poor Protestants are fit Objects for her Majesty's Bounty, and that if Her Majesty shall be graciously pleased to allow them the same as is already granted to the others, for their subsistence, and that they be transported with the Rest to New York, We further humbly Offer that before their Departure they be likewise made free Denizens of this kingdom, for their greater incouragement in the made free Denizens of this kingdom, for their greater incouragement in the incouragement in the injoyment of the Priviliges accuring by such letter of denization.

We are, Sir Your most humble Servants.
Herbert
Pr. Meadows
Jno Pulteney

1709 Letters regarding the Palatines

Report of Board of Trade respecting the Palatines. August 30, 1709. [New York Entries, G. 387.]

To the Rt. Honourable The Ld High Treasurer of Great Britain.

My Lord,
(The first part of the letter concerns the proposition of settling the Palatines in Jamaica.)

If it be though advisable that these poor people or any number of them be settled on the Continent of America, We are of opinion that such settlement, especially if made at Her Majesty's charge shou'd be in Provinces under Her Majesty immediate Government, and we know no place so proper as Hudson's River on the Frontier of New York, Whereby they will be a **good barrier between Her Majesty's Subjects and the French & their Indians in those parts, and in process of time by intermarrying with the neighbouring Indians (as the French do) they may be Capable of rendring very great Service to Her Majesty's Subjects there; and not only very much promote the Fur Trade, but likewise the increase of Naval Stores, which may be produced in great plenty at New York, wherein M(r) Bridger Her Majesty's Surveyor of the Woods on that Continent may be Directed to instruct them.**

Lastly we take leave to Observe to Your Lord that in Virginia and some other parts of the said Continent, where the Air is clear and healthfull, wild Vines do naturally grow and afford plenty of Grapes, which if cultivated and improved by husbandry wou'd produce good wines. Wherefore if some of these Palatines who are Vine Dressers were settled there, and imployed in that sort of Husbandry, and new proffitable Trade might be Introduced to the Benefit of this Kingdom.

We are, My Lord, Y(r) Lord (p's) most humble Servants.
Dartmouth
M. Smith
Ph. Meadows
J. Pulteney.
Whitehal, August the 30th, 1709.

December 23, 1709.

Report of the Board of Trade on the Plans for Settling the Palatines.
[New York Entries, G. 473.]

To the Queen's Most Excellent Majes(ty)

May it please Your Majesty;

In obedience to Your Majesty's Commands signifyed to us by the Right Hono(ble) the Earl of Sunderland, we have considered the Proposals made by Colonel Hunter, **for settling 3000 Palatines at New York, and Employing them in the Production of Naval stores, and there upon humbly Represent to Your Majesty.**

That the Province of New Yorke being the most advanced Frontier of Your Majesty's Plantations on the Continent of America, the Defence and Preservation of that place is of the utmost importance to the Security of all the Rest; And if the said Palatines were seated there they would be an additional strength and Security to that Province, and only with regard to the French of Canada, But against any Insurrection of the Scattered Nations of Indians upon that Continent, and therefore we humbly Propose that they be sent thither.

By the best Information we can gett, the most proper Places for the seating of them in that Province, so as they may be of benefit to this Kingdom by the Production of navel Stores, are in the **Mohaquest (Mohawk) River, and on Hudson's River, where are very great numbers of Pines fit for Production of Turpentine and Tarr, out of which Rozin and Pitch are made**.

First in relation to the Mohaques River; your Majesty was pleased by Your Order in Council of the 26th of June 1708, to confirm an Act past at New York the 2d of March 169 8/9 for vacating several Extravagant Grants, whereby large Tracts of Land are returned to Your Majesty, and among the rest.

A Tract of Land lying on the Mohaques River containing about 50 miles in length and four Miles in breadth, and a Tract of land lying upon a Creek which runs into the said River, containing between 24 and 30 Miles in length. This last mentioned Land, of which Your Majesty has the possession is claimed by the Mohaques, but that claim may be satisfyed on very easy Terms.

The Objection that may be made to the Seating of the Palatines on the fore-mentioned Mohaques River, is the Falls that are in the said River between Schenectedy and Albany, which will be an Interruption to the Water carriage, but as that may be easily helped by a short land carriage of about 3 miles at the most, We do not see that this objection will be any hindrance to the seating of them there, In case there be not an opportunity of doing it more conveniently in some other part of that Province.

There are other large Tracts of Lands on Hudson's River, which are resumed to Your Majesty by the foresaid Vacating Act, viz(t)

A Tract of Land lying on the East side of that River, containing 12 miles in breadth, and about 70 miles in length, and on the other Tract on the West side, containing 20 miles in Breadth and 40 miles in length.

By all which it appears that there are Lands Sufficient in Your Majesty's gift, for the proposed settlement of the said Palatines, in case the same have not been regranted by Your Majesty's Governor or the Commander in Chief there, since those lands were so resumed, which we do not hear has been done.

We therefore humbly Offer that that Governor or Commander in Chief be directed upon their arrival, to seat them all either in a Boddy or in different Settlements upon those or other Lands as he shall find most proper, And that they be Encouraged to settle and work in Partnership, that is 5 or more families to unite and Work in Common.

That the Governor be likewise Directed to grant under the Seal of that Province, **without fee or Reward, 40 Acres per head to each family, after they shall have repaid by the produce of their labour the charges the publick shall be at in settling and subsisting them there, in the manner as is herein after proposed; To have and to hold the said Lands, to them and their heirs for ever, under the usual Quit rent to commence and be payable after seven years from the date of each respective Grant; and further that in every such grant there be an Express Proviso that the Lands so granted shall be seated and planted within a reasonable time to be therein prefixed, or in failure thereof; such Grant to be void and to revert to the crown**; And for the better preventing those people from falling upon the Woollen Manufactures, it will be proper that in every such Grant, a clause be incerted, declaring the said Grant to be Void, if such Grantee shall apply himself to the making the Woollen or such like Manufacture.

As these People are very necessitous they will not be able to maintain themselves there, 'till they can reap the benefit of their labour which will not be 'till after one year, at the soonest,

We therefore humbly Offer that be subsisted, The men and women at the rate of 6d sterling a hear pr day, and the children under the age of 10 years at 4 d sterling a head pr day,which as we are informed will be Sufficient.

When their houses shall be built, and the ground cleared for making their settlements they may then be employed in the making of Turpentine, Rozin, Tarr, and Pitch, and that this will be beneficial not only to the said Palatine but to this Kingdom. We take leave to observe; That one Man may make by his own labour six tunns of these Stores in a Year; and we have been informed that a number of men assisting each other may in proportion make double that quantity; so that supposing 600 men be imployed in this work, they may produce 7000 Tuns of these goods a year, and if in time a greater quantity of those stores should be made there, than shall be consumed in Your Majesty's Dominions, We hope the overplus may turn to a very beneficial Trade with Spain & Portugal.

(The rest of the letter talks about making the naval stores, how to do it and how many "teachers" they might require, supervisors, store house or commissary, keeping accounts, shipping of the naval stores etc..)

Lastly We humbly offer that the said Palatines upon their arrival there be Naturalized, without Fee or Reqard, that they may enjoy all such Privileges and Advantages as are Enjoyed by the present Inhabitants of that Province.
All which is most humbly Submitted.
Stamford
LDartmouth
Ph. Meadows
Jo Pulteney
R. Monckton
Cha. Turner
Whitehall
Decemb(r) 5th 1709.

Covenants for the Palatines, Residence and Employment in New York.

This is the all important covenant the Palatines said was not the same as the one read to them in England before they boarded ship.

Whereas we the underwritten Persons Natives of the Lower Palatinate of the Rhine, have been subsisted, maintained and supported since our Arrival in this Kingdom by the great and Christian Charity of Her Majesty the Queen, and of many of her good subject; and Whereas her Majesty has been graciously pleased to order and advance a Loan for us, & on our behalf of several very considerable sums towards the transporting maintaining & settling of us and our respective Families in Her Majesty's Province of New York in America, and towards the Imploying of us upon lands, for that intent and purpose, to be allotted to us, in the production and Manufacture of all manner of Naval Stores, to the evident benefit and Advantage of us and of our respective Families, and Whereas her Majesty has been likewise graciously pleased to give her Royal Orders to the Hon(ble;) Colonel Robert Hunter, who has now Her Majesty's Commission to be Captain General and Governor in Chief of the said Province, and to all Governors of the said Province for the time being, that as soon as we shall have made good and repaid to Her Majesty, her Heirs or Successors, out of the Produce of our labours in the Manufactures we are to be Employed in, the full sum or sums of mony in which we already are, or shall become, indebted to Her Majesty, by the produce of our labour in the Manufacture of all manner of Naval Stores on the Lands to that end to be allotted to us, that then he said Coloonel Robert Hunter, or the Governor or Governors of the said Province for the time being shall give and grant to us and to our Heirs for Ever, to our own use and Benefit, the said Lands so allotted as aforesaid, to the proportion or amount of Forty Acres to each Person free from all Taxes, Quit Rents, or other manner of services for seven years, from the date of such Grant, and afterwards subjected only to such Reservations as are accustomed and in use in that Her Majesty's said Province.
Now Know all men by these Presents that we the said underwritten Persons in a grateful sense just Regard and due consideration of the Premises, do hereby severally for ourselves, our Heirs, Executors and Administrators, covenant, promise and grant to and with the Queen's most Excellent Majesty her heirs and Successors, that We with our respective Families will settle

ourselves in such place or places as shall be allotted to us in the Province of New York on the Continent of America, and abide and continue Resident upon the Lands so to be allotted to us as aforesaid, Continent of America, and abide and continue. Resident upon the Lands so to be allotted to us as aforesaid, in such Bodyes or Societys as shall be thought usefull or Necessary either for carrying on the Manufacture of things proper for Navall Stores or for the Defence of us and the rest of her Majesty's Subjects against the French or any other of her Majesty's Enemies, and that We will not upon any Account or any manner of Pretence quit or desert the said Province, without leave from the Governor of the said Province first had and obteyned for so doing, and but that we will to our utmost power employ and occupy our selves and our respective families in the producing and Manufacturing of all manner of Naval Stores upon the Lands so to be allotted to us, or on such other Lands as shall be thought more proper for that purpose and not concern ourselves in working up or making things belonging to the Woollen Manufacture, but behave ourselves in all things as becomes dutifull and loyall subjects and gratefull and faithfull Servants to Her Majesty, Her Heires and Successors, paying all due Obedience to the said Honourable Colonel Robert Hunter or to the Governor or Governors of the said Province for the time being, and to all Magistrates and other officers who shall from time to time be legally appointed and set over us; and towards Repayment of Her Majesty, her heirs and Successors, all such sums of money, as she or they shall at any time disburse for our support and maintenance till we can reap the Benefit of the Produce of our labours, We shall permit and suffer all Naval Stores by us Manufactured to be put into Her Majesty's Store houses which shall be for this purpose provided, under the care of a Commissary, who is to keep a faithful Account of the Goods which shall be so Delivered, and We shall allow out of the neat Produce thereof so much to be paid Her Majesty, her heires and Successors as upon a fair account shall appear to have been Disbursed for Subsistance of us, or providing Necessaries for our families. In Witness, &c

Board of Trade to the Earl of Sunderland.
[New York Entries, H., 3.]
To the Right Hon(ble) the Earl of Sunderland.
My Lord.
      Pursuant to Her Majesty's pleasure signified to us by Your Lordships Letter of the 10th Instant, we have prepared the Draughts of Instructions to Colonel Hunter for the Government of New York and New Jersey as also those relating to the Acts of Trade and Navigation, together with Two Additional Instructions for Her Majes(tys) Royal Signature, and transmit the same to
      Your Lorship with our Report thereupon to be laid before Her Majesty, and are,
      My Lord,
      Your Lorships most hum(ble) Servants
      Stamford
      Dartmouth
      Ph. Meadows
      J(n) Pulteney
      Rob(t) Monckton.
      Cha. Turner.
      Whitehall
      Decemb(r) 23, 1709.

1710 Letter regarding the Palatines

Resprsentation of the Lords of Trade respecting Naval Stores, &c.

To the Queen's Most Excell(t) Majesty

May it please your Majesty.
      Our proposal of the 5th of Decemb(r) 1709 for **setling three thousand Palatines at New York, and for employing them there in the production of Naval Stores having been approved of by your Majesty, and the said Palatines transported thither accordingly**, We have now received from M(r) Hunter Your Majesty's Govern(r) of that Province, an Account of what Progress has been made in that settlem(t) and have likewise been informed thereof as well by letters from M(r) Bridger (Surveyor of Your Majesty's Woods on the Continent of America) who

was directed to go from New England to New York, to instruct them in the said manufacture, as by the discourse we have had with M(r) Dupre, the Person sent over by your Majestys said Governor to solicit a further subsistence for the said Palatines, Whereupon we beg leave humbly to lay before your Majesty.

That the said **Palatines did not arrive at New York till June last, when the season for preparing the Trees for making Tar was over**, Whereby nothing could be done that year towards the production of Naval Stores. However that there might be no loss of time the Governor went with the said M(r) Bridger to view several Tracts of Land upon Hudson's River, and on the Mohaques River. The latter was judg'd too remote, and therefore the Governor purchased for two hundred twenty six pounds sterling, a Tract of land containing six thousand acres, lying on the East side of Hudson's River, which is about a hundred miles from New York.

On that land the greatest number of the said **Palatines are setled in three towns, where they have already erect(d) their Huts.**

Opposite thereto and belonging to Your Majesty on the West side of the said River, lyes another Tract of Land, extending about a mile in length to the side of that River on which Land the rest of the Palatines are seated in two towns.

Which said settlements are very commodious, as well in regard of the fertility of the soil, as that they are adjoyning to the Pine Lands, and that ships drawing fifteen foot water may come up to them.

M(r) Dupre has informed us that when he came away the number of the Palatines so setled was Two thousand, Two hundred, twenty seven, who were then employed in clearing the ground, for Indian Corn & Gardens; And are this Spring to be set on work in preparing the Trees for the Production of Tar and other Naval Stores.

Your Majesty's said Govern(r) and Surveyor do say, That this great and usefull undertaking of providing this Kingdom with Naval Stores cannot fail of success if duly encourag'd and supported from hence, there being Pines enough for a constant supply of Tar for the use of all the shipping of Great Britain.

In order to produce Tar the Trees must be rinded in the Spring, after which it is necessary that they stand two years that the Sap may be lost, and only the Gummy substance remain to be run into Tar, by burning the Trees after a particular manner; Wherefore 'till the Palatines can make Tar, in order to reimburse Your Majesty what has already been or shall be further advanc'd for their use, the Governor proposes y(t) they be subsisted at the rate of six pence p(r) Day, for Persons above ten years of age, and four pence a head p(r) Day for children under Ten Years; To defray which expence and other charges incident to the said undertaking (as is more particularly set forth in an Estimate now lying before the Lords of Your Majesty's Treasury) he Craves an allowance of Fifteen Thous(d) Pounds a Year.

In regard it was so late before the said Palatines were seated, as before mention'd, and for that the weather in that Country is usually very hard during the Winter season, they could not by their labour contribute towards their own Lively hood-during any Part of the first year, which Time to that purpose be reckoned lost; Therefore the **Governor proposes that the said allowance of fifteen thousand pounds a Year, be made for Two years to be computed from Midsummer 1710 w(th)in the first of which two years, (though a great part of their labour will be employed in the Spring, to prepare Trees for making Tar)** He computes they will be so far able to contribute towards their own lively hood, that the said sum of Fifteen thousand pounds will in a great measure answer the rest of that year's expence on account of the said undertaking, And that within the latter of the said two years the produce of their lands will contribute towards their support to such a further degree that the second fifteen thousand pounds will be sufficient to answer the second years expence, and to make good the deficiency of the former year.

(The rest of the correspondence does not pertain to the Palatines.)

All which is most humbly submitted.
STAMFORD
R MONCKTON
PH: MEADOWS
CHA: TURNER
J. PULTENEY
GEO : BAILLIE
ART: MOORE

Order in Council in relation to a Standing Revenue.
[New-York Entries, H. 298]

1711 Letters regarding the Palatines

Mr. John Cast to Governor Hunter.
[Translated from the French.]
[New York Papers: Aa: 35.]
My Lord

The deportment of the Palatines continues the same as I had the honor to report to Your Excellency in my last. No person comes here except for tools, either for agricultural purposes, or for altering their huts into houses. After having distributed what I had, I put off the others until the first arrival from New York. Some ask for seed, so that the labor they have expended on their land may not be in vain. I given them to understand that the people of the country, not anticipating this demand for seed, will find it difficult to supply the requisite quantity; that the seed they have brought from Germany, London and even New York will possibly be sufficient for this year, inasmuch as it is more easy for each one to find what he needs, than for us to lay up a supply for the entire people, in the distribution of which each takes what he does not require.

In other respects the people contemplate present settlement for a couple of years. They persuade themselves that Canada will he taken this campaign, and that upon the conquest of that country, as a security for their settlement, they will be established on the lands destined for them. In this opinion they are confirmed by the reports of those who have wintered at Albany; who say, that the inhabitants up there are accordingly very apprehensive of losing the profit they derive from the Indians, and the hay they annually cut on said lands.

Some days ago, five Palatines were sitting around the fire conversing on the prospect of their settlement. They all agreed, that the selection of the Levingston lands was well planned-that their situation between New-York Sopes and Albany was very convenient; that the proximity to the river is of great advantage, and that the exemption from the fear of enemies affords peace and a home to their families. But the desire to possess a good deal of land, upset and demolished, in a moment afterwards, all these advantages. The more moderate and sensible, to remove this, said to them-

What, if, in return for all your pretended rights, the Governor will not give you any other lands than those in the rear of our villages, and be determined that we pass our whole lives here? What can you then do? Nothing, continued the same man, but drawdown by the displeasure of the Governor, evils we do not experience here, and deprive ourselves of the good we now enjoy. For in fine (he continued) as it is our duty, and we must absolutely work for the Queen, it cannot be otherwise than that Her Majesty will put us in a position to earn our obread; for she will not keep us always in this way.

Earn our bread, said another. **We came to America to establish our families-to secure lands for our children, on which they will be able to support themselves after we die; and that we cannot do here.** What is to be done in that case but to have patience? replied the first. "Patience and Hope make fools of those who fill their bellies with them." Whereupon the whole five burst out a-laughing and changed the conversation.

I asked Mr. Kocherthall in what way his people behave ? He tells me all are at work and busy, but manifestly with repugnance, and merely temporarily-that the tract intended for them is, in their minds, a Land of Canaan-they agree, that it is a very dangerous place to settle at present, and for this reason it is that they are willing to have patience here for a couple of years. But they will not listen to Tar making. He thinks this repugnance can be overcome, as was that to cultivate their gardens; and that the future will furnish with difficulty what the present time would have easily guaranteed, did the people conform to the intentions of their superior.

I have considered it my duty to give Your Excellency communication of all that precedes, for your information. I have no other object in the world, for the remainder of my days, than to serve faitlifully, disinterestedly, impartially, without seeking any other *Meum* than what can be useful to your Excellency. God preserve me from painting the people in blacker colors than they deserve. But in drawing their portrait I have avoided flattery also. I consider it, of the utmost importance to avoid the one and the other. Thus, by reporting purely and simply what occurs from day to day, whether good or bad, Your Excellency will be able to infer what is to be hoped and what is to be feared.

After the change which has just taken place among the people, I have remarked further, that many heads of families are solicitous for a better form of Magistracy. They frankly say, our affairs will never prosper as long as we are our own masters; each follows his own evil inclinations, and if there be no bridle to act as a check, the man who is well to do will be forced and constrained to defend himself, and to go constantly armed to his work.

Not only is each emulous to be the first to finish his garden, but likewise eager to work so as to be no longer dependent on the inhabitants of the country. For they openly confess, that they have learned sufficiently by experience, that not only do the settlers want to accustom them to work for their daily food, or at most for a'little provisions extra, and [but] have reason to be jealous of their settlement, inasmuch as they see themselves already obliged to lower the price of their articles (ouvrages) in order to retain customers. The mechanics among the Palatines understand this so well, that they do all in their power to set themselves to work, and we assist them as far as our means permit. It is the agricultural portion of them alone that contemplate the possession of a large quantity of land ; these however form the mass of the people to whom I should wish to give occupation after their gardens are completed. It is impossible that they can all find employment among the farmers. At New York, force had to be used to make them cut wood for a shilling a cord, with 1 s. a week for butter and salt. Here they are mighty glad to labor for 1 s. a day. Thus doth folly change with circumstances.

The people, especially those of Queensbury, perniciously abuse the favor Your Excellency extended to them, by saying, If any one happened to have a spot unfit for cultivation, let him have another. Seven belonging to Queensbury have, of their own authority, appropriated other places unto themselves, fell into dispute about them, and two of them have fought each other with axes. The Overseer of the village demands that they be punished so as to prevent other similar assaults. To do what I can, I am this moment on the point of setting out with the Surveyor to examine the lots and the cause,of the dispute, in order to stop the quarrel and apply a remedy to these abuses.

I have drawn up the necessary notices for the dissolution of the two Marriages mentioned by Mr. Hayer to Your Excellency, and have presented them to Mr. Livingstone who says, he is not a Magistrate of that country where the Palatines live, that his jurisdiction is between his Manor and Albany, that application must be made to Mr. Dirck Wessellse ten Broeck. The interested parties desiring the prosecution of these proceedings, I shall address myself accordingly, without giving any explanation for fear of displeasing the honest people, and affording greater encouragement to the wicked in their wickedness; for the good are a long time wishing for the establishment of an effective police which they do not find in the person of an absent judge.

Mr. Wagner whom I deputed to present Captain Gerlach to the people of Annsbury in placo of Wormbз, deceased, informs me that they absolutely refuse him as Captain; in fact he immediately returned to his village without pretending any thing. The people of Annsbury since tell me that the majority of them belong to the New York company, and are thereby too much convinced of the malversations he committed in the distribution of the provisions, to wish to fall again into the same misfortune. Singular persistency in an accusation which has never lifted its head during his sojourn at New York.

> I am with profound respect,
> My Lord,
> Your Excellency's most humble
> and most obedient Servant
> March 27, 1711.
> JEAN CAST.

Secretary Clarke to the Lords of Trade.
[New-York Entries, H. 398.]
To the R(t) Hon(ble) the Lords Commiss(rs) for Trade & Plantations.

My Lords

His Excellency Collonel Hunter being called on by the season of the year to **set the Palatines to work on preparing the Pine Trees,** left me his commands in case he should not return before this Packet sailed to acquaint Your Lordships that he is upon that service, desirous by his presence to encourage and to be a witness to their first labours.

He has also commanded me to inform your Lordships of some other things relating to this Government.

(The rest of the letter pertains to other matters.)

New York, May 28th 1711 GEO: CLARKE

Secretary Clarke to the Lords of Trade.
[New York Entries, H. 402.]

To the R(t) Hon(ble) the Lords Commiss(rs) for Trade and Plantations.

My Lords
 I have said nothing more of the Palatines in my other letter then that His Excellency was gone up to set them to work on preparing the Pine Trees, not having then received any clear account of their deportment, but since I closed that I have had one full and particular which it will require more time to give it your Lordships, especially at length & with the Copys of some Papers requisite to a thorough prospect of their proceedings than I now have, for I expect to be called on every minute, for this however I will endeavour to be as particular as I can now.
 About a fortnight agoe his Excellency having received information from their Overseers and other Officers, that these people had taken a resolution neither to work in making Pitch and Tarr nor to remain on the land they are settled upon for that purpose, but even by force if they could not otherwise effect it, to remove to Schohary and that they had actually hindred the Surveyors from laying out more Lots to them strengthening each other in these Resolutions by a secret association, his Excellency was forced to send for a Detachment of sixty from the Garrison of Albany to meet him at the Manor of Levingston which is about two miles from their settlement on the West Side of the River so soon as his Excellency arrived there he sent to all the villages on that side of the River to know how they dared disobey his orders and hinder the Surveyors and other Officers to do their duty.
 By their Deputys they returned for answer, that when the Surveyors came to lay out the land, the People called them out, told them 'twas worth nothing, they would have no more, so that it 'twas needless to survey it & that they would have the lands of Schohary which the Queen had ordered them by their contract.
 His Excellency replyed that he had often told them that if any man by chance had a bad lott, the Surveyors, on application would lay him out another, as they were ordered, that those who had cleared what was given them might, upon application to the Surveyors, have more: and if what he had already purchased was not sufficient he would purchase more, provided it lay on the River, and near the Pines, that they might ffollow the manufacture that they were destin'd for and obliged to by their contract. That as to the lands of Schohary its the malice of those who would have them for their slaves that put them on demanding it, for that those lands the Indians had not yet parted with, nor were they fit for their labour, no Pine being within twenty miles of it, that it would be impossible to subsist them there, or defend them against y(e) French and French Indians, and besides they had obliged themselves to settle on such lands, as he should assign them, and then desired their final answer, which was that they would have the lands appointed them by the Queen; Whereup" his Excellency, in writing, told them that since neither their duty allegiance or regard to Her Majesty's unparalleled charity and goodness in taking them up, and providing for them when they were starving, and abandon'd by all ye world besides, had been of any force to keep y(m) within the bounds of their duty, and since they had no regard to a solemn contract signed by them he was come to require and enforce the execution of it, Copys and Translations of which they had in their own language. Then his Excell(cy) desired that what passed between them, Copies whereof were then given y(m), might be communicated to the people, and their last resolution and final answer the next day at four in the evening.
 A few Minutes after the Deputys were gone his Excellency was inform'd that a body of three or four hundred of them were then passing the brook, the Deputys, among wliom were the Captains, returned to him and in appearance seemed softened, and then went to the people who were drawn up in the hill above the House, towards whom his Excellency marching with the detachment, one of the Comissarys who had been with them told him they wanted to pay their compliment to him, so his Excellency walk'd up to them, and ask'd them what they meant by appearing in arms, they told him what they had told the Comissarys, whereupon his Excell(cy) ordered them home to their habitations, and being gone about a mile they discharged all their Firelocks, but their saying they came to pay their Compliment was only a Pretence, for they told

two of their Officers, as they were going home, that they came to releive their Deputys in case they had been confined.

The next day the Deputys came according to order with their answer, which begins indeed with a desire that his Excellency would assist them, that they may be settled in the lands of Scohary, but they soon forget that humble stile, and told his Excellency they had rather lose their lives immediatly than remain where they are, that they are cheated by the contract, it not being the same that was read to them in Engl(d), there they say it run thus, that seven years after they had had forty acres ahead given them, they were to repay the Queen by Hemp, Mast Trees, Tar and Pitch or any thing else, so that it may he no damage to any man in his Family. Upon these terms they will perform the contract, but to be forced by another contract to remain on these lands all their lives, and work for her Majesty for the Ship's use, that they will never doe, what does it signify they say to promise them this land, that they shall make Pitch & Tar, They will be obedient to the Queen but they will have the promise kep't, that W Cast read to them in High Dutch in England, and upon that land which was promised them they will be there and, if they cannot, they desire three or four men may goe for England, and lay their case before the Queen, they say likewise there are a great many things promised them, as clothing, household goods, working Tools, w(eh) they desire to have; They say further their people dye for want of care and proper remedys and desire money to subsist themselves, and lastly they say that M(r) Cast told them he'd make them slaves, and therefore desire his Excellency to appoint another in his room.

Whilst his Excellency was talking with the Deputys he received Information that there was a great body of men in arms on the other side of the Brook, and having by that time a reinforcement of Seventy men more, he marched the detachment immediately and passed the Brook, the Palatines were run home to their houses, His Excellency marched to the first Village and ordered them to bring in all their Arms, which they did immediately except a few; He could go no farther that night but the next morning march'd to y(e) other three Villages on the same side of the River and disarmed them all, and then returning to M(r) Livingston sent orders to the Villages on the other side to bring in their arms that day to the Store house to be transported to him, which I believe they have done, if they refused His Excellency in case of necessity had sloops ready to transport the Detachment thither.

Its hardly credible that men who reap so great a benefit as they doe by these people, not only by the consumption of their Provisions, but by the increase of strength, should yet be so malicious to possess them with notions so injurious to themselves & prejudicial to Her Majesty's Interest, but yet it is so, and I belleve almost the only cause of their present discontents, the Land they live on is generally good, producing so great a crop that those Farmers and men of skill in husbandry who are. honest enough to wish success to these peoples labours wonder how they could be wrought upon to complain of it, but great pains have been taken to magnify the goodness of that at Scohary above this, and to perswade them that, if they once settle where they are, their is no prospect of their ever removeing, but if they refuse to doe that and insist on their being planted on. the other, the Gov (r) must give way to it, and by these means it is that they are arrived to this pitch of disobedience which I hope will wear off now they are disarmed of their Firelocks, the power by which they hoped to force a compliance to their unreasonable humours.

His Excellency has published a Declaration revoking all military Commission and putting them intirely under the command of their overseers and Directors, as the Queen's hired Serv(ts) and all the good people amongst them who have been meerly misled and fright'ned by the turbulent to join in these tumults, are better satisfyed with that rule of Government.

Whatsoever else they complain of I dare be bold to affirm, there are not many Planters in the Province so happy, so healthfull and so well cloth'd as they, nor could it well be otherwise considering how well they have been used, they have by their own choice three flesh and four flower days a Week, a pound of beef a head or equivalent in pork and pease, as long as they lik'd them, besides three quarters of a pound of the finest, or a pound of the coarser sort, of bread, which they please, and as good Beer as any man in the Province drinks of at his table ; of flow(r) they have a pound a head, with bread and beer; there is not one of their houses that is not hung round with Provisions and as to their clothing every one has had of Shoes, Stockins, Kerseys, Shaggs, and other sort of Woollen, such a quantity last winter as their occasions required, and now against the summer a sufficient quantity of linnen, the remainder is kept for their use to supply them as they want, which by such management will goe twice as far as by making one general distribution of the whole; of Tools they have had as many as they want, and a great many more have been made for them here, as particularly two hundred barking irons; as to their dying indeed, many did at their first coming, tho none for want of care or proper Applications, but by diseases contracted on board, since they have been planted in the country they liave had as good a share of health as any people in the world, but all sickness was likewise provided against there by Doctors & Medicines, the want of any thing I am sure is no cause of their turbulent behaviour, whatever the care and plenty they have lived in is.

The 24th Ins(t) **M(r) Sacket, who has been acquainted with the methods of preparing the Trees, was to visit the Woods in order to divide the work amongst the people and then to teach the overseers how to bark the Trees, that they may instruct the people, so that now I suppose they are all at work, and his Excellency has great hopes for thorough reformation.** M(r) Bridger has given over all thoughts of attending this work on any other consideration then that of being hired to it, his Excellency wrote to him to tell him the season of the year approach'd and that it was high time he should be here, he answered if his Excellency would defray his expences he would; The Governor little expected such an answer considering the Salary of two hundred pounds a year sterling allowed him as Surveyor of the Queen's Woods, that by Her Majesty's Royal Letter, under her signet and sign manual, he is expresly commanded to attend that work, and that no Salary is proposed to be allowed him for it by Your Lordships Representation to her Majesty, this put him upon making some farther enquiry after some who had been in the Eastern Countrys, and acquainted themselves with the method of preparing Pine Trees and at length he met with this M(r) Sacket, who undertakes it, and I have very good hopes he will be able to effect it, for he talks more reasonably on that head, then any man I have yet met with, however his Excellency was willing to have M(r) Bridger too, because he was assigned to that work, and for that purpose wrote him two positive orders, in each mentioning Her Majesty's Commands to him, but he still refuses unless on the afore mentioned considerations.

Had he come his Excellency would have reposed but little trust in him, for the method which he formerly proposed to bark the Trees (as he publish'd it in print) would not doe, it has been try'd in Jersey without effect, and to the considerable damage of some men there, nor had he himself better success in Connecticut, as his Excellency is likewise informed from thence; had he been unacquainted with the method of this work he ought to have been engenious in confessing it, that his Excellency might sooner have enquired after some who are acquaint(d) with it, and not have laid hold on that frivolous pretence to conceal his ignorance which however is more excusable than his disobedience to the commands of so gracious Queen, whose bread he has so long, and, as it appears, so unworthily eaten.

This is what, My Lords, I have in command to doe myself the honour to lay before Your Lordships with respect to the Palatines, whatever may have escaped from the haste I am in, for fear of losing the opportunity of the packet, as likewise the Copyes of wliat may be necessary for your Lordship's further information, his Excellency will doe himself the honour to send you by the next.

As to what farther relates to the Indians I inclose you an Caopy of a Letter from the Commission(rs) of the Indian Affairs, and of one from Collonel Schuyler to his Excellency who designs to be at Albany the first of June to meet the Sachems.

I humbly ask pardon for the confus(n) which the want of time may have occasioned in this; and that you will give me leave to subscribe myself as I am, with all possible honour,

> My Lords
> Your Lordships most humble
> and most obedient Servant
> Geo: Clarke.
> New York
> May 30th 1711.

Governor Hunter to the Lords of Trade.
[New York Entries, H. 428.]

To the Right Honb(le) the Lords Commiss(rs) for Trade and Plantations.
My Lords,
(The first part of this document is not included because it pertains to other matters.)
As to the Palatines, the tumults raised among them, by the ill arts of such as had a minde to crush the design have had a quite contrary effect, for since that time,

and a new modell of management, they have been very busy and very obedient; I have now prepared near a hundred thousand Trees, and in the fall sett them to work about the second preparation. M(r) Sackett who has the direction of that work, and seems perfectly well to understand it, has prepared some thousands in a manner, to produce a quantity of Tarr next spring, but that being little better than an Experiment, I doe not much depend upon it. M(r) Bridgers having basely declined, nay endevoured to betray this service, has promoted it soe that I think Providence favours it, for the Gentleman now employed, has been three years amongst the Tarr workers, in the Eastern Contry's, and his manner is soe different from M(r) Bridger's, that I have good reason to conclude, that he knew little of the matter, and would have served only to have thwarted the other, and obstructed the design; I believe if he were strictly examined, he would discover upon what inducements he has acted soe treacherously; **I yelded to his importunity and let him go to Boston in the Winter, he promising a speedy return, hearing nothing from him in the spring when I expected him to attend that work, I wrote to him to meet me at the Palatine Settlements, which by a letter he refused, pretending want of sufficient encouragement.** I wrote to him againe with positive orders to repair thither as he was directed by Her Majesty's special letter, told him that I had applyed to your Lordships for an additional salary for him and put him in mind that he had never been refused money when he called for it, but all to the same purpose I protest to your Lordships whilst he attended to that work he lived as I did, and to my knowledge he did not expend the value of a Crowne, and had several sums of money to the value of about thirty pounds from me during that time. I have had by this packet a letter from M(r) Lownds directing me to enquire into some abuses of his, with relation to the Queen's Woods. I have not had time to make a particular enquiry and have only heard in General that instead of preserving, he has wasted them, by giving deputations to such as have saw-mills for certain yearly sums of money paid him by them by which means all the valuable Timber in these parts is destroyed.

That your Lordships may informe yourselves whether wee be in the right in the pursuite of this Manufacture, **I will give you an account of M(r) Sacketts method of preparing the Trees. In the Spring when the sapp is up, hee barks the North quarter of the circumference about two foot in length, where the sun has least force to draw out the Turpentine; in the Fall before the sapp falls down, hee Barks the South quarter about two foot and four inches next spring, the East quarter for the former reason, about two foot and eight inches, and in that fall the remaining quarter near three foot, after which the part above what is bark'd being full of Turpentine, is cut down splitt and put into kills for Tarr.**

That noe hands may be idle, wee Imployed the Boys and Girls in gathering knotts, whilst their Fathers were a barking, out of which he has made about three score barrells of good Tarr, and hath kills ready to sett on fire for about as much more so soon as he gets casks ready to receive it- .

Now Mylords, tho' I have met with discouragement unspeakable, yet concluding it impossible that the wisdome of Her Ma(tys) Councills should let drop soe beneficial a project, and soe considerable a branch of Trade, when it is in soe hopeful a way, I have launched out all the money and credit I could raise in the pursuit of it, tho' I have as yet no returns to my first bills I have drawn on Mylord Treasurer for about half a year's subsistance for that people ending the 24th of June last, according to the enclosed scheme mark'd D, which I beg your Lordships would be pleased to second with your recommendations. I have made the best Bridge in all North America, over the River between the Pine Woods and their Settlements, have laid in Timber and all other materials for building the Storehouse upon the place and am about the purchase of a convenient- house without the gates of New York on the Harbour for a General Storehouse. Least I should tire your Lordps I shall refer you to my next for more particular accounts of this and all other matters.

(Remainder of document not included, it pertains to other matters.)
Signed
ROB: HUNTER
12 Sept. 1711.

Messrs. Perry, Keill and Du Pre to the Lords of Trade.
[New-York Entries, H. 467.]
To the Right Hon(ble) the Lords Comm(rs) for Trade and Plantations—

My Lords.

In obedience to Your Lordships commands, we underwritten, in behalf of His Excell(cy) Robert Hunter Esq: Gov(r) of New York humbly offer the following answers to the several objections and questions made us concerning the settlement of the Palatines in that province, viz(t).

1st Objection:-That there was no need of the Palatines to set the Manufacture of Naval Stores on foot because others might have done as well.

2nd Objection:-That the Governor did not settle the Palatines on the most convenient place for raising such stores.

3rd Objection:-That the Gov(r) was fallen into bad hands, when he contracted with Coll: Robert Levingston, he being represented to have defrauded the Crown of great sums of money when he subsisted the forces at Albany.

4th Objection:-That the Palatines might have hired themselves to day labour, and have earn'd their living.-

QUERIES:-

1st How long the Palatines are to be subsisted by the Govern(t)?

2nd What Quantity of Tar they are likely to make yearly?

3rd In what manner and in what time the sums advanced by the Queen shall be repaid ?

In answer to the 1st Objection.

We-own, others can raise Naval stores as well as Palatines, provided they be sent upon that design; but since few people in that Country can be spar'd from other labour, there is no considerable quantity of those commodities to be expected, but from the Palatines: And we humbly conceive that the contract made with them, was thought the most effectual means, to set that Manufacture upon a lasting foot, they having thereby oblig'd themselves, to make it their sole business-

To the 2nd Objection.

The Gov(r) before his departure from England did design to setttle the Palatines in the Maquaa's Country, but after he had viewed the same, he judged it impossible for the following reasons-viz(t) 1st Because the purchase thereof from the Indians was not clear. 2nd That it is too much exposed to the incursions of the French and their Indians. 3rd and chiefly, because those lands are distant from the River near 20 miles and Schenectady, besides a Waterfall of 600 foot high, hath the same inconveniency, upon which account the carriage of any thing would cost as much if not more than its worth.-

Now the Gov(r) having found no lands at the Queens disposal, except a tract of 6300 acres on the West side of Hudson's river, which being too small for such a number of families and M(r) Levingston having offered to part with 6000 acres of his lands situated on the other side of the said River distant eight miles above the aforesaid tract at a reasonable rate, His Excell(cy) accepted the offer and purchased it for £200 sterling, so that both settlements are distant about 100 miles from the City of New York on each side of a River navigable by ships of burthen, who may take in their loadings at the said settlements. And for a further demonstration, that this situation was the most proper for answering the ends of the settlement, we humbly refer your Lordships to the draught of-that Country: Within 3 miles or less of the respective settlements there are large tracts of Pine lands the owners whereof have given leave to make use of the trees-M(r) Levingston having reserv'd a sort fit for his saw-mills for planks and Timber and which are of no use for Tarr.

To the third Objection.

M(r) Levingston was always known, to be a careful, industrious and diligent man, who by these more, than by any other means, hath got a considerable estate. It is true that he was accused by a faction in that Country of having defrauded the Gover(t) of great sums when he subsisted the forces at Albany, .but it is as true that he bath honorably clear'd himself, having fairly pas't his accounts before a Committee of Council, upon which he obtained an act of Assembly for releasing him and his Estate that was under a sequestration, until he had so past his accounts; and the reason which induced Gov(r) to deal with him, was not so much his choice as advantage, because the said Levingston made most reasonable and fair offers, and because he was capable of making the largest advances and had most conveniencies for that purpose as Brew house and Bake house. However the Gov(r) did therein act with all the caution and the care imaginable, and the contracts were drawn up by M(r)Mompesson Chief Justice of the province, and made as plain and binding as possible, so well with regard to the purchase of the land as to the Bread and Beer he undertook for, at the rates the Magistrates of the City of New York should from time to time set upon them, and with this express condition, that if the Palatines or their overseers had any legal objection against either the Bread or Beer, he did oblige himself to take it back and give better in lieu thereof. That M(r) Levingston undertook this with a prospect of advantage is so certain, that it might have created an ill opinion of him if it were otherwise.

To the fourth Objection.

The Palatines could not have hired themselves to day labour, without disbanding themselves after their arrival at New York which His Excell(cy) could not have given his consent to, without disobeying the Queen's Instructions, which are positive for settling them in a body, and for subsisting them, until they could subsist of the product of their labour; And we do humbly conceive the Gov(r)could never have answered it to the Queen, and to this Hon(ble) Board, if contrary to his instructions he had suffered the dispersion of them; Whereby all hope of making any benefit by that useful Manufacture had been lost, especially after he had received £8000 from the Govern(t) in part for their subsistence, towards that end. Besides: My Lords, any one who is not altogether a stranger to that Country knows that not above 5 or 600 could have disposed of themselves in that manner, and even half of them could not have found imployment, but in plowing and harvest time; so that above one thousand of them, must either have starved or become a burthen to the Country.-

We shall in the next place humbly offer in answer to your Lords.

Queries:

1st That the Gov'(r) affirms that after Christmas 1712. the Palatines shall be able to subsist of the product of their lands.

2nd That many experiences have demonstrated, that one Man may easily make 60 Barels of Tar in a year; so that computing the number of working hands to be 500, these will raise 30000 barrels in the whole, and so on yearly after the year 1713.

3rd That a Barrel of Tar is sold at New York for 85 sterling so that the whole product will yearly amount to £12,000.

And if the Queen will be graciously pleased to allow them, for an encouragement suppose one mojety out of the yearly product being, £6000. there will remain a yearly sum of £6000. towards discharging the money advanced by the Queen for their settlement and support; so that computing the whole expence to be 40000, they may repay the Queen in seven years or less after the year 1713.

My Lords.

We humbly ask leave to observe further that tho' Tar be only here mentioned, it is not the only thing designed; but as the Gov(r) hath carryed with him Pots and other utencils necessary for boiling Pitch and Rozin the children from 8 years and upwards will be usefully imployed therein, And that Coll: Hunter by a letter to me Micajah Perry gives direction to send him a considerable quantity of Hemp-seed, saying that he hath given orders for preparing lands to sow it in, and dressing of Hemp is a work tliat may be done in the depth of Winter, when people can not stir out of doors, by which means they will have constant imployment-And if this design be duly encouraged and supported, as the Gov(r) hopes it will, it will infallibly compleat and make it a standing Manufacture of Naval stores.

All which is humbly submitted to Your Lordps. prudent consideration by your Lordps. ettc.

11 Dec(r) 1711 MICAJAH PERRY, JOHN KEILL, JAMES DU PRE.

1712 Letters regarding the Palatines

Lords of Trade to the Lord High Treasurer
[New-York Entries, H. 482.]
To the Most Hon(ble) the Lord High Treasurer of Great Britain.

My Lord.

Pursuant to Your Lordp's desire signify'd to us by M(r) Lowndes the 26th Nov(r) last we have considered the observations made by the Earl of Clarendon upon two letters from Coll Hunter to the Earl of Dartmouth relating to the Palatines at New York upon which we observe to your Lordship.

That in August 1709. when the Palatines were in this Kingdom, it was referred by Her Maj(ty) to this Board to consider how to dispose of the said Palatines who thereupon proposed that such of them as should not be otherwise provided for, be sent to be settled on Hudson's River in the province of N. York.

In Nov(r) following when Coll: Hunter was appointed Gov(r) of New York a proposal of his for taking over with him 3000 of the said Palatines, to be employed in the producing of Naval Stores in that province, was referred to this Board, and on the 5th Dec(r) they reported the advantage it would be to that province to have such a number of those people settled there, and the benefit that would accrue to Her Maj(ty) and this Kingdome by establishing a trade for Naval Stores in Her Majt(ys) dominions. The said Report further contained a scheme for settling, maintaining and imploying the said Palatines and Her Maj(ty) having been pleased to approve thereof and Coll. Hunter desiring to have instructions in relation to the said Palatines, that Rep(tn) was turned into an Additional Instruction and signed by Her Majesty.

And lest the Palatines should at any time fall off from the imployment design'd for them, Her Maj(ty) was pleased to direct that they should oblige themselves by a contract in writing to attend that work, and an instrument for that purpose having been drawn (with the advice of Her Maj(tys) then Attorney General) was signed by the Palatines accordingly, a copy of which is herewith laid before Your Lordship. In which they promise that the neat produce of the Naval Stores they shall make, shall be applyed towards the repayment of what Her Majv shall disburse for their support & maintenance.

We take leave further to observe that in the forementioned representation of 5th Dec(r) 1709. there is one clause which proposes: "That as these people are very necessitous they will not be able to maintain themselves till they can reap the benefit of their labour, which will not be till after one year at the soonest, they be therefore subsisted the Men & women at sixpence ster: a head p(r) day and the children under ten years of age at four pence steri:"- This Representation having been turned into an instruction as aforesaid, seem to be a consent on Her Maj(tys) behalf, that she would subsist the Palatines as is therein proposed and the directions the then Commiss(rs) for trade had to prepare the forementioned contract signed by the Palatines, imply that Her Maj'y would do it for the first year.

After their arrival at New York the Gov(r) sent over an account of what had been done towards their settlement and imployment upon which this Board laid before Her Maj(ty) in Feb'y last a full State of that matter, giving the reasons why it was necessary to allow £15000 a year for their subsistance for two years to be computed from midsummer 1710, a copy of which Representation is herewith laid before Your Lordship.

When the Palatines arrived at New York they were in number 2227, and by the Acc(t) transmitted over by Coll: Hunter, & laid before your Lordship the 13th Nov(r) last the number that had been subsisted from the 26th March to the 24. June last was about 1894:

We have no acc(t) from the Gov(r) of the application of the 10000 pounds, which has been issued to him otherwise than that he informs us that " besides the £8000 for which he had bills over with him he had drawn other bills for £4700, all which money, he writes, has been expended in settling these people, and that he had transmitted an acc(t) thereof to the then

Lords Comss(rs) of the Treasury whereby, he says, it does appear that he has disposed of that money with good management.

In order to our laying this matter more fully before your Lordp. and to propose some method how Her Maj(ty) shall be repaid, we take leave to offer that computing by the number of trees already prepared they may make 30000 Barrels of Tarr the first year 1713. which at New York is 8 shill: Steri: pr Barril and will come to £12000-And that if Her Majesty should be graciously pleased to allow them one mojety it would be sufficient encouragement for them to go on with their work, and by this means Her Maj(ty) would be repaid in about six years time as as more fully set forth in a memorial herewith laid before Your Lordship-

In case Her Maj(ty) shall be graciously pleased to approve hereof, we are of opinion, that it will be necessary a person be appointed by Her Maj(ty) to receive the Tar at New York into a storehouse to be provided there to ship the same for this Kingdom, and to Slate and keep particular accounts of the whole, both in relation to the past as future expence to be laid from time to time before Your Lordp. as is more particularly set forth in the above mentioned Representation of 5Dec(r)1709.

Upon the whole as it does not appear to us there has been any mismanagement in subsisting the said Palatines by Coll: Hunter and that his Credit is very deeply ingaged in that service, and in consideration that the whole design of producing Naval Stores in Her Maj(tys) Dominions by the Palatines must fall and the money already expended be intirely lost unless they are subsisted for two years as aforementioned, we are humbly of opinion that they be supported in such method as your Lordship shall think proper-We are-Mylord. Your Lordp's most obedient humble servants

> WINCHELSEA,
> GEO: BAILLIE,
> PH. MEADOWS,
> ARTH MOORE,
> CH. TURNER,
> FR. GWYN.
> Whitehall Febr(y) 1, 17 11/12.

Governor Hunter to the Lords of Trade.

(First part of letter is not shown, it pertains to other matters.)

...................As. to the Palatines I doe assure your Lordships that their work comes fully up to our expectation, the trees they are prepar(g) and which will receive the last barking next fall promisse extreamly well, and M(r) Sackett tells me he does not in the least doubt but that the experiment he is making of some trees to fell at a years preparation will answer very well and as soon as this parking (which they are now about) is over hee will try it, of which I will inform your Lordships, by the first opportunity after it, as to that small quantity of tar which I formerly mentioned to your Lordships, I must beg leave again to observe to you, that it was made from the Knotts which the children gather'd together whilst their Fathers were working on the trees, this tar may have y(e) burning quality, but is as good fro pitch as the other. N. your Lordships want to be informed out of what fund I provide the cask for the tar, formerly told your Lordships, that out of the sixpences and four pences a day for these peoples subsistance, I hoped to pay all the contingent charges, except such as are mentioned in a list sent by M(r) Du Pre, and this of the cask is one of those charges I shall pay out of the subsistance.

I have not had any complaints of late of the Palatines they work chearfully, and seem resolved to goe through what they are employed about, being greatly incouraged by the proposall of receiving one half of the proffits of y(e) tarr to their own use, whilst the other half goes towards the payment of the charge her Majesty is put to about them I am so much indisposed now to goe to them, but as soon as I am able to de[s]ign to goe up and visit their works and M(r) Sackett being with them he will take care that noe part of this Barking season be mispent.

(........................ the letter covers other topics.)
It is signed by Robt Hunter, New York June 23d 1712.

Governor Hunter to the Lords of Trade

(First part of letter is not shown because it pertains to other matters.)

...............As to the Palatines my substance and credit being exhausted, I had no remedy left but by a letter to the managers of the work, to inimate to that people that they should take measures to subsist themselves during the winter, upon the lands where they were planted, and such as could not, might find it by working with the inhabitants leaving with their commissaries their names and the names of the places or landlords where they are employed during that time, that they may be in readiness upon the first publick notice given to return to work, which they have obliged themselves by contract to pursue; upon this intimation some hundreds of them took a reolution of possessing the lands of Scharee, & are accordingly march'd thither have been suisy in cutting a road from Schenectedy to that place, and have purchased or procured a quantity of Indian corn toward their winter subsistance, it being imposs(ble;) for me to prevent this, I have been the easier under it, upon these considerations that by these means the body of that people is kept together witin the Province, that when it shall please her Majesty to resume the design of Prosecuti;ng that work, that body at Schoharee may be employ'd in working in the vast pine woods near to Albany, which they must be obliged to do, having no manner of pretence to y(e) possession of any lands but by performing their part of the contract relating to that manufacture, and that in that situation they serve in some measure as a frontier to, or at least an increase to the strength of Albany and Schenectaday, but if the war continues, or should by any misfortune break out again, it will be neighter possible for them to subsist, or safe for them to reamin there; considering the ill use they have already made of arms when they were intrusted with them. The tar work in the mean time was brought to all the perfection that was possible in the time, the trees have received their last preparation, and staves prepar'd for the barrels, the magazines almost finish'd, and the road between it and the pine woods almost compleated M(r) Sacket, who has had the direction of that work ever since M(r) Bridger did basely desert it, assures me, that the trees promise beyond expectation, the best of it in oru present circumstances is that the longer they should stand now the more tar they will yield, providing it do not exceed a year or two.

The reasons of the difference between the method of preparing the trees which your Lordships have transmitted to me, and that we follow, are obvious; the sun has much more force here than in Moscow, which obliges us to consult and follow the seasons of the year in our several barkings; I myself have observed that where by mistake the trees have been first rinded on the side where the suns heat had most influence, the ground near it was filled with turpentine dreined by it from the tree.

My friends in England who know nothing of the matter press mightily the send over a quantity of tar to convince the world of the solidity of the project to your Lordships I refer them, who are sufficiently apprized of the time absolutely requisite to produce the first quantity in the manner it is done in all other Countries from whence we have had it, and shall conclude this subject with this reflection, if the production of that quantity of tar requisite for the Navy in her Majesty's own Plantations be a real advantage or rather at this time indispensable necessary to Great Britian, if the world is convinced that tar is made out of Pitch pine, of which we are here sufficiently perswaded, our trees yielding as much turpentine, (which is the same substance) as any in the world, if a sufficient Number of hands duely instructed and employ'd are the instruments and mean of producing it, which are now here at a great expence and so employ'd, if all this, be true as undeniable it is, then I shall still conclude it impossible that this design as can be dropt, when it is brought so near to the Pitch of perfection.

(...................................rest of letter discusses other matters.)

Signed Robt Hunter
New York
Oct(r) 31st, 1712.

1720 Petition Regarding The Palatines and Their Settling in Schoharie.

Petition of Johannes Wilhelm Schefs, Agent for the Palatines. [New York Papers, Cc., 86.]

To the Right Honble the Lords, Com(rs) of Trade & Plantations,
        The humble Petition of William Scheef, in behalf of himself & the Germans commonly called Palatines Dwelling in Schorie in New York.
        Sheweth That there are at present about one Hundred & sixty Families, consisting of about One Thousand Souls, in that part of New York, called Schorie, in which they have built Hutts, Houses & some Mills for grinding of Corn where, also they have improved the Ground; & have cleared away (besides an other mentioned in their Case) [a road] that runs down from their Habitations as far as Albany being about twenty four Miles in Length, for a free communication with Albany
        That there are also about five Hundred German Families, consisting of about Three thousand Souls dwelling in dispersed habitations in the said Province of New York.
        That the said German Families have impowered your Petitioner as also John Conrad Weiser; (1) to implore the Kings gracious favour for granting the free possession of the said Valley of Schorie to the said 160 Families, or as many others as should find Room to settle therein; And to pray that His Majesty would be pleased to extend His bounty to the remaining 500 families, by securing a settlement for them, either above, below or round about, the valley of Schorie in those parts, formerly in the possession of M(r) Godfrey Dellius or in Mackworth (2) Land
        But your Petitioner (hearing with grief that John Conrad Weiser has petitioned your Lordships, for obtain(g) a tract of land called Chettery(3)) most humbly entreats your Lordships, to dismiss the said Weiser's Petition as being directly contrary to our Instruct(ns) & the inclinations of our people who earnestly desire to lead a quiett & peaceable life and are utterly averse to expose their tender Children, and child bearing Women to another Transportation by Water as still remembering the loss of most of their young children at their going from home to America; all which may appear in our case,(4) now laying before your Lordships, which is signed by M(r) Weiser himself
        If your Lordships should think fit to remove the said 160 families to any other part of the said Province of New York, They hope their Houses, their Mills, & their labour in clearing the Ground and making the said way of 24 Miles shall be appraised by impartial persons to be chosen by each party, & the value thereof made good unto them before their Removal from thence
        And considering, that the grant of the valley of Schorie supposed to be given to some Gentlemen of Albany, being made some time after the said Germans had seated themselves therein at first to one & afterwards to two other persons, was as they humbly conceive against the Plantation Laws for the truth of which they humbly appeal to the proceedings of the

        Footnote (1) JOHN CONRAD WEISER, son of Jacob Weiser, was a magistrate of the village of Great Anstach, in the Duchy of Wirtemburg, in Germany, and married Anna Magdalena Uebele, by -whom he had fifteen children. She dying in 1709, he left his country, and landed, - with the major part of his family, in New York, in June, 1710. Thence he was sent, -with a number of other Palatines, to Livingston Manor, -where he again married in 1711. Government having withdrawn all assistance from the Palatines, in 1713, they sent John Christ. Fuchs, Hartman Winedecker, John Peter Kneskern, John Christ. Gerlach, Hans George Schmidt and Mr. Weiser, as deputies to the Mohawk Indians for permission to settle in Schoharie, whither about 150 families removed in 1114. The lands having been granted to others, great confusion ensued, as the Palatines refused to hold under the patentees, and appealed to the Government in England, to which country Captain Weiser, William Scheff and -- Walrath proceeded, to lay their Case at the foot of the Throne. They secretly embarked at Philadelphia in 1718, but on the voyage fell into the hands of pirates who robbed them of their all and then set them free, when they put into Boston to procure necessaries. On arriving in London thay found themselves penniless and forced to contract debts. The consequence was, Weiser and Scheff were thrown into prison, from which they were afterwards released only by a remittance from New York. Scheff and Weiser quarreled whilst in London. The former returned to America in 1721 and died shortly after. Weiser returned in 1723. Some of the Palatines removed to Stone Arabia, some remained at Schoharie, but the major part of them crossed the forests to the head waters of the Susquehanna where they built canoes and floated down that river to Swatara, on the head waters of which and of the Tulpehocken they settled on Indian lands now comprising part of Berks and Lebanon counties. Captain Weiser died on the 13th July, 1760. Abridged from
Collections of the Historical Society of Pennsylvania, I., 1-6. - ED.

(2) Mackwaa, i. e., Mohawk.
(3) Swatara, Penn. See note 1.
(4) See ante, p. 553.

Assembly of the Province, and those of the Governor & Council; In case they shall be maintain(d)
in the said Valley of Schorie they will cheerfully pay all such charges for the support of the government as other subjects there are used to do.

Therefore Your Petitioner humbly Prays your Lordships will be pleased to confirm the said 160 Families in the Possession fo the Valley of Schorie & the mountainous parts thereof, & allot to the other 500 Families such Lands somewhere near about the valley of Schorie as your Lordship in your great wisdom shall think fit.

And that your Lordships would further vouchsafe to grant a Coppy of Colonel Hunters Memorial relating to our Case that the underwritten may have an opportunity to vindicate his principals from any mismanagement alledged ag(st) his Collegue M(r) Weiser
And Your Petitioner as in duty bound shall ever pray &c &c.
Nov: 1. 1720
(signed) Johan Whilm Schefs.

1720 Letters regarding the Palatines settling in Schoharie.

Brigadier Hunter to Secretary Popple.
[New-York Papers, Cc., 12.]
London y 26 July. 1720.

Sir

I have the honour of a Petition from. Wyser and ether Palatines with their Lordp(s) commands relating to it.

Such of that people as were sober & industrious remain on the Lands where I settled them at first & which I was obliged to Purchase for them on Hudsons River for the ends proposed by those who sent them Viz(t) the manufacture of Naval Stores; these are well inabled to subsist themselves the rest have been wanderers. About forty Familys of them went and took possession of Lands granted to several persons at New York and Albany against repeated orders: In compassion to the innocent women and children I prevailed with the Proprietors of these Lands to make them an offer of the Lands free from all rent or acknowledgement for ten years & ever after at a very moderate Quit Rent. The Majority accepted of the conditions but durst not or could not execute the agreem1 for fear of the rest who had been tampering with the Indians who had resigned their claims to their Lands to the Crown, but I have some reason to beleive that in the mean time it is compleated or speedily will be so

Their Lordships know that all the Lands of any value were granted away before my Administration There is still a great Tract of Land but very remote on the Frontiers formerly graunted to Domine Dellius of Fifty miles square & resumed by Act of Assembly which may be graunted to them, if they are willing to transplant themselves thither In a body so as they may be secure from the attempts of the French Indians their nearest Neighbours, but their neighbourhood with our Indians has given much trouble & may give more. If their Lordships think fit to make them an offer of that settlement a letter to the present Governor for that purpose will do the thing & free their Lordships from further trouble if they are willing to accept of the offer but

Query how far such grant may avail them until his Majesty has approved of the Naturalization Act or whether the Gov(t) can grant them letters of Denization to enable them to hold Lands, there being no such powers mentioned in his letters patent. I am with the greatest respect.

Sir, Your most obedient
- humble Servant
Sg(t) RO HUNTER.

Petition of the New York Palatines to the Lords of Trade.
[New York Papers, Cc., 11.]

The Case of the Palatines, and others Germans, in the Province of New York in America sheweth.

That, In the year 1709. The Palatines, & other Germans, being invited to come into England about Four Thousand of them were sent into New York in America, of whom about 1700. Died on Board, or at their landing in that Province, by unavoidable sickness That before they went on Board, they were promised, those remaining alive should have forty acres of Land, & Five pounds sterling p(r) Head, besides Cloths, Tools, Utensils & other necessaries, to Husbandry to be given at their arrival in America

That on their landing their they were quartered in Tents, & divided into six companies, promise but having each a Captain of their own Nation, with a promise of an allowance of allowance fifteen Pounds per annum to each commander

That afterwards they were removed on Lands belonging to M(r) Livingstone, where they erected small Houses for shelter during the winter season

That in the Spring following they were ordered into the woods, to make Pitch & Tar, where they lived about two years; But the country not being fit to raise any considerable quantity of Naval Stores, They were commanded to Build, to clear, & improve the ground, belonging to a private person

That the Indians have yielded to Her late Ma(ty) of pious memory a small Tract of Land called Schorie for the use of the Palatines, they in fifteen days cleared a way of fifteen miles through the woods & settled fifty families therein

That in the following Spring the remainder of the said Palatines joined the said fifty families so settled therein Shorie

But that country being too small for their encreasing families, they were constrained to purchase some Neighbouring Land of the Indians for which they were to give Three hund(d) pieces of Eight

And having built small Houses, & Hutts there about one year after the said purchase some gentelmen of Albani, declared to the Palatines, that themselves having purchas(d) the said country of Schorie of the Gov(r) of New York they would not permit them to live there, unless an agreement were also made with those of Albany; But that the Palatines having refused to enter into such an agreement, A Sheriff & some officers were sent from Albany to seize one of their Captains, who being upon his Guard ; The Indians were animated against the Palatines; but these found means to appease the Savages by giving them what they would of their own substance.

That In the year 1717 the Governour of New York having summoned the Palatines to appear at Albani, some of them being deputed went thither accordingly, where they were told, that unless they did agree with the Gentlemen of Albany, the Governor expected an order from England to transport them to another place, And that he would send twelve men to view their works & improvements to appraise the same & then to give them the value thereof in money But this not being done the Palatines to the number of about three Thousand, have continued to manure & to sew the Land that they might not be starved for want of Corn & food

For which manuring the Gentlemen of Albani have put in prison one man and one woman, & will not release them, unless they have suffic(t) security of One Hundred Crowns for the former

Now in order that the Palatines may be preserved in the said Land of Schorie, which they have purchased of the Indians, or that they may be so settled in an adjoining Tract of Land, as to raise a necessary subsistance for themselves & their families, they have sent into England Three Persons one of whom is since dead humbly to lay their Case before His Maj(ty) not doubting but that in consideration of the Hardships they have suffered for want of a secure settlement, His Majestys Ministers and Council will compassionate those His faithful Subjects; Who, in the first year after their arrival willingly and cheerfully sent Three Hundred men to the expedition against Canada, & afterwards to the Asistcince of Albani which was threatened by the French and Indians, for which service they have never received One Penny tho' they were upon the Establishment of New York or New Jersey nor had they received one Penny of the five pounds per head promised at, their going on board from England Neither have their commanders received anything of the allowance of fifteen pounds per Annum, and tho' the arms they had given them at the Canada expedition which were by special order from Her late Majesty, to be left in their possession, have been taken from them, yet they are still ready to fight against all the enemies of His Mat(y) & those countrys whenever there shall be occasion to shew their hearty endeav(rs) for the prosperity of their generous Benefactors in England as well as in America

Therefore they hope from the Justice of the Right Honble the Lords Commissioners of Trade and Plantations, to whom their Petition to their Excellencies the Lords Justices has Been referred That they shall be so supported by their Lordships Report, as to be represented fit objects to be secured in the Land they now do inhabit or in some near adjoining lands remaining int he right of the Crown in the said Province of New York

And they shall ever pray as in duty bound &c

2 Aug: 1720.

Minutes of the Board of Trade respecting the Palatines.
[Journal, XXX., 3A1.]
Whitehall Tuesday 6th Sept(r)1780

At a meeting of His Majesty's Commiss(rs)for Trade & Plantations.
PRESENT- " Earl of Westmorland
M(r) Doeminique
Sir Charles Cooke
M(r)Bladen

New York.

Gen(l) Nicholson attending as desir'd, as also M(r) Jeremy Long who appears in behalf of the Palatines & other Germans at New York, whose Petition & case, as also a letter from Brigadier Hunter on the same subject are mention'd in the Minutes of the 21st of July and 2d of August last, the said case and Letter were again read; And Gen(l) Nicholson being ask'd what he knew of the Allegations set forth in behalf of the said Palatines; He said that he understood the Number of the Palatines first sent over to New York, was about 3200 ; -That he knew nothing of any promises made to them;-That he had about 300 of the said Palatines with him in the expedition to Montreal, who were subsisted during that Expedition, but that he knows of no Engagements concerning their Pay;--That he is a stranger to their settlement at Schories-That as to the Arms made use of in the Expedition, he knows of no direction for leaving what the Palatines had in their possession, but that there was an Order for leaving some of them in the Plantations as Stores for the Magazines there-And M(r) Long above mentioned being unable to make proof of any of the Particulars set forth in the said Case of the Palatines; he was acquainted that Copies of the several Papers relating to their Petition, shou'd be transmitted to M(r) Burnet Gov(r) of New York, and the settlement of such of them as desire to remove to proper places, recommended to him, tho it was observ'd to M(r) Long that it seem'd sev(l) of the said Palatines had behav'd themselves very undutifully to His Majesty and his late Governor of that Province.

Charles Cooke

1722 Letters from Governor Burnet regarding the Palatines

Governor Burnet to the Lords of Trade.
[New York Papers, Cc., 96.]

New York 21st Nov(r) 1722

My Lords

I now send your Lordships all the Propositions made to the Indians at Albany by the Governors of Virginia & Pensylvania as well as my own, with the several Answers of the Indians: which I hope have laid such a foundation for a good understanding between the several Provinces in their Management with the Indians as will make them look upon us as a much more powerful people than the French of Canada while they see us united in our Proceedings, whereas the frequent occasions they have had to observe that the Provinces acted upon separate Interests, have been the cheif cause of their unsteadiness and of their fearing the French more than us

The Governor of Virginia having the year before complained to me that the five nations made frequent inroads into that Province contrary to their ancient Treatys made at Albany with Lord Howard of Effingham, Governor of Virginia forty years ago, & which were several times renewed I did then purpose that they should not exceed certain Bounds in their Hunting or warlike expeditions to the Southward so as to keep clear of Virginia to which Proposal the Indians did consent but expected that the Government of Virginia should send them some Person of distinction to renew the Covenant Chain, as they call it that is to give them a fine present to refresh their Memorys Upon my acquainting Coll Spotswood of this he did at last prevail with the Assembly in Virginia to provide for the necessary charge of this Embassy and accordingly came himself to treat with them on this view, first obtaining my approbation with that of the Council of New York, for every single point he proposed, And this is the subject matter of his two days Propositions to the Indians and of their answers in which they perfectly agreed to what he proposed for the Particulars of which I humbly beg leave to refer your Lordships to the Papers themselves which I have distinguished by Titles on the Back

The Governor of Pensylvania found it necessary to give these Indians a meeting upon an unfortunate accident of an Indian of the five Nations, being killed in Pensylvania by a Christian, for whose death he had not sufficient evidence The Offender continued a Prisoner till the Indians desired his enlargement and declared themselves satisfied and this is the subject, of the conference between S(r) William Keith and the five Nations

Though I doubt not but Coll Spotswood & S(r) W(m) Keith will give your Lordships an account at large of these Proceedings, yet as they were transacted in this Province in my own sight. I thought it my duty to do it myself likewise

I had likewise received a Proposal some time ago from the Government of Boston, that they might send Deputys to treat with the five Nations in order to engage them against the Eastern Indians, but finding a great averseness in the Council of this Province that their Deputys should treat with the five Nations unless the particulars were first regulated with the Goverment here & the Government of New England not agreeing to send commissioners to treat with us previously upon the heads to be proposed to the Indians, I found no way but to take this matter wholly upon myself and I accordingly proposed to the Indians the very terms desired by the Government of Boston and have effected the interposition of the five Nations, by messengers now gone from them to Boston & from thence to the Eastern Indians; for which I have the thanks of Governor Shute for making this affair succeed, when he had little reason to expect it, from the indiscretion of some Persons sent from Boston to Albany, which attempted to treat with the five Nations of Indians without the knowledge of this Government which had raised the jealousy here to that Degree, that I had no small difficulty to bring the Council to agree with me in that affair, which however I did at last.

And this is the main matter that is new in my treaty with the Indians of the five Nations and I did also enforce what I had recommended to them the year before to avoid all Dependance on Canada, and hearkening to their emissarys and to encourage the Trade from hence with the far Nations which has had good success, and is in a fair way to encrease their being now a constant company resident on the Lake Ontorio, and who have in presence of the French at Niagara sold goods by our Indians hands for half the value that the French used to extort by which they are likely to loose ground to us in that Trade every year. In my last Speech I did in the presence of the two other Governors take notice of the present strong Union and good intelligence, there is between all the Provinces, which shewed itself in their acting in concert in every thing and that they looked on themselves as concerned equally in what was done to any one of them and so renewed the old Covenant in behalf of the whole British Interest, for the particular of all which I must likewise take the liberty to refer your Lordships to the Papers themselves, all which I have annexed together, with my propositions to the River Indians, as we call them who live interspersed among the Inhabitants and are not so numerous or warlike as the five Nations and much more under command, I have also sent their answer to me

When I was at Albany I expected to have fixed the Palatines in their new Settlement which I had obtained of the Indians for them at a very late purchase, but I found them very much divided into Parties and the cunningest among them fomenting their Divisions on purpose that the greatest number might leave the Province and then the great Tract of Land lately purchas(d) would make so many considerable estates to the few Familys that should remain- And with this view they told me that they found the Land was far short of what the Indians had represented it to them and that not above twenty Familys could subsist there which I shewed them was a mere pretence by naming a Tract where 130 Familys live and flourish, which by their own confession was less and no better soil than theirs however since I found it was their humour to undervalue what had been done for them I thought it best to wait till they should of themselves be forward to settle this new Tract rather than to shew too much earnestness in pressing them to it. But as about sixty familys desired to be in a distinct Tract from the rest & were those who had all along been most hearty for the Government I have given them leave to purchase land from the Indians, between the present English settlements near Fort Hunter & part of Canada on a Creek called Canada Creek where they will be still more immediately a Barrier against the sudden incursions of the French, who made this their Road when they last attacked & burned the Frontier Town called Schonectady-The other Palatines have since my return to New York, sent some of their body to desire a warrant of Survey for y(e) New Tract already purchased, which convinces me that I had done right, in not being too ernest in that affair when I was at Albany And indeed in my dealings with those people I find very little gratitude for favors done them, & particularly that those who were best taken care of & settled on good Lands by my Predecessor are the most apt to misrepresent him and this is managed by a few cunning persons among them that lead the rest as they please, who are for the generality a laborious and honest but a headstrong ignorant people

I have now sent your Lordships one private act for the sale of some houses and Lands belonging to Gilbert Livingstone which will not be effectual till confirmed by his Mat(y) & as all the Partys concerned to this act, and it is the only way the Debt to the revenue can be paid by this Gilbert Livingstone, who was the later Farmer of the Excise I hope your Lordships will favor me with an effectual & speedy recommendation of this Act to His May(y) for His Royal Approbation I intend by the next opportunity to send y(e) Lordships all the other Act pass(d) in this session of the Assembly at New York with some account of them. I should apprehand being tiresome to your Lordships had not your favorable construction of all my former importunity emboldened me to subscribe myself with a great deal of Cheerfulness as well as with the sincerest respect.

Your Lords mo Obed(t) Servant
Signed (d) W. Burnet

Mr. Colden's Account of the Climate of New York.

Date on this is uncertain; it appears in the 1723 documents.

[New-York Papers, Co., 118.]
An Account of the Climate of New York. by. C Colden Surveyor Gen(ll) of the Province

The City of New York lyes nearly in 40. degr: & 40 min: of North Latitude and about five hours west from London-The climate partakes of the extreem climates Sometimes the summer is as hot as in the Torrid Zone, and the Winter often is not less cold than in the Northern Parts of Europe-The Heat & cold depends very much upon the winds and for that reason in the same season of the year are very various, In the Summer when the wind blows from the Northwest which frequently happens) the air is agreeably cool but in the winter it is piercing cold A Southerly and South Westerly wind if it continue any time in Summer, becomes very hot, and if we want winds, which sometimes happens in July and August, the Air becomes sultry Southerly winds in Winter make the cold very moderate We have much less rain or Snow than in England & the Heaven is seldom overcast with Clouds-The Northwest wind being so extreemly cold, even so far South as North Carolina, I beleive is owing to the high ridge of Mountains which lye to the Westward of Virginia, Maryland, Pensylvania and this province, tho it be generally attributed to the great Lakes which lye to the North westward of this Province, for it is observed in all other countrys that the winds which come from any great quantity of water are not so cold as those that come from Mountains and are always accompanied with rain or moisture whereas the Northwest winds here are very drye besides the winds from the Lakes must be stopt in their course, by these high Mountains which lye betwixt us & the Lakes This is confirmed by what I am told by those who have continued some time in the Sinnekees Country near lagara, on the west side of the mountains, that the Northwest winds there are always accompanied with rain as the easterly winds are here

Tho there be so great a variety of weather in this Country the Height of the Mercury in the Barometer does not suffer so great changes as in England I have had a Barometer by me about six years & never observed the Mercury Lower than 29 inch & 7 or 8 tenths of an inch & it is generally betwixt 30 & 30 1/2 Inches high, tho I have sometimes observed it 31- Inches high which is as high as it is ever observed in England, or I think any where else, but it is so high only in the time of very hard Frost

The Spring is much later than in England, we perceive but very little of it before the latter end of April, March is generally cold and windy, tho for the most part the latter end of February be mild and warm-The winds in March are generally Northerly and they as well as the cold, is owing to the melting of the snow to the Northward of us for these winds are always preceded by some warm weather, either in the latter end of February or beginning of March-The lateness of the Spring is owing to the whole country being covered with wood, so that the Sun cannot easily dissolve the snow which lyes under the Trees or warm the earth-The lateness of the Spring makes it short the hot weather succeeding the cold very quickly-In the Spring the people are subject to Pleuresies and inflammatory fevers, as in all other Countrys upon the breaking up of hard winters, but not so much as in Pennsylvania, and in the countrys to the Southward-The country people and such as are most exposed to the cold are most liable to these Distempers perhaps the reason of the Southern Countrys being more subject to Pleurisies, is that in those countrys the poorer sort are not so well cloathed & have not such warm houses as in this.

The Summer begins in the end of May, and continues hot to the beginning of September July & August are the most sultry months, and very often rainy, The air in these two months is always full of moisture, so much that the Doors and windows are observed then to be more swelled than at any other time of the year & Iron rusts so much that it is difficult to keep any Instrument clean, which is made of that Metal tho the weather be extreemly hot at the same time A far greater quantity of Dew likewise falls in these months than at any other time, arid begins to fall a considerable while before Sun set the Mornings are frequently foggy especially near the Rivers & Marshes, after sun rising this proceeds from the quantity of vapour which falls in the night, & is easily raised but is generally dissipated before ten in the morning-The heat in these months is a great deal more uneasy than in June Tho a greater quantity of the Sun's Rays fall upon the earth in that month than in these

This is owing to the quantity of vapour in the air which retains the heat and becomes in a manner scalding for it is always observed that the heat is a great deal more uneasy before rain (tho' the sun does not shine clear) than it is after a shower when it shines with its greatest brightness, and a burning glass before rain does not burn so vehemently as it does after rain. If the air continues sultry after rain we expect more rain speedily or a great quantity of Dew that night. The air is frequently fanned in the hot months with sudden Gusts of Nortwest winds they commonly rise in the afternoon and blow violently for half an hour or little more with heavy showers of rain & thunder claps & leave the air agreeably cool & serene when the Country was first settled these Gusts were very frequent hardly a day in the hot seasons passing without them but now since the country began to be cleared the summer is not so sultry and these Gusts are not so frequent-They are likewise much more frequent in the Provinces to the southward of us than in this.

The Thermometer (mind is of Mr Patricks make) in the Summer within doors where the sun can not reach is generally about 20 tho at sometimes it is above 15 & other times below 30- In June I tryed the difference betwixt what it was in the house & the open air where it was exposed to the suns rays, betwixt 2 and 3 in the afternoon which is generally the hottest time of the day and found the Spirit -rise 36 degrees or parts marked in the Thermometer above what it was in the House The Thermometer in the house stood at 26, & exposed to the sun rose 5 degrees above the place marked 3.

The months of July Aug & beginning of September are the most sickly months in the year more people being sick and more children dying than in all the rest of the year The Epidemical Diseases are intermitting Fevers, Cholera Morbus & Fluxes The intermitting Fevers are not near so frequent in this Province as in those more to y(e)Southward, but I think fluxes are more frequent in this Town than in Philadelphia Two reasons may be assigned for this first, the poor people at this time eat abundance of Water Melons and other such kind of fruits more than they do at Philadelphia The other is that the Water in the Town is not neer so good as there being brackish & so hard (as it is commonly termed,) that it will not dissolve Soap.

The fall in this country (and all over the main of America) is most agreeable from the beginning of September to the middle of November The weather being mild and dry The Sckie always serene, and the People healthy

We reckon the winter from the middle of November to March tho' the violent Frosts do not usually begin till about Christmas & then to the middle of February it is extreemly cold the great River during that time being frozen so hard, that horses and Sleds pass dayly upon it- However it does not every year freeze within several miles of the City but in that time there is often so much Ice floathing that it is not safe for Vessels to go to sea or come in The Winter is above 6 weeks longer at Albany than at New York that place being 140 miles further up Hudsons

River-It is likewise longer at Philadelphia than here tho' that Town be above a degree & a half more to the South ward This is owing to that place's being situated upon a Fresh water River which more easily Freezes and to its distance from the Sea

The Thermometer in the month of January is generally about 80 I observ(d) it twice at 100. & once at 103. Then the frost & cold was excessive, all Liquors except Spirits Froze-I found Madeira Wine which is a very strong wine frozen in the morning in a Room where there had been a good fire all day untill eleven o clock at night Hudsons River was then frozen over at the Town, where it ft about two miles broad, and the water very salt, so that people passed over on the Ice in Crowds, but the Ice did not continue fast at this place above 3 days-In the beginning of Winter People are in danger of Rheumatic pains and in February to Bastard Pleurisies.

The air of the Country being almost always clear and its Spring strong we have few consumptions or diseases of the Lungs I never heard of a broken winded horse in this Country. People inclined to be consumptive in England are often perfectly cured by our fine air, but if there be ulcers formed they die in a little time

The Climate grows every day better as the country is cleared of the woods, and more healthy as all the people that have lived long here, testifie, this has even been sensible to me tho' I have been but about 12 years in the country-I therefore doubt not but it will in time become one of the most agreeable & healthy Climates on the face of the Earth As it is I prefer it to the climate of England and I believe most people that have lived any considerable time here & are returned to England will confirm this. FINIS.

The Board of Trade List of First Party of Palatines in London, May 3, 1709

This list is the first of four lists of Palatines compiled up to June 16, 1709 by Reverend John Tribbeko and Reverend George Andrew Rupterti. The four lists include only the first 6,000 of the Germans to arrive in that year. The lists which contain information on the age and occupation of the head of the family, numbers and age of the members of the family and religion, may be found in the Public Record Office, C. O. 388/76, 56 ii, 64, and 68-70. They have been published without change in the New York Genealogical and Biographical Records (New York, 1909 and 1910), XL, 49-54, 93-100, 160-167, 241-248; XLI, 10-19. They are also published in L. D. MacWethy, The Book of Names especially Relating to the Early Palatines and the First Settlers in the Mohawk Valley (St. Johnsville, New York, 1933) in an alphabetical order and an abridged form. In the latter version there are errors, which are excusable because of the nature of the material but the bad alphabetizing of the names is not to be regarded so lightly.

Only the first of the four Board of Trade Lists (that of May 6, 1709) is included here because that group of 825 persons is unmentioned in the Embarkation Lists from The Netherlands. They were sent, as related in Chapter III, before the arrangement, by which the British government financed their passage to London, was well worked out. This first Board of Trade List given below has been carefully alphabetized, but the information given as to occupation, religion and age has not been included here for a number of reasons: 1) it is accessible elsewhere, 2) it would crowd an already lengthy Appendix, 3) it would not conform to the Embarkation Lists which it is intended to supplement here. The abbreviation w. denotes the presence of the wife.

Adeler, Henry-w. 1 son
Albenz, Christoph
Albrecht, James-w.
Andrew, Benedict-w. 1 son
Anke, Joseph
Bahr, John-w. 3 sons
Bauer, Christian-w. 2 sons, 3 daus
Bauer, Christina
Bauer, George
Baumann, Michael-w. 1 dau
Becker, Gerhard-w.1 son, 1 dau
Bekell, Philip-w. 1 son, 5 daus
Beller, Jacob-w. 1 son
Berg, Frederick-w. 1son, 1 dau
Bergleuchter, Anton
Berstler, Adam-w 2 sons, 1 dau
Bettinger, Anna Christina

Bien, John
Blesinger, Danue. -w. 2 daus
Bohm, Johannes
Bolker, Charles--w.
Bollon, Christoff-w. 1 son, 2 daus
Boos, John Henry - w.
Bretschi, Lorentz
Bruchly, John Henry -. 2 sons
Buehler, John- w. 3 daus
Buff, George -w. 1 dau
Cathrina-servant maid
Clemens, Gerhard - w 2 sons
Closterbeker, John-w. 1 son, 2 daus
Daninger, Jacob - 2 sons, 2 daus
Daun, George - w. 1 dau
Degen, Felix
Denias, Philip

deRocheford, Peter-w. 2 sons, 2 daus.
Dieterich, John-w. 1 son
Dision, David-w. 1 son
Drechsler, John Peter-w. 1dau
DuBois, Abraham -w. 3 sons, 1 dau
Durbecker, John Adam-w. 2 daus
Durk, John Adam-w. 1 son, 2 daus
Ebert, Hartman--w.
Emichen, Ernst-w. 4 sons
Ende, John Philip am-w. 1 son, 1 dau
Ends, Matthew-w. 1son
Engelsbruecher, Nicol-w. 1 dau.
Erkel. Bernard-w.
Eschelmanns, Anna-1 son
Escherich, John
Eyech, John Valentine
Faubell, John-w. 1dau
Fodder, John-w. 2 sons, 1 dau
Frey, Conrad-w. 2 sons, 2 daus
Friede, Cathrina
Fuhrman, Jacob -2 daus.
Galathe, Jacob
Galathe, John Jacob, w. 1 son, 1 dau
Garrinot, Peter-W.
Geisell, George -w. 2 sons
Gerhard, John George-W. 2 sons, 4 daus
Gessienger, Henry-w. 1 dau
Glaents, John- w. 1 son
Gnaedi, Benedict-w. 1 son, 1 dau
Goebell, Paul-w. 1 son, 1 dau
Gothzeit, William-w. 1 son, 1 dau
Graeff, Jacob-his parents live in
Pennsylvania
Gring, Jacob-w. 1 dau
Gruondner, Matthew
Guth, Henry
Haas, John-w. 2 sons, 2 daus
Hagder, John
Hagenback, Frederick-w. 2 sons
Hahrlaender, Conrad-w. 2 sons
Hakl. John George -w. 1 sons, 3 daus.
Hartman, John George-w. 1 son
Hassmer, John
Haun, Andrew-w. 5 sons, 2 daus
Hebenstreit, John Jas.- w.
Heffen, Bartin
Heidman, Peter-w. 3 dau
Helffert, Peter-w.
Henrich, Lorentz-w. 1 son, 1 dau
Herman, Daniel-w. 1 son, 1 dau
Herman, Jacob
Herman, Niclas
Herman, Peter-w 2 sons, 1 dau
Herman, Valentine-w. 1 son
Hermann, Niclas
Hesse, John-w. 2 daus
Heyde, Peter-w. 1 son
Hirtzbach, Anton-w. 3 sons, 1 dau.
Hirzeach, Martin-w. 2 sons, 2 daus
Hobler, Abraham -w. 1 sons, 1 dau

Hocky, Andrew
Hocky, Peter
Hoffart, John Adam-w.
Hoffsaetter, Philip
Hohenstein, Christian-w. 2 sons, 1dau
Hoherluth, George Adan -w. 2 sons, 2 daus
Hornigh, John George-w. 2 sons, 2 daus
Hubscher, Andrew-w. 1 son, 4 daus
Hubmacher, Niclas-w. 1 son, 2 daus
Huebner, Anton-w. 2 sons, 1 dau
Jacobi, John Thomas-w. 2 sons, 1 dau
Jalathe, John William-w. 2 sons, 1 dau
Kaff, Bazar-w. 3 sons
Kaldauer, Valentine-w. 2 sons, 3 daus
Keyser, George Frederick -w. 1 sons, 2 daus
Kinfeller, Frederick-w. 1 son, 1 dau
Kirchofen, Francis Ludwig
Klaemer, Ludwig-w. 1 son, 2 daus
Klein, John Jacob -w. 1 son
Klein, John -w. 2 sons
Klein, Michael, sister-in-law of
Klein, Michael-w. 2 daus
Klein, Peter-w. 1 son, 1 dau
Klug, George-w. 1 son
Klug, George, his sister and son, a boy of
15 years
Koenig, John Adam
Kolb, Arnold
Kolb, Henry-w. 3 daus
Kueffer, John -w, 2 daus
Kuhlwein, Philip
Kuhner, Jacob-w. 3 sons, 1 dau.
laForge, John Wm. w.
Lang, Johan-4 in family
Lang, Philip-w 1 son 1 dau
Lauber, Jacob-w. 3 daus
Le Dee, John-2 daus
LeFevre, Abram-w. 1 son, 1 dau
Leibengut, John Wendell-1 son
Leucht, Lewis-w. 1 son
Lichtnegger, Gottlob August
Lucas, Frncis-w. 2 sons, 5 daus
Lup, Henry-w. 3 sons, 1 dau
Machtig, Jacob-w. 2 sons, 2 daus
Martins, Gertrud-1 son
Mason, Niclas
Mendon, Jacob
Meningen, John-w. 2 sons
Messer, Sylvester-w. 2 sons, 2 daus
Mey, David-W.
Meyer, Hartman-w. 1 son, 2 daus
Meyer, Henry-w. 2 daus
Meyer, Henry-sister of
Moor, Austin
Moor, John
Moor, John William
Mueller, John Jacob-w 6 sons, 1 dau
Mueller, Valentine
Muller, Daniel
Nagel, John-w. 1 dau

Neidhofer, John Quirinus-w. 1 son, 1 dau
Notzel, Rudolf-w. 3 daus
Obender, Samuel-w. 1 dau
Oberholtzer, Mark-w. 3 sons, 2 daus
Pelle, Peter
Penning, Daniel
Pens, Benedict-4 in family
Pfeiffer, John Jacob-w. 1 sons, 1 dau
Presler, Valentine-w 3 sons, 2 daus
Rath (Bath), John-w. 1 son, 1 dau
Raths, Jane
Rausch, George
Rebell, Jacob
Reiser, John Peter-w. 5 sons
Reuling, Jacob-w. 1 dfau
Rheine, John am-w.
Rider, Niclas-w.
Riedel, George-mother-in-law of
Riedell, John George-w. 1 son, 1 dau
Rohrbach, Christian-w. 1 dau
Rose, Anna-1 son, 2 daus
Rose, Catherine-1 dau
Rudolff, John
Schaeffer, John-w. 1 son
Schaeffer, John -w. 4 sons, 2 daus
Schaeffer, John Conrad
Schaeffer, Joseph-w. 2 sons, 4 daus
Schletzer, Jeremy-w. 2 sons, 3 daus
Schlingluff, John -w. 3 sons
Scholttenhofer, Christof-w. 2 sons
Schmitzer, John Martin-w. 1 son
Schneider, Philip-w. 2 sons, 1 dau
Schneider, John Michael-w. 1 son, 1 dau
Schoen, Maria Cathrina-3 sons, 1 dau
Schrager, Andrew-w. 2 daus
Schuetz, John -w. 4 daus
Schwaegerin, Apollonia
Schwengel, John-w. 1 son, 3 daus
Seibert, Conrad-w. 1 son, 1 dau
Seibert, Martin-w. 1 son, 1 dau
Sheuer, John Adam-w. 2 sons, 1 dau
Shonweiss, John-w. 1 son, 2 daus

Shwab, Peter-w. 1 son, 1 dau
Shwartz, Matthias-w. 2 sons, 1 dau.
Shwartze, John-w. 1 son, 1 dau
Smith, Henry-w. 4 sons, 1 dau
Smith, Jacob-w. 2 sons, 1 dau
Smith, John-w. 4 sons, 6 daus
Spuehler, Jacob -w. 1 son
Staehler, Peter
Stutz, Eberhard-5 in family
Stutz, John Eberhard-w. 2 sons, 1 dau
Turch, Caspar
Tanner, Cathrina-1 dau
Thevoux, Daniel-w. 1 son, 1 dau
Thomas, John George-w. 2 sons, 1 dau
Thor, Conrad am w. 1 dau
Trombauer, Niclas-w. 1 son, 2 daus
Truat, John -w. 2 sons
Trumph, John Michael-1 son
Vogt, Abraham-w. 1 son, 3 daus
Vogt, John-w. 1 son
Volweider, Jacob-w.
Wagner, John -w. 2 sons, 3 daus
Wagner, Mary Elizabeth
Walter, John George-w. 3 sons, 2 daus
Warambour, Mary-4 sons, 1 dau
Wayner, Henry-w. 2 sons, 1 dau
Weber, John Engel-w. 5 daus
Weber, John Jacob -w.
Weinrich, Balzar-w. 3 sons, 1 dau
Weitzell, John-w, 2 sons
Wenig, Peter-w. 1 dau
Wentzen, Peter
Werner, Christoff-w, 1 dau
Willich, Peter-w. 2 daus
Winter, Maria Cathrina-1 dau
Zeber, John-w. 2 sons, 2 daus
Zeisler, Lorentz-w. 2 sons, 1 dau
Zeitz, John Peter
Ziegler, Michael
Zimmerman, John Wolff-w. 2 sons, 4 daus
Zinkhan, Conrad-w. 1 son, 2 daus
Zitel, Jacob-w.

THE EMBARKATION LISTS FROM THE NETHERLANDS

These lists comprise the enumeration of five separate sailings of Palatines from The Netherlands, as sent by the Rotterdam Commissioners, vanToren and van Gent, to Minister Dayrolle, who forwarded them to England. The lists were found in the Public Record Office, T 1/119, 6-10, 19-26, 68-72, 58-65, 79-82, also data given in the lists below was compiled from the following sources: Public Record Office, London; Library of Congress, Washington, D. C., has transcripts and Photostats of British documents, especially of the Colonial Office; Documentary History of the State of New York, edited by E. B. O'Callaghan, Vol. III (Albany, 1850); Documents Relative to the Colonial History of New York by John Romeyn Brodhead, edited by E. B. O'Callaghan, II vols. (Albany, 1851-61).

The Embarkation Lists are not complete. They do not include those Palatines who paid their own way to London or were sent by private charity in August and October 1709.

So far as possible the enumerations have been retained in exactly the form in which the Dutchmen made them. This was considered most desirable for genealogists, who will use them to greatest advantage. For the ordinary reader, it may be necessary to explain further that **"vrouw"** means wife; **"weduw"**, widow; **"moeder"**, mother; **"swister,"** sister; **"knegt,"** servant, **"Wede"** is an abbreviation for widow. Of course, each sailing list has been alphabetized.

When names are immediately below without a last name, they are the names of children which happen to be mentioned, and they are not included in the additional number of children ending the line.

SECOND PARTY SAILING MAY 23, 1709

Aldemos, Philip
Altum, Hans & vrouw, 2 ch.
Aman, Johannes
Amand, Johannes & vrouw
Arm, David & vrouw
Johan Arm, Izaak, Kristina, David, & 2 ch.
Atam, Hans & vrouw, 1 ch.
Back, Johs & vrouw
Anna Margreta, Ane Marya & 1 ch.
Balbar, Kryn & vrouw, 2 ch
Bampert, Johans & vrouw
Anna Krita, Gysbert, Frans Adam & 2 ch.
Barban, Hans Wolf and vrouw
Anna & 2 ch.
Bastiaen, Andries
Batyn, Nocholaas & vrouw, 2 ch
Baur, Elias
Beck, Johannes
Beck, Thobias & vrouw, 5 ch.
Bergs, Hans
Berkman & vrouw
Anna Elisabet Betha, Anna Margreta, Anna
Barbera, Johannes Berkma [sic], & 1 ch.
Borthram, Pr
Besser, Johan Peter
Better, Johan Peter & vrouw, 1 ch.
Bickman, Jacob & vrouw
Andries Vredrig, Justina Madeleena, Anna
Christina, Abraham, Maria Dorta, & 2 ch.
Bilar, Johan & vrouw, 3 ch.
Binder, Johannes & vrouw, 3 ch.
Binder, Valentyn & vrouw, 1 ch.
Bischop, Lodewyk
Blaum, Herman & vrouw
Gerrard, Anna Cartel, & 1 ch.
Bolla, Jacob
Bols, Johan
Bols, Jorig & vrouw
Jurig Bols & 2 ch.
Bornman, Hans Peter & vrouw, 2 ch.
Bortran, Pieter
Bos, Kasper & vrouw, 1 ch.
Bos, Philip & vrouw
Hans Bos, Mighiel Bos, & 3 ch.
Bouwer, Elias
Bouwer, Kritiaan & vrouw
Elisa Margreta & 1 ch.
Brensard, Johan Jurrey & vrouw, 3 ch.
Bresly, Johan & vrouw, 3 ch

Brug, Johannes
Buckjo, Abraham
Buckjo, Izaak
Buckjo, Jacob & vrouw, 3 ch
Buckjo, Johan Jorge
Burdin, Johan
Nog een vrouws persoon
Bus, Daniel & vrouw
Margriet [child]
Cartuir, Peter & vrouw
Johannes & 2 ch.
Cauer, Jacob Mittell & vrouw, 3 ch.
Clos, Henrig & vrouw
Maria Dore, Maria Clos, & 4 ch.
Codevina, Stema
Couis, Magdeleena
Couis, Maria
Cous, Hans & vrouw
Johannes & 2 ch
Crisser, Hans Musil & vrouw
Hans Musil, Katrina, & 2 ch.
Cuits, Johan Kristoffel
Darsel, Philip & vrouw
Abram Dars, Maria Susanna, & 3 ch.
Daslum, Lampare & vrouw
Maria Lysa
deWaal, Antony & vrouw, 3 ch
Diderig, & vrouw, 2 ch. [sic]
Diderig, Hans & vrouw, 6 ch.
Diderig, John Peter & vrouw, 3 ch.
Dilbern, Johan & vrouw, 1 ch.
Dinant, Hans Pieter & vrouw
Susanna, Hans Philip, & 4 ch.
Dinges, Paulus & vrouw, 3 ch
Dirll, Bernhard & vrouw
Anna Elisa, Magdaleena, Maria Croda, Hans
Fildin, Jorg Henry, & 3 ch.
Divin, Annda
Dobys, Jorig & vrouw
Dopper, Leborges & vrouw
Johan Peter, Angeniet, & 2 ch.
Dor, Peter & vrouw, 3 ch.
Doub-dysul, Peter
Duister, Johannes & vrouw, 4 ch.
Duits, Pieter
Ebrosard, Johannes & vrouw
Jacob, Sirnner, Hanrich, & 1 ch.
Eemig, Johan Nicolaes
Eger, Daniel

Einbag, Hans Jurig & vrouw, 2 ch.
Elenberger, Jurig & vrouw
Jurig
Ewold, Koenraet & vrouw, 4 ch
Falee, Hans & vrouw, 3 ch.
Falthum, Peter & vrouw
Henrig, & 1 ch
Feske, Jacob & vrouw
Daniel, Jacob
Fischbac, Johannes & vrouw
Johannes & 2 ch.
Fraus, Peter & vrouw, 9 ch
Freeder, Johan & vrouw, 5 ch
Frei, Jo Hendrik & vrouw, 2 ch
Frenger, Michel
Fridl, Jacob & vrouw
Froes, Hans Jacob & vrouw
Froth, Fredig & vrouw, 3 ch
Froug, Jurig & vrouw, 2 ch
Fusror, Henrig & vrouw, 4 ch.
Gewte [blotted] Jacob & vrouw, 5 ch.
Gocu [?], Ulia
Godvried, Ester Sosannah
Katrina, Rosemonda, Nicolaas, & 2 ch.
Gramli, Soloma
Greef, Andreg
Griet, Hans Jurig & vrouw
Maria Bern, Hans Lenart, Johan Jurig, Hans
Miggel, Hans Peter, & 3 ch.
Groos, Philippus & vrouw
Geertruy, Anna Madeleena
Groots, Philipps, 2 ch.
Haber, Barthel & vrouw
Susanna & 3 ch
Haen, Marthin & vrouw
Haiser, Johannes & vrouw, 3 ch
Haldeman, Ulrigh & vrouw
Hans Henrig & 3 ch
Halig, Koenraet & vrouw
Johan Diderig, Johan Phillippus, & Anna
Katrina
Hannal, Camurs & vrouw, 2 ch
Hardwick, Mattys & vrouw
Harman, Bastiaan
Harnas, Johannes & vrouw, 1 ch
Hart, Simon & vrouw, 3 ch
Hartman, Hans Jurig & vrouw, 1 ch
Hartogin, Anna Elisabet
Hartong, Kasper
Hartwig, Kasper & vrouw, 3 ch.
Heller, Hans Atam & vrouw
Johannes
Heller, Jacob & vrouw, 1 ch
Helm pr & vrouw
Simon, Leenhart & 5 ch.
Helwig, Hendrik & vrouw, 1 ch.
Hendrig, Wendel & vrouw, 4 ch
Henkel, Hans Jurig & vrouw
Henrig, Johan & vrouw, 2 ch

Hepman, Williger & vrouw
Haningel, Maria Geertuit, & 1 ch.
Herber, John Jacob
Hermickel, Hendrig & vrouw
Maria Beck & 2 ch.
Heve, Johannes & vrouw, 1 ch.
Hivang, Henrig & vrouw, 2 ch.
Hobbersin, John Jurig
Hoest, Jacob & vrouw
Michel, Johannes
Hofer, Simon & vrouw
Hofman, Gabriel
Hofman, Johan Kasper
Holzir, Hans & vrouw, 1 ch.
Hureuter, Willem & vrouw, 3 ch.
Imig, Paulus & vrouw
Jaeger, Daniel & vrouw
Jacob, Hans & vrouw, 1 ch.
Jacob, Hans & vrouw
Anna & 1 ch.
Jacob, Kristiaan & vrouw, 3 ch.
Jong, Elisabeth
Pieter Jong, Katrina, Maria Katharina,
Hendr. Pieter
Jonge, Jacob
Joost, Johan & vrouw, 2 ch
Jorden, Koenraed
Jorgen, Hans
Jorter, Andries & vrouw, 3 ch.
Joseph, Jurig
Jourg, Hans & vrouw, 2 ch
Judik, Maria, 1 ch.
Jung, John & vrouw
Jurig, Abraham
Kaeiman & vrouw, 2 ch [sic]
Karty, Johan
Kast, Balter & vrouw
Marita, Anna Mary, & 2 ch
Katrina [sic]
Keizer, Mattheus & vrouw
Anna Elisabet
Kelger, Peter
Keller, Johns & vrouw, 1 ch
Keller, Nicolaas & vrouw
Kernar, Wolf & vrouw, 2 ch
Kernerin, Anna Maria
Kernreiter, Johannes & vrouw, 3 ch
Kerry, Falentyn & vrouw, 5 ch
Keulen, Koenraet
Keyzer, Henrig & vrouw, 3 ch
Kilberin, Barbera
Klein, Jacob
Kleus, Johannes & vrouw
Harler, Margriet
Klinger, Nicolaes & vrouw, 4 ch
Kliuwe, Johs
Kloutt, Henrig & vrouw, 2 ch
Koen, Koenraet & vrouw
Hans Veldekoen, Hans Deterkoen, Hans
Jurgekeon, & 1 ch.

Koen, Mattheus & vrouw, 1 ch
Koenraed, Johan
Koenraet, Martyn & vrouw
Anna Katrina, John Joris, & 2 ch.
Kont, Nicolaas & vrouw
Kop, Henrig & vrouw
Hans Peter, Ursela & 2 ch
Korin, Johannes & vrouw, 2 ch
Krems, Johannes & vrouw
Anna Kristina & 1 ch
Kreps, Pieter & vrouw
Salme, Johannes, Rudolf, & 2 ch.
Kriget, Arnold & vrouw, 2 ch
Kris, Henrig & vrouw, 3 ch
Kristaan & vrouw, 4 ch [sic]
Kristoffel, Johan & vrouw
Andreas, Hans Sellim, Johan Henrig, & 3 ch.
Kroevenag, Penetik & vrouw
Mary Sebille, Juliaen, Anna Eva, & 3 ch.
Krol, Hans Jurig & vrouw, 1 ch
Kroohart, Michel
Kuiber, Daniel
Kurby, Michel & vrouw, 2 ch.
Lang, Jacob & vrouw, 2 ch
Lang, Johannes & vrouw
Barbera, Peter, Catharina, & 2 ch
Langbrin, Kristoffel
Laurens, Peter & vrouw
Anna Margreta, Maria Margreta, Anna
Rosina & 1 ch.
Leiser, Castiaen & vrouw
Johan Jacob, Anna Margraet, Anna Lys,
Anna Castiaens, Hans Jurig & 5 ch.
Lenhart, Hans & vrouw, 1 ch
Listahoris, Lucas & vrouw
Litig, Hans Jagol
Litig, Hans Koenraet
Litig, Jacob
Litig, Kristoffel
Lodwig, Antony
Loedolf, Johannes & vrouw, 4 ch
Loedolf, Koenrad
Loet, Hans Peter & vrouw
Balthazer Loet & 2 ch
Lott, Johs & vrouw, 9 ch
Lourens, Johannes & vrouw
Anna Lys, Anna Margriet, Magdelena, & 3
other children
Lusa, Maria
Lutig, Johan
Luts, Hans Adam
Luts, Jan Jurig & vrouw, 4 ch
Luttig, Kristiaan
Luur, Johan & vrouw
Kornelus & 2 ch.
Maartsen, Hans Jurig & vrouw
Mary, Magdeleena, Anna Katrina, Hans Jurig
& 2 ch.
Maerten, Matthys & vrouw
Maria, Katharina, Barbera, & 1 ch

Marines & vrouw [sic]
Martyn, Thoms
Mathell, Willem & vrouw, 1 ch
Meder, Johan & vrouw
Meier, Johannes & vrouw
Johan Koenraad, Johannes, Anna Devoda,
Maria Lisaba
Melck, Mighel & vrouw, 1 ch
Melries, Johannes & vrouw, 2 ch
Messer, Pieter,
Jacobus & 1 ch
Michel, Johan & vrouw, 1 ch
Milbert, John Martin & vrouw
Miller, Falentyn & vrouw, 1 ch
Miller, Hans Jacob 2 ch
Miller, Johannes
Miller, Johannes & vrouw
Jacob Miller & 4 ch
Miller, Peter & vrouw
vrous swister & 2 ch
Miller, Smich & vrouw
Johan Nickel, Willem, Johannes, Katrina & 1
ch
Miller, Steve & vrouw
Philips
Minkeler, Kelioen & vrouw
Anna Margreta
Misselman, Daniel & vrouw
Swagers Moeder & 3 ch.
Miyn, Joseph & vrouw, 1 ch
Mockel, Ulrig * vrouw, 2 ch
Montria, Paulus, & vrouw, 4 ch
Moon, Klemen & vrouw, 4 ch
Morrer, Jacob & vrouw, 4 ch
Anna Appel, Susan, & 2 ch
Morrits, Mattheus
Mossel, Jacob & vrouw
Hans Develt, Anna Maria, Johannes Mossel,
& 1 ch [The last two are probably sister and
brother of Jacob Mossel, since their names
are given after those of the children in the
family.]
Muding, Pieter & vrouw
Maria & 1 ch
Muldering, Maria Katharin over
Mulnier, Johannes & vrouw, 2 ch
Muver[?], Hans Jurig & vrouw, 3 ch
Naebour, Andries & vrouw, 3 ch
Nicolaes & vrouw [sic]
Ode, Johannes & vrouw, 5 ch
Omstad, Veldin
Ooster, Arent & vrouw
Pallaueborg, Koenraed & vrouw, 1 ch
Pelmug, John & vrouw, 3 ch
Peter, Johan & vrouw, 1 ch
Peter, Johan & vrouw, 2 ch
Peters, Frans Henrig
Petri, Johan Henrig
Phat, Henrig & vrouw, 4 ch
Phat, Masel & vrouw

Philips, Johan & vrouw
Kristina, Anna Dors
Pogeman, Jacob & vrouw, 2 ch
Ponis, Julius & vrouw
Johannes & 1 ch
Poort, Pieter
Porst, Joris & vrouw, 2 ch
Pyn, Marten & vrouw
Reiner, Hans Jurig & vrouw
Johan Peter
Reiner, Barbera, Elisabet, & 3 ch.
Reitwel, Jacob
Reynart, Hans & vrouw
Katrina
Reynart, Michel, Margreta, & 3 ch.
Reynart, Pieter & vrouw, 4 ch
Rieslin, Mathys & vrouw, 3 ch
Ritwell, Fredrig & vrouw, 1 ch
Roost, Johan & vrouw
Anna Maria
Rop, Johannes
Roth, Hans Peter & vrouw, 2 ch
Roug, Kasper
Rustiw, Andries & vrouw, 4 ch
Ruth & vrouw, 5 ch [sic]
Ruth, Kristiaan & vrouw, 1 ch.
Scheever, Hendrig & vrouw, 2 ch
Scherp, Jacob & vrouw, 2 ch
Schipper, Jurig
Schneider, Bernhard & vrouw
Ariaan, Anna Bara, & 1 ch
Scholtes, Johannes & vrouw, 1 ch
Schoolmeester, Suurlotte
Schreets, Mighiel
Schruner, Isaak & vrouw
Siake, Susan
Sigmund, Johannes
Simbluv, Johannes & vrouw, 1 ch
Sleephaan, Johannes
Sluyber, Sacharias & vrouw, 3 ch
Smies, Theodorus & vrouw, 1 ch
Smith, John Willem & vrouw
Margreta & 3 ch
Smith, Kasper
Magdeleena, Maria Barbera, Nocolaus, Peter
& 4 ch.
Smith, Sigmud
Snel, Mathys
Snitzer, Jacob & vrouw, 2 ch
Soerl, Michal & vrouw, 2 ch
Soets, Diderig & vrouw
Hans Pieter & 2 ch
Sous, Hans Pieter
Sous, Johannes & vrouw
Hans Pr
Sous, Maria, Magdaleena, Maria Lucina
Spanemer, Jurig & vrouw
Maria Rosina, Manna Maria & 2 ch
Spinler, Kasper & vrouw
Liliana, Dorethea, Zimon & 1 ch

Sprosser, Anthony & vrouw
Spykerman, Sebastiaen
Spys, John Peter
Staan, Johannes & vrouw
Stambag, Jacob & vrouw
Steenbergen, Hans Jacob & vrouw
Johan Adam, Anna Katrina, & 2 ch.
Stevvel, Frans & vrouw, 3 ch
Stoffer, Andries, 2 ch
Stol, Johannes
Stoppelbeen, Pieter & vrouw, 2 ch
Suller, Hans Jorig & vrouw
Anna & 1 ch
Swarts, Kristiaan
Swik, Mathys & vrouw
Anna Margriet, Hans Jurig, & 2 ch
Tebalt, Jurig
Terber, Johan Adolf, 4 ch
Toup, Michel & vrouw
Ulrig, Kristoffel & vrouw
Daniel, Anna Maria, Elisabet, Katharina & 3
ch
Urzel, Hans Migel & vrouw 1 ch
van Kunter, Klaas & vrouw, 5 ch
Vereter, Hans Jurig & vrouw
Anna Lotsia & 2 ch
Ving, Andreas & vrouw, 1 ch
Vinis, Hans Jacob & vrouw
Johannes, Elizabet, Nocolaes, & 2ch
Vink, Hendrik Lodwig
Vink, Johan Cristof
Vink, Johan Godvyd
Voerman, Hans Michel & vrouw
Magdleena & 2 ch
Voes, Andries & vrouw
Anna Lys & 3 ch
Voes, Johannes & vrouw, 2 ch
Vogel, Spravger Jochem
Volhand, Englehart & vrouw
Vrick, Hendrik & vrouw
Vriesig, [Wiesig?], Kasper & vrouw 2 ch
Vuer, Jacob
Wagenaar, Andries & vrouw, 2 ch
Walrenis, Peter & vrouw, 3 ch
Wanbag, Nicolaes & vrous
Hans Peter & 4 ch
Webel, Hans Jacob & vrouw
Orzel & 4 ch.
Weier, Johan Jorig & vrouw, 2 ch
Weistemar, Velten
Johan Philip, Anna Barber, & 2 ch
Wentel, John Jurig
Werner, Mighel & vrouw
Anna Geertruyt
Wever [blotted], Philip
Wihart, Jacob & vrouw
John Hendrig & 3 ch
Wilhelm, Johan & vrouw, 2 ch
Willem, Hans

Willi, Johan Hanrus & vrouw
Johan Gristia & 2 ch
Wilsing, Maria
Winbold, Burg
Windel, Johan
Wittel, Geertruy, 3 ch
Wolf, Michel
Woltman, Leenhard & vrouw, 3 ch
Wonderlig, Kristiaan

Wortman, Johannes & vrouw
Anna Margreth, Hendr. Wortman & 2 ch
Wustum, Peter
Wyneberger, Jacob & vrouw
Johannes & 3 ch
Wyterman, Ulig & vrouw
Koenraet, Frans Seler
Zegeler, Henrig & vrouw
Andries, Kasper, & 1 ch.
Zsimet, Joost & vrouw, 2ch.

Embarkation List from The Netherlands
Third Party--Embarked June 5 to June 10, 1709

Abal, Michel & vrouw, 2 ch
Abelman, Jacob
Abelt, Hans Jacob
Aberrs (Aberse), Ulrig
Achber, (Nachber?), Falenteyn & vrouw, 2 ch
Adam, Johan's soujuger
Aeier, Hans Jacob
Aelbert, Jacob
Aelbert, Johan
Albersmit, Wilhelm
Alleman, Simon
Alsemusch, Philippus & vrouw, 4 ch
Altfatter, Felten & vrouw
Althenser, Mattys
Altlind, Arnold & vrous, 6 ch.
Andries, Hans Mighel & vrouw, 1 ch
Andries, Peter & vrouw, 3 ch
Anweillersz, Johan & vrouw, 3 ch
Aochn, Johan & vrouw, 8 ch
Appel, Johan Hoog & vrouw, 5 ch
Arbonus, Kasper & vrouw, 1 ch
Assenbier, Frans Willem & vrouw
Atzperger, Anna Maria
Balniger, Frans & vrouw, 3 ch
Barbara, Maria & child
Barkman, Joost & vrouw, 2 ch
Barrabam, Andries & vrouw
Bast, Michel & vrouw, 6 ch
Bauer, Anna Margreet
Beckman, Michel & vrouw, 4 ch
Beisch, Johan & vrouw, 3 ch
Bek, Johannes & vrouw
Bekker, Michel
Bekker, Mighel & vrouw 2 ch
Bekker, Johan Peter
Bekker, Simon & vrouw, 8 ch.
Bekker, Antony & vrouw, 2 ch
Belts, Leenart
Bender, Henrig & vrouw, 3 ch
Berger, Kornelis Reusner & vrouw, 3 ch
Bergman, Andreas & vrouw, 2 ch

Bes, Johan & vrouw
Beschop, Berhard
Beschop. Henrig & vrouw, 2 ch
Beyscher, Johan & vrouw, 4 ch
Bieler, Henrig
Biettleman, Hans Michel & vrouw, 3 ch
Birber, Sacharias & vrouw
Blasch, Koenraet & vrouw, 5 ch
Bles, Penetek & vrouw, 3 ch
Bloms, Kristiaen & vrouw
Blosch, Jacob
Boey, Wendel & vrouw, 5 ch
Bol, Gerards, & vrouw
Bom, Frans & vrouw 6 ch
Bonderskel, Johan & vrown, 5 ch
Bonn, Frans & vrouw, 3 ch
Dorits, Juliannes & vrouw, 3 ch
Borniger, Kasper & vrouw, 3 ch.
Borsig, Rudolph
Bos, Hans Janz
Botermer, Joseph & vrouw, 2 ch
Bouwer, Johan
Bouwer, Tomas & vrouw, 9 ch.
Braem, Bastiaen & vrouw, 3 ch
Brand, Koenraet
Brandlyn, Kasper & vrouw, 2 ch.
Braum, Andries & vrouw, 4 ch
Brekedir, Barent & vrouw, 4 ch
Brekhamer, Throk & vrouw, 4 ch
Brill, Johannes & vrouw, 3 ch
Brom, Johannes Joost & vrouw, 7 ch.
Brosch, Frederig, & vrouw, 2 ch
Brouwer, Diderick
Brummer, Johannes & vrouw, 2 ch
Brunk, Johan Michel
Buisch, Johan Rain & vrouw, 1 ch
Buks, Johan Bernhart & vrouw, 5 ch
Bumer, Simon
Bun, Johannes & vrouw, 3 ch
Bungert, Hans Willem & vrouw, 2 ch
Bungert, Jacob & vrouw, 2 ch.
Bungert, Mattys & vrouw, 2 ch

Burger, Fryt, & vrouw, 2 ch
Busch, Herman & vrouw, 6 ch
Ceubel, Hans Dienes & vrouw
Chiernte (?), Mischael & vrouw, 2 ch
Chreiter, Kristoffel
Chrisfilips, Domink & vrouw, 5 ch
Chrisfilips, Hans Wilhem & vrouw, 4 ch
Chrisfilips, Jeurg, & vrouw, 1 ch
Ci-----[blotted], Johan & vrouw, 1 ch.
Cirbb, Philippus Jacob & vrouw, 5 ch
Citider, Martin & vrouw, 5 ch
Cloos, Peter & vrouw, 5 ch
Copal, Barnhart (minister) & vrouw, 1 ch
Crieg, Johan Just & vrouw, 4 ch
Danner, Urban & vrouw, 4 ch
Daull, Mattys
Daumer, Johan
Deis, Peter & vrouw, 1 ch.
Deur, Koenraet
Deutger, Paulus & vrouw, 2 ch
Dich, Martin & vrouw, 5 ch
Diderick, Jacob & vrouw, 7 ch
Diderick, Johan & vrouw, 1 ch
Didert, Andries & vrouw, 1 ch
Diel, Johan & vrouw
Dielman, Hans & vrouw
Dies, Johan & vrouw
Diredurf, Henrig
Ditir, Hans Bernhart
Dog, Frans Henrig & vrouw, 3 ch
Dolmet, Johan & vrouw, 5 ch
Domnis, Mattys & vrouw, 5 ch
Dorff, Reys & vrouw, 2 ch
Dulies, Koenraet & vrouw, 5 ch.
Durding, Koenraet
Ebregt, Johan & vrouw, 2 ch
Eding, Bastiaen & vrouw, 1 ch
Eeger, Dirk & moeder
Eker, Jacob & vrouw
Emmell, Johannes & vrouw, 2 ch
Emrig, Peter & vrouw, 1 ch
Engel, Adam & vrouw, 3 ch
Engel, Martin & vrouw, 4 ch
Engel, Robbt & vrouw, 5 ch
Eperhart, Johan Mighel & vrouw, 4 ch
Eralter, Hans Jacob
Erbs, Hans Henrig & vrouw, 3 ch
Evathi, Barbara 2 ch
Eweling, Johan & vrouw, 4 ch
Falig, Arholt, & vrouw, 2 ch
Filips, Paulus & vrouw, 5 ch
Flehr, Johan & vrouw, 2 ch
Flies, Nicolaes
Floer, Johan & vrouw, 3 ch
Flohr, Johan Peter
Folleg, Peter & vrouw, 5 ch
Forer, Hans & vrouw, 1 ch
Frank, Johan Marten
Frank, Michal
Frantz, Johan Koenraet

Fredig, Gerard
Fredrig, Johan Nicolaes & vrouw, 4 ch
Fremmen, Johan Jurg & vrouw, 5 ch
Fres, Tomas & vrouw, 1 ch
Freysen, Johan Rikes & vrouw, 5 ch
Frib, Hans Peter & vrouw, 1 ch
Fuhrman, Mattys & vrouw
Fuyken, Orghel & vrouw, 2 ch
Ganner, Jacob nog twe gebroeders
Gants, Johan Nicolaes
Geiser, Johan Paltzer
Genedig, Johan & vrouw, 3 ch
Genir, Jacob & vrouw, 7 ch
Gerard, Hans Peter & vrouw
Gerhart, Valenteyn & vrouw, 5 ch
Get, Peter
Gilig, Andreas & vrouw, 1 ch
Gitz, Frederigh & vrouw, 3 ch
Glaser, Hans Jurg & vrouw, 2 ch
Gloos, Valenteyn--Anna Maria
Gneyzer, David & vrouw, 4 ch
Goestamt, Johan Philip
Gorg, Hans & vrouw, 3 ch
Gottel, Jacob & vrouw, 7 ch.
Graef, Hans Jacob Mark & vrouw, 4 ch
Grousch, Han Miggel & vrouw, 2 ch
Grejster, Johannes & vrouw, 3 ch
Greyloff, Urby & vrouw, 2 ch
Grieschman, Johan Heinrig
Grosch, Falenteyn & vrouw
Grosch, Joggen & vrouw
Grosch, Philips Leinhart & vrouw, 5 ch
Grosch, Wilhem & vrouw, 2 ch
Groschman, Johan & vrouw, 3 ch
Gross (?), Bendrick & vrouw
Gross, Johan & vrouw
Gross, Johan Jorg & vrouw, 2 ch
Grysman, Henrig
Guint, Anders, 1 ch
Gulk, Johannes & vrouw, 3 ch.
Hack, Johan Koenraed & vrouw, 2 ch
Hairtinam, Koenraet & vrouw, 1 ch.
Haister, Martin & vrouw, 6 ch.
Halles, Johan Willem & vrouw, 4 ch
Hamer, Johan Peter
Hansz, Schrenhart & vrouw, 4 ch
Harna, Jacob & vrouw, 2 ch
Hart, Johannes
Hasch, Anna Elisabeth
Hasch, Nicolaes & vrouw, 4 ch
Hasen, (Hafen?), Willem
Haubt, Kristoffel
Haus, Johan Adam
Hebus, Johan & vrouw, 3 ch
Heck, Sebastiaen & vrouw, 3 ch
Hegt, Kasper & vrouw, 7 ch
Heimsein, Paul & vrouw, 1 ch
Heister, Johan Jacob & vrouw, 6 ch
Heistrebach, Nicolaes & vrouw, 4 ch.
Helscher, Kristoffel & vrouw

Herbener, Henrig & vrouw, 4 ch
Herber, Johan Kasper
Herman, Philippus & vrouw, 1 ch
Hernan, Frederig, & vrouw, 2 ch
Herst, Jacob & vrouw, 2 ch
Hertman, Koenraet & vrouw, 3 ch
Hes, Fredrig & vrouw, 3 ch
Hes, Andries
Hetin, Anna Maria
Heyg, Alexander
Heyll, Balser & vrouw, 5 ch
Heyll, Mattheys Jurg & vrouw
Heym, Johs & vrouw, 5 ch
Heymerley, Johan Jacob & vrouw, 4 ch
Heyster, Herman & vrouw, 4 ch
Hiebis, Henrig & vrouw
Hiel, Ruldolf & vrouw
Hielman, Johan
Hirt, Stoffel & vrouw, 4 ch
Hisirber, Johannes & vrouw, 4 ch
Hobst, Tomas & vrouw
Hoentz, Nicolaes & vrouw
Hoeper, Jacob & vrouw, 3 ch
Hofen, Wilhem & vrouw, 2 ch
Hoffenbraut, Johan & vrouw, 2 ch
Hoffner, Jeuly Mayer
Hofman, Henrig & vrouw, 3 ch
Hofmenin, Katarina
Hoigt, Wirchart & vrouw, 2 ch
Hol, Migel
Holgaerden, Hans Peter
Hollander, Johan Melchior (?)
Hollerin, Anna Katrina
Holwaserz, Antony, 1 ch.
Homberg, Kryn
Hoppf, Hans Jurg & vrouw
Horents, Michel & vrouw, 4 ch
Horling, Johan Koenraet
Horts, Walter & vrouw, 3 ch
Hortz, Hans Fletter & vrouw, 2 ch
Hosserlwegh, & vrouw, 4 ch
Huberin, Margreta
Hun, Mattys
Huns Koenraet &: vrouw, 2 ch
Husman, Johannes & vrouw, 5 ch
Isler, Nicolaes & vrouw, 5 ch.
Jacob, Hans
Jacob, Hans & vrouw, 10 ch.
Jacob, Johan & vrouw, 3 ch
Jacobi, Johan Adam & vrouw, 8 ch
Johan Henrig & vrouw, 4 ch
Jsbraut, Hans Wolf
Junik, Hans Ari
Junik, Johan
Jurg, Hans & vrouw
Jurg, Johan
Jurig, Johan & vrouw, 2 ch
Kaisser, Johs & vrouw, 6 ch
Kak, Peter & vrouw, 4 ch
Karb, Johan Philip & vrouw, 5 ch

Kaulil, Frederig & vrouw, 2 ch
Keichel, Johan
Keiger, Johan
Keil, Henrig & vrouw, 2 ch
Keler, Peter & vrouw, 1 ch
Kelil, Johan
Keller, Jacob & vrouw, 6 ch
Kerger, Johan & vrouw, 1 ch
Kersner, Philip & vrouw, 3 ch
Keuler, Hans Peter
Keyserin, Anna Maria
Kien, Hendrig & vrouw, 2 ch
Kirches, Paulus
Kiselback, Johan & vrouw, 3 ch
Kister, Fredrig & vrouw, 2 ch
Kister, Palters & vrouw, 3 ch
Klaas, Peter
Klaser, Kitter & vrouw, 3 ch
Kletters, Johan & vrouw, 2 ch
Kleyn, Hans Willem & vrouw, 3 ch
Kleyn, Koenraet
Kleyn, Lodewyk
Kleyn, Ludwig
Kleyn, Michael & vrouw, 5 ch
Kleyter, Hans Jurg & vrouw, 1 ch
Klippingen, Johan Peter
Klos, Willem & vrouw, 5 ch
Kloter, Johan Paul & vrouw, 4 ch.
Kloter, Paulus & vrouw, 5 ch
Klun, Jacob & vrouw, 1 ch
Klyn, Johan Palser & vrouw, 4 ch
Knaus, Hans Kristoffel & vrouw, 2 ch
Knegt, Miggel & vrouw, 4 ch
Knykers, Johan & vrouw
Kock, Martin
Koeman, Bastiaen & vrouw, 1 ch
Koenraet, Koenraet & vrouw, 2 ch
Koenraet, Kristoffel
Koenraet, Mattys
Koenraet, Mattys
Koenraet, Nicolaes
Kohler, [Jacob?] & vrouw, 9 ch.
Koll, Frans & vrouw, 3 ch
Koller, Martin
Koller, Simon & vrouw, 3 ch
Konig, Johan Joost & vrouw, 2 ch
Korier, Karel Henrig & vrouw
Koris, Johannes & vrouw, 4 ch
Kormer, Nicolaes & vrouw, 4 ch
Kost, Johan Jurg & vrouw, 4 ch
Kount, Philippus
Kraft, Valenteyn & vrouw, 5 ch
Kramer, Johan & vrouw, 1 ch
Kramer, Philippus & vrouw
Kraud, Johan
Kraut, Peter & vrouw, 4 ch
Kreegelman, Leenhart & vrouw, 3 ch
Krestoffel, Mattys & vrouw, 3 ch
Krestoffel, Mattys & vrouw, 4 ch
Kreyser, Lodewyk

Krimp, Krederik

_____, Kirstiaen (no other name given) & vrouw, 1 ch

Kristina, Anna

Kroon, Hans Jurg & vrouw, 1 ch

Krouwel, Loret & vrouw, 1 ch

Kruel, Herman

Krymaiser, Jacob & vrouw, 3 ch

Kuseteler, Hendrig & vrouw, 2 ch

Kulk, Johan Peter

Kumel, Peter & vrouw, 6 ch

Kuminer, Hans Peter & vrouw, 2 ch

Kummer, Hans Peter & vrouw

Kunen, Nicolaes & vrouw, 2 ch

Kunteman, Kasper & 2 ch.

Kurger, Henrig--Elisabeth

Laam, Frans & vrouw, 3 ch

Lambreg, Hans Jurg & vrouw, 5 ch

Lamoth, Johan Daniel & vrouw, 2 ch

Land, Andanig & vrouw, 5 ch

Lang, Eles

Lang, Kristiaen & vrouw, 4 ch

Lang, Peter & vrouw, 2 ch

Lank, Hans Philip

Lant, Philippus & vrouw, 3 ch.

Laurens, Mattys

Laurmen, Eva

Layper, Johan & vrouw, 3 ch

Lecobs, (or Lecolis), Peter & vrouw, 2 ch

Leenhart, Hans Peter & vrouw, 1 ch

Leinweber, Johan & vrouw, 2 ch

Lenard (no family name given) & vrouw, 2 ch

Lepus, Mattys

Lersas, Hans Philips & vrouw, 1 ch

Lesch, Johan Henrig & vrouw, 3 ch

Leschemis, Jeremias & vrouw, 3 ch

Lesorin, Magdalena

Lesser, Kristoffel & vrouw, 4 ch

Libern, Ludwig & vrouw, 1 ch

Liespel, Maria

Lippert, Johan Walter

Los, Johan Adam

Lots, Johan & vrouw, 2 ch

Lou, Johan Michel & vrouw, 2 ch

Lourens, (only name given) & vrouw, 7 ch.

Lout, Henrig & vrouw, 3 ch

Luth, Hans Jacob & vrouw, 2 ch

Lutz, Peter

Lutz, Jeorg & vrouw, 1 ch

Lutz, Peter & vrouw, 4 ch

Lutz, Peter & vrouw, 4 ch

Lybok, Reinhart & vrouw, 3 ch

Madelaer, Michel, & vrouw, 4 ch

Maes, Johan Philip & vrouw, 5 ch

Maeyer, Just Tomas & vrouw, 2 ch.

Mager, Nicolaes & vrouw, 3 ch

Maier, Andries

Maller, Bastiaen & vrouw

Maltsberger, Philippus & vrouw, 1 ch

Marea, Eve & 1 ch

Margriet, Anna

Maria, Anna

Marks, Joseph & vrouw

Marman, Hans Joost & vrouw

Marstall, Kristoffel

Marsteller, Henrig & vrouw, 5 ch

Marstil, Kirstoffel

Marten, Adam & vrouw, 3 ch

Marten Stoffel & vrouw, 4 ch

Martin, Nicholaas & child

Martheys, Hendrig & vrouw, 6 ch

Mattys, Johannes & vrouw, 3 ch

Mattys, Peter's (Wede.), 3 ch

Mattyskolk, Johan & vrouw, 6 ch

May, Peter & vrouw, 4 ch

Mayer, Kristoffel & vrouw, 1 ch

Meeis, Matys & vrouw, 1 ch

Meier, Paulus & vrouw, 5 ch

Meinhober, Philippus & vrouw

Meis, Henrig & vrouw, 3 ch

Meliger, Frans & vrouw, 2 ch

Menges, Hans & vrouw

Menias, Johan & vrouw, 4 ch

Mensch, Antony & vrouw, 2 ch

Mensch, Johan Jurg

Mentizeberges, Diderig & vrouw, 7 ch

Merks, Peter

Merschel, Peter & vrouw, 2 ch

Mese, David & vrouw, 2 ch

Messer, Koenraet & vrouw

Metor, Dangel & vrouw, 4 ch

Mets, Andreas & vrouw, 4 ch

Metsler, Philippus & vrouw, 6 ch

Meyer, Johan & vrouw, 3 ch

Meyer, Hans Jacob

Meyer, Henrig & vrouw, 3 ch

Meyer, Johannes & vrouw, 5 ch

Michel, Otto Henrig & vrouw, 1 ch

Miesch, Paul & vrouw

Migel, Hans & vrouw, 2 ch

Migel, Otto Henrig & vrouw, 1 ch

Miler, Hans Jurig

Millerin, Susanna

Ming, Kristoffel & vrouw, 2 ch

Mink, Hans Hendrig & vrouw, 5 ch

Mink, Hendrig, & vrouw, 4 ch

Mites, Hans Bartel & vrouw

Mitteler, Engel Bertus

Mitteler, Juliaen & vrouw

Moelleremt, Kasper & vrouw, 2 ch

Mohr, Jonas & vrouw, 1 ch

Moht (Mohr), Kristoffel & vrouw

Monbouwer, Hans Adam

Monik, Jacob & vrouw, 3 ch

Mosch, Emgen & vrouw

Moul, Hans Henrig & vrouw, 5 ch

Muillensz, Georg Philip & vrouw, 5 ch

Mukket, Johannes & vrouw, 1 ch

Mullendyk, Herman & vrouw, 2 ch

Muller, Johan Adam & vrouw, 3 ch
Muller, Johan Philips
Mullerin, Margreta
Muncanas, Joseph & vrouw
Muse, Johan Jacob & vrouw, 6 ch
Muster, Lambaert & vrouw, 2 ch
Nagel, Hans Jacob
Nagtegael, Koenraet & vrouw, 2 ch
Nasar, Hans Migel & vrouw, 4 ch
Nau, Peter Hans & vrouw, 3 ch
Nauthil, Sacharianen & vrouw, 4 ch
Neey, Hans Michel & vrouw, 6 ch
Nepeler, Johan
Neuman, Lodewyk & vrouw, 5 ch
Neumeiyer, Frans & vrouw, 2 ch
Neusch, Andreas
Neymeyer, Arts & vrouw, 4 ch
Nidermeyer, Andries & vrouw, 4 ch
Noll, Johan Danyell
Nols, Bernhart & vrouw
Olthanier, Hans Jurg & vrouw, 6 ch
Olthanier, Hans Jurs's moeder
Ordenier, Nicolaes & vrouw, 4 ch
Ott, Johan & vrouw
Pachman, Johan & vrouw, 2 ch
Pack, Jacob & vrouw, 1 ch
Palerwaltman, Johan
Paul, Johan Daniell, 4 ch
Peckert, Koenraet & vrouw, 3 ch
Pergen, Jorig & vrouw, 5 ch
Peschart, Koenraet & vrouw, 3 ch
Peter, Johan Adam
Petrey, Hans Jacob & vrouw, 6 ch
Petri, Jacob & vrouw, 6 ch
Potri, Nicolaes & vrouw, 3 ch
Petry, Henry & vrouw, 5 ch
Petteren, Johannes & vrouw, 3 ch
Pettig, Johan Dederig & vrouw, 1 ch
Pfeffer, Hans Peter & vrouw, 2 ch
Philips, Hans Jacob
Philyps, Hans
Pinter, Johan Foost
Pirk, Johan
Pith, (sic) Jacob & vrouw
Pitts, Joseph & vrouw, 2 ch
Pittig, Henrig & vrouw, 5 ch
Plak, Kristiaen
Pliemelin, Krestman & vrouw, 4 ch
Poller, Philippus & vrouw, 5 ch
Prang, Herman
Prauw, Arnold & vrouw, 1 ch
Praux, Felten & vrouw, 3 ch
Preg, Michel & vrouw, 1 ch
Preker, Paulus & vrouw, 3 ch
Pscheere (no other name given)
Pudum, Lucus & vrouw, 2 ch
Puths, Wilhem
Putsch, Johannes & vrouw, 1 ch
Rab, Killiaen & vrouw, 3 ch
Ram, Nicolaes & vrouw, 4 ch

Reiger, Henrig
Rein, Antony & vrouw, 2 ch
Reygert, Kaspert & vrouw, 2 ch
Kaspert Reygerts vrouws moeder, 4 ch
Reynard, Johan & vrouw, 2 ch
Reynhart, Hendrig & vrouw, 1 ch
Reyser, Michel
Ribel, Johan Nicolaes & vrouw, 6 ch
Rickert, Koenraet & vrouw, 3 ch
Rieckker, Johan Tiell
Rief, Hans Pieter
Rigel, Jacob & vrouw, 5 ch
Rigell, Kasper & vrouw, 1 ch
Ritter, Philip & vrouw, 5 ch
Rob, Hans Jurg
Roe, Hans Jacob & vrouw, 2 ch
Ros, Frederig & vrouw
Rot, Philyppus & vrouw, 4 ch
Roth, John Joost & vrouw, 3 ch
Ruchsal, Jacob & vrouw, 3 ch
Rupert, Rudolph
Russer, John Peter
Sainmoft, Sailalt & vrouw, 7 ch
Samuel, Jonas
Sarborger, Frans & vrouw, 4 ch
Sarborger, Hans David & vrouw, 2ch
Sardis, Isaek & vrouw
Sauffert, Felten & vrouw, 1 ch
Schafer, Philip & vrouw, 2 ch
Schaffer, Bernhard & vrouw, 3 ch
Schaffer, Johan & vrouw, 3 ch
Scham, Hans Jurg & vrouw
Schammel, Peter & vrouw
Schant, Johan & vrouw, 2 ch
Schar, Peter
Schbut, Ellrug & vrouw, 3 ch
Schefer, Lourens
Scheffer, Hans Adam & vrouw, 6 ch
Scheffer, Hans Peter & vrouw
Scheffier, Matteys & vrouw, 2 ch
Schellenperge, Koenraet & vrouw, 2 ch
Schellenperger, Hans Jeorg & vrouw, 1 ch
Schenkelberger, Hans Jacob & vrouw, 5 ch
Scherhinger, Johs, & vrouw, 3 ch
Scherman, Valentyn
Schermig, Andries & vrouw, 2 ch
Scherver, Joost & vrouw, 4 ch
Schesting, Johannes & vrouw, 2 ch
Schetmak, Johan
Scheureder, Handerig & vrouw, 1 ch.
Scheyt, Mander & vrouw, 1 ch
Schier, Hans Ulrig, 2 ch
Schiloser, Johan & vrouw, 2 ch
Schimell, Johan Nicolaes
Schimtin, Eva Maria
Schlegt, Johan & vrouw, 2 ch
Schimell, Johan Nicolaes
Schimtin, Eva Maria
Schlegt, Johan & vrouw, 1 ch
Schlepusch, Hans Peter

Schleyer, Johan & vrouw, 3 ch
Schlug, Johan & Paulus
Schluk, Martin * vrouw
Schmick, Nicolaes & vrouw, 6 ch
Schmiet, Nicolaes & vrouw, 3 ch
Schminch, Johan
Schmit, Hans Jacob & vrouw, 1 ch
Schmit, Esmist
Schmit, Johan Adam
Schmit, Hans Migel & vrouw, 5 ch
Schmit, Hans Peter & vrouw, 5 ch
Schmit, Mattys & vrouw, 2 ch
Schmit, Nicolaes & vrouw, 3 ch
Schmit, Philippus & vrouw, 4 ch
Schmit, Johan & vrouw, 3 ch
Schmit, Kasper & vrouw, 4 ch
Schneide, Johan & vrouw, 2 ch
Schneide, Johan & vrouw, 3 ch
Schneider, Koenraet & vrouw, 2 ch
Schnel, Mattys & vrouw, 5 ch
Schneyer, Hans George & vrouw, 2 ch
Schober, Kristiaen & vrouw, 2 ch
Schoeck, Nicolaes & vrouw, 2 ch
Schoenmager, Henrig & vrouw, 1 ch
Schoenmager, Henrig & vrouw, 1 ch
Schreiner, Hans Jacob & vrouw, 4 ch
Schriber, Albertus
Schwan, Johan
Schul, Martin & vrouw, 4 ch
Schwarts, Jurg & vrouw, 8 ch
Schwartz, Jacob & vrouw
Schwartz, Jacob en knegt & groohm
Schwel, Roedolf & vrouw, 3 ch
Schwin, Johs & vrouw
Seipert, Johan Henrig & vrouw, 4 ch
Seldvau, Mattys & vrouw, 5 ch
Serberger, Hansatt & vrouw, 2 ch
Sermis, Johan & vrouw, 2 ch
Sescher, Johan & vrouw, 1 ch
Sigeler, Kristiaen & vrouw, 2 ch
Sikert, Basser & vrouw, 2 ch Johannes 1
Silbus, Hans
Sildere, Johan
Sillo, Klaud & vrouw
Simen, Johan Adam & vrouw, 3 ch
Simmerman, Johan Jurg & vrouw, 3 ch
Simon, Philippus & vrouw, 1 ch
Sinder, Henrig, Johan, 5 ch
Singraff, Henrig & vrouw, 4 ch
Smeyer, Johannes & vrouw, 4 ch
Smit, Andries & vrouw, 5 ch
Smit, Daniel & vrouw, 2 ch
Smit, Hendrig & vrouw, 5 ch
Smit, Johannes & vrouw, 4 ch
Smit, Kasper & vrouw, 1 ch
Smit, Michel & vrouw, 5 ch
Snegel (Fregel?) Johan Nicolaes & vrouw, 3 ch.
Snyder, Koenraet & vrouw, 2 ch
Souwerman, Samuel

Spath, Mattheys & vrouw, 2 ch
Spengeler, Fredrig & vrouw, 2 ch
Spengeler, Johan Frans & vrouw
Spies, Werner 7 vrouw, 6 ch
Spolgt, Johan & vrouw, 3 ch
Spropssel, Jeorg & vrouw, 2 ch
Staenhauwer, Kristian & vrouw, 6 ch.
Staes, Hans Bernhard & vrouw, 2 ch
Stauck, Johan & vrouw, 1 ch
Steinbekker, Hans Philip & vrouw, 1 ch
Stek, Herman & vrouw, 2 ch
Steyner, Migel & vrouw, 4 ch
Sticker, Johan
Stikker, Michel
Stil, Willem & vrouw, 4 ch
Stoffel, Johan & vrouw, 5 ch
Stog, Hans Ledendig & vrouw
Stok, Johan Henrig & vrouw
Stork Hans Henrig & vrouw, 5 ch
Strab, Lourens & vrouw, 6 ch
Straetbarger, Baltzar & vrouw, 1 ch
Straup, Johan & vrouw, 1 ch
Straysmil, Jacob & vrouw, 5 ch
Streyt, Ludwig & vrouw, 4 ch
Strib, Hans Peter & vrouw, 3 ch
Sturpert, Kasper
Stury, Alexander
Stuts, Johan & vrouw, 4 ch
Suchs, Johan Tilbs & vrouw, 5 ch
Sukors, Johan
Suller, Mattys & vrouw, 4 ch
Tainck, Kasper & vrouw, 2 ch
Tanis, Ary & vrouw, 5 ch
Teister, Daniel & vrouw, 2 ch
Tex, Johan Wilhem & vrouw, 1 ch
Tharsch, Henrig & vrouw, 2 ch
Thomas, Gerhart
Tibere, Peter
Tibre, Jean & vrouw, 2 ch
Timmerman, Matys & vrouw, 2 ch
Titemer, Hans Martin & vrouw
Torer, Hans & vrouw, 2 ch
Treattemam, Martin
Trift, Matteus & vrouw, 2 ch
Trip, Mattys & vrouw
Katarina Margreet, 2 ch
Tsmallenberger, Zill & vrouw, 1 ch
Ubel Kristiaen & vrouw, 3 ch
Ullerig, Hans Jeorg & vrouw, 3 ch
Ullersz, Henrig, & vrouw, 2 ch
Unis, Johan & vrouw, 2 ch
Van Staek, Peter
Vapeneiker, Nicolaes & vrouw
Vasch, Godevrig & vrouw, 2 ch
Vaugh, Johannes
Velinger, Hans Ulrig & vrouw
Veller, Johan & vrouw, 4 ch
Vendel, Johan Nicolaes & vrouw, 3 ch
Vergen, Henrig Peter & vrouw, 2 ch
Vevel, Daniel

Vhoris, Johannes
Voerman, Nicolaes
Vogt, Daniel & vrouw, 3 ch
Vogt, John & vrouw, 3 ch
Volkenburg, Johan Felden & vrouw, 2 ch
Volpertin, Anna Margreta, 3 ch
Vondermul, Philippus & vrouw, 9 ch
Von Reyn, Kristiaen & vrouw, 1 ch
Vootenfloor, Joh & vrouw, 4 ch
Vossina, Antony & vrouw
Vosseyen, Goyert & vrouw, 5 ch
Vrisal, Frederik & vrouw, 1 ch
Wagenaer, Berhart & vrouw, 2 ch
Wagenaer, Koenraet & vrouw, 6 ch
Wagenaer, Lodewig & vrouw, 6 ch
Wagenaer, Velden & vrouw, 3 ch
Wagenaer, Windel & vrouw, 4 ch
Walkker, Johan Henrig & vrouw
Walpnet, Jacob & vrouw, 3 ch
Walter, Hans Jacob& vrouw, 2 ch
Waschpaelt, Johan & vrouw, 7 ch
Wasser, Rudolf & vrouw, 2 ch
Weber, Martin & vrouw, 2 ch
Weber, Mighiel & vrouw, 2 ch
Weber, Philip & vrouw, 1 ch
Weber, Nicolaes & vrouw, 2 ch
Weber, Valenteyn & vrouw, 1 ch
Wedz, Anna Maria, 2 ch
Weer, Frederig & vrouw
Wegman, Matys & vrouw, 7 ch
Wehr, Kristiaen & vrouw, 2 ch
Weickel, Velden & vrouw, 5 ch
Weiller, Andries & vrouw, 3 ch
Weiller, Johan & vrouw
Weiner, Simon & vrouw, 5 ch
Weitseerges, Magdelena
Wekiter, Philip & vrouw, 2 ch
Wekkert, Johan Milgert
Weller, Kasper & vrouw, 2 ch
Wendel, Peter & vrouw, 2 ch
Wens, Johan

Wensch, Johannes & vrouw, 3 ch
Wensell, Lourens & vrouw, 6 ch
Wensz, Balzer
Weper, Henrig & vrouw, 4 ch
Werner, Hendrig
Wesbak, Wendel & vrouw, 4 ch
Westheser, Johan Jacob 1 ch
Wetteg, Barht & vrouw, 2 ch
Wever, Henrig & vrouw, 6 ch
Weyngert, Johan Melchier
Wiekel, Johan & vrouw
Wilbert, Hans Marten & vrouw, 5 ch
Wilhelm, Henrig & vrouw
Wilhelm, Johan Simon & vrouw, 2 ch
Winter, Melger, & vrouw, 1 ch
Wintter, Henrig & vrouw, 5 ch
Wissenmiker, Kasper
Wollten, Philip & vrouw, 3 ch
Wolf, Johan Jurg & vrouw, 4 ch
Wolf, Johan
Wolf, Petrus
Wolf, Koenraet & vrouw, 1 ch
Wolffler, Peter & vrouw
Wolfskel, Hans Jurg & vrouw
Wolleben (John) & vrouw, 5 ch
Woller, Philip & vrouw, 3 ch
Wollfslager, Melchior
Wolter, Adam & vrouw, 8 ch
Wou, Hans Frederig
Wupf, Hans Jacob & vrouw, 1 ch
Wyngert, Koenraet & vrouw, 3 ch
Wynman, Andries & vrouw, 3 ch
Zebersz, Joseph
Zeyps, Balter & vrouw, 4 ch
Zingeler, Nicolaes & vrouw, 4 ch
Zink, Rudolf & vrouw, 4 ch
Zolzeber, Albertus & vrouw, 5 ch
Zutinger, George Peter & vrouw, 3 ch
Zyck, Koenraet
Anonymous (6)

Embarkation List from The Netherlands
Fourth Party -- Embarked June 10 to June 19, Sailed June 21, 1709

Adam, Jacob & vrouw
Adler, Paulus & vrouw, 5 ch
Albiger, Wilhelm & vrouw
_____, Anna Maria (no other name given)
Arnolt, Philippus & vrouw, 2 ch
Atter, Johan & vrouw, 4 ch
Backer, Ferdinant & vrouw, 2 ch
Baltzer, Hans Jacob & vrouw, 3 ch
Bambra, Johan
Barbara, Anna & 3 ch
Barkman, Izaac & vrouw, 3 ch
Bart, Henrik & vrouw, 5 ch

Bartel, Henrik & vrouw, 5 ch
Basseler, Frants & vrouw, 3 ch
Baug, Fredrig & vrouw, 4 ch
Baug, Johan & vrouw, 6 ch
Baum, Abram & vrouw, 5 ch
Baur, Johan Mikel
Baue, Kristoffel
Bechtel, Jacob & vrouw
Becker, Johan & vrouw, 1 ch
Becker, Johan & vrouw
Becker, Johan & vrouw, 2 ch
Beehr, Nicholaas & vrouw, 1 ch

Beller, Hans Jacob & vrouw, 2 ch
Bensch, Jacob & vrouw, 2 ch
Berdolff, Jacob & vrouw, 4 ch
Bergen, Hans & vrouw, 2 ch
Besser, Jurg & vrouw, 4 ch
Besser, Kasper & vrouw, 3 ch
Beyer, Tomas & vrouw, 3 ch
Birck, Henrig & vrouw, 3 ch
Birk, Lys
Birk, Mattys & vrouw, 6 ch
Bleezen, Kristiaan & vrouw
Bohr, Mattys & vrouw, 2 ch
Bornwaster, Herman & vrouw, 1 ch
Bots, Fredrig & vrouw, 3 ch
Boumain, Anna Maria
Bovlentzer, Johan & vrouw, 2 ch
Brandeau, Johan Weyant & vrouw
Brando, John Willem & vrouw, 1 ch
Braun, Johan Jurg & vrouw, 5 ch
Braun, Johan Niklaas & vrouw, 6 ch
Bresch, Klaas
Briti, Jacob & vrouw, 2 ch
Brohen, Nicolas & vrouw, 1 ch
Brotheder, Joost & vrouw, 5 ch
Brull, Joost & vrouw
Buchler, Michel & vrouw, 6 ch
Buderman, Johan & vrouw, 7 ch
Buenner, Jeurg Baltazev
Bug, Henrig & vrouw, 3 ch
Buger, Kasper
Bugspul, Augustyn & vrouw, 7 ch
Bulffer, Wendel & vrouw, 2 ch
Bumer, Jurg Baltzaser
Bummery, Bongratsgi & vrouw, 3 ch
Burger, Johan & vrouw, 2 ch
Burobesch, Herman & vrouw 1 ch
Busch, Daniel & vrouw
Busekart, Daniel & vrouw, 8 ch
Bustz, Joost
Butting, Everhard
Camerd, Johan & vrouw, 4 ch
Creitzin, Elizabeth & 6 ch
Dames, Mattys
Daniel, Antony & vrouw, 7 ch
Danck, Johan Jurg & vrouw, 3 ch
Decker, Johan & vrouw, 1 ch
Dedler, Johan Jacob
de Witz, Frantz
Dieer, Philippus
Diel, Henrig
Dimer, Johan & vrouw, 5 ch
Dimkel, Andries & vrouw, 4 ch
Doni, Johan Martin & vrouw, 2 ch
Drisel, John & vrouw, 1 ch
Drissell, Willem, & vrouw
Eberhart, Michel & vrouw, 4 ch
Egh, Hans Jacob & vrouw, 1 ch
Egh, Hans Jurg & vrouw
Eigman, Henrig & vrouw, 1 ch
Eiller, Johan Henrig & vrouw, 3 ch.

Einel, Stoffel & vrouw, 1 ch
Engle, Jacob & vrouw
Engle, Johan & vrouw, 3 ch
Engle, Johan Willem & vrouw
Engeler, Peter & vrouw, 2 ch
Erberg, Ary Mag Ronolt & vrouw, 4 ch
Ermitter, Frants & vrouw, 3 ch
Eschweiler, Jacob & vrouw, 3 ch
Eschweiler, Tomas & vrouw, 2 ch
Eulembag, Hans Jurg & vrouw, 2 ch
_____, Ewertry (no other name)
Faver, Adam
Felt, Gerhart & vrouw, 6 ch
Feuhert, Emig & vrouw, 2 ch
Focks, Johan Peter & vrouw, 2 ch
Fogelsberger, Peter & vrouw, 1 ch
Folhart, Johan & vrouw, 5 ch
Forbert (Sorber?), Hans Jurg & vrouw, 1 ch
Formen, Kristoffel & vrouw, 1 ch
Forster, Johan Mikel
Freyhausch, Joseph & vrouw, 1 ch
Frisch, Johan & vrouw, 4 ch
Frits, Niklas & vrouw, 7 ch
Frobus, Jorug & vrouw, 5 ch
Fukendem, Bernhart & vrouw, 4 ch
Fux, Johan Jorig & vrouw, 6 ch
Gablen, Johan
Gevell, Henrig & vrouw, 4 ch
Gevell, Johan Andries & vrouw, 1 ch
Geerlach, Johan Koenraet & vrouw, 4 ch
Geisch, Johan
Gesel, Johan Philippus & vrouw, 6 ch
Gessner, Koenraet & vrouw, 2 ch
Gib, Michel & vrouw
Ginter, Kristiaan & vrouw, 4 ch
Gottman, Kasper & vrouw, 8 ch
Grausch, Katrina & 2 ch
Gritnig, Hans & vrouw, 2 ch
Grosch, Diderig & vrouw
Grosch, Willem & vrouw, 3 ch
Grybel, Johan Bernhart & vrouw, 4 ch
Gutir, Johan Philip & vrouw, 2 ch
Gysbert, Johan Joost & vrouw, 4 ch
Haas, Michel
Hag, Johan Henrik & vrouw, 5 ch
Hagedoren, Peter & vrouw, 5 ch
Hanheimer, Paulus & vrouw, 3 ch
Haub, Leickert & vrouw, 2 ch
Heer, Johan & vrouw, 3 ch
Heitwig, Frants
Helfrig, Henrig & vrouw, 2 ch
Heller, Wolff
Henrig, Andreas
Hensch, Hans Adam & vrouw, 2 ch
Hensell, Jacob & vrouw, 1 ch
Herdel, Adam & vrouw, 1 ch
Herman, Bastiaan & vrouw
Herman, Johan Joost & vrouw, 2 ch
Hermans, Jan
Herschbag, Diederig & vrouw, 2 ch

Hetirm, Koenraet & vrouw, 1 ch
Heud, Jacob & vrouw, 1 ch
Heus, Johan Mikel, Katrina
Hodel, Izaak & vrouw, 1 ch
Hodrigzedel, Laurents
Hoffman, Johan Philippus & vrouw, 1 ch
Hoffman, Koenraet & vrouw, 3 ch
Hoffman, Sofia
Hofman, Jacob & vrouw, 1 ch
Holts, Andreas
Holts, Hans Peter
Honig, Lucas & vrouw, 9 ch
Hontsz, Koenraet & vrouw, 2 ch
Hornung, Gerhart & vrouw, 2 ch
Hubig, Lisa Margreta & 3 ch
Huerig, Joost & vrouw, 6 ch
Hupter, David & vrouw, 2 ch
Jacobs, Barth
Jerger, Karolus & vrouw, 2 ch
Jeorg, Hans & vrouw, 1 ch
Jeurg, Johan Mikel
John, Johan Elia
John, Johan Philips
_____, Jud (no other name given)
Julig, Johan Henrig
Kalbour, Johan Kasper
Kargard, Peter & vrouw, 1 ch
_____, Katrina (no other name given)
Kauts, Andreas
Kers, Adam & vrouw, 3 ch
Keseler, Kasper & 2 ch
Kessler, Frans Niklaas & vrouw, 2 ch
Keusel, Hans Jacob & vrouw, 5 ch
Klaas, Johan & vrouw, 2 ch
Klein, Johan Willem & vrouw, 3 ch
Klein, Philip & vrouw, 3 ch
Kleman, Pieter
Klepper, Koenraet & vrouw, 3 ch
Kloosch, Simon & vrouw, 1 ch
Knauer, Sacharias
Koenraet, Johan
Kog, Johan Mattys & vrouw, 5 ch
Kog, Johan Philips & vrouw, 2 ch
Kokkin, Anna Lys
Koog, Johan & vrouw, 1 ch
Korlus, Lucas & vrouw, 3 ch
Krants, Koenraet & vrouw, 1 ch
Krauwer, Hans Jacob
Kreuber, Mattys & vrouw, 5 ch
Krisman, Hans & vrouw, 4 ch
Kro, Johan Jeorg & vrouw, 3 ch
Kruitsch, Johan & vrouw, 5 ch
Kufaber, Johan Adam & vrouw, 4 ch
Kulen, Peter
Kun, Herman & vrouw, 3 ch
Kurts, Hans Jurg & vrouw, 1 ch
Landolt, Samuel & vrouw, 3 ch
Lang, Hans Wolf & vrouw, 3 ch
Lang, Mortis & vrouw, 5 ch
Laurens, Diderig & vrouw, 3 ch

Lauv, Johan & vrouw, 3 ch
LaVore, Johan & vrouw, 1 ch
Leenhart, Johan & vrouw, 5 ch
Leib, Johan & vrouw, 4 ch
Leig, Simon & vrouw, 3 ch
Lenarker, Peter & vrouw, 8 ch
Lenenbaig, Stoffel & vrouw, 2 ch
Lerner, Mattys & vrouw, 5 ch
Lesch, Burchent & vrouw
Leschner, Michel & vrouw, 2 ch
Liesen, Anna Eva & 3 ch
Linck, Martin & vrouw, 5 ch
Linenbaug, Peter & vrouw, 2 ch
_____, Lodewig (no other name given)
Lodewyk, Antony & vrouw, 3ch
Ludt, Castman & vrouw, 2 ch
Ludwig, Johan Henrig & vrouw, 2 ch
Luts, Johan & vrouw, 6 ch
Lutz, Hans & vrouw
Luwy, Hans Nickel & vrouw, 4 ch
Lys, Mattys & vrouw, 7 ch
Mag, Johan Jurg
Maier, Hans Adam & vrouw
Mansbeil, Kasper & vrouw, 1 ch
_____, Maria Barbara (no other name)
_____, Maria Magdleena & 2 sisters (no other name)
Martin, Peter & vrouw, 3 ch
_____, Mary Barbara (no other name)
Matterm, Abram
Mattheus, Martin & vrouw, 4 ch
Mattys, Laurents & 1 ch
Maur, Johan & vrouw, 5 ch
Maus, Michel
Maybag, Dirk & vrouw, 3 ch
Megel, Hans Wendel & vrouw, 2 ch
Meister, Koenraet
Menimeier, Frants
Mest, Abram & vrouw, 12 ch.
Mets, Simon & vrouw, 3 ch
Metseger, Johan & vrouw, 1 ch
Meurin, Margreta
Meyer, Arent
Meyer, Bartel & vrouw, 4 ch
Meyer, Henrig & vrouw, 2 ch
Meyer, Henrig & vrouw, 3 ch
Meyer, Paulus & vrouw, 1 ch
Michel, Henrig & vrouw, 3 ch
Michel, Niklas & vrouw
Miller, Antony & vrouw
Miller, Jacob & vrouw, 3 ch
Miller, Johan Jacob & vrouw, 1 ch
Miller, Johan Willem
Miller, Peter & vrouw, 5 ch
Miller, Samuel
Mitelig, Herman & vrouw, 2 ch
Mohr, Augustyn & vrouw, 4 ch
Moll, Kasper & vrouw, 1 ch
Morheisser, Niklaas & vrouw, 3 ch
Motji, Johan & vrouw, 4 ch

Moze, David
Muller, Gerlag & vrouw, 1 ch
Muller, Hans Martin & vrouw, 4 ch
Muller, Henrig & vrouw, 3 ch
Muller, Jacob & vrouw, 2 ch
Muller, Michael & vrouw, 2 ch
Muller, Peter & vrouw, 3 ch
Mummenthal, Jacob & vrouw
Munster, Johan Peter & vrouw, 5 ch
Muts, Diderig & vrouw, 3 ch
Mutsch, Fredrig & vrouw
Nadoor, Johan
Nobel, Jacob & vrouw, 3 ch
Nou, Wendel
Nudig, Hans & vrouw, 5 ch
Nusch, Lodwyk, & vrouw, 3 ch
Nutzberger, Mattys & vrouw, 4 ch.
Oberhubel, Jacob & vrouw, 3 ch
Odilioswal, _____ & vrouw [sic]
Ohll, Peter & vrouw, 7 ch
Ostwalt, Johan & vrouw, 4 ch
Paf, Johan Andries & vrouw, 5 ch
Paltzer, Henrig & vrouw, 3 ch
Paul, Henrig & vrouw, 7 ch
Pellesheim, Johan Peter & vrouw, 1 ch
Peter, Jacob & vrouw
Peter, Klaas & vrouw, 6 ch.
Peter, Klaas, & vrouw, 7 ch
Peter, Philip; & vrouw, 1 ch
Piccisch, Adam & vrouw, 2 ach
Ping, Melger
Pinehimer, Barth & vrouw, 4 ch
Ponts, Niklaas & vrouw, 3 ch
Pribl, Michel
Propper, Johan Just & vrouw, 3 ch
Pull, Johan Peter & vrouw, 5 ch
Raads, Pieter
Red, Johan & vrouw, 5 ch
Redel, Johan Henrig & vrouw, 3 ch
Reiter, Henrig & vrouw, 2 ch
Reiter, Johan Lodewyk & vrouw
Reutter, Nicolas
Reyer, Henrig & vrouw, 3 ch
Richart, Francois & vrouw, 1 ch
Rieter, Hans & vrouw, 3 ch
Rigel, Kristiaan
Romer, Johan & vrouw, 3 ch
Roos, Kristoffel
Rosenboom, Pieter & vrouw, 4 ch
Rosor, Martinus Fredrik & vrouw, 2 ch
Rosebach, Peter & vrouw, 2 ch
Rot, Peter & vrouw, 5 ch
Rubel, Johan & vrouw, 1 ch
Ruch, Nicolas & vrouw, 5 ch
Russing, Mattys
Saar, Johan & vrouw, 7 ch
Salbach, Johan & vrouw, 2 ch
Salbach, Johan Emend & vrouw
Sanse, Peter
Sauns, Johan Peter

Schalosch, Peter & vrouw, 3 ch
Scheffer, Andries & vrouw, 4 ch
Schein, Michel Meing
Schellengerger, Koenraet
Scheller, Johan & vrouw
Schelling, Johan & vrouw
Schesbli, Joost Koenraet
Schesselmin, Henrig & vrouw, 1 ch
Schester, Serbus & vrouw, 1 ch
Schilt, Johan Henrig & vrouw
Schithel, Jacob & vrouw
Schits, Marten & vrouw, 1 ch
Schling, Henrik & vrouw
Schmit, Adam & vrouw, 3 ch
Schmit, Henrig & vrouw, 7 ch
Schmit, Jeorg Mikel & vrouw
Schmit, Johan & vrouw, 3 ch
Schmit, Johan Peter
Schmit, Johan Peter & vrouw, 5 ch
Schmit, Niklaas & vrouw, 1 ch
Schmit, Peter & vrouw, 5 ch
Schneiter, Ulrigh & vrouw, 2 ch
Schnitzerling, Johan & vrouw, 3 ch
Schnenmaker, Barth & 5 ch
Scholler, Peter & vrouw, 5 ch
Schommer, Johan
Schonwolff, Johan
Schopfer, Hans Jacob & vrouw
Schoutner, Diebelt & vrouw, 4 ch
Schreits, Mattys & vrouw, 6 ch
Schreling, Peter & vrouw, 6 ch
Schreyer, Johan & vrouw, 1 ch
Schreyts, Johan & vrouw, 3 ch
Schumacher, Johan
Schumes, Ebrehart
Schwarts, Hans Jacob
Schwed, Jacob & vrouw, 7 ch
Seimer, Simon & vrouw, 5 ch
Sibel, Falenteyn
Siles, Mickel & vrouw, 4 ch
Silesy, Katrina & 1 ch
Siller, Johan & vrouw
Sipler, Kristiaan
Sittig, Herman & vrouw, 5 ch
Sleiger, Johan Jurg & vrouw, 4 ch
Sliger, Johan Michel & vrouw, 5 ch
Smit, George Volpert & vrouw, 7 ch
Smith, Hans Miggel & vrouw
Smit, Johan & vrouw
Smit, Johan Adam & vrouw, 3 ch
Smit, Karel & vrouw, 6 ch
Smith, Kasper & vrouw, 1 ch
Sneyder, Frants
Snor, Johan Nickel & vrouw, 3 ch
Soffer, Niklaas & vrouw, 3 ch
Sontag, Frants & vrouw, 4 ch
Sorg, Mattys & vrouw, 3 ch
Speiherman, Johan Henrig & vrouw, 2
Schstaal, Johan Diderig & vrouw, 1 ch
Steem Johan & vrouw, 5 ch

Steeren, Mattys
Steffen, Johan & vrouw, 4 ch
Steiner, Michel & vrouw
Steun, Johan & vrouw, 3 ch
Stouts, _____ [illegible] & vrouw
Stroser, Daniel & vrouw, 1 ch
Suner, Johan Michel & vrouw, 6 ch
Sweeber, Bastiaan
Sweeber, Hendrik
Sypel, Hans Jurg
Talheimer, Henrig & vrouw, 2 ch
Telers, Johan
Thenster, Sibmasers
Thirffenbach, Hans Koenraet & vrouw, 3 ch.
Thirffenbachrin, Anna
Tiell, Ananias & vrouw, 2 ch
Tiell, Herman & vrouw, 1 ch
Tiell, Johan & vrouw, 2 ch
Tielman, _____ (no other name)
Tillman, Hans Koenraet & vrouw, 4 ch
Tubenbeeker, Johan
Ulrig, Johan Elias & vrouw, 3 ch
Valendin, Velden & vrouw, 7 ch
Veesch, Johan Ada & vrouw, 5 ch
Veldents, Henrig
Vinschbag, Kristiaan & vrouw
Visser, Pieter & vrouw, 2 ch
Vogt, Henrig & vrouw, 1 ch
Volks, Arnold & vrouw, 4 ch
Vorster, Jurg & vrouw, 4 ch

Wadenpoll, Jacob & vrouw, 2 ch
Walter, Johan & vrouw, 2 ch
Walter, Kasper & vrouw, 10 ch
Weber, Diderig & vrouw, 2 ch
Weins, Bastiaan & vrouw, 3 ch
Weiroug, Peter & brouw, 4 ch
Weyant, Johan Martin & vrouw
Weyant's Swager & 1 ch
Weysgerber, Johan & vrouw, 2 ch
Wiggert, Hans & vrouw, 5 ch
Wighalm, Mattys & vrouw, 3 ch
Wilhelm, Jan & vrouw
William, Johanna
William, Paul
Wilmer, Anton & vrouw, 1 ch
Wind, Henrig & vrouw, 3 ch
Wind, Peter & vrouw, 5 ch
Windt, Henrig & vrouw, 4 ch
Winkel, Henrig
Wisser, Jacob & vrouw, 1 ch
Wob, Philippus
Woger, Nicolas & vrouw, 2 ch
Wulgraaf, Muller
Zeb, Leonart & vrouw, 4 ch
Zeerbisch, Johan Peter & vrouw, 9 ch
Zerber, Johan Martin & vrouw, 4 ch
Zerber, Philip
Zeyt, Mattys & vrouw, 1 ch
Zigler, Andries & vrouw, 4 ch

Embarkation List from The Netherlands
Fifth Party-Embarked July 3 to July 10, Sailed July 15, 1709

Adolf, Peter & vrouw, 1 ch
Albert, Lodewyk & vrouw, 2 ch
Andries, Koenraet & vrouw, 7 ch
Andries, Peter & vrouw, 1 ch
Anna Katrina, 2 ch
Anna Magdeleena (Wede.), 1 ch
Anna Mary, 2 ch (no other name)
Appel, Andreas
Appleman, Hans Peter & vrouw, 3 ch
Arnolt, Hans Gorg & vrouw, 6 ch
Arnolt, Johan & vrouw, 5 ch
Atorf, Ty & vrouw, 4 ch
Aust, Johan Philips
Autfetter, Felten & vrouw, 1 ch
Baar, Johan
Baptist, Johan
Barbera, Anna
Barbera, Anna, 1 ch
Batelman, Mattias & vrouw, 2 ch
Baur, Kasper & vrouw, 3 ch
Bauwer, Peeter & vrouw, 3 ch
Becker, Johan & vrouw, 3 ch

Becker, Zoden & vrouw, 6 ch
Beesch, Ludwig & vrouw, 1 ch
Bender, Henrig & vrouw, 3 ch
Bender, Johan Bernhart & vrouw, 4 ch
Bender, Koenraet & vrouw, 2 ch
Benedik, Peter
Benter, Baltes & vrouw, 5 ch
Bentram, Geerlof
Ber, Andries & vrouw
Ber, Hans Peter & vrouw
Berderum, Philips
Berg, Kasper
Berlag, Koenraet & vrouw, 4 ch
Berman, Johan & vrouw
Berner, Mattys & vrouw, 2 ch
Bernhart, Peeter & vrouw, 3 ch
Bert, Johan & vrouw, 3 ch
Bert, Johan & vrouw, 4 ch
Bert, Willem
Besser, Niklaas, & vrouw, 3 ch
Beus, Ferdinant & vrouw, 1 ch
Bevit, Johan & vrouw, 4 ch

Beyer, Hans Peter & vrouw, 2 ch
Beyer, Henrig & vrouw, 5 ch
Bickel, Hans Michel & vrouw, 2 ch
Bienlein, Hans
Biettel, Willem
Biltstein, Hans Jacob & vrouw, 4 ch
Bintslin, Anna Kornelia
Birck, Johan & vrouw, 4 ch
Bitz, Hans Gorg & vrouw, 4 ch
Blank, Niklaas & vrouw, 2 ch
Blittersdorf, Koenraet & vrouw, 3 ch
Blomreeder, Willem & vrouw, 3 ch
Bok, Joseph
Bol, Gerland & vrouw, 8 ch
Boller, Philips & vrouw, 5 ch
Born, Gorg & vrouw, 5 ch
Born, Hans & vrouw, 1 ch
Borninger, Kasper & vrouw, 3 ch
Bouman, Jacob & vrouw
Bouman, Joost & 2 ch
Bouwerman, Miggel & vrouw, 3 ch
Braedvis, Godvried
Branck, Emanuel
Brandeurf, Joost & vrouw, 4 ch
Braun, Bastiaan & vrouw, 3 ch
Braun, Ulrig & vrouw, 4 ch
Bretta, Mary
Breyn, Johan Belzar
Brick, Maria Elizabeth
Brounet, Hans Philips & vrouw, 3 ch
Brouve, Hans Jacob & vrouw, 4 ch
Brown, Johan & vrouw, 1 ch
Bruckin, Katrina, 5 ch
Brug, Carla
Buch, Fredrig & vrouw, 4 ch
Buch, Hans Georg & vrouw, 5 ch
Buk, Dunges & vrouw, 1 ch
Burckert, Mattys & vrouw, 2 ch
Burger, Hans Jacob & vrouw, 3 ch
Burket, Kasper & vrouw, 2 ch
Buster, Henrig & vrouw, 6 ch
Cebi, Kristiaan
Cloos, Peeter & vrouw, 5 ch
Collet, Michel & vrouw, 7 ch
Copiak, Mattys
Dal, Andreas & vrouw, 1 ch
Daub, Michel & vrouw, 1 ch
Debesman, David
Decker, Hans Schiedt & vrouw, 1 ch
Dederin, Maria
Deis, Johan & vrouw, 3 ch
Deis, Marcus & vrouw, 3 ch
Deisinger, Hans Jorg
Deisinger, Peter
Dem, Joost & vrouw, 4 ch
Denemarker, Kristoffel & vrouw, 3 ch
Dennerey, Jacob & vrouw
Derner, Hans Jacob & vrouw, 2 ch
Diel, Kristiaan & vrouw
Dielsneyder, Johan & vrouw, 4 ch

Dierig, Neeltje
Dieschell, Hans Gorg
Diets, Johan Jorg & vrouw, 6 ch
Dikert, Henrig & vrouw, 4 ch
Dilshinit, Johan
Dorst, Robbert & vrouw
Doup, Diderig
Drom, Andries & vrouw, 5 ch
Drous, Kirstiaan
Dubous, Michel
Duffing, Willen & vrouw, 4 ch
Egeler, Johan & vrouw
Egred, Louwis
Elhart, Johan & vrouw
Elizabeth, Anna
Elkener, Hans Adam & vrouw, 4 ch
Elroot, Johan Dider & vrouw, 1 ch
Emmell, Johan & vrouw, 1 ch
Engel, _____ & vrouw (no other name)
Engel, Johan
Engle, Margreta (Wede), 2 ch
Engle, Philip & vrouw, 4 ch
Erbs, Hans Henrig & vrouw, 3 ch
Escher, Jacob & vrouw, 2 ch
Eva, Anna
Faech, Johan & vrouw, 4 ch
Feel, Jacob & vrouw, 3 ch
Fink, Johan Willem & vrouw, 6 ch
Fink, Kasper & vrouw, 2 ch
Finkin (Wede.) 2 ch
Finsinger, Philips & vrouw, 1 ch
Fisel, Adam & vrouw, 3 ch
Flip, Jorg & vrouw, 3 ch
Foght, Hans Peter
Frans, Johan & vrouw, 5 ch
Fransnus, Johan Paul & vrouw
Fredig, Cartes & vrouw, 5 ch
Fredig, Hans Adam & vrouw, 1 ch
Fredrick, Koenraet & vrouw, 2 ch
Freymeier, Michel & vrouw, 5 ch
Freonet, Philip & vrouw
Frolug, Valentyn & vrouw, 2 ch
Frowberg, Mattys
Furiger, Fredrig & vrouw, 2 ch
Gardner, Peeter & vrouw, 5 ch
Geerlof, _____ & vrouw, 3 ch (no other name)
Geerlof, Johan Krist & vrouw, 3 ch
Geerlof, Peeter & vrouw, 4 ch
Geertrug, Anna
_____, Geertruy (Wede.) 3 ch. (no other name)
Gees, Jurg & vrouw, 1 ch
Geis, Niklass & vrouw, 4 ch
Gems, Jorg Adam & vrouw
Gerber, Jacob
Geres, Jurg & vrouw, 5 ch
Gerhart, Falentryn & vrouw, 5 ch
Gerhart, Johan & vrouw
Gerheim, Johan & vrouw, 3 ch

Gerlin, Johan
Gertner, Jacob 1 ch
Giseling, Johan Hendrig
Goettel, Daniel & vrouw, 7 ch
Goftig (Gostig), Korn, & vrouw, 4 ch
Gonan, Johan Hendrik
Goplat, Kasper
Grausch, Jacob's (Wede.), 3 ch.
Grausch, Johan Peeter & vrouw, 4 ch
Grefter, Simon & vrouw, 5 ch
Grug, Hans Gorg & vrouw, 5 ch
Grunnig, Bendik & vrouw, 4 ch
Gudtud, Peter & vrouw
Haas, Hend
Haas, Paulus & vrouw, 2 ch
Haber, Ditmut & vrouw, 6 ch
Hag, Mattys & vrouw, 2 ch
Haman, Adries & vrouw
Hannes, Willem & vrouw, 2 ch
Hans (Haus), Blein & vrouw
Harbag, Andreas & vrouw, 2 ch
Hardwig, Johan Jacob & vrouw, 2 ch
Haring, Godvryd
Harman, Johan
Hatenkrowst, Philip
Hattler, Ulrig & vrouw, 9 ch
Hausman, Ludwig & vrouw
Heipt, Philippus & vrouw, 3 ch
Helmet, Philips & vrouw, 6 ch
Helsch, Maarten & vrouw, 3 ch
Hemberg, Johan
Henrig, Andreas & vrouw, 3 ch
Herschner, Steve & vrouw
Hertzeel, Jacob & vrouw, 1 ch
Hes, Johan
Hes, Koenraet & vrouw, 3 ch
Hes, Tomas & vrouw, 3 ch
Hes, Ulrig & vrouw, 2 ch
Het, Koenraet & vrouw, 3 ch
Heu, Fredrig & vrouw, 3 ch
Heu, Kasper & vrouw, 3 ch
Heul, Mattys Gorg & vrouw
Heyt, Joost & vrouw, 1 ch
Hiebesch, Johan
Hilsch, Kristoffel & vrouw
Hober, Krist
Hoch, Michel & vrouw, 2 ch
Hoepert, Hans & vrouw
Hoffman, Albert & vrouw, 6 ch
Hoffman, Henrig & vrouw, 1 ch
Hoffman, Mattys & vrouw, 2 ch
Hoffman, Michel
Hoffrin, Katrina
Hoof, Hans Peter & vrouw, 5 ch
Hoofman, Joost & vrouw
Hoost, Johan Felten & vrouw, 4 ch
Horlakker, Hans Jurg
Horn, Kasper & vrouw, 3 ch
Horsch, Peter & vrouw, 1 ch
Houser, Hans & vrouw, 3 ch

Houtrug, Jorg & vrouw, 3 ch
Huniaben, Willem
Illes, Roypert & vrouw, 4 ch
Jacob, Johan
Jacob, Johan
Jager, Beltes & vrouw, 1 ch
Janse, Willem
Jeger Kristiaan & vrouw, 1 ch
Jemal (Wede), 5 ch
Joggem, Johan & vrouw, 1 ch
Joosten, Johan & vrouw, 6 ch
Jorg, Hans
Josep, Anna
Jung, Johan
Jung, Johan & vrouw
Jung, Johan Peter
Jung, Klaus & vrouw, 3 ch
Jungst, Johan Henrig & vrouw, 3 ch
Jurg, Johan & vrouw, 2 ch
K_____[blotted], Johan Jacob & vrouw, 4 ch
Kamd (Kame?), Gorg & vrouw, 5 ch
Kamp, Koenraet & vrouw, 3 ch
Kanhorner, Margreeta, 1 ch
Karn, Michel & vrouw, 2 ch
Karol, Jacob & vrouw, 5 ch
Kas, Andries Laurens & vrouw, 1 ch
Kasner, Andreas & vrouw, 5 ch
Katrina, Anna
Katrina, Maria
Katrina (Wede), 1 ch
Kayg, Anna Katrina, 3 ch
Kebels, Andries & vrouw, 1 ch
Keelman, Michel & vrouw, 3 ch
Kees, Johan Peter & vrouw, 3 ch
Kel, Peeter & vrouw, 3 ch
Kell, Niklaas & vrouw
Keneman, Jurg Karel
Kenmer, Hans Nikel
Kerbel, Kasper & vrouw, 7 ch.
Kerbel, Peter & vrouw, 1 ch
Kerger, Johan & vrouw, 1 ch
Kermerroot, Johan & vrouw, 6 ch
Kerver, Niklaas & vrouw, 2 ch
Kessen, Houpvig & vrouw
Kever, Hans Philip & vrouw, 7 ch
Kever, Philip & vrouw, 1 ch
Kieselbag, Johan & vrouw, 3 ch
Kigel, Henrig & vrouw, 1 ch
Kindr, Bendik & vrouw, 3 ch
Kittert, Mattys
Klaar, Anna
Klaas, Bartel & vrouw, 2 ch
Klam, Daniel & vrouw, 3 ch
Klapper, Johan Willem & vrouw, 3 ch
Klaus, Bernhart & vrouw, 4 ch
Klein, Jeronimus & vrouw, 3 ch
Klein, Mattys & vrouw, 1 ch
Klein, Peeter & vrouw
Klein, Peter & vrouw

Kleinkor, Korn & vrouw, 1 ch
Kletters, Johan & vrouw, 2 ch
Kloe, Barlin & vrouw, 2 ch
Klop, Johan Nikel & vrouw, 4 ch
Klopper, Johan Willem & vrouw, 3 ch
Knap, Hans Nikel & vrouw, 3 ch
Kneskern, Johan Peter & vrouw
Knevel, Andries, 2 ch
Knever, Paulua & vrouw, 6 ch
Koen, Dinges
Koenraet, Hans
Koert, Michel & vrouw, 8 ch
Kog, Niklaas & vrouw, 2 ch
Konig, Johan Joost & vrouw, 2 ch
Kop, Jacob & vrouw, 4 ch
Kreber, Peeter & vrouw
Kreffulm, Jacob
Kreider, Bernhardt
Kremer, Peter
Kreps, Joost
Krilion, Johan & vrouw, 1 ch
Krist, Johan & vrouw, 3 ch
Kroutner, Mattys
Krow, Koenraet & vrouw
Kruis, Jacob & vrouw, 2 ch
Krum, Johan Herman
Krys, Mattys & vrouw, 3 ch
Kumenstein, Johan Nikel & vrouw, 4 ch
Kun, Philippus & vrouw, 6 ch
Kuntz, Koenraet & vrouw, 3 ch
Lab, Georg & vrouw, 2 ch
Labag, Adam & vrouw, 5 ch
Labag, Adam & vrouw, 5 ch
Lang, Abm. & vrouw, 3 ch
Lang, Johan & vrouw
Langevelt, Hend.
Lank, Peter & vrouw
Lankr (?) Felten & vrouw, 4 ch
Leber, Willem & vrouw, 2 ch
Lei, Hans Henrig & vrouw
Leidecker, Henderick & vrouw
Leitner, Johan Adam & vrouw, 2 ch
Lenken, Jan Willem & vrouw
Lepper, Philippus Herman & vrouw, 5 ch.
Lergerseiler, Johan Willem & vrouw, 1 ch
Lesering, Antony
Leuven, Mary Katryn
Level, Johan Koenraet & vrouw, 3 ch
Licks, Willem Bernhart & vrouw
Lieger, Johan Adam
Lingelbach, Baltes & vrouw, 3 ch
Lingoret, Bernhart & vrouw, 1 ch
Lochrugs, Ulrig & vrouw, 1 ch
Locks, Hans Nikel & vrouw, 3 ch
Lodewyk, Hendrik & vrouw, 4 ch
Logrugs, Mattys, & vrouw, 3 ch
Losch, Mattys & vrouw, 3 ch
Louck, Hans Michel & vrouw, 1 ch
Louck, Johan
Luber, Gabriel & vrouw, 3 ch

Ludwig, Andreas
Ludwig, Johan & vrouw, 6 ch
Ludwig, Mattys & vrouw, 4 ch
Lukas, Hans Gorg & vrouw, 7 ch
Lutz, Peter & vrouw, 4 ch
Lys Katryn
Lysbet, Anna
Maester, Paulus & vrouw, 1 ch
Magdleena (wede.), 5 ch
Man, Herman & vrouw, 3 ch
Mandenagt, Willem
Mangel, Johan Jurg
Margreet, Anna
Margreet, Anna
Maria, Anna
Maria, Anna (Wede.), 1 ch
Maria (Wede.) (no other name)
Maria (Wede), 1 ch (no other name)
Martman, Ludwig
Mary, Anna
Masge, Niklaas & vrouw, 7 ch
Matser, Johan & vrouw, 3 ch
Mattys, _____ & vrouw, 2 ch. (no other name)
Mattys, Peter & vrouw, 5 chMattys, Webbers
May, Johan Peter & vrouw, 2 ch
Meesterin, Margreeta, 2 ch
Meier, Koenraet & vrouw
Meinhober, Philippus & vrouw
Meinsinger, Koenraet & vrouw, 1 ch
Melbreg, Adam & vrouw
Melbreg, Johan
Melsers, Stoffel & vrouw, 2 ch
Meltsberger, Philips & vrouw, 2 ch
Mengel, Hans Jorg & vrouw, 5 ch
Mengje, Fredrig & vrouw, 8 ch
Menin, Johan
Menst, Peter & vrouw, 2 ch
Mese, Mattys & vrouw, 5 ch
Mets, Andreas & vrouw, 4 ch
Metsgennen Doretta
Mey, Johan Dinges (Wede), 1 ch
Myer, Bastiaan
Myer, Henrig & vrouw, 2 ch
Mikkeler, Johan & vrouw, 1 ch
Mikle, Henrig & vrouw, 3 ch
Miller, Johan
Miller, Niklaas
Minsinger, Bastiaan & vrouw, 3 ch
Mitler, Joost
Miyn, Johan & vrouw, 7 ch
Moor, Johan Koenraet & vrouw, 1 ch
Moor, Johan Krist & vrouw, 6 ch
Moor, Philip Willem & vrouw, 2 ch
Morial, Hendrk.
Morees, Frans
Mous, Miggel & vrouw
Muleri, Ula
Muller, Anna Mary
Muller, Hans Georg & vrouw, 1 ch

Muller, Jacob & vrouw, 5 ch
Muller, Johan & vrouw, 4 ch
Muller, Johan Benedik & vrouw, 3 ch
Muller, Johan Henrig & vrouw, 4 ch
Muller, Johan Jacob & vrouw
Muller, Johan Joost & vrouw, 6 ch
Muller, Johan Mikel & vrouw, 1 ch
Muller, Johan Sebastiaan & vrouw
Muller, Johan Tys & vrouw, 2 ch
Muller, Johan Tys & vrouw, 2 ch
Muller, Michel & vrouw, 6 ch
Muller, Miklaas & vrouw, 5 ch
Muller, Peter
Muller, Peter & vrouw, 3 ch
Muller, Philip & vrouw, 2 ch
Muller, Philippus & vrouw, 8 ch
Mulleryn, Anna Mary
Museler, Jacob & vrouw, 4 ch
Negs, Jacob & vrouw, 7 ch
Niesch, Gorg Willem & vrouw, 2 ch
Niklaas, Juties & vrouw, 7 ch
Niklaas, Peeter & vrouw, 2 ch
Nol, Herbert & vrouw
Nonius, Johan Peter
Obel, Johan & vrouw, 1 ch
Obreschur (?), Johan Hendrig & vrouw, 7 ch.
Octer, Kristoffel
Odilja (Wede.) 3 ch
Ogs, Hans Mikel & vrouw, 2 ch
Oosterman, Johan & vrouw, 5 ch
Openheizer, Philip
Patturf, Peter & vrouw, 5 ch
Paulus, Johan Henrig & vrouw, 1 ch
Paulus, Michel
Peerelman, Johan & vrouw, 3 ch
Peerschoor, Hans Jacob & vrouw, 6 ch
Peeter, Andreas
Peeter, Johan
Peeter, Mattys
Peffer, Miggel & vrouw, 2 ch
Pender, Jacob
Penenstehl, Niklaas & vrouw, 2 ch
Perriger, Jacob & vrouw
Peter, Ludwig
Petorius, Gerhart & vrouw, 7 ch
Pettemer, Fredrig & vrouw, 4 ch
Pieleman, Pieter & vrouw, 1 ch
Plein, Jacob & vrouw, 5 ch
Poel, Mikel & vrouw, 2 ch
Poel, Nikel & vrouw, 2 ch
Prak, Hans Michel & vrouw, 1 ch
Prettert, Jeunes & vrouw, 2 ch
Printz, Daniel & vrouw, 3 ch
Prouk, Peter & vrouw, 3 ch
Prunck, Peter
Rageutzwey, Huybert & vrouw, 3 ch
Ram, Niklaas & vrouw, 4 ch
Range, Martin & vrouw
Ras, Michel & vrouw, 1 ch

Rau, Johan Jacob & vrouw, 2 ch
Rechten, Tunes & vrouw, 1 ch
Reder, Laurents
Regebag, Johan & vrouw, 8 ch
Reinbalt, Mattys & vrouw, 2 ch
Reinhart, Kasper & vrouw, 3 ch
Reinhart, Koenraet & vrouw, 3 ch
Reiter, Mattys & vrouw, 2 ch
Reiter, Samuel, 3 ch
Remmer, Johan Willem & vrouw, 5 ch
Rensten, Henrig
Riger, Johan Philips & vrouw, 4 ch
Rensten, Henrig
Riger, Johan Philips & vrouw, 4 ch
Ringer, Jacob & vrouw, 1 ch
Risch, Hans Jorg & vrouw, 5 ch
Rodenberger, Johan
Rodenmeyer, Tobias
Roel, Maria Katrina
Roel, Niklaas & vrouw, 2 ch
Roer, Laurens & vrouw, 3 ch
Roeterscheg, Johan Jurg & vrouw, 3 ch
Roll, Jorg Willem & vrouw, 3 ch
Roschkop, Martin & vrouw, 3 ch
Rover, Hans Jacob & vrouw, 1 ch
Rubert, Arnold
Ruff, Johan & vrouw, 3 ch
Rutz, Matteus & vrouw, 6 ch
Sacks, Bastiaan & vrouw, 4 ch
Sairburger, Hans Jurg & vrouw, 1 ch
Sairburger, Hans Michel
Saly, Dominic & vrouw, 6 ch
Schaff, Bartel & vrouw, 1 ch
Schaft, Bartel & vrouw, 1 ch
Schart, Johan & vrouw, 3 ch
Schart, Johan Daniel
Scheefer, Geerard & vrouw, 2 ch
Scheefer, Niklaas & vrouw
Scheenberger, Johan
Scheever, Johan Hendrig & vrouw
Scheffener, Reinart & vrouw, 2 ch
Scheffer, Jacob & vrouw, 2 ch
Schehart, Michel & vrouw, 2 ch
Schel, Jacob & vrouw, 3 ch
Schelter, Kasper & vrouw, 4 ch
Schenk, Hans Koenraet & vrouw, 2 ch
Schenk, Hans Nikel & vrouw
Scherdel, Koenraet & vrouw, 4 ch
Scherver, Philippus
Scheser (Schever?), Hans Hendrik
Schester, Philip & vrouw, 5 ch
Scheucher, Michel &v rouw, 5 ch
Scheue, Gilles & vrouw, 3 ch
Scheugh, Mattys & vrouw, 4 ch
Schey, Hans Peter & vrouw, 3 ch
Schilderin, Margreet, 3 ch
Schilling, _____ & vrouw, 3 ch [sic]
Schimberger, Henrig
Schinberger, Bartel
Schinberger, Susan

Schmit, Michel
Schmitz, Johan & vrouw, 2 ch
Schneider, Peter & vrouw, 2 ch
Schner, Johan & vrouw
Schniter, Peter & vrouw
Schnitspan, Korn & vrouw, 5 ch
Schnug, Johan Adam
Schnug, Willem
Schober, Peter
Schoek, Niklaas & vrouw, 2 ch
Schoenmager, Jorg Willem & vrouw, 4 ch
Schoenmager, Mattys
Schoffer, Jacob & vrouw, 8 ch
Schog, Johan Hendrig & vrouw, 1 ch
Schog, Kristiaan & vrouw, 6 ch
Schoof, Johan
Schoetis, Johan Jurg & vrouw, 2 ch
Schover, Kristiaan
Schram, Pieter & vrouw, 3 ch
Schreeder, Onelgert & vrouw, 7 ch
Schreider, Philip & vrouw, 5 ch
Schriber, Jacob & vrouw, 7 ch
Schrout, Levi
Schudelbag, Martin & vrouw
Schug, Miklaas & vrouw, 8 ch
Schulerd, Koenraet & vrouw, 3 ch
Schuller, Hans Jacob & vrouw, 1 ch
Schultheisch, Johan
Schumager, Daniel & vrouw, 3 ch
Schupman, Herman & vrouw, 7 ch
Schus, Johan & vrouw, 4 ch
Schuts, Philips & vrouw, 4 ch
Schwarts, Jurg & vrouw, 4 ch
Schwer, Adam :& vrouw, 1 ch
Seder, Johan & vrouw, 1 ch
Sies, Hans Peter & vrouw, 6 ch
Sikart, Mattys & vrouw, 4 ch
Simon, Benedik & vrouw, 4 ch
Simon, Laurents
Simon, Peter
Simon Sagarias & vrouw, 3 ch
Sitig, Krist & vrouw, 1 ch
Slesser, Hendrik & vrouw, 5 ch
Sligt, Hans
Slosher, Andreas, 2 ch
Smit, Hans Peter
Smit, Johan Andreas & vrouw, 4 ch
Smit, Joost
Smit, Niklaas & vrouw, 4 ch
Smit, Thomas
Sneider, Arnold & vrouw, 3 ch
Sneider, Jacob
Sneider, Johan & vrouw, 3 ch
Sneiter, Henrig & vrouw, 3 ch
Sneyder, Johan & vrouw
Sneyder, Johan Willem & vrouw, 1 ch
Sneyder, Kasper & vrouw, 6 ch
Sneyder, Kristiaan & vrouw, 3 ch
Sneyder, Miggel, & vrouw, 4 ch
Sneyder Juriaan & vrouw, 1 ch

Snyder, Johan & vrouw, 3 ch
Soelst, Johan Jurg & vrouw, 1 ch
Sommer, Hans Jacob & vrouw, 1 ch
Sool, Johan & vrouw, 5 ch
Sool, Kiritiaan & vrouw, 6 ch
Spengeler, Johan Frans & vrouw
Sporin, Anna Katrina
Stal, Martin & vrouw, 1 ch
Stall, Henrig & vrouw, 4 ch
Stamber, Melger & vrouw, 1 ch
Stauber, Jacob & vrouw, 1 ch
Steen, Elias & vrouw, 3 ch
Steever, Mattys & vrouw, 2 ch
Steier, Johan Mikel
Stein, Martin
Stein, Michel & vrouw, 3 ch
Steiner, Jorg & vrouw
Stekle, Benedik & vrouw, 5 ch
Sterm, Kristiaan & vrouw, 1 ch
Stern, Jacob & vrouw, 2 ch
Stern, Philip & vrouw, 1 ch
Stik, Mattys & vrouw, 3 ch
Stor, Miggel & vrouw, 4 ch
Straes, Andreas & vrouw, 2 ch
Straetsborger, Baltes & vrouw, 1 ch
Stree, Herman
Streit, Kristiaan & vrouw, 5 ch
Stook, Kristiaan & vrouw, 2 ch
Stub, Maarten, 3 ch
Stubinger, Hans
Swal, Johan Geerard & vrouw, 1 ch
Swart, Hans Adam & vrouw
Swartbag, Hartel & vrouw, 7 ch
Switseler, Henrig & vrouw, 4 ch
Tamboer, Henrig & vrouw, 3 ch
Tewisman, Emrig & vrouw, 2 ch
Toos, Serris & vrouw, 5 ch. [sic]
Theis, Johan
Theis, Thomas
Thomas, Peeter & vrouw, 2 ch
Tietruy, Hans Willem & vrouw, 5 ch
Timmerman, M. & vrouw, 1 ch
Timmerman, Willem, 2 ch
Tipenhove, Hans Jurg & vrouw, 3 ch
Tomas, Hans Willem & vrouw, 2 ch
Tomas, Johan & vrouw, 6 ch
Tomas, Mattys
Triespeisser (?), Johan
Tys, Mattys & vrouw, 5 ch
Tzoll, Hans Jacob
Ulrig, Albregt & vrouw, 1 ch
Ulrig, Hans
Umdrucht, Jacob & vrouw, 5 ch
Urban, Michel & vrouw, 4 ch
Vaar, Daniel & vrouw
van Bergen, Hans Peter & vrouw, 2 ch
Vasbender, Bertram & vrouw, 3 ch
Vegt, Simon & vrouw
Vesser, Hans Jurg & vrouw, 2 ch
Visser, Garrard & vrouw, 3 ch

Visser, Hans & vrouw, 2 ch
Visser, Hendk & vrouw
Visser, Johan & vrouw, 1 ch
Vos, Johan
Vulman, Laurens
Vulman, Mattys & vrouw, 4 ch
Waal, Kristoffel & vrouw, 6 ch
Wagenaar, Johan Hendrik
Wagenaar, Niklaas & vrouw, 3 ch
Wagman, Ab. & vrouw, 2 ch
Wagnaar, Willem
Wagner, Johan & vrouw, 1 ch
Wagner, Niklaas & vrouw, 4 ch
Wagner, Philippus & vrouw 2 ch
Walen, Johan
Walter, Johan Henrig & vrouw, 4 ch
Wannemager, Peter & vrouw
Weber, Baltes
Weber, Hans Jacob & vrouw, 4 ch
Weber, Jacob & vrouw, 1 ch
Weber, Johan Henrig & vrouw, 1 ch
Weber, Johan Koenraet & vrouw, 5 ch
Weber, Mattys
Weber, Niklaas & vrouw
Weber, Philip
Weber, Simon & vrouw, 2 ch
Wechel, Hans Michel & vrouw, 2 ch
Wedebag, Peter
Weilant, Peeter & vrouw, 2 ch
Weiller, Johan & vrouw, 1 ch
Weinberg, Koenraet & vrouw
Welsaker, Stoffel & vrouw, 1 ch
Welter, Matteus
Wendesheimer, Stoffel & vrouw, 5 ch
Weyech, Matteus, & vrouw, 5 ch

Weyspaart, Jurg & vrouw, 3 ch
Wiesener, Johan & vrouw, 6 ch
Wilhellem, Henrig & vrouw, 5 ch
Willem, Jorg & vrouw
Wilmy, Jacob & vrouw, 2 ch
Winsman, Henrig & vrouw, 3 ch
Wintik, Johan Jacob
Wisner, Johan & vrouw, 6 ch
Wistenroot, Anneke
Wolfskel, Hans Gorg & vrouw
Wolft, Bertram & vrouw, 4 ch
Wolkin, Anna Barber, 2 ch
Wolleben, Hans Felten & vrouw, 3 ch
Wolleben, Hans Miggle & vrouw, 1 ch
Wolleben, Johan
Worms, Kristiaan & vrouw, 4 ch
Wormster, Bastiaan & vrouw, 2 ch
Woust, Felix
Wugin, Lizabet, 1 ch
Wyngaertenaer, Peter & vrouw, 3 ch
Wys, Johan Hendrig & vrouw, 4 ch
Wyskerver, Johan Hendrif & vrouw, 4 ch
Wyst, Koenraet & vrouw, 3 ch
Yslant, David & vrouw, 1 ch
Zamer, Maarten & vrouw, 5 ch
Zeiger, Jurg & vrouw, 2 ch
Zeiter, Andries & vrouw, 3 ch
Zeiter, Ahsn & vrouw
Zekel, Willem & vrouw
Zetgen, Henrig Peter & vrouw, 2 ch
Ziel, Marcus & vrouw, 1 ch
Zigler, Koenraet & vrouw, 1 ch
Zosin, _____ & vrouw, 4 ch. [sic]
Zouwe, Mattys & vrouw, 5 ch

SIXTH PARTY--EMBARKED JULY 27
SAILED JULY 28, 1709

Ache, Johan
Achenbag, Johan
Agenbag, Anna Margreta
Aggenbag, Johan Jacob & vrouw & 4 ch
Allebad, Andrass & vrouw
Allebag, Elizabet
Antomin, Anna Margreta & 1 ch
Appel, Johan
Ar, Johan Willem & vrouw, & 6 ch
Arendorff, Johan Henrig & vrouw & 1 ch
Arnold, Johan & vrouw
Arommenuil, Geerhart
Aterbag, Jurg & vrouw
Bang, Kristiaan & vrouw, & 3 ch.
Bast, Joost Hendrig & vrouw, & 5 ch
Bauerin, Anna Maria
Baume, Frants Heller & vrouw, & 4 ch

Beck, Simon & vrouw & 8 ch
Becker, Albert & vrouw & 1 ch
Becker, Hans Henrig
Becker, Johan & vrouw, & 3 ch
Bele, Johan Jacob
Belger, Johan & vrouw, & 1 ch
Belts, Johan
Berdram, Johan & vrouw
Berg, Johan Henrig
Berks, Martin & vrouw
Berlee, Frans & vrouw & 2 ch
Berner, Johan & vrouw & 3 ch
Bernhard, Josep & vrouw
Bernhart, Johan
Bernhart, Johan & vrouw & 2 ch
Bernhart, Johan & vrouw & 2 ch
Bescher, Henrig & vrouw & 3 ch

Besme, Henrig & vrouw, & 3 ch
Besme, Henrig & vrouw & 3 ch
Best, Johan Hirg & vrouw & 1 ch
Beyer, Mikel & swister
Beyer, Sagond & swister
Blasch, Johan & vrouw & 2 ch
Botser, Anna Maria
Botser, Johan Herman & vrouw & 8 ch
Bremer, Jacob & vrouw & 4 ch
Bron, Mattys & vrouw & 2 ch
Bruch, Hans Henrig & vrouw & 4 ch
Brusel, Johan Nikel & vrouw & 4 ch
Brustel, Johan Gorg & vrouw & 4 ch
Brustel, Johan Melgior & vrouw & 3 ch
de Hed, Kristoffel & vrouw & 4 ch
Deiritsbacher, Michel
Deisch, Andreas & vrouw & 4 ch
Deiwig, Simon & vrouw & 3 ch
den Decer, Peter Jansz & vrouw & 5 ch
Detweider, Jacob & vrouw & 2 ch
deWolf, Godvried & vrouw & 3 ch
Dickl, Johan & vrouw & 4 ch
Diel, Johan Jurg & vrouw & 1 ch
Diepel, Johan Peter & vrouw & 3 ch
Dilcher, Herman & vrouw & 3 ch
Dilser, Koenraet's (Wede.) & 1 ch
Diltey, Hans Jacob & vrouw & 5 ch
Dinges, Hans Jacob & vrouw & 4 ch
Doll, Hans Adam & vrouw, & 2 ch
Domels, Barber & 2 ch
Dorman, Johannes & 2 ch
Dorreman, Geertruy
Draks, Johan Jacob & vrouw & 4 ch
Dreschel, Johan Jurg & vrouw
Dreshauser, Willem & vrouw & 3 ch
Eberhartin, Anna Barber
Ebers, Daniel & vrouw & 3 ch
Eberts, Johan Peter & vrouw & 2 ch
Eeisenberg, Antonius
Ekman, Daniel & vrouw & 1 ch
Emaus, Bonefacius & vrouw & 5 ch
Engelsman, Jurg &v rouw & 3 ch
Erlang, Johan & vrouw & 4 ch
Feigsfint, Mattys
Feiseler, Andreas & vrouw & 2 ch
Ferdener, Hans Jurg & vrouw & 1 ch
Feschler, Johan Wendel & vrouw & 3 ch
Feysters, Herman &v rouw & 2 ch
Fiedel, Fredrik & vrouw & 3 ch
Fischbag, Diderig
Fischbag, Johan Bast & vrouw & 2 ch
Fischbag, Joost
Fisser, Andries & vrouw & 7 ch
Fleuter, David
Folant, Johan Willem & vrouw & 3 ch
Fosch, Martin's (Wede.) & 3 ch
Frants, Anna & 2 ch
Frants, Henrig & vrouw & 7 ch
Frants, Paulus
Fredrig, Hans Felten & vrouw & 5 ch

Frits, Jurg Willem & vrouw & 3 ch
Funck, Anna Katrina
Funck, Peter & vrouw & 4 ch
Furster, Michel & vrouw & 3 ch
Fyk, Anna Katrina
Gerserin, Geertrug
Getter, Henrig & vrouw & 2 ch
Giseler, Johan Henrig & vrouw & 1 ch
Gleich, Sovia
Gnalder, Andries
Godwig, Antonius & vrouw
Goltman, Koenraet & vrouw & 5 ch
Greff, Philips Jacob & vrouw & 2 ch
Greidter, Joggem
Grein, Anna Katrina
Grosch, Johannes & vrouw & 5 ch
Gruwer, Hans & vrouw & 3 ch
Guth, Johan
Haan Johan Jurg & vrouw & 7 ch
Haberstig, Henrig & vrouw
Halte, Hans Felten & vrouw & 2 ch
Hamon, Johan Willem & vrouw & 4 ch
Harger, Sondag
Hartman, Fredrig & vrouw & 2 ch
Hartwig, Hans Gorg & 2 ch
Haus, Johan's (Wede.) & 3 ch
Heck, Henrig & vrouw & 3 ch
Heger, Johan Fredrik
Heidelberger, Hirchel & vrouw & 2 ch
Heil, Hans Jacob
Held, Henrig & vrouw & 3 ch
Hell, Johan & vrouw & 4 ch
Helman, Adam
Henrig, Johan & vrouw & 3 ch
Herberts, Jacob & vrouw & 2 ch
Herling, Henrig
Hesche, Niklas & vrouw & 1 ch
Heydee, Peeter & vrouw & 1 ch
Heyer, Johan Jurg & vrouw
Hindterschit, Michel & vrouw & 3 ch
Hitserin, Kristiaan
Hock, Johan & vrouw & 3 ch
Hoff, Johan Melgior & vrouw & 6 ch
Hoffman, Henrig & vrouw & 2 ch
Hoffsteittler, Kristiaan & vrouw & 5 ch
Hoperhempt, Fredrik & vrouw & 2 ch
Hummel, Herman & vrouw & 1 ch
Huppers, Henrig & vrouw & 8 ch.
Ingold, Hans & vrouw & 5 ch
Jacob, Johan
Jacob, Johan
Jacob, Johan & vrouw & 2 ch
Jacobi, Philip & vrouw
Jacobsz, Roel
Joggem, Mattys
Joost, Kristoffel & vrouw & 1 ch
Jorg, Antony & vrouw & 6 ch
Josten, Margreta & 1 ch
Jung, Johan Eberhard & vrouw & 1 ch
Junge, Johannes' (Wede.) & 5 ch

Jurg, Johan
Kartneer, Johan & 3 ch
Kastner, Johan & 7 ch
Keil, Johann & vrouw & 2 ch
Keiming, Johan Markus & vrouw & 3 ch
Keiseham, Johan Joost's (Wede.) & 1 ch
Keldereich, Abram & vrouw & 3 ch
Kell, Jurg, Andries & vrouw & 1 ch
Keys, Johan Philip & vrouw & 1 ch
Kirch, Johan Deisch
Klein, Johan & vrouw & 2 ch
Kleisch, Kristoffel & vrouw
Klengs, Johan & vrouw
Klegs, Johan Gorg & vrouw & 3 ch
Klegs, Johan Henrig & vrouw & 4 ch
Knuppelberg, Paul
Koch, Johan & vrouw
Koenraed, Johan Anders & vrouw & 5 ch
Koenraed, Salmon & 2 ch
Kog, Hans Henrig & vrouw & 5 ch
Kogh, Jurg & vrouw & 4 ch
Kolb, Jacob & 2 ch
Kolbin, Maria Tys
Kolle, Hans Jacob
Koltman, Koenraet & vrouw & 5 ch
Koog, Johan Antony
Koog, Johan Willem & vrouw & 1 ch
Koselich, David
Kramerin, Susanne
Kristhaus, Johan & vrouw & 6 ch
Krooschler, Johan Koenraet
Kum, Hans Jacob & vrouw & 5 ch
Kumpff, Johan Peeter & 5 ch
Kurts, Johan Kristoffel &v rouw & 2 ch
Lamain, Franto & vrouw & 4 ch
Laue, Johan Peter & vrouw & 4 ch
Lents, Henrig
Lents, Willem & vrouw & 5 ch
Leuben, Peter & vrouw & 2 ch
Leyger, Koenraet & vrouw & 2 ch
Leyger, Koenraet & vrouw & 2 ch
Leyn, Eberhart Hieronimus & vrouw & 4 ch
Lind, Gerhard
Loost, Andries & vrouw & 3 ch
Luck, Anonius
Margreet, Anna
Mattern, Marcus
Matthys, Hans
Maul, Fredrig & vrouw & 2 ch
Maul, Hendk & vrouw
Maul, Johan & vrouw & 7 ch
Meisser, Johan Jurg & vrouw & 4 ch
Melsch, Johan & vrouw
Merlee, Willem & vrouw
Mescherling, Benedik
Mets, Johan & vrouw & 2 ch
Metsch, Maria Tys
Meyer, Antony & vrouw & 3 ch
Meyer, Johan Jacob & vrouw & 6 ch
Meyer, Kristiaan

Meyer, Leendert & vrouw & 1 ch
Meyer, Simon & 2 ch
Meyer, Weyand & swister
Michel, Johan & vrouw & 2 ch
Michel, Kasper & vrouw & 3 ch
Miller, Hans Gorg & vrouw & 1 ch
Moll, Johan Wiand
Mons, Paulus & vrouw & 2 ch
Mouts, Kleman & vrouw
Muller, Hans Merde
Muller, Jozep
Muller, Thys & vrouw & 1 ch
Musche, Maria Tys
Nagel, Herman
Net, Jurg, Fredrig & 1 ch
Nier, Johan Gofvried & vrouw & 2 ch
Niesch, Anna
Niesch, Anna Margreta
Niesch, Hans Henrig & vrouw & 5 ch
Niesch, Jacob
Niesch, Thomas & 1 ch
Noigt, Johan Philip & vrouw & 1 ch
Obber, Valentyn & vrouw & 2 ch
Obers, Peter & vrouw & 1 ch
Order (?), Johan Adam & vrouw & 2 ch
Ort, Hans Jacob & vrouw
Peeter, Johan & 2 ch
Peeter, Johan Koenraet & vrouw & 1 ch
Peifer, Johan Willem
Penel, Antony & vrouw & 3 ch
Petri, Johan Jacob
Petrin, Elizabet & 1 ch
Petrosines, Remedius & vrouw
Petry, Arent & vrouw & 1 ch
Petry, Kristiaan & vrouw & 1 ch
Philip, Johan & vrouw & 3 ch
Philips, Johan Fredrig & vrouw & 2 ch
Plenter, Frants
Poller, Kristiaan
Poppelsdorff, Kasper & vrouw & 3 ch
Prints, Johan & vrouw & 4 ch
Provo, Hans Peter & vrouw & 3 ch
Raminger, Daniel & vrouw & 1 ch
Raubel, Jacob
Rauch, Johan Kasper & vrouw & 3 ch
Reck, Samuel
Reinhart, Jozep & vrouw & 6 ch
Reinhelt, Jurg & vrouw
Repscher, Johan Peter
Repscher, Philip & vrouw & 3 ch
Restein, Johan & vrouw & 1 ch
Retschhuff, Johan Paul
Ritsel, Johan & vrouw & 6 ch
Ritter, Johan Michel
Rogge, Hans
Ronche, Thys & vrouw & 1 ch
Rosenberger, Johan Philip
Roth, Johan Engelbert
Roth, Joost & vrouw & 3 ch
Rutsel, Kasper & vrouw & 1 ch

Salbag, Anna Margreta
Sampt, Johan Sudot & vrouw
Sargusch, Philip & vrouw & 5 ch
Sattler, Johan Jacob & vrouw & 1 ch
Schalt, Johan Peter & vrouw & 6 ch
Schantsman, Koenraet & vrouw & 3 ch
Scheefer, Hans Jacob & vrouw & 4 ch
Scheefer, Johan Andries & vrouw & 2 ch
Schefer, Johan Mikel & vrouw & 6 ch
Scheff, Johan Willem & vrouw
Scheffer, Johan Gorg
Scheffing, Johanna
Scheifer, Gerhardus
Scheifer, Hans & vrouw & 3 ch
Schenkelberger, Herman & vrouw & 4 ch
Schepp, Antony
Schesdons, Kristoffel & vrouw & 3 ch
Schet, Johan Henrig & 1 ch
Schilfer, Ludwig & vrouw & 2 ch
Schitsin, Anna & 7 ch
Schneider, Gorg
Schneider, Henrig & vrouw & 1 ch
Schneider, Johan Jacob
Schneiter, Johan Henrig
Schnider, Valentyn & vrouw & 6 ch
Schniter, Johan Diderig & vrouw & 6 ch
Schut, Anna Geertruty
Schog, Johan Henrig
Schonholts, Ulrig &v rouw & 3 ch
Schonwolf, Johan Bernhardus
Schredt, Johan & vrouw
Schreiner, Jacob & vrouw & 3 ch
Schriber, Tielman
Schu, Johan & vrouw & 4 ch
Schwab, Hans Otta & vrouw & 1 ch
Schwachin, Maria Durt & 1 ch
Scharts, Antony & vrouw & 3 ch
Sedle, Johan
Seel, Koenraet & vrouw & 2 ch
Seger, Johan Henrig & vrouw & 1 ch
Sehn, Johan & vrouw & 4 ch
Seinter, Gorg
Selter, Kristoffel & vrouw & 3 ch
Sempt, Peter Adam & vrouw & 6 ch
Siegman, Hans Peter & vrouw
Smit, Bernhart & vrouw
Smit, Hans Martin & vrouw & 2 ch
Smit, Johan & vrouw
Smit, Johan Elias
Smit, Johan Joost & vrouw & 4 ch
Sneider, Hans Willem & vrouw & 6 ch
Sneiter, Johan Wilhellem
Soeg, Henrik & vrouw & 3 ch
Solinger, Peter
Spanjert, Johan & vrouw & 4 ch
Stang, Hans Jacob & vrouw & 3 ch
Steibing, Johan Peter & vrouw & 2 ch
Steinebag, Kristoffel & vrouw & 2 ch
Steinbag, Willem & vrouw & 4 ch

Steir, Joost & vrouw & 3 ch
Stelzer, Kasper & vrouw & 5 ch
Steyg, Miggel
Stier, Peter Adolph & vrouw & 3 ch
Straup, Mattys
Stul, Johan Henrig
Stumpf, Hans Gorg & vrouw & 2 ch
Stuner, Johan Michel & vrouw & 2 ch
Sweever, Margretta & 3 ch
Tiedberger, Hans & vrouw & 3 ch
Teilhauzer, Jacob & vrouw & 7 ch
Tilenz, Johan Martin
Timmerman, Johan Peter
Timmerman, Koenraet
Ulrig, Fredrig Hartman &v rouw & 2 ch
Ulrig, Johan & vrouw
Vater, Henrig Michel & vrouw & 3 ch
Visbag, Joost
Vischbag, Johan Jacob & vrouw & 7 ch
Vischer, Sebastiaan & vrouw & 2 ch
Volk, Johan & vrouw & 1 ch
Wabel, Hans Jacob & vrouw & 5 ch
Wabel, Miklas & vrouw & 3 ch
Walje, Jacob
Wanmager, Koenraet & vrouw & 8 ch
Wanniger, Johan & vrouw
Wapag, Herman & vrouw & 4 ch
Weber, Michel
Weil, Hans Jacob & vrouw & 3 ch
Weischgerterin, Maria Katrina
Weiser, Johan Koenraet & vrouw & 8 ch
Wendel, Johan Jacob & vrouw & 1 ch
Wendel, Peter & vrouw & 3 ch
Wepel, Valentyn & vrouw
Werner, Hans & vrouw & 2 ch
Weyants, Benedik & vrouw & 1 ch
Widt, Johan Joost & vrouw & 1 ch
Wierstein, Hans & vrouw & 3 ch
Wiesner, Gorg & vrouw & 2 ch
Wilhellem, Andreas' (Wede.) & 4 ch
Wilhellem, Johan Joost & vrouw & 3 ch
Willem, Antony & vrouw & 2 ch
Willem, Johan & vrouw & 3 ch
Willemse, Adriaan & vrouw & 4 ch
Winter, Thomas & vrouw & 4 ch
Witsch, Niklaas & vrouw & 2 ch
Witse, Johan Ulrig & vrouw & 2 ch
Wolff, Hans
Wolff, Johan Richard
Wolfin, Anna & 2 ch
Wolfin, Eva
Wurst, Leenhart & vrouw & 1 ch
Yung, Johan, Mikel & vrouw
Zambag, Mathys & vrouw & 5 ch
Zelts, Adam & vrouw & 1 ch
Zimmerman, Jacob & vrouw & 3 ch
Zoot, Fredrig & vrouw & 4 ch
Zuber, Ulrig & vrouw
Zufungs, Gorg & vrouw & 3 ch

Further Classification of London List by Occupation, by Religion.

From: The Book of Names
Especially Relating to The Early Palatines and the First Settlers in the
Mohawk Valley
Compiled and Arranged by Lou D. MacWethy
Published by The Enterprise and News
St. Johnsville, NY., 1933

Occupation	1st	2nd	3rd	4th	Total
Hs. & V	113	113	456	262	944
Hus.	32	83			115
Hrd.	3			1	4
Wheelwrights	1	5	5	3	14
Smiths	11	9	15	12	47
Saddlers	1	1	2	1	5
Millers	5	4	9	10	28
Bakers	2	10	11	11	34
Brewers	1	12			13
Butchers	3	3	8	1	15
Clo. & Lin. weavers	8	15	27	15	65
Tailors	3	19	18	16	56
Shoemakers	5		20	12	37
Stocking weavers	1		2	3	6
Tanners	1		2	3	6
Carpenters	8	14	44	22	88
Joiners	3			5	8
Masons	2	9	36	7	54
Coopers	3			12	15
Bookbinders	1				1
Miners			2		2
Schoolmasteres		3	5	3	11
Coopers & Br.			23		23
Turners		4	2		6
Laborers		2			2
Silversmiths		2			2
Hunters			3	2	5
Wool weavers			2		2

Potters		3		3
Tilemakers		1		1
Brickmakers		2	3	5
Surgeons		2	1	3
Figuremakers		1	1	2
Locksmith		2	1	3
Hatters			2	2
Glazers			3	3
Bricklayers			4	4

	By	Religion			
Lutheran	55	132	243	132	562
Reformed	125	145	282	140	692
Catholic	25	63	258	177	523
Baptist	9			1	10
Mennonite		1		2	3

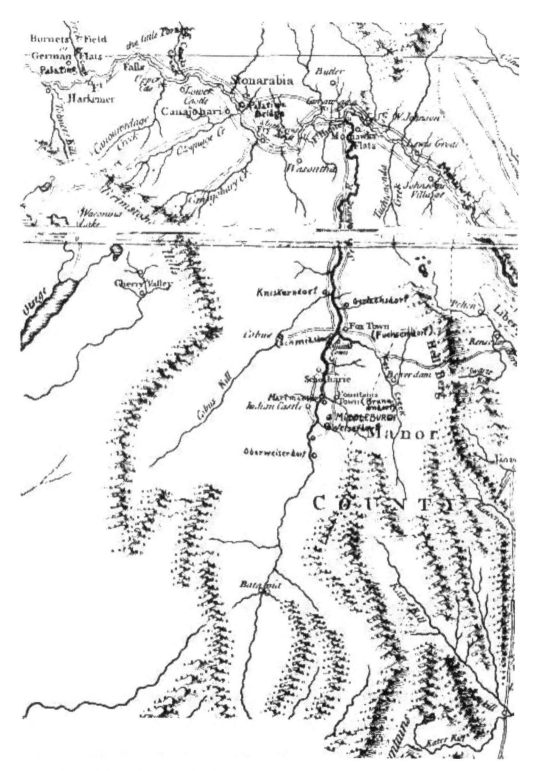

Map of Central New York, showing the Palatine settlements in New York. Courtesy of New York Historical Society.

Our Early Citizens
Names of Those Taking the Oath of Allegiance from 1715 to 1773
Compiled from the Colonial Laws by Lt. Com. L. F. Bellinger, U. S. N., Retired

PALATINE NATURALIZATIONS
By L. F. BELLINGER

As a boy I understood perfectly why foreigners desired to become citizens of this land of the free and home of, for, and by the brave, but never did understand there could be any question of property rights, and thought if a man bought property, it belonged to him regardless of his nationality, present or past. Later in life I learned that in Haiti, foreigners cannot acquire real estate, and the same is true in Japan at present. It appears that about 1700 one who was naturalized in one of the American Colonies; was by no means naturalized in all of them. Also, there were certain questions about owning property and buying property which seem queer to us. First, it was necessary to obtain a legal permit or license before any purchasing of lands from the Indians could be instituted. Undoubtedly there were "costs" connected with the issuance of these permits. Next, after the land was deeded by the Indians, aliens were always in trouble with the Colonial Government about quit-rents, and transfers of the land to others, that did not cause trouble to citizens of the colony, and a law was passed July 5, 1715 to remove some of these troubles. Fifty years or so later it was necessary to fix up the 1715 law so the property belonging to the first naturalized citizens could be received and held by their children born in the Colony of New York.

It is of interest to note how the scare of loss of land and the passage of new laws and privileges brought about surges in the desire for naturalizations.

It is noteworthy that some of our ancestors failed to save up the necessary 19 or 20 shillings in six months or a year as the requirement was, and their names had to go on later special acts for their benefit.

After all that trouble of theirs to acquire the land, how many in your "Descendants" column live now on the land that troubled their ancestors so much? Count 'em Mr. Editor!

Following this is given a list of names of the Palatines in the valley, as far as I can pick out names with which we are all more or less familiar.

I have tried to put in parenthesis a more modern spelling than is given in the books from which I quote. It may help some to determine ages and names that were in existence at the date specified, and may also reduce the number of those needing to be grafted to the "Family Tree."

As an example we have here evidence that Benton's statement is incorrect, as far as the Herkimer family not arriving until the 1722 immigration. Here is George Herkimer. His son, Johan Jost was evidently not yet 21, and his grandson General Nicholas was not born until about 1726, all of which is consistent. Similarly, Benton argues that Rudolph Staley of Staley's Patent did not arrived until the 1722 immigration, because he was not one of the Burnettsfield Patentees; yet we now have him as "Roelof Steel" over 21 on the date specified.

John Jacob Ehl shows up as the first of his tribe apparently.

Peter Bellinger now shown to be over 21 in 1715 appeared only as a sponsor at a Kocherthal record birth in 1715, from which the argument was that he was at least 15 years old when acting as sponsor. He signed deed to land in 1782 and 1784 and lived to be over 90 therefore. He was the father in law of Adam Helmer, the famous scout, the father of Colonel Peter Bellinger, the father of "Hoffrich" Bellinger of the "Mohawk Dutch Marines," and the father in law of Lieut. Timothy Frank. Longevity in Peter's family was hereditary. Colonel Peter lived to be 87, one daughter to 96, another daughter to 100, and the son of Colonel Peter lived to 93.

Note--All the names which appear in the Annals of Albany are given. Selection was made from the large number in "Colonial Laws." New York Palatines naturalized in Albany, N. Y. (Taken from Munsell's "Annals of Albany," pp. 40, 43, 46, 48, and 49). At a Mayors Court held in the City Hall of Albany, Oct. 11, 1715.

The following persons to wit.

Juryh Herck Heemer
Petrus Van Driesen

Jan Lansingh
Claes Van Der Volgen

Jan. Janse Bleecker
Peter Kneskern
Hans Jury Kast
Warnaer Deygert
Nicholas Wever
Johannis Feeck
Frederick Scheffer
Reynhaert Scheffer
Jurry Beenner
Anthony Bchyet
Jackob Kop
Nicholas Korning
Jacob Weever
Christian Houys

Johannis Keyser
Hendrick Klock
Jacob Snell
Peter Freeck
Poelof Steel
Hendrick Seix
Leendert Helmer
William Schief
Paul Dinser
Johan Frederick Bell
Phillips Helmer
Nicholas Schieffer
Jacob Freeck

Did in open Court take the oaths by law appointed to be taken instead of oaths of allegiance & supremacy subscribe the test and make repeat and swear to & subscribe the abjuration oath pursuant to the directions of an act of general assembly entitled an act declaring yet all those of foreign birth theretofore inhabiting within this colony and dying seized of any lands tenements and hereditaments shall be forever hereafter deemed taken & esteemed to have been naturalized and for naturalizing all protestants of foreign birth now inhabiting within this colony.

To whom certificates are forthwith to be given according to the directions of ye said act.

At a Mayors Court held at the City Hall of Albany ye 22th day of November 1715.

The following person to witt

Adam Vroman
Evert Janze
Johan Andries Drom
Hans Pieter Heyser
Johannis Rousman
Hans Michall Drock
Pieter Vonk
Johan Coenraet Petrie
Jacob Bsheere
Peter Smith
Hendrick Nies
David Hoefler
Johan Smitt
Johan Joseph Proper
Johan Pieter Proper
Johan Fred'k Proper
Ananias Tiel

Andries Bartel
Philip Bartel
Jacob Schieffer
David Chierts
Johannis Schiets
Jacob Schoemaker
Christophel Hagedorn
Hend. Ch'l. Wiederwax
Johan And. Wiederwax
Hans Adam Schiets
Andries Vink
Frederick Kietman
Johannis Beerman
Thomas Schoemaker
Hans Jury Thomas
Frederick Bellinger

At a Mayors Court held in ye City Hall of Albany ye 3d day of January, 1715/6

The following persons to witt

Johannis Heiner
Johannis Kessler
Johannis Miller
Jacob Moussler
Johannis Jury Heyn
Baltus Annasbach
Hans Jury Moussier
Dewaeld Pryl
Christian Vink

Johannis Skans
Johan Christ Smit
Melgert Volts
Johan Hendrick Loucks
Jacob Timmerman
Jury Taxstieder
Hans Hendrick Clock
Philip Scheffer
Harme Segedorp

111

Christian Former

Symon Herhardt

Omy de la Crangle

Hendrick Jung

Tebald Young

At a Mayors Court held at ye City Hall of Albany the 17th day of January 1715/6.

The following persons to witt

Hendrick Heydorn

Jurick Mower

Hendrick Sneyder

Coenraed Barringer

Johannis Vinger

Niccolas Smith

Coenraed Smith

Johan Adam Smith

Niccolas Smith

Hans Hendrick Hock

And. Lod'k. Casselman

Abraham Berk

Peter Smith

Samuel Muller

Philip Loucks

Michiel Heyntie

Hendrick Winter

Christiaen Lang

Mathys Coens

Johan Jurch Shmit

Johannis Wm. Pulver

Peter Clop

Hans Jurch Row

Peter Philips

Niccolas Philips

Christiaen Haver

Johan Hend. Plas

Killiaen Mineklaer

Josias Mincklaer

Coenraet Schuerman

Adam Ding

Johan Christ. Miller

Jurich Kelmer

Christ. Dederich

Jurich Emrig Scherp

Peter Stoppelbert

Niccolas Hes

Johan Wm. Shoe

Johannis Shoe

Martinus Shoe

Coenraet Ham

Johan Hend. Plas

Philips Vingler

Jury Houck

Philips Heypt

Marte Server

Hendrick Michiel

Hendrick Michiel Jun'r.

Anthony Michiel

Jonas Shinkel

Johan Hendrick Shinkel

William Rees

Claes Van Pettn

Patron Anders

Johan Jurch Muller

Johannis Leek

Daniel Janze

Jacob Best

Abraham Langer

Jacob Bayer

Johans Christman

Harma Betser

David Kesselaer

Jacob Sneyder

Johan Wm. Siemon

Johan Jacob Server

Peter Lautman

Philip Wm. Moor

Niecolas Bonnesteel

Johannis Hes

Peter Burger

Johan Casper Rouch

Johan Willem Dalis

Hendrick Coenraet

Baltus Stiever

Franz Dompsback

Jost Hend Dompsback

Ulrigh Jacobi

Firdinard Menti

Martin Tiel

Fiet Miesick

Johan Wm. Hambough

Christiaen Diederigh

Daniel Buch

Johan hend. Buch

Enrich Bliss

Daniel Post

Johan Hend. Post

Michel Herder

Peter Betser

Willem Sneyder

Hendrick Lodwick

January 31--The following persons (to witt)

Johan Lodoph Corning

Johannis Scholdies

Hans Jury Stomf

Johan Harme Spickerman

Abraham Loucks

Johan Coenraet Jefback

Uldrich Dandler
Jacob Eswine
Adam Starn
Diedrich Loucks
Philip Clom
Peter Belinger
William Nelles
Niccolas Eckhar
Johan Pieter Diegert
Marten Stiep
Hans Jury Herckhemer
Philips Bender
Johan Jacob Besharn
Johan Willem Foex

Johannis Coens
Jurch Scherts
Christian Berck
Hans Marte Weytman
Frederick Willem Leer
Hans Casper Liepe
Adam Hoft
Andries Hoft
Lodwick Wanner
Christian Nelles
Peter Waggenaer
Johan B. Sterenbergen
Adam Kleyn
Sefreen Deygert

February 14--The following persons (to witt)

Dirck Wessels Ten Broeck
Uldrich Weyniger
Willem Linck
Johan Sneyder
Hans Gerhard Weyniger
Johannis Graet
Jacob Coens
Philip Coens
Jurich Loundert
Jurich Reyfenburger
Willem Hagedorn
Casper Ham
Hans Michiel Edich
Hans Michiel Edich Jr.
Niccolas Stickling
Johan Joest Sneyder
Jacob Krough
Niccolas Steyger

Johannis Daet
Hans Bernhardt Daet
Jacob Cerman

February 28--The following persons (to witt)

Isabella Staats
Geertry Isabella Lydyus
Maria Adrianata Lydyus
Hendrick Meyer
Johannis Krem
Jeron Van Flyeren
Johan Pieter Lodwick
Jury Mathys
Peter Ham
Johan Adolph Warraven
Lawrence Herder

Colonial Laws, N. Y. Vol. 1, page 858. General act of naturalization passed July 5, 1715, "declaring that all persons of foreign birth hereafter inhabiting within this colony and dying seized of any lands, tenements or hereditaments shall be forever hereafter deemed taken and deemed to have been naturalized and for naturalizing all Protestants of foreign birth now inhabiting within this colony."

These special acts became of no effect if oaths were not taken and fees paid within six months, then nine months and later one year from the passage of these special acts. One of these, June 17, 1726, prescribed no time limit another passed Oct. 14, 1737 had special provisions about removing from the colony of New York.

"Colonial Laws," Naturalization of Individuals
Volume 2, July 27, 1721.

Johannes Hausz (House).

October 14, 1732.
John Jacob Ell (Ehle).

Naturalization of Individuals, Colonial Laws
Volume 2, December 16, 1737.

Conrad Franck
Andreas Klebsatel
Jorg RihtMeyer (Richtmyer)
Philip Schuttes

Volume 3, May 3, 1755.

John Godfrey Miller
Michael Hoffman
Jacob Tiefendorph
Hendrick Heger
Solomon Myer
Jacob Myer

Volume 4, July 3, 1759.

Daniel Christian Fueter (Feeter)
John Ludwig Dunckel
Matthews Schaffer
George Kass
Lucas Vetter (Vedder)
Andreas Sneider
Nicholas Schaffer
William Gerlach
John Andiel Miller
Johannes Elgenbrood
Hermanus Eell (Ehle)
John Thomas Miller
Peter Freidrick
Gerlach Meyer
John Shauman
Felix Meyer
William Sneider

Volume 4, September 11, 1761.

Frederick Franck
Hannes Wohlgemuth
Jacob Schneyder
Ludwick Kraan (Crane)
Jorg Dieffendorf
Hannes Dieffendorf
Felix Mayer
Hendrick Dieffendorf
Jacob Mayer
Andreas Keller
Hans Geerlag Mayer, Jr.
Hannes Eigenbrook
Johan Geerlag Mayer
Hendrick Hess
Hannes Jordan junr.
Michael Sneyder
Hendrick Mayer
Casper Jordan junr.
Solomon Mayer
Joseph Mayer
Jacob Seeber
Johannes Schall
Hendrick Eckler

Henry Bell
Jacob Miller
Jacob Abel
John Sherp (Sharp)
Michael Poltz (Folts)
Jacob Sherp(Sharp)
Michael Sherp (Sharp)
Cornelius Miller
Christopher Ring
Johan Hess
John Volmer (Fulmer)
Michael Polfer (Pulver)
Peter Polfer (Pulver)

John Peter Hillegas
Frederick Franck
Johannes Eigenbrood
Martin Smith
Felix Keller
Jacob Keller
Ruldolph Keller
Henry Keller
Jan Joost Koch
William Gerlach
John George Yordan
Johannes Wolgemooth
Casper Clock
Jacob Algajer (Algire)
Michael Hoffman
Carl Hoffman
Jury Hoffman

Andreas Dusler
Johannes Valentine Caspasus
Stephanus Frank
Johannes Ehl
Johan Hendrick Smith
Wilhelmus Smith
Godfried Shoewaker
William Seeber
George Sbrecker (Spraker)
Martin Sbrecker
Coenrood Sbracker
Johannes Schal
William Seeber
Johan Nicholas Smith
Johannes Smith
Jacob Seeber junr.
Chrisitan Schel
Coenraad Smith
Phillip Frederick
Augustus Eckler
Abraham Ecker
George Ecker
Jacob Sever

December 31, 1761

George Snyder

Volume 4, March 20, 1762.

Frederick Schall
Isaac Paris
Isaac Paris Junior.
Abraham Rosekrans
Adam Kiltz
Peter Kiltz
Johannes Kilts
Johan Nekel Kiltz
Hendrick Reimesnyder
Harme Schever (Schaffer)
John Eisenlord
Christian Young
Peter Nicholas Somner

Henrich Schneider
Jacob Fry
Jurry Fry
Philip Miller
Andries Frank
Christophel Frank
Philip Shapher
Stephen Jordan
Peter Fox
Golliep Bowman
Abraham Bowman
Johannis Joost Weeder (Veeder)

Volume 4, December 20, 1763

Johannes Weaver
Frederick Hillecas
Henry Widerstein
Christian Schell
Johannes Schell

Lawrence Schuler
Nicholas Timmerman

December 31, 1768

October 20, 1764

Hermanus Myer
Henry Widerstein
Christian Schell
Johannes Schell

Coenrad Shol
Philip Smith
John Smith
Henry Smith
Jacob Flander
Johannes Shol
Leonhart Cratser (Kretser)
Christoffel Miller
Michael Salsbergh

December 19, 1766

Volume 5, January 27, 1770

Jacob Seber
Augustus Eckler
Conraat Smith
George Ecker
George Sharpe
Jacob Becker

Frederick Waggoner
Adam Garlogh
Peter Young
Peter Gronce (Grantz or Crontz)
William Petrie

February 1*, 1771

John Smith
Jacob Meyars
Christian Schultz
William Showman
Jacob Waggoner
John Smith
Adam Plank

Michael Myar
Francis Fry
Johan Adam Frank
Andreas Schough (Shoe or Shuh)
Lewis Fueter (Feeter)
Frederick Myer

Volume 5, March 24, 1772

Michael Berringer

March 8, 1773

Michael Warner
Jacob Waggoner
Michael Witterick (Widrig)
George Witterick
Philip Bellanger
George Ough (Ochs or OX)
Faltin Miller (Valentine M--)
Baltus Breitenbger
George Bower
Niccholas Keller
John Kellar Junior
Jacob Myer
Hendrick Schafer
Adam Hartmen
John Eisenlord
Simon Bydeman
John Conradt Smith
Francis Fry

Jacob Myer
Leonard Kratzer
Coenradt Hoining (Horning)
Philip Smith
Henry Smith
Samuel Millur
Jacob Flander
Johan Jost Volz
Johan Daniel Gros
Adam Dumm (Thumb or Thume)
Nicholas Dumm
Nelicher Dumm (Melchoir or Matthew D.)
Henry Becker
Jacob Joran (Yerdon)
Peter Eigebrode
John Smith
Christian Graf
John Fisher

Source Material:

From: <u>The Book of Names</u>
Especially Relating to The Early Palatines and the First Settlers in the Mohawk Valley. Compiled
and Arranged by Lou D. MacWethy
Published by The Enterprise and News
St. Johnsville, NY. , 1933
(Used with permission)

Colonial Census of 1710

List of Palatines Remaining in New York. Figures denote age, you will note in some cases, it says
"dead"! Perhaps the "X" indicates the estimated age.

From vol. III Documentary History of New York

Almerodin Anna, Wid. 67
Ableman, Peter, 42
Abelman, Anna Margraeta, 32
Badner, Johan Paul, 19
Bronck Matheis, works in ye Govr. Gard 50
Bronck, Anna Christina, his daughter, 22
Bronck, John Hendrick his son, 16
Baumin, Magadlena wid., 29
Baumin, Johan Niclaus, 15
Bornwaserin, Maria Cath. wid. 26
Baschin, Frances, Wid, 40
Baschin, Margaretha, 20
Beijerin, Susanna wid., 30
Bieferin, Susanna Maria, 1
Batzin, Anna Cath, 38
Batzin, John Ludwig, 7
Bruiere, Jeane, 18
Bruiere, Jacque, 15
Bruiere, Susannah, 6
Buers, Ludwig, 32
Buers, Maria Cath, 28
Beuer, Catharine, 3

Benderin, Anna Maria, wid., 44
Benderin, Eve Catharina, 12
Benderin, John Matheus, 8
Brilmannin, Helena, orph, x, 17
Bressler, Valtin, 41
Bressler, Christina, 36
Bressler, Anna Eliz, 14
Bressler, Anna Gertrude, 12
Bressler, Andreas, 9
Bressler, Anthony, 5
Bressler, Maria Agnes, 1/2
Baer, Johannes, 40
Baer, Anna, 27
Baer, John Fred, 10
Baer, John Jacob, 4
Cramerin, Anna Maria, Wid., 38
Cramerin, her eldest son x, 18
Cramerin, Maria Eliz, 12
Cramerin, John Hendrich, 7
Cramerin, Anna Catharina, 5
Cramerin, Juliana Maria, 1 1/2

Castleman, Christian, 36
Castleman, Anna Judeth, 27
Castleman, Eva Maria Cath, 12
Dietrich, Anna Eliz, orph., 20
Deitrich, Anna Gertrude, 12 (possible transposition of letters)
Daunermarker, Christopher, 28
Daunermarker, Christina, 28
Daunermarker, Cath. Eliz, 8
Danemark, Anna Hargt., Wid., 58 (possibly Margt., also last name? grouped as a family in book)
Dausweber, Melchoir, 55
Dausweber, Maria Christina, 20
Dausweber, Anna Maria, 17
Deible, Johannes, 38
Deible, Anna Catharina, 7
Dorner, Johannes, 36
Dorner, Anna Margaretta, dead, 40
Erbin, Anna Catharina, wid., 44
Erbin, Eliz. Catha, 9
Elich, Andreas, 37
Elich, Anna Rosina, 23
Elich, John George, 3
Engelle, Johannes, 31
Engelle, Anna Christina, 12
Engelle, Anna Maria, 8
Engelle, Anna Eliz, 4
Erkel. Bernhard, 53
Erkel, Anna Maria, 43
Falck, Arnold, 36
Falck, Anna Eliz., 35
Falck, Johannes, 6
ffucks, John Peter, 31
ffucks, Anna Margt, 24
Fucks frau, Johanna Eliz. 22
ffelton, John Wm., x, 30
ffelton, Christina, 28
ffelton, Anthoni, 11
ffelton, Anna Clara, 17
Frederich, Conrad, 52
Frederich, Anna Maria, 45
Frederich, John Peter, 14
Frederich, John Conrad, 13
Feversback, Deitrich, 21A
Garlack, Peter, 37
Garlack, Magdalena, 39
Garlack, Margaretta, 12
Greisler, Johan Philip, 40
Greisler, Catharine, 40
Greisler, John George, 11
Greisler, Johannes, 7
Gossinger, Johan Henrich, 31
Gossinger, Anna Eliz, 27
Gossinger, Anna Margt, 2
Gablin, Anna Maria, 34
Gablin, Anna Maria, 7
Galete, Maria, wid., 38
Galete, Sarah Margaret, 7
Galete, Jacob, 4

Grauin, Anna Cath., 40
Grauin, Anna Eliz., 18
Grauin, Anna Sophia, 10
Grauin, Johannes, 11
Grauberger, Philip Peter, 29
Grauberger, Anna Barbara, 33
Hoffman, Hermanus x, 30
Hoffman, Maria Gertrude x, 30
These two remained at Hackensack at John Lotz's.
Heidin, Anna Maria, wid., 50
Hauch, Lucas, dead, 44
Hauch, Anna Magda, 45
Hauch, Maria Cathar, 16
Hauch, Maria Margt, 16
Hauch, John Jacob, 13
Hauch, John George x, 12
Hauch, Maria Eliz x, 11
Hauch, Johannes, 4
Hebmannin, Maria Cath, wid., 40
Hebmannin, Anna Engle, 21A
Hebmannin, Gertrude, 14
Hebmannin, Anna Magdalena, 11
Hartwig, Caspar, 39
Hartwig, Anna Eliz, 39
Hartwig, Johan Bernhard, 8
Hartwig, Johan Lorentz, 6
Hartwig, Magdalena, 10
Henneschid, Michael, 36
Henneschid, Anna Catharina, 30
Henneschid, Caspar, 11
Henneschid, John Peter, 1
Henneschid, Maria Sophia, 6
Hellich, Conrad, 30
Hellich, Anna Marie, 26
Hellich, Johannes, dead, 1
Heisterbach, Nichaus, 53
Heisterbach, Johan Jacob, 4
Heisterbach, Christina Cath, 10
Jung, Johannes, 32
Jung, Anna, 35
Jungens, Nichlaus, works in ye Govr Gard, 38
Jungens, Anna Magdalena, 25
Klein, Hinronimus, 38
Klein, Maria, 38
Klein, Amalia, 12
Klein, Anna Eva, 14
Klein, Anna Eliz., 6
Kornman, Peter Jacob, dead, 51
Kornman, Anna Conigunda, dead, 52
Kornman, Anna Conig, 24
Kornman, John Christopher, 12A
Kunatz, Johannes, 40
Keiser, John Matheus, 23
Kuhner, Benedictus, 36
Kuhner, Anna Felice, 40
Kuhner, Jacob A., 4
Kuhner, Eva Barbara, 9
Korning, Ludolf, 50

Korning, Otillia, 50
Korning, Catharina, 16
Korning, Anna Dorothea, 15
Korning, Conrad, 7
Lucas, Frantz at New Rochelle at Mr.
Chadden, 38
Lucis, Maria Eliz. his daughter, 20
Lucas, Frantz, 13
Lucas, Anna Maria, 8
Lucas, Anne, 7
Lucas, Anna Catharina, 4
Leicht, George Ludwig, 66
Leicht, Anna Margatta, 58
Leicht, Johan Henrich, 24
Leicht, Anna Eliz. 20
Lein, Conrad, 56
Lein, Maria Marga, 46
Lein, Juliana, 18
Lein, Margretha, 14
Lein, Anna Maria, 12
Lein, Abraham, 10
Lein, Conrad, 7
Lickard, Bernhard, 25
Lickard, Justina, 32
Lohrentz, Johannes, 43
Lohrentz, Anna Margaretta, 39
Lohrentz, Magdalena, 13
Lohrentz, Anna Barbara, 11
Lohrentz, Alexander, 1/2
Lintzin, Apollonia, wid., 40
Lintzin, Anna Catha, 16
Lintzin, Anna Margt, 13
Lintzin, Anna Eva, 6
Lauking, Anna Elizabeth, 42
Lenhard, Johan, 5
Lenhard, Eva Catharina, 12
Lampertin, Eliz., wid., 47
Leampetin, Erhard A., 13
Lampertin, Frantz Adam A., 11
Melchlin, Sittonia, wid., 41
Melchlin, Anna Maria, 11
Melchlin, Anna Eliz, 8
Mengelsin, Anna Maria wid., 27
Mengelsin, John Carolus, 3
Mengelsin, Anna Maria, 5
Mengelsin, Juliana, 1 1/2
Meyin, Maria, wid., 45
Meyin, Anna Eliz., 9
Monen, Maria, 23
Monen, John Phillips, 2
Maulin, Anna Eliz, wid., 42
Maulin, Anna Catharina, 13
Maulin, Anna Ursula, 16
Maulin, Anna Maria, 5
Maul, Frederick, 31
Maul, Anna Ursula, 31
Maul, John Jacob, 4
Maul, John Paul, orph., 12

Morellin, Anna Eva, wid., 48
Morellin, Anna Apolonia, 18
Morellin, Anna Barbara, 11
Mullerin, Elizabeth, Wid., 42
Mullerin, Jacob, 15
Mullerin, Melchoir, 13
Mullerin, Nichlaus, 6
Mullerin, Anna Engell, 3
Mullerin, Catharina, wid., 36
Mullerin, Hans George, 1/2
Meserin, Margaret, wid., 50
Meserin, Johannes, 15
Meserin, Susan Cath, 10
Neff, Fred'ch, dead, 34
Neff, Johan, dead, 8
Newkirk, Johan Henrich, 36
Newkirk, Anna Maria, 33
Newkirk, Johannes, 11
Newkirk, John Henrich, dead, 8
Offin, Magdalena, wid., 32
Offin, Johan Jacob, 8
Offin, Anna Barbara, 6
Planck, Johannes, 43
Planch, Maria Margt, 32
Planck, Johanna Eliz, 14
Planck, Ludwig Henrich, 6
Nollin, Elizabeth, Wid. x, 66
Niesin, Maria, wid, 38
Niesin, Maria Magdalena, 15
Onin, Maria Barbara, 36
Pseffer, Michael, 32
Pseffer, Anna Maria, 28
Reichin, Anna Maria, orph., 17
Reichin, Anna Margt, dead, 8
Reichin, Hans Thomas A, 12
Romer, George x, 30
Romer, Eliz x, 26
Roschman, johannes, 33
Roschman, Anna Eliz. 30
Roschman, Maria Cath, 9
Rosin, Umbert, 45
Rusin, Anna Conegunda, wid., 44
Rusin, Anna Catharina, 14
Rusin, Anna Margaretta, 10
Rusin, Maria Catharina, 8
Rorbaalin, Anna Eliz, Wid., 34
Rorballin, Anna Morga, 11
Richter, Andreas, 47
Richter, Anna Maria, 45
Richter, Andreas, 16
Richter, Anna Barbara, 9
Schmidt, Henrich, 54
Schmidt, Anna Eliz, 54
Schmidt, Clements, 24
Schmidt, Wilhelm, 20
Schmidt, Hans George, 13
Schmidt, John Niclaus, 9
Schmidt, Anna Maria, 18

Schumacher, Daniel, 30
Schumacher, Anna Maria, 36
Schumacher, Hans Niclaus, 8
Scherin, Maria Margt wid., 23
Schutzin, Maria Cath, wid., 40
Schutzin, Hans Valentine, 17
Schutzin, Maria Catherina, 12
Schutzin, John Henrich, 3
Stuckrath, hans Wm., 37
Stuckrauth, Anna Margaretta, 28
Stuckrath, Anna Clara, 10
Stuckrath, John Marcus, 1/2
Schultzin, Anna Eliz., wid., 22
Strud, Christina, 40
Strud, Maria Ursula, 28
Strud, Catharin, 13
Strud, Anna Maria, 11
Strud, John Jacob, 9
Strud, Maria Catharine, 13
Simendinger, Ulrich, 38
Simendinger, Anna Margaretta, 36
Scahtz, John Deitrich, 38
Scahtz, Magdalena, 42
Scahtz, Hans Peter, 14
Starenburger, Johan Jacob, 45
Starenburger, Catharina, 33
Starenburger, Johan Langsert, 14
Starenburger, Anna Cathar, 12
Starenburger, John Adam, 5
Schmidtin, Margaretta, wid., 27
Schmidtin, Johan Daniel A., 4
Salbachin, Elizab., 15
Sieknerin, Anna Apolonia wid., 44
Sieknerin, Johannes dead 9
Sieckerin, John Jacob, 7
Storr, Michael, 38
Storr, Anna Marg, 48
Storr, Eliz. Catharina, 12
Sacksin, Anna Maria, wid., 30
Schneider, Johan Wm. x, 28

Schoneborin, 25
Teffa, Daniel, 30
Teffa, Marianna, 11
Teffa, Abraham, 7
Trilhauser, Johannes, x, 23
Vogdt, Simon, 30
Vogdt, Christina, 26
Werner, Christopher, 35
Werner, Maria Magdalena, 23
Werner, John Matheus, 3
Wickhaus, Peter, 32
Wickhaus, Eliz Catharina, 31
Wickhaus, Maria Catha, 15
Wannermacher, Johan Dietrick, 28
Weisin, Susannah, 36
Wenerick, Baltzar, 40
Wenerick, Elizabeth, 30
Wenerick, Hans George, 9
Wenerick, Johan Maltheis, 6
Wenerick, Maria Eliz., 17
Wenerich, Benedictus, 32
Wenerich, Christina, 33
Wenerich, Frantz, 5
Wenerich, Johannes, 1/2
Weidnecht, Andreas, 40
Weidnecht, Margaret, 40
Weidnecht, George Fred, 13
Weidnecht, Anna Eliz, 9
Wormserin, Anna, Widow, 36
Zwickin, Vernonica, wid., 39
Zwickin, Veronica, wid., 39
Zwickin, Marcus, 31
Zwickin, John Martin, 6
Zwickin, Anna Margaretta, 14
Zangerin, Johanna, wid., 33
Zangerin, Peter, 13
Zangerin, Johannes, 7
Zangerin, Anna Catharina, 10
Zolner, Hans Adam, 52
Zolner, Maria, before Baumersin, 40

Volunteers for Canadian Expediton 1711 List
List of Palatines who volunteered for the expedition against Canada in 1711.

Queensbury

Bergman, Andreas
Bellenger, Fred
Breigle, Geo.
Dopff, Jno. Peter
Dillenback, Martin
Dachstader, George
Eckard, Nicklaus
Feeg, Johannis
Finck, Frantz
Feller, Niclaus
George, Wm., Lieut.
Haber, Christian

Hagedorn, Cristo
Hoffman, Hen.
Hagedorn, Peter
Jung, Henrich
Kuhn, Jacob
Kuntz, Mattheus
Kisler, Johannis
Leyer, Johan
Muller, Geo.
Mathais, Geo.
Munsinger, Jno. Jac.
Mathous, Henr.
Nelles, William
Nehr, Carl

Reinbolt, Mattheus
Reisch, Jno. Jacob
Reichert, Werner
Schurtz, Andreas
Schaid, Antho.
Schaffer, Fred
Sien, Jno. Pet.
Schnell, Jacob
Schaffer, John
Wisner, Johan Cond, Capt
Widerwachs, Hen.
Weber, Niclaus
Webber, Jacob
Zaysdorf, Johannes

356 men, women and children in this Town.

A True Copy from the Original
HENRY MAYER.

Haysbury

Dales, John Wm
Bacuh, Christian
Cup, Jacob
Dientzer, Paulus
Foltz, Melch.
ffucks, John Christopher. Was he "Capt."
Gottel, Niclaus
Hayd, Peter
Hammer, Henr.
Habuch, Jno. Wm.
Ittich, Mich
Kyser, Johan
Laus, Phillip
Langen, Abraham
Laux, Niclaus
Reitchoff, Paulus
Schaff, John Wm.
Segendorf, John
Schultz, Jno. Jacob.

243 Men, Women & Children

Hunterstown, 16 July 1711

Anspach, Baltz
Bell, Frederick
Bender, George
Goldman, Cond.
Hills, Christ.
Huppert, David
Koch, Geo. Lud.
Kerchmer, Grol
Keller, Conrad
Kobell, Jacob
Kneskern, Jno. Peter, Capt.

Musig, Veil
Roschman, Johannes
Schawerman, Conrad
Sex, Henrick
Schulties, Johannes
Schaffer, Reinhard
Schmidt, Jno. Geo.
Schumacher, Tho.
Schmidt, Peter
Schwall, Johan
Stahl. Rudol
Uhl. Carl
Uhl, Jno. Hen.
Warno, Jacob

336 Men, women and children

Annsberg

Bruckhart, Ulrich
Busch, Danl
Bitzer, Herman
Blass, Johannes
Bonroth, Johannes
Bernhard, Johannes
Bast, Jacob
Bellinger, Hen.
Bellenger, Marcus
Orendorff, Jno. Hen.
Conradt, Jno. Hen.
Dings, Jacob
Dill, Jno. Wm.
Ess, Jacob
Fischer, Sebastian
Fehling, Hendrick
Hayd, Niclaus
Kuhn, Samuel
Kuhn, Conrad
Kradt, Johan
Kammer, Johan Wm.
Kuhn, Valtin
Linch, Jno. Wm.
Mentegen, Ferdo
Maisinger, Cond.
Netzbach, Jno. Mart
Petry, John Jost
Rieffenberg, Jno. Geo.
Rauch, Casper
Ruffener, Thos
Ruhl, Niclaus
Schaffer, Gerhard
Spies, Peter
Schue, Johannes
Schneider, John Wm.
Stuper, Hen. BAlt.
Schneider, Johan
Schaffer, Phill
Schmidt, Ludw.
Sittenich, Christ

120

Schmidt, Jno. Hen.
Schmidt, Adam Mic
Theis, Jno. Phill
Windecker, Hartman, Capt.
Winter, Henrich
Weis, Johannes
Walbourn, Jno. Adn
Zeller, Hans Hen.
Zeller, Johannes
Zerbe, Jno. Phill
Zerbe, Martin

A True Copy from the Original HEN. MAYER.

250 Men

Index--To The Rev. Kocherthal's Church Records
(Pages 15 to 50 inclusive)
Key to Alphabetical References
The numeral following each name refers to the page number. The letter refers to the status of the individual. As Follows:

- c Child
- d Died
- m married
- p Parent
- s Sponsor
- r Received in Holy Communion

Example--Flegler, Zacharias, p. 24, p. 26, s 25, m 41, m 43. From this we learn he was a parent on page 24 and 26, acted as a sponsor at a baptism on page 25 and was married to a second wife on page 41 and to his third on page 43.

- Aigler, Christian, p18, s18, s 19
  - Andreas, c18
  - Maria Eva, p18
- Aigner, Peter, p26, p47
  - Anna Margretha, p26, p32, p37
  - Johann Peter, p32
  - Johann Fridrich, c32
  - Johann Balthasar, d47
  - Susanna Margretha, c26
- Aignor, Peter p37
  - Johann Balthasar, c37
- Asmer, Philipp, 44
  - Anna Barbara, m44
- Anspach, Maria Barbara, c37
  - Anna Maria, p37
  - Balthasar, p37
- Arsen, Wilhelm, 16
  - Elizabeth 16
- Arnold, Christina, r40
- Albertson, Johann s23

- Amstach, Johann Peter, c28
  - Anna Maria, p28
  - Balthasar, p28
- Artopoeus, Johann Adolph, s17
- Bakus, Johann Reichart, p35
  - Maria Barbara, c35
- Backus, Maria Elisabeth, s23
  - Elisabeth, p24
  - Johann Peter, c24
  - Agnes, m41
  - Sebasian, 41
  - Reichart and his wife Elizabetha Catharina, s30
  - Elisabeth Catharina, s23, p35
  - Anna Margretha, s38, r40
  - Johann Reitz, s21, p24, s38, r39
  - Johann Reitz, child of, d47
- Baender, Johann Henrich, c35
  - Johann Valentin, s16
  - Veltin, p35
  - Jerf, s34
  - Johan Georg and his wife, s23, s21
  - Anna Margretha, s16, p35
  - Anna Maria, s31, s32
- Baggs, Andreas, s22
- Ball, Johann, 43
  - Maria Ottila, m43
- Bardorf, Martin, s35
- Bardorst (orf), Catharina Elisabetha, r39
- Barthel, Elisabatha, s28, m46
  - Andreas, r39
  - Henrich, p46
  - Johan Andreas, s28

- o Maria Margretha, s28
- o Philip Balthasar, r39
- Bast, Johann Henrich, p21
  - o Anna Dorothea, p21
  - o Anna Maria c21
- Bason, Niclaus, s24
- Batz, Anna Catharina, m43
  - o Fridrich, 43
- Bauch, Christian, p17
  - o Anna Dorothea, p17
  - o Anna Margretha, c1;7
    Christian and his wife, p31
- Baumann, Maria Catharina, p35
  - o Adam, m43
  - o Anna Maria, m42
  - o Anna Margretha, s23
  - o Johann Adam, p35
  - o Henrich, 42
  - o Margretha, s35
- Baunert, Johann Georg, r40
- Beck, Johanna Maria, r40
- Becker, Elisabetha, m42
  - o Anna Juliana, c33
  - o Anna Catharina, m42
  - o Anna Elisabetha, p22, p25,
    s28, s29, p33
  - o Conrad, m46
  - o Catharina, s49
  - o Hermann, s49
  - o Johann Michael, 42
  - o Johann Henrich, 42
  - o Johann Peter, p25
  - o Johann Jacob, m45
  - o Johann Christian, c25
  - o Johannes, p22, c22
  - o Johann, s22, 42, p45
  - o Peter, s32, p33
  - o Sebastian, p46
- Beer, Johann, m43
- Bernhard, Anna Elisazetha, c29
  - o Anna, p29
  - o Jost, s234
  - o Johann, s19
  - o Johannes, p29
  - o Johann Ulrich, s20
- Berenhard, Elisabetha, s17, c17
  - o Anna Maria, p17
  - o Johann, p17
- Barnard, Johannes, p48
  - o Maria Margaret, c48
  - o Anna Eulalia, p48
- Bertram, Martha, s20
- Behr, Hermanus, s49
- Bellinger, Marcus, s27
  - o Johann Henrich, s20
  - o Peter, s21

- Bell, Johann Jacob, c23, p23
  - o Anna Maria, p23, s34
  - o Johann Fridrich, p23
- Bellross, Christoph, m43
- Behringer, Johann Henrich, c27
  - o Conrad, s26,p27
- Beringer, Anna Elisabeth, p21, p27
  - o Conrad, p21
  - o Maria Elisabetha, c21
- Berg, Johann Christian, r40
  - o Johann, r39
- Berman, Jacob s21
- Bertold, Anna Margretha, 48
  - o Adam, 48
- Bertsch, Jan, s36
- Beruer, Johann s30
- Best, Christina, p49
  - o Jacob, s25
  - o Johann Hermann, c49
  - o Johann, p49
- Bestuh, Daniel, s28
- Bitzer, Peter, s30
  - o Maria Catharina, s28
- Bitzwig, Anna Maria, s28
- Blanick, Maria Catharina, 317
- Blast, Anna Maria, m43
  - o Adam, 43
- Blettel, Johann Jacob, p 15
- Boeshaar, Anna Catharina, p34
  - o Johann, c34
  - o Jacob, p34
- Boemer, Johann Adam c21
  - o Elisabetha, p21
  - o Hans Jorg, p21
- Bohenstihl, Nichlaus, p28
  - o Anna Margretha, p28
  - o Susanna Margretha, c28
- Bohl, Lastar, 42
  - o Anna Sophia, m42
- Bois, Wilhelmina, p20
  - o Henrich, p20
  - o Pieter, c20
- Bond, Rachel, s22
  - o Jannike, p22
  - o Johan p22
  - o Mattheus, c22
- Border, Maria, s26
- Borner, Johann Georg, m41
- Brack, Michel, p29
  - o Anna Maria, p29
  - o Johann Michel, m46
  - o Maria Catharina, c29
- Brandau, Anna Christina Elisabeth,
  c36

- Elisabeth Catharina, p36
- Elisabeth Catharina, s36
- Elisabetha, p28
- Hannes, s50
- Johann Fridrich, c28
- Johann Wilhelm, p22, s26, p28, p36
- Johannes, c22
- Liesbeth, c50, p50
- Maria Elisabetha Catharina, p22
- Nicklas, p50
- Wilhelm, s38
- Bransan, Johann Wilhelm, s50
- Brauchler, Anna Magdalena, C27
  - Johann Jacob, c27
  - Johann Henrich p27
  - Magdalena, p27
- Braun, Johann Philip, r39
- Bredfort, H., 48
- Brein, Maria, c18
  - Elisabetha, p18
  - Johann, p18
- Brendel, Anna Agatha, p16
  - Anna Margretha, c16
  - Caspar, p16
- Bretsch, Catharina, p24
  - Anna Maria, c18
  - Catharina, p18
  - Johann Ludwig, c24
  - Ludwig, p18, s21, p24
- Brehjis, Margretha, m44
  - Christoph, 44
- Brick, Anna Maria, c26
  - Johann, p26
  - Maria Barbara, p26
- Brigel, Johann George, s29
- Brinck, Matteus, m42
- Brucker, Margretha, r39
- Bruckhard, Ulrich, r40
- Bruen, Margretha, 16
  - Christian, 16
  - Johan, 16
- Brunck, Niclaus, c25
  - Anna, p24, m46
  - Christina, s38
  - Mattheus, p24, d47
- Bruschl, Elsgen, p35
  - Margretha, c35
  - Weinsan, p35
- Buck, Maria Gerdaut, s26
- Burckhard, Anna Elisabeth, c49
  - Amalia, p36, p49
  - Anna Maria, s25
  - Anna Margreth, s29, m45

- Elisabetha, d47, m44
- Johanens, c49
- Johann Martin, s33, r40
- Johann, 44, p45, p46
- Johann Conrad, c36
- Johann Peter, s29, m46, p49
- Peter, s33, s36, p36
- Burgard, Peter, p50
  - Maria, c50
  - Mattie, p50
- Busch, Anna Maria s17
- Butt, Anna Catharina, s21
- Buvnat, Paul, s20
- Cast, Johann (see Kast), s34
- Castlemann, Anna (see Kasselman, Kessel, Kissel), p19
  - Anna Maria Judith, p17, p25, p36
  - Anna Elizabeth, s16, m44
  - Anna Maria, p29
  - Christian, p25, p17, p36, p29
  - Dietrich, s21
  - Eva Cathatina, c17
  - Johann Ludwig, r40
  - Johann Dietrich, p19, 44
  - Johann Peter, c29
  - Maria Justina, c25
  - Sophia Magdalena, c36
  - Wilhelm, C19
- Caputz, Dorothea, s28
- Caputzgl, Margretha, s27
- Castin, Anna s22
- Caujun, Fransa 46
  - Belicka m46
- Chisem, Anna, p18
  - Annike, p25
  - Christina, c25
  - Henrich, p18, s21, p25, 46
  - Jan s25
  - Margretha, s21
  - Robert, c18
- Chamborary Johann, s17
  - Barbara Elisabetha, s17
- Christian, Andreas Christian, c35
  - Elisabeth, p35
  - Pieter, p35, m44
- Christman, Johann, s30
  - Gertraut, s34
- Clerk, William s18
- Clotter, Paul 41
  - Susanna, m41
- Coblentzer, Elizabeth Margretha, m41
  - Johann Peter, 41
- Congreve, Carolus, 15

- Connrath, Johann, r39
- Conrad, Anna Catharina, s34
  - Johann Henrich, s23, s34, m46
- Conterman, Anna Eva, c26
  - Andreas Frantz, p33, m45
  - Elisabetha, c33
  - Johann Fridrich, p26, p33, p45, d47
  - Jacob, c33
  - Maria Barbara, p26, p33
  - Sibylla, p33
- Corhof, Maria Catharina, r39
- Crump, Johann m42
- Cun, Anna Catharina, c31, p31
  - Veltin, p31
- Cuntz, Maria Catharina, p21, s24
  - Anna Margretha, p19
  - Johann Jacob, m45
  - Johan David, c19
  - Johann, p21, s24
  - Ludwig, c21
  - Matheus, p19, s20, p45, p46
  - Philip, s29
  - Philipp Henrich, m46
- Curring, Johann Ludolph s23
  - Anna Catharina, m43
  - Catharina, s19
  - Lodolst, 43
  - Ottillia, s34
  - Rololph, s22
- Dachsetter, Anna Elizabeth, 321, p34
- Dachstetter, Georg, p34
  - Johann Fridrich, c34
- Dausweber, Anna Magdalena, p22
  - Johann Melchoir, p22, 41, m42
  - Maria Barbara, m41
  - Maria Regina c22
- DeBois, Abraham, c18
  - Pannicke, p18
  - Pieter, p18
- Decker, Arianicke, s24
  - Gabriel, c50
  - Georg, Johann, p24
  - Geritt, p50
  - Gertrud, p50
  - Johanna, c24
  - Joris, s24
  - Jurg, Jan, p49
  - Margaret, c49, p49
  - Maria, p24
- Demuth, Alexander, 44
  - Anna, s30
  - Anna Maria, s26, s33, s36, r39

- Anna Maria Dorothea, s21
- Dietrich, r39
- Georg, s29
- Gerg, s27, m44
- Johann Fridrich, r40
- Destuh, Daniel and his wife Barbara, s33
- Deteutscher, Janike, p27
  - Rudolph, c27, p27
- Diehl, Hananias, s17
- Diestenbach, Anna Barbara, p27
  - Johann Conrad p27
- Dietrich Agnes, s28, s33
  - Anna Catharina, c50
  - Anna Margareta, p21, c48, s48
  - Anna Maria, c37, p37
  - Catharina, c50
  - Christian, s28, p45, p50
  - Eva, p48, p50
  - Friderich, p50 (2), p48
  - Hans Wilhelm, s48, s49
  - Johann Christian, s25, s35, p37
  - Johann Wilhelm, p21
  - Jorg Wilhelm, c21
  - Margareta, m45, p50
  - Margrete, s49
  - Maria, c50
  - Maria Cathrina, s50
- Dihl, Ananias, p26, p36
  - Elisabetha, p26, p36
  - Johann Henrich, c36
  - Johann Peter, c26
- Dillenbach, Anna Margretha, c23
  - George Martin widower, m44
  - Jorg Martin, p23, m44
  - Sata Catharina, p23
- Dings, Jacob s18
- Dippel, Anna Barbara, s17, m42
  - Anna Catharina, p21, p26, c26, s34
  - Anna Eva, c21
  - Anna Maria, r40
  - Johann Peter, p21, p26
  - Peter, s27
  - Philipp, 42
- Distenbach, Dorothea, c27
- Dobus, Abraham, p37
  - Jann, c37
- Doerner, Anna Margretha, r39
- Dolest, Anna Margretha, s33
- Dopf, Anna Maria, s27
  - Johann, p36
  - Margretha, m44
  - Peter, 44

124

- Dopp, Johann Peter, s34, c36
- Dorn, Anna Margreth, p29, p36
  - Latzarus, p29, p36
  - Maria Barbara c29
  - Michael, c36
- Dreschler, Anna Catharina, c27
  - Catharina, p27
  - Peter, p27
- Driesen, P. V., 35
- Drum, Maria Catharina, s29
- Duntzbach, Anna Elizabeth, s26
  - Elisabeth, s35
- Eberhard, Anna Sibylia, p22, s49
  - Johannes, p22, s49
  - Johann Georg, c22
  - Johann m43
- Ebert, Anna Catharina, r40
- Eckhard, Adam, p22, p27, p34
  - Anna, p27, p34
  - Anna Elisabetha, c27
  - Anna Catharina c22
  - Johann, Georg, r39
  - Johann Peter, c34
  - Elisabetha, Catharina, p22
  - Maria Barbara, r39
  - Magdalena, s24, s34
- Ehmann, Thomas, m43
- Elmer, Johannes, Peter, r39
- Eigner, Peter, s37
- Eichler, Andreas, s50
- Elsaesser, Paul, 42
  - Gertrauda, m42
- Elswa, Faemige, p18
  - Benjamin, p18
  - William c18
- Elig, Hans Jurge, s50
  - Andreas, s18, p18
  - Anna Rosina, p18
  - Christian c18
- Ellich, Andreas and his wife Anna
  - Andreas, s 35, s36, s29, p35, m45
  - Anna Sophia, p35
  - Johann Wilhelm, c35
  - Sophia, s32
  - Souphia, d47, s35, s36
- Emerich, Margreth, p38
  - Anna, c33
  - Anna Catharina, c24
  - Anna Elisabetha, s23
  - Anna Margretha, p19
  - Anna Margretha, s24, s24, p26, p23, s37
  - Catharina, s49
  - Elisabetha, p24, c26

- Hannes, s50
- Johann Michael, p24, m43
- Johann s24
- Johannes, and wife, p26, p33, p38, c38, s38
- Johanna Catharina, c19
- Johann Peter, 43
- Johann s24, s25
- Johannes, p19
- Maria Martha m43
- Endters, Johann Wilhelm, c34
  - Bertram, p34
  - Maria Christina, p34
- Engel, Johannes, r 39
- Erhard, Maria Catharina, c20
  - AnnaMargretha, p20
  - Simeon, p20
- Eschenreuter, Anna Margretha s30, r39
- Esswein, Thomas, 42
  - Anna Elisabetha, m42
  - Elisabetha, s17
  - Jacob, p27, p38
  - Johann Wendell, s27
  - Margretha, p27
  - Veronica, c37
- Falck, Anna Elisabeth, p25, p28
  - Arnold, p25, p28, s32 (2), d47
  - Gertraut, c28
  - Johann Peter, c25
- Falckenburg, Agnes, c28
  - Anna Gertraut, c19
  - Elisabetha, Maria, p19, p28
  - Gertrud, s49
  - Hans Veltin, s21
  - Johann Hieronymus, c28
  - Johann Valentin, p19, p28, s25
  - Veltin, s26
- Falckner, Justus, Rev. 15, 16
- Feegen, Elisabetha Barbara, m44
- Feegan Johann 44
- Feg, Catharina, r39
- Feeg, Anna Margaretha, c31
  - Anna Maria, s17, 131, p31
  - Johann, p45
  - Johann Peter, p31
  - Johannes, p17
  - Leonard, m45
  - Maria Margretha, p17, c17
- Fees, Christina, s49
  - Henrich, s49
- Fehling, Henrich, p31
  - Maria Kunigunda, p31
  - Niclaus, c31

- Fehlinger, Anna Kunigunda, p25
  - Johann Jacob c25, p25
- Feller, Catharina Elisabeth, p35
  - Johann Niclaus, c35
  - Johann Philipp, p35, m46
  - Maria Elisabetha, c23, p23
  - Niclaus, p23, p46
- Fidler, Elisabeth, s34
  - Johann Gottfrid and wife, s34
- Finck, Andreas, p23, s30
  - Frantz, m44
  - Jacob, c23
  - Johann Adam, 44
  - Maria, p23
- Finckel, Anna Catharina, p23
  - Johann Philipp, c23, p23
- Fischer, Andreas, c51
  - Johann, m40, s22
  - Johannes, 15, p16, s18, p51
  - Margretha, c16
  - Maria, p16, s22
- Fisher, Maria, p16, s22, r39
- Fischering, Maria Barbara, p51
- Flegler, Anna Magdalena Elizabetha, c24
  - Eve Anna Elizabetha, p24, s25, p26
  - Elisabetha, s21
  - Simon, c26
  - Zacharias, p24, p26, s25, m41, m43
- Forster, Margretha, r40
  - Susanna Margretha, s32
- Fowles, William s16
- Franck, Johannes, s22, m43
- Francke, Johann s19
- Frey, Catharina, s34
  - Henrich and wife, s31
- Freymeyer, Anna Eva, c20
  - Anna Elisabetha, p20
  - John Michael, p20
- Friedrich, the wife of Conrad, s18
- Fridrich, Johann Adam and wife Regina, 29
  - Johann Adam, s21
  - Johann conrad, r39
- Fritz, Maria Elizabetha, s24
- Frehd, Maria Margretha, s28
- Friderich, Maria, Regina, s22
- Friderich, Regina, s21
- Froehlich, Anna Catharina, c24
  - Anna Elisabetha, p24
  - Appollonia, s19, p24, s27, p33

- Bernhard, c33
- Johannes, c24
- Johann Valentin, p24, s33
- Stephan, p24
- Veltin, s30, p33
- Fuchs, Christoph, p23
  - Anna Maria, r39
  - Johanna Elisabetha, p23
  - Johann Philipp, s23, c23
- Fuhrer, Johann, s21, s27, m44, d47
  - Anna Maria, c49
  - Catharina, p48, p50
  - Henrich, c50
  - Johannes, s28
  - Valntin, p49, s32
- Fuhrer, Valentin, p50
- Fulz, Catharina, s19
- Fux, Christina, s30
- Gans, Anna Catharina, c19
  - Gertrud, p19
  - Johann, p19, m41
- German, Anna Catharina s27
  - Anna Catharina, s26
  - Jacob, s27
- Gerlach, Anna Margretha, s22
  - Conrad's widow, s18
  - Johann Peter s23
- Gerystler, Catharina, s25
- Gesteler, Anna Louisa, s21
- Giesser, Sibylla, m43
  - Johann, 43
- Giller, Barbara, p19
  - Franz, p19
  - Joseph, c19
- Gisler, Anna Lucia, p23
  - Johann Hermann, c23
  - Peter, p23, p33, s36
- Glock, (See Clock, Klock), Henrich, p20
  - Johannes, c20
  - Maria Margretha, p20
- Glopp, Anna Magdalena, p31
  - Johann, Peters, m43, s20
  - Peter, s24, p31
  - Susanna c31
- Gockel, Anna Christina, r39
- Goebel, Anna Margretha, s16
- Gottel, Daniel, r39
- Gormann, Jacob, s33
- Gratt, Gabriel, s50, (2)
  - Gabriel, s50
  - Greetje, s50
- Grad, Anna Elisabetha, c26
  - Johann, p26, s26
  - Wiaburga, p26

- Graad, Maria Margretha, s50
- Gransche, Elisabetha, s22
  - Omyla, s22
- Grauberger, Anna Barbara, s23, p21
  - Johann Fridrich, c21
  - Philip Peter, s19, p21, s22
- Greisler, Anna Catharine, p27, c27
  - Catharina, p24
  - Johann Hieronymus, c24
- Greissler, Johann Philip, p47, p27
- Grems, Anna Apolonia, p16
  - Johannes, p16
  - William c16
- Greysler, Johannes, r40
- Groster, Anna Catharina, s31
- Gulch, Ana Catharine, p52
  - Melchoir, p52
- Guchin, Heinrich, c52
  - Magdalena, c52
- Gunterman (See Countryman, Konderman,) Andreas, r40
  - Anna Barbara, s22
- Guss, Mattheus, s22
- Haas, Anna Barbara, c18
  - Anna Catharina, r39
  - Anna Elisabeth, c17
  - Anna Sabina, c26
  - Catharina, p22
  - Jannike, c22
  - Johann Niclaus, s27
  - John, p22
  - Maria, Sabina, p26
  - Niclaus, p17, p26
  - Rosina, p18, p25
  - Sabina, p17
  - Simon, p18, p25, s26
  - Zacharia, c25
- Haber, Christian, m44
- Haeger, Johann Fridrich, s22, s24, s38
  - Johann Fridrich, Rev., m46
- Hagedorn, Johann Peter, s17
- Hagedorn, Johan Peter, s26
  - Maria, Gartraut, r39
  - Peter s32
- Ham, Catharina, p49
  - Johannes Peter, c49
  - Peter, p49
- Hambuch, Johann Wilhelm, 30, m46
- Hambuck, Johann Wilhelm, s27
- Hamm, Anna Catharina, c27
  - Anna Catharain Sibylla p27
  - Peter, p27
- Hammer, Hans Henrich, s20

- Hanor, Johann, m41
- Hanti, (Or Meauti), Conrad, s36
- Hartman, Anna, s28
  - Anna Maria, m41
  - Conrad, 41
  - Johann Hermann, s30
- Hassmann, Elisabeth, r40
- Hastmann, Elisabetha, s29
- Hauck, Anna Elisabeth, p34
  - Anna Margretha, c34
  - Georg p34
- Haug, Lucas, 43
  - Magdalena, m43
- Haupt, Anna Catharina, r39
  - Cathrina, c28
  - Gertraut, p28
  - Philipp, p28
- Hauss, Christian, m42
- Hayner, Johannes, s20
- Heckman, Maria Gertraut, r40
- Heidorn, Henrich, m43
- Heil, Anna Catharina, s29
- Heller, Johann Philipp, s27
- Helm, Johann Peter, s20
- Helmer, Anna Catharina, m42
  - Antonius, 42
- Hemer, Elisabeth, s35
- Hemler, Elisabetha, p31
  - Johann Gottfrid, c31
  - Leonard, p31
- Henrich, Frantz, c30
  - Johann Lorentz, s36
  - Lorentz, p30
  - Regina, p30
- Hendrickson, Abraham, c18
  - Isaac, p18
  - Judith, p18
- Herchemer, Jerg, s31
- Herdel, Anna Margretha, p23, s26
  - Anna Margretha, s19, s26
  - Elisabeth, s32, s38
- Herder, Johann Michael, s23
- Hertel, Adam, s19, p23, s25, p28, m46
  - Adam, child of d47
  - Adam, wife of, d47
  - Eva Maria, c28
  - Margretha, p28
- Hertel, Maria Elisabeth c23
- Hess, Anna Catharina, p29, c34, p34
  - Anna Maria, c29
  - Catharina, s26
  - Johann, s19, p29, s26, p34, m43

- o Niclaus, s18
- Hettich, Anna Maria, p17
  - o Conrad, p17
  - o Johannes, c17
- Hettman, Gartraut, s34, (2)
- Heu, Litcken, 16
- Heydorn, Henrich, s28
  - o Maria Barbara, s29
- Heyl, Catharina, m45
  - o Johann Wilhelm, p45
- Heypert, Anna Elisabetha, r39
- Hill, Carolus 40
  - o Maria, m40
- Hochdihl, Jacob, 46
- Hoener, Johann and his wife Catharina, s34
- Hoerner, Margretha, m42
- Hoenig, Anna Elisabeth, c35
  - o Magdalena, p35
  - o Michael, p35
- Hof, Adam, p35
  - o Anna Catharina, p35
  - o Johann Phillipp, c35
- Hofmann, Anna Elalia, p17
  - o Anna Mara, s17, c17
  - o Dietrich, p17
  - o Esther, p25
  - o Herman, s23
  - o Jannike, c25
  - o Jacob, p20
  - o Maria Elisabetha, p20
  - o Mattheus, c20
  - o Zacharias, p25
- Hoffman, Ester, 29
  - o Rennalt, c29
  - o Zacharias, p29
- Hofmann, Gabriel, p19
  - o Jospeh, c19
  - o Susanna, p19
- Horning, Gerhard, s27
  - o Sophia, s29
- Hornung, Anna Sophia, m45
  - o Gerhard, d47
  - o Sophia, s2r (?this doesn't look correct)
- Hostmann, Anna Catharina, p24, r39
  - o Conrad, p20
  - o Eva Margretha, p20
  - o Gabriel, m43
  - o Gabriel, m43
  - o Johann Peter, c20
  - o Sebastian, c24
- Huen, Anna Gertrauda, m41
  - o Dietrich, 41
- Huenschick, Michael, s24

- Humbel, Elisabetha, m43
  - o Jerg, 43
- Humel, Anna Margretha, p38
  - o Hermann, p38
  - o Peter, c38
- Hummel, Hermann, p33
  - o Johann Georg, c33
  - o Margretha, p33
- Hopfer, Anna Catharina, p27
  - o David p27
  - o Jacobina Maria, r39
  - o Sophia, c27
- Ifland, Anna Maria, s31
  - o Johann David, s19
- Ittich, Johann s31
- Jan, a negro, p32
- Jaefer, Christina Elisabetha, s20, p30
  - o Johann, c30
  - o Wendell, p30
- Janson, Maria, p22, 16
  - o Peter, 16, p22, c22
- Jorg, Johann Niclaus, c18
  - o Maria, p18
  - o Wilhelm, s18, p18
- Jung (Young), Anna Elisabeth s35
  - o Anna Margretha, p20, p32
  - o Anna Veronica, p30, p36, p50, p49
  - o Catharina Elisabetha, c30
  - o Elisabetha, s30, s21 (2)
  - o Eva Maria, c36
  - o Gertrudt, c49
  - o Henrich, p20, p32, s35
  - o Johan Henrich, Anna Margreth, twins, c32
  - o Jacob, widow of p22
  - o Jan Matthias, p50
  - o Jerg Hans, 44
  - o Johann Adam, c34
  - o Johann Eberhard, s24
  - o Johann Mattheus, s20, s26, s29, p30, p36, m44, p49
  - o Johann Quirinius, d47
  - o Johannes, c50
  - o Magdalena, s19
  - o Magdalena, wife of Niclaus, s24
  - o Maria Catharina, c20, p34
  - o Niclaus, s24, d47
  - o Theobald, p34
- Kaehl, Jorg Wilhelm, s26
- Kanikill, Peter Samuel, 16
  - o Emicke, 16
  - o Johannes, 16
  - o Samuel, 16
- Kaputzgi, Jacob, s33

- Anna Magdalena, s33
- Anna Margretha, p40, m46
- and wife, s29
- Anna Dorothea, r40
- Johann Jacob, p46
- **Kehl, Anna Sibylla Catharina, s21**
  - Gerdraut, s26, s36
  - Georg Wilhelm, s29, s33
  - Jorg Wilhelm, s21
  - Jerg Wilhelm, s36
  - Sibylla Catharina, s38
- **Keller, Frantz, p29, s30**
  - Barbara, p29, s30
  - Johann Wilhelm, c29
- **Kernick, James s38**
- **Kestler, Anna Margretha, p31, p34**
  - Anna Catharina, c31
  - Johann, p31, c34, p34
- **Keyser, Anna Margretha, c35, p35**
  - Johann, p35, m42
- **Kiever, Christina, p49**
  - Balthasar p49
  - Catharina, c49
  - Henrich, c49
- **Kilmer, Eva Margretha, p49**
  - Georg, p49
  - Johann Wilhelm, c49
- **Kistler, Eleonora Catharina, s20**
  - David, s20, s32
- **Klein, Adam, p31**
  - Amelia, s25, s33
  - Anna Maria, s27, m46
  - Anna Maria Clara, c31
  - Anna Catharina, p31
  - Elisabeth, s49
  - Johann, s26, s38
  - Hieronymus, s22, s24, s28, p46, s48
  - Maria, s28, s32, s50
  - Maria Margretha, s25, s26
- **Klug, Johann Georg, p17**
  - Johannes, c17
  - Susanna p17
- **Klumm, Anna Margretha, c33**
  - Johann Georg, c19
  - Philipp, p19, p33
  - Veronica, p19, p33
- **Kniestberg, Anna Maria, c32**
  - Elisabetha, Barbara, p34
  - Elisabetha, p32
  - Johann Godtfrid, c34
  - Johann Peter, p32, p34
- **Kobel, Jacob, p23, s23**
  - Anna Maria, p23
  - Johann Henrich, c23
- **Koch, Anna Maria, s19**

- Jorg Ludwig, s19
- **Kocherthal, Christian Joshua, Rev., c52**
  - Benigna Siblla, s29, s30, s35, s36, c52
  - Joshua, p16, s25, s30, p52
  - Louisa Abigail, c16
  - Susanna Sibylla c52
  - Sibylla Charlotta, p16, d47, p52
- **Koerner, Anna Magdalena, p19, p26**
  - Catharina Elisabetha, c26
  - Johann Adam, c19
  - Johann Niclaus, p26
  - Niclaus, p19
- **Kohl, Georg Wilhelm, s50**
  - Gertruda, s19, s50
  - Jurge Willem, s50
- **Koop, Johann Adam, s34**
  - Anna Sophia, s17
- **Kornmann, Anna Kunigunda, m42**
- **Korb, Gebje, p50**
  - Hendrick, p50
  - Jannetje, c50
- **Kraemer, Antoni, p29, r42**
  - Anthon, r39
  - Gertaut, p29, s33
  - Johannes, c29, s34
- **Krantz, Johann Henrich, p22, p24**
  - Anna Catharina, p22, s24, p24, p29, p36
  - Conrad, 43
  - Elisabetha, s28, s36, m43
  - Henrich and his wife, s32
  - Johann, m41
  - Johannes, c24
  - Johann Wilhelm, c36
  - Maria Elisabetha, c29
- **Kraus, Jacob, d41**
  - Anna Maria, m41
- **Kreystler, Johann Georg, r40**
- **Kreiser, Catharina, p17**
  - Johann Philipp, p17
  - Johann Henrich Valentin, c17
- **Kuester, Anna Maria, s20, s32, m46**
  - Johann Wilhelm, s28, p46
  - Johann Balthasar, s21, s35, s37, r39
  - Wilhelm, s24
- **Kuster, Catharina Susanna, r40**
- **Kuestler, Susanna, s26**
- **Kugel, Anna Margretha, m43**
  - Johann, 43
- **Kuhlman, Catharina, s38**
  - Johann, s30

- Kuhn, Veltin, p20
  - Anna Catharina, p20
  - Johanna Elisabeth Margretha, c20
- Kun, Elisabetha, s37
- Kunz, Johann Wilhelm, s49
- Kuntz, Margretha, s17
- Kurtz, Lorentz Henrich, s17
  - Maria Margretha, s17
  - Margretha, s35
- La Fransche, Entike, s25
  - Johann, s24
- Lambert, Anna Elisabetha, s27
- Lamed, Anna Elisabeth s17
  - Johannes, s17
- Lamert, Johann, s26
  - Wife of Johann, s38
- Land, Anna Margretha, s31
- Landgrast, Jerg and his daughter Anna Elisabetha, s32
- Landmann, Peter, p47, m47, r39
- Lang, Abraham and wife s37
- Langry, Maria Catharina, wife of Abraham s20
- Last, Anna, p31
  - Anna Dorothea, c31
  - Johann Georg, p31
  - Johann Just, s31
- Lastner, Johann Peter, p21
  - Juliana Elisabetha, c21
  - Magdalena, p21
- Lauck, Abraham, p20, p30
  - Anna Christina, c30
  - Catharina, p20, p30
  - Elisabetha, m43
  - Jacob, 43
  - Maria Catharina, c20
- Launert, Anna Catharina, c3
  - Anna Margretha, p30
  - Jerg, s30
  - Hohann Georg s34, m45
  - Philipp, s28, s29, p30, p45
- Laur, Arnold, 42
  - Maria Agnes, m42
- Lauer, Johann Mettheus, r40
- Laux, Anna Elisabetha, s28, s30, p30
  - Dietrich and wife, s32
  - Johann Adam, c31
  - Johann Dietrich, p31
  - Johann Just, s34, p45
  - Johann Peter, r40
  - Johann Wilhelm, c30
  - Maria Elisabetha, m45
  - Maria Margretha, r39
  - Niclaus, p30

- Leer, Anna Margretha, c22
  - Johann, p34
  - Johannes, p22
  - Ottilia Helena, c34
  - Sibylla Catharina, p22, p34
- Lehmann, Anna Elisabeth, c36
  - Anna Margretha, c30
  - Clemens, p27, p30, p36, m44, d47, p50
  - Johann Wilhelm, c27, s27, s35
- Lehman, Wilhelm and wife Maria, s32
- Leich, Elisabeth, p19
  - Georg Ludwig, m43
  - Johann Eberhard, c24
  - Johann Henrich, p19
  - Ludwig, p24
  - Maria Martha p24
  - Philip, c19
- Leick, Anna Catharina, c34
  - Johann p34
  - Maria Barbara, p34
- Lein, Conrad, p23
  - Johann Peter, c23
  - Margretha, p23
  - Margretha, r39
- Leitz, Johannes, s48
  - Maria Barbara, s48
- Leman, Anna Maria, c50
  - Gertrud, p27, p30, p36, p50
  - Maria Eva, s50
  - Willem, s38, s50
- Lerck, Wilhelm, s26
  - Henrich, s38
- Lesch, Johann Adam, s17
- Lescher, Bastian, s37
- Liboscha, Maria Johann, 51
  - Susanna, 51
- Linck, Anna Eva, p26
  - AnnaGerdraut, c26
  - Wilhelm, p26
- Lisemus, Anna Maria, s23
- Lispenaer, Abigail, s16
- Listenus, Anna Barbara, r40
- Listenius, Anna Maria, p19, m44
  - Bernhard, p19
  - Christianus, c19
- Loehn, Anna Margretha, p34
  - Johann, c34, p34
- Loeshaar, Jacob s23
  - Maria Elisabetha, p16, c16
  - Sebastian, p16
- Loiner, Abigail p48
  - Robert, c38
  - William, p48

- Loockstad, Elisabetha, p18
  - Georg, p18, m41
  - Georgius, c18
- Lorentz, Alexander, c127
  - Anna Margretha, p17
  - Henrich and his wife s23
  - Johannes p17
  - Henrich, s18
- Losch, Elisabetha, r39
- Loscher, Conrad, r40
  - Johann Bastian, s48
  - Johann Georg, r39
- Losting, Andreas, c22
  - Cornelia, p22
  - Peter, p22
- Louck, Abraham, m42
- Lucka, Maria Elisabetha, s17
- Luckhard, Bernhard, child of d47
- Ludwig, Susanna Catharina, s37
- Lueckhard, Bernhard, p24, p28, s33, p33
  - Johann Bernhard, p18
  - Johann Daniel, c28
  - Johann Peter, c33
  - Johann Wilhelm, c18
  - Johannes, c24
  - Justina, p18, s22, p24, s25, p28, p33
- Lued, Johan Leonard, s16
- Leutken, Daniel, s16
  - Daniel, M. D., 15
- Luti, Elisabetha, p27
  - Marcus, c27
  - Samuel, p27
- Lutt, Anna Catharina, s33, m46
  - Barthas, r39
  - Johann Balthas, s35
- Lutz, Anna Magdalena, m43
  - Johann Christoph, 43
- Maemig, Ferdinand, p46
  - Maria Elisabetha, m46
- Maerten, Johann Conrad, p24, p28
  - Johann Fridrich, c24
  - Johann Henrich, c28
  - Maria, p24
  - Maria Elisabeth, p28
- Manck, Anna Veronica, s26
  - Eva Catharina, s21, s30
  - Jacob, child of, d47
- Mancken, Anna Veronica, m44
  - Jacob, 44
- Manges, Johann, s26
- Mann Henrich, s23
  - Johann Henrich, p19
  - Johann Peter, c19

- Maria Elisabetha, p19
- Mannich, Maria Elisabetha, r39
- Martenstock, Albrecht, p33
  - Albrecht, Dietrich, p21, c21, p28, p38, m41, 48
  - Daniel, c33
  - Elisabetha, p21, p28, p33, s37, p38, 48
  - Johanna Maria Sophia, c28
  - Maria Christina, c38
- Martin, Conrad, s26
  - Maria, s26
- Matthes, Anna Maria, s27, m45
  - Maria Apollonia, m41
  - Peter, 41, p45
- Matteus, Henrich, p46
  - Sabina, m46
- Mattheus, Conrad, c34
  - Georg, p34
  - Jerg, s20, p31
  - Johan Jacob, c31
  - Maria Catharina, p31, p34
  - Maria Sibylla, s21
- Mauck, Jacob, s19
- Mauer, Anna Catharine, p23
  - Anna Margreth, c23
  - Johann Georg, r39
  - Peter, p23
- Maul, Anna Catharina, s36
  - Anna Elisabetha, c37
  - Anna Julian, s21
  - Anna Margaretha, c40
  - Anna Maria, c23
  - Anna Ursula, p23, p32, p37
  - Christoph, s23, s30
  - Fridrich, s21, s24, s25, s27, s28, p37, s50
  - Johann Fridrich, p32
  - Johann Joacob, s49
  - Johannes, c32
  - J. Fridrich, p23
  - Ursula, s36
- Mauer, Anna Catharina, 30, p30
  - Dorothea, s27
  - Johannes, c30
  - Johann Peter, s19
  - Jorg, s27
  - Peter, s24, p30, s37
- Mayer, Anna Gertraut, p38
  - Catharina, c38
  - Christian p38
- Mehs, Henrich, s17
- Meinhard, Burckhard, and wife, s18
- Mendes, Maria Christina s31
- Menges, Anna Eva, s21, p29, s33, p36

- o   Anna Elisabetha, c29
- o   Gerdraut, c36
- o   Johannes, p29
- Mengis, Johann, s17, s33, s35, p36
- Merckel, Anna Barbara, p21, p24, p33
  - o   Eva, c33
  - o   Elisabetha, c38
  - o   Fridrich, p21, p24, p33
  - o   Johann Adam, c21
  - o   Johann Fridrich, p38
  - o   Johann Jacob, s31
  - o   Maria Elisabetha, c24
- Mertin, Margaretha, s22
- Mertz, Anna Catharina, m41
  - o   Elisabetha, r40
  - o   Johann, 41
  - o   Sophia Elisabeth Margaretha, r39
- Meyer, Anna Christina c35
  - o   Anna Maria, c21, m45
  - o   Christian, p19, p26, s25, p30, p35
  - o   Gerdraut, s36
  - o   Johann and wife Barbara, s32
  - o   Johann Fridrich, p45
  - o   Johann Peter, c30
  - o   Maria Barbara, s35
- Meyrer, Anna Gertraut, p19, p26, p30, p35
  - o   Anna Kungunda, p21, p31
  - o   Henrich, p21, p31
  - o   Johann Henrich, c31
  - o   Johann Wilhelm, c26
  - o   Maria Elisabetha, c19
- Meyser, Johann Michel, s34
- Mossig, Johann Heinrich, c28
  - o   Maria Catharina, p28, s37, p38
  - o   Susanna, c38
  - o   Veit, p28, p38
- Mohr, Anna Catharina, c21
  - o   Anna Margretha, p21
  - o   Heinrich, p21, s27
  - o   Johann, r39
  - o   Philipp, s21, s33, s37
- Moor, Anna Margreth, p30
  - o   Catharina Elisabeth, c30
  - o   Christina, p28
  - o   Elizabeth, p31
  - o   Henrich, s28, p30
  - o   Johann, p31
  - o   Johann Georg, c31
  - o   Philipp, r40
  - o   Philipp Henrich, c28

- o   Philipp Wilhelm, p28, s30, s35
- Motasch, Juliana, s21
- Michael, Georg Andreas, c28
  - o   Maria Barbara, p28
  - o   Niclaus, p28
- Michel, Anna Barbara, p32
  - o   Elisabetha Margretha, c32
  - o   Henrich, p45
  - o   Johann Henrich, r40
  - o   Johann Niclaus, p32
  - o   Susanna, m45
  - o   Susanna Gerdraut, r39
- Mickler, Anna Margretha, p23
  - o   Jacob, c23
  - o   Killiam p23
- Migrigri, Letischa, 16
  - o   Peter, 16
- Mueller, Anna s27
  - o   Anna Catharina, s27
  - o   Anna Eva, s36
  - o   Anna Elisabetha, s20
  - o   Anna Elisabetha, m44
  - o   Anna Margretha, s23
  - o   Anna Maria, s21, m41
  - o   Catharina, p32
  - o   Christian, m45
  - o   Eva, s33
  - o   Elisazetha, s16, s17, c37, m43
  - o   Georg, 43
  - o   Johann, s16, s22, s34, 44
  - o   Johannes, s21, (2), c32, C49
  - o   Johann Christian, p37
  - o   Johann Georg, 41, p45
  - o   Johann Philipp c17
  - o   Margretha, p37
  - o   Maria Catharina, m43
  - o   Maria Elisabeth, s36
  - o   Philip, p17, s19, s20, s30, p32, 43
  - o   Samuel, s27
- Muller, Anna Sibilla, s48
  - o   Bartel, r39
  - o   Christiana Clara, r40
  - o   David, s36, p49
  - o   Margrete, p49
- Muenckler, Anna Margretha, c27, p27
  - o   Anna Maria, c27
  - o   Killian, p27
  - o   Mustirr, Catharina, m41
  - o   Johann Jacob, 41
- Naeher, Carl,
- Naehrung, Johann Henrich, 16
- Neher, Anna Constantia, p32
  - o   Johann Fridrich, c32

- Netzbacher, Anna Margaretha, c30
  - Barbara Elisabetha, p23
  - Johann Henrich, c23
  - Johann Martin, p23
  - Martin, p25, p30
- Netzbaecher, Anna Barbara, p25
  - Anna Maria, c25
- Neukirch, Anna Benigma, c30
  - Anna Maria, p25
  - Maria Catharina, c25
  - Johann, s32
  - Johann Henrich, p25, p30
- Neus, Abraham, p17
  - Anna Elisabetha, C17
- Neurich, Anna Maria, s23, p30
- Noecher, Anna Constinia, p35
  - Anna Maria, c35
  - Carl, p35
- Noll, Bernhard, s28, s33
- Nuess, Johann Heinrich, r39
- Oberbach, Anna Maria, c25, s50
  - Christina, s27
  - Elisabetha, s19, p25, s33, p33
  - Elisabetha Magdalena, s33
  - Jerg, s30, 47
  - Johann Christian, c25
  - Johann Georg, s19, c30
  - Johann Peter, c20, p20, s20, p25, s25, p30
  - Maria Christina, s19, p20, p25, p30, c33, c36
  - Peter, s20, p25, p33, s36
- Oemich, Anna Catharina, p38, r39
  - Jerg Adam, s32
  - Johann Adam, r39
  - Lorentz, c38
  - Niclaus, p38
- Ohmich, Anna Catharina, p29
  - Anna Maria, c29
  - Niclaus and his wife, s28, p29
- Ohrendorf, Henrich, p35
  - Anna Margretha, p35
  - Maria Elisabetha c35
- Onderling, Anna, m44
- Ormen, Richard, s33
- Peeter, Anna Maria, s19
- Persch, Anna, s22
- Petri, Anna Gertraut, c31, s31
  - Anna Margretha, s19
  - Cordula, p31
  - Philipp, s19, m44
  - Johann Just, p31
- Pfester, Andreas, r39

- Pfester, Anna Maria, p18, s32
  - Johannes, c18
  - Michael, p18, s18
- Pfuhl, Anna Catharina, c25
  - Anna Sophia, p25
  - Peter, p25, m42
- Philipp, Anna Catharina, s37
  - Magdalena, s26, s49
- Philip, Catharina s37
  - Johann Peter, s49
  - Peter, s49
- Planck, Christina, c30
  - Johann, s18, p18, s24, c25, p25, p30, d47, (2), p47
  - Johann Elisabetha, r39, m47
  - Johann Michael, c18
  - Killian, p22
  - Maria Margretha, p18, c22, p25, p30
- Plass, Elisabetha, p28
  - Johann, p26, s28
  - Johann Wilhelm, c26
- Pletel, Jacob, p51
- Plettel, Elizabetha, 15
  - Johannes, 15
- Pletelin, Ana Elisabetha, p51
  - Anna Sara, c51
  - Catharine, c51
  - Margretha, c51
- Plettol, Elisabetha, m41
  - Jacob, 41
- Pliest, Johann Emerich, s29
- Plirs, Johan Emmerich, s22
- Poehler, Johann Henrich, r39, m41
- Porster, Maria, wife of Jacob, s20
- Practer, Helena, 16
  - Joseph, 16
- Presler, Valentin, s17
- Propeet, Maria Barbara, r39
- Propert, Anna Maria, s37
- Propper, Anna Elisabetha, s49
  - Johann Jost, s49
- Prusie, Gertraut, s25
  - Gabrial, s25
- Prusti, Gabriel, s27
  - Gertraut, s27
- Pulfer, Anna Catharina, s19
- Pulver, Johann Wendel, s27
- Rau, Catharina, c48, p48
  - Catharina Elisabetha, s26, s27
  - Fridrich, r40
  - Friderich, p48
  - Gerdraut, s28

- Johann Georg, r39
- Johann Niclaus, s35
- Michael, s48
- Niclaus, s28
- Rauersee, Gertraud, p20
  - Hermann, p20
  - Meinhard, c20
- Rauh, Catharina Elisabetha, m46
  - Niclaus, p46
- Rausch, Anna Christina, r39
- Rauscher, Martin r39
- Rautenbusch, Anna Barbara, m42
  - Johann, 42
- Rauw, Anna Maria, p50
  - Catharina, c50
  - Michael, p50
- Reckfel, Anna, r39
- Rees, Andreas, s35
  - Benjamin, p35
  - Cathariana, s35
  - Gertraud, p35
  - Henrich, c35
- Reichard, Hans, 43
  - Johann Bernhard, c22
- Reichart, Anna Constantia, m45
  - Anna Maria, s19, p22, p26, s35, m43, 48
  - Elisabetha, Catharina Backus, p29
  - Joseph, s19, p22, p26, s28, s34, s35, m42, p45
  - Johann Mattheus, c29
  - Johann David, c26
  - Johann, p29
- Reisdorst, Anna Margretha, s33
- Reiter, Henrich and his wife, s23
- Reitschaft, Johann Paul, m41
- Rennau, Henry, s16, p51
  - Heinrich, c51
  - Johanna, s16, p51
  - Lorenz, c51
- Reuter, Anna Juliana, p19, p27, p36, 48, s49
  - Eva Catharina, p36
  - Henrich, p19, p27, s28, p36, s36, 48
  - Johanna Elisabetha, c19
  - Johann Herman, s49
  - Johann Fridrich, c27
  - Juliana, s24, s32
  - Liesabeth, s50
- Richter, Andreas, p27, 44
  - Anna Barbara, r40
  - Anna Maria, m44
  - Anna Maria, s24
  - Elisabetha, s24, p27

- Johannes, c27
- Risch, Johann, Jacob, s17
- Risom, Anna s18
  - Hensic, s18
- Ritscher, Anna, p36
  - Johann Conrad, p35
  - Maria, c36
- Rohrbach, Anna Catharina, 29, s30, m46
- Rohrbauch, Anna Catharina, s27
- Roos, Catharina, s22
  - Ephraim, m44
  - Wilhelm, s22, 44
- Roschmann, Anna Elisabetha, c26, p26, s27, r39
  - Johann, p26, s29
  - Johannes s27
  - Maria Catharina, r40
- Rose, Andreas, s18
  - Peter, 16
- Rosenquest, Alexander, s17
- Roth, Johann, 15
- Ruebenich, Elisabetha, m41
  - Mattaeus, 41
- Rued, Johann Georg, s31
  - Johann Michael, r39
  - Johann Peter, r39
- Rueger, Anna Margretha, p21, p24
- Rueger, Johann Philipp, p21
  - Johannes, c21
- Ruehl, Anna Catharina, c24, 35
  - Anna Dorothea Margretha, p33
  - Gottfrid, s21
  - Gottfried, p24
  - Gottfrid and wife, s31
  - Niclaus, p33
  - Niclaus, s31
- Rusch, Anna Magdalena, r39
- Rusmann, Elisabeth, p49
  - Johann, p49
  - Johannes, c49
- Saalbach, Johann Smith, s48
  - Maria Margretha, s48
- Saderland, William and wife, s16
- Saltmann, Anna Margretha, p38, c38
  - Georg, p38
- Saltzmann, Amalia, r40
- Salzmann, Georg, m46
- Savoy, Anna Elisabetha, c34, p34
  - Joseph, p34
- Schaarmann, Anna Catharina, m41
  - Conrad, p29
  - Henrich, 40, m42, p45

- o   Johann Henrich, s22, 29
- Schauermann, Johan Emerich, c29
  - o   Maria Salomo, p29
  - o   Sibylla, m45
- Schaefer, Elisabetha, 16
  - o   Maria Margretha, p16
  - o   Maria Catharina, s20
- Schaeffer, Johann, s31
- Scheffer, Johannes, s50
- Schaeffer, Justis Henrich, 16, p16
- Schaib, Anna Catharina, p38
  - o   Catharina,, s28
  - o   Fridrich, c38
  - o   Hieronymus, p38
- Schaester, Agnes, p21, p25, p29, s35, p38
  - o   Anna Elisabetha, s20
  - o   Anna Margretha, s20, s31, r39
  - o   Anna Maria, p17, p29, s35
  - o   Dorothea, p32, p37, d47
  - o   Elisabeth Catharina, c37
  - o   Elisabetha, c37
  - o   Fridrich, s34
  - o   Georg, m45
  - o   Gerhard, p17, r40
  - o   Henrich, s29, s37
  - o   Jacob, p45
  - o   Jerg, s27, p29
  - o   Jerg Philip, c29
  - o   Johann Adam, c29
  - o   Johann Henrich, c21, s35, r39
  - o   Johan Niclaus, s20
  - o   Johann Philipp, c25
  - o   Johann Werner, s30
  - o   Johannes, c38
  - o   Jost Henrich, p21, p25
  - o   Just Henrich, p38, m41, 48
  - o   Justus Henrich, 29
  - o   Maria Catharina, s20
  - o   Maria Sophia, c17
  - o   Valtin, r40
- Schaster, Anna Sibylla, r40
  - o   Margretha Elisabeth, r39
  - o   Maria Margretha, s22, m45, 48
- Schester, Johann, s21, p35, c35
  - o   Johann Veltin, s35
- Schall, Maria Elisabetha, s23
- Schauser, Michael, 42
- Schister, Philipp, p45
- Schampnor, Daniel, p20
  - o   Johanna, p20
  - o   Paul, c20
- Schauer, Johann Michael, r40

- o   Magdalena, m42
- Schedp, Jacob, s23
- Schef, Anna Maria, s50
- Scheff, Anna Margreta, p50
  - o   Lisabeth, c50
- Scheib, Anna Catharina, p26
  - o   Anna Catharina, p32, s33
  - o   Anna Maria, c26
  - o   Hieronymus, p26, p32, s33
  - o   Maria Elisabeth, c32
- Scherp, Anna Barbara, p48
  - o   Anna Maria, s48
  - o   Jacob, s48
  - o   Johan Jacob, c48
  - o   Jurgen Henrich, p48
- Scherer, Theobald, wife of, Justina s27
- Schest, Johann Wilhelm, s34
- Schleicher, Anna Catharina, m41
  - o   Anna Margretha, p17
  - o   Catharina Elisabeth, s25
  - o   Johann Adam, c17
  - o   Johann, Georg, p17, 41
- Schlemer, Anna Eva, c21
  - o   Mattheus, p21
- Schlemmer, Anna Elisabetha, c33
  - o   Anna Veronica, p21, s23, p26, p33
  - o   Maria Catharina, c26
  - o   Maria Gerdraut, c26
  - o   Mattheus, p21, s26, p26, s29, p33, s33
- Schley, Anna Maria, m46
  - o   Johann Michel, p46
- Schlitzler, Maria Elisabetha, s21
- Schmid, Adam, s25
  - o   Adam Michael, s17
  - o   Anna Catharina, s25, p25
  - o   Anna Elisabetha, p19, c25, s32, r40, p50
  - o   Anna Maria, m44
  - o   Bernhard, s28
  - o   Christina, p49
  - o   Conrad, s29
  - o   Elisabeth, p37
  - o   Elisabetha Margretha, p23, p29
  - o   Eva, p37
  - o   Georg, s25
  - o   Georg Adam, s19
  - o   Henrich, s25, 44
  - o   Johann Adam, r40
  - o   Johann Georg, p19, c23, r39
  - o   Johann Henrich, p25, c37, m41, 44

- Johann Peter, p23, s28, s29, p37
- Johannes, Peter, c49
- Johannes, c29
- Jorg Ludwig, c19
- Justus Adam, p49
- Ludwig, m42
- Margaretje, c50
- Maria Barbara, r39
- Maria Catharina, r40
- Nicklas, s27, s36, p37, 40, r40, p50
- Peter, p29, m41, m46
- Susanna, Catharina, c37
- Wilhelm, s49, p50
- Wilhelmus, c50

- **Schmidt, Gertrauda, m41**
  - Maria Elisabeth, s50, p50
- **Schmid, Paul, s49**
- **Schnell, Johann Just, s31**
- **Schneider, Agnes, c35**
  - Anna, p27
  - Anna Barbara, p30
  - Anna Catharina, m45
  - Anna Margretha, s37
  - Anna Maria, s23, c28, s38
  - Antoni, p33
  - Anthonipous, m45
  - Dietrich, p45
  - Elsie, s48
  - Henrich, p27
  - Jacob, p30
  - Johann Dietrich, p45
  - Johann Georg, 30, s33, m47
  - Johann Henrich, c30
  - Johann Samuel, c27
  - Johann Wilhelm, s26, p28, s30, p47
  - Johannes, s38
  - Margreth, s34, p35
  - Susanna Margretha, s28
- **Schnitt, Johann Jacob, p17**
  - Johanna Elisabetha, c17
  - Maria Elisabetha, p17
- **Schott, Helena, s18, p21**
  - Hargreth, c21, s25
  - Wilhelm, s18, p21
- **Schraemmle, Johann Henrich, s23**
- **Schramm, Anna Maria, p35, p37, s49**
  - Catharina, s35
  - Friderich, s32, p35, p37, s38, m46, p48, s49
  - Henrich, s23, s28, s33, p46, s50
  - Johann William, c35
  - Johann Henrich, c37
- **Schram, Margretha, s26, s50**

- Maria, c48, p48
- **Schreib, Catharina, s28**
  - Hieronymus, s25
- **Schreiber, Albrecht, p20**
  - Anna Margretha, c20
  - Eva, p20
- **Schuch, Gerdraut, s26**
- **Schuertz, Andreas, p37**
  - Anna Catharina, s26, c37, m45
  - Jerg, s37
- **Schuett, Anna Maria, p29**
  - Hericus, c18
  - Peter, c29
  - Salomon, p18, p29
- **Schuetz, Benjamin, c25**
  - Johan Michael, 15, p25
- **Schuetze, Jannicke, 15, p25**
  - Maria, 15, p25
- **Schumacher, Anna Barbara, 18, s19**
  - Anna Maria, p24
  - Barbara, r39
  - Daniel, p24
  - Dorothea, s30
  - Jacob, s34
  - Johann Jost, c24
- **Schuemann, W. Harmannus, 15**
- **Schut, Catharina, s50**
- **Schultz, Anna Elisabetha, m43**
- **Schutz, Conrad, s32, s34, p45**
  - Susanna, s31
  - Georg, 43
- **Schuertz, Catharina Appolonia, p37**
- **Schurtz, Eva, s20**
  - David, r40
- **Schuh, Eva, s38**
- **Schuenemann, Herman, m43**
- **Schultheis, Elsabetha, s31**
  - Johann, m42
- **Schultheiss, Johann George, s19**
- **Schwisser, Anna Catharian, p51**
  - Johanns, c51
  - Lorens, p51
- **Schweitzer, Laurenz, p16**
  - Catharina, p16
  - Johann Heinrich, c16
- **Seegendorf, Adam, p46**
  - Anna Gertraud, m46
- **Segendorf, Hermann, p34**
  - Johann Georg, c34
  - Maria Catharina, s27
- **Segendorst, Hermann, s20**
  - Maria Catharina, s27

- Shen, Anna Gertraud, wife of Peter, s25
- Seibert, Jerg Adam, c32
  - Anna Maria, p32
  - Johann Martin, p32
- Sexer, Anna Magdalena, r39
- Seybold, Georg, s34
- Simon, Anna Elisabetha, c32
  - Anna Maria, p20, p32
  - Johann Michael, m41
  - Johann Wilhelm, p32
  - Johann Ulrich, c20
  - Wilhelm, p20
- Sittig, Christian, s20
- Sixt, Anna Elisabeth, s34
  - Christina, p30, p34
  - Christina, Elsabeth, c30
  - Elsabeth, s30
  - Gertraut, c34
  - Henrch, p30, s30, p34
- Soller, Adam, d47
- Soeller, Johann Adam s21, m42, m44
- Speickermann, Anna Catharina, s26
  - Catharina, s28
  - Anna Elisabetha, p20, p28
  - Anna Maria Catharina, c28
  - Johann Hermann, s26, m41
  - Philip Peter, c20
  - Sebastian, p20, p28, s30
- Spohn, Anna Catharina, p31
  - Anna Margretha, c25, s25
  - Anna Maria, p25, p36
  - Adam, s23, p25, s32, p36, m44
  - Henrich, p31
  - Johann Henrich, c23, m43
  - Johann Niclaus, c31, m43
  - Johann Peter, p23
  - Maria Catharina, p23
  - Maria, Elisabetha, c36
  - Werner, 44
- Sponheimer, Anna Margaretha, c1?
  - Anna Maria, p16, s22
  - Johann Georg, p16, s22
- Spoon, Adam s28, p32, s50
  - Anna Maria, p32, s50
  - Maria Eva, c32
- Spoor, Annika, p30
  - Isaac, p30
  - Johann, c30
- Springstein, Catharine, 16, p18, p37, c37
  - David, s18
  - Georg, 16, p18, p37
  - Gertrauda, 16, c18
  - Maria, 16

- Melchoir, 16
- Samuel, 16
- Stahl, Anna Agatha, s26
  - Anna Elisazetha, s21
  - Anna Maria, c20
  - Anna Ursula, p20, 028
  - Johann, p20
  - Johannes, s27, p28, s32
  - Johann Henrich, c28
- Stehl, Maria Dorothea, s34
- Staring, Anna Margretha, c19
  - Niclaus, p19
- Starring, Adam and wife, s31
  - Anna Maria, p32
  - Johann Adam p32, m44
  - Maria Catharina, p19, c32
- Steigher, Catharina, s26
  - Johann Niclaus, r40
- Stein, Anna Maria, c21, p21
  - Maria, s19
  - Martin p21, m43
- Steis, Elisabetha, Magdalena, r39
- Sternberger, Jacob, p22, r39
  - Johann Lampert, r39
  - Philippus Hieronymus, c22
- Steuber, Balthas, s26
- Storr, Anna Kunigunda, c19
  - Elisabetha, p19
  - Elisabetha, Ottilia, s22
  - Michael, s17, p19
- Straub, Johann, s22
  - Johannnes, s24
  - Maria Elisabetha, s22, s24
- Straup, Johann Jacob, c34
  - Johann Wilhelm, c26
  - Johannes, p26, 29, p34, p38
  - Maria Elisabetha, p26, c34, c38, p38
- Streid, Anna Catharian p49
  - Friderich, s28, s38, p49
- Sertie, Anna Christina, s36
  - Anna Maria, r39, c49
  - Catharina, r39
  - Ludwig, 43
  - Magdalana, m43
  - Ursula, r39
- Stubenrauch, Anna Catharina, p23, s24
  - Georg Henrich, c23
  - Henrich, s24
  - Jorg Henrich, p23
- Stuber, Anna Elisabeth, r40
- Stueber, Maria Catharina, r39, m41
- Stueckenrad, Johann Wilhelm, s18
- Stump, Johann George, s20, s34

- Stupp, Anna Elisabetha, c31
  - Catharina, p31
  - Martin, p31
- Sutz, Amilia, c33
  - Andreas, c24
  - Dietrich, p24, s37
  - Johan Dietrich, p45
  - Johan Peter, s25, m45
  - Magdalena, s36, p24
  - Anna Margreth, p33
  - Peter, p33
- Taeter, Anna Maria, p33
  - Jerg, p33
  - Maria Magdalena, c33
- Tales, Anna Margretha, p27
  - Johann Wilhelm, c27, p27
- Taus, Anna Albertina, r39
- Tesch, (or Yesch), Johann Henrich, s29
- Testu, Maria Barbara, s28
- Thaeter, Anna Maria, p36
  - Georg, s28, p36
  - Gerg and his wife Anna Maria, s29, m47
  - Johann, p45
  - Johannes, c36
  - Lorentz, s38
- Thais, Johan Philipp, r39
- Theis, Christina, s25
- Thibaux, Elias, c17
  - Job, c17
  - Maria, p17, c17
  - William, p17
- Thomas, Anna, p31
  - Anna Eva, s23
  - Jerg, p31
  - Johann Henrich, c31
  - Johan Peter, s31
- Thonius, Anna Catharina, m47
  - Anna Demuth, s20
  - Anna Maria, s25
  - Stephan, p47
- Thonus, Christina, s25
- Thonusen, Margretha, s30
  - Peter, s30
- Tobich, Johann Peter, r39
- Tonese, Peter, s35
- Tonius, Christina, s35
- Tonnius, Anna Christina, s33
- Tambauper, Magdalena, s21
- Traut, Elisabetha, s32
- Terber, Anna Maria, m42
  - Johann, 42
  - Sebastian, s24, s39

- Thombauer, Anna Christina, c22
  - Anna Elisabetha, c32
  - Johan Niclaus, p32
  - Magdalena, p22
- Trombour, Dietrich, c37
  - Johannes, c38
  - Magdalana, p32, p37, p38
  - Niclaus, p22, p27, p38
- Turck, Isaac, 52
- Uhl, Christina, s36
- Van Orde, Temperans, s49
  - Willem, s49
- Voess, Christina, s37, s38
  - Henrich, s37
- Volck, Andreas and wife, s18, p18, 15, p22, p51
  - Anna Catharina, 15, p18, s18, p51
  - Anna Maria, c18
  - Carloss, 15
  - Catharina, p22
  - Georg Hieronymus, c51
  - Johannes, c22
- Volckin, Anna Gertrauda, c51
  - Maria Barbara, c51
- Vollbart, Anna Gartraud, r39
- Voltz, Anna Eva, s20
  - Melchoir, s20
- Von De Bogard, Jacobus, s20
- Von Husum, Anna, p22
  - Jannicke, c22
  - Maria, s22
  - Rennier, p22
  - Volkart, s22
- Von Kleck, Pieter, s20
- Von Loon, Albert, p23
  - Alberth, s25
  - John, c23
  - Maria, p23, s23
  - Marion, s25
- VonNordstradt, Jan, m46
- Von Schaak, Arend, p25, p36
  - Jannike, c25
  - Maria, p25, p36
  - Margreth, c36
- Von Thesen, Abraham, s18
  - Jacobina, s18
- Vorst, Jacob, p18, c18
  - Maria, p18
- Vorstung, Abraham, p25
  - Clara, p25
  - Isaac, c25
- Vosburg, Cornelia, p32
  - Gertraud, s32
  - Jacob, c32

- o   Jan, p32
- o   Peter, s32
- Voshel, Anna Catharina, c19
  - o   Peter, p19
  - o   Maria, p19
- Waegelin, Anna Maria, p29
  - o   Johann Georg, c29
  - o   Johann Michael, p29, s36, m41
- Wagner, Maria Margretha, s22
  - o   Peter, s19
- Waid, Gertraud, m46
- Waidnecht, Johann Michael, s17
- Walbuer, Maria Elisabetha, r39
- Waldron, Maria Elizabeth, s35
- Wallrath, Anna Maria, p20
  - o   Christina Elisabetha, c20
  - o   Gerhard, p20
  - o   Johann Adam, s34
- Wambach, Catharina, s50
  - o   Wilhelm, s50
- Wanner, Agnes Barbara, p31
  - o   Anna Barbara, p34
  - o   Johann Ludwig, p31
  - o   Johann Michael, c31
  - o   Ludwig, p34
  - o   Maria Dorothea, c34
- Wanemacher, Anna wife of Dietrich, s19
  - o   Anna Margretha, p17
  - o   Johann Dietrich, p17, p22
  - o   Johann Michael, c17
- Wannenmacher, Anna Kunigunda, s18, p22
  - o   Elisabetha, Ottilia, c22
  - o   John, m42
- Warmer, Aliken, p33
  - o   Cornelius, p33
  - o   Jan and wife, s33
  - o   Johannes, c33
- Warno, Sibylla, r39
- Weberin, Eva Elisabetha, c51
  - o   Eva Maria, p51
- Weber, Anna Elisabetha, 15, p16, p51
  - o   Jacob, 15, p16, s23, s31, s32, p51
  - o   Johann Herman, 15
  - o   Johannes, c16
  - o   Ottilia, s32
- Weerich, Maria Elisabeth, r39
- Weid, Anna Catharina, s30
  - o   Gertraut, s25
- Weidnecht, Andreas, s21
  - o   Margretha, s21

- Weidmann, Anna Margretha, C29
  - o   Anna Ursula, p29
  - o   Martin, p29
- Weigand, Anna Catharina, s16, p51
  - o   Anna Maria, 15, 16, s38
  - o   Georg, s18, c51
  - o   Michael, s16, p51
  - o   Tobias, c51
- Weigandin, Ana Maria, c51
- Weight, Goodith, p18
  - o   Isaac, c18
  - o   William, p18
- Weishard, Margretha, s18
- Weisser, Conrad, s34
- Weller, Anna Juiana, p22, p25, p29, p33, s33
  - o   Hieronymus p22, c25, p25, s28, p29, p33, s38, d47
  - o   Johann Friderich, c22
  - o   Johann Heinrich, c33
  - o   Johann Hieronymmus, s23
  - o   Johann Wilhelm, c29
- Wenerich, Benedict, p17
  - o   Christina, p17
  - o   Johannes, c17
- Wennerich, Johann George, r40
- Wenn, Anna p24, p32
  - o   Anna Elsabetha, c24
  - o   Duerch, p24, m44
  - o   Rebecca, c32
  - o   Richard, p32
- Wenne, Jannetje, s50
- Weniger, wife of Ulrich, s30
- Werner, Anna Gertraud, m44
  - o   Appolonia, c19
  - o   Christoph, p19
  - o   Johanna Elisabeth, s19
  - o   Magdalena, p19
  - o   Maria Magdalena, r39
  - o   Michael, s36, 44
- Whoerner, Ludwig Ernst, 42
- Wickhaus, Elisabetha, Maria, p19
  - o   Maria Magdalena, c19
  - o   Peter, p19, s21
- Widerwachs, Andreas, r40, p48
  - o   Anna Barbara, p48
  - o   Anna Cecelia, p20
  - o   Johann Georg, c20
  - o   Johann Henrich, p20
  - o   Henrich, s23, s28
  - o   Maria Catharina, s25
- Widerwachs, Johann Bastian, c48
- Wihler, Edwart, p45
  - o   Robert, M45
- Whihs, Johann, s17

139

Palatine Heads of Families
From
Governor Hunter's Ration Lists
June, 1710 to September, 1714
Compiled from the records in London and Presented to the descendants of the Palatines by
BOYD EHLE. C. E.
From: The Book of Names
Especially Relating to The Early Palatines and the First Settlers in the
Mohawk Valley
Compiled and Arranged by Lou D. MacWethy
Published by The Enterprise and News
St. Johnsville, NY., 1933

Historians in general and descendants of the Palatines in particular have long felt a desire for a more complete list of those Palatine emigrants who settled in New York and along the Hudson under the patronage of Queen Anne of 1710. Documentary History of New York, Vol. III gives a census of those in New York, also those in West Camp, but no mention is made of those in East Camp although it is known that there were unlisted settlements on the east side. During the summer of 1931 Mr. Boyd Ehle through his London agents caused a search of the records there with the result that the ledger accounts of Governor Hunter were consulted and all the names of heads of families drawing rations were copied. Mr. Ehle has arranged them in alphabetical order and indicated their place of residence by the symbols to be found following the name in case where residence is known as follows:

E---East Camp. Soldiers in Canadian Exposition of 1711.

W---West Camp.

N. New York City.

These locations are from the census reports in Doc. Hist., Vol 3. Those not designated are presumed to have been residents of east Camp. No census of this camp has been discovered, but by eliminating those of known location the balance must belong to East Camp.

This kindly service on the part of Mr. Ehle is duly acknowledged by the Enterprise and News on behalf of the descendants of the Palatinate. Surely no kindlier service can be imagined and not only those living today but those who will follow will find reason to be grateful for the thoughtfulness of Mr. Ehle in preserving the precious knowledge for the descendants.

London Letter

The letter accompanying the Ration Lists fromt he London compilers will be of interest and is here given:

Colonial Office Class 5

Vols. 1230-1231.

(Badly classified--1731 is first int he point of order).

These two folio volumes, clearly written and bound in undressed calf are the statement of Gov. Hunter's account against the Government for the subsistence to the Palatines 1710-1713 each having the certificates and the seal of New York in red wax, as noted in Dr. Andrew's Guide. The first is the Journal or account book, No. 1231, the other (1230) is the ledger, each name being posted up in alphabetical order. Both these show the number drawn for by the heads of families or the recipient thus:--2 adults 2 young (i.e. under 10 years): 3 adults 1 young; 1 adults, as the case may be.

Vol. 1231

This journal, as it is called is divided under the following headings:

p. 1. "New York 30 June 1719.

"The Palatines hereafter named for themselves and their families Subsistence, Debtors to the Queen's most Sacred Majesty . . . . . for 4 days subsistance distributed. . . from 27 June to this day at the rate of 6d for persons above 10 years of age and 4d per diem for children under 10 years. . ."

(Then follows names and sums of money to cash).

p. 4 New York 1st July 1710. Similar heading for 4 days 28 june to this day.

p. 10 New York 4th July 1710. Similar heading 4 days 1st July to this day.

p. 14 New York 4th August 1710. Sililar heading 25 days 10th July to this day.

p. 29 New York 4 October 1710. Sililar heading. 61 days 5th August to this day.

p. 45. Mannor of Livingston 31 December 1710. The Platines hereafter named for themselves and their families subsistance debtors to the Queens most Sacred Majesty for Subsistance distributed to the said Palatines from the time of their several arrivals at this place and ye other side Hudson River (the first being ye 6 October) to this day make 89 days.

p. 55 Mannor of Livingston 25 March 1711. . . . for 84 days from 1 January 1711.

p. 66 Mannor of Livingston 24 June 1711. . . .91 days from 26 March.

p. 78 Mannor of Livingston 29 September 1711. . . .97 days from 25 June abating 14 days during which time they had little or no provision.

p. 91. Mannor of Livingston 24 December 1711. . . . .86 days from 30 September.

p. 103. New York 24 December 1711. . . .from 5th October 1710 at New York to 5 October last . . . . .N. B. Those families charged with small sums were sent up to the Settlement last fall, others with large sums were subsisted at New York in the spring following and not sent up till April and May. And the remainder being Widows and Orphans have been sussisted to this time.

p. 117. Mannor of Livingston 25 March 1712. . . . for 92 days from 25 October 1711 to this time.

p. 129 New York 25 March 1712. . . 172 days from 6 October 1711 to this day.

p. 130 Mannor of Livingston 24 June 1712. . . . .91 days from 26 March.

p. 143 Mannor of Livingston 13 September 1712. . . .81 days from 25 June.

A few names added under heading "New York."

P. 155 (no place given) 23 September 1713 for unequal time subsistance from 13 September 1712 to this day.

p. 156 The book is then apparently made up 27 August 1714 and certified and sealed 2 September 1714.

Palatine Heads of Families
Location (N), New York City.
(E) East Camps, Columbia Co., N. Y.
(W), West Camps, Ulster Co., N. Y.
Abelman, John Peter, (N)
Anspach, Johann Balthasar (E)
Anthess, Conrad (his widow)
Arnold, Jacob (W)
Arthopeus, Johan Aloph
Asmer, Philip
Baches, Agnes
Bahr, Johannes, (N)
Bahr, Jacob (widow)
Ballin, Anna Catherin
Barthel, Henrich
Barthelin, Anna Dorothea
Barthin, Anna
Bason, Nicolas
Bast, Johann Henrich
Bast, Jacob, (E)
Bast, Georg
Battorfin, Anna
Batzin, Anna Catherin, (N)
Bauch, Christian, (E)
Baum, Mathias (son of Johan Jost)
Bauman, Adam
Baumannin, Anna Margaretha
Baumarsin, Anna Maria
Bayerin, Anna Margretha
Beck, Adreas Friderich
Becker Peter (W)
Becker, Johan Friderick, (W)
Beckerin, Maria
Beckerin, Elizabetha, Sr. (W)
Beckerin, Elisabetha Jr.
Beckerin, Anna Catharina
Beckerin, Anna Dorothea
Beckerin, Magdalena
Bellin, Elizabetha
Bellinger, Niclaus
Bellinger, Johannes
Bellinger, Marcus, (E)
Bellinger, Henrich, (E)
Bellinger, Elizabetha
Bender, Georg (E)
Bender, Valentin (W)
Bender, Peter, his widow
Benderin, Anna Maria (N)
Berck, Christian
Berg, Johannes
Berg, Abraham
Bergman, Andreas, (E)
Beringer, Conrad
Berleman, Johannes
Berner, Georg Ludwig
Bernhart, Johann Just
Bernhart, Johann Jost
Bernhard, Johannes, (E)
Bernhard, Ulrich (E)
Bertin, Gerhard Berter and Anna
Bertram, Jacob
Betzer, Herman (E)
Beryer, Johan Jacob
Beyerin, Susanna
Bierman, Johannes
Blass, Johannes, (E)
Bohler, Johan Henrich
Bohm, Henrich
Bollin, Sophia
Bonn, Franz le Febure
Bonnenstiel, Niclaus
Bonroth, Phonnes, (E)
Borne, Jacob
Borsch, Ludwig

Borst, Jacob
Boshaar, Jacob
Boshaar, Johann Jacob
Bousche, Daniel
Brackin, Anna Catharina
Brack, Johan Michael
Bradaw, Wilhelm (W)
Bradorff, Jost
Braun, Johann Jost
Braun, Johann Paul
Brendel, Caspar
Bressler, Valentin, (N)
Bretter, Anthoni
Bregel, Georg (E)
Brillin, Anna Margretha
Brillemannin, Helena, (N)
Bronnwasser, Anna Gertrude
Brong, Mattheus (N)
Bruchle, Henrich
Bruyere, Susanne
Bruyere, Jeanne (N)
Boff, Johann Georg
Buck, Martin
Brucher, Ulrich
Burckhard, Johannes
Bouche, Daniel
Busch, Daniel, Sr. (E)
Borsch, Elizabeth
Capulscher, Joann, Jacob
Cast, Johannes
Castner, Johann Conrad
Castner, Johann Peter
Champanois, Daniel
Christman, Hanns
Christmannin, Elizabeth
Chevenius, Bernhard
Conrad, Henrich, (E)
Conradin, Anna
Dachastatter, Georg (E)
Dahles, Johan Wilhelm (E)
Danler, Ulrich
Dannemarcker, Christoph (N)
Darrey, Conrad
Dather, Lorentz
Datt, Johann Bernhard
Dansweber, Melchoir, (N)
Deffer, Daniel, (N)
Demuth, Jacob (N)
Demuthin, Anna Catharina
Demuthin, Anna Maria (W)
Demuthin, Agnes
Deubig, Johann Paul
Dietrichin, Anna Elizabetha (W)
Drerenbach, Conrad and his mother Anna
Diewel, Johannes, (N)
Diewel, Johann Peter (W)
Deuchert, Werner (E)
Dill, Annanias
Dill, Wilhelm (E)
Dillin, Anna Clara

Dillenbachin, Barbara and son Martin (E)
Dilteyin, Catharina
Dinant, Peter
Dings, Jacob (E)
Dorn, Lazarus
Dorner, Johannes, (N)
Dorner, Jacob
Dornheiser, Jacob
Dontzbachin, Anna Elisabetha
Dontizbach, Franz
Dopff, Johan Peter (E)
Draurh, Ludwig, his widow
Drechsler, Peter
Dreuthin, Catharina
Dreuthin, Elisabetha
Drumm, Andreas
Drumbaur, Niclaus
Duntzer, Paulus
Eigenbrodt, Elizabeth
Eberhard, Johannes, (W)
Eckling, Johann Georg
Eckhard, Adam
Eckhard, Niclaus (E)
Eckhardin, Gertrude (W)
Ehemann, Tomas (W)
Ehlig, Andreas (N)
Eigler, Christian
Elasser, Paul
Emichen Johan Ernst
Emich, Johan Niclaus
Emmerich, Johannes
Emmerich, Johan Michael (W)
Emrichin, Anna Maria (W)
Engel, Johannes (N)
Engelin, Maria Elizabetha
Englebert, Johan Peter
Engesbrucher, Niclaus
Engelsbrurger, Tilleman
Enners, Bertram
Erbin, Catharina, (N)
Erckel, Bernhard (N)
Erhard, Simon
Eschenreuter, Henrich
Eschoffin, Catharina
Eschideins, Thomas, his widow
Ess, Jacob, (E)
Esswein, Jacob
Eygner, Peter (W)
Eygerin, Jeremia
Faeg, Peter
Faeg, Johannes (E)
Fahling, Henrich (E)
Falck, Arnold (N)
Falckenburg, Johann Wilhelm (W)
Fasius, Valentin
Fasius, Johannes
Feller, Niclaus (E)
Fewersbach, Dietrich (N)
Fiddler, Gottfriend, (W)
Fills, Wilhelm Philip

Fills, Philip
Finck, Johann Wilhelm
Finck, Frantz (E)
Finck, Andreas
Finckin, Magdalena
Foltz, Melchoir
Finckel, Johan Philip
Fischer, Peter
Fischer, Sebastian
Fulger, Zacharias
Forster, Johan Georg
Franck, Johannes (W)
Fred, Johan Georg
Freil, Christopher
Frey, Henrich
Freyerin, Barbara
Freymeyer, Michael
Friderick, Conrad (N)
Friderick, Hanns Adam (W)
Frillin, Maria Elizabeth
Fritz, Johann Wilhelm
Frolich, Stephen (W)
Frollich, Valentin
Fuchs, Johann Christoph (E)
Fucks, Johann Philip
Fucks, Johann Peter (N)
Fuhrer, Johannes
Funck, Peter
Fuhrman, Jacob
Gieserin, Sibilla
Galdach, Anna Maria (N)
Gantz, Johannes
Gebelin, Anna Margretha
Georg, Johann Anthoni
Georg, Johann Wilhelm (E)
Georgin, Anna Elizabetha
Gerlach, Peter, (N)
Gerlach, Johann Christ (W)
Gerlachin, Otilla
German, Jacob
Gesinger, Henrich (N)
Getel, Daniel, his widow
Getmannin, Barbara
Giesler, Peter (W)
Glump, Philipp
Getmannin, Maria Barbara
Glock (Klock) Henrich
Goldman, Conrad (E)
Gondermann, Johann Friderick
Grad, Johannes
Grauberger, Philipp Peter
Graw, Gerlach, his widow
Grawsin, Anna Maria
Greisler, Johann Philipp (N)
Gresserin, Maria Elizabetha
Griffon, Marie
Griot, Jean
Grucko, Arnold
Gruco, Johann Peter
Hammin, Gertrude

Haas, Simon
Haas, Niclaus
Haber, Christian (E)
Hahn, Johann Georg
Hagedorn, Peter
Hagedorn, Johann Peter (E)
Hager, Johann Friderick
Hagerin, Maria
Haintz, Urbanus
Hambuch, Johann Wilhelm (E)
Hamer, Johann Henrich (E)
Hamm, Peter
Hamm, Conrad
Harter, Johann Niclaus
Harter, Johann Michael
Hartman, Johann Hermann
Hartman, Peter
Hartmanin, Anna Maria
Hartwig, Caspar (N)
Hartel, Adam (W)
Hasel, Wilhelm
Haselin, Johan Henrich
Hassman Dietrich
Haupt, Philipp
Haugh, Lucas, his widwo
Haug, Plaichard
Haus, Johann Christian
Hayd, Niclaus (E)
Hayd, Peter (E)
Haydin, Maria Cunigunda
Hayder, Henrich
Hebmann, Michael, (N)
Heel, Jacob
Heydelbert, George Jacob
Heyner, Johannes
Heytersbach, Niclaus (N)
Helmer, Philipp (W)
Helmer, Peter
Hemmerle, Anna Barbara
Henneschield, Michael (N)
Henrich, Lorentz
Herman, Jost
Herner, Ludwig Ernest
Hertzel, Jacob
Hertzog, Henrich, his widow
Hess, Johannes
Hess, Niclaus
Hefferick, Johannes
Heffick, Johannes Conrad
Heusen, Johan Peter
Heydin, Anna Maria
Heydorn, Henrich
Hildebrand, Anna Catharina
Hirchemer, Georg
Hoff, Johan Adam
Hoff, Andreas
Hofferlin, Anna Maria
Hoffin, Margaretha
Hoffmann, Gabrial
Hoffman, Herman (N)

Hoffmann, Jacob
Hoffmann, Conrad
Hoffmann, Heinrich (E)
Hoffmannin, Anna Eva
Hoffmannin, Anna Catharina
Homburger, Thomas
Honingen, Michael
Horne, Johan
Horne, Caspar
Hornich, Niclaus
Horning, Gerhard
Hothenrothin, Veronica
Huckin, Barbara
Huls, Christoph
Hummel, Georg
Hummel, Herman
Huner, Benedict
Huppert, David (E)
Hussmann, Johann Adam
Hussman, Herman
Iffland, Johann David
Ingold, Ulrich
Ittich, Johann Michael
Jacobi, Ulrich
Jager, Wendel
Jager, Christian
Jamin, Peter
Jung, Johann Eberhard
Jung, Peter
Jung, Henrich, (E)
Jungin, Maria
Jung, Johannes, (N)
Jungin, Anna Elizabeth
Jung, Theobald
Jungin, Juliana
Jungens, Niclaus, (N)
Kabsin, Anna Sibilla
Kahl, Johann Wilhelm
Kamer, Johann Wilhelm (E)
Kang, Johan Peter
Kaschelin, Anna Margretha
Kasselmann, Christian (N)
Kasselmann, Dietrich
Kast, Johann Georg
Kayser, Johann Wilhelm (W)
Kayser, Johann Matheus (W)
Kayserin, Maria
Kasin, Eva Catharina
Keller, Christian, his widow
Keller, Frantz (N)
Kercherin, Anna Maria
Kessler, Johannes, (E)
Kesselerin, Anna Maria
Kefler, Henrich
Kieffler, Johan William
Kiesler, David
Kirtzenberg, Elizabetha
Klapperin, Anna Agatha
Kleinin, Helena
Kleins, Peter, his widow

Klein, Hyeronimus, (N)
Klein, Johannes
Klein, Johann Jacob
Klein, Johan Herman
Klein, Henrich
Klein, Adam
Klapp, Peter
Klotter, Henrich
Klotterin, Susanna and Caspar
Klug, Johan Georg
Knab, Ludwig
Kneibin, Helene Sophia
Kneskern, Hans Peter (E)
Kobel, Jacob (E)
Koch, George Ludwig (E)
Koch, George Ludwig (E)
Kocherthal, Joshua (W)
Kohlmeyerin, Catharina
Kolsch, Anna Eva
Kolsch, Johan Henrich
Konig, Marcus
Kopff, Jacob
Kornmann, Peter Jacob, (N)
Korn, Johann Henrich
Korner, Niclaus (W)
Krafftin, Anna Ursula
Kramer, Johannes
Kramer, Anthoni, (W)
Kramer, Anna Maria & Michael (N)
Krantz, Johann Henrich (W)
Krantz, Conrad
Krembs, Johannes
Kugel, Johannes
Kuhlmer, Johannes
Kuhlmann, Georg (W)
Kuhn, Johann Jacob (E)
Kuhn, Samuel (E)
Kuhn, Conrad & Valenin (E)
Kuhn, Valentine (E)
Kohner, Benedict (N)
Kuntz, Jacob 1st
Kuntz, Jacob 2nd
Kuntz, Johannes (W)
Kuntz, Mathias
Kuntz, Matheus
Kurtz, Johan Christop
Labach, Johannes
Laib, Johann Caspar
Lahmeyer, Johannes
Lambertin, Elizabetha (N)
Lamet, Johannes
Lancker, Johannes
Lampmann, Peter
Landgraff, Georg
Langin, Magdalena
Langer, Abraham (E)
Lantin, Anna Catharina
Lappin, Agnes
Lauck, Johan Jacob, his widow
Lauck, Abraham

Laucks, Johann Niclaus (E)
Laux, Philipp (E)
Laux, Johann Philipp
Laux, Johan Jost
Laux, Johannes
Laux, Georg
Laux, Dietrich
Laux, Johann Dietrich
Lawer, Peter
Lehemann, Wilhelm
Lehr, Johannes (W)
Leicht, Henrich (N)
Leicht, Ludwig (N)
Leick, Johannes
Lein, Conrad (N)
Lenckin, Marla Catharina, her son
Lepper, Philipp Hermann his widow
Lesch, Balthasar
Lescherin, Magdalena
Leyer, Johannes (E)
Lickard, Bernhard (N)
Lincken, Johan Wilhelm
Linsin, Apolonia (W)
Loscher, Sebastian
Lohin, Anna Catharina
Lucas, Georg
Lucas, Francois
Ludwig, Johann Henrich
Lutzin, Magdalena
Lutzin, Anna Barbara
Madebachin, Elnora
Maisinger, Conrad
Maisinger, Sebastian & Niclaus
Manck, Jacob (W)
Mann, Henrich (W)
Marterstock, Albrecht Dietrich (W)
Marvin, Maria Magdalena
Mathesin, Ann
Mattheus, Johann Martin
Matheus, Andreas
Matheus, George (E)
Matheus, Henrich (W)
Maul, Johann Friderich (N)
Maul, Johannes & Widow (N)
Maul, Christoph
Mauer, Georg
Mauer, Johan Georg
Mauer, Peter (W)
Mauser, Johan Georg
Mausin, Eva
May, Christoph,his widow
Mayin, Otillia
May, Peter
Mengilin, Anna Maria (N)
Menges, Johannes
Metgen, Ferdinand
Merckel, Frederick (W)
Mertzin, Anna Catharina
Mess, Henrich
Messerin, Anna Margretha (N)

Meyer, Christian (W)
Meyer, Henrich
Meyer, Friderick
Meyer, Henrich
Meyerin, Elizabeth
Meyin, Meyin (N)
Meyin, Barbara
Meysenheim, Anna Gertrud
Michael, Hans Henrich
Michael, Johan Georg
Michael, Niclaus
Milch, Johan Eberhard
Milges, Johan Wilhelm
Minckler, Killian
Mittler, Johannes
Mohin, Maria, (N)
Moor, Henrich (W)
Moor, Johan Christ
Moor, Philipp Wilhelm
Morelin, Anna Eva (N)
Motsch, Johannes
Muller, Adam
Muller, Johann Christoph
Muller, Johann Wilhelm
Muller, Johannes, 1st
Muller, Johannes, his widow
Muller, Johannes, 2nd
Muller, Adam
Muller, Philipp 1st (W)
Muller Philipp 2nd
Muller, Phillip 2nd, his widow
Muller, Johann Conrad
Muller, Johann Henrich
Mullerin, Christina
Muller, Samuel
Muller, Johann Georg (E)
Mullerin, Catharina (N)
Mullerin, Anna Maria
Mullerin Anna Margretha
Mullerin, Anna Margretha
Musinger, Jacob
Musig, Johan Jost
Musig, Viet (E)
Neff, Georg Friderick, (N)
Nehr, Carl (E)
Nelles, Johan Gerog (E)
Nellesin, Maria Elizabeth
Nelles, Johan Wilhelm (E)
Nerbel, Johan Georg
Ness, Georg Wilhelm his widow
Netzbackes, Johan Martin (E)
Newkirch, Johan Henrich (N)
Netthaber, Quirness
Neiss, Abraham, his widow (N)
Noll, Bernhard
Nollin, Anna Margaretha
Oberbach, Peter (W)
Oberbach, Georg
Oberbach, Johann Peter
Oberer, Johan Jacob his widow

Oberin, Anna
Off, Jacob (N)
Ohrehdorff, Henrich
Pach, Daniel, his widow
Peter, Philipp
Peterin, Anna Gertrude
Petri, Gertrude
Petri, Johan Jost (E)
Pfeffer, Michael, his widow (N)
Pfeiffer, Severin, his child
Pfeiffer, Henrich, his widow
Pfuhl, Johan Peter
Philips, Peter
Planck, Johannes, (N)
Piles, Emerich
Poffner, Johannes Paul
Propperty, Johann Jost
Prunet, Paul
Pulver, Johan Wilhelm
Rabel, Daniel
Rainault, Peter
Rainault, Pierre
Rauch, Niclaus
Raudenbusch, Johann, his widow
Rausch. Caspar, (E)
Ray, Niclaus
Rawin, Anna Joh & Georg
Reich, Balthasar
Reichard, Joseph (W)
Reiffenberg, Johann Georg, (E)
Reinbold, Matheus (E)
Reisdorff, Johannes
Reitzbackes, Johannes (W)
Retischuff, Johan Paul (E)
Reuther, Henrich
Rickardt, Conrad
Richter, Andreas (N)
Richausin, Christina
Reidtin, Anna Chatharina
Reidt, Johann Reonhard
Riegel, Christoph
Riehl, Gottfried, (W)
Rietich, Johann Peter
Reitichin, Amalia
Reisch, Jacob (E)
Ritznig, Johannes
Rohrbachin, Anna Elizabeth
Romsch, Christian
Romer, Georg (N)
Roos, Andreas (W)
Roschmann, Johannes (N)
Rosenbaum, Bernhard
Rosenweig, Agnes Gertrude
Rothin, Anna Catherin (N)
Rouch, Friderich
Rues, Ludwig
Ruffner, Thomas
Ruger, Johann Philipp
Ruch. Niclaus
Salbach, Johannes

Salbach, Johann Edmund
Saxin, Anna Gertrude
Saxin, Anna Maria (N)
Schaff, Wilhelm (E)
Schaffer, Friderich (E)
Schaffer, Johannes
Schaffer, Joseph
Schaffer, Georg (W)
Schaffer, Reinhard (E)
Schaffer, Johann Werner (E)
Schaffer, Jacob (W)
Schaffer, Jost Henrich
Schaffer, Gerhard (E)
Schaffer, Johann Niclaus
Schafferin, Elizabeth
Schafferin, Maria Elizabetha
Schafferin, Maria Margretha (N)
Schaib, Hyeronimus (W)
Schaid, Anthon
Schantz, David
Schawerin, Magdalena
Schawerman, Conrad (E)
Schell, Christian S 115
Schell, Johannes S 115
Schellin, Anna Margretha
Schellin, Anna Gertrude
Schenckel, Jonas
Schenckelberg, Christina
Scherl, Jacob
Scherer, Johann Theobald
Scherer, Ulrich, his widow
Schermann, Henrich (N)
Schienck, Michael
Schlicherin, Anna Margretha
Schleffer, Philipp (E)
Schieumer, Mathias, (W)
Schley, Johann Peter
Schmidt, George Adam
Schmidt, Adam his widow
Schmidt, Johann Adam
Schmiden, Elizabetha
Schmidt, Johann Georg (E)
Schmidt, Georg Volbert & Adam
Schmidt, Henrich, Sr. (N)
Schmidt, Henrich, Jr.
Schmidt, Johann Henrich (E)
Schmidt, Ludwig (E)
Schmidt, Martin
Schmidt, Johann Wilhelm
Schmidt, Niclaus
Schmidt, Peter (E)
Schmidt, Valentin
Schmidt, Ulrich
Schmidin, Gertrude
Schmidin, Anna Barbara
Schmidin, Margretha, Ada & Michael (N)
Schneiderin, Catharin & Peter
Schneider, Jacob
Schneider, Henrich
Schneider, Jacob

Schneider, Johannes 1st (E)
Schneider, Johannes 2nd (N)
Schneider, Johann Wilhelm, Sr. (N)
Schneider, Johann Wilhelm, Jr.
Schneider, Johann Dietrich
Schneider, Johann Wilhelm (E)
Schnell, Jacob (E)
Schottin, Anna Maria
Schramm, Henrich
Schreiber, Albertus
Schremle, Henrich (W)
Schuch, Johann Wilhelm
Schuch, Johannes (E)
Schucherin, Anna Catharin
Schultheis, Johannes (E)
Schultheir, Johann Georg
Schultheisin, Anna Barbara
Schultzin, Anna Elizabetha
Schumacher, Jacob
Schumacher, Thomas, (E)
Schumacher, Daniel (N)
Schumacherin, Anna Eva
Schunemann, Hermann
Schuppmann, Herman
Schultz, Michael & Andreas (E)
Schultz, Johann Adam
Schutz, Adam
Schutz, Philip 1st
Schutz, Catharina & Philipp 2nd (W)
Schwalb, Johannes, (E)
Schwedin, Anna Elizabetha (W)
Schwitzler, Henrich
Seber, Jacob S 115
Segendorff, Johann Adam (E)
Seibs, Henrich, his widow
Sein, Johann Peter (E)
Selher, Johann Adam
Seuberb, Johann Martin
Sex, Henrich, his widow (E)
Sibelin, Anna Getha
Signer, Johannes, his widow (N)
Simendinger, Ulrich (N)
Simon, Philipp, his widow
Simon, Whilhelm
Simonin, Anna Margretha
Simonin, Maria Magdalena
Sittenich, Christian (E)
Spanheimer, Johann Georg (W)
Speder, Johannes
Speichermann, Sebastian
Spickermann, Johann Herman
Spies, Peter (E)
Spoon, Henrich
Spuler, Jacob
Stahl, Henrich
Stahl, Johannes
Stahl, Rudolph (E)
Stahl, Joseph
Stayger, Niclaus
Stayger, Stephen

Stambuchin, Anna Margretha
Staringer, Niclaus
Stein, Martin
Sterenberger, Jacob (N)
Stier, Jost
Stockelin, Anna Maria
Stoppelbein, Peter
Storr, Michael (N)
Straub, Johannes, (W)
Streithin, Magdalena (W)
Streith, Christian (N)
Stickhauser, Balthaser
Stubenrauch, Georg Henrich (W)
Stuber, Henrich Balthaser (E)
Stuber, Jacob
Stuckrad, Johann Wilhelm (N)
Stumpff, Johan Georg
Stupp, Martin
Stuz, Johan Dietrich
Taschen, Hubert
Theis, Johan Philipp (E)
Thiel, Adolph
Thomas, Henrich
Thomas, Andreas
Thomas, Henrich Peter
Thomas, Johann Georg
Taberin, Anna Maria
Trilheuser, Johannes (N)
Uhl, Carol
Uhl, Henrich
Ulrich, Johannes Elias
Umbertro, Valentin
Vandeberg, Cornelius
Velten, Johann Wilhelm
Vogt, Simon (N)
Volbert, Jacob, his widow
Vollandin, Anna Regina
Wagner, Johann Christ
Wagner, Peter
Walrath, Gerhard
Walborn, Johan Adam (E)
Wallrath, Henrich Conrad
Wannemacher, Dietrich (N)
Wannemacher, Peter
Wanner, Ludwig
Warembourg, Maria
Warno, Jacob (E)
Weber, Henrich
Weber, Valentin
Weber, Niclaus (E)
Weber, Jacob (E)
Weber, Wigand
Weberin, Otillia
Wegle, Michael
Weydknecht, Andreas (N)
Weidschopff, Johann Peter
Weillin, Catharina
Weis, Stephen
Weis, Mathias
Weisborn, Georg

Weiser, Johann Conrad (E)
Weisin, Susanna (N)
Weller, Hyeronimus (W)
Wendeling, Anna Juliana
Wennerich, Balthasar (N)
Wennerich, Benedict
Werner, Michael
Weydin, Gertrude
Wickhausen, Peter (N)
Widerwachs, Henrich (E)
Wies, Melchoir
Wilhelm, Paul
Wilhelm, Anthony, his widow
Wilhelm, Niclaus, his widow
Windecker, Hartman (E)
Winniger, Ulrich
Winther, Henrich (E)
Wisener, Johannes
Wittman, Johan Martin
Wittmachin, Maria Catharina
Wolleben, Peter (W)
Wohleben, Philipp (W)
Wohleben, Christoph
Wohleben, Valentin (W)

Wohleben, Michael
Wohleben, Anna Catharina
Wolbach, Engelbert
Wolbert, Niclaus
Wolffin, Anna Gertrude
Wolffin, Maria Clara
Wolffin, Maria Catharina
Wormbs, Christian
Woschel, Peter Anthoni
Woschel, Augustin
Wulffen, Gottfried
Wurhmserin, Anna (N)
Wust, Conrad
Zangerin, Johannes (N)
Zehe, Johannes (E)
Zeller, Johann Henrich
Zeller, Johannes, (E)
Zerbe, Philipp (E)
Zerbe, Martin
Zimmerman, Johan Jacob
Zipperle, Bernhard
Zufeld, Johan Gerog
Zwickin, Veronica (N)

847 names

A Review of the Food List
By Boyd Ehle
The Book of Names
Especially Relating to The Early Palatines and the First Settlers in the
Mohawk Valley
Compiled and Arranged by Lou D. MacWethy
Published by The Enterprise and News
St. Johnsville, NY., 1933

Differences in the name spelling are noted below.

List --------Variations
Bauman-Bowman
Bernhard-Barnhart
Beyer-Baer-Behr
Boshaard-Boshart
Brach-Brock
Braum-Brown
Busch-Bush
Cast-Kast
Christman-Cristman-Chrisman
Dachstatter-Dagsstatter-Dockstader
Deuchert-Deichert-Dygart
Dillenbach-Dillebag-Tillebagh-Dillenbeck

Echard-Eacker-Aker
Fahling-Fehling-Failing
Fischer-Fisher
Franch-Frank
Frolich-Fraley-Fraleigh
Friderick-Frederick
Fucks-Fox

Gerlach-Garlob-Garlock
Giesler-Geesler-Keesler
Conderman-Conterman-Countryman
Glock-Klock-Clock
Harter-Herter
Hartwig-Hartwick
Hayd-Haight
Henrich-Henry
Hirchemer-Herkomer-Herkimer
Hoffman-Huffman
Horne-Horn
Huls-Hultz
Ittich-Ittig
Jager-Yager
Jung-Young
Kasselman-Casselman
Kayser-Kaiser-Keyser
Kneskern-Knieskern
Koch-Cook
Kolsch-Kolesch
Krembs-Crems-Gramps
Laib-Lipe
Lancker-Leninger
Laucks-Laux-Loucks
Manck-Mang

149

Meyer-Mayer-Maiers
Muller-Miller
Nehr-Heher
Nelles-Nellis
Noll-Knoll
Petri-Patrie-Petrie
Pfeiffer-Piper
Reichard-Richard
Rouch-Rauch
Shawerman-Showerman
Scherer-Shearer
Scherman-Sherman
Specher-Spraker
Schienck-Schenck
Schmidt-Smith
Schneider-Snyder

Schnell-Snell
Schultheis-Shults
Schumacher-Shoemaker-Schoonmaker
Salzman-Saltsman
Sutx-Suits
Seybert-Seibert-Sibert
Spoon-Spohn
Staringer-Staring-Starin
Stompff-Stumf
Thiel-Tiel-Teall
Wagner-Waggoner
Wannemacher-Wannemaker
Zehe-Zeh
Zimmerman-Timmerman
Zeller-Zoller

The list also enables some corrections to be made in local history that Hendrick Frey came with the Palatines in 1709 instead of in 1689 as stated by Simms in his Frontiersmen. This correction is also confimed by the London List. It is also noted that Herkimers appear in this 1709 emigration which is a correction to Benton's History of Herkimer county. The Zollers also appear in the 1709 list which is a variation from the family tradition.

It will be noted that many family names have "in" added which is merely the German way of indication of female members of the family and does not indicate another family.

Yours truly, BOYD EHLE

Those Who Fought
The meaning of Militia is - " The military force of a nation."

Pension Applications. Some records are presented in an almost complete form because they are interesting. In reading the applications, you will note that just about every season a man would sign up for a different service. Usually the time of service was during the good weather, about nine months. These records are from a variety of services, Continental, New York Line, Levies, Rangers, Militia.

To read the Pension Applications, scan them until you reach an interesting part and then read more thoroughly. Supporting pieces which were "annexed" were not usually included, the material was duplicative. In some cases, a letter from the research done years ago was included in the pension papers, and this was included in these instances especially when the application itself was not in good condition. When the application could not be read, you will find ??? in place of a missing word.

Pension Application for Daniel Frederick Bakeman
(Last pensioned soldier and last pensioned widow of the Revolution. These two were not married, they are separate cases.

This application is almost impossible to read. It appears the application was made June 17, 1867 when the soldier was 107 years of age and lived in the County of Wyoming. He died April 5, 1869 aged 109 years. He served four years in the Revolutionary War, the last four years of the war. His application really does not tell much about where he served, if at all. It is a very short application and not really legible.

He served in Col. Marinus Willett's Regiment. He said the papers were burned about 70 years ago and he has no proof of service. Apparently he was not questioned too closely and of course he could produce no witnesses. His pension was $500.00 per annum commencing 1st July 1866.

Included in the papers is the following letter. Please note the two were not husband and wife, and are separate cases.

August 23, 1933
Mr. John Nix
6683 Hollywoof Blvd.
Hollywood, California

Dear Sir:
Reference is made to your request for verification as to the last of the Revolutionary War pensioned soldiers to survive and the last pensioned widow of a Revolutionary War soldier to survive.

Daniel Frederick Bakeman who died April 5, 1869 at Freedom, New York, was the last to survive of the pensioned soldiers of the Revolution. His formal application for pension was executed June 17, 1867, and at that time he stated that he was one hundred seven years of age and was living in Freedom, New York.

Esther S. Daman or Damon who was the widow of Noah Daman or Damon and who died November 11, 1906 in Plymouth Union, Vermont was the last pensioned widow of a Revolutionary War Soldier to survive.

This is in answer to your request made to the War Department and transmitted to this office.
Very truly yours,
A.D. Hiller
Assistant to Administrator

Pension Application for Barent Becker

State of New York
Schoharie County
On this fifth day of February in the year of our Lord one thousand eight hundred and thirty-three, personally appeared in open court before the judges of the Court of Common Pleas of the County of Schohaire in the state aforesaid, Barent Becker a resident from the Town of Middleburgh in the said County of Schoharie and State aforesaid, who being first duly sown according to law doth on his oath make the following declaration in order to obtain the benefit of the Act of Congress passed June 7th 1832.

That he entered the service of the United States under the following named officers and served as herein after sated.

That in the year 1780 this deponent lived in the town of Schohaire and County of Albany now called the Town of Middleburgh situate in the County of Schohaire, that in the month of October of said year to wit 1780, the particular day this deponent does not recollect, he this deponent volunteered as a militia man in the service of the United Sates and was stationed at the Middle Fort in the Town of Schohaire and County of Albany, since changed into the Town of Middleburgh and County of Schoharie.

That this deponent as such volunteered and served under one Col. Peter Vrooman.

That this deponent does not recollect the names of the under officers, that this deponent together with others, volunteered in services for the defense of said Middle Fort and to repel the attack of one John Johnson who with about eight hundred men was endeavoring to take and get possession of said Middle Fort. That Col. Peter Vrooman succeeded one Major Woolsey in the command of the militiaman stationed at said fort.

That said Major Woolsey had about surrendered said Middle Fort into the hands of the British and Tories under command of said Johnson when the aforesaid Col. Peter Vrooman took command of the soldiers then stationed and defended said fort and prevented it from falling into the hands of the British.

That this deponent is confident and therefore expressly declares that he served faithfully as such volunteer full two months being from the middle of October until the middle of December 1780.

This deponent further declares that on the first of April 1781 he this deponent enlisted into the army of the Revolution for the period of nine months. That he served faithfully in that part of the State in New York then called Schohaire in the County of Albany but since called the County of Schohaire. That he served under on Captain Hale.

That said Captain Hale's Company was stationed principally at the Middle Fort aforesaid. That said Fort during the nine months service of this deponent was commanded by one Col. Peter Vrooman. That during said term of service. He this deponent was in the battle fought against the British and Indians near the head of the Delaware River. That this deponent was under the command of Capt Hale in said battle. That this deponent was one of a scouting party who surprised said party of Indians and Tories at a place then called Harpersfield.

That there was a battle took place between the scouting party of which this deponent was one, and the Tories and Indians at said place. That the party to which this deponent belonged as aforesaid, were repulsed with the loss of two men. That said scouting party restrained until they met Col. Peter Vrooman with his army. That then the army under command of Col. Peter Vrooman advanced to the attack of said party of Indians and Tories but upon reaching the place then called Harpersfield near the head of the Delaware River, they discovered that said party of Indians and Tories had retreated and left that place. That then Col. Peter Vrooman with the Soldiers under his command returned to the said Middle Fort. That this deponent during said nine months service was frequently out as one of a scouting party sent out to discover the situation of the enemy forces. That at the expiration of his said term of service to wit, the first of January 1782, he this deponent was honorably discharged but that his discharge is now lost and cannot be found.

And this deponent further declares that in the month of May 1782 he this deponent was ordered out as a militiaman and served under Captain George Rytchmeyer and in Col. Peter Vrooman's Regiment.

That this deponent was stationed the principal part of the time at the Middle Fort in Schoharie aforesaid.

That he frequently served as sentry at said Middle Fort and was frequently sent out in scouting parties in various parts of the counties of Tryon and Albany.

And this deponent further declares that he faithfully served as such militiaman for the full period of seven months being from the first of May until the first of December 1782.

And this deponent further declares in answer to the Interrogatories presented by the War Department that he was born in the Town of Schoharie and County of Albany. Since changed into the Town of Middleburgh and County of Schoharie.

That he was born about the year 1762 but he cannot state positively how old he is, but to the best of his information and belief he is now about 70 years of age. That he has no record of his age and his parents have long been dead nor does he know of the existence of any church or other record of his age.

And this deponent further declares that he is now infirm and in indigent circumstances; that he has for a long time been affected with a Rheumatic affliction, which has deprived him of the use of his limbs and entire incapacitated him for any kind of labor, and this cut him off from his only source of support.

That petitioner hereby relinquishes every claim whatever to a pension or annuity except the present and declares that his name is not on the pension roll of the agency of any state.

Sworn to and subscribed the day and year aforesaid.

John Gobhard, Clerk
Signed by Barent, Becker

Pension Application for Francis Becraft

State of New York
Schoharie County

On this twelfth day of November in the year of our Lord, one thousand eight hundred and thirty two personally appeared in open court before the judges of the court of open and Examiner??? Held in and for the county of Schoharie and state aforesaid now sitting Francis Becraft, a resident of the town and county of Schoharie and State of New York aged seventy three years and five months, who being first duly sworn according to law, doth on his oath make the following declaration in order to obtain the benefit of the act of Congress passed June 7, 1832. That he entered the service of the Untied States under the following named officers and served as herein stated.

He entered the service as a volunteer in the month of August, he thinks it was, in the year 1778, in Captain William Deitz's company in Colonel Peter Vrooman's regiment. The company was then commanded by Lieutenant Mattice Shultes, Captain Deitz having been a few days before taken prisoner by the Indians, and his father, mother, wife and all his children murdered and scalped by the Indians and he taken to Canada. The company was stationed at Merdman's Fort at a place called Beverdam in Albany County in the State of New York about ten or twelve miles from the lower fort in Schoharie, that he joined the company there and continued to serve in it for the space of three months and was discharged at the fort in the month of November, that his discharge was not in writing that when he entered the service he lived at a place now called Rensselaerville in the county of Albany and the state of New York.

That in the spring of the year 1779 in the month of April he thinks it was, he again entered the service as a volunteer in the same company and regiment and was stationed at the same fort above mentioned that he continued to serve in the company till sometime in the month of November when he was discharged at the place aforesaid.

That again in the spring of the year 1780, he entered the service in the same company and regiment and was stationed at the same place as before and continued in the service till sometime in November when he was discharged. That during the term of service they were a good part of the time employed in building another fort at Beverdam aforesaid about two miles from the one where they were stationed.

In the spring of the year 1781 sometime in the month of April he thinks it was he entered the service again as a volunteer in the same company and regiment as before said, that they were stationed at the many forts in Beverdam aforesaid in the county of Albany aforesaid, that he continued to serve in said company till late in the fall when he was discharged at the fort aforesaid. That he was not in any battle but his chief employment was standing guard on the frontier.

That again in the spring of the year 1780 he again enlisted in the same company and regiment aforesaid at the place aforesaid and continued to serve the said company for about a month when they were all discharged.

That he was in the service in Captain Deitz's company then commanded by Lieutenant Shultes at Beverdam aforesaid in all about two years and six or eight months according to the best of his recollection.

He was born in Hudson in the county of Columbia and state of New York the 12th day of June 1760. That his age is recorded in the church book (the words "High Dutch" are crossed out) at the city of Hudson, Columbia County and state of New York.

That he was living in a place now called Rensselaer Kill in the county of Albany and State of New York where he first entered the service that he has lived since the Revolutionary War in the town of Bern in Albany County till about twenty years ago, he moved to the town and county of Schoharie and state of New York where he has lived ever since and now lives.

That he entered the service each time as a volunteer. He does not recollect the names of any regular officers who were with the troops when he served or of any continental or militia regiments other than the regiment he belonged to. He never received a written discharge.

That he is known to the following persons in his present neighborhood who he thinks can testify to his character for veracity and their belief of his services as a Soldier of the Revolution. To wit: Ezer Nethaway, Peter Nethaway, Robert Burton, Christian Wever, Christian Shafer, John Ingold, Julies W. Throop and others.

He hereby relinquishes every claim whatever to a pension or annuity except the present and declares that his name is not on the pension roll of the agency of any state. ETC.
Francis Beacraft (his mark)

Pension Application for Adam Bellinger

The interesting part about this pension is Lena applied for the benefit with an affidavit from her daughter Ann. In order to establish her age, Ann cites remembering the Great Eclipse in 1806. Here are some interesting excerpts in the pension application. The county where the pension application was made was not legible.

On this 9th day of July 1844 personally appeared before the subscriber, a judge of the court in and for said county, Lena G. Bellinger, a resident of Shelby and said county, aged seventy seven years, who being first duly and sworn to obtain the benefit of the pension made by the act of Congress, passed July 7, 1838, entitled "An Act Ggranting Half Pay and Pensions to Certain Widows"--

That she is the widow of Adam Bellinger who was a soldier in the War of the Revolution; that her husband the aforesaid Adam Bellinger served at Stone Arabia on the Mohawk River at the time of the War of the Revolution; and was a long time in the boating service, for this army on the Mohawk River; and he was in the army as a private in the War of the Revolution under various officers from 1778 or 1779 to the close of its disturbance; Capt Jacob Dievendorf, Capt Peter Suits, Capt House, Col. Clyde, Col. Waggoner, and perhaps Col. Willett, but as to officers, she cannot be sure, but she believes the above named were at least some of those mentioned by her husband, and under whom he must have served. He was in the Battle of Johnstown.

She further declares that she was married to the said Adam Bellinger near Little Falls on the Mohawk River, she believes by Rev. Mr. Rosencrantz in the fall of 1786 seven hundred and eighty six, that her husband the aforesaid Adam Bellinger, died in September 1822 eighteen hundred and twenty-two. That she was not married to him prior to his leaving the service, but the marriage took place previous to the first of January seventeen hundred and seventy five. Viz, prior to the time above stated that she has no family record.
Lena Bellinger (her mark)

Anna Eve Garter of Shelby in said county, aged forty-six years, being born in 1798 seven hundred and ninety eight, after being duly sworn according to law, deposeth and saith that widow Lena G. Bellinger who is applying for a pension as the widow of Adam Bellinger, late a soldier in the War of the Revolution was this deponents father and that this deponent is the fifth child of her said father and mother that she has no doubt of her age, being as stated, that she was of sufficient age at the time of the "Great Eclipse" in 1806 to recollect it distinctly; that she can recollect that she was at that time eight years of age, that she has from a child always understood and believed that her said father resided near the Mohawk River serving the War of the Revolution and that he served in that war as a soldier; that her said father died in September 1822, eighteen hundred and twenty-two, leaving as his widow the said Lena G Bellinger, who still remains his widow.

Anna Eve Bellinger (her mark)

Pension Application for John Borst

State of New York
Schoharie County

On the third day of October 1832 personally appeared before the Justice of the Court of Common Pleas the County of Schoharie now sitting John Borst a resident of the Town of Sharon in the aforesaid County of Schoharie, aged 77 years who being first according to law doth on his oath make the following declarations in order to obtain the benefit of the Act of Congress dated June 7th 1832.

That he entered the service of the United States under the following named officers and served as herein stated.

That the said John Borst enlisted for his term of service of nine months on the first of April 1779 in Schoharie in the State of New York in the company commanded by Captain DuBois in the (Levies) Regiment Commanded by Colonel DuBois (Jim Morrison has this labeled as Colonel Lewis, Dubois' Regiment) in the State of New York with the Continental establishment that he served his term of enlistment out faithfully in first Schoharie, Cobleskill and in the fort in Schoharie and in that vicinity that he was honorably discharged on the first of January 1780 in the fort in Schohaire in the State of New York.

He said that he hereby relinquishes every claim whatever to a pension or annuity except the present and declares that his name is not on the Pension Roll of the agency of any state for any purpose, the interrogations to this applicant he answered that he was born at Cobles Kill and lived ??? and Sharon and ???

That he has not any record of his age, that has been informed and believed the same to be true that he is seventy seven years old that he served in Cobleskill at the time when he enlisted in Captain Dubois' company and Captain Mimtrusk??? Who had served the troops in Colonel Dubois' regiment that he was discharged in Middle fort in Schoharie in the State of New York as he has stated in his declaration.

Sown and subscribed this day and year aforesaid.

John Borst (his Mark)

State of New York
Schoharie County

On the 31st day of December 1838 personally appeased in open Surrogate Court in County named, now sitting held by Jacob Houck Junior Surrogate in the County of Schoharie Christina Borst widow of John Borst deceased, a resident of the Town of Sharon in the County of Schoharie aged 66 years who being first duly sworn according to law doth on her oath make the following declaration in order to obtain the benefit of the provision made by the Act of Congress passed July 7th 1838 entitled an act granting half pay to certain widows.

That she is the widow of the said John Borst, deceased, according to the best knowledge and belief that her husband John Borst deceased was enlisted as private solder in the Army of The Revolutionary War, that he was a pensioner of the United States until to his death that his pension certificate granted and dated March 7th 1833.

She the said Christiana further declares that she was married to the said John Borst on the 13th day of December 1789 before the Rev. Mr. Braffer? Minister of Dutch Reformed Church in Schoharie that her name at the time of marriage was Christina Plogger.

That her husband the aforesaid John Borst died on the 2nd day of July 1834 in the Town of Sharon in the County of Schoharie, that she was not married to him prior to his leaving the service that the marriage took place previous to the first day of January seventeen hundred and ninety-four viz at the time afore stated. She further declares that she never was afterward married that she remains the widow of the said John Borst, deceased, to this day.

Signed with her mark, Christine Borst.

Declaration:

In order to obtain the benefit of the provisions made by the Act of Congress passed July 7th, 1838 entitled An Act Granting Half Pay and Pensions to Certain Widows and the Acts and Resolutions Amending the Same.

State of New York
Schoharie County

On this 3rd day of August 1843 personally appeared before John Westout, Judge of the Court of Common Pleas in and for the County of Schoharie and State of New York, Christina Borst a resident of Cobleskill in said county aged seventy years and upwards who being first duly sworn according to law doth on her oath make the following declaration in order to obtain the benefits of the provisions made by and Act of Congress passed July 7th 1838 entitled An Act Granting Half Pay and Pensions to Certain Widows and the Acts and Resolutions Amending the Same.

That she is the widow of Johannis Borst sometimes called John Borst and sometimes written John Borst Jr. or Johannis Borst Jr. late a resident of the Town of Seward in the County of Schoharie and State of New York who was a pensioner of the United States and who departed this life on the 2nd day of July 1834.

That she is unable to state the particulars of his said husband's services in the War of the Revolution, as she was not married to him until after the said War of the Revolution. She has however frequently heard her said husband say that he did serve during said war and was stationed some of the time at Fort Edward, Fort Stanwix and Herkimer.

That in consideration of said services her said husband was previous to his death enrolled upon the pension list of the United States and received a pension as this deponent was informed of thirty dollars per annum that she has never seen the certificate of her said husband entitling him to said pension and has heard her said husband say that he had never seen the certificate it having been retained by the man who obtained the pension for him but who said the amount was thirty dollars and who annually paid over to him that amount after deducting his fees.

And this deponent has frequently heard her said husband complain that he did not receive by the way of pension as much as was supposed his services entitled him to.

And declarant further saith that he maiden name was Christianna Plogger. That she was married to the said Johannis Borst on the 13th day of Dec. 1789 by a minister of the High Dutch Reformed Church by the name of Coonradt L. Broeffle in the Town and County of Schohaire in the presence of Johannes Koening, Mariah Nichol, Mariah Borst and Henry Borst. That her husband the said Johannis Borst died as aforesaid on the 2nd July 1834. That she is the mother of five children by the said Johannis Borst the start of whom (Mariah) was born 20th Dec. 1790. That she was not married to the said Johannis Borst previous to his leaving the service but that her marriage took place before the first January 1794 to wit at the time before stated and that since the death of the said Johannis Borst as aforesaid she has remained his widow single and unmarried and is still unmarried.

Signed with her mark, Christianna Borst.

Subscribed and sworn the day and year aforesaid before me and I certify that the declarant Christianna Borst is unable (here the page ends).

Letter included in the pension application folder.
Rev. and 1812 War Section
May 1, 1926
Mrs. L. C. Schermerhorn
29 Beuna Vista Ave.
Hawthorne, N.J.

Madam:

I have to advise you from the papers in the Revolutionary War Pension claim W. 20736, it appears that John (Johannis) Borst was born at Cobleskill, New York of German extraction. The date of his birth is not stated.

While residing at said Cobleskill, he enlisted April 1, 1779 and served nine months as a private in Captain Dubois' Company, Colonel Dubois' New York Regiment.

He was allowed pension on his application executed October 3, 1832, while a resident of Sharon, Schoharie County, New York, aged seventy-seven years.

He died July 2nd 1834.

Soldier married December 13, 1789 at Schoharie, New York, Christina (Christiana) Plogger. She was allowed pension on his application executed December 31, 1838, while a resident of Sharon, New York, aged sixty-six years. In 1843 she was living in Cobleskill, New York.

They had five children, three sons and two daughters; only name stated being Mariah (the eldest) who was born; December 20, 1790, she married Jacob Near, and was living in Cobleskill, New York in 1844.

Respectfully,
Winfield Scott
Commissioner.

In a handwritten note the following was written.

I only used the nine months service as claimed by soldier as the other services claimed by widow and witnesses, were never proven nor accepted by this bureau.

Pension Application for John Boyer

The deposition given by Mr. Boyer states he served in Fort Plain, on the north side of the river. Perhaps he had been away from the state too long, but Fort Plain is on the south side of the river.

State of Indiana
Decatur County

On this 24th day of October 1832, personally appeared in open court before the Honorable Judges of the Decatur Circuit Court in and for the County of Decatur now sitting John Boyer a resident of the County of Decatur and State of Indiana aged seventy-two years the 17th day of October 1832 who first being duly sworn according to law doth on his oath make the following declaration in order to obtain the benefit of the act of congress passed June 7th 1832.

That he entered the service of the United States under the following named officers and served as herein stated, that he was drafted to serve in the United States service about the month of September 1779 in the regiment commanded by Peter Bellinger in Captain Samuel Gray's Company and was stationed at Fort Herkimer in the State of New York and served three months and then was discharged until further orders.

That he enlisted in the service of the United States at the Town of Palatine State of New York under Captain Samuel Gray for during the war in the boat service and was stationed on the Mohawk River in the State of New York and followed the Mohawk River from Schenectady to (can't read) enlisted the forepart of January 1780 and was dismissed from service until further orders in the forepart of December following that he volunteered in the service of the United States for nine months in April 1781 in the State of New York and entered the service in Montgomery County then the County of Tryon, Town of Johnstown and joined the regiment commanded by Colonel Willett in the company commanded by Captain Garrett Putman and was stationed part of the times as a guard at Fort Plain on the North Side of the Mohawk River that he was at the Battle at Johnstown and followed the enemy up the Mohawk River to Fort Herkimer and fifth day after the Battle at Johnstown overtook the enemy at Jersey Field and had a skirmish with the enemy and took Lieutenant Wrightman a British officer and nine men. Then followed the British to West Canady Creek where we overtook them and fired on them and killed a British officer by the name of Butler and took twenty-two prisoners and was in the service until about the first day of January following.

And further sayeth that he was born in the Town of Palatine then county of Albany, State of New York on the 17th day of October 1760 and remained in said state until 1823 then removed to the State of Indiana, Decatur County where he now resides.

He hereby relinquishes every claim whatever to pension or annuity except the present and declares that his name is not on the pension roll of any agency or state and that he has no documentary evidence of his service and that he knows of no person whose testimony he can produce who can testify to his service and that he has a record of his age in an old him book (hymnbook) but it is so decayed that is it unilegible and that he had no direct recollection of any of the regular officers. Sworn to and subscribed the day and year aforesaid.
Signed with His Mark (John Boyer)

Pension Application for Valentine Boyer

State of New York
Oneida County

On this day of April, personally appeared before the Hon. Ralph McIntosh, Justice of a Court of Record and Special Surrogate in and for the County of Oneida and state aforesaid. Elizabeth Boyer of the Town of Lenox, County of Madison and State of New York to me made known, aged eighty seven years who being first duly sworn according to law, doth on her oath make the following declaration in order to obtain the benefits of the provisions made by act of Congress passed July 7th 1838, entitled "An Act Granting Half Pay and Pensions to Certain Widows."

That she is the widow of Valentine Boyer deceased, who was a private in the company commanded by Captain John Keyser in a regiment commanded by Jacob Klock in the War of the Revolution.

That he entered the service aforesaid in about the month of _____ A.D. 1776, and continued in active service in said War until the third day of December 1782, as this declarant was informed by her said husband Valentine Boyer deceased and which she truly believes to be true. That she well remembers when said Valentine entered the service or left his home for that, ??? which was, to wit, at the time above set forth and that she was informed afterwards by said

Valentine as well as others who went with him from the same place to wit, Munkier??? in the County of Montgomery and State of New York, that being the place of his residence and when he was drafted or enlisted, that on or about the third day of May A. D. 1781, her husband Valentine Boyer was taken prisoner by the British officers and remained so imprisoned at Bucks Island in Canada for a period of 19 months, and who suffered greatly by the abuses practiced upon him by the British authorities. When on the third day of December A. D. 1782, he was released and honorably discharged as will more fully appear by the proof hereunto annexed. That the number of his certificate of discharge as filed by the proper officer of the United States was No. 38052.

She further declares that she was married to said Valentine Boyer on the 20th day of March in the year of seventeen hundred and eighty. That her husband the aforesaid Valentine Boyer died on the 20th day of August A. D. 1832; that she was married to said Valentine Boyer prior to his leaving the service to wit, at the time above stated as will more fully appear by proof hereunto annexed where reference is made for greater certainty.

And she doth further declare that she is physically disabled to appear in open court is the reason why she appears before the Hon. Ralph McIntosh, Justice of a Court of Record and ??? in and for said County of Oneida in his office in the Village of Vernon in said county and she makes this ???

Signed Elizabeth Boyer (her mark)

Pension Application for George Bush

This soldier fought under Col. Cox in the Battle of Oriskany. Col. Cox supposedly was one of the men who said General Herkimer was afraid of the enemy and this spurred him into action when he should have given more thought to the coming action.

State of New York
County of Montgomery

On the 19th day of September in the year of our Lord one thousand eight hundred and thirty two, personally appeared in open court, before the Judges of the Court of Common Pleas of said County, now sitting, George Bush, a resident of the Town of Minden in the County and state aforesaid, aged eighty seven years in June last, when being first duly sworn according to law, doth on his oath make the following declarations in order to obtain the benefit of the act of Congress passed June 7th 1832. That he entered the service of the United States under the following named officers and served as herein after mentioned.

That in 1776 thinks in the month of June, he enlisted in the services of his country during the pleasure of Congress under Capt John Winn, Lieutenants Severinus Clock and thinks Peter Serarding, that under the above named officers he served in scouting from Cooperstown in the County of Otsego down the Unidilla and Susquehanna Rivers and to the north of the Mohawk River to the head of the West Canada Creek, that some of the time he and those of the same company were stationed at Cooperstown on duty and on guard while others of the company were out scouting in other directions. That he continued so to serve about five months and then procured one William Sixbury to take his place and he was discharged.

That afterwards and about the first of January 1777 he was drafted and called in to service in a company Commanded by Capt Nicholas Wiser, the Regiment was Commanded by Col. Ebeneezer Cox, That they soon thereafter left the Mohawk River at Canajoharie when to Ticonderoga when they with some regular troops, were commanded by Gen'l Hays, remained there in the building fortifications and works for the better defense of County until the forepart of April following when we were discharged and that about a week thereafter he arrived at Springfield the place of his then residence.

That afternoon and about the last of July in the same year on a call of the Militia to meet the enemy, he was again called into service and marched under the Command of the said Captain to Fort Plain when they joined services other companies under Command of Colo. Ebeneezer Cox and then marched up the Mohawk River to Oriskany in the County of Oneida, then Commanded by Gen. Herkimer. That he was then engaged in the Oriskany Battle and was employed in the battle, marching to and from the place of battle and until he arrived home at least two weeks.

That about the middle of July 1778 he was called out from near Fort Plain when he then directed by Capt. Adam Lipe and marched to Springfield on receiving the alarm that the Indians and Tories were destroying that settlement that they arrived at that place, about fifteen miles from Fort Plain, after it was destroyed and then pursued the party of Indians and Tories well to what was called Young's Lake, did not come up with them and then returned to Fort Plain, that he was out on duty at that time about six days.

That in November following when the alarm came that the Indians and Tories were destroying Cherry Valley he was called out and marched to that place, about fifteen miles south of Fort Plain when we arrived after it was destroyed, many men, women, and children murdered and the party had moved off that he stayed assisting in burying the dead and then returned to Fort Plain and that he was out in that service about a week.

That in the month of October 1780 he was again called out with the company to which he then belonged Commanded by Capt. Sefrinus Cook in the Town of Palatine, where he then left to assist Col. Johnson who had the Command of some nine months in an attack upon Sir John Johnson who was then destroying up the north side of the Mohawk River with a party of British troops, Indians, and Tories, that he was engaged in the battle under Col. Johnson against Sir John in Stone Arabia near the Mohawk River when Colo. Johnson was killed and that he was out in service at that time before at and after the battle about two weeks.

That soon after he was drafted by a draft of every third man out of Capt Cook's Company. The men drafted were marched under Command of Capt. Cook to a place called the Royal Grant in the County of Herkimer, north of the little falls and about thirty miles from where he resided in Palatine. That they were then stationed and kept on duty better than two weeks and that he was in service at that time about twenty days.

That in the month of July 1781 he was again called out by his said Capt. Cook, marched with some troops and Militia Men. Commanded by Colo. Willet to a place called Turlock in the Town of Sharon in the County of Schoharie, there engaged with, fought and routed about three hundred Indians and Tories. Commanded by a Tory by the name of Dockstader and that he was in service at that time a week or more.

That besides the service of him in the Revolution above mentioned, he was called out by his officers at many times and to many places up and down and north and south of the Mohawk River in cases of alarm by the expected depredations of the Indians and Tories during the war. That it is entirely out of his power to state the times and places they were so frequent, indeed the savage depredations were almost constant during the summer and fore seasons from 1777 to 1781.

That the service he did during those years which he cannot particularly state but, as he fully believes, amount to at least six months actual duty in the service of his country and that in the most severe and perilous times.

That he has no documentary evidence and that he knows of no person, whose testimony he can procure, who can testify to all his service.

That he was born in Germany in June 1745, came to the Province of New York about nine years before the Revolution. That he has no record of his age.

That he was living in Springfield in the County of Otsego and state aforesaid. When called into service, that during the war he moved to Minden in the County of Montgomery then to Palatine in said county where he lived to the end and about fifteen years after the war, then moved to Minden aforesaid, where he has lived since.

That he was called into service at the time and in the manner above mentioned.

That he cannot state the names of officers of regular troops, Continental or other Regiments or the general circumstances of his service, other than as the same is by him above stated and that he never received a written discharge.

That George D. Ferguson and Peter Young are the names of persons to whom he is known in his present neighborhood, who can testify as to his character for veracity and their belief of his services as a soldier of the Revolution and that there is no clergyman residing in his vicinity.

He hereby relinquishes every claim whatever to a pension or annuity except the present, and declares that his name is not on the pension role of the agency of any state.

Sworn and subscribed the day and year aforesaid. George D. Ferguson, Clerk

George Bush (his mark)

Letter included in his pension application.

August 31, 1937
Miss Harriet M. Willsey

111 East 3rd Avenue
Johnstown, New York

Dear Madam;

Reference is made to your letter in which you request the Revolutionary War record of your ancestor, George Bush, who was born in 1745.

The record has been found of a George Bush who was born in 1745; it may be that of your ancestor. The data given were found in his claim for pension, S. 12355, based upon his service in the Revolutionary War.

George Bush was born in June 1745, in Germany, the exact place of his birth and the names of his parents are not shown. He emigrated to the Province of New York about nine years before the Revolutionary War. At the time he entered service, he resided in Springfield, Otsego County, New York, also resided in Minden and Palatine, in Montgomery County during the period of the war.

George Bush enlisted in June 1776, served as private at various times until July 1781, amounting in all to eleven months and two weeks, under Captains John Winn, Nicholas Weser, Adam Lipe, Severinus Clock, and Colonels Ebenezer Cox, Johnson and Willett in the New York troops; during the period of his service, he was in the Battles of Oriskany, Stone Arabia and Sharon Spring, and was engaged on alarms along the Mohawk River, protecting the inhabitants from the Indians and Tories.

The soldier continued to reside in Palatine, New York, about fifteen years after the war, then moved to Minden, New York.

George Bush was allowed pension on his application executed September 19, 1832, at which time he resided in Minden, Montgomery County, New York where he and continued to reside. The soldier made no reference to wife or children.

In order to obtain the date of last payment of pension, name of person paid, and possibly the date of death of this pensioner, you should write to the Comptroller General, General Accounting Office, this city, and furnish the following:
George Bush
Certificate # 24026
Issued October 25, 1833
Rate $37 per annum
Commenced March 4, 1831
Act of June 7, 1832
New York Agency

Very truly Yours,
A.D. Hiller

Pension Application for Asa Camp, Sergeant

This soldier had some very interesting service, Bunker Hill, White Plains, Valley Forge, served on a naval vessel, which was captured, commanded the guard that dug Major Andre's grave and served at Fort Frederick, which was across the Mohawk River from East Canada Creek.

State of New York
Tioga County

On this 20th day of November 1832, personally appeared in open court before the Judges of the Court of ??? at the once ??? in Owego in and for the said County of Tioga and now in (blotted), Asa Camp a resident of Owego in the County of Tioga and State of New York aged seventy-four years who being first duly sworn according to law doth on his oath make the following declaration in order to obtain the benefit of the act of Congress passed June 7, 1832.

That he entered the service of the United States under the following named officers and served as herein stated.

In the year 1775 He enlisted at South Springfield, Springfield County, Massachusetts under Captain Wolbridge for a term of eight month. The company was attached to the regiment commanded by Colonel David Brewer. He saw the Battle of Bunkershill.

After his discharge which was at the end of the eight months, and in the year 1776 at Brimsfield before mentioned he enlisted and for four months in a company attached to the regiment and commanded by Colonel Holman. The men of the company officers he has forgotten. He marched to New York and was engaged in the Battle at White Plains. At the end of the four months he was discharged and went to Boston whereby went on board an armed vessel called the *Revenge* commanded by Captain Freeman. This was in 1777.

Off the banks of Newfoundland they were engaged by a British vessel which they escaped after a severe battle and arrived at Martinique. Where they took in a cargo of cannon and balls and tools for intrenching???

On their return voyage the vessel was captured by the British and carried with it over first to the island of Burtola, and afterwards to New York from whence he made his escape and returned home, having been absent for seven months. He then enlisted for three months to go to Bristol to guard that place. There was but a single company there and he has forgotten many of the officers.

On the year 1778 he removed into the State of New York, to the County of Albany (then) and the Town of New Concord where he enlisted for a term of nine months into a company attached to the regiment of Colonel Courtland of the Continental Line, the major's name was Fish. He has forgotten the names of the Company Officers. He joined the Regiment at Valley Forge in the State of Pennsylvania. After serving with him the nine months, he returned to New Concord and there in 1779 enlisted under Captain Allen for nine months. The company was attached to the regiment of Col. John Harper from which he received a warrant as the Orderly or first Sergeant of Captain Allen's Company, which post he continued to hold during the nine months for which he enlisted.

That the regiment marched to the German Flatts on the Mohawk River. That he was sent with a Corporal and three men to Germantown to take command of a picket fort there, which he things was called Fort Fredericks. That while there the fort was attacked by a party of Tories and Indians who were however without artillery. He replied to them that there were Yankees in the fort and if they got it, they would get it by the hardest that an attack was made by them on the fort, which was resisted by his party until the enemy desisted and left the place. That he understood from a deserter after the battle that the party of assailants numbered two hundred and fifty of whom the little garrison killed nine and wounded thirteen.

In the year 1780 he enlisted for nine months under Capt. Funday (Fonda) whose company was attached to a regiment commanded by Colonel Willett. He received from the Colonel a Sergeant's warrant and served under his command five months when a division of the company took place and he was attached to a company in the Regiment of Col. Wisenfell called the 4th New York Regiment and there being no sergeant's post vacant in the company he acted as a corporal during the remainder of the nine months during which time Major Andres, the British spy was convicted and he commanded the guard or party which dug the grave of the officer.

Beside the regiments and officers already mentioned he was acquainted with the 1st of New York Regiment under the command of Colonel Van Schaick. He received a written discharge in to instances, one of them from Col. Courtland both of which are lost. He has also lost his warrants appointing him to be sergeant as aforestated they having probably been destroyed by his grand children.

He was born at Rehoboth in Massachusetts on the 14th day of September in 1759. He has always since his recollection understood he has no proof of his age. He has lived in the State of New York since the War of the Revolution and for the last 45 years has resided in the Town of Owego in Tioga aforesaid where he now resides. He is known to Elezar Danke, John R. Drake, John Hollengack, and Charles Brumsilly in his present neighborhood and who can testify as to his character for veracity and their belief in his services as a solder of the Revolution.

He hereby relinquishes every claim whatever to a pension or annuity except the present and declares that his name is not on the pension roll of the agency of any state.
Signed Asa Camp.

The following letter was included in the pension application.

September 17, 1936

Marion B. Brown
912 Fifth Avenue
New York City, New York

Dear Madam:

Reference is made to your letter in which you request information regarding your ancestor, Asa Camp, who served in the New York Regiments, and received a pension.

The date which follows were found in pension claim S. 22673, based upon service of Asa Camp in the Revolutionary War.

Asa Camp was born September 14, 1759 in Rehoboth, Massachusetts; the names of his parents were not given.

While a resident of South Brimfield, Massachusetts, he enlisted early in 1775 and served eight months as private in Captain Salbridge's company, Colonel David Brewer's Massachusetts Regiment; he enlisted in 1776, served four months as private in Colonel Homans' Massachusetts Regiment, name of his captain not given, during which he was in the Battle of White Plains. He went then to Boston, shipped out in 1777, on the small vessel, "*Revenge*". Captain Freeman, was in an engagement off the banks of Newfoundland with a British vessel from which they escaped, but were captured on their return from Martinique, carried to "Burtola" Island and to New York, where he made his escape, length of this service seven months. He served next three months guarding Bristol, names of officers not given. In the year 1778, Asa Camp moved to New Concord, Albany County, New York; he enlisted and served nine months as private in Colonel Cortland's New York Regiment, a part of the time at Valley Forge and afterwards, at Rochester, New York. He enlisted in 1780, served as orderly sergeant and corporal in Captain Allen's Company, Colonel John Harper's and Weisenfels' New York Regiment, was in command at Fort Frederick on the Mohawk River when it was attacked by a party of Indians, and commanded the guard that dug Major Andre's grave. He enlisted in 1782, and served nine months as private in Captain Fonda's Company, Colonel Willett's New York Regiment.

After the Revolutionary War, Asa Camp continued to reside in New York State.

He was allowed pension on his application executed November 20, 1832 at which time he resided in Oswego, Tioga County, New York; he stated then that he had resided in that county forty-five years. The soldier made no references to wife or children, he referred to grand-children, but did not give any names.

In order to obtain the date of the last payment of pension, name of person paid, and possibly the date of death of Asa Camp, you should apply to The Comptroller General, General Accounting Office, Records Division, this city, and cite the following:

Asa Camp
Certificate #28871
Issued August 12, 1834
Rate $90.59 per annum
Commended March 4, 1831.
Act of June 7, 1832
New York Agency

Very truly yours,
A.D. Miller,
Executive Assistant
To the Administrator

Pension Application for Adam Casler

State of New York
County of Montgomery

On the 19th day of September in the year of our Lord one thousand eight hundred and thirty two personally appeared in open court before the judges of the Court of Common Pleas of said county now sitting Adam Casler a resident of the Town of Minden in the country and state aforesaid aged 67 years in October last who being first duly sworn according to law doth on his oath make the following declaration in order to obtain the benefit of the Act of Congress passed June 7th 1832. That he entered the service of the United States under the following named officers and served as hereafter stated.

That in the year 1781 he resided in Schenectady and on or about the first of April in that year he enlisted for nine months time entered the service of the United State in the War of the Revolution under Captain Stephen White, Lieut. John Thornton, Ensign (blurred) Moore. That after being stationed in the City of Schenectady the company was then marched to Ballston in the

County of Saratoga where they were kept on duty with scouting from place to place to protect the inhabitants and county from the murdering and cruelty of the Indians and Tories until about the last of September following when they were marched to Fort Plain in the County of Montgomery where they formed a body of men under command of Colo. Marinus Willett where they remained until the twenty fourth day of October when they were with the men under Col. Willett's command marched to Johnstown and on the day following they met the enemy under command of Colo. Walter Butler and Major Ross, fought the Johnstown Battle defeated and drove the enemy, that they pursued Butler with the men he had forced him westward to the West Canada Creek where Butler was killed after which they returned to Fort Plain remained there until in the month of December when they were marched to Fort Dayton in Herkimer County where they continued in service until the first of January when they were discharged and he in three days thereafter reached his residence in the City of Schenectady, the place of his enlistment.

He had no documentary evidence of his service and that he was born in the Town of Herkimer in the County of Herkimer in the State of New York in October 1764.

That he has no proof of his age. That he was living in the City and County of Schenectady when called into service but lived since the Revolutionary War and now lives in the Town of Minden, County and state aforesaid.

That he entered the service enlisting as above stated.

That he cannot state the name of officers with troops Continental and Militia Regiments or the general circumstances of his services other than as he had above stated the same.

And that he never received a written discharge.

Her hereby relinquishes every claim whatever to a pension or annuity except the present and declares that his name is not on the pension with the agency of any state.

Sworn and subscribed the day and year aforesaid.
Geo. D. Ferguson, Clerk
Adam Casler (his mark)

State of New York
Montgomery County
John A. Casler of the Town of Minden in said County being further duly sworn doth declare and say that is one of the sons and the administrator of the Estate of Maria Casler widow of Adam Casler, Deceased.

That said Adam Casler was at the time of his death a pensioner of the United States, as deponent understood and believes at the rate of $30 per annum under the Acts of Congress passed 7th June 1832 and that he died on the 20th? March 1845, having a widow Maria Casler, him surviving.

That said Maria Casler was allowed a pension of the United States at first at the rate of $25 per annum which was afterwards increased to $30 per annum. That she departed this life on the twenty fourth day of September 1848 leaving her surviving several children as particularly certified to by the surrogate of said county whose certificate accompanies this declaration and affidavit.

That the services in the War of the Revolution which said Adam Casler was pensioned for, was rendered in and with the New York States troops of Levies, that he also served in the Company of Batteaux commanded by Captain Samuel Gray for the term of at least nine months for which last named service no pension was awarded. (These men were considered "private contractors" and not in service to the United States."

This deponent has given an affidavit stating the services of his father in said company of Batteaumen and wants now to say in addition that tradition of said services is clear and distinct in the mind of this deponent and that he has heard this same repeated again and again, and many years ago that among this particular fact bearing upon the subject he will recollect that Nicholas Kasler under _____ of this deponent received a full pension for his services in the War of the Revolution and part of his services for which he was thus pensioned was rendered in said company of Batteauman.

That this deponent heard said Nicholas represent to his father the said Adam the last named fact and enquired of said Adam why he had not applied to have his pension increased on account of said Batteaux services.

The said Adam replied thereto that he was told that said Batteaux services was not deemed military within the meaning of the said act and therefore he had not thought it of any use to apply for aforesaid. That the widow of Peter Sitts as deponent has been credibly informed and believes has been pensioned from such Batteaux service and that he this deponent distinctly heard said Nicholas Kasler say that he and the said Adam Kasler served in the same company of Batteaux men together to wit, the company of said Samuel Gray. Uriah Smith, John Potter and John Casler and others have testified to the identity of his father the said Adam Casler as the same person who served with Nicholas Kasler, Peter Sitts and others in the said company of Captain Samuel Gray.

And this declarant now hereby opens this claim of said Adam from the 4th March 1831 under said act of 1832 to the tenth day of March 1845 when he died, for an increase of his stipend by reason of said Batteaux services and also from the 20th day of March 1845 to the 24th September 1848 for the increase of the stipend under the Acts of Congress passed 17th June 1844 and 2nd February 1848.

Subscribed and sworn this first day of March 1852.
Jacob Graff Justice of the Peace
Signed, John A. Kesslar

Pension Application for John Casler

Some of the application papers are not legible for this service record.

State of New York
Jefferson County

On the 26 day of February 1830 personally appeared in open court of Common Pleas in the said county of Jefferson in the State of New York bring a court of ??? John Casler resident in said county aged sixty eight years on the eighth day of September last past, who being first duly sworn according to law, doth on his oath, make the following declaration in order to obtain the provision made by the acts of Congress of then 18th March 1818 and the first May 1820,

That said John Casler enlisted into a company of Rangers in the then country of Montgomery in the State of New York for and during the Revolutionary War, that he served in the said company of Rangers about one year and a half, that he then discharged from the said company of Rangers under Lawrence Gross was then first lieutenant, Peter Schremling second lieutenant and John Winne was Captain of the said company of Rangers to which he the said John Casler belonged.

That in 1778 he the said John Casler enlisted for the term of from the first day of March 1778 until the first day of January 1779 on the Mohawk River in the then County of Montgomery in the State of New York in a company commanded by Captain Peter Ale (Ehle?) in a regiment commanded by Colonel Christopher Yates in the boat or naval service in the Continental establishment, that he continued to serve in the said boat and naval service until the said first day of January 1779 when he was regularly discharged at Saratoga on the North River in the State of New York.

That after he was discharged from said boat or naval service on the first day of January 1779 he returned home to the County of Montgomery.

That in March 1779 he again enlisted in the boat or naval service in a company commanded by Captain John Denny or Dana in the line of the State of New York on the Continental establishment that he left the County of Montgomery and went onto the North River in the State of New York and continued to serve in the said corps for the term of from March 1779 until the first day of January 1780 when he was regularly discharged from the said service at Fish Kill on the North River (Hudson River) in the State of New York.

That in 1782 in April or May he again enlisted for the term of from the first April or May 1782 until the first day of January 1783 in a company commanded by Captain John Deers in a regiment commanded by Colonel Marinus Willett in the State of New York on the Continental establishment that he continued to serve in the said corps until the said first day of January 1783 when he was regularly discharged from the service at Fort Plain in the State of New York.

That he hereby relinquishes every claim whatever to a pension except the present, that his name is not on the roll of any state except the State of New York and that the reason whey he was delayed making a earlier application for a pension is that in 1818 or 1819 he applied to William Robinson a Judge of the Court of Common Pleas for the County of Jefferson in the State of New York to procure a pension for him, that the company papers never made out as he supposed, signed by him this deponent, forwarded to the proper department at Washington as he was informed by Judge Robinson and the papers were returned by said Robinson and the papers never returned to said Robinson and the pensions was not obtained and this deponent supposed until within a short time ago that he was not entitled to a pension.

Also in pursuance of the Act of the first May 1820, I do solemnly swear that I was a resident citizen of the United States on the 18th day of March 1818 and that I have not, since that time by gift, or sale in any manner whatever disposed of my property or any part thereof with intent ??? so to diminish it, as to bring myself within the provisions of an Act of Congress entitled "An act to provide for certain persons engaged in the land and naval services of the United States in the Revolutionary War. Passed on the 18 day of March 1818 that I am not nor has any person.......................etc.

The following letter is included in the pension application papers.
June 15, 1939
Mr. G. W. Alisia
215 South George Street
Charles Town, West Virginia

Dear Madam:
    The data which follow is regard to John Casler were obtained from the papers on file in pension claim A 12681, based upon his service in the Revolutionary War.
    John Casler was born September 8, 1761, the place of his birth and names of parents were not stated. His signature by mark appears Casler, also.
    While residing in Canajoharie, in what was then Tryon County, but later Montgomery County, New York, John Casler enlisted in the spring of 1775, and served one year six months as private in Captain John Winne's New York company or Rangers. He was called out August 1, 7777, to go to Oriskany, served one month as private in Captain Robert Crouse's company, Colonel Cox's New York regiment, was in the battle of Oriskany in which both his captain and colonel were killed, then served one month in Captain Adam Lipe's company, Colonel Fairlie's(?) New York regiment, and was in the battle of Stillwater in which Burgoyne was captured. He enlisted March 1, 1778 in the batteaux service under Captain Peter Ale (Ehle) and Colonel Christopher Yates and served to January 1, 1779. He enlisted in March 1779 and served as private in Captain John Denny's company, Colonel Hay's New York regiment and was discharged January 1, 1780. He served four months in 1781, exact date not stated, at Schoharie in Captain Hale's New York company. He enlisted in April 1782 and served as private in Captain Tearee's company, Colonel Marinus Willett's New York regiment, and was discharged January 1, 1783.
    The name of soldier's wife is not shown in the claim. In 1830, while a resident of Jefferson County, New York, John Casler referred to two sons but did not designate their names.
    In 1833, one Nicholas Casler was living in Limerick, Jefferson County, New York, his age, or his relationship to soldier not stated.
    In order to obtain the date of last payment of pension, the name and address of the person paid and possibly the date of death of John Casler, you should write to the Comptroller General, General Accounting Office, Records Division, this city, and cite the following data:
John Casler
Certificate #22604
Issued April 24, 1854
Rate, $30 per annum
Commenced March 4, 1831
Act of June 7, 1832
New York Agency
        Very truly yours
        A.   D. Hiller
        Executive Assistant
        To the Administrator

Pension Application for John Darrow

This pension is a great one to read! John was a "waiter" to his father and saw battles in the northern part of the state.

State of Pennsylvania
Susquehanna County
    On the tenth day of September 1832 personally appeared in open court before William Thomson and David Dimvik, associates, Judges of the Court of Common Pleas of said county now sitting John Darrow of Middletown township in the County of Susquehanna and State of

Pennsylvania aged sixty eight years who being first duly sworn according to law, doth on his oath make the following declaration in order to obtain the benefit of the act of Congress passed June 7th 1832.

That he entered the service of the United States under the following named officers and served as herein stated to vizt:

That in the month of May 1777 at the Town of New Concord in the County of Columbia and State of New York, he entered the service of the United States as waiter to his father, George Darrow, Adjutant of a Regiment of Volunteers, commanded by Colonel McKinstry. The regiment to which he belonged marched from New Concord to Bennington in Vermont, was stationed at that place about four weeks when the Battle of Bennington was fought in which his father was engaged but he being but a boy remained during the engagement in the war of the main army. The battle commenced in the afternoon. The American were forced to retreat before the enemy to a place called Bemus Heights, was stationed at Bemus Heights as near as he can recollect about five weeks during which time the Battle of Bemus Heights was fought. During the engagement he, with other waiters was constantly employed in carrying water to the men engaged with the enemy. The Americans remained master of the field. The British retreated the same night to Saratoga. The whole of the American forces proceeded then on the following morning to Saratoga; found them entrenching themselves and preparing to make a bold defense. The American Army immediately commenced throwing up entrenchments , planting batteries and redoubts and in the meantime reinforcements came in until he enemy were literally surrounded. Frequent skirmishes took place between the armies. The armies lay at that place as near as he can recollect, about a month, when a smart action took place between a part of the American Army commanded by General Arnold and the enemy and on the next day the whole British Army under General Burgoyne surrendered prisoners of war.

That he went with his father to Albany to guard the prisoners who were taken to that place. After the arrival of the army at Albany and about the first of November he with his father were discharged and returned to New Concord having been in the service five months.

And the said John Darrow further saith that in the month of March 1781 at the Town of New Concord in the County and state aforesaid he enlisted in a company commanded by Captain James Cannon for the term of nine months. Marched to Albany where he remained about three days. The company to which he belonged was then attached to a regiment under the command of Colonel Marinus Willett which regiment marched to Fort Plain on the Mohawk River. He remained with the regiment at Fort Plain until as near as he can recollect to about the first of November when a battle was fought between a party of British troops and the Americans at Johnstown In which he was engaged. The enemy were repelled and driven from the fields and sometime in the month of December 1781 he was discharged by Col. Willett at Fort Plain and returned back to New Concord.

And the said John Darrow on his oath, further saith that in the latter part of March 1782, at the town of New Concord in the County and State aforesaid, he enlisted as a volunteer in a company commanded by Captain Whelps for the term of nine months, went to Claverack and that the company to which he belonged was attached to a regiment of State Troops under the command of Colonel Van Schaick. He marched immediately to West Point on the North River (Hudson), was stationed at West Point according to the best of his recollection about four months. That then the company to which he belonged was removed to a place called Smith's Clove (as near as he can recollect) about eight miles distance from West Point back from the river. He remained at that place in garrison until the expiration of the term of his enlistment and was then discharged about the first of January 1783 and returned to New Concord.

And the said John Darrow on his oath further saith that he does not now recollect the names of regular officers under whom he served (other than herein stated) except General Gates and General Arnold who commanded at Saratoga, both of whom he well knew. He further states that he has no documentary evidence and that he knows of no person whose testimony he can procure who can testify to his services.

He hereby relinquishes every claim to a pension or annuity except the present and declares that his name is not on the pension roll of any state.
John Darrow (signed by him)

From the file W25511 we learn John was born December 1763, son of George Darrow, name of mother not given, in New Concord, Columbia County, New York. John Darrow married May 2, 1781, Martha, date, maiden name, and place not given nor names of her parents. He died in Middletown Township, Pennsylvania July 4, 1854 at the residence of his son-in-law, again the name was not given. The widow, Martha Darrow, was allowed pension on her application executed September 1, 1884 at which time she was eighty-nine years old and a resident of Bridgewater Township, Susquehanna County, Pennsylvania.

Pension Application for Philip Failing

This soldier went into the Militia as a substitute for three men in succession. One of the men Philip substituted for was his brother who wanted to be at home to support the family after their father was taken prisoner by the Indians.

It is interesting the men Philip was serving with decided they did not have to obey an order and since there was no commissioned officer around, they simply returned to Palatine. He was at Fort Paris during the Battle of Stone Arabia and when Col. Brown was killed. He was near Major McKean at the Battle of Turlough (Sharon) when he was shot and killed. Philip was also in the Battle of Johnstown and participated in the chase to find Walter Butler.

State of New York
Steuben County SS
      On this sixteenth day of October one thousand eight hundred and thirty two personally appeared in open court before the Court of Common Pleas of the said county now sitting Phillip Failing a resident of the county and state aforesaid aged sixty seven years and upwards who being first duly sworn according to law doth on his oath make the following declarations in order to obtain the benefits of the Act of Congress passed June 7, 1832 that he entered the service of the United States under the following named officers and served as herein stated.
      That in the summer of the year 1779 he entered a company stationed at Palatine in the then County of Tryon now Montgomery where he had previously resided, that the said company was Commanded by a Capt. Christian House and was attached to a Regiment commanded by Col. Jacob Klock, that he entered said Company at first as a substitute and that he served in said three successive weeks that one of said weeks he was a substitute for Jacob Failing, in second of said weeks as a substitute for Conrad Heliker and the third week as a substitute for Yari Laper that during the third of said term of three weeks he remained at the said Town of Palatine and was engaged together with the said company in scouting the County of Tryon with a view of cleaning it of Indians and Tories by whom it was at that time very much infested.
      That after the said time had expired he remained in his place of residence in the said Town of Palatine until sometime in the spring or summer in the year 1780 when he was engaged from time to time in the said County of Tryon under the Command of the said Capt. House as the service of the County remained without any regular settlements.
      That he was some of this engaged in scouting under the Command of the said Capt. over two or three or more days as he was from time to time reprised, that he was at times engaged in the said last mentioned service until the month of June in the years aforesaid when he enlisted in a Company Commanded by Captain John Bigbread which was attached to the regiment commanded by a Col. DuBois as he thinks that his recollection as to the name of the Colo. is indistinct that the said Regiment was under the Command of General Van Rensselaer that said enlistment was for the term of four months, that he remained with the said company at Palatine aforesaid sometime when he was detached with about twenty soldiers to drive some cattle to the German Flatts now Herkimer for the support of the forces there stationed at the latter place that on the evening of their arrival at Herkimer they received orders to go up the Mohawk the next morning for the purpose of guiding the boats then passing up that river to Fort Stanwix with the provisions for that place that there was no commissioned officers with that part of the company to which he belonged then at Herkimer and the men refused to obey the said orders except himself and one other supposing they were not bound to do so and returned to Palatine and rejoined the said Company.
      That he with one other person of said company in pursuance of the said orders marched with other forces up the river on the service aforesaid, that they continued their march until about three o'clock of that day when they discovered the enemy consisting of about 700 Indians and Tories who were scattered through the woods around them. That they remained at the place where they discovered the said enemy, for about ten days behind a small breastwork thrown up for that purpose, that at the expiration of the said ten days they were relieved by a body of five or six hundred more under the immediate Command of Gen. Van Rensselaer, that in the said body was the company to which he was originally attached and which he rejoined at that place.

That upon such reinforcement arriving the enemy retreated and the whole force under the Command of Gen. Van Rensselaer marched to Fort Stanwix that after delivering the said provisions they returned immediately to Palatine that he remained at and about Palatine some time when they moved to Herkimer where they lay several weeks and until the enemy returned in considerable force to Stone Arabia within the bounds of the said Town of Palatine that they then received orders to march for that place to the relief of Col. Brown then stationed there and immediately started for that place where they arrived the following day in the afternoon, that on the forenoon of the day of their arrival, Col. Brown had attacked the enemy and was entirely defeated and was himself killed. That on their arrival they pursued the enemy and overtook them near the Mohawk, engaged them and completely defeated them, driving them through the Mohawk and retook from them all the cattle and provisions they had seized and captured one cannon which they had with them and returned to Herkimer where her remained until his discharge. That during the said period he was part of the time under the Command of a Major Penscoter that he served a half month over the time for which he originally enlisted owing to the unsettled state of the county that he did not when he was discharged as aforesaid receive a written discharge.

That in the spring of the year 1781 he again enlisted at Palatine aforesaid in a company commanded by Lawrence Gros, attached to the regiment under the command of Col. Marinus Willett for the term of nine months and joined the said company at Fort Plain, that he had said (living) quarters of the said Regiment were at that place and that he was employed scouting about the countryside the most of the time until in the month of July when the enemy consisting of about 300 Indians were discovered strongly posted in a thick cedar swamp in Durlough (Turlough) now in the Town of Sharon, Schoharie County and information of that fact was immediately conveyed to Col. Willett that Col. Willett immediately ordered out the forces as in his command and started out in the edge of the evening to attack the Indians in their encampment that on their route they were joined by Major McKean with a small force.

That the night was very dark and they traveled through the woods until near daylight when they came near the encampment of the enemy that the force was then divided into two parties, one of which was under the Command of Col. Willett and the other under the Command of Major McKean and stationed in two parallel lines behind the trees and brush that the applicant was under the Command of Major McKean and that after they were so stationed two men were sent out to draw the Indians from their camp that the men went up in sight of the Indians who immediately pursued them and were led by the men between the two lines where they were attacked and entirely beaten that the applicant during the forepart of the engagement was placed near Major McKean and was by close by his side when he received a wound from a ball of which he died the following evening.

That they then returned to Fort Plain where they remained until the month of August when they were again employed in scouting and also in cutting the grain in Dorlough which belonged to the Tories and conveying it to Fort Plain, that in the later part of the month of August a party of about 500 British Tories and Indians came from Canada to Johnstown and posted themselves there. That the applicant was engaged in the battle at that place against this force, that Col. Willett and Col. Harper commanded the American forces at that place, that he recollects distinctly having seen Walter Butler lying dead on the shore of the West Canada Creek which he had been killed by an Indians while he was retreating from the Battle of Johnstown that from Johnstown he returned to Fort Plain where he remained until the said term of nine months had expired when he was discharged at that place, that he did not receive a written discharge.

That he returned to Palatine aforesaid and in the year 1782 he was out at different times during the summer and fall of that year under the command of Col. Willett but that he is unable to state how often or how long he was engaged that he did not enlist but turned out whenever there was a call made upon him and when the emergency had passed, returned again to his home.

That he was born at the said Town of Palatine on the 16 February 1765. That he has the original record kept by his father of the pages of the family now in his possession. That from Palatine he removed to Canajoharie in the County of Montgomery after the close of the war and remained there about twenty years when he removed to Jasper in present place of residence where he has resided ever since that time. That the annexed affidavit of Jacob Failing is the only evidence of his services that he has been able after a diligent search to procure. He hereby relinquishes every claim whatever to a pension or annuity except the present and declares that his name is not on the pension roll of the agency of any state. This in his present neighborhood he is acquainted with Andrew Simpson, Andrew Craig, John Deck, Rev. Samuel Dacy, Adam

Brutzman, Nicholas Brutzman, William Hunter and others, who can testify about his character for truth and veracity and their belief of his services as a soldier of the Revolution.
Subscribed this day aforesaid and sworn. (Signed, Philip Failing)

State of New York
Montgomery County
   Jacob T. Failing and Conrad Hellegas both of the Town of Oppenheim in said County being severally sworn by me the subscriber a Justice of the Peace in and for said county according to law do depose and swear as follows: That is the said Jacob I Failing for himself aforesaid on his oath that he is aged about seventy two years and that he is the brother of Philip Failing who has, as he has been told by him made application for a pension. That the said Philip and he during the Revolutionary War when not in actual service lived together. That he well remembers that said Philip served in the United States service during the Revolutionary War, that his memory is poor in consequence cannot precisely state his said brother's services but gives the same to the best of his recollection. Vizt, that he recollects that he said Jacob was drafted as a private out of the company whereof Christian House was Capt., in the Regiment whereof Jacob Klock was Colonel, that he was to serve in Remensnyderbush and that said Philip became his substitute in this service. This was according to the best of his recollection in the year 1779 but the day and months he cannot recollect, that his brother Philip went as such substitute after an absence of about 8 days returned home, and then said and told him he had served in Remensnyderbush as so he has always since understood was the fact, he thinks it was in the fall of that year this service was done but to undertake to swear so positively he cannot.
   That he also remembers that some men were drafted out of the Company whereof Christian House was Capt., in the Regt. whereof Jacob Klock was the Colonel in the year 1780 according to his recollection that his brother Philip became his substitute, that by reason of his brother's becoming his substitute as aforesaid is that their father was taken by the Indians a prisoner and that the family of his father depended on said Jacob to take care and provide for them which he did and that said Philip was younger and considered not so capable to take care of the family of their father. It was sometime he thinks in the summer of that year that said Philip became Jacob's substitute as mentioned, but the particular time he cannot swear, he remembers that said Philip left home for last mentioned service and was gone sometime, he should say between 4 & 5 months and on the return of said Philip in home he stated then and often since then to the said services in that last mentioned service in the company whereof in Bigbread or Breadback said Captain of the company.
   That he said Jacob was engaged as a soldier in the pursuit of Major Ross by the forces under the command of Col. Willett that he saw his brother also in the service at said time under Capt. Lawrence Gross in the United States service, this was the thinks in the fall of 1781. He so saw his brother in last mentioned service, that his brother during the war was since often told him he served nine months under Capt. Gross and so he has also heard from others and believes the same. That he has no doubt from the absence of his brother from home that he served for the period of nine months as last mentioned that he understood from said Philip that he had enlisted in said company as a private and said Jacob further says that his brother was often absent from the house and said to be in the service of the United States, besides the periods before mentioned, but he cannot say that he saw him in the service except at Fort Plain in the year 1782 and except the times before mentioned by him to have seen him.
   That he saw said Philip in the service of the year 1782 at Fort Plain in Minden in the service in said fort in standing guard and doing duty and that he saw him often during said year in said fort in the service. He has heard said Philip often relate of his being engaged in the Turlock Battle in that Battle at Johnstown and in the skirmish with Sir John Johnson.
   Conrad Hellegas for himself says, that he was a Soldier of the Revolution and is aged about 72 years that he believed in the Revolutionary War that Philip Failing then a resident of Tryon County now County of Montgomery and who now resides, as he is told, in the Town of Jasper in the County of Steuben served in the United States services in the Revolutionary War. That according to the best of his recollection he was drafted out of the Company whereof Christopher Fox was Captain once and afterwards John Hess Capt and after him Peter Waggoner Junr., was Capt of said company in the Regt whereof Jacob Klock was Colonel but cannot swear which of said captains named by him was at the time he was so drafted the captain of said company and cannot recollect said, that when he was so drafted he received a bounty of money and he did not serve, but procured said Philip Failing as his substitute as a private, that said Philip was quite young at the time and he was fearful he would not be accepted as his substitute,

but he was, because he was smart and lively for his age. That he cannot recollect for how long he was drafted, that he was drafted according to his recollection in the year 1780 or 1781 in the spring of that year, but cannot say what month or day. He knows that said Philip went as his substitute and served as he understood for the period he was to serve that in consequence of the loss of his memory by reason of his age, he cannot state further or more particularly the service rendered by said Philip during the Revolutionary War, but recollects that he always understood in the war and after that said Failing had done a great deal of service and had been a true and good soldier of which he never heard a doubt expressed.

Sworn and subscribed this 20th day of June A.D. 1833 before me.

(Signed, Jacob Failing and Conrad Hellegas.)

State of New York
Steuben County

On this eighth day of March in the year eighteen hundred forty four personally appeared before the Judges of the Court of Common Pleas in and for Steuben County, Margaret Failing a resident of the Town of Jasper in the said town of Steuben aged seventy eight years on the first day of March and who being first duly sworn according to law doth on her oath make the following declaration in order to obtain the benefit of the provision made by the act of Congress passed July 7, 1838, entitled An Act Granting Half Pay and Pensions to Certain Widows. That she is the widow of Philip Failing who was a private in the Revolutionary Army and served during three summers under Col. Marinus Willett and Capt Bigbread as she has been frequently informed by her said husband during his life time that she does not know the other officers under whom he served that he was in an action at Johnstown and in the action at Durlaugh sometimes spelt Turlock she cannot state the precise time he left the service but that her said husband Philip Failing was a pensioner of the United States and drew at the rate of fifty dollars and sixty six cents reference being made to the paper on file in the Pension Office with more fully approved. She further declares that she was married to the said Philip Failing on the fifteenth day of April in the year seventeen hundred and eighty eight that her husband the aforesaid Philip Failing died on the seventeenth day of May eighteen hundred and forty two. That she was not married to him prior to his leaving service but the marriage took place previous to the first of January seventeen hundred and ninety four vizt at the time above stated she further states she has no documentary evidence of the facts above stated except the pensions certificate of the said Philip Failing and the records taken from the German Psalm book, that her marriage took place in what was called the Town of Palatine in the Country of Montgomery.

Signed, Margaret Failing (Her Mark)

State of New York
Steuben County

Adam Failing being duly sworn says that he resides in the Town of Jasper in said county and has resided there nineteen years that he was born in the County of Montgomery on the 25th day of March 1795 that he is the son of Philip and Margaret Failing that the German Psalm Book from which annexed leaves were taken has been in the family of the said Philip and Margaret ever since his recollection that the entries there made have also been there since his earliest recollection that he does not know by whom they were so made, that said leaves contain the record of the births of the children of the said Margaret and Philip that he had (blotted, I think it says sister Catherine) and Daniel his brother older than himself. This deponent further says that the said Philip resided with this deponent until his death which took place the 17 day of May eighteen hundred and forty two. That said Philip and Margaret always lived together as man and wife and were so treated by their friends and acknowledged their children that he has never lived apart from his said parents, they having resided with this deponent ever since he came to man's estate and that the said Margaret is still a widow.

Subscribed and sworn this 8 day of March 1844 before me, Harrison Finck Judge of said county.

(Signed) Adam Failing

Pension Application for Christian Fink

Fink saw a lot of interesting service around the area. He was involved in the boating services and was an assessor and collector, it appears to have been for the war effort, or else it probably would not have appeared on his pension application.

(The first part is just like all the others.)

That he entered the service of the United States under the following officers and served as herein stated. That he was enrolled in the year 1775 when he was sixteen years of age in a company commanded by Capt. Keyser, Col. Clucks (Klock's) regiment some of the other officers attached to the same regiment were Lieutenant Col. Woolever and Major Esellort (Eisenlord?).

From this time he was enrolled till the termination of the war he served as a volunteer or rather in the capacity of a Minute Man. The first active service that he performed was in a company commanded by Capt. Tillenbaugh (Dillenbach) when he was ordered to Caughnawaga a distance from Palatine of about sixteen miles where he continued about one week.

He was upon two or three occasions ordered to Rome and Fort Stanwix a distance from Palatine of about fifty miles. While at Rome he was once ordered under the command of a sergeant by the name of Conall Garoll? to proceed to Wood Creek and bring up a number of boats loaded with whiskey and provisions on these occasions he was absent from three to four weeks. He was twice ordered to Fort Planck where he remained about three weeks performing camp duties on one occasion he was ordered from Fort Plank to Cherry Valley at the time it was burnt by the Indians and Toreys, he was there about four weeks.

He was in the Battle of Johnstown where he was absent about one week. He was in the Battle of Oriskany commanded by Capt. Tillenbaugh; and after he was killed he was commanded by Capt. Cook. He was absent this time about three weeks a distance of forty seven miles from Palatine.

In the year 1777 he was ordered to transport a quantity of provisions to Albany and after he had arrived in that place he was ordered to Stillwater and arrived there soon after the surrender of Burgoyne at this time he was absent about four weeks a distance from Palatine about seventy seven miles.

He was twice ordered to transport a quantity of provisions from Albany to West Point where he was absent from three to four weeks. He once lay at Bowen's Creek with Col. Cluck's regiment about three weeks. He was once ordered to Springfield at the time it was burnt when he was about one week. At the time that General Sullivan marched into the western part of the State of New York he was ordered out with a wagon and horses to transport boats and provisions from the Mohawk River to the Otsego Lake. He was absent at this time about three weeks under the command of Capt Cook.

He was employed as a assessor and collector to collect clothing for the army the time that he was employed as such assessor and collector he cannot state with any degree of certainty.

He likewise lost a horse in the service for which he never received any compensation. He has no documentary evidence of his services and knows of no other person whose testimony he can procure other than the affidavit of George Shultries hereto annexed said Schulthies is about the same age was borned and brought up in the same neighborhood whose services were of the same nature and was a fellow soldier with him in most of all the excursions and engagements.

He once had a certificate from Capt. Fink certifying that he had enlisted a man for the term of three years to serve in Col. Cluck's (Klock) regiment in his stead to discharge himself from his liability of being drafted during that period as his services were of more value acting in the capacity of a minute man or volunteer.

Christian Finck (His Mark)

Pension Application for Asabel Foote

Commonwealth of Massachusetts
County of Berkshire

On this twenty-eighth day of August A.D. 1836, personally appeared in open court, before the Honorable William P. Walker, Judge of the Court of Probate, within and for said County of Berkshire, no sitting, Asabel Foote, a resident of the town of Lee in the County of Berkshire and Commonwealth of Massachusetts, aged sixty-nine years, who being first duly sworn according to law, doth, on his oath make the following declaration in order to obtain the benefit of the act of Congress, passed June 7, 1832.

That he entered the service of the United States under the following named officers, and served as herein stated. On the third day of July in the year A.D. 1777, enlisted in the company commanded by Captain Ford in the regiment commanded by Col. William Brown of Pittsfield in the Line of the State of Massachusetts, then a resident of the Town of Lee.

We went immediately to Albany where we stayed over a week and we were put into companies. From Albany we marched to Schohaire for the purpose of guarding the town from the British and Indians, and where we acted as scouts. In the town there were three forts, designated by the terms, upper, middle and lower forts. I was placed part of the time in one of them and part of the time in another.

The Indians made no attacks upon the forts, but our scouting parties had frequent skirmishes with them. We was dismissed and commenced our return home on the 20th of November of that year having served during that enlistment. I served four months, I remained at home until July of the next summer when I was drafted in Capt. Marsh's company in Stockbridge in Col. Brown's Regiment.

We marched to Albany from thence to Schoharie after we had been at Schoharie some time the Indians came down upon it I was then on guard and was the first to give the alarm about break of day. They had with them a howitzer and four-pounder for the purpose of firing in upon our fort. Shells and balls we had then but seventy men in the fort. They commenced then firing upon us for the purpose of burning our magazine. They fired into the fort with a dozen shells which set our magazine on fire three times. Some of our men was lost and mortally wounded. We had in the fort some rifle men from Virginia companies who were not subject to the command of our officers one of them shot down three different men who had been sent by the enemy with a flag of truce and we supposed to demand our surrender.

The enemy remained till over night fall when they were off and then commenced their firing upon one of the other forts from thence they went to Stonerarbias then called Stone Robby to which place we followed them. They had arrived a short time before on our way many cattle lay dead until hardly an animal to be seen living, houses smoking in ruins and when we arrived at Stone Robby, many of the men was laying in their gore yet unburied. We were informed that the Indians had placed ten of the number in sight a short distance from that fort and that Colo. Brown had ordered his men to pursue them. They retired and led Col. Brown into an ambuscade in a notch where they were upon them and slaughtered almost all of them. Col. Brown fell the first fire and was deposited in his grave the day before we arrived.

I remained in the service until the last of Nov. And served a few days and four months. I remained at home until the first of August 1781 when a call was made upon the Town of Lee to furnish a certain number of men three years more. I was drafted and entered the company commanded by Captain Kellum in the regiment in which Maj. Ashley of Stockbridge was Major. The Colo. I do not recollect. I went to Stockbridge from thence to White Plains and thence directly to West Point where I remained until the last of the next March when I was relieved by another person and returned home. While I was there Gen. Washington was there and at Weat Point many times. General Gates was also there. I was under the Continental officers this campaign, but at the time I served, I was in the Line of the State of Mass.

(Then he lists the time he served and it added up to 16 months.)

I was born in Colchester Ct. in the year 1763, 22 April. I have a record of my age in my family. I entered the service always in the town of Lee where I then lived and where I have lived ever since.

I never had a discharge. I know of no person living who can testify to my services during the Revolution.

I am acquainted with the Rev. Alva Hyde of Lee and Stephen Couch, the former of whom I have known more than forty years.

(Here the record ends.)

Pension Application for Peter Fox, Corporal

This application is interesting because he mentions some of the local fortified homes and the reason he feels Col. Klock did not respond earlier to the Cherry Valley massacre. Peter helped palisade some of the homes for protection. He went with General Herkimer to the conference with Joseph Brandt just before the Battle of Oriskany, Battle of Stone Arabia, Battle of Johnstown and several smaller skirmishes.

State of New York
Montgomery County

On this fifteenth day of February one thousand eight hundred and fifty one personally appeared before me a justice of the peace within and for the county and state aforesaid. David S. Shull who being duly sworn according to law deposes and says that he resides at Stone Arabia in said county and he is a member of the Dutch Reformed Church of Stone Arabia that he had the records of said church in his possession and upon examination of said records he finds that Peter Fox was married to Maria Richter on the 17th of January A.D. 1796 by the Rev. D. C. Pick, who was for several years the regular pastor of said church and was authorized by law to solemnize marriages. The record of the marriage is in the words and figures following viz:

Married on the 17th Jan 1796 Peter Fox
Married to Maria Richter by D.C. Pick

And that the above is a true copy of said record.

D. S. Shull

Subscribed and sworn to before on this 15th day of February 1851. And I certify that deponent is entitled to full credit.

James W. Hamilton
Justice of the Peace

State of New York
Montgomery County

On this 19th day of Sept in the year 1832 personally appeared in open court now sitting, Peter Fox a resident of the town of Palatine County of Montgomery aged seventy three years, Sept. this instant month has been first duly sworn according to law doth on his oath make the following declarations in order to obtain the benefit of the act passes June 7th 1832 that he entered the service of the United States under the following officers and served as herein stated vizt:--

That this claimant declares that he belonged to the Regt of Militia commanded by Col. Jacob Klock and Peter Waggoner Lieut Col in the company commanded by Christopher W. Fox that he was born in the month of Sept. in the year one thousand seven hundred fifty nine as appears by family record that he this applicant was involved and kept himself in readiness armed and equipped in compliance with the order of his superior officers and the laws of this country from the year 1776 to the conclusion of the war, that he been satisfied that he was called out on duty and that he hath performed services but the particulars he doth not recollect.

That this applicant declares that early in the war he was ordered to march under Capt Fox with his company to George Saltsman in Palatine. They remained for about eight days, scouting and guarding against the incursions of the common enemy and at another time for about ten days at George Gettman's, the farms like the preceding, also palisaded at Fort Snell and like service under Capt Fox and his company, also at Fort Plank the farms in about fort. Also at Frederick Eregliers? – the like, does not recollect when under Capt Fox—also under command of Capt Henry Miller for about ? weeks, stationed at a place now called St. Johns Ville was Town of Oppenheim according to his belief about two weeks the like services Febr'y into the fore part in March 1779.

That he went and marched to now formerly Herkimer then Tryon County to Fort Dayton there remained for about three weeks and performed the like duties and services to the best of his knowledge in the year 1779. That this applicant further declares that he was ordered out to march to German Flatts, now County of Herkimer in May with his capt. under Col. Klock. There stationed for a number of days. From thence marched to Andrustown south from German Flatts to the lakes but did meet no enemy at that time having been out for about two weeks.

Also ordered out to march to Young's Lake where the enemy generally would have recourse to harbour at the house of Adam Young but not discovering nor met any Tories or Indians from Canada. Those he believes in the year 1778.

That the applicant further declares that in the latter part of July men ordered out under Captain Christopher W. Fox to march to Fort Stanwix and on this march from Herkimer under the command of General Nicholas Herkimer, which on our way at about four miles this side of the Fort those engaged in that memorable Battle at Oriskany when claimant sustained his ground until that part of Gen'l St. Leger's army retreated and left them.

That previous to Oriskany Battle, under the command of Gen'l Herkimer after he hath been drafted out of Capt Fox's company, marching down the Susquehanna River to Unadilla those with Capt Brandt who had a large number of warriors at his command with him and after several days, Genl Herkimer and Capt Brandt held a conference at Genl Herkimer's encampment. In coming then leaving after, he had been out for at least three weeks. In June and July 1777 and the former when the battle was fought at Oriskany happened the 6th of August 1777 same year.

That this applicant further declares that in October 19th in the year 1780 that the battle generally called Col. Brown's Battle (Battle of Stone Arabia) in the Town of Palatine after Sir John Johnson with his incendiaries which caused a general conflagration or nearly the whole old settlement of Stone Arabia and up along the Mohawk River, applicant declares that he went in pursuit of the enemy and there in Battle at Klocks and Failings Flats. Then continued in battle until the enemy took flight.

This claimant further states that he volunteered in what is called Landman's Battle against a large party of Indians and Tories from Canada the Indian chief killed and several wounded which occurrence happened July 29th 1781.

That this applicant further declared that in October 25th 1781 same year again in battle then under the immediate command of Col. Marinus Willett against Major Ross and Capt Butler and supposed about 500 of their incendiaries from the enemy retreating which battle culminated with the loss of many killed on both sides and many taken prisoner on both sides.

This applicant further declares that himself and eight others engaged for three months service by Col. Jacob Klock under Major Christopher W. Fox in the year 1780 for running scout on snow shoes during the winter enlisted to guard against the incursions of the enemy that this applicant states that he hath served faithfully under Capt. Christian Gettman for and during the term of three months, which company was divided into three groups. When out, in rotation continually, also in July 1781 when (there is a little notation in tiny print and the only thing I can make out is Fort Timmerman and pursuing the enemy for about thirty miles).

That this applicant further declares that he was ordered out immediately after the cruel scalpings and butchering and inhuman murdering at Cherry Valley to march there. He believes he was under the command of Col. Klock but he feels satisfied that Col. Klock's Reg't was ordered out previous not knowing at which place the enemy would approach situate and they were at now Town of Canajohary for several days from there marched to Cherry Valley.

That this claimant further and last declares that often and very frequently hath been under orders to watch and to guard against the invasions of the daily expected enemy at their principal fort vizt: Fort Paris with the Militia soldiers were so trained and instructed whose serving and hearing therefore of the alarming cannon generally each one not waiting for his corporal to be warned but would without any hesitation or equivocation shoulder his arms in hastening to the fort and prepared to march out on any occurrence or emergency which formed or thought expedient by their superior officers.

That this claimant declares that after lapses of time it has rendered it impracticable to describe or remember all the duties and services performed during the Revolution but sufficient for his honor the Secretary of the War Department to be satisfied that he this claimant was always in compliance in the orders of his superior officers and also conformable to the resolution passed May 27 1775 hereupon it is resolved that the Militia of New York armed and trained man in constant readiness to act at a moments warning.

And that in conformity to the preceding resolution passed by the old Congress as early there the year and date above mentioned. That this applicant not only in obedience to the orders and directions of his superiors, officers and the court of his country, but also, did consider it a duty incumbent on him to have kept himself always well armed and equipped and in constant readiness so when called upon always willing on a minutes warning to march out on each and every emergency in defending the rights and liberties of his country.

And further this applicant saith:--

That he hereby relinquishes every claim whatever to a pension or annuity except the aforeseth and declares that his name is not on the pension roll of the agency of any state.

Sworn to and subscribed the day and year aforesaid
Signed, Peter Fox
Geo D. Ferguson, Clerk

Pension Application for Peter Getman.

This soldier saw service as a scout and was at the Battle of Stone Arabia.

State of New York
County of Montgomery

On this 20th day of September 1832, personally appeared in open court before Aaron Horning, Abraham Morrell, Samuel A. Pickert, John Hand and Henry I. Dievendorf, Judges of the Court of Common Pleas now sitting Peter Getman, a resident of Ephratah in the County of Montgomery and State of New York aged sixty eight years and eight months who being first duly sworn according to law doth on his oath make the following declaration in order to obtain the benefit of the act of Congress passed June 7th 1832.

That he entered the service of the United States under the following named officers and served as herein stated, and in the month of April 1777 he was enrolled in the Militia Company of Captain Henry Miller in Col. Klocks Regiment and marched with said company to the Royal Grant and was there stationed to guard the then new settlement from the numerous marauding parties of Tories and Indians that were at that time infesting the country with Butler and Brant as their emissaries. That he continued in said Miller's Company until the spring of 1780.

That in April of that year he enlisted into the company of Captain John Casselman. This was a Company of Rangers raised by order of the Committee of Tryon County and attached to the regiment of Col. Jacob Klock the officers in this company were at the time the applicant enlisted was John Casselman, Captain; Adam Empie, Lieut; and George Getman, Ensign.

That the services rendered while in this company were the company was divided and a part stationed at Fort Paris under Captain Casselman a part at the forts on the Mohawk River under Lieut. Empie and a part at the block house in the north settlement of Palatine under Ensign Getman from which station parties called scouting parties were sent to range and watch the movements of the hostile Indians and Tories and to give an alarm in case of danger that this applicant enlisted in said company for two years and served the full period of his said enlistment that while in this company he was the whole time in actual service, going on scouts both in summer and winter or when not in this service was with the company at the forts or in the service as ordered by the captain or other superior officers.

That he was at the Battle at Stone Arabia and saw Col. Brown after he was slain, and assisted at the funeral. This was in October 1780. That this applicant was also (while in Capt. Casselmans Company) at the Battle of Johnstown on the 22nd October 1781.

That when his term of service expired in Capt. Casselmans Company in March 1782, the applicant enlisted into a company of nine months, the men under the command of Capt Finch in Col. Willett's Regiment.

That he enlisted into said company about the 1st April 1782 at the Block House in Palatine and marched from there to Fort House, near the East Canada Creek and from there to Fort Herkimer and was there stationed doing duty at garrison and going on scouting parties from the Fort at Herkimer to Fort Stanwix and the Oneida Lake and into the interior and then wilderness towards the river St. Lawrence until the 1st Jan'y 1783 when he was discharged and returned to his home at Stone Arabia. He knows of no more or other testimony than the affidavits herewith annexed, all from his fellow soldiers and who served with (him) in the Revolutionary War.

He hereby relinquishes every claim whatever to a pension or annuity except the present and declares that his name is not on the roll of any agency or any state.

To the questions directed to before omitted, he answers,

1st he was born in the now Town of Ephratah, County of Montgomery and State of New York on the 5th day of January 1764. He has a record of his age made by his father in his Bible, it is now at the house of Mr. Philip Empie in the Town of Ephratah. He lives at Stone Arabia (now Palatine) when he entered the service. After the Revolutionary War he continued to live with his father at Stone Arabia about four years. He then married and settled in now Ephratah, then Palatine about four miles from his father then removed to Manheim Herkimer County, lived there seven years and has resided since that time in Ephratah his present place of residence. He was first enrolled as a Militia Soldier in Capt Henry Millers Company and afterwards enlisted into the company of Captains Casselman and Finch as stated above.

He served with Col. Willett, Col. Klock, Major Finck, Col. Brown and the officers in the stations along the Mohawk River and In Tryon County.

Sworn to and subscribed at this 20th Day of September 1832.

Signed Peter Getman.

State of New York
County of Montgomery

On this 16th day of March 1847, personally appeared in open court before the judges of the county courts in the aforesaid county, Elisabeth Getman (or Kitman) a resident of the Town of Ephratah in the County of Fulton formerly Montgomery aforesaid aged Eighty Four years on the 28th day of February last past, and she being duly sworn according to law, doth on her oath make the following declaration in order to obtain the benefits of the pension made by the act of Congress passed 7 July 1838, entitled "an act of granting half pay and pensions to certain widows" and acts explanatory of amending and extending the same. That she is the widow of Peter Getman who served in the war of the revolution as herein after stated.

That she was married to said Peter Getman on the tenth day of March in the year one thousand seven hundred and eighty five by the Reverend Mr. Rees, at his house, Pastor of the Lutheran Church at Stone Arabia. That previous to her said marriage she resided in Dillenburgh (Tillaboro) in the District of Palatine NY and her maiden name was Richter (or Rightor).

That her husband the said Peter Getman died on the twenty second day of May one thousand eight hundred and forty-five. That since his death she has remained single and unmarried and is still his widow and unmarried.

That said husband Peter Getman was a pensioner of the United States under the act of June 1832, at the rate of $80 per annum on account of his services in the War of the Revolution. Declarant is unable to specify said services, but remembers hearing her said husband say many years ago before any pension laws were passed that he served at the Stone Arabia when that place and other along the Mohawk Valley were destroyed by the British and their Indian & Tory allies, that he served under Captain Kisselman or Casselman on several occasions, under Captain Finck and Colonel Willett also at Ticonderoga and Johnstown and Fort Herkimer and other forts along the said valley. That her husband the said Peter Getman was a son of Christian Getman Captain of a Company of Rangers during said war.

And this declarant further saith that she had children by said Peter Gitman as follows: A son named Peter who was born on the 29th day of July one thousand seven hundred and ninety two, another son named Arendt who was born on the 7th November one thousand seven hundred and ninety four, a daughter named Mary born 19th September one thousand eight hundred and eighty six, Anna born September 4th one thousand seven hundred and eighty eight and further declarant said.

Subscribed and sworn this day and year first aforesaid In open court as aforesaid. Elizabeth Getman (her mark)

State of New York
County of Montgomery

I, Charles Junkes of the town of Palatine in said County, do hereby certify and depose that I am pastor of the Reformed Dutch Church of Stone Arabia in said town that as such I have the custody of the records of said church.

That on examining the record of Baptisms, I find the following entry in fair legible figures and records word for word and figured for figure viz-

1792	Eltern	Kinder	Gevattern
n. 29: July B 5 Aug	Peter Gettman Elizabeth, nat: Richter	Peter	Peter Richter Catharina Gettmann
1794			
n. 7 November B 7 Nov	Peter Gettmann Elizabeth (Richter)	Arendt	Arendt Brower Cornelia Richter

(From which it appears that "Peter" a son of Peter Gettmann and Elizabeth his wife, whose maiden name was "Richter" was baptized according to the rites of said church and by the then pastor thereof on the fifth day of August, in the year of our Lord, one thousand seven hundred and ninety two and said son is noted as having been born on the 29th day of July in said year last named 1792.)

It further appears that another child of said Peter Gettman and his wife Elizabeth named "Arendt" was born on the seventh day of November one thousand seven hundred and ninety four and baptized on the 9th day of said month of November last named.

Signed Charles Junkes

Pension Application for Henry Gramps

Henry was a Minute Man, his service began in 1775. He fought in Oriskany, the Battle of Stone Arabia, Klock's Field, Landman's Battle and the Battle of Johnstown.   In his opinion, the name of Van Rensselaer should be forever disgraced for misleading Col. Brown and leading to his death.

State of New York
Montgomery County
      On the sixth day of Sept. 1832 personally appeared before me Henry Dieffendorff, the judges of the Court of Common pleas in and for the County of Montgomery of said State of New York.
      Henry Gramps, a resident of the Town of Palatine in the County of Montgomery, said State of New York, aged exceeding seventy nine years, that he was born on the 2nd day of May 1753. Being first duly sworn according to law doth on his oath make the following declaration in order to obtain the benefit of the act of Congress passed June 7th 1832. That he entered the service of the United States under the following named officers as far as he can recollect vizt in the Regiment of Militia Commanded by Col. Jacob Klock and Peter Waggoner Lieut. Col and Capt Andrew Dillenbeck's company in the then County of Tryon now County of Montgomery aforesaid.
      That the Old Congress on the 27th Day of May 1775 it was resolved that the Militia of New York be armed and trained in a constant readiness to act at a moment's warning this claimant saith and states that he hath furnished himself with sufficient arms and accoutrements as therefore required at least from that time to the close of the war, and always kept himself in readiness at a moment's warning.
      That immediately after the commencement of the war, sometimes in mass and of these and frequently drafted the Militia of our Brigade and were particularly ready to which this claimant did belong to had to shoulder their arms, march with his accoutrements and provisions in marching at a distance away from his abode or place of residence in order to guard against and to repel the incursions of the common enemy.
      That this claimant regrets that after such an elapse and length of time he is not being enabled to document or describe the number of days, months or years or any particular duty or service as performed on behalf of his country, United States. But that he sufice it sufficient by making it appear in the following declaration to his Honor the Secretary of the War Department that he has proved a faithful subject of his country from the beginning to the close of the war, will put his application beyond any doubt.
      First he recollects he was drafted with others in the Militia to go in pursuit of men who burnt by Herkimer. (Much of the next is not legible, he speaks about sometime in 1775 , going to Herkimer to stop someone from going to Canada with about 100 Militia.) That all the Militia of Col. Klock's Regt, then belonged to Capt Andrew Dillenbenbagh's Company, called out to march to Caughnawaga now Montgomery County there joining Gen. Schuyler with his Militia from Albany and Schenectady and there marched to Johnstown to cause surrender of Sir John. Not knowing the particular object of Sir John's but apparently as the intended or counter intended either to march off to join the British in Canada, otherwise expecting that they would commit depredations by injuring the friends of Whigs who felt in favor of American Independence which the foregoing happened in the winter of 1775. Continued for about two weeks when they returned.
      This claimant further states and declares that he did perform services for various occasions and in many and at different times and emergency to guard against the incursions of the common need daily in reported enemy until the forepart of summer in the year 1777. When draft of the Militia was made they went with Gen Herkimer vizt the General of the Brigade to which the claimant did belong to Unadilla down the Susquehanna River there with Capt. Brandt the Indian Chief with a large body of Indians supposing at least five hundred Indian Warriors. But after four days, Capt. Brandt with two of his warriors came into camp, testing and considering not to take battle. About six weeks gone from home.
      From year 1777 in July marching then on command of Gen. Nicholas Herkimer on his way to Fort Stanwix when sent back by the general himself with others to guard General's family and neighbors around Indian Castle while others went into Battle of Oriskany with General himself then remained until after battle when General returned after battle, wounded and died. When after this claimant returned home to his family.

This claimant further declares that as the believes on the 22nd day of May 1780 that he was ordered out under Capt. Severenus Cook. Some others and company to which he belonged previous, threatened Caughnawaga, then Town of Johnstown where Sir John Johnson with a large party of his incendiaries which came from Canada hath taken the most unexpectable part of its inhabitants on in the night or daybreak, murdering and scalping, marking prisoners of men, women and children, taking them along into the woods after being pursued by the Militia. Then under the Command of Col. John Harper to the Village of Johnstown and after arriving at Johnstown Village the last the claimant saw of the enemy there leaving the last residence vizt, the Hall, marching across the farms once owned by the said Sir John the last force of them at that time.

This claimant also declares that in October 19th the same year 1780 immediately after the Battle in Palatine, generally called Brown's Battle (Battle of Stone Arabia) in which Col. Brown fell victim to the enemy, Sir John Johnson at the head of the incendiaries came from Canada at which engagement forty five of our own slain and slaughtered before retreating both the Militia and Brown's was, he declares, that in pursuit of Sir John with his incendiary came for about eight miles there in battle on Failing's and Klock's Field or Flats that he the claimant continued in battle until the enemy was put to flight.

O let that name be disgraced for ever and accompany the character of General Van Rensselaer, who first misled the brave Col. Brown who was slain in the first engagement, in Stone Arabia when chiefly all the buildings and grain was burnt and again when in pursuit of the incendiary crew on the same day in the afternoon where in the power of the general with sufficient force to have caused a total surrender of the enemy, making a halt at a distance some short of one mile. Leaving it to the courageous, vizt Col. DuBois with some of his nine month men and the Militia who fought the Battle on Failing's and Klock's Field connected with some of our own Indians whereas if General Van Renssalaer had been marching on with the force under his then command the common enemy would have entertained no possible hopes to have escaped but constrained to capture and surrender.

That this claimant further declares that in July 29th 1781 engaged in battle also there in the said Town of Palatine against a large party of Indians and Tories in the woods, then has he believes under the command of Lieut. Jacob Sammons who he believes had the command of our Militia when the enemy were attacked and taken on surprise. Generally called Landman's Battle being near Landman's farm in the woods, on a holy Sabbath day. The chief of the Indians killed and serveral wounded and set to flight.

And again in Oct. 25th 1781, same year, engaged in Battle at Johnstown then under the immediate Command of Col. Marinus Willett against Major Ross and a large party from Canada the 1st of which not certain but supposed at least five hundred which happened to have posed a serious conflict. A number of lives lost on both sides and prisoners taken from both sides, first our field piece taken by the enemy and again retaken when he this applicant was present in retaking this cannon with the loss of several lives by the enemy around about the field piece as well as some of theirs was slain.

This applicant further declares and states that he went with the Militia to Cherry Valley when ordered out when the general murders and butchering and depredation was committed and fear penetrated on the inhabitants of this town by the Indians and Tories, vigt on men, women and children that we soon came there only and evidentially after the worst acts had been done aiding and assisting in carrying away the horrid mangled dead bodies on waggons vizt men, women and children in some instances many whole families were connectively carried to such places as directed. This claimant further declares that he thinks in the latter part of summer 1783 in the then Town of Palatine aforesaid, same county, now Town of Oppenheim again a large party of Indians and Tories from Canady estimated about 300 on surprise and unexpectedly laying waste by burning, killing and destroying and burnt at a distance around and about Fort Timmerman although Town of Oppenheim but now is called St. John's Ville.

When this claimant went in pursuit of the common enemy he thinks they were under the immediate Command of Col. Willett at a distance of about thirty miles but not overtaking the incendiaries. The number of days he does not recollect while gone from home.

This claimant further says that in the summer of 1780 to the best of his knowledge the militia ordered out to guard the boats and boat crew attending the same. The company of boats was Commanded by Capt. Samuel Gray from Fort Schuyler to Fort Stanwix conveying provisions for the supply of the garrison, Capt Gray was appointed to this command of a company of boatmen at two different seasons for 9 months this claimant always turned out for each seasons transporting provisions from Schenectady to Fort Stanwix and elsewhere whenever he was required at this particular period well ascertained that a large party or number from Canada vizt of the common enemy were watching and determined to make an attack on Capt Gray's Company and boats dispersing and disappointing Col. Ganswvoort, Col. Willet and soldiers in not receiving their expected supply at the fort.

When General Van Renssalear and Colonel John Harper with the Militia sent the boats at Fort Schuyler, the enemy passing down along the Mohawk River laying waste and burning and destroying all the south side of the river now Town of Minden about 35 miles below Fort Schuyler when the boats and Company all guarded safe to Fort Stanwix but day afterwards on they returned down along the Mohawk River but number of days gone this claimant does not remember.

That this applicant further declares that he has been drafted several times to march with others of the Militia to the Royal Grant watching and guarding frontier. Also at different times to Herkimer. (this part is missing)………guarding and watching against the incursions and depredations of the enemy and at various and different other places impossible to recollect after and elapse of fifty years and more, and this applicant further says and declares that he hath resided a little better than half a mile from Fort Paris, where the inhabitants generally round about the fort and a number at a distance from one to ten miles would and did move, and of the times all around the fort, into the fort and so continued, he may safely say the fort being erected and build in the year 1775, that from the commencement of the year 1777 then services performed in watching and guarding the fort, would at a moderate calculation average twelve months to the conclusion of the war.

That his claimant further said and declares that he had been in the Town of Palatine, then County of Tryon now County of Montgomery when he hath resided continuous for and during the war and was since and he hereby relinquishes every claim whatever to a pension or annuity except the present and declares that his name is not on the pension roll of the agency of any state.

Henry Gramps (his mark)

He died on March 23, 1837

Pension Application for John P. Gramps, Sergeant
(Jim Morrison has this veteran listed as a Sergeant, the application lists him as a private.)

Mr. Gramps mentions that he fought against Lieut. Jacob Klock from Canada. Here is mentioned the officer, apparently Colonel Jacob Klock's son, who must have turned Tory and was mentioned in William Feeter's pension application as the American officer who turned Tory.

State of New York
Montgomery County SS
Declaration

In order to obtain the benefits of the actions of the act of Congress of the 4th of July 1836. On this 23rd day of August 1838, personally appeared before me, David F. Sacia a Judge of Montgomery County Courts, being a court of record, Nancy Gramps, widow of John P. Gramps deceased of the Town of Palatine, County and State aforesaid aged seventy eight years last, who being first duly sworn according to law, doth on her oath make the following declaration in order to obtain the benefit of the provisions, made by the Act of Congress, passed July 4th 1836 that she is the widow of John P. Gramps who was a private soldier in the Militia in the Company Commanded by Lieut. Andreas Dillenbagh until 6th Agusut 1777 when the said Lieut. Dillenbagh was slain at the Battle of Oriskany as always understood, under the Chief Command of General Nicholas Herkimer and in the Regt. Commanded by Col. Jacob Klock.

Deponent further saith, that immediately after Lieut. Dillenbagh was slain at Oriskany Battle, scout Severenus Cook succeeded in taking Command and continued in being the command of the same company from and after this aforesaid 6th day of August 1777 from year to year until the final termination of the War of Revolution, excepting three different tours in rendering Batteau Service, for the saith claiment said, that she had heard her husband often and frequently observe that he had been enlisted in the Batteau Service at the different services, first as understood under the Command of Capt. William Gettenson the said claiment believing from the early part in spring until late in fall, in the year 1777.

Said claimant further saith that her husband often and frequently told and saith that he hath been enlisted under the Command of Capt. Samuel Gray two tours, vizt in the years 1779 and 1780, that early in Spring 1779 commencing in transporting with bateaux, provisions and other necessaries from Schenectady up along the Mohawk River to fortify the garrison at Fort Stanwix, and some other forts situated up along the said river until the time of General Clinton's expedition down the Susquahanny. Capt. Gray with his boatmen and boats as understood from Otsego Lake floating from the Susquehanny was with that section of the Army then under the Chief Command of General James Clinton to Tioga Point there awaiting the arrival of General Sullivan with the main army at the time when General Sullivan and General Clinton then disposed the Indians and Tories to the west in destroying their crops and habitations and that they the said company vizt Capt. Gray with his Company of Batteaux men did not return to their various places of residence until forepart in winter, calculated to have rendered at least the length of 9 months United States service during said tour in 1777 and 1780.

Claimant further saith that she has likewise often and frequently heard her husband observe and say that he again was enlisted under the said Capt. Samuel Gray early in spring in a Company of Boatmen and they had commenced early in spring and continued in transporting provisions and other necessaries from Schenectady up along the Mohawk River to supply the garrison at Fort Stanwix and other forts situate up along the said Mohawk River and that by the statements of her deceased husband he at least must have rendered nine months service to the Untied States during said tours, vizt 9 months in the year 1780.

Claimant further saith that it is impracticable for her to remember or recollect all and the imnumerous tours which she heard her deceased husband relate to the United States during the war, shall only relate one or a few tours in each and every year from the year 1776 from year to year to the final termination of the Revolution.

Jan. 1776 as instructed not only by her husband but also by others that her husband was ordered out in mass under the General Command of General Herkimer with the whole Brigade of then Tryon Militia when joined General Schuyler at Caughnawaga from thence to the Village of Johnstown causing surrender of Sir John Johnson with as stated 400 associates of Johnson.

Claimant further saith that same year in fall, again ordered out in mass, the whole brigade, again under the Command of General Herkimer at the time of the general conflagrations at Balstown, ordered to Tripes Hill (Tribes Hill) when returned to Stone Arabia, saith continued from first to last 3 weeks.

Claimant further saith that the Militia were often alarmed, and called out frequently drafted and fortified and ?? that her deceased husband could not (Several lines are not readable) 1777 ??? (passage not legible) Capt. William Tatcor? and understood that the Capt with his company of boatmen have rendered their bateau service to the United States in the service from Spring until late in fall, but cannot specify the precise length of time but should suppose nothing short of eight months.

1778 Claimant further saith that this was a severe and destructive year to general parts of the then County of Tryon, she believing in June the incursion and general conflagration at Springfield, again in October at the time of the incursion and general conflagration at Herkimer in the south side of the Mohawk down to Fort Herkimer and on the north side of the said Mohawk River down to Fort Dayton, all made desolate.

And again sometime in November at the time of the overt sufferings at Cherry Valley not using the mother with the child unborn in her womb when to claimants own observations and knowledge, Col. Jacob Klock's Regt in each and every one of these foregoing mentioned occurrences were ordered out and satisfied that the deceased solder at his turn had kept back by looking and doing his share his fellows a private, militia, soldiers, advancing towards the common enemy and that he in sharing the sure faith with all others ~ besides various occurrences have transpired during the course of this year which has drawn the Militia from their places of residence, drafted, sometimes in consequence of alarms, and watching and rendering garrison duty.

1779 and 1780 claimant further saith that her husband from the early part in spring until forepart in the winter, was engaged, and enlisted under the Command of Capt. Samuel Gray in rendering boat service as aforesaid vizt eighteen months in the course of the two years vizt 18 months.

The applicant further declares that Capt Gray with his company of boat men during the latter years vizt 1780 have met with some Tories attacks in consequence of the enemy from Canada when on the 19th day of October same year, that claimant has reason to believe that her deceased husband with Captain Walthous? of the same company of bateaux man were engaged twice in battle first under the command of Col. Brown in Stone Arabia in what is called Col.

Brown's Battle against Col. John Johnson with his incendiary associates army from Canada when Col. Brown was slain in battle, when the said John P. Gramps again with his Capt and some other of his company, pursuing the enemy at a distance of about eight miles again engaged in battle on Klock & Failing's field under the Command of Col. Lewis DuBois when the enemy withdrew themselves in confusion ~ and same reason in July, Capt Gray was waylaid by Capt. Brandt and detained for ten or eleven days when released by Col. Klock's and Col. Clyde's Regiments.

Also in May previous when on their way to Fort Stanwix, stopped at Fort Hunter with their boats by Sir John Johnson saith with 800 Indians.

1781 The applicant further declares that he said husband latter part in July was engaged in what is called Landman's Battle against a large party of Indians and Tories headed by Leiut. Jacob Klock from Canada the Americans Commanded by Capt Henry Miller, Capt Samuel Gray and Lieut. Jacob Sammons, when the enemy took flight.

Claimant further saith that from the early part in spring until late in fall her deceased husband almost continually kept on the alert, after often and frequently called out in consequence of the incursions of the enemy as claimant may know by what her husband did frequently observe to her, besides personally recollect that frequent serious occurrences have been perpetrated by the common enemy at the time of the general conflagration at and all around Fort Timmerman when her deceased husband beyond any doubt under the command of Col. Willett went in pursuit of the enemy, again engaged in Johnstown Battle under the command of Col. Willett against Major Ross with his incendiary associates from Canada and again after the battle pursuing the enemy to the West Canada Creek under the command of Col. Willett, when Capt. Butler and others of the British was killed and a number of prisoners taken of the British.

1782 During the course of this year, claimant saith and declares that a number of serious occurrences have exhibited itself, murdering, burning and many prisoners taken to Canada, that from the early part in spring until late in fall, the militia were continually kept on the alert and that the deceased soldier has done his full equal part of duty on behalf of the United States during said January.

1783 The applicant further states and declares that at the time of Col. Willett's expedition to Oswego that her husband drove his team of black horses and sleigh and personally knows that her husband did start and went with and under Col. Willett on the expedition to Oswego and not returned until March when Col. Willett with his men returned again.

She further declares that she was married to the said John P. Gramps on the 17th day of January 1783, and that he went under Col. Willett to Oswego on his expedition in February and not returned tunil some time later the same year 1873, that her husband the said John P. Gramps died on the 5th day of August 1819 and that she has remained a widow ever since that period as will more fully appear by reference to the proof hereto annexed.

Sworn to and subscribed on the 23rd day of August 1838 before me.

Nancy Gramps (her mark)

D. F. Salcia Judge

State of New York
Montgomery County

On the 11ath day of August 1838 personally appeared before me John W. Hawer, a Justice of the Peace in and for the County of Montgomery, aforesaid Delia Ehle, widow of John C. Ehle, deceased of the Town of Minden, County and State aforesaid aged seventy years past, who has been duly sworn according to law deposeth and saith, that she has been personally acquainted saith John P. Gramps and Nancy Bellengger sister to the said deponent.

And deponent further saith that the she perfectly recollects and remembers that the said John P. Gramps and Nancy Gramps otherwise then Bellinger were legally and lawfully joined in lawful matrimony in January 1783 by the Rev. Doct. John Daniel Gros D.D. that she was present when the marriage ceremonies was performed that at the time of the marriage she observed seeing them joining hands in hands until the marriage covenant was concluded.

Deponent further saith that according to the best of deponents knowledge or belief that the said John P. Gramps and Nancy his wife have lived and cohabitated together in becoming husband and wife until the 5th day of August 1819 when he the said John P. Gramps died when the said Nancy Gramps became the widow of the said John P. Gramps and yet remaining his widow to this present day and is yet living and not intermarried again.

And deponent further saith that the said John P. Gramps as she always understood hath been a faithful and enterprising Revolutionary Militia Soldier from the early part of the war until the termination of the war.

Deponent further saith that the said deceased soldier which she well recollects that in the month of February 1783 after he had joined in lawful wedlock with her sister, Nancy that her husband had been with slay (sleight) and horses and go under the command of Marinus Willett at the time of his campaign to Oswego that she well recollects his pair of black horses (?) before his Marry, and deponent further saith the reason why she happened to remember or recollect the same occurrence were perculariy, because they had only been there for a such a short period before considered it an unpleasant (?) and further deponent saith not.

Sworn to and subscribed this 11th day of August 1838 before me John W. Hawen, Justice of the Peace.

Delia Ehle (her mark)

This letter was included with the pension papers. The copy is very bad.

June 10, 1937

Mrs. George Hildebrand
111 Prindle Avenue
Johnstown, New York

Dear Madam:

Reference is made to your letter in which you request the Revolutionary War records of John P. Gramps pension number W17959. Lieutenant Johannes Bellinger, killed at the Battle of Oriskany and Jacob James Kronkhuit, variously spelled.

Because of the great demand for Revolutionary War data and the limited clerical force available for furnishing and information, it is impossible to comply in full with each request pertaining to soldiers of that war. The record of John P. Gramps is furnished you herein, the data for which were obtained from the papers on file in pension claim, W. 17959, based upon his military service in the Revolutionary War.

John P. Gramps (the name appears also, as Gremps and Grumps) was born in Tryon County, New York. The names of his parents and date of his birth are not shown.

While a resident of Stone Arabia, Tryon (later Montgomery) County New York, John P. Gramps belonged to a company of Militia under the command of Lieutenant Andrew Dillenbagh and Colonel Jacob Klock. He entered the service in January 1776, under the above named officers and served at various times on tours throughout the entire war. Lieutenant Dillenbagh was killed at the Battle of Oriskany, August 6, 1777 after which Lieutenant Serverinus Cook or Klock took command of that company. Soldier served also under Captain Henry Miller and Colonels Lewis DuBois and Marinus Willett. It was stated that he participated in the Battles of Oriskany, (not legible) Stone Arabia, Klock's Field and Johnstown and in may incidences with the Indians and Tories in mid-Tryon County and along the Mohawk River. He was in a battle called "Landman's" Battle and marched to Cherry Valley at the time of the massacre at that place. He also served three tours as batteauman, one tour on the Hudson River under Captain William Ederson (can't really read the name) in 1778 and two tours on the Mohawk in 1779 and 1780 under Captain Samuel Gray. This service lasted from the time the ice broke up in the river until late in the fall of each year. In 1779, the boats conveyed the troops under General James Clinton to Tioga Point on the Susquehanna River where they joined the army under General Sullivan and west under that officer in the campaign against the Indians. In 1780, the boats carried (not legible) to their necessary supplies from Schenectady to Fort Stanwix and other forts along the Mohawk. In January 1783 he went under Colonel Marinus Willett on an expedition to Oswego Fort and drove his team of black horses and sleigh and did not return until sometime sin March of that year. The entire length of his service was over two years.

John P. Gramps married January 17, 1782, Nancy, daughter of John Bellinger. The date and place of birth of Nancy and the name of her mother are not shown. They were married by the Reverend Johan Daniel Gros, D.C., pastor of the Reformed Dutch Church of Canajoharie, New York.

The soldier died August 5, 1819 at Stone Arabia New York and his widow died at Palatine, New York September 5, 1838, aged seventy-eight years.

The widow was survived by the following heirs:

Catharine or Caty Gramps, who married Aaron Vedder. In 1838 they were residing in Palatine, New York she aged forty-eight years and he sixty-ones years.

Peter Gramps, of Van Buren County, Michigan.

Elizabeth Gramps, widow of Daniel Fenny? Of Fort Plain or Minden, New York.

Lenny? Gramps, wife of Samuel Cook, of Danube, Herkimer County, New York

Mary or Mariah Gramps, wife of John Koop? Of Virgil New York.

Edward Shults of Van Buren County, Michigan and John A. W. Shults or (not legible) children of Nancy Gramp and her husband Christopher Shults both Deceased.

The pension which was due Nancy Gramps was allowed for the benefit of her surviving heirs.

In 1838, Delia Ehle, a sister of Henry Bellinger Gramps was aged about seventy years and resided in Minden, New York. She was the widow of John Ehle.

Solder had a brother, Peter Gramps, also a cousin, Hendrick Gramps. There are no further data in regard to Peter or Hendrick.

(Not legible) Vedder, a brother of Aaron Vedder, husband of Caty Gramps, daughter of this soldier was living in Montgomery County New York in 1840, and stated that the Herman?) was born in 1773.

Very truly yours.

A.   D. Miller

Executive Assistant to the Administrator

Note: the pension was awarded, $80 per annum.

Pension Application for Samuel Gray, Adjutant

State of Illinois

County of Kane

On this 11th day of September 1840 personally appeared in open Court being a Court of Records in the County of Kane and State of Illinois, Nicholas Gray, Samuel S. Gray and Jacob Gray, all of the county and state aforesaid who being duly sworn doth depose and swear that they together with Samuel Gray, Adam Gray, John Gray. Andrew S. Gray, Mary Loucks (wife of William Snell) all of the State of New York are all and the only children of Samuel Gray late of Palatine in the County of Montgomery and State of New York deceased, that they have good reason to believe that their father the said Samuel Gray served at least two years in the grade of an officer during the Revolutionary War as will show fully appear by reference to the records in the War Department of the United States and the Comptrollers Office of the State of New York and the evidence in addition thereto to be procured in the State of New York that their father the said Samuel Gray died on the _____ day of March 1832 and as they age advice? and verily believe without having applied for or received that compensation to which he was entitled by the Act of Congress passed 7th June1832 and in fact he could not have done so having died previous to its passage. They therefore in accordance with the provisions of said Act of June 7th 1832 and in connection with the aforementioned Samuel, Adam, Andrew S., William, Mary and Catharine hereby make application for the amount that would have been due their father the said Samuel Gray viz from the 4th day of March 1831 until the day of March 1832 on which day he died.

Signed, Jacob Gray, (2 other signatures not legible)

State of New York

Montgomery County

On this 10th day of March 1841 personally appeared before the Court of Common Pleas of the said County of Montgomery now sitting, John Gray, Andrew S. Gray, William Gray and Catherine Snell (wife of William Snell) residents of the Town of Palatine in said county who being duly sworn do depose and swear that they together with Nicholas Gray, Daniel S. Gray and Jacob Gray of Kane County State of Illinois, Adam Gray of Erie County New York, and Samuel Gray and Mary Loucks (wife of George Loucks) of Jefferson County in State of New York are all the only children of Samuel Gray late of Palatine in said County of Montgomery deceased. That they have reason to believe that their father the said Samuel Gray served two years and upwards in the grade of a commissioned officer in the Militia of the State of New York in Colonel Jacob Klock's Regiment and in the Battalion Service of the Militia, states during the War of the Revolution as with may fully appear to record in the War Department of the United States in the Comptrollers Office of the State of New York and the attestation of surviving widow here with accompanying.

That their father the said Samuel Gray died on the 19th day of March 1832 and without having applied for or received the confirmation to which he would have been entitled under the Act of Congress passed 7th June 1832. That they therefore in accordance with the provisions of said act and in connection with the aforesaid Samuel Gray, Nicholas Gray, Daniel S. Gray, Jacob

Gray and Mary Loucks and Adam Gray hereby make application for the amount that would have been due their father the said Samuel Gray. Vizt from the 4th day or March 1831 to the 17th day of March 1832 in which day he died.

Signed Andrew S. Gray, William Gray, John Gray (the above says Jacob) and Catherine Snell.

Jim Morrison shed some interesting light on this pension application. He said that often those who served in the boating services were excluded because they were considered a private operation and therefore did not serve in the military part of the war. Being a Captain in the boating service was akin to being a foreman.

Pension Application for Daniel Hart

Hart served during the attack on Canada and when his enlistment was over, he had no way to get home, so he had to re-enlist. After his return from Canada, he was kept very busy as a scout or ranger. This is a very interesting service record.

He entered the service of the United States under the following named officers and serviced as herein stated.

That sometime in the month of July in the year 1775, he enlisted voluntarily in the Company of New York State troops (or Yorkers as they were then called) commanded by Capt Gates in the Regiment of Col. Van Schaick and in which Peter Gansevoort was Major. That the name of the lieutenant was Andrew Finks, the name of the Ensign not recollected, the name of the orderly sergeant was John Guitte?.

That he enlisted in the Town of Palatine in what was then Tryon County (now Montgomery) New York where he resided at the time of entering the service. That immediately after his enlisting he was marched to Albany with his company where he lay a short time, and then they marched to join the Regiment or Battalion of Col. Van Schaick which they did or near Saratoga and then marched to the north for the purpose of invading Canada which they did under Gen'l Montgomery.

They went by way of Lake George to Ticonderoga where they lay a few days and then went to Isle au Noix and from there to St. John where they had an engagement or skirmish with the British and laid siege to the place. That he was in the Battle at Chamblee when the fort was taken by the Americans. After the detachment in which he was engaged went down the Sorrel to a place (the name of which he does not now recollect) and there took a quantity of stores and then returned to Chamblee and St. Johns.

After St. Johns was taken he marched to Montreal with his company and lay there until his time was out which was about the first of July 1776. Their time was about out before they got to Montreal but then the soldiers were persuaded to go on. In Montreal they were discharged or dismissed. Their captain did not go to Montreal and the company went with Lieut. Fink who was in command.

The length of time they enlisted was between five and six months from the time he entered the service before he was discharged as aforesaid. After being discharged in Montreal he again enlisted (being unable to get home) together with a number of his comrades about the middle of Aug. in a company commanded by Capt Brisbe at Montreal in the Continental NY troops he thinks. He lay at Montreal during the winter and served in said Beeber's Company and the Lieutenant was Allen, the other officers of the company not recollected.

They were attached as he believes to Col. Elmore's Regiment and were under the command of Gen'l Wooster. That they marched from Montreal back to Albany in the spring and were discharged in Albany sometime in the month of May. It was three months and a half or four months from the time he enlisted in Capt. Beeber's Company in Montreal until he was discharged in Albany. They marched together until they reached Albany where those who would not enlist were obliged to leave their guns and receive five dollars for it. He did not again enlist but returned to his family residence, he received pay of his gun.

His first period of service was in what was called the Second Battalion of Yorkers (or New York Men) commanded by Col. Van Schaick, but he does not remember any other regiment officers than here stated or any other of the companies with whom he served during this expedition.

In the spring of the year 1777 a company of Rangers (as they were then called) was raised in Palatine in the county of Tryon New York (now Montgomery County New York) for the purpose of scouting and acting as spies upon the Indians who frequently attacked the settlements.

The company was principally raised of men from Stone Arabia (a settlement in Palatine), that he enlisted in said company in the spring but cannot recollect the precise day or month and that he enlisted for nine months the time for which the company was raised. The company was divided in four parties each of which was to be out a week and then one of the other parties relieved them or took their place and changed through the season.

In his portion of the time when he was out he traversed the county in watching and observing the Indians from Stone Arabia through Johnstown and Mayfield to Sacondaga Lake and back, these served as principal places of watching although they were put in other directions occasionally and he remembered going down the Susquehanna a short distance at one time when the Indians that murdered a family in Springfield or Cherry Valley and then retreated down the Susquehanna. They were in readiness to march whenever called upon and raised for that purpose.

He does not know to what Regiment they belonged, one Klock was colonel of the militia in that section at the time but whether they belonged to his regiment or not, he cannot say that when they were not out on duty they remained at their own residences in Palatine. That the company in which he enlisted and served as aforesaid was the company of Capt. Christian Gettman and the Lieutenant was James Billington and the Ensign was Jacob Sammons and the orderly sergeant John Smith the same one who is mentioned as being orderly sergeant in the company of Capt. Gates when on the Canada expedition.

During this nine months service he went out with his company which was called out by Gen'l Herkimer and went with Lieutenant Billington. Capt Gettman did not go out at this time, and the company to relieve Fort Schuyler (Fort Stanwix). While out at this time they had the engagement with the British and Indians usually called Oriskany Battle at which Gen'l Herkimer was wounded and Lieutenant Billington killed or taken prisoner as he never saw him after, that they were defeated and came back and the company dispersed.

After this battle he returned home and served as before in the Rangers and was in the party of Capt. Gettman and served out the whole of the said nine months in the manner aforesaid, at what time his period of his service expired, he cannot recollect as he does not know when it commenced but is positive he enlisted for nine months and served out the whole of his time. Again in the spring of the year 1778 a company of Rangers was raised in the Town of Palatine for the like purposes as the company in the year 1777. He enlisted in the Town of Palatine in said company in the month of April or May.

That the company was then commanded by Capt John Casselman and Lieutenant Sammons, that same who was Ensign the year before in Capt Gettmans company and the company was divided in four parties and each party was out a week at a time and so through the season. They were stationed along the same route they watched the year before and were to look out for Indians and give notice. They were frequently around Sacondaga Lake and they generally went out through Dillebaugh (Tilleborough) to Sacandaga and back home through Mayfield and Johnstown.

That he was in actual service during both the seasons in his depositions mentioned more than one quarter of the time besides being at all times ready and able to be called out as he frequently was. That he does not know to what Regt they belonged or whether they belonged to any. That he served out the whole of said nine months and at expiration thereof the company was dispersed.

Daniel Hart (His Mark)

Pension Application for Daniel Herrick

This soldier guarded the Arsenal at Albany, guarded prisoners of war, served in Fort Plain, Herkimer, Johnstown and was in the chase after the Battle of Johnstown which resulted in Walter Butler's death.

State of New York
Delaware County

On this twenty-fourth day of January in the year of our Lord one thousand eight hundred and thirty-three, personally appeared before the under named, Amos Douglass, one of the Judges of the Court of Common Pleas of the County of Delaware in the State of New York, being a court of record constituted and declared by the Act of the Legislature of the State of New York, Daniel Herrick, a resident in the Town of Davenport in the County of Delaware and State of New York, aged seventy (blotted) years who being first duly sworn according to low doth on his oath make the following declaration in order to obtain the benefit of the Act of Congress passed June 7th 1832.

That he entered the service of the United States under the following named officers and served as herein stated.

He enlisted in the spring season, the month he does not recollect, in the year one thousand seven hundred and seventy-eight in the Town of Kinderhook, in the then County of Albany but now in the County of Columbia and State of New York as a volunteer into a company commanded by Captain Van Ness whose Christian name he does not recollect, for the term of four months and immediately after the enlistment, the company marched to the City of Albany and were stationed there for a short time, but were not attached to any regiment. And then the said company under the command of Captain Van Ness escorted some prisoners of war who were taken at the surrender of General Burgoyne from Albany to Hartford, in Connecticut and then returned to Albany, and after the company returned to Albany we were stationed to guard the arsenal where they kept guns, powder and military stores were deposited and at the expiration of our term of service the company were discharged by said Captain Van Ness, but did not receive any written discharge. The company was not attached to any regiment or any other company. This deponent does not recollect the name of any other officer of said company beside the Captain.

That he enlisted in the spring season, the month he does not recollect, in the year one thousand seven hundred and (blotted) in the town of Kinderhook, in the then County of Albany but now in the County of Columbia and State of New York as a volunteer for the term of nine months into a company commanded by Captain Stephen White, first Lieutenant John Thornton as second Lieutenant Mores, in the militia of the State of New York and were stationed there to guard and defend the place against attacks by the British or Indians and until the fall season when the company marched to Fort Plain in the County of Montgomery on the Mohawk River and was united with a company which was stationed there to defend that place, in the regiment commanded by Colonel Marinus Willett.

And having heard that the Indians had attacked or were preparing to attack Fort Herkimer we marched to Fort Herkimer to defend it and the Indians not being at that place we returned to Fort Plain. And then having received information that the Indians and British were at Johnstown in Montgomery County we marched to that place, and the day before we arrived at Johnstown there had been a battle between the Americans and British and Indians in which the Americans were victorious and we then returned to Fort Herkimer on the Mohawk River in the month of October or November, and at Fort Herkimer two soldiers out of every company in Colonel Marinus Willett's regiment were detached and were united with the Continental Army at that place and this deponent was one of the soldiers so detached, but does not recollect the names of the officers who commanded the company to which he was attached or officers of the regiment.

And then the army pursued the British and Indians to Canada Creek near the Mohawk River and there was a battle with them where Captain Butler of the British Army and nine Indians were killed, and the enemy was defeated and then we returned to Fort Plain and in the latter part of the fall or forepart of the winter season just before the nine months service, for which he enlisted had expired, this deponent, on account of feeble health was discharged by Colonel Marinus Willett, the commanding officers but did receive any written discharge.

And the deponent further says that he has not any documentary evidence of his service and that he does not know of any person whose testimony he can procure who can testify to his service.

And in answer to the interrogatories put by the said Judge, this deponent says that he was born in the said town of Kinderhook in the County of Albany but now in the County of Columbia and State of New York in the year one thousand seven hundred and sixty two in the month of April and that he has not any record of his age, only the traditional information of his parents and relatives which he believes to be correct.

And that he lived in said Town of Kinderhook when he enlisted into the service as above mentioned and about a year after the war he moved into Schodack, in the then County of Albany but now in the County of Rensselaer and lived there about five years, the then moved into the Town of Harpersfield in the said County of Delaware and lived there about twenty-five years he then moved into said Town of Davenport and has lived there about fifteen years, where he now resides.

That he enlisted into said service as a volunteer and that he does not recollect the names of any Continental or Militia officers besides those above mentioned and that he did not receive any written discharge from the service and that Daniel R. Campbell and Charles Spoor of the Town of Davenport in the County of Delaware are and have been well acquainted with this deponent as much as twelve years past and who can testify as to the character of this deponent for veracity and their belief of his services as a so9ldier of the Revolution.

Here hereby relinquishes every claim whatever to a pension or annuity except the present and declares that his name is not on the pension roll of the agency of any state.
Signed Daniel Herrick (his mark)

Pension Application for Christian Hess, Sergeant

Application was made by his widow for a pension benefit and after her death, by her daughter for herself and other siblings. The pension law covered children of officers receiving a pension.

On this eighteenth day of October in the year of our Lord eighteen hundred and thirty eight personally appeared before me John B Dygert Esquire a judge of the court of common pleas of said county Elizabeth Hess resident of Brighton; in the county of Monroe in said state and ninety four years who living, by me first sworn according to law doth on her oath make the following declaration in order to obtain the benefit of the provisions made by the act of Congress passed July 4, 1836. That she is the widow of Christian Hess late of Pittsford in the County of Monroe deceased who was a private a part of the time and a sergeant a part of the time during the Revolutionary War in the army and Militia of the United States.

That her husband enlisted first about commencement of the war and for service nine months under Captains Eyesler and Bigbread and that during his term of service and in the month of April she was married to him, that after he served out this term, he soon or immediately after went to Stone Arabia now in the county of Montgomery in said state and enlisted again as she was then informed, understood and believes for three years, but this deponent has forgotten the names of his officers on this occasions though she thinks the name of one was Willett, Willims or Wilkis or some such name.

That he was absent from home on this occasion in the service nine or ten months and then returned home and stayed some five days perhaps two or three and then went off again to serve and in this way he served occasionally returning home and remaining a few days until about or to the final close of the war, but whether he enlisted for any other term or terms than those she stated, she cannot state through he was off in the service as have stated that during the Revolutionary War, the place of residence of this deponent and her said husband was in part of the time in Schuyler in the County of Herkimer and State of New York and a part of the time in Stone Arabia aforesaid.

That when the nearness of the enemy rendered it necessary this deponent went to the nearest fort for protection, that he said husband was absent when Stone Arabia was burnt in the service, but this deponent was then there and went into this fort after that on such occasion she went into Fort Plain that the record of his making his statement before an officer in Herkimer county is because his relatives reside in that county as well as the persons or most of the persons now living who know of the service of her late husband, that she is not able owing to her advanced age and bodily infirmity to attend court to make her declaration and she further declares that she was married to the said Christian Hess in the month of April in the first year of the war but on what particular day of the month or in what particular year she is not able to state, that her husband the aforesaid Christian Hess died on the fifth day of August 1804 and that she has remained a widow ever since that period as will more fully shown by reference to the proof here to annex that she and her husband resided in Herkimer County aforesaid to the county of Monroe aforesaid about forty years since.

Sworn to and subscribed on this day and year shown written before

Elizabeth Hess (her mark)

State of New York
County of Livingston

In Open Court

On this 31st day of January A.D. 1855 before the county court held within and for the county and state aforesaid personally appeared Catherine Stilwell aged Sixty Nine years a resident of the Town of Livona in the County of Livingston and state of New York who being duly sworn according to law doth on her oath make the following declaration in order to obtain the benefits of the provisions of the Act of Congress of the 7th June 1832 granting pensions to certain survivors and the Widows and children of Officers and soldiers who served in the War of the Revolution.

That she is one of the children alive of Elizabeth Hess deceased who was once the wife and afterwards the widow of Christian Hess deceased who was a private as she has been informed and believes in Colonel Willett's Regiment for which service the said Elizabeth Hess declarant's mother received a pension to an amount less than thirty dollars per annum as she has been informed and verily believes that where and when he entered the service and how long he served and where and when he was discharged and under what officers he served except said Col. Willett or in what battles he was engaged, declarant has not know.

Declarant further states that she has heard her said father Christian Hess and her said mother Elizabeth Hess frequently say and declarant states that fact to her that said Christian Hess his said father served in said war as a sergeant in Col. Graham's Regiment but when and where he entered the said services and under what officers he served except Col. Graham or in what battle he was engaged in or how long he served and where and when he was discharged declarant does not know but she believes that he served as such sergeant in said regiment more than two years. That she has no documentary evidence of his service but for the proof of his service she must rely on the proofs and records now on file in Washington.

That her said father Christian Hess died on the 23rd day of August in the year 1808 according to the best of her recollection in the town of Opurietta? In the County of Monroe in the State of New York and left a widow surviving him the said Elizabeth Hess of died in the town of Pirrington in the said county of Monroe on the twenty second day of February in the year on thousand eight hundred and forty three.

That the following are the only surviving children of the said soldier Chirstian Hess and are the surviving children of the declarants mother the said Elizabeth Hess to wit Chatharine Stilwell, and declarant Augustus Hess, Joseph Hess, Daniel Hess and Elizabeth Allen.

The declarant makes this declaration in behalf of herself and the said other children for the purpose of obtaining an increase of the said Elizabeth Hess's pension for more service than she is receiving and for service which the said Christian Hess performed in the said Col. Graham's Regiment as a Sergeant or otherwise or in any other regiments and capacity while serving or applied for by her mother the said Elizabeth Hess or by any other person.

Catherine Stilwell (Signed)

Pension Application for Daniel Hess

This soldier saw a lot of interesting service and most of his pension record is presented here. He mentions that he fetched ammunition for the regiment and brought it back to Col. Jacob Klock's house. Some of the local fortified homes were picketed (or palisaded) by Hess and others as part of his service. During the Clinton Sullivan Campaign, he helped with the horses in bringing supplies and baggage.

State of New York
Montgomery County

On the fifth day of September A.D. 1832, Daniel Hess made the following deposition.

David Hess now a resident of the Town of Oppenheim aged 76 this 13th November last made the following declaration in order to obtain the benefit of the Act of Congress passed June 7, 1832. That by reason of his age and consequent loss of memory and the great length of time that has elapsed he cannot possibility state the precise period of his service hereafter stated but states that to the best of his recollection as follows.

That as he can remember on the 15th March 1775, he entered the company where John Hess was Capt and Wormuth was Lieut and George Waggoner Ensign in the Regiment where Jacob Klock was Col in the Brigade where Nicholas Herkimer was the General.

That he then resided in the Town of Palatine. He served as a private in said company and that the whole company of Capt Hess's were engaged from 15 March 1775 to 20 March 1775 for at least five days at the now village of Palatine where there was a small fort (so called) that he served during said time in said company as a private (to which he belonged) for at least 5 days in company was stationed at said case and that he was ordered out by the officers of his company that he has no evidence he knows of that he can for service as to this time of service.

On the 4 May 1775, he was drafted out of said John Hess Company as a private with about 15 others to fetch ammunition from Albany that when drafted he took supplies from the then Town of Palatine to Albany guarding wagons to Albany. At Albany the wagons were loaded with ammunition which they guarded back to the house of Col. Jacob Klock where the ammunition was lodged that he cannot remember which of his officers accompanied them if any, that one Jacob Klock appeared to have the command of the wagons and he thinks commanded or assumed the command of the guard for the wagons. That he knows they took with them a private from this time he was drafted as last mentioned to the 15 May 1775 for a least he thinks ten days and that he has no evidence of this service that he can procure except that of Peter Eigenbrod.

7 March 1776 he still belonged to Capt Hess's Company and that the Hess said company was called out into the service and he also that he in said company marched to the then Town of Palatine where he resided to Caughnawaga at near house of Vedder's Mills at said place and was stationed with said company to 22 March 1776 for at least 14 days as a private that Capt Hess commanded said company that scouts were sent out he then said he served at aforesaid for at least a fortnight as aforesaid, that there were others of the militia at said place and thinks one Capt Fox company that he knows of no testimony he can use ? to his service in this time out.

5th day of October 1776 the said company of Capt Hess were ordered into service that said company marched from the then town of Palatine where he resided to German Flatts and that house of Mr. Harmen Dygert's and said company were then principally stationed to 16 of same month that he served on this time for at least 11 days as a private in same company that he thinks the Indians had burned some of the dwelling houses of the German Flatts people and while at the German Flatts.

One Helmer, a scout, came in and reported that they had seen Indians who had shot one of the scouts and fired on the others, the inhabitants were alarmed and fled to the fort that the Indians did not succeed to kill any of the inhabitants that he can remember except one of the scouts as aforesaid and that scouts were sent out and that he has no testimony he knows of he can procure on his service on this tour.

That as near as he can recollect to date on the 15 June 1776 he was drafted out of Capt John Hess's company with Louis ?? after being drafted they were first with Commander Christopher Fox, called on Capt Hess, marched from the then town of Palatine where we went to Fort Dayton that the while at Fort Dayton aforesaid in ? said fort, Col Dayton was at the fort that he says from the time he was drafted to July 15, 1776 at Fort Dayton in marching to the fort that while at said place Gen Herkimer held a treaty with the Indians when there were quite a number of troops there, that he served at this time as a private for at least one month that he was as to this his services the ? of Lodowick Kring armed being the only Indians he ? at the start he says (can't read a lot in here) that on the 10th day of August 1776 the company of Capt Hess served at least he thinks 5 days at that ? of Lt Col Waggoner where this was a small fort in the ? That he served as a private at this time in said company but ? is near he can recollect from 10 Aug 1776 to the 14th of same month for at least 5 days as a private in said company in this service, he remembers that Henry Miller, a private in said company, was in the service accidentally shot by one Geo Waggoner but recovered of said wound that he does not know of anyone he can procure as to this part of his service.

That was summoned into service with the company of said John Hess was Captain was ordered out while company he belonged as a private that he thinks they were out and served for at least ten days he thinks at this time as a private, they were marched from the town of Palatine where he resided to German Flatts on account from alarms, that hey were stayed out one ? ? ? to Herkimer, served at least the thinks 10 days that he has no knowledge and knows of no one he can procure as to the evidence of his service on last tour.

That he can recollect he worked in building or making a sort of fort of Capt John Hess's dwelling it was commonly known as Fort Hess that one Christopher Fox then or afterwards a committee at Fort Hess started in building it under his Capt. John Hess and a number of privates of said Hess company were also engaged in assisting to fortify said home for a fort that he labored he thinks from May 4, 1777 in building said fort for at least 16 days and he was then a private in said company and that he cannot swear that he was ordered into service by his officer or whether the neighbors voluntarily did this work and cannot say that he was strictly engaged as a soldier in this service when so to work he had aforesaid that pickets were built among other things for fortifying said fort that Capt Hess ordered this work and those engaged but if he cannot be allowed for this service the ? is to be disregarded that he has as to this service the testimony of Peter Eggabroadt ?? from which he thinks it possible that this service was rendered by order of his officers and cannot swear from his recollection to that effect as he does not recollect.

That as much as he can recollect he served as a private in said company aforesaid from June 17, 1777 to 26 the of same month for at least 14 days at Fort Hess that he was a private in his company that according to the best of his recollection the whole company was ordered out and marched to said fort that he was left with some others to guard Fort Paris and the rest of this company proceeded to Johnstown with some others that he thinks remained at Fort Paris guarding same by the order of his captain, that whether he was drafted out of said company to remain at said Fort he is not positive but thinks those must have been a draft and that he thinks were drafted and stayed at said fort for at least the period aforesaid and then returned home, that he has no witness as to this service and has no one of same he can procure.

That to the best of his recollection he served as a private from the 10 July 1777 to 27th of same month for at least 7 days as follows and he was drafted into said company commanded by John Hess Capt to go to Schenectady to fetch ammunition and that proceeded from the town of Palatine in batteaus or boats on the Mohawk River to Schenectady there got ammunition loaded in their bateaus, or boats and he thinks he was ordered on the return and this ammunition was brought to Col Jacob Klock. That some of these went along the bank of the river on foot guarding the batteaus and he thinks they must have been engaged on this time out at least one week that he cannot recollect no one he can inquire as to the recruiting of the service.

That according to the best of his recollection he served as a private from 2 Sept 1777 to the 7th of same month as follows. In the said company of Capt Hess were ordered out into service That this company served for as Herkimer and other troops which he understood they secured intelligence that the Indians were in their rear, the troops or some of them returned part of the way, when it turned out that the report was unfounded that the company and troops then were ordered on their way to Oriskany and this applicant and others returned home. His officers ordered or requested him to return home.

Col Klock gave him a letter to deliver it to his captain that the company of Capt Hess waited some time 2 or 3 days and some others waiting for re-enforcements at Herkimer, that he served on this tour at least 5 days, that said company was engaged in the battle called the Oriskany Battle that he this applicant was not in the battle by reason of his returning as aforesaid, that he believes this letter to Col. Klock's son, that the only testimony as to this his service he can produce that the following is that of Peter Eggebradt hereto aforesaid.

That according to his recollection served as a private from the 18 May 1778 to 21 May 1778 in said Company of Capt Hess as follows: said company served and was stationed at the house of Mr. Failing in the Town of Palatine and part of the house of Mr. Zimmerman nearby, that the company was stationed at said place and standing sentry and scouts were sent forth as it was reported that the Indians intended to attack the said place in that he serviced during said patrol for at least 13 days, that he has no evidence to this service and knows of no one he can procure for this evidence thereof.

That to the best of his recollection he served as a private in said company for at least one day in the summer of 1778, that he thinks 7th July of this year is near as he can think of same that the said Hess Company were engaged, they provided to same Col. Klock's residence in this neighborhood for which a Ser? Huss? had been killed by the Indians and more engaged, he thinks but one day, that he has no evidence knows of no one he can procure as to the certitude of this service.

That according to the best of his recollection; he served as a private in said company from July 10 1778 to 16th of same month for at least 6 days, that the whole company were engaged, proceeded to Springfield where they found the building burnt and he thinks two Indians had been there and that he served as a private and then resided in the said Town of Palatine that Capt Hess commanded said Company that he has no evidence and knows no one he can procure of this service.

That as near as he can bring to his recollection he served from; 20 Sept 1778 to 27th of the same month as a private in same company for at least 7 days that the company was engaged that the company went to Bowman's Creek and were there stationed that the services were rendered he thinks the same season that Cherry Valley had burned but whether it was a little before or after he cannot positively state it was about the time, about this time his Lieut Wormuth was killed by the Indians that he has no evidence and knows of no one he can procure as to this service.

That he served as near as his memory is as a private in this company aforesaid from 1 March 1779 to 13 of same month at least for 13 days that this whole company was engaged, that they were marched to Remensnyder's Bush to a small fort and stationed there. Scouts were daily sent out that at said fort two persons were taken prisoners by a body of Indians, he remembers there was 6 now on the ground and it may be that he rendered this service in Feb? but thinks it was as aforesaid that the resided in the Town of Palatine about this time Peter Waggoner was made a Capt of said company in the place of Ens. Hess but that particular time he cannot positively state that he has no evidence as to this service and knows of no one he can procure.

That as near as he can recollect he served as a private 1 or 2 days at least one day in the said company sometime in the month of April of 1779. He thinks and that the company was marched to Krings Bush in Palatine where a house had been burned down supposed to have been done by some Indians and when they got there they found the Indians had been those burned and said house and taken as boy as prisoner by the name of Smith that he served a least one day at this time that he had no evidence and knows of no one he can procure as to this service.

That according to the best of his recollection he was ordered either by his officers or some of the committee men to go to and harness teams to aid General Clinton in carrying his baggage, ammunition and go to Otsego he thinks he rejoined Gen'l Sullivan's Army, that he was engaged in bringing teams as the aforesaid for at least 6 days from 1 June 1779 to 7 of same month including the time in going to make his return, that he went twice to get teams the first he did not get enough when he was ordered a second time that he cannot have been engaged he thinks in this business at least 6 days including the time of going to make his returns and he belonged at this time as a private to the same company aforesaid that he resided at this time in the Town of Palatine aforesaid that he has no evidence of the rendition of this service and knows of no one he can procure, that he went some ten miles to procure teams.

He belonged at this time as a private to the same company aforesaid he thinks commanded by Capt. Peter Waggoner from 15 June 1779 to 25th of the same month for at lease 10 days or more the whole company were engaged in this service that they were marched to near Utica where there were some Batteaux or boats which they assisted in reaching to Fort Stanwix, that these and more troops at this time waiting for reinforcement that he was engaged as a private on this time for at least 10 days.

He thinks in this service he saw an officer by the name of Major Morris, he has no evidence or knows of no one he can procure as to the rendition of this service. 8 days, he may be mistaken as to the time this service was rendered by him.

That he near as he can recollect he served as a private for two days, he thinks as near as he stated in the month of September 1779, day 10 and 11 of same month, under Capt Waggoner he thinks the whole company were engaged it was the time that Capt Rechtor was shot and wounded by the Indians in Dillenborough (Tilleborough near Ephratah) in the then Town of Palatine whom they found wounded and some others also were killed by a part of Indians, he is not positive as to the time and may be mistaken though he has the day he rendered this service he has no evidence of this service and knows of no one he can procure.

That as near as he can recollect he served as a private from May 7 1780 to 15 May 1780 in Fort Countryman a house fortified as a fort in Minden and he was drafted at this time with others. Eight of said company were stationed at the fort, served there for at least 14 days as a private that he cannot remember who had the command of this fort, that they were stationed in said fort and guarded houses, that he may he mistaken as to the time when this service was rendered but is positive that he served at said place that he has no evidence of this service and knows of no one he can procure.

That as near as his memory serves him he also served as a private under Capt. Peter Waggoner from Sept 9 1780 to 22 of same month that the company was marched to Utica guarding boats to Fort Stanwix that they guarded or assisted in guarding said boats to Fort Stanwix that in this service Gen'l Van Renssalaer commanded that he served as a private in this service for at least 13 days that he has no evidence and knows of no one he can procure and but that of Peter Eggabroat ???

That as near as he can remember he was in Fort Hess 15 Oct 1780 and had been nine days previously under Capt. Peter Waggoner that Sir John Johnson and his men marched and past said fort that they fired from the fort on Sir Johnson's forces and they returned fire that some rounds were discharged that an Indian was killed by those in the fort that after Sir Johnson had passed on he went and found the Indian's musket and whom they carried off that some of those in the fort went with Gen'l Van Rensselaer in pursuit of Sir Johnson. That he thinks he served in said Fort for at least 5 days at this time that he has no evidence and knows of no one he can procure on this since (seems to be something missing here) and further says that he may be mistaken as to the time stated by him as aforesaid when his aforesaid services was rendered but is positive that he served in times before herein specified by him and to the best of his recollections for the length stated by him and that he has no evidence of said services and has stated same according to the best of his recollections and belief that he for one year resided in the County of Herkimer.

Until lately that he now resides in the Town of Oppenheim the said County of Montgomery that he resided in the County of Herkimer (blotted) a person to sign but his papers for a pension but by reason of his age and he is residing out of said county, his papers were not completed which are the reasons of his not applying sooner and further says that he is in indigent circumstances and that when the services herein stated by him as (blotted) done he resided in the then Town of Palatine in the now County of Montgomery where he has resided the greater part of his life and most of the time he resided in Herkimer County that he has no documentary evidence and has procured all the evidence he could as to his said services.

I hereby relinquish to any claims whatsoever to a pension or annuity except the present and do swear that my name is not on the pension roll of this state or any state that he swears ?? a never was discharged from the service he can recollect but surely verbal ones.

Interragoratories.
He states he was born 13th day of November 1757 in the Town of Palatine in the County of Montgomery and that he was living in the Town of Palatine when he entered service.
This part is very repetitious.
He provided two fellow soldiers of the Revolution to verify his claim, Rev. Charles A. Smith and Peter C. Fox

He died November 4, 1832.

Pension Application for Christian House

The pension file for Christian House contains the following letter from a previous inquiry.

June 18, 1936
Mrs. James A Venable
1434 Iroquois Ave.
Detroit, Mich.

Madam:
I have to advise you from the papers in the Revolutionary War pension claim W 7759 it appeared that Christian House was born October 14, 1756, place not stated.

He enlisted in 1775 and served nine months as private in Captain Jacob Sauer's New York Regiment; and immediately after enlisted and served nine months in Captain John Winn's New York Company.

He enlisted at Canajoharie in March 1777 and served in Captain Robert McKean's Company, Colonel Goose VanSchaick's New York Regiment, he was at the taking of Burgoyne, the Battle of Monmouth, and was taken prisoner in July 1779 near Fort Stanwix, and carried to Canada, from where he made his escape in June 1781, and returned to his regiment, and was discharged at close of war.

He was allowed pension on his application executed April 9, 1818, while a resident of Florida, Montgomery County, New York. He died March 11, 1844.

Soldier married December 22, 1822 at Minden, Montgomery County, New York, Mrs. Huldah Schuyler (widow of John Schuyler). She was allowed pension, on account of the services of Christian House, on her application executed May 19, 1855, while a resident of Minden, New York, aged eighty years.

In 1819, soldier's son-in-law, is referred to, his name is not stated, nor that of his wife. There is no further data on file as to family.
Respectfully,
Winfield Scott, Commissioner

State of New York
Montgomery County
Christian House of the Town of Florida in the County of Montgomery afore said being duly sworn doth depose and say that he served under the Continental establishment for the Revolutionary War from the time of his enlistment till the end of the war and that he entered the services in the year seventeen hundred and seventy five he thinks and enlisted under the command of Capt. Jacob Sauer first for nine months and at the expiration of the nine months he this deponent enlisted under Capt. John Winn for nine months more and served the time out faithfully this deponent then enlisted under Capt. Robert McGee for during the war and then this deponent served under commander till the close of the war and then received his honorable discharge which discharge this deponent was lost.
This deponent further said he was in several battles, namely, the Monmouth Battle and the taking of Burgoyne and several at this engagement not mentioned.
This deponent further said that by reason of his advanced age and extreme age he is unable to provide evidence from a distance that are now living to prove the facts above stated and this deponent further said that by reason of his reduced circumstances in life and old age than stands in need of assistance from his country for support and further said not.
Sworn and subscribed before me on this 9th day of April 1818.
Benedict Smath? Judge of Com. Pleas
Christian House (his mark)

State of New York
Montgomery County
Christian House, this applicant, in the annexed papers named being duly sworn says that he this deponent in the month of March in the year of our lord 1777 at Canajoharie in the said county and state enlisted in a company commanded by Robert McKean and in Robert McGee's as mistakenly wrote in his first declaration hereto annexed in the regiment commanded by Goose Van Schick as Colonel in the first New York regiment in the line of the state in the Continental Army of the United states the Revolutionary War, for and during the war and continued in said regiment until the month of July 1779 when he was taken prisoner by the British near Fort Stanwix now Town of Rome in the County of Oneida in said state and was taken from thence to Canada and remained there as prisoner until about the month of June 1781 when he affected his escape and returned from Montreal and came to his regiment at and between Stillwater and Albany in said state and then in consequence of his being a prisoner of war his officer gave him a permit to return to his home and there remain until farther orders of that he was not thereafter called upon for any service although he continued were ordered.
Subscribed and sworn to this 2nd day of August 1819, before me, Aaron Haring, First Judge of Montgomery County.
Christian House (his mark)

Pension Application for Cornelius House

Some of the early pensions depended on a veteran having no assets and being unable to support himself. You will find a list of this soldier's assets and debts. Note the amounts of the debts. It is too bad early pensions were dependent on the soldier's income and assets.

State of New York
Montgomery County
Court of Common Pleas
1820 on this fourteenth day of June, personally appeared in Open Court in the Court of Common Please of the County of Montgomery being a court of records constituted and established by the constitution and laws of the State of New York in the said county who being first duly sworn according to law doth on his oath declare that he served in the Revolutionary Was as follows.

That he was enlisted to service during the war in a regiment of artillery commanded by Col. Lamb in the Line of the State of New York in Captain Doughtery's Company sometime in the beginning of the year 1780 according to the best of the declarants knowledge said belief in which he served till regularly discharged in 1783 and that he has received a pension certificate under the seal of the War Office No. 1050 and I the said Cornelius House do solemnly swear that I was a resident citizen of the United States on the 18th March 1818 and that I have not since that time by gift, sale or in any manner disproved of my property or any part thereof with intent thereof.

As to diminish it as to bring myself within the provision of an Act of Congress entitled An Act to provide for certain persons engaged in the land and navel service of the United States in the Revolutionary War, passed on the 18th March 1818 and I have not nor has any person in trust for me any property or secured contractor debts due me, nor have I any income other than what is contained in the schedule hererto annexed and by me subscribed. Scheduled out 6 acres of land on which I reside in the Town of Johnstown on which is a small swelling house, one plough and one old wagon. One grindstone, some household furniture, one scythe, one loom, one calf, two horses, one iron pot, one Bible.

(His Mark) Cornelius House.

Sworn to and declared on the 14th day of June 1820 in open court before me, John Carthy (Clerk)

And the declarant Cornelius House further saith that he has no mechanical trade but his occupation is that of a common labourer. That his is much afflicted with rheumatism in his left shoulder, hip and knee and is not able to perform hard labour and is frequently in consequence of the rheumatism in such a situation that he cannot labour at all.

That his family residing with him consists of two daughters to wit, Jane House of the age of about thirty years and Nancy House of the age of about twenty seven years and a step daughter named Pother Wilkley aged about fifty eight years who has been confined to her bed for upwards of twenty years past in consequence of weakness or some inward complaint and is yet so confined without any probability of relief. That his daughters the said Jane and Nancy or one of them must always remain at the house to attend to his aforesaid step daughter. That one of them occasionally works out but this declarants get no part of their earnings. And the declarant further states that he is now justly indebted in the following sums of money for the six acres of land in the schedule of his property mentioned about. $70.00

To Nicholas T. Goodan	12.50
To Jacob Wilson	10.00
To Jane House	10.00
To Cornelius Putman	4.75
To Henry Fonda	4.50
To Douw Wemple	8.00
To Benjamin Sammons	2.37 ½
To Wm Taylor, merchant at Caughnawaga	3.61
To Oliver Bannister	5.00
To Thomas Sammons	7.00
To Myndert Staring	1.75
To Jacob M. Gardinear	3.00
	$142.17

Montgomery Common Pleas June four 1820.

It is the opinion of the court that the total amount in the value of the property exhibited in the schedule within contained is 154 dollars and 70 cents.

State of New York
Montgomery County
Clerks Office

I, John McCarthy Clerk of the Court of Common Pleas in and for said County do hereby certify that the foregoing oath and the schedule thereunto annexed are truly copied from the record of the said court and I further certify that it is proved to the satisfaction of the said court by the oat of credible witnesses and that it is the opinion of the said court that the total amount in value of the property exhibited in the aforesaid schedule is one hundred fifty four dollars and seventy cents. In testimony whereof I have hereto set my hand and affixed the seal of the said Court on the 14th day of June 1820.

John McCarthy

Montgomery County for: Cornelius House for the Town of Johnstown in the County of Montgomery and State of New York being duly sworn, deposeth and saith that he is listed as a Matross? Or private soldier in a company of Artillery commanded by Captain Doughty belonging to a Regiment of New York Artillery commanded by Col. Lamb sometime in the year one thousand seven hundred and eighty in the Revolutionary War between the United States and Great Britain. That he served in said Regiment from; the time of his enlistment as aforesaid until the Army of the United State was disbanded at the close of the war in the year one thousand seven hundred and eighty three, when he was honorably discharged. And this deponent further saith, that he is in reduced circumstances in life, and in need of assistance from his Country for support; and has never received any pension on account of his services. (his mark) Cornelius House. Sworn the 2d day of April 1878 before me, Simon Veeder, one of the Judges of the Court of Common Pleas for the County of Montgomery.

Montgomery County, State of New York SS

Personally appeared before me, Simon Veeder, one of the Judges of the Court of Common Pleas of the County of Montgomery aforesaid, the said, Cornelius House, in the written deposition named and made oath that he was enlisted as in the written deposition mentioned and mustered at New Windsor in the State of New York and that he was discharged from the Army at the close of the war as in the said deposition mentioned at West Point in the State aforesaid. That he was in the battle at Yorktown in Virginia under General Washington, at the taking of Lord Cornwallis. And this deponent farther saith that his discharge is not now in his possession, but that sometime after the close of the Revolutionary War, he delivered it to a man by the name of Michael Rawkins to draw some arrears of pay then due to this deponent and that the said Michael Rawkins (since deceased) never turned it to the deponent nor does he know where the same now is.
(his mark) Cornelius House
Sworn the 15th day of May 1818 before me.
Simon Veeder, one of the Judges of the Court of Common Pleas for the County of Montgomery.

State of New York
Montgomery County SS.

On the tenth day of June, in the year of our Lord, 1823, personally appeared in open court being the Court of Common Pleas of said county in said state and being a court of record by the Constitution and laws of said state, Cornelius House, resident in said county aged sixty years on the first day of March last past who being first duly sworn, according to law, doth on his oath, make the following declaration in order to obtain the provision made by the act of Congress of the 18th of March 1813, and the first of May 1820.

That he, the said Cornelius House enlisted for the term of, for, and during the Revolutionary War on or about the month of November in the year of our Lord 1780 in the State afore said, in the company commanded by Captain Doughty, in the Regiment commanded by Colonel John Lamb in the Line of the State of New York (New York Line) aforesaid on the Continental establishment, that he continued in service in said corps until the month of June 1783 when he was discharged from said service at West Point in the State of New York.

That his name has been placed on the pension list and dropt there from on account of his property. And in pursuance of the act of May 1820. I do solemnly swear that I was a resident citizen of the United States, on the 18th day of March 1818 and that I have not since that time, by gift, sale or in any manner disposed of my property or any part thereof with intent thereby so to diminish it as to bring myself within the provisions of an act of Congress entitled an act of provide for certain persons engaged in the land and naval service of the United State in the Revolutionary War passed on the 18th day of March 1818, and that I have not, nor has any person in and for me, any property or any securities, contracts, or other debts due to me, nor have I any income other than what is contained in the schedule hereto annexed, and by me subscribed to wit, six acres of land, on which I reside in Johnstown, Montgomery County, New York State, on which is a small dwelling house, one plough, some old iron of a wagon, one grind stone, a few articles of old and nearly worn out household furniture, one scyth, one loom, one calf, two horses, one iron pot, one Bible.

That since the exhibition of my last schedule the following changes have been made in my property, that the land stated in my said first inventory, I held by article of assignment from

John Davis, by which it was stipulated I should pay two hundred and fifty dollars and then receive a conveyance for it, that I was unable to pay the money within the time stipulated, the said John Davis declared the contract forfeited and all my rights at an end, and he then sold, conveyed it to Nicholas Yordon and I occupy it as a tenant at which under an obligation to pay of the seasonable use and occupation of it. That at the other articles dated except the furniture I have sold for the purpose of supporting myself and family and I just own one old mare.

That I am by occupation a farmer, but I am unable to do scarcely any labor at that, in consequence of old age and severe rheumatic complaint under which I labor daily and cannot fully open one of my hands by reason of it. That I have one daughter residing with me, named Nancy aged thirty years and she is able to support herself by her labor, that I am unable to support myself by labor.

(his mark) Cornelius House

Sworn in Open Court, 10th June 1823, Henry J. Yates, Clerk

State of New York
Montgomery County SS

I Henry J. Yates, Clerk of the Court of Common Pleas of the said county, do hereby certify, that it appears to satisfaction of the court that the said Cornelius House did serve in the Revolutionary War, as stated in the preceding declaration against the common enemy for the term of nine months under one engagement, on to Continental establishment. I also certify that the foregoing oath, and the schedule there to annexed, are truly copied from the records of said court, and I do further certify, that it is the opinion of the said court, that the total amount of value of the property exhibited in the aforesaid schedule is fifteen dollars. In testimony hereof, I have hereunto set my hand and affixed the seal of the said court on this the 10th day of June 1829.

(Signed) Henry J. Yates, Clerk.

Pension Application for George House

This pension revealed some shocking information, something which appears in no history book I have ever seen. He tells about Sergeant Weefer disobeying Captain Winn and the captain hitting him with his musket and killing him. Captain Winn was caught and put in jail but somehow he managed to get out. After this he was demoted from captain to quartermaster. How he managed to do this, history does not tell us.

State of New York
Herkimer County

On the twelfth day of February 1833 personally appeared in open court before the Judges of the Court of Common Pleas in and for the County of Herkimer, sitting George House of the Town of Warren, County of Herkimer, State of New York aged seventy six years of age who being first duly sworn according by law doth on his oath aforesaid and make the following declarations in order to obtain the benefit of the Act of Congress passeth the seventh day of June 1832, do make the following declarations that he enlisted in the services of the United States under the following named officers and serviced as herein after stated.

And this deponent further saith that he was born in the Town of Canajohary, County of Tryon, now the Town of Danube, County of Herkimer, State of New York and that when he first entered the service of the United State he resided in the now Town of Minden as aforesaid and County of Montgomery that aforesaid.

This deponent further saith that he does not recollect the year he first enlisted into the service of the United States but says according to the best of his recollection that he enlisted in the month of July under Capt John Winn, Lieutenant Lawrence Gross, the enlistment took place in the now town of Minden by Sergeant Elias House, for during the war this deponent further saith that he thinks that this enlistment took place shortly after the commencement of the war and was enlisted as a private soldier.

This deponent further saith that after being so enlisted as aforesaid that deponent was ordered to go to Canajohary and after arriving at that place was passed muster and took the oath of allegiance, this took place in the presence of my officers of the company to which I belonged to wit, Capt. John Winn, Lieutenant Lawrence Gross and Second Lieutenant Peter Shremling and after the company being so organized was commissioned our march proceeded to Springfield, Otsego County from there to Cooperstown in said county, remained there sometime during which time I was sent out in scouts among the detachment to Unadilla, German Flatts, says others on arriving at German Flatts we received a paper for us to carry to our officers in order to show that we were at that place on the aforementioned scouts.

This deponent further saith that sometime in the winter of said year we left Cooper Town from there to Springfield there we remained until the spring following thence the company recontinued their march from thence to Johnstown from thence to a place called Philadelphia Bush, there we lay sometime in going out on scouts at diverse and different places to wit to Sacandaga, Lake George about fifty miles, to Sandy Hill, Saratoga.

This deponent further states on arriving at Sandy Hill aforesaid the company there present were ordered on parade and Sergeant Jacob Weefer disobeyed the order of Capt. John Winn when said Capt. gave said Weefer (Weaver) such a mortal shove with a musket which caused wounding by Weefer's which he surviving only few days.

In consequence of the death of said Weefer, Capt. John Winn fled and left his company and was pursued by a group of men and was taken on the Susquehanna River and brought back to Canajohary there the deponent stood guard over his body a number of days and until he the said Capt. was taken to Albany there confined in the Goal of that County.

This took place sometime in fall of said year and then this deponent quit the service the company being much disorganized and scattered that they all quit it and this deponent proceeded home, this deponent further saith to the best of his recollection he serviced under said Capt. John Winn, Lieutenant Lawrence Goss, Second Lieutenant Shremling, not less than one year and five months, this deponent further saith that when he enlisted under said Capt John Winn he enlisted for during the war and that they enlisted as Rangers and were known as a company of Rangers and during our term of service we rendered no other service than Ranging and Scouting from place to place until the company became abandoned as aforesaid.

This deponent further saith that the year after the Battle of Oriskany early in the spring of said year he this deponent, enlisted in the service of the United States for the term of nine months under Capt. Dickson of Cherry Valley as a private soldier this enlistment took place in the Town of Springfield Otsego County. After my enlistment I proceeded to Albany under the command of said Capt Dickson after arriving there the company under the command of Capt. Dickson and another company commanded by Capt. Gray was ordered to take possession of a number of boats said to have been taken from ??? something like twenty in number and we proceeded down the river with said boats to a place called Tarry Town, there we remained some time in ferrying soldiers across the river this was General Washington's Army which we ferried across the river, thinks in the Jerseys from thence back to Albany there I remained on duty in boating up the river and back until the close of the year and on the ??? before new year I received a written discharge by Capt. Dickson which said discharge is since lost, this ended my nine months term of enlistment.

And this deponent further saith that he enlisted in the service of the United States the third time for the term of nine months, I was entered into the company commanded by Capt. Samuel Gray as a private soldier this enrollment took place early in the spring of afore mentioned succeeding year the year after the above mentioned this deponent says cannot recollect the year this enrollment took place but days he was enlisted at or near Fort Windecker now Montgomery County and after being so enlisted I was ordered to go to Schenectady and on arriving there we were set a boating on the Mohawk River up and down the river and we returned that kind of service during the summer season under the command of Capt. Samuel Gray, Colonel Brown who was afterwards killed at Stone Arabia, Montgomery County and was discharged as this deponent thinks at Schenectady by Capt. Samuel Gray by a verbal discharge. This ended my enlistment of nine months.

This deponent further saith that he enlisted the fourth time early in the spring of the following year, cannot give the year when the enlistment took place but says that this enlistment was at some place along the Mohawk thinks it Canajohary for the term of nine months under Capt. Lefler Company as a private soldier and commenced my service at Schenectady and continued my service with boating service during the whole summer season and ended my term of nine months enlistment and received a verbal discharge by Capt Lefler. This deponent does not know but this last enlistment may not be this third enlistment in place of the fourth.

This deponent further says that he enlisted a fifth time in the war for a term of nine months as the deponent thinks in the year 1781 at Fort Windecker by or under Capt Lawrence Gross as a private soldier and under the immediate (this word is spelled amidite, sometimes emidite) command of Colonel Marinus Willett. I remained at said Fort Windecker the time of about two and a half months during which time I had the command of said fort which command I received from Capt Lawrence Gross and after remaining as long as before stated, I went across the Mohawk River in order to get permission to supply the fort when I was taken prisoner by enemy's Indians and conveyed to Canaday there was passed by then eleven months and got my liberty to go about and scout from place to place and afterwards made my escape and came back the whole time of my absence was about one year and two months.

This deponent further saith that he served in the War of Revolution not less than the period mentioned below and the following grades to ???

The four years and ten months I served as a private enlisted soldier and for such service I claim a pension.

This claimant further saith that eleven months out of the above estimate of Revolutionary service I was a prisoner of war among the enemies Indians in Canaday.

This deponent further saith that his second, third and fourth enlistment as above mentioned to war under Capt. Dickson, Capt. Samuel Gray and Capt. Lefler was rendered in the War of the Revolution exclusively in the boating service, this service was rendered financially in the Mohawk River from the City of Schenectady to Fort Stansicks (Stanwix) and places intermediate except my second enlistment above mentioned was rendered in the boating service in the North River as before stated. (Note, the Hudson was called the North River in the early days.)

This deponent further saith that my services on the Mohawk River as a boatman consisted in carrying military goods, stores, ammunition, arms,??? Cannons, from Schenectady to Fort Stanwicks and other forts intermediate. (in between)

This deponent further saith that his first enlistment commenced soon after the commencement of the War of the Revolution and that he this deponent entered into the United States Continental troops for during the war and the company to which he belonged was known as a company of Rangers does not at present does not recollect other such company was attached to our regiment or not said company because seemed to be the Ranger thru in the country and go on scouts from place to place in the company. I served one year and five months until said company became disbanded.

This deponent further saith that the several companies commanded by Capt. Dickson, Capt. Samuel Gray, Capt. Lefler and Capt. Gross afore mentioned served under the immediate command of Colonel Willett.

This deponent further saith that he was born in the now Town of Danube, Herkimer County State of New York does not recollect the year positively but believe in July 1757, says that he has no record of his age, says that he resided in the now Town of Danube, Herkimer County State of New York when he first enlisted in the service of the United States in the War of Revolution and since the war he resides in the aforementioned town from thence to the Town of Stark, Herkimer County from then to the Town of Springfield, Otsego County, New York from thence to Warren my present place of residence, Herkimer County.

This deponent further says that he entered in the War of the Revolution as a private soldier says had not never been drafted he was neither a volunteer nor a substitute.

This deponent further saith that the regular officers who were with the troops where I served were Colonel Willett, Colonel Brown, Capt. John Winn, Capt. Dickson, Capt Samuel Gray, Capt. Lefler, Capt Lawrence Gross. Said Gross was Lieutenant under said John Winn, Lieutenant Shremling, General Herkimer, Colonel Cox and Major Finck.

This deponent further says that he had got but one written discharge that was from Capt. Dickson which is lost and all other discharges were verbal.

This deponent further says that the following persons are to me personally known and reside in my immediate neighborhood who can testify to my character and their belief of my services as a soldier in the War of the Rrevolution to wit, Peter Bellinger, Joakim Van Volkenburgh, Henry House, John Duesler.

This deponent further says that he never received any annuity or pension from government or under any law of the United States providing for the officers and soldier of the Rrevolution hereby relinquish every claim to a pension or annuity except the present passeth June 7th, 1832. And declares that my name is not on any pension list of any agency or any State.

This deponent further says that he has not obtained the evidence of a clergy neither is there any clergy now living in this deponents knowledge who can testify to this deponents age.

This deponent further says that he has no documentary evidence showing any of the service of this deponent in the War of the Revolution.

(Signed with His Mark) George House

Sworn in open court February 12th 1833. Julius T. Nelsoir?, Clerk

We, Thomas Hall of the Town of Stark, Herkimer County and John Duesler of the Town of Danube, County of Herkimer both of the State of New York do hereby certify that we are well acquainted with George House who has sworn and says further the above declaration we believe him to be seventy six years of age, that he is reputed and believed in his neighborhood where he resides to have been a solder of the Revolution, that we concur in that opinion.
(Signed with His Mark) John Duesler, (Signed) Thomas Hall
Sworn and subscribed in open court February 12, 1853.
Julius T. Nelsoir?, Clerk

State of New York
Herkimer County
Town of Danube
     Came before me 1833 Feb 12, Abhm George N. Schuyler, Esqr, one of the Justices of the Peace in and for the County of Herkimer, State of New York, David Schuyler, now of the Town of German Flatts, County of Herkimer. That County of Herkimer in State aforesaid who being duly sworn depose and saith, that he has been personally acquainted with George House present applicant for a pension and a resident in the Town of Warren, county aforesaid before the War of the Revolution during the said War and since the War of the Revolution.
     This deponent further saith that in the year 1781 or 1782 he this deponent and said George House enlisted as a private soldier in the service of the United State in the War of the Revolution in the company commanded by Capt. Lawrence Gross at Fort Windecker for the term of nine months, early in in the spring of said year in the then County of Tryon and now County of Montgomery and that aforesaid.
     This deponent further saith that after being so enlisted this deponent and said George House was stationed by order of said Capt. Gross at said Fort Windecker in order to guard said fort and that after remaining at said fort about two and half months by order of said Capt and under the immediate command of Colonel Willett myself and said George House were sent to cross the Mohawk River in order to procure provisions and supplies for said fort.
     When said George House and this deponent were taken prisoner of the enemies' Indians and taken to Canaday then was kept by them as prisoner for more than one year when said George House was set at liberty to go from place to place when at a suitable opportunity said George House made his escape and returned to his country.
     This deponent further saith that during the time we were taken prisoners as before mentioned I was in company with Said George until we arrived in Canada and after arriving there I more or less saw him every month or more thru one year and until said George House made his escape as before mentioned.
     This deponent further saith that it was perfectly understood during the whole War of the Revolution that said George House was and had enlisted in the service of the United States almost every summer during the whole war and that said George House had been in the boating service for several summer seasons on the Mohawk River as well as on the North or Hudson River and that in the early part of the war said George had enlisted in the Company of Rangers under the Command of Capt. John Winn.
     This deponent further saith that eh was well satisfied that said George House served during the ??? part of the War of the Revolution from the reason that said George had entered several different terms for nine months in the vicinity of Fort Plank or Tryon County and that from the many conversations on the subject of his different enlistments and the general talk at that time and since, do not herefore hesitate in making the above statements.

State of New York
Herkimer County
     Came before me, Cornelius Ten Eyck Van Horn Esqr, one of the Justices of the Peace in and for the County of Herkimer in State of New York. Christian House of the Town of Stark, Herkimer County that aforesaid who being duly sworn before and saith that he was well acquainted with George House present applicant for a pension before the War of the Revolution during the war of the Revolution and since the War of the Revolution.

This deponent further saith that shortly after the commencement of the War of the Revolution he this deponent for George House aforesaid on duty and serve as a private soldier in a company of Rangers then spying at Cooperstown Otsego County under the command of Capt John Winn and Lieutenant Lawrence Gross and an other officer by the name of Shremling the first two officers to wit, Capt John Winn and Lieutenant Lawrence Gross are well and had been personally known to this deponent and to further state at the time this deponent saw said George House in the militia service of the United States and under the command of said Capt. John Winn and he, this deponent, was informed after making the necessary inquiries that said George House was an enlisted soldier into the company then laying those that the company to which he enlisted was a company of Rangers and that said George House had enlisted in said company for during the war, does not recollect the precise year when the deponent saw House as aforesaid.

The deponent further saith that at the time when this deponent was with General Washington's Army and was crossing the North River at Tarry Town near White Plain that he this deponent saw said George House employed in the boatery service in ferrying the army across the North River (Hudson) and that some inquires was informed by said George House that he said House was enlisted in the Boating Service under Capt. Dickson and that his said Enlistment was for nine months.

This deponent further saith that at an other time when this deponent was in the service of the United States it was of the Revolution at Fort Stanwicks in guarding the fort and that during which time he this deponent saw said George House employed in the boatery service carrying military goods and arms, ammunition, provisions up the Mohawk River to said fort to supply said fort. This deponent further saith that he this deponent lay and was stationed at said Fort Stanwicks for something like one year in guarding said fort under the immediate command of Lieutenant Colonel Van Slyck, Major Craim Cast? and Andrew Fink.

This deponent further saith that during which time I this deponent frequently saw said George House in the course of the summer season on the boating service and that he this deponent saw said George House often in the course of the summer does not hesitate on saying that said House was constantly employed during the summer season and that Said house had been an enlisted soldier of the term of nine months in the boating service does not know the officers under where he served but recollects to have seen said House under the command of same ??? an officer commanding said boat and further saith not.

(Signed with his mark) Christian House
Sworn and subscribed this 15th day of February 1835 before me.
Corn'l V.E. Van Horne, Justice.

I hereby certify that I am personally acquainted with the before named Christian House and that his evidence may be relied upon as being just and true.
Corn'l V.E. Van Horne, J.P

Pension Application for Hendrick House, Otsego County RWPA W 21383

Hendrick spent time serving in Fort Windecker which was on the south side of the river, a bit west of St. Johnsville. He served in the Battle of Johnstown.

State of New York
Otsego County
On the seventeenth day of October 1832 personally appeared on open court before the Judges of the Court of Common Pleas in and for the County of Otsego now sitting Henry House of the Town of Springfield in County of Otsego State of New York aged seventy seven years of age who being first duly sworn according to law, doth make the following declaration in order to obtain the benefit of the Act of Congress passeth June the Seventh 1832 that he entered the service of the United States under the following officers and served as herein stated.

This deponent further states that he was born in the Now Town of Minden Montgomery County, State of New York that he has record of his age but says from information that he was born the seventh day of April 1765.

This deponent further saith that at the age of sixteen years of age he enlisted in the War of the Revolution at Fort Plank then the Town of Canajoharie, County of Tryon now the Town of Minden, Montgomery County this enlistment took place early in the Spring of the year 1781 and this deponent has reason to believe from circumstances at Fort Plank aforesaid and enlisted in the company commanded by Capt. Lawrence Gross under the immediate command of Colonel Marinus Willett. This deponent further states that after being enlisted aforesaid and passeth muster he was ordered to Fort Plain from thence to Fort Windecker. Those at that fort I was stationed to guard and stand sentry on stouts? Here we remained and served as aforesaid until sometime in the fall of said year and more particularly until the Battle of Johnstown now Montgomery County and did also the taking of Butler at the West Canaday Creek.

This deponent further saith that he was in the aforementioned Battle of Johnstown aforesaid that he served there shortly before the battle commenced and that he the deponent was engaged throughout the whole of said battle and in the morning of the next day I went in pursuit of said Butler and was present at the taking of said Butler and saw his dead body lay on the ground with his scalp taken off and was nakit (naked).

This deponent further saith that after the battle aforesaid I remained a short time at Fort Windecker from there to Fort House from there To Fort Tayton (Dayton) from thence Fort Herkimer and so on from place to place thence to Fort Herkimer again there received my discharge. This discharge was a letter sent by Capt Lawrence Gross to the officers commanding the Fort to discharge men there that had enlisted.

Gross of the officers commanding this fort, discharged me and others who had enlisted the same time. This enlistment-nine months my enlistment.

This deponent further says that during this aforesaid enlistment I was commanded by the following officers to wit, the Battle of Johnstown I was commanded by Col. Marinus Willett, Capt Lawrence Gross, Capt. Putman at other places Lieutenant Loltkill, Lieutenant Hutton, Capt Lawrence Gross.

This deponent further saith that he rendered services to the United States in the War of the Revolution in what summer season at Fort Plank the year previous to the above enlistment this was militia service and during which time rendered no other service, did no other ??? employed at not other kind of work there to guard, stand sentry and go on Scouts this service rendered under the immediate command of Major Coapman, Capt. House, Lieutenant Miller, this summer season service amounts to, as this deponent believes, to six months actual service.

This deponent further saith that the year after my aforesaid enlistment thinks in that year 1782, I rendered services to the United States in the War of the Revolution as a Militiaman in Fort Plank as aforesaid this season I commended early in the spring of said year under command of Captain House and Major Coapman and I continued my service as aforesaid in guarding said fort Montgomery County and going on scouts at different times and different durations this summer season almost wholly employed in the season of the fort and going on scouts as afore said and that I rendered no other services the whole summer season than as aforesaid of my Country obliged the orders of my officers as above stated this summer amounted to six months actual service and further says not.

This deponent further says that he was born in the now Town of Minden on the seventh day of April 1765.

Says that he has no record of his age.

Says that he enlisted when he entered the service at Fort Plank since the war resided in the now Town of Danube, Herkimer County from there to Springfield to my present place of residence

Says that he was drafted, never was a volunteer, never a substitute.

Says that officers under which I served are the following to wit, Colonel Marinus Willett, Captain Lawrence Gross, Capt. Putman, Lieutenant Loltkill, Major Coapman, Captain House.

Never received any written discharge.

Says the following persons reside in my immediate neighborhood who can testify to character for veracity and their belief of my service as a soldier in the War of the Revolution. To wit, Geo House, John Dusler, Jacob Young, Jacob Van Valkenburgh, John Allen.

This deponent further saith that he never received any annuity or pension under any law of the United States providing for the Revolutionary officers and soldiers hereby relinquishes every claim whatever to a pension or annuity except the present and declares that his name is not on the pension roll of this or of any state. (Signed) Hendrick House.

Sworn and subscribed in open court the 17th day of October 1832, Horace Lathrop, Clerk

State of New York
Otsego County SS

On this fourteenth day of September 1838, personally appeared before Circuit Court of the fifth Circuit, Nancy House, a resident of Springfield in said County of Otsego, aged seventy years, who being duly sworn according to law, doth on her oath make the following declaration in order to obtain the benefit of the provision made by the Act of Congress passed July 7, 1838 entitled "An Act Granting Half Pay and Pensions to Certain Widows". That she is the widow of Henry House, who was a private soldier in the Army of the Revolution, that he served in Capt. Gross and Capt. House Company for a more particular description reference may be had to the evidence in the War Department, that the said Henry House was an applicant for a pension.

That this deponent received the same from the 4th March 1831 to the 5th day of June 1834. The day of his death, under the of 1832. (looks like a word was left out of the application) She further declares that she was married to the said Henry House on the fifteenth day of February 1789; that her husband the aforesaid Henry House died on the fifth day of June 1834. That she was not married to him prior to his leaving the service but the marriage took place previous to the first day of January seventeen hundred and ninety four, vizt at the time above stated.

Sworn to and subscribed on the day and year above written before me in open court. (Signed with her mark) Nancy House

Jesse Nose? Clerk

I certify that from age and infirmity Nancy House the foregoing applicant is unable to write her name and therefore makes her mark. Jesse Nose?, Clerk

Pension Application for Henry House S45385

This soldier just got out of Debtor's Prison and he has a daughter sick with consumption (TB) and near her end. To help care for her he had to hire a nurse. Very sad story.

State of New York
Schoharie County SS

On the ninth day of February in the year of our Lord one thousand eight hundred and twenty one, personally appeared in the open court of Common Pleas of the County of Schoharie, said court being a court of record, Henry House aged fifty eight years, the fourteenth day of March last, a resident of the Town of Schoharie in County aforesaid, who duly sworn according to law doth on his oath declare that he served in the Revolutionary War as follows to wit, that he entered about the month of July or August but on what particular day or month he cannot say in the year 1777, into a company commanded by Captain Johnston, whose Christian name is not recollected in the fifth regiment then commanded by Colonel Lewis DuBois, in General James Clinton's Brigade, in the New York Line, that he faithfully served upon the Continental establishment exceeding nine month, that is to say from the above mentioned time of enlistment until the expiration of the War or until the ninth of June in the year 1782 according to the best of his recollection when he was discharged honorably at a place called at Snakes Hill in the County of Orange in the State of New York.

The services he performed and battles in which he was engaged are more particularly set forth in an original declaration by him made and which has been or he believes transmitted to the War Department of the United States at Washington bearing date April 10th 1818, to which he begs leave to refer, that he has been placed upon the pension list and received a pension and that the number of his certificate is 7,114.

And I do solemnly swear that I was a resident citizen of the United States on the 18th day of March 1818, and that I have not since that time by gift, sale or in any manner disposed of my property or any part thereof with intent thereby to diminish it, so as to bring myself within the provisions of and Act of Congress entitled "an act to provide for certain persons engaged in the land and naval service of the United States in the Revolutionary War, passed on the 10th day of March 1818.

And that I have not nor has any person for me, any property or securities, contracts of debits due to me, nor have I any income other than what is contained in the schedule hereunto amended, and by me subscribed. A true and perfect schedule of the read and personal estate of Henry House (necessary and bedding excepted.)

The said Henry House has no real estate whatsoever, nor interest therein.

His personal estate consists (necessary clothing and bedding excepted) of one chair, the cart of which was one dollar only the said Henry House having been a debtor for almost one year in the County of Schoharie until the Ninth day of December, last when he was discharged from imprisonment upon assigning and delivering up to his assignees. All his estate for the use of all his executors, excepting the necessary wearing apparel of himself and his family, his arms and equipments according to an act of the Legislature of the State of New York entitled "An Act to Abolish Imprisonment for Debt in Certain Cases" passed April 7th 1819.

I, the said Henry House, do further in manner aforesaid, swear and declare that I never learned a trade, but am a common laborer that for ten months last past, I have been able to labor but a small part of the time, and for two of the ten months, not at all, on account of the rapid declination of my health.

I have no wife, but sired children, who need from me, aid to obtain a comfortable support, one of whom particularly a daughter is very low with the consumption (TB) as is said by physician, and is apparently very near her end, to attend whom I have been obliged to employ a nurse, but am utterly unable to compensate her.

Sworn and subscribed (Signed) Henry House
This ninth day of February 1821.

Pension Application for John S. Kasselman

This man applied for his pension August 8, 1832 and died August 20, 1832.

State of New York
Montgomery County
On this ninth day of August in the year of our Lord one thousand eight hundred and thirty two personally appeared before David? Haring first Judge of the Court of Common Pleas of the County of Montgomery and State of New York John S. Kasselman, a resident of the Town of Johnstown in the County and State of New York aforesaid, aged seventy years, who being first duly sworn according to law, on his oath make the following declaration in order to obtain the benefit of the Act of Congress passed June 7, 1832.

That he entered the service of the United States under the following named officers and served as herein stated.

Your applicant says that in November in the year 1777 he was drafted as a Militia Man in the Company of Captain John Breadbig, entered upon duty in the spring following of 1778 and served at the following places, the times when he went out and when discharged, this applicant does not recollect. The first time he went to a place now called St. Johnsville, Montgomery County does not recollect how long he was out at this time.

The second time he was drafted as a waggoner in Sullivan's expedition and was out five or six weeks. He also served a term at Fort Plank now Minden, Montgomery County, and the length of time he was out at this time he does not recollect. In Fort ??? he served five or six weeks and also served two months as a at a place then called Remensnider's Bush. And also served two months in Fort Dayton situate in Herkimer and there in the County of Tryon as was Remen Snyder's Bush at that time in Tryon, but now Oppenheim, Montgomery County. And also, another term at Fort Herkimer for four or five weeks. And also served one month and a half at Dillenburgh, (Tillaborough) situate at that time in Tryon and now Montgomery County. Your applicant says that he served three different winters during the Revolutionary War in carrying provisions and implements of was from Albany to Fort Stanwicks, a month or five weeks each winter.

Your applicant says that he was at Fort House, at that time Tryon County and now in Oppenheim, about one month. (This is now in the Town of St. Johnsville. When Fulton and Montgomery Counties split, part of Oppenheim to the south was in Montgomery County and became the Town of St. Johnsville.)

(Part of next line is missing) months, in the year 1781 and that he went out sometime in the months of April or May and served the full term of nine months under Captain Lawrence Gross, this company was attached to Colonel Marinus Willett's Regiment and that they went to Herkimer and then to the battle called Turlough, in Sharon, Schoharie County.

In the year 1779 I served at Fort Keyser, then in Tryon County since Palatine, Montgomery County and served at this fort in all about three or four months. Your applicants says that he was out during the Revolution on scouts and alarms at different and divers times also and above the number so herein before specified. Your applicant says that at this time he was called into the service, he resided at now Palatine, Montgomery County.

Your applicant says that he was born at Palatine aforesaid in the year seventeen hundred and sixty two and has no record of his age.

Your applicant says that he was acquainted with the following regular officers, Colonels Gansevoort, Willett, Capt Andrew Finck. Your applicants says that he is acquainted with the following persons residing in his neighborhood who can testify as to his character for truth and veracity and their belief of his services as an officer of the Revolution. David Zeilly, George Walter, Peter Wormwood. Your applicant says that he has the documentary evidence.

And your applicant says that he hereby relinquishes every claim whatever to a pension or annuity except the present and declares that his name is not on the pension roll of the agency of any state. Your applicant says that he was in the Turlough Battle and has served during the whole time he was out at least two year and nine months.

And this applicant says that Captain Hess was his Captain one time when stationed at now Herkimer. George Klock, Colonel. That Capt. Breadbake and Lieutenant Zeilly were his officers most of the time and that at one time a Lieutenant Finch was his officer. That most of the time nearly all of the beginning of the service in Col. George Klock (He must mean Col. Jacob Klock, George was never a Colonel) of the latter part of the time under Col. Peter Waggoner and as to the rest of his officers he is unable to relate except that Jellis Fonda was his Adjutant for awhile of which was for the nine months service and at the frequency of calls for service for several years and this great distant period when performed and the alarms and I was daily changes of command and the constant shifts of tours renders it now out of his power to name all his officers.

John S. Kasselman (signed by him)

Montgomery County.

On this twentieth day of September in the year of our Lord one thousand and eight hundred and thirty two personally appeared before the judges of the Court of Common Pleas of Montgomery County now sitting at Johnstown in said County, David I. Zeiley a resident of Palatine in the County aforesaid, aged sixty two years and upwards, who doth depose and say that John S. Casselman the above named applicant for a pension, lived with John Zeiley his father, to learn the art of farming, about the beginning of the Revolutionary War and until the end of this war and that during the time the said Casselman lived with Zeiley in the year 1778, the said Casselman entered the service of the United States as a Militia Man and served at different times during two years, he does not know at what time of the year 1778 he entered the service at this time he was under Capt. Bredbig of the Regiment Commanded by Col. Jacob Klock.

This deponent further says that the said Casselman returned to his father's house several times during the two years and that in the year 1781 he was again drafted for nine months and he served out that time.

Deponents says that he knows that the above named applicant was engaged in the Battle at Tourlock in the County then called Tryon now called Schoharie, also in the Battle at Johnstown in Montgomery County

This deponent further says that in the year 1782 the said Casselman was in the service of the United States at different times, but how long he does not recollect. And this deponent says that the said John S. Cassleman died in the year 1832 on the twentieth day of August and he was present at his funeral, and that said Casselman was a man of truth and veracity and that he was reputed to be a man of truth and veracity in the neighborhood where he the said Casselman resided.

And this deponent further says that the said John died leaving five children by the names of John F. Casselman, Jonas Casselman, two sons, Maria, the wife of John F. Dockstater, Nancy wife of Lodewick Beck and his unmarried daughter Betsey.

And this deponent says that these are all the children that the said John left and he further says that they are all more than twenty some years of age and upwards and this deponent further says that he died having no widow and further this deponent says not.

David I. Zeiley (signed by him)

Letter from Governor Clinton to Colonel Klock

Poughkeepsie Sept'r 25th , 1778
Sir,

By my Orders to you of the 6th April last, you was directed to raise two Companies of sixty men each, including non Commissioned Officers, from the Militia of Tryon County to be stationed on the Western Frontier for the Protection of the Inhabitants af't the Incursions and RavAges of the Enemy &ca.

And by my subsequent Orders, you was directed to Call into actual service and constantly keep out one fourth Part of the Militia for the same Purpose, & similar Orders to the last were also issued at the same Time to the Commanding Officers of the Militia of Albany County.

But, as I have not been favoured with a Line from you on that Subject, or any Return of the Men you may have had in Service in Consequence of these Orders, I am altogether ignorant whether they have been complied with by you. The deaily Depradations committed by the Enemy on the Frontier Inhabitants & particularly the late melancholy one at the Flatts, leads me to believe they have not, as I am persuaded had my Orders been fully & faithfully carried into Execution most of the Distresses experienced by those Unhappy People might have been prevented.

I am, therefore, again to repeat my above Orders to you, & the absolute necessity of their being faithfully & without Delay carried into Execution; & it is my further Orders that the Militia for this Service be so stationed as to afford the most equal & perfect Security to all the Frontier Settlements & that you make Returns to me from Time to Time of the Numbers you have out, where stationed &c.

I have Reason (from his Excell'cy Genl. Washington's Letter in answer to mine contain'g a Representations of the Distresses of the frontier Inhabitants) to expect some small Succor, (however illy to be spared), from the main army; but as some time must elapse before they can arrive the utmost exertions of the militia are absolutely necessary. I am Sir Your most Obed't
G. C.
To Colo. Clock

Tryon County Asks for Assistance

Letter to Governor Clinton

Canijohary Tryon County Sept 28th 1778.
Sir,

We beg leave to represent to your Excellency the most deplorable Situation of this County. The Enemy have from Time to Time desolated and destroyed the Settlements of Springfield; AndrewsTown and the German Flatts, by which at least one hundred and fifty Families are reduced to Misery and Distress. People who before were in flourishing Circumstances are thus by one wanton Act brought to Poverty.

Notwithstanding we have repeatedly wrote our Situation down and asked relief, we have obtained none except Colo. Alden's Regiment, which is stationed at Cherry Valley where they remain in Garrison. Woeful Experience teaches us, that the Troops in Cherry Valley are by no means a Defence for any other Part of the Country. We should long e'er now have desisted from requesting any farther Support were we not convinced that unless we obtain Relief, the Enemy are strong enough and we fear will in short make another Attempt to lay waste this Country.

Strange as it may appear to your Excellency, it is no less true, that our Militia by Desertion to the enemy and by Enlistments into our Service, are reduced to less than seven hundred Men. Indeed if these 700 would do their Duty and act like Men, we might perhaps give the Enemy a Check, so as to give Time to the Militia from below to come up, but, Sir, they are actuated by such an ungovernable Spirit that it is out of the Power of any Officer in the County to command them with any Credit to himself—for notwithstan'g the utmost Exertaion the Officers have nothing but Blame in Return.

From the Information we are able to collect from Prisoners and otherwise, we learn that the Enemy, when at the German Flatts were 500 or upwards strong commanded by a Capt. Caldwell. That they intended soon to make another Incursion, and that a Reinformcement of 5 or 600 men on its March from the western Nations of Indians to join the Enemy, Indians being frequently seen and our People fired upon, seems in our opinion to indicate a speedy Return of the Enemy.

We have, therefore, now to request of your Excellency, to order up a sufficient Force, in order to make a vigorous Impression on the Enemy's Quarters, and to drive those murdering Villians out of our Country. Your Excellency may be assured that we shall exert every nerve to collect what Men we possibly can.

We sent the Bearers, Colo. Fisher and Peter S. Deygert, Esq. To give your Excellency what farther Information you may desire to know, and to join us in supplicating your Excellency to afford us immediate Succour. We have the Honor to be Sir Your Excellency's most Obedient and very Hble. servants.

Jacob Klock, Sam'l. Campbell, Pieter Weizger, Sam'l. Clyde, Christopher W. Fox, John Hess, Jacob Defendorff, Christ. Stofel Fox.
To Gov'r Clinton

The Governor Holds Officers To Blame

Poghkeepsing Oct'r 12th, 1778.
Gentlemen,

I have received your Letter of the 27th ult but have not seen either Col. Fisher or Mr. Dygert whom you mention as Bearers and to whom you refer me for more particular Infoamtion.

When we are acquainted that W. Chester, Orange, Ulster & Albany & Charlotte Counties are equally exposed to the Ravages of the enemy with yourselves and that the Militia of Dutchess which is the only remaining County have been during the Summer frequently called to strengthen

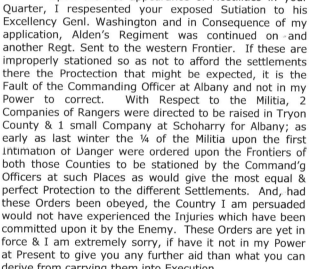

the Posts in the Highlands, you will readily perceive that your Safety must in a great Measure depend upon your own Exertions & the aid which can be afforded you by the County of Albany.

Upon the fist appearance of Hostilities in your Quarter, I respesented your exposed Sutiation to his Excellency Genl. Washington and in Consequence of my application, Alden's Regiment was continued on and another Regt. Sent to the western Frontier. If these are improperly stationed so as not to afford the settlements there the Proctection that might be expected, it is the Fault of the Commanding Officer at Albany and not in my Power to correct. With Respect to the Militia, 2 Companies of Rangers were directed to be raised in Tryon County & 1 small Company at Schoharry for Albany; as early as last winter the ¼ of the Militia upon the first Intimation of Danger were ordered upon the Frontiers of both those Counties to be stationed by the Command'g Officers at such Places as would give the most equal & perfect Protection to the different Settlements. And, had these Orders been obeyed, the Country I am persuaded would not have experienced the Injuries which have been committed upon it by the Enemy. These Orders are yet in force & I am extremely sorry, if have it not in my Power at Present to give you any further aid than what you can derive from carrying them into Execution.

I will, however, make it my Business to lay your distressed Situation before the Legislature, and I wo'd fain hope that they will put it in my Power to raise a sufficient Body of men to carry on offensive operations at't the Enemy & thereby give more Security to the Frontier Settlements. It is not for me to determine whether it is from the refractory spirit of the men, or neglect of the Officers, that my orders have not been executed. No Returns have been made to me by any of the officers in consequence of my repeated orders; neither does it appear to me that Courts Martial have been held upon the conduct of the refractory & disobedient. In these Instances the officers are certainly to blame & merit all the Censure they have received. I am &c.
G.C.
To Col. Klock.

The three previous letters are from: Public Papers of George Clinton

I wonder where the Governor thought all these men were to be found? Manpower was getting scarce in the valley about this time. About a year later the regiment was down to 258 men and two years later about 100 men, if the accounts are correct. The regiment was spread very thin and had a huge area to cover. The longer the war went on, the less the men felt like joining up to fight and the fewer men were available to fight.

In addition, Colonel Jacob Klock was in a bit of trouble from the time of the Cherry Valley Massacre. He did not respond as promptly to the call for help as he should have and did not stay long enough to be of much help at the scene even after the massacre. Thereafter, he was not in charge of as many troops as previously, Colonel Frederick Visscher was given the responsibility for most of the troops.

There was a garrison of troops at the fort in Cherry Valley, but Brant and his troops were possibly still in the area. Could they not get out of the garrison? Klock was in another spot at the time with his men and no doubt it took time to get the message and then respond to the call for help. They were in Cherry Valley by the evening the day after the massacre.

Probably about this time, Colonel Klock was very weary of warfare. He served in the French and Indian Wars and in fact was captured during this war. According to calculations, he had to be up in years during the Revolutionary War, in his 60s or 70s no doubt, he had two sons and a son-in-law who joined the enemy and all around him he saw devestation and death with no end in sight.

Who would want to stay the course under those conditions? It could not have been an easy or pleasant time for anyone who lived in the valley during this time.

Pension Application for Witter Johnston

Johnston went with Herkimer when he met with Joseph Brant before the war. He fought at Oriskany and at the Battle of Johnstown.

State of New York
County of Delaware SS

On this eighth day of October on thousand eight hundred and thirty two, personally appeared in open court before the Judges of the Court of Common Pleas now sitting at the Court House in Delhi in the County aforesaid. Witter Johnston a resident of the Town of Sidney in the said county aged seventy nine years who being first duly sworn according to law doth upon his oath make the following declaration in order to obtain the benefit of the act passed the 7th June 1832.

That he entered the service of the United States as a volunteer in the year 1777 and served as herein stated, viz.

For several years prior to the year 1777 he resided with his father's family in the Town of Sidney aforesaid. They were driven off in the fore part of the summer of that year by the Indians under Brant and went to Cherry Valley. Shortly after which Gen'l Herkimer was sent with a party of Militia down the Susquehanna River in order to check Brant's deputation. He volunteered as a private in the Militia who attended General Herkimer during this expedition and went with him to the place of his former abode and was present at the time Brant and Gen'l Herkimer under a flag of truce and held a conference. This meeting took place in the immediate vicinity of the farm upon which he had before resided. Gen'l Herkimer returned immediately after the conference with his forces to Cherry Valley.

Soon after this Gen'l Herkimer again marched with the Militia for the purpose of relieving Fort Stanwix when he again volunteered his services and served during that expedition on a Company of Militia commanded by Capt. Whittaker in Col. Cox's Regiment. In this expedition Gen'l Herkimer was mortally wounded and Col. Cox was killed.

He returned with the Militia from the termination of this expedition again to Cherry Valley and was occasionally engaged during the latter part of the season in exploring or scouting parties and remained with his father's family (his father being the officiating chaplain at that time for the troops stationed there), during the winter ensuring an additionally performing garrison duties and still under the command of Capt. Whittaker and continued actively on scouting through the spring performing garrison duties and laboring with the troops in fortifying the place until sometimes in the summer of the ?? time. He cannot state when he had engaged as an adjutant deputy commander for the garrison and remained in that capacity up to the time when Cherry Valley was captured and destroyed by the enemy.

At that time Col. Alden commanded the regular forces stationed at there and was killed in the attack and the Lieut. Col. (Stacy or Statia) taken prisoner. Immediately upon that event he went to Schenectady and remained there until the spring of the year 1780 when he moved to the Town of Florida in Montgomery County. In the course of this season he again volunteered in the Militia in a company commanded by Capt. McMaster's and was stationed at Fort Plain.

When Sir John Johnson made his invasion into the Mohawk River when they immediately marched against him in a Regiment commanded by Col. Fisher and followed him until after he fled from the Mohawk until he reached the head water of the Unadilla River when the pursuit was abandoned.

In the course of the third expedition he engaged in the battle immediately preceding Sir John Johnson's across the Mohawk.

In the fall of the year 1781, he again volunteered in Capt. David McMaster's Company (in the Town of Florida, south side of the river opposite Amsterdam) Col. Willett then having the command of the Militia and marched to Johnstown around there during the battle on the British Tories and Indians under the command of Major Ross and and from there to Fort Herkimer and from thence marched to the north through what was called Jersey Plains (Jerseyfield) until they again fell in with Ross's party and captured his rear guard and pursued them until they crossed the North Canada Creek, where the Tory Capt. Butler was killed in a skirmish and followed until the next night when the was abandoned and he again returned to Florida and remained there until the month of April 1782.

That in making the preceding statement he had no list to refer to and had made the same from memory alone. He cannot therefore state nor will he undertake to state how long he was actually engaged in the Militia during the time aforesaid.

He further stated in the month of April and he verily believed on or about the first of April 1782 he again entered the service as a Second Lieutenant, Capt. French's Company (of New York State Troops) in the regiment commanded by Col. Marinus Willett and served in said Company nine months. Then he was transferred to the company of Capt. Peter B. Tierce in the same regiment and served in said company until the fourth day of January 1782. To the best of his knowledge and belief when he was discharged at the City of Schenectady. During the latter part of this time however and while he was in Capt. Tierce's Company the Regiment and redirected to a Battalion under the command of Major Van Benschoten and he then ranked as an Ensign. A considerable part of his time while thus serving as a Lieutenant and spent in exploring parties on our then frontiers.

He was with Col. Willett in February 1783 in his expedition against Fort Oswego and was one of the Corps that escorted Gen. Washington from Fort Herkimer to Fort Stanwix. His field officers were Col. Willett, Major Van Benschoten and Andrew Fink, under whom he served for one year and nine months as a Lieutenant and Ensign as aforesaid, but he cannot designate the time he served in each capacity. He first entered the service as a Lieutenant as a nine months man and without having the service at the extension of that time again engaged as he believes for three years.

During his services as aforesaid he marched through what was then called Caughnawaga, Johnstown, Canajoharie. Curry Town and at Fort Herkimer, Fort Schuyler, Fort Plain, Fort Plank, Stone Arabia, and in fact traveled to most all of our then frontier settlements and posts upon the frontier west of Schenectady.

He was acquainted with the following Militia officers during his services, his being commissioned as aforesaid viz. Col. Cox, Col. Fisher and Col. Campbell. After being commissioned (believes Col. Willett and Majors Van Benschoten and Fink) He recollected among those with whom he served and who were in service. Captains, Finck, Tierce, O'Conner, Young, Newel, Wright, Connor, Henry and Hamilton, some of these were nine months men among those he continued in Militia Regiment after the nine months were Captains Tierce, F. Connor, Newel, O'Conner, Harrison, according to the best of his recollection.

Among the Continental Troops with whom he served the winter of 1783 and summer of 1783, (names were crossed out.)

(There is about a whole page I simply can't read.)

The pension application file contains the April 1783 Muster Roll for Captain Peter B. Tierce's Company of Lieutenant Colonel Marinus Willett's Regiment.

Officers

Captain Peter B. Tierce
Lieutenant John Thornton

Lieutenant Witter Johnston
Sergeant William Robertson
Sergeant James Shaw
Sergeant Henry Boonsteel

Sergeant Abraham Shutts
Corporal Benjamin Holmes
Corporal Absolum Solmon
Fifer John Myres

Privates

Peter Adamy
Henry Bulson
Andrew Buckley
David Culver
Mathew Calkins
Christopher Coats
Bartley Coselman
Henry Devoe
Zadock Hawley
John Helsinger
Peter Hoser
John McCoy
Samson Vanble
John Ouderkirk
Thomas Archer
Charles Cox (Deserted 25 April 1783)

Jacob Oar
Moses Parr
Peter Roberson
Samuel Joy
James Van Atter
Ryneart Van Sickler
Ebeneezer Welch
John Wormwood
Henry Young
John Casler
John Hunter
Richard Kenton
Henry Stillman
Charles Bullock
Prospect Carpenter
Peter Lawrence
Henry Lewis
Henry Chambers (sick in hospital in Albany)
Henry Casler
Newman Babcock (Deserted 25 April 1783)
Daniel Clyde (Deserted 25 April 1783)
Christopher Hall (Deserted 25 April 1783)

An order dated August 27, 1783, Fort Rensselaer is included in his file. It asked Witter to muster his company again because a desertion had taken place after Thorton had last made out the must roll. He also advises Witter to get tents and to pay his liquor bills.

A copy of the written order is included following.

Fort Renselaer August 29th 1783

D. Sir/

I take this opportunity to inform you that You will be pleased to make out Two Muster Rolls as a desertion took place after I had maid mine out, & not having time to Recopy the Same, as you may observe in this Roll I now send you the Casualties is herein expressed Excepting those men that will be on Command at Fort Renselaer with me. what men I know not certainly by name at present but those that are absent you may put them under my Command at this post unless you receive further intelligence Endeavour to get your Number of Tents according to your No of Men & furnish them in every respect with what is due to them — as some Tents are better than others try to get the best. The Liquor Bills you will receive & take care of being unwell, am detain'd here for further orders. I am Dr Sir

Your Obedient Servt

Jno. Thornton

To Lieut. Johnston

Pension Application for John Kern

This pension is lengthy. Apparently in the first attempt, Mr. Kern was too brief and was denied his pension. In the second attempt, he fixed the problem and gave lots of interesting testimony and procured witnesses.

State of New York
Montgomery County

On this nineteenth day of September in the year of our Lord, one thousand eight hundred and thirty two personally appeared in open court before the judges of the Court of Common Pleas in and for said county now sitting John Kern, a resident of the Town of Oppenheim in said county aged about seventy three years and upwards who being first duly sworn according to law doth on his oath make the following declaration in order to obtain the benefit of the Act of Congress passed June 7th, 1832.

He was born, as he believes, in the year 1759 in the Town of Palatine in said County of Montgomery and that he resided there when called into service and resided there after the war until about twenty years since when he removed to the said Town of Oppenheim in the said county where he now resides.

He entered the service of the United States under the following required officers and served as herein stated.

That he arrived at the age of sixteen years he was enrolled as a private in the company of Militia to wit: the company of Captain Christian House, in the Regiment of Colonel Jacob Klock. His other company and field officers whom he recollects are Lieutenant Colonel Peter Waggoner, the Lieutenant John Bellinger.

That he was kept on duty and out on scouting parties to the West Canada Creek to Cherry Valley, Springfield and various other places at different times and that he continued to serve in that manner regularly every year under Captain House until the year (blotted) when he enlisted as a private in a company of Militia commanded by Captain John Bigbread and Lieutenant Helmer for the term of nine months and that he was stationed at Fort Herkimer in the County of Herkimer. That he was kept on duty at the fort and out scouting south to Anderstown and to the forks of the Unadilla River and in various other directions and at different times until the expiration of the nine months when he was discharged and returned home, when he immediately was called out again under Captain House and served until the conclusion of the war. (The deposition copy ends here.)

State of New York
Montgomery County

I, Ashabel Loomis, Esq. One of the Justice of the Peace in aforesaid county do hereby certify that, Jacob Zimmerman, of the Town of Oppenheim in said county recognize named is well known to me and that he is a respectable honorable person, who on being duly sworn by me according to law doth depose that he is about seventy six years of age, that he served in the Revolutionary War and part of the time in the company commanded by Christian House in the Reg't commanded by Colonel Jacob Klock, that his memory by reason of old age is poor and that he cannot remember the service rendered by any particular person in said company during said war, only to say that they were immediate with him for some particular circumstances happened in said service to fix it upon his memory.

That he was some acquainted with John Kern in said war, and knows that he served in said company as a private, but the amount of such services he cannot state but distinctly recollects before the year 1780 (when this deponent according to he recollection was taken prisoner) the said John Kern was being deposed, an applicant for a pension as he has been informed, and believes resides in the Town of Oppenheim engaged as a private until company dismissed. He saw said Kern serving in the ranks on a tour of service of said company to Herkimer of that this service has rendered before the year 1780 when this deponent was taken a prisoner but what particular time or year he cannot state and thinks the company most probably have been engaged about four days and further says not.

Signed by Jacob Zimmerman.
Sworn this 5th day of February 1834 before me,
Ashbel Loomis
Justice of the Peace

State of New York
Montgomery County

Be it known that on this 8th day of April A.D. 1834, personally appeared before me, a Justice of the Peace in the Town of Oppenheim in said county, John Kern, a resident of the same town and about 74 years, who on being duly sworn by law, the said justice according to law, does in order to admit his pension application, depose and say on his oath that by reason of his old age and consequence of his memories and the infirmities occasioned by his age and the attack of the numb palsey, he cannot positively state the precise length of his services hereafter mentioned, not the precise date of entering and leaving each term of service and he can state such to the best of his memory and now therefore he is some respect mistaken as to the period of his service, vizt, he as a private was engaged on a time of service therefore (then) Town of Palatine in the then County of Tryon now County of Montgomery in said sate where he then resided to the German Flatts in the now County of Herkimer as near as he can recollect from the 15 May 1776 to the 17th May 1776 for at least five days including going to and returning to said place.

That he then belonged and served as aforesaid in the Company of Infantry whereof Christian House was the Capt., John Zimmerman Lieut., Henry Zimmerman Ensign in the Reg't whereof Jacob Klock was the Colonel, commanded by General Nicholas Herkimer, that the said company was engaged as aforesaid, was ordered into service by his officers and verbally discharged thereupon that he thinks the affidavit of Jacob Zimmerman which is hereto deposed.

He further says that he was again engaged as a private on a time of service from the then Town of Palatine aforesaid where he then continued to reside to the German Flatts in that same company and same officers, he thinks commanding said company as last above mentioned, he thinks the whole Reg't were engaged, Gen'l Schuyler was along and held a treaty with the Indians ??? place. He served he thinks from 25 June 1776 to 5 July 1776 for at least 10 days in said time, thinks that as the whole company was engaged he was ordered into service by his officers, and he was verbally discharged. Thereupon for the time of service, the history of the town has been consulted, that he knows no evidence he can procure as to this service but is positive that he served.

And further says that he was again engaged as a private in a tour of service from the same place last as aforesaid and he still continued to reside and to go to the place so called Caughnawaga in the then county of Tryon, now Montgomery from some day in March 1776 (the particular day he is unable to give) to some day thereafter for at least 10 days in the same company and the same officers, he thinks commanded said company as last aforesaid, he remembers that the (can't make out a section here) was also engaged at another service at said time in said company, they were stationed some time at the house of Vedder at said place and then his service was rendered about the commencement of the War of the Revolution. This service was before the first above so mentioned service according to his recollection, his officer's ordered him into this service in the spring of 1776 aforesaid, as to the service is rendered the (can't read a section)

And further, says that he was again engaged as a private on a tour of service from the same place last aforesaid where he still resided to the house of Jacob Failing in the same town he then resided in the same company commanded by the same officers he thinks, as last aforesaid from Sept 10, 1775 to the 17th of the same month for at least the period of seven days. That said company was stationed the said Failing's house where in the front most there had been a fort and pathway of the Indians in going to Johnstown.

This service he thinks was the first he rendered in said war. But he cannot positively say as to the time when his service was rendered, and may be mistaken in such respect this he knows that he served at said place for about the period aforesaid. Said service may have been rendered early in the ensuing spring, cannot state positively to the service except that he served.

And furthers says that he was again engaged at as a private on a tour of service from the then Town of Palatine aforesaid where he resided at the time to Fort Remensnyder (so called) in the company aforesaid commanded by Capt House in Col. Jacob Klock's Reg't to which he belonged as a private. He was drafted, he thinks, into this out of said company and was marched to said Fort ??? stationed doing duty for at least the period of ??? days viz, as nearly as his memory serves him from ??? 1780 to 16th August 1780 as a private. Capt'n House commanded the engagement according to his recollection. He thinks the Indians had killed a few days before, some women and children in the neighborhood of said fort, which was the reason of his serving in said fort at the time and he was verbally discharged, and that he has not been able to procure any evidence of this tour of service and knows of no one left except Jacob Youger hereto annexed which affidavit is so far as his memory serves him correct.

And further says that when the Oriskany Battle was he again served on a tour of duty as a private from the then Town of Palatine to the Oriskany near Utica, that he belonged to Capt. Christian House's Company and Klock's Reg't of Militia as a private. That the company and regiment had been principally gone to relief of Fort Stanwix and he believes was left behind on the account of what reason he has forgotten and that after the troops had gone he and some others under Lieut. Zimmerman of said company marched in pursuit of the troops and had proceeded as far as, or nearly so, where Utica now is when they met some of the militia who had fled from the battle and who informed them that all was lost and that they then returned home. That this service was under or near as he can state from Aug't 1, 1777 to Aug't 6, 1777 for at least 5 days. And he was verbally discharged and knows of no one he can procure as to this service.

And further says that on the 15th Sept 1777 he was still a private in the company whereof Christian House was the Captain in this the company whereof Jacob Klock was Colonel where he still continued to reside in the said Town of Palatine and was drafted out of said company with others, that he and those to be drafted went to Fort Plank in the Town of Minden and these served under a captain of the name he thinks of Jacob Zielly for at least eight days and he thinks longer to 23rd Aug't 1777 he thinks he was discharged (can't read) he served as a private. That he knows of no evidence he can procure as to this service.

And further says that as near as he can state from memory he enlisted as a private on the 25 March 1778 for nine months in the company whereof John Bigbread (Breadbig, so many men had difficultly with this name) was captain and the regiment he cannot state, nor names but of one Helmer was a Lieut. (he thinks) in said company but the other officer's names he cannot remember.

Said company, he thinks, acted as rangers and served the state in his last declaration that he served said nine months as a private in said company and was probably verbally discharged as he has no written discharge and does not believe that he received one that he has procured the evidence of Cornelius Van Camp which is annexed, that he might probably procure an additional evidence but for his age, and is afflicted with the numb palsy. He thinks he was discharged the first of Jan'y 1772. That when he so enlisted he resided in the said Town of Palatine.

That Cornelius Van Camp served in said company and also John Dockey, now deceased, and he has annexed that affidavit of Jacob Youker as to the service, to that of Dockey given in his life time as to this service. He remembers one Lassitte? was an officer in said company, but the rank he cannot recollect.

And further says he was engaged as a private on a tour of service from the now Town of Oppenheim, then Town of Palatine when he still continued to reside in the company whereof Christian House was Capt., Reg't whereof Jacob Klock was Colonel to Fort Klock where he was stationed with others. He was drafted, he thinks and served at said fort for at least 8 days according to the best of his memory. From June 1779 to the day he cannot state to some day in same month as private for at least 8 days. That Capt. House and Lieut. Zimmerman (which he has forgotten) commanded them. He was drafted out of said company, that he received only a verbal discharge from this service, that he has no evidence of this his service and knows of none he can procure save that of Theobato Moyer hereto annexed.

And further says that on the 10th Aug't 1780 (as near as he can recollect) he was called out by his officers into their service and he then resided in same Town aforesaid. And in the company whereof Christian House was Capt. in Col. Jacob Klock's Reg't was guarding along the Mohawk some boats to Fort Stanwix or near it under Gen'l Van Rensselaer that he served as a private in said company for at least 10 days to Fort Stanwix and back and was verbally discharged that he has procured the affidavit as to this service of Theobatlo Moyer which is annexed and was discharged as near as he can recollect the date of the same month verbally, thinks they did not go quite to Fort Stanwix, but may be mistaken, when on this tour.

And further says that in the spring of the year, he thinks in April 1779 (the particular day he cannot state) he was called by his officers into their service as a private for one week and then resided in same Town aforesaid and in the company of Christian House was Captain, Col. Jacob Klock's Reg't. That he was marched there to the house of Audolph Walrath with whom he was well acquainted, and was there stationed for the period, of said company to which he belonged, served their time of service. Said Walrath resided in the now County of Montgomery from the time he commenced this service he served at least 6 days as aforesaid as a private that he has no evidence he can procure as to this service but knows that he served at said place.

That he also served as a private in the company whereof Christian House was Capt. in Re'gt of Col. Jacob Klock on a tour of service when Walter Butler was killed at West Canada Creek from Sept ? 1781 as near as he can recollect to 25th of same month including going and returning at least 5 days as estimate and he was present when Butler was killed. He has no evidence of this service or knows of no one he can procure, he then resided in Palatine aforesaid and was verbally discharged and ordered out by his officers.

And further says that as near as the can recollect that 15 June 1780, he together with others were drafted out of Capt. Christian House Company, Col. Jacob Klock's Reg't to serve in a Fort at Stone Arabia in Palatine called, he thinks Fort Paris, that he and those drafted under the command of the officers of said company (whose name he cannot bring in memory) went to said place and there were stationed one ??? and then were discharged and returned home to the said Town of Palatine in he thinks 22 of same men having served as a private at least 6 days that he knows of no evidence to can procure as to the proof of this service.

And further says that as near as his memory serves him he went on the 10th Sept 1776 a private in the company whereof Christian House was Capt., Col. Jacob Klock's Regt, that he resided in the same place aforesaid and that a draft was made of about 12 men out of said company, that he was then drafted and he and those drafted were to take some Tories, two of whom where named Frey, from where he then escorted them to West Point that they then proceeded with some Tories to Albany on foot and at Albany went on boats down the river to West Point and when they delivered said Tories to the officer. The officer gave them something to eat and drink that then they again returned home. That he served at least he thinks 14 days when they returned home. That he cannot recollect the Sergeant or Corporal's name that commanded on this tour who belonged however to said company that he may be mistaken as to the time this service was done but is positive that he served on such a tour of duty and for about the period at least as aforesaid. That he knows of no evidence he can procure as to the proof and time of this service, that he served as a private on said tours and was discharged he thinks the last of 1776.

That he did other services in the said war repeating in short tours but cannot on account of his loss of memory give an intelligible account of those and also recollects that he served 3 months as a substitute for his brother in Capt McKean's company but he has been told that he cannot be allowed for said service under his present declaration, rather than process a new, he wants to relinquish said services and hereby relinquished it. That he is poor in feeble health and very infirm and is maintained by others and that he wants to rather receive a smaller pension and thinks he hasn't long left.

(In the deposition he goes on to say his wife is aged also and has the numb palsy. Then he adds some people he served with were killed in the war, that no clergyman lives in his area to vouch for his veracity and character. He applied for pension 19 Sept 1832.)

This application was successful and he received his pension but he died December 2, 1935.

John Kern signed with his mark

Pension Application For Lodowick Kring

Kring fought in Oriskany, Stone Arabia and Johnstown Battles. He was involved in helping to fortify the valley farms and building forts. He helped transport boats from Canajoharie to Lake Otsego.

State of New York
Montgomery County

On this twentieth day of September one thousand eight hundred and thirty two, personally appeared in open court before Caring Abraham Morrell, Henry I Quackendorph, John Hand, and Samuel A. Gilbert, Judges of the Court of Common Pleas in and for said county now sitting Lodowick Kring, a resident of the town of Ephratah, County of Montgomery and State of New York, aged seventy three years two months and four days, who being first duly sworn according to law doth on his oath make the following declaration in order to obtain the benefit of the Act of Congress passed June 7, 1832.

That he entered the service of the United States under the following named officers and served as herein stated. That the first officers that he served under were Colonel Jacob Klock, Lieutenant Colonel Peter Waggoner, Major John Frey, Captain Nicholas Richter, Lieutenant Johannes Shull, Ensign Honyost Shull. That he was enrolled in the summer of 1774 under the aforesaid officers but was not called into actual service until the summer of 1776.

That the company that he belonged to was marched down the Mohawk River under the order of General Herkimer and that we patrolled in the ice while then General Schuyler sent an expedition to Sir John Johnston in Johnstown and then the said Sir John Johnson did surrender together with all his forces without exchanging a shot from either side, that he the said deponent continued in said service through this first part of the time until about the first of August that he the said deponent enlisted into a company of Rangers commanded by Captain Christian Getman, Jacob Sammons 1st Lieutenant and James Billington 2nd Lieutenant for and during the war until he was discharged.

And this deponent and Jacobus Gray that while in this company, they were ordered to Ticonderoga a distance of about 16 miles and forty five miles and we went down by way of Albany. The time we started from our homes was about Christmas in 1776 and stayed there until the latter part of March and that it was the 24th 1777 that they got back to Johnstown.

The officers that we were under at Ticonderoga were Colonel Ebenezer Cox and Major E??? After he the said deponent returned from the expedition they then were discharged, there having been a resolution passed at Kingston the 27th of March 1777 to discharge the several companies of Rangers in the State of New York of which there is a copy annexed to this declaration.

And this deponent further says that this spring (after discharge as Ranger) he volunteered to go with Colonel Van Schaick and Colonel Dayton who were stationed at Johnstown to the German Flatts while at this place General Schuyler arrived there and gave orders to go farther west to build forts.

That Colonel Dayton and Colonel Van Schaick started from this place and proceeded up the Mohawk and that he the deponent returned with General Schuyler as far as Canajoharie acting as a guard for him and this deponent further says that he had but just got back when the received orders to march to Oriskany to defend that post. And he together with the company that he was with in war, put under march immediately and was in that memorable battle on the 6th day of August 1777 and this deponent further says that after the Battle of Oriskany the regiment to which he belonged commanded by Colonel Jacob Klock returned to Fort Paris at Stone Arabia except the dead and wounded, and this deponent further says that he was in actual service the whole of the year from its commencement to its close.

And this deponent further says that he continued in the service through the year 1778. That is to say, not on duty all the whole but frequently called out to defend and protect the inhabitants that were living along the frontier from the depredations that were making by the Indians and Tories were scattered through the woods and country.

That in the fall of this year he went to Cherry Valley in company with his fellow soldiers to aid and assist the inhabitants at that place from depredations of the same nature and this deponent further says that in the spring of 1779 opened the scenes of war in a more hostile manner than was. On the 20th of April the captain was wounded at his farm after small skirmish with the Indians and Tories at this skirmish there was one killed and two wounded. Our officers in the said company which was commanded by Captain Richter and this deponent further says that the inhabitants there moved with all their affects to Fort Paris a distance of about 8 miles leaving but one family behind which was a Tory.

And this deponent further says that after he was removed to Fort Paris he the said deponent volunteered with a team to transport boats from Canajoharie to Lake Otsego by land a distance of about 20 miles and that it was sometime in the summer before he returned to Fort Paris. This service was performed under General Clinton and this deponent further says that after he returned from this expedition he continued in the service the remainder of the summer and fall performing various kinds of duty such as guarding forts, running scouts, standing century and etc., at different places part of the time at Fort Paris, part of the time at Fort Plank, part of the time at Fort Herkimer, and that while at the latter place, myself together with two other soldiers while running scouts took ten head of cattle and brought them to the fort which the enemy had undertook to drive off.

And this deponent further says that in the spring of 1780 (belonging to said Klock's Regiment) he continued in the service guarding the residents along the Mohawk at different forts as before stated, stationed principally at Fort Paris. And this deponent further says that sometime in the first of August this year he together with a number of other soldiers volunteered to the assistance of Col. Willett of Fort Plain who was then in an engagement with Butler and Brandt, however not arriving on time. The engagement having ended we returned again to Fort Paris and remained there until the battle at that place running scout and guarding the frontiers.

While at this place we had an engagement on the 19th October 1780 with John Johnson. Col. Brown commanded the American forces who was slain together with thirty of forty of his little band.

And this deponent further says he continued in the service all the fall and winter running scout probably here at which he took the duty of a soldier that had to ??? and county was infected with parties of Indians and Tories and we watched inhabitants and whenever they would find one at labor on his farm, the party would sally forth and take prisoners and in this manner a great many of them whereabouts were pacified.

The running of Scouts remained this way in a measure, parties of three or four would start one morning and the same number the next morning and continue sending out until the frost returned and in this measure a number of Tories and Indians were taken prisoners.

And this deponent further says that in the year 1781 in the morning on the 22nd of October he together with a number of his fellow soldiers mounted horses at Fort Paris and rode to Johnstown a distance of about 10 miles having received the order the night before. We were not there a great while before the battle commended. It was a pretty hot engagement that followed. The American forces were commanded by Col. Willett and the British by Major Ross and Butler, the Americans having gained the victory.

The day following the battle the Americans the deponent together with others pursued the enemy to West Canada Creek and finally took the British commander Butler who was shot at the place, and this deponent further says that he continued in the service until the close of the war and that he the deponent further says that he believed the service that he rendered during the war far exceeds four years. He hereby relinquishes every claim whatever to a pension or annuity except the present and declares that his name is not on the pension roll of the agency of any state.

To the questions directed to be answered he said the following.

That he was born in the County of Orange, Town of Orange, year 1759, on the 5th day of July

That he has no other records of his birth except (can't read the rest of this).

That he lived in the County of Montgomery (can't read the rest of this).

That he still lives in the County of Montgomery.

That he rendered the service as a volunteer until ?? in to Captain Christian Getman and after he returned from Ticonderoga and that he continued as a volunteer through the whole of the service and that in the aforesaid declaration

The names of some of the officers that I was acquainted with; General James Clinton, General Philip Schuyler, General Nicholas Herkimer, General Morgan, Col. Klock, Col. Willett, Col. Brown, Col. Cox, Col. Bellinger.

That he once had a discharge and that it is lost.

That I am acquainted with Samuel Waters, William Smith, John F. Empie, Peter Getman and a great many others that will attest to my veracity.

Sworn to and subscribed this day and year aforesaid.

(Signed) Lodowick Kring.

Capt. John Lefler's Company of Batteaumen, 1778

April 24	Bacehus, John
April 24	Bakely, Jesse
Aug 6	Casselman, Bartel
May 12	Countryman, Adam
April 24	Countryman, Frederick
April 24	Countryman, John Jr.
May 12	Golyer, James M.
May 14	Favill, John
April 24	Flander, Henry
May 4	Kreamer, Jost
April 24	Kretzer, Leonard

April 24	Leather, Christian
April 24	Nellis, George
May 12	Polmentier, Daumont
April 26	Putman, Arent
April 24	Putman, Adam
April 24	Putman, Victor
April 24	Spraker, John
April 24	Sypher, John
May 12	Tygert Sefrinus
April 24	Van Slyke, Samuel
April 24	Wafle, Henry
April 24	Wolf, Jacob
April 24	Young, Jost
May 12	Young, John
Aug 22	Young, Peter
June 4	Young, Richard
April 24	Zoller, Casper

Pension Application for Jeremiah Mason

This applicant had a problem, he was too young to serve and therefore denied any pension.

War Department
Pension Office
Dec 12, 1832

Sir

The papers transmitted by you in support of your claim to a pension under the act of 7 June 1832 have been examined. In your declaration you allege that you enlisted in 1780 and served 2 ½ or 3 years in Col. Willett's regt, having previous to that time performed military service upon emergency. The account of your age made you 13 in 1780. No boy at that age could perform military duty in the ranks and the regulations respecting enlistments forbid the reception of such. Your claim is therefore rejected and your papers retained on file.
TO: Mr. Jeremiah Mason, Johnstown

State of New York
Montgomery County

On the 21st day of September personally appeared in open court before the Judges of the Court of Common Pleas now sitting Jeremiah Mason a resident in the Town of Johnstown and County of Montgomery and State of New York who aged 66 years the first day of May next, who being first duly sworn according to law, does on his oath make the following declaration in order to obtain the benefit of the Act of Congress, passed June 7, 1832.

The following named officers and the time he entered the service of the United States is hereby fully stated and set forth.

That he entered the service in the year 1780 as was as he can recollect in the month of May the day he cannot state.

That he was enrolled in Captain Tierce's Company. The other officers of the company does he does not recollect. That during the time he served, there were several field officers who had the command of the Regiment in which he was, to wit: Colonel Willett, Colonel Levingston, Colonel Deighton, some previous to he enrollment and some subsequent.

That he resided at Johnstown during the hole of the war, and previous to his being enrolled was called out frequently in case of emergency, and was out with this during the whole time of the war until he was enrolled in the military in 1780.

That is parents resided in the Town of Johnstown and in the village, and that his father and brothers were also in the army.

That he was in the battle fought by Colonel Willett at the Johnson Hall in Johnstown and was one who helped bury the dead after the battle. That he was in the regiment that lay at Johnstown from the April or month of May 1780 until that Major Ross, the British officer who commanded at Johnstown was the British side where Willett commanded and the battle fought.

That he still remained as a soldier of the said battle until there was ended and he cannot tell how long it was after the battle he remained in the service but according to the best of his knowledge thinks that eh was in the service, enrolled about two years and a half or three years, but cannot tell which, thinks it was not far from that aforesaid time.

That during the aforesaid time he was frequently and out in scouting parties in search of Tories and Indians, who were probing around that place and destroying the inhabitants when and opportunity occurred.

That he was stationed at Johnstown to defend and protect that place from the enemy. That some time in the year 1781 or 1782 that news came of peace being had between British and our people but that it was not very certain, and that they continued in the service a long time after that on account of the Indians and Tories frequently returning and attacking the inhabitants. That he volunteered when he was enrolled.

That he continued under the captain he was in whose company he was enrolled until he following winter 1781 and than the company was commanded by another captain whose name he does not recollect. That he was under the command of several officers whose names he does not recollect.

That he has no documentary evidence of his services.

That he was born as the thinks in the year 1765 or 1766, at the County of Summerset, New Jersey. That he has no record of his age but ??? kept by himself.

That he lived in the Town of Johnstown and County of Tryon (now Montgomery County). That he has resided since that time in the said Town of Johnstown and County of Montgomery. That he never received a discharge from his services.

I hereby relinquish every claim whatever to a pension or annuity except the present and declare that my name is not on the pension roll of the agency of any state.
Signed, Jeremiah Mason

Pension Application For Daniel McGraw

Some pension applications are full of news, and this one certainly is. McGraw's Captain, Pettingall, was killed at Oriskany. He saw a lot of action during the war and seems to have taken it all in his stride. Daniel helped transport the British troops to Albany after their surrender at Saratoga. He also mentions guarding Veeder's Mill outside of Caughnawaga because it supplied flour for the American Army.

State of New York
Montgomery County

On the 10th day of March (1834), personally appeared in open court before the judges of the Court of Common Pleas of the County of Montgomery now sitting at the Court House in said county, Daniel McGraw a resident of the Town of Amsterdam in the County of Montgomery aforesaid and state of New York aged seventy nine years, who being first duly sworn according to law doth on his oath make the following declaration in order to obtain the benefit of the Act of Congress passed June 7th 1832.

That he entered the service of the United States under the following named officers and served as herein stated.

That in the year 1775 this deponent resided in the Town of Florida in Montgomery County and belonged to Captain Samuel Pettingall's Company in Col. Frederick Fischer's (Visscher's) Regiment of Militia of the State of New York.

That some time in the summer of 1775 the exact time he cannot now remember, this deponent was drafted from Captain Pettingall's Company and was ordered to Sacandaga and stationed on guard under the command of Captain Pettingall, who then commanded the forces at that place. That William Snook, a Lieutenant of the company was also there on duty, and the deponent then served eight days and was discharged and returned home with his captain and the others of the company who had been ordered out.

That in the spring of the year 1776 this deponent was drafted from said company and marched to Sacandaga and was first under the command of Col. Frederick Fisher and was employed in building a block house at Sacandaga and served there ten days and was then discharged.

That in the fall of the year 1776 this deponent was drafted and marched to the block house at Sacandaga and was there placed on guard under the command of Captain Walter Vrooman and served at that time twenty days.

That sometime in the year 1776, or in the spring 1777, this deponent was drafted and went to Tripes Hill and stationed on guard to watch the Tories and Indians, and went out on scouting parties for the same purpose under the command of Captain Pettingall and was in service at that time eight days and was then discharged.

This deponent in the year 1777 in the fall of the year was ordered out under the command of Captain Snook who had succeeded to the command of the company, formerly commanded by Captain Pettingall. He having been killed in the Oriskany Battle and marched to Ballstown in the County of Saratoga and took thirty Tories. One of the Tories he recollects had been accidentally shot through the thigh by some of their own men. This deponent served in that enterprise ten days and returned home and was discharged.

That in the latter part of the year 1777 he was drafted from Captain Snook's Company and stationed at Fort Johnson below Tripes Hill under the command of Captain Mabee; Lieutenant McMasters was also and officer under Captain Mabee, and the forces were placed on guard watching Tories and Indians, and this deponent served eight days and was then discharged.

That sometime in the fall of 1777 this deponent was drafted from Captain Snook's Company and stationed at the Stone House near Fort Hunter under the command of Lieutenant Benjamin Newkirk on guard and continued there six days and was then discharged.

That in the same fall of 1777 this deponent was drafted from Captain Snook's Company and placed on guard on Switser Hill at the house of one John Kitts under the command of Captain Snook to watch the movements of the British and Tories and continued there eight days in service and then discharged.

That in the fall of the year 1777 this deponent was drafted from Captain Snook's Company and stationed on guard at the house of Ephraim Wemple in Florida about two miles below Fort Hunter on the Mohawk River under the command of Ensign Van Horne and continued in service four days and then discharged.

That in year 1777 in the fore part of the month of September this deponent was drafted from Captain Snook's Company and stationed at Stilwater in the County of Saratoga under the command of Col. Veeder and Major Newkirk previous to the surrender of General Burgoyne. The American Army lay at Bemis Heights and this deponent served at that time thirty days and was ordered back to Mo9ntgomery County some few days previous to the Battle at Stillwater on account of some false alarms in Montgomery. That some few days after this deponent had returned to Montgomery he heard of the surrender of Burgoyne and soon returned to the British camp on a pass made for teams to transport the British prisoners and baggage to Albany. And this deponent on this occasion volunteered, furnished himself with a supplied horses and waggon and spent fourteen days in transporting British prisoners and baggage from Burgoyne's camp to Albany.

That in the fall of the year 1778 this deponent was drafted from Captain Snook's Company and placed under the Command of Captain Snook at the house of Jellis Fonda at Caughnawaga on guard to watch the movements of the enemy and continued in service six days and discharged.

And in the same fall, 1778 this deponent was again drafted and stationed at Veeder's Mills near Caughnawaga under command of Captain Snook to prevent the enemy from burning the mill, which was the principle mill for supplying the American Army at that place with flour and served there eight days.

That late in the fall of the year 1778 this deponent was drafted from said company and stationed at the Black House in Sacandaga on guard under the command of Captain Andrew Wemple and served then twenty days. John Wemple was Lieutenant and Conradt Steene was Ensign and was then discharged. That some time in the year 1778 he cannot recollect the particular time this deponent was ordered out by Captain Snook with others of his company and went to Curry Fly now called Duanesburgh in Schenectady County to take some Tories who were looking about at the place as spies. This deponent was about four days in this service.

That in the year 1778 the particular time does not remember, this deponent was ordered out by Col. Veeder to go on a scouting party through Stone Arabia in Palatine to Canajohary and tarried at the house of one Rooff a number of days. The party were only three in number and had no commanding officer. This deponent served eight days at this time. That in the same year this deponent was sent on a scouting party to the North River, north of Sacandaga by Col. Veeder and was absent eight days and then returned to Johnstown and found the company of Captain Snook who then say other with his company.

That in the year 1778 about the commencement of the wheat harvest this deponent was ordered out by Captain Snook with a part of his company and marched up the Mohawk River near the pace called the Nose at the house of Abraham Yates and was stationed there on guard and sent out on scouting parties at this time he served six days.

That during the same year the particular time he cannot remember he was ordered out by Captain Snook and marched to Currytown in company with his captain and stationed on guard at the house of one Lewis and continued in that service seven days and was then discharged.

And very soon thereafter this deponent was again ordered out by Captain Snook and marched up the Mohawk River to the house of one Robert Yates and stationed on guard under the command of his captain for the term of six days and from thence he was ordered by his captain to go through Currytown and turned west about six or eight miles to the house of one Hartman. The place was then called Hartman's Dorf and lay there three days on guard.

From thence he went by the order of the captain up the Mohawk River as far as Fall Hill at the house of Warner Dygert and lay there on guard four days under the command of Captain Snook and was discharged and returned home.

That during the year 1778 this deponent was ordered out by Captain Snook and stationed at the house of one Mart Van Alstine near Canajoharie on guard under the command of his capt. for the term of at least forty days.

That he was also stationed in like manner under the command of his captain at the house of one Gosen Van Alstine at Canajoharie Village on guard for the space of thirty days.

That in the year 1779 this deponent was ordered under the command of Captain Snook and marched up the Mohawk River to Fort Plain and stationed there on guard thirty days; during the same year he was drafted and stationed at Fort Plank under Captain Snook on guard thirteen days.

He was also drafted and stationed at Fort Windecker in the year last aforesaid under the command of Captain Snook on guard four days on alarm. In the same year 1779 the deponent was drafted from said company and marched to Fort Herkimer under the command of Captain Snook and served there on guard ten days.

This deponent then marched from Fort Herkimer in the Company of Captain Snook, the whole of the American forces were then under the command of George Clinton (I am sure this is not correct!) who had come from Albany and pursued on west in pursuit of Sir John Johnson and Col. Butler, whom it was then supposed was seven or eight hundred strong. The march was principally through the woods and the British took two companies of Rangers belonging to the Americans and this time the deponent served thirteen days and then returned home. That some time in the year 1779 he cannot state the exact time this deponent was drafted to go to Oneida to build a fort. And went as far as Connoley's Tavern when the company was rendezvoused under Captain Robert Yates who did not arrive and the expedition was given up and this deponent returned home. He served five days at this time.

That in the winter 1777 this deponent was ordered out by Captain Snook to meet at Col. Fisher's with a view to draft a corps of men to go to Ticonderoga. This deponent met at Col. Fisher's and a body of men was raised as volunteers and ordered on to Ticonderoga but the deponent after the company was formed by??? and returned home having served at that time six days.

That in the year 1778 this deponent was ordered out by Captain Snook and marched with others of the company up the Mohawk and crossed below Fort Plain on the north side of the Mohawk River and stationed at the house of one Garret Walradt on guard under the command of Captain Snook. This deponent served then seven days and was then discharged.

That in the latter part of the year 1779 or 1780 cannot say which this deponent was ordered out by Captain Snook and marched up the Mohawk and crossed on the north side and stationed on guard three days under command of Captain Snook and then discharged.

That in the year 1781 at the time Warrensbush was burnt now called (a line is missing here) joined Captain French's Company and they marched for Johnstown and found Col. Willett's forces at Johnstown and arrived there just as the battle was over between the British and American forces. Willett commanded the Americans and Major Ross the British, at this time the deponent served four days.

That in the year 1780 in the month of May when the Village of Caughnawaga was burnt by the British the deponent volunteered and went to Johnstown and joined the forces commanded by Major Newkirk and Sir John Johnson commanded the British the Americans found themselves too weak and made no attack on the British. This deponent served four days and was discharged.

In the year 1778 Captain Snook's Company was ordered out and marched to Stone Arabia on an alarm at that place. The deponent believes that Col. Veeder commanded the American's at this time. This deponent served six days and was then discharged.

That in the year 1780 Captain Snook's Company was ordered to the German Flats and stationed on guard and this deponent served twelve days. He believes that Col. Dayton had the command. This deponent had volunteered. From the German Flats they were ordered as far back as Fort Dayton and lay there ten days under the command of Col. Dayton and dismissed.

That in the year 1778 this deponent was ordered out with Captain Snook's Company and marched to Stone Arabia a second time on an alarm and placed on guard and served eight days under the command of Col. Veeder's.

That in the same year Captain Snook's Company was ordered out a third time on an alarm and at Stone Arabia at the house of one Countryman under the command of Col. Veeder this deponent served six days and was discharged.

That with the same year said company was ordered out a fourth time on an alarm and stationed at the house of one Cook? in Stone Arabia under the command of Col. Veeder. This deponent served at this time nine days and was discharged.

(There doesn't appear to be any more of the deposition of this soldier.)

Following is the deposition by his brother John to support Daniel's claim.

State of New York
Montgomery County
John McGraw of the town of Florida in the said county being first duly sworn doth depose and say that he is aged eighty one years and upwards and a brother of Daniel McGraw and has known him from a boy.

That said Daniel lived within one mile of this deponent during the whole of the Revolutionary War. That in the year 1775 the same Daniel belonged to Captain Samuel Pettengall's Company in Col. Frederick Fisher's Regiment of Militia in the State of New York of which deponent also belongs.

That in the year 1775 as near as he can recollect Daniel McGraw was stationed at Sacandaga, guard at that place and was drafted from Captain Pettingalle's Company and continued there as guard a number of days, but the precise number days he cannot now remember.

This deponent further testified that in the forepart of the season in the spring of the year 1776, the said same Daniel at Sacandaga, having been drafted from said company with deponent and others and was engaged in building a new block house at which time this deponent believes that Col. Fisher, then commanded and this deponent and the said Daniel continued in service at that time while the fort was finished and was then discharged and returned home. But the number of days said Daniel was engaged in building said fort he cannot now remember but believes it to be nearly two weeks.

That in the fall of the year 1776 this deponent and said Daniel were again drafted from said company and stationed at Sacandaga on guard under the command of Walter Vrooman that he cannot testify as to the number of days then employed, but believes it was upwards of two weeks and then discharged.

That this deponent well does think that the said Daniel at one time was drafted and stationed on Tripes Hill to guard the Tories and Indians but is unable to remember who then commanded or how many days the said Daniel served.

That some time in the year 1777 the deponent recollects that said Daniel was stationed below Tripes Hill at Fort Johnson on guard under command of Captain Mabee to watch the Tories and Indians. Then said Daniel served between one and two weeks at this time and was then discharged.

That the same fall this deponent remember that said Daniel was drafted and placed on guard at the Stone House not far from Fort Hunter and in the command of Benjamin Newkirk but that deponent cannot remember how long he served as this deponent did not stay there all this time that said Daniel did serve. That during the same fall of 1777 the same Daniel was drafted from Captain Snook's Company and stationed on Switser Hill at the home of John Kitts to guard the British and Tories does not remember who commanded but (next line was not copied) but recollects said Daniel served at that time between one and two weeks and was then discharged.

This deponent also remembers that said Daniel was stationed at the house of Ephraim Wemple in Florida under the command of one Van Horne who was either an Ensign or Lieutenant and the same fall of 1777 but does not have any distinct recollection how long he served at that time in.

That in the fall of 1777 served in the battle with Burgoyne's army said Daniel was drafted and went to Stillwater and was stationed there under the command of Col. Veeder, he recollects that Major Newkrik was also there and thinks it was in the month of September but not certain. But he well remembers that it was before the surrender of General Burgoyne to the American Forces, he cannot testify how long said Daniel served this time but he remembers that said Daniel stayed in several days longer than this deponent. That after the surrender of Burgoyne's army the deponent well recollects that said Daniel was supplied with wagon and team to transport British prisoners and baggage from Stillwater to Albany but this deponent was not present when the service was performed and cannot say how long said Daniel served in that capacity.

That in the fall of the year 1778 this deponent remembers that it was reported in the neighborhood that said Daniel was stationed at the house of Jelles Fonda in Caughnawaga and at Veeder's Mills from Caughnawaga on guard at their places but this deponent was not present and cannot testify from his own knowledge he knew that he was absent from home at the time and reported to be in the service as stated.

That in the fall of 1778 this deponent recollects the same Daniel was drafted and stationed at the block house at Sacandaga and was stationed there between two and three weeks but will not say precisely and was then discharged.

This deponent remembers that during some of this service stationed at Sacandaga Captain Wemple commanded.

That some time in the year 1778 this deponent was drafted with said Daniel from Captain Snook's Company and stationed at the house of Abraham Yates on the south side of the Mohawk River as a scouting party. This deponent does not remember how many days said Daniel served at this time. The deponent also recollects that said Daniel served six days at the house of one Lewis in Currytown and was commanded by Captain Snook and was then discharged in the year 1778.

He also testifies that said Daniel was several times ordered out and stationed at the house of one Mart Van Alstine near Canajoharie in 1778 as this deponent was stationed then with said Daniel during a part of this time and knows that a portion of service was rendered by him and this same Daniel served forty days at the home of Mart Van Alstine. This deponent also testifies that said Daniel was stationed also at the home of one Gosen Van Alstine in Canajohaire on guard several times under command of Captain Snooks and performed service at this place at least to the number twenty five days.

The deponent testifies that some time in the year 1779 said Daniel was ordered out by Captain Snook and marched to Fort Windecker on an alarm and served then four days at the least with this deponent.

The witness also remembers that said Daniel served at Fort Herkimer in the year 1779 under the command of Captain Snook between one and two weeks. That the armed forces left Fort Herkimer and pursued Sir John Johnson and Col. Butler that the said Daniel was ordered with forces and they pursued principally through the woods. Once the same Daniel served at this time, eight or ten days as near as he can recollect and was then discharged.

That in the year 1778 the witness recollects that the said Daniel was drafted under command of Captain Snook and stationed at the house of one Robert Walradt on the north side of the Mohawk River opposite Fort Plain for upwards of a week. The company was then discharged.

That in the year 1780 Caughnawaga burnt and Samuel McGraw with the witness volunteered and joined the Americans at Johnstown commanded by Major Newkirk. The same Daniel served several days at that time but cannot state precisely how many.

That in the year 1780 the witness testifies that I and Daniel served in Captain Snook's Company on an alarm at Stone Arabia for upwards of a week, and in the year 1780 he was ordered to the German Flats and stationed him on guard under command of Col. Dayton and then returned back to Fort Dayton and they then were dismissed, under this engagement the said Daniel served upwards of three weeks to the best of his recollection.

That the witness testifies that he knows this said Daniel McGraw was ordered out as many as four different times and stationed at Stone Arabia on alarm at Stone Arabia in the year 1778. But the number of days he served he is unable now to remember.

That some time in the year 1779 the witness testifies that same Daniel was drafted under the command of Captain Snook's Company on guard at the house of one Andrew Wemple near Caughnawaga and placed under the command of Captain Wemple and said Daniel served then one week as near as he can recollect. (The next part is missing.)

This deponent further testifies that said Daniel was stationed on guard at Fort Hunter under Captain Putman in the year 1781 and served a number of days but cannot relate to how many. The witness further testifies that in the year 1781 as near as he can recollect said Daniel was stationed at the house of Samuel Gardinier in Glen under the Command of Captain Snook and also at the house of John Wemple in or near Gagnawage under the same captain on guard that said Daniel served at those places the days to the best of his memory and belief.

And this witness further testifies that he knows that the same Daniel has been repeatedly stationed and drafted at the Johnstown Fort during the years of 1777 and 1778 on various and different occasions but is unable to state the months and days with accuracy and precision as this fort was always kept as a guarded fort during the whole war and regular drafts from the militia were made from time to time to keep the same defended.

The witness recollects that Walter Vrooman, Joseph Printup, Henry Snook and Jacob Sammons were officers who commanded at the Johnstown Fort during the Revolutionary war. And further this deponent says not.

John McGraw (Signed with his mark)

Pension Application for John McGraw

This soldier was very articulate and gives great details about his service. He certainly was kept busy and saw a lot of action.

State of New York
Montgomery County

On the nineteenth day of September in the year of our Lord one thousand eight hundred and thirty two personally appeared in open court before the judges of the Court of Common Pleas of the County and State aforesaid now sitting at Johnstown, John McGraw, aged eighty years. Who being first duly sworn according to law doth on his oath make the following declaration in order to obtain the benefit of the act of Congress passed June 7, 1832. That he entered the service of the United States under the following named officers and served as herein stated.

That in the latter part of the year 1775, this deponent belonged to a company of Militia in the Town of Florida in the County and State aforesaid when Samuel Pettingell was Captain in a Regiment commanded by Col. Frederick Fisher (Visscher) of the New York State Militia. That this deponent received orders from his captain to prepare himself with a gun, bayonet and cartridge box to fight for liberty and freedom.

That this deponent prepared himself accordingly and sometime in the forepart of the year 1776 as near as he can recollect, he was drafted from Captain Pettingell's company to go to Sacandaga at a Block House built by the Americans at this place for the purpose of preventing the Tories, British and hostile Indians from passing to and from the part of the country to Canada.

That this deponent with William Snook the Lieutenant of the Company and Henry Snook, William Pettingell, Joseph Pettingell, Daniel Pettingell and Hugh Connolly, privates in said company and probably others which he does not now remember, marched from the Town of Florida to Sacandaga and lay in the fort as a guard at that place until relieved by another draft from the same company.

That he had been drafted and went to Sacandaga four or five times in like manner and served his several tours at that place, sometimes would be stationed there a week, at others a fortnight, three weeks and a month, as occasions in the service required, but he cannot be particular as to the precise time he did serve there, he judges however, that he served in all of the Sacandaga Block Houses as much as two months at least.

That in going from Florida to Sacandaga they usually rafted the Mohawk River at Tripes Hill, and some times at Amsterdam, and marched to the Block House at Sacandaga principally through the woods and that place as but little improvement in roads had been made, to that section of country as well as to avoid any surprises by the enemy.

And this deponent further says, that in the year 1777 he was drafted in like manner from Captain Pettengill's Company as many as five times and served regular tours at Johnstown in a picket fort around the Johnstown Jail.

That he several times of service at that place would vary from one to four and five weeks before he got relieved.

That Captain Walter Vrooman commanded at the fort a principle part of the time.

That one Beekman was Lieutenant and one Hatch a Sergeant.

That the object in keeping a force at that plain was that the Americans apprehended an attack from the enemy coming through from Canada by the way of Sacandaga, Johnstown being the residence of Sir John Johnson, a Tory who had done much injury during the war.

That in the month of August 1777 Captain Pettingell's company was ordered out and the whole of Col. Fisher's Regiment to march for Oriskany in the County of Oneida at the time the battle was fought between the Americans and the British at that place and that this deponent was excused from serving at that place in consequence of a lame knee.

That in the Oriskany Battle Captain Pettingill was mortally wounded as this deponent was informed and believes, and Lieutenant Snook afterwards took command of the company and was appointed captain.

That after the Oriskany Battle a certain number was drafted from Captain Snook's Company to join General Gates forces at Saratoga, among which was this deponent, that one Thomas Van Horne commanded the draft from same company, he the being Lieutenant of said company.

That they marched from Florida to the City of Schenectady and from thence down the Mohawk River and marched over into Saratoga near Stillwater and there found General Gates Army.

And a few days before the battle between the forces commanded by General Gates, and those of the British commanded by General Burgoyne, this deponent was ordered to the town of Florida on business by Major David McMaster who commanded the forces at Stillwater to which this deponent was attached in the Militia. And this deponent did not return as this news arrived, that the battle had been fought and that Burgoyne and his army had been taken.

And this deponent further says that sometime in the year 1778 as near as he can recollect, Col. Fisher's Regiment was ordered out including Captain Snook's Company and marched to Stone Arabia in the Town of Palatine upon an alarm of high alert in that quarter, and were there about ten days as near as he could judge and was then ordered by another ??? of militia.

That in the year 1779 this deponent was drafted from Captain Snook's Company to march to the German Flats. He recollects that Captain Snook was among the number and that Robert McGrady, Cornelius Van Horne, William Phillips, Daniel McGraw, Conradt Steen, Justin Rosey and Henry Snooks, privates in said company were also among the number drafted.

That they marched up the Mohawk River on the south side to the German Flats and joined some Militia at that place, who had been called out in consequence of the Indians having scalped some of the Americans at that place. That this deponent was then absent about three weeks.

That this deponent had been ordered out in the years 1778, 1779, and 1780 on various occasions and stationed at Fort Plain, Fort Plank, Fort Windecker, Fort Dayton and the German Flats to protect the Americans from the incursions of the British and Indians. That from the repeated and number of occasions this deponent had been called and stationed at the before mentioned places in the American service, and from the great length of time, he is unable to state particularly how long he served in each of those places in a ???. He recollects that he has been at Bowman's Creek in the Town of Canajoharie and served on regular tour on guard at that place.

That at the time the battle was fought at Johnstown between the American forces commanded by Col. Willett and the British troops then commanded by Major Ross, Captain Snook's company was ordered out and sent to their relief and arrived the next morning after the battle was over and thinks that the Americans followed Major Ross about two days journey, Major Ross marched northward towards Canada but that Capt Snooks Company found the (blotted) and pursued Ross as before mentioned and then returned (blotted).

The deponent further says that he has been stationed at Tripes Hill to stand guard at that place, an attack was expected from the Tories, he cannot remember the year but thinks it was the latter part of the war, nor the length of time, but he remembers that Captain Snook Commanded at the time

Captain Snook's Company was also called out sometime the latter part of the war, and was stationed apposite Fort Plain in the now Town of Oppenheim (now St. Johnsville) as he believes on the north side of the Mohawk River and helped guard at that place.

They crossed the Mohawk River a little above Caughnawaga and marched up the river on the north side and found some of the American forces been marched by McMasters, he cannot recollect how long they were stationed there.

He has also been placed on guard at a stone house a little below Fort Hunter to watch and movements of the Tories and Indians but how long, cannot recollect.

That this deponent further says that during the whole war he kept himself in readiness to march any moment he was called upon to serve his country, and from the various services which he remembered he thinks he can safely state that he served the country as much as two years estimate at least and probably much longer, but his memory fails him and he cannot detail the events of the war with much ???

And this deponent further says that he was born in the town of Florida in the county and state aforesaid in the year 1752 and resided in the same place when he entered the service and has so resided ever since. That he has a record of his age in his family Bible written in German in his possession, that when called into service he had been personally drafted or called upon by his superior officers and always held himself in readiness to obey the call and served the country on his own account that he has stated the names of the principle officers engaged in the services as near as he can recollect and the concerned terms of his services. He has no documentary records in his possession nor any written discharge and hereby relinquishes every claim whatever to a pension or annuity except the present, and declared that the name is not on the pension roll of the agency of any state or of the United States and this deponent records is proved by Henry Smith, Garnet Newkirk, Daniel McGraw and George Stine and he also thinks is proved by Nicholas Hill and Henry Snook who can testify as to the veracity of this deponent and of their belief as to this deponent's services as soldier of the Revolution.

John McGraw (his mark)

Sworn to and subscribed this day and year aforesaid, Geo D. Ferguson, Clerk.

Pension Application for George Mour

Hand written note in file:

Mour, George

His name appears on a list of applicants for invalid pension returned by the District Court for the District of New York, submitted to the House of Representatives by the Secretary of War on April 25, 1794, and printed in the American State Papers, Class 9, Page 74.

Rank: Private
Regt: Col Vischer's
Disability: Wounded in both shoulders in an action with the Indians.
When and where disabled: Aug. 7, 1777, Oriskie (Oriskany)
Residence: Mohawk Town
To what pension entitled: Full
Remarks: There are no militia rolls in this office.
Evidence transmitted by the District Court complete.

(Geo. Mour Petition)

George Mour came before me, one of the Justices for the County of Montgomery and made oath that he is the same George Mour who was placed on the Pension List under the Act of Congress passed the 23rd March 1792 and that he now resides in Charlestown Montgomery County and has resided there, previous to the late War.

Sworn before me
This _____day of 1794_____
A Copy of the above certificate must be sworn too every six months on the fifth of March 1795

Herkimer County on this third day of April 1820 before me, the subscriber, a Justice of the peace for the said County of Herkimer personally appeared George Mour who on his oath declares that he is the same person who verily belonged to the company commanded by Captain Robert Yates at the time when he this deponent was wounded at the Oriskany Battle in the Regiment commanded by Colonel Frederick Visscher in the service of the United States, that he the deponent belonged to the company commanded by Captain Garret Putman in the regiment commanded by Colonel Marinus Willett at the time he was discharged from the service, that his name was placed on the pension list under the act of Congress passed the 23rd March 1792, that

he is ignorant of ever having received a certificate of such, his being placed on the pension list that he has regularly drawn a pension semi-annually since the year 1795 that he always has drawn the said pension by virtue of a copy of the annexed papers duly executed, that he received the annexed paper from the person, who kept the pension office in the City of New York at the time he received his first payment as a directory to him in drawing his pension thereafter which has always been deemed a sufficient evidence of his being placed on the pension list and has always heretofore entitled him to an enabled him to draw the pension therein mentioned, that he now resides in the town of Danube in the County of Herkimer and that his disability occasioned by the wounds he received in the Oriskany Battle still existed that he did at the time he was placed on the pension list resided in Charlestown in the County of Montgomery.
Signed George Mour (his mark)

Pension Application for Peter Mower

State of New York
Oneida County

On this ____ day of September 1832 personally appeared in open court, the court of Common Pleas of said county, now sitting, Peter Mower aged sixty seven years, a resident of said county who being first duly sworn according to law, doth on his oath make the following declaration in order to obtain the benefit of the act of Congress passed June 7, 1832.

That he entered the service of the United States under the following named officers and served as herein stated.

That he was born at Claverack, NY July 1765. He has no record of age or certificate. Enlisted at Charlestown, Montgomery County NY where he entered service. Since the war has lived at Danube NY now at Annsville, Oneida County. That he enlisted in Capt. Garret Putnam's Company, Col. Marinus Willett's Regt in forepart of April 1781 when he was discharged at Fort Plain on the Mohawk River and received a written discharge signed by Capt. Putnam which has been lost.

That in April 1782 he enlisted again in Capt. French's Company, Col, Willett's Regt for nine months and served therein until Jan'y of 1783, 9 months and immediately enlisted for three years in Capt Peter Tierce's Company. Lieutenant John Thorn, Col. Willett's Regt and continued to serve until the 3rd of 4th day of January 1786 when he was discharged from service at Schenectady. His service was performed along the Mohawk River and in the region about.

He hereby relinquishes every claim whatever to a pension or annuity except the present and declares that his name is not on the pension roll of the agency of any state.
Signed Peter Mowor (his mark)

Other pension papers reveal that his wife applied for a pension 13 of April 1855, Magdalena Mower, aged 78 years, a resident of Annsville, widow of Peter Mower, deceased. They were married in Fort Plain the 19 day of March 1794 by Rev. Pecke, minister and her name before marriage was Magdalena Foterly. Peter died at Annsville 4 of August 1851.

Pension Application for Timothy Murphy

In this case, the application is a request for Widow's Benefits and is impossible for me to read but there was a letter included in the application which doesn't tell a lot about Murphy's service. The marriage mentioned here is his second marriage after his first wife died. Murphy died from throat cancer.

September 8, 1929
Timothy Murphy R 16668

Mr. W. U. O'Brien
3878 Carron Place
New York

Dear Sir:

Reference is made to your request for information relative to Timothy Murphy, a Revolutionary War soldier who served in Colonel Daniel Morgan's Rifle Corps.

The data which follow were taken from papers on file in pension claim, R 16668, based on the military service of the only Timothy Murphy that is found in the Revolutionary War records of this office.

On October 18, 1860, Mary Murphy, a resident of Davenport, Delaware County, New York, aged seventy-seven years, applied for pension as the widow of Timothy Murphy. It was alleged that Timothy Murphy served during most of the Revolutionary War and that in 1780 he was serving as private in Captain Isaac Bogart's company in Colonel John Harper's New York regiment. The claim was not allowed, as proof of the alleged service was not furnished in accordance with the requirement of the pension law.

It was stated that solder and Mary Robertson were married April 22, 1811, at Middleburgh, Delaware County, New York. The following persons were present at the marriage, all of whom were dead in 1860; James Robertson, Elizabeth Robertson and Peter Robertson, their relation to the widow not shown.

Timothy Murphy died June 17, 1818, at Middleburgh, New York and he and the said Mary had the following children: George who was the eldest and died when about five years of age, and Charles, Timothy and Alexander who survived their father but the dates of their deaths were not shown.

In 1860 one John Robertson (relationship not shown) aged seventy-five years and a resident of Worcester, Otsego County, New York, stated that he had been acquainted with the soldier, Timothy for a number of years before he died.

The date and place of birth of Timothy Murphy and the names of his parents are not shown.

Very truly yours
A.D. Hiller
Executive Assistant to the Administrator.

Pension Application for Martin Nestle

State of New York
Montgomery County

On this sixteenth day of February 1821 personally appeared in open court being a court of record called a Court of Common Pleas of the said county of Montgomery and having by the Constitution and laws of the said state common law jurisdiction and passed of the power of fine and imprisonment Martin Nestle aged about sixty one years being resident in the Town of Oppenheim in the County of Montgomery aforesaid who being first duly sworn according to law doth on his oath declare that he enlisted into the United States Service in the War of the Revolution on the Continental Establishment sometime in the summer or fall of the year 1781 at a place called Stone Arabia in the Town of Palatine in the county and state aforesaid that he enlisted into the service as aforesaid for and during the war in a company commanded by one Captain Fleming and which belonged to a New York Regiment of Artillery under the command of one Colonel Lamb.

That he served in the said regiment as a private soldier against the common enemy from the time of his said enlistment until the end of the said War of the Revolution and that he received his discharge in writing from the said service at Stony Point on the Hudson River about thirty six miles north of the City of New York, sometime in the summer or fall of the year 1783 that the discharge of this deponent which he received from the said service as aforesaid was many years ago left with our Fort Spreaker in said town of Palatine whose dwelling has since been consumed by fire and probably said discharge with it for which has since been made for it among the papers of said Fort Spreaker and it could not be found.

That this deponent cannot procure said discharge not having it in his power or possession and believes it to be lost or destroyed and that he has no other written evidence in his power of his said services, that he was in the Battle of Johnstown which in the said service.

And I Martin Nestle do solemnly swear that I was a resident within the United States on the eighteenth day of March one thousand eight hundred and eighteen and that I have not since that time by gift sale or in any manner whatever disposed of my property or any part thereof with intent thereby to diminish it as to bring myself within the provisions of an act of Congress entitled an act to provide for certain persons engaged in the land and naval service of the United States in the Revolutionary War passed the eighteenth day of March one thousand eight hundred and eighteen and that I have not nor has any person in trust for me any property or securities contracts or debts due to me nor have I any income other than what is contained in the schedule hereto annexed and by me subscribed.

That I am poor and in reduced circumstances in life not having any property except my wearing apparel and some little house with furniture and that my family and myself sometimes suffer for the want of provisions and ??? and that I actually had the assistance of my bounty for service that the foregoing declaration on oath is made in order to obtain the benefits of an act of Congress entitled an act to provide for certain persons in the land and naval service of the United States in the Revolutionary War.

Martin Nestle (his signature.)

Pension Information for Jacob Noble

The interesting part about this one is that it is from Massachusetts, Colonel John Brown's Regiment.

January 25, 1934
Mr. Charles H. Lovett
225 Sheridan Road
Winnetka, Illinois
Dear Sir:

Reference is made to your request for the Revolutionary War record of Jacob Noble.

The data furnished herein were obtained from papers on file in the pensions claim, W 21853, based upon the military services of Jacob Noble.

While a resident of Westfield, Hampden County, Massachusetts, he enlisted and served with the Massachusetts troops as follows: from about May 16, 1776, until December 1, 1776, as private in Captain John Gray's company in Colonel Woodbridge's regiment; from September 21, 1777, until October 11, 1777, in Captain David Moseley's company in Colonel John Moseley's regiment; from July 20, 1780, until October 22, 1780 as sergeant in Captain Levi Ely's company in Colonel John Brown's regiment and was in the battle of Stone Arabia; also served about three weeks and was engaged in guarding prisoners taken at Westfield.

He married at Westfield, Massachusetts, November 29, 1792, Eunice Moseley of that place. It was not shown that she was related to the officers of that surname under whom Jacob Noble served.

Jacob Noble died at Westfield, Massachusetts August 2, 1828, aged sixty-nine years. It was stated that he was a native of Westfield but the exact date of his birth was not given.

His widow, Eunice, was allowed pension on her application executed October 2, 1828, at which time she was sixty-seven years of age and was living in Westfield.

(The rest of the letter is missing and there is no more in his file.)

Pension Application for John Nobel

John was very young, not yet 13 years old, when he was a fifer in his father's company and he saw a lot of interesting service, the battles in the Saratoga area and finally the battle where Col. Brown was killed in Stone Arabia.

State of Vermont
Rutland County

On this 19th day of July A.D. 1832, personally appeared in open court before the Judge of the Probate Court of the Rutland District now sitting, John Nobel, a resident of the County of Rutland and State of Vermont, aged 70 years, who being first duly sworn according to law, doth on his oath make the following declaration, in order to obtain the benefit of the Act of Congress, passed June 7, 1832.

That he entered the service of the United States under the following named officers, and served as herein stated. In 1775 he resided in Pittsfield, Mass, and although not quite 13 years old, he stood as a minute man in a company commanded by his father, James Nobel, and marched immediately after the Battle of Lexington in a company as fifer to Ticonderoga, which was taken by Col. Ethan Allen, a day or two before he arrived. He was under Col. Benedict Arnold, Lt. Col. Easton, Maj. Brown, Lt. Dickinson, Ensign Hitchcock, there to Crown Point.

Went with Gen'l Montgomery under Lt. Col. Eason to St. John, Montreal, Chambly, and Sorrel, which places he assisted in taking. Was taken sick at Sorrel and returned to Crown Point and was discharged there in December, having served eight months.

In 1777 when Burgoyne came down, he volunteered and marched in August to Stillwater and until he met the enemy when they fell back with the rest of the army, he served in Capt. William's company, Col. Brown's Reg't, was at Saratoga when Burgoyne was taken and was soon after dismissed having served three months.

In 1778 or 1779, he forgets which (year) he enlisted into Capt. Raymond's Company, Col. Brown's Regiment and marched to Hudson thence to Albany where he served three months in guarding stores, when he was discharged.

Does not remember his other officers except Adjt White.

In 1780 in July he enlisted in Captain Ford's Company, Col. Brown's Reg't and was ??? to Maj. Root, marched to Albany, Fort Plain, Fort Stanwix, guarding provisions and protecting the inhabitants, was in the Battle At Stone Robby (Stone Arabia) with the British, Tories and Indians, when his colonel, Brown, was killed and where he was discharged. After his time was out, the day the battle was fought, then 21 October, but he remained in service about ten days longer until the army was driven beyond Canada Creek. He was also frequently called out on alarms and served a few days at a time amounting to at least one month. He never received any written discharge.

Maj. Elenore commanded a Reg't at Crown Point when he was there. Ethan Allen commanded then the troops. He knew Genenerals Montgomery, Schuyler, Arnold, Starks, Lafayette and many others.

He has no documentary evidence, and knows of no person whose testimony he can procure who can testify to his services, except what accompanies this. He was born in Hebron, Connecticut, on 25 October 1762, his age is recorded in his Bible. Since the Revolutionary War he has lived in Benson, Addison, then lived in Chenango, NY seven years, then moved to Newell where he now lives and where he has lived since 1807.

The clergyman of Newell has recently been dismissed, but he is known to most of the inhabitants of that place.

He hereby relinquishes every claim, etc………………

Letter in the Pension Application
February 26, 1940

Dr. J. E. Brunett Buckenham
Chestnut Hill
Philadelphia, Pennsylvania

Dear Sir:

Reference is made to you letter in which you request the War of 1812 record of John Noble, who received a pension, claim No. S21900, on his application dated July 19, 1832.

The John Noble cited by you was a Revolutionary War soldier, and his record as shown in pension claim S 21900, based upon his service in the Revolutionary War is as follows:

John Noble was born October 25, 1762, in Hebron Connecticut. He was the son of James Noble who died in 1817.

While residing in Pittsfield, Massachusetts, John Noble enlisted in the spring of 1775, as a Minute Man in the company of his father, Captain James Noble. Immediately after the Battle of Lexington he marched with said company as a fifer in Colonels Benedict Arnold's and Easton's regiments, was in the expedition to Canada and at the taking of St. John's, Montreal, Chambly and Sorrel, and was discharged in December 1775 having served at least eight months, enlisted in July or August 1777, served three months as private in Captain Roswell Williams' company, Colonel Brown's Massachusetts regiment and was at the surrender of Burgoyne; enlisted in 1778 or 1779, and served three months as a private in Captain Raymond's Company, Colonel Parsons' Massachusetts regiment, was in the Battle of Stone Arabia and was discharged about the last of October 1780, having served three months and ten days. He was frequently called out on alarm and served at least one month. (End of copy of letter.)

To the Honorable Secretary of War
Dear Sir.

Having received information through the politeness of the Hon'r Williams that members from the district in which I live in Rutland County, that the pension granted to those persons who applied to Mr. Temple for assistance in obtaining this pension was suspended until such information could be obtained from said pensioners as should convince the War department that no fraud was committed in obtaining the certificate for the pension. I would now informe the War Department that I am one of the numbers who obtained my pension certificate through the agency of Mr. Temple, who then stood high in the estimation of the people in the Rutland County and even in this state generally.

I would further state that as near as I can now know that I went to Rutland in the month of July 1832 and made out my Declaration, as I now believe before the Hon'r Charles Williams Chief Judge of the Supreme Court of the State of Vermont.

Mr. Temple did the writing or wrote the Declaration but had nothing to do about obtaining my testimony. One of my witnesses was James Nobel of Benson in said Rutland County, he was sworn to the truth of his testimony and I now believe before Isaac Ginswold of said Benson, my other testimony was taken in Owell the town in which I live and the witness was Mr. Assonoor Austin of Said Owell and sworn before Thosmasto Hermnand Esq, or the ??. My other testimony was Luther Brown Esq. And Ivan Smith Esq. Who were both sworn before Norwell Bottom Esq. Or said Owell. Also I believe that Aaron Angier and George Hibbard both of said Owell testified.

Something about my age and character and the opinion of people in my vicinity regarding my revolutionary services, the said Aaron Angier and George Hibbard was sworn as I now believe in Rutland but before whom I now do not recollect.

The necessary certificates accompanying my pension papers I believe was made by the Hon'r Robert Pierpoint then and now Clerk of the Supreme Court of the State of Vermont.

The amount per annum of my pension as certified by the Secretary of War is fifty-nine dollars and thirty cents, the last payment which I have received was the 4th of September 1834. I missed money at bank in Owell the town where I now live and have lived something over twenty-seven years. Unknowing to this state I gave a power of Attorney to Miny McCarbin Cashier of Owell Bank to draw my half years pension at the Burlington Bank where I had a right to apply for my pension as it pertained to my services.

I commenced my first tour of service immediately after commencement of hostilities at Lexington I believe the latter part of April or first of May 1775. I served under my father Captain James Noble and a part of the time in Col. Arnold's and a part of the time under Col. Eason who was the Lieut Col. Until Col. Arnold left to repair to Boston to commence his month through the woods to Quebec.

When I entered the service I belonged to Pittsfield in the State of Massachusetts. I began my service in marching by Whitehall then Skeneborough for the purpose of joining Col. Arnold and Col. Allen in taking Ticonderoga. The fort was taken a day or two before we arrived. Was then ordered to Crown Point there remained until General Montgomery marched for Canada I believe in September 1775. I then went on with the regiment of Col. Eason to St. Johns and from there we was ordered to Chamblee and was then taken sick as I now believe the latter part of November and I was soon after sent back to Crown Point and there remained until I was discharged and which as I believe was the first of January making the term I served for my first tour eight months or over. I was enlisted as a soldier or fifer and belonged to the Bay State Troops.

I again enlisted in said Pittsfield under Capt. Roswell Williams as I now believe in the month of July 1777 and was assigned to Col. John Brown's regiment and immediately ordered to Stillwater to join the army under General Gates. I there remained until General Burgoyne retreated to Saratoga. We pursued on to Saratoga and there remained until General Burgoyne surrendered the 17th of Oct, 1777 and as soon after dismissed and returned home.

I again enlisted as near as I now believe in the summer of 1778 for the term of three months under Capt. Raymond of Richmont in said Bay State and Col. Parson's company. We was enlisted for the purpose of marching to the southward, we marched to Hudson on the North River (Hudson River) and was then ordered to Albany to Guard the Continental Stores as for their safety.

I remained at Albany until my time expired and was then dismissed and returned to Pittsfield, again in the month of July 1780 I enlisted for the term of three months under Capt. William Ford of said Pittsfield, Col. John Brown's Regiment. I enlisted as a waiter to Maj. Oliver Root of said Pittsfield. We was immediately marched through Albany to a place called Fort Plain and from there we were marched twice to forts to which took general provision to the places. In the Battle at Stone Arabia, the place where Col. John Brown was killed, I believe the 21st October in which Battle I was personally engaged. The enemy retreated and was followed to Canada Creek.

I served ten days over my term of three months and was then dismissed and returned home after that tour. I was called out a number of times in the militia and served in all to the amount of one month or more. All my services was performed from Pittsfield in the State of Massachusetts where I was then a resident. I was 72 years the 25th day of October 1836.
??? February 7th 1835

To the Hon'r the Secretary of War.
Signed, John Nobel

Pension Application for Peter J. Quackenboss

R8538
State of New York
Montgomery County

On this nineteenth day of September in the year of our Lord one thousand eight hundred and thirty two personally appeared in open court before the judges of the Court of Common Pleas of Montgomery County now sitting at the Court House in Johnstown in and for said County, Peter J. Quackenboss, a resident of the Town of Glen in the County and State aforesaid, aged seventy eight years who being first duly sworn according to law doth on his oath make the following declaration in order to obtain the benefit of the Act of Congress passed June 7, 1832.

That he entered the service of the United States under the following named officers and served as herein stated.

That in the year 1776 this deponent belonged to a company commanded by Captain Jacob Gardinier in Col. Frederick Fisher's Regiment of the New York State Militia and held himself in readiness as a minute man to be called upon at any moment with three days provision and sufficient ammunition for the same time; that said company was very frequently called out for military exercise and improvement in the early part of the Revolution. That some time in the year 1777 as near as he can now recollect, but the day and month cannot remember. This deponent marched with a part of Captain Gardinier's Company from the now Town of Glen to Sacandaga in the Town of Northampton about twenty five miles to a Block House near Sacandaga and that this deponent and the others in the American Service was engaged in building a new block house which was called Fort Fisher, to prevent the Tories and Indians from going to and from this quarter of the country to Canada. After building Fort Fisher which occupied them about six or eight days they returned home.

That some time during the same year this deponent was ordered to Johnstown to oppose the British forces Commanded by Sir John Johnson at that place. General Schuyler Commanded the American forces; and the Americans took about six hundred prisoners from Sir John Johnson which included himself and about all his forces. The Americans taking all these arms and ammunition permitted Johnson and his men to go upon parole of honor. And this deponent returned home to the Town of Glen.

That sometime about the first of August 1777, this deponent was marched from the Town of Glen to Oriskany in the County of Oneida (this can't be right!) in Captain Gardiner's Company of Militia to oppose the Tories of General St. Leger. Captain Gardinier's Company including the Regiment Commanded by Col. Frederick Fisher, marched on the south side of the Mohawk River as far as the Indian Castle a little above Fort Plain and then found the forces Commanded by General Herkimer.

Near the place General Herkimer Commanding took a number of Tories and left them at Fort Dayton with a guard to take care of them, and continued on his march, crossed the Mohawk River at Herkimer near the West Canada Creek and continued up the Mohawk River near Utica and then recrossed the river and passed up the south side of the Mohawk River through Whitestown and camped near Oriskany Creek.

The next day about nine o'clock in the morning the battle commenced between the forces under the Command of General Herkimer and the British. Herkimer's forces were surrounded by the British by falling in ambush and suffered considerably. General Herkimer became mortally wounded. Captain Gardiner was wounded having been pierced in two places with the bayonet near the hip joint. Col. Cox and Captain Davis, both died of their wounds. And Peter Covenhoven was shot with a ball near the knee.

After the battle the American forces returned down the Mohawk to Montgomery on the same route as they advanced. The deponent well recollects that Col. Willett and Gansevoort Commanded the other part of the American Army at Oriskany in opposing the forces of Gen'l St. Leger.

And this deponent further says that some time before General Burgoyne came from Canada by the way of Lake Champlain and the Hudson River with his Army, but the month or year the deponent cannot now remember, he was ??? to go to Fort Edward on the Hudson River for the defending of this place. That he took his own team, went by Schenectady and through the County of Saratoga to Fort Edward and was then employed about eight weeks as near as he can recollect in carting provisions from Fort Edward to Lake George for the benefit of the American Troops. General Schuyler then commanded at this place.

And this deponent further says that he was at Cherry Valley at the time the American forces were out of that place. That he went in Captain Gardinier's Company arrived at Cherry Valley just after the battle was over and assisted in aiding the sick and wounded, burying the dead. That it is impossible for him to remember the year from his advanced age. But he recollects that Brant an Indian and Walter Butler commanded the enemies forces, and this deponent well recollects that he had been ordered out and stationed at Cherry Valley as a guard and that place, some two or three weeks previous to the time the forces were cut off at that place. That Major John Newkirk and Captain Jacob Gardinier Commanded the Americans before the battle was fought that after having been stationed there some time about two weeks, he had permission to come home and his captain also and soon after heard that Cherry Valley was attacked by Brant and Butler and this deponent then returned to Cherry Valley to assist in the defense of that place. Arrived just as the battle was over as before related.

And this deponent further says that a battle was fought between the British and Americans at Turlock, now called the Town of Sharon in the County of Schoharie and a company of men commanded by Captain Garret Putman marched to the relief of the Americans at that place and the deponent went with the company from Glen to Schoharie to aid and assist in the defense of that place but the battle had ended principally by the time Captain Putman arrived, Captain McKeen and American officer died of his wounds. Col. Willett commanded the American forces and this deponent assisted in taking care of the sick and wounded. This deponent cannot remember the year the aforesaid battle was fought but believes it to have been in the year 1781.

And this deponent further saith that some time after the Oriskany Battle this deponent cannot say whether it was the next or the year then after; he was ordered out with the rest of the Militia belonging to Col. Frederick Fisher's Regiment to march to Fort Plain in Montgomery County. Captain Jacob Gardinier was Captain of this deponent's company. Col. Volkert Veeder commanded the regiment in consequence of Col. Fisher having been scalped by the Indians and unable to do duty.

While the deponent was absent at Fort Plain embodied with the Militia at that place, Sir John Johnson with the hostile Indians, British and Tories, burnt Schoharie and marched down to the Schoharie Creek and Montgomery County and burnt all the houses along the Mohawk in the Town of Glen and kept a very few owned by the Tories. This deponent's house was burnt with all his furniture and provisions. And he and his family lived three days without any thing to eat except one loaf of bread. That this deponent returned from Fort Plain as soon as he heard that his house had been burnt.

And this deponent further saith that he stood for three summers sentinel at Fort Hunter near Schoharie Creek by taking his regular tour of duty at that place when not otherwise employed in the service.

And this deponent further saith that he was engaged more of less during the whole Revolution standing Sentinel, going on express; and engaged in scouting parties and that while this deponent was stationed at Schoharie Creek he took five men prisoners from Major Ross' Tories at the time.

The battle was fought at Johnstown between the Americans and the British. Col. Willett commanded the Americans at Johnstown; and Major Ross the British forces. The British marched from Curry town down through Warrensbush, now the Town of Florida near the Schoharie Creek and crossed the Mohawk River a little below the Schoharie Creek and proceeded to Johnstown.

And this deponent further says that he was born in the now Town of Glen as he has understood and believes in the year 1754. That he has no record of his age as the same was burnt in the Revolution when his house was burnt by the British and Indians. That he lived in the now Town of Glen when he entered the American Service. And has lived in the same place ever since the war where he now resides. That this deponent was drafted part of the time while engaged in the American Service and volunteered the residue. That he never received any written discharge. That in the foregoing account he has stated the principle officers engaged in the service as near as he can recollect and the circumstances of his service. He expects to be able to prove some of his service by contemporary ??? William Forgason, Cornelius Newkirk and Myndert B. Wemple. That he has no documentary evidence.

And hereby relinquishes every claim whatever to a pension or annuity except the present and declares that his name is not on the Pension Roll of the agency of any state or of the United States. And this deponent expect to prove by Abraham Van Horne, and Myndert Wemple who can testify as to the veracity of the deponent and of their believe as to this deponent's service as a soldier of the Revolution.

(Signed with his mark) Peter J. Quackenboss

Testimony was provided by Myndert B. Wemple, William Forgason, Cornelius Newkirk, William Wallace, Nicholas A Gardinier, Howland Fish, John Hand and John Sanford. This pension was DENIED because he did not specifically state the times of service.

June 10, 1833, he tried once more to apply for his pension. He was successful.

State of New York
Montgomery County

Peter J. Quackenboss, this applicant who signed the annexed declaration for a pension in further specification and supplement to said declaration being duly sworn doth depose and say:

That in the year 1777 he was engaged in building a new block house called Fort Fisher at Sacandaga. Six days at the least in the manner particularly described and set forth in his former declarations.

And this deponent further preparation of his said declaration saith that in 1777 he was ordered to march to Johnstown to oppose the British forces commanded by Sir John Johnson in a manner now particularly set forth in his declaration. He was under the command of Captain Jacob Gardinier in Col. Fisher's Regiment. He was actually engaged in this service at Johnstown twenty days at the least. The month that this service was rendered this deponent does not remember.

And the deponent further says that in the month of August in the same year, 1777 as near as the can recollect, it was at the first of August in the same year, 1777. This deponent was ordered out in Captain Gardinier's Company to march to Oriskany in the County of Oneida to oppose the forces of the British under the command of General St. Leger, as is now particularly detailed in his former declaration. The battle which was fought at Oriskany was generally known by the name of the Oriskany Battle, that from the time this deponent left his home for said expedition in going to and returned from the Oriskany Battle, he was engaged in that service twenty six days at the least.

This deponent further says in specification of his former declaration, that forward to the time that General Burgoyne came from Canada by the way of the Lake Champlain and the Hudson River in the manner particularly set forth in his former declaration. He this deponent and others from the County of Montgomery were pressed into this public service as stated in his said declaration.

And that this deponent was engaged in this service at the least the term of seven weeks.

Three hundred wagons and teams as near as he could judge were pressed into said service. And one Christopher Yates had the command of the teams in regard to their employment. And then deponent was ordered out under Captain Gardinier and was stationed at Cherry Valley on duty for two weeks at the least before the battle was fought at Cherry Valley, he had permission to return home and his captain also as is particularly set forth in his former declaration. They heard Cherry Valley was attacked by Brant and Butler and this deponent and Captain returned back to Cherry Valley and found the American Troops as the battle was over. In the last service the deponent was engaged eight days at the least.

And this deponent further says that he was engaged at the time of the Turlock Battle at a place now called the Town of Sharon in the County of Schoharie the term of ten days at the least, the manner of circumstances of that service is particularly detailed in his former declaration. This deponent also further declares that he was stationed at Fort Plain in the public service of at least fourteen days, a detailed amount of that service is made in his former declaration to which he refers.

And this deponent further declares that he was stationed for three successive summers at Fort Hunter near Schoharie Creek as a sentinel. He will not be positive as to the several years he was stationed here but believes it to be in the years 1780, 1781, 1782 to the best of his recollection.

That the first year he was stationed at said fort he commenced service as early as the 20th May and continued as late as the 1st of October at least.

In the second year he commenced as early as the first of June and continued in service until as late as the 1st of September at the least.

And in the third year he commenced as early as the 15th May and continued in service as late as the 18th September at the least, making the amount of service at Fort Hunter eleven months and six days. That while at Fort Hunter he continued constantly at the fort except he left the fort as often as twice a week on scouting parties to watch the movement of the British and Indians and he thinks that he was absent at the time of the Turlock Battle. That during this deponent's service at Fort Hunter, Garret Putman had command of the fort part of the time who held the rank of Captain. Captain Whelfs a Frenchman also had command of the fort during some part of the time; and that which this deponent was engaged in the public service as stated in his declaration and in this supplement thinks he was not employed in any other pursuit.

And deponent further declares that he has omitted to state in its regular order twenty days which he served at Sacandaga before the new block house was built on guard at this place in Captain Gardinier's Company in Col. Frederick Fisher's Regiment. This service was rendered in the latter part of the year 1776 or 1777. He cannot remember which, at a place a little north of the new block house.

And this deponent further declares by reason of forgetfulness he omitted on is former declaration to state that he served at least twelve days at Stone Arabia in the Town of Palatine in Captain Gardinier's Company in Col. Fisher's Regiment upon an alarm at that place. The service was rendered sometime in the year 1777 to as best of his recollection, as the thinks it was near the time of the Oriskany Battle.

And this deponent also omitted in his first disclosure to state that he was ordered out by Captain Gardinier with ten or twelve other men to go and take on Yerry Cuck a mulatto and a noted Tory and Spy who traveled between Canada and this country to obtain information for the British. The party surrounded a house then in the Town of Charleston in this county occupied by a man named Van Zail and they found Cuck in the house under the floor concealed whom they took. Cuck was well armed and attempted to shoot but was shot dead by the party under Captain Gardinier. And Captain Gardinier and his men made a prisoner of John Van Zail and delivered him to the Commanding Officers at Johnstown.

In this service this deponent was engaged four days at the least, making the final amount of his service seventeen months and twenty days.
(Signed with his mark) Peter J. Quackenbush

The following is the marriage proof presented.

I, Douw Van OLinda, of the Town of Mohawk County of Montgomery and the State of New York hereby certify that I am at present the minister of the Reformed Protestant Dutch Church of Caughnawaga in the Town of Mohawk and County of Montgomery and as such minister I have the custody of the church records. That I have examined the records and find in the records of marriages in the hand writing of Dominie Romeyn, on what is generally understood to be his hand writing he being the minister of said church at the time the following entry~
"1774 July 19 Peter Quackinbus met Susanne Bradt"
I certify the above to be a true extract from the records word for word and letter for letter by which it appears that the said Peter Quackenbus and Susanne Bradt were lawfully married at that time.

(Signed) Douw Van OLinda

Sworn to before me this 11th day of March 1853
John Everson, Justice of the Peace

In pursuance of a law passed the 27th of April, 1784, entitled "An act for the settlement of the pay of the Levies and Militia, for their service in the late War, and for other purposes therein mentioned," the following certificates have been issued, bearing interest at five per cent per annum, viz:

Date	Name	Rank	No. of Cert'e issued	£	s	d
1779. Dec 3	Peter Quackenbos	Serg't	11210	4	18	8
1780. " 3	Do	"	11244	5	17	4
" Oct 24	Do	Private	29862	1	3	1/3
" July 5	Do		29890		8	10 1/2
" Aug 4	Do	Corporal	29927		17	7 1/2
" "	Do	Private	29940		16	—
1779 Sept 1	Do	"	29948		17	2 1/3
" Nov 3	Do	"	31525		16	2
1780 May 27	Do	"	31548		10	8
" June 5	Do	"	31557		7	1 1/3
" May 17	Do	"	31575		8	10 7/
1779 Nov 4	Do	Corporal	31621		19	7

Pension Application for John Reed

State of New York
Lewis County

On this twentieth day of September in the year one thousand eight hundred and thirty two personally appeared in open court before the Court of Common Pleas of the County of Lewis now sitting John Reed, a resident of the Town of Lowville in the County of Lewis and State of New York aged seventy years in December next who being first duly sworn according to law doth on his oath make the following declaration in order to obtain the benefit of the Act of Congress passed June 7, 1832.

That in the year 1781 he enlisted under Captain Gross in the Regiment of New York State Troops commanded by Colonel Willett, Adjutant Fonda for nine months and served during that period.

That he entered the service in the spring and was discharged at the expiration of his term of service. That he was stationed at Fort Plain NY, marched to Fort Stanwix and laboured in repairing the Fort and was at Fort Herkimer.

That from the year 1777 to the year 1782 he served in the New York Militia under Captain Henry Miller, Lieutenant Samuel Van Atten in the regiment commanded by Colonel Clock, several tours every year except the year 1781 when he served in the State Troops above mentioned.

That he cannot state the time of entering and leaving the service of the length of time he served in each year, but is confident that the whole time he served in the Militia considerably exceeds three months. That in his services in the Militia he was stationed on the Mohawk River. That he marched at one time to Fort Stanwix while serving in the Militia aforesaid.

That while performing the above services his father and mother were both killed and scalped by the Indians.

And he further states that he was in the Battle at Johnstown in the year 1781 was also in a Battle at Turlow near Bowman's Creek was also at West Canada Creek at the time Colonel Butler was killed.

That he entered the service as a volunteer at all the times above specified.

That he resided at the time of entering the service in the Town of Palatine, Montgomery County, New York. That he has no documentary evidence and knows of no person whose testimony he can procure who can testify to his service.

Here hereby relinquishes every claim whatever to a pension or annuity except the present and declares that his name is not on the pension rolls of the agency of any state.

John Reed (his mark)

Sworn to and subscribed the day and year aforesaid.

Pension Application for George Saltsman

This application is simply not legible. However, the letter in the back of the file gives the summary of the service.

June 26, 1931
Mr. John C. Ferres, Second
114 South Market Street
Johnstown, New York

Dear Madam:

You are advised that it appears from the papers in the Revolutionary War pension claim W 22152, that George Saltsman, the son of Michael Saltsman, was born December 13, 1763 in Palatine, Tryon County, New York.

While residing in said Palatine, he enlisted in 1779 and served as private at various times with the New York Troops in Captains Henry Miller's and John Diffendorff's Companies under Colonels Jacob Klock, Harper, Brown, Willett and Wagoner, was in the battles of Stone Arabia and Johnstown and several skirmishes with the Indians, and served until in 1783, amounting in all to one year, one month and twenty seven days.

He was allowed pension on his application executed September 19, 1832, at which time he was living in Palatine, New York.

He died February 14, 1838 in said Palatine where he had always lived.

The soldier married, February 20, 1787 in Palatine, New York, Savina Lebern or Lepper, of Palatine New York.

She was allowed pension on her application executed December 28, 1838, aged seventy three years and a resident of Palatine.

In 1838, their son-in-law, William Gray, was aged forty-seven years and living in Palatine, New York.

The names of children are not shown.

Very truly yours,
E. W. Morgan
Acting Commissioner.

Pension Application for Benjamin Sammons

Benjamin served in the Albany Militia and went to Lake George, he fought in the Battle of Klock's Field, and guarded at Continental Store House.

State of New York
Montgomery County SS

On this 19th day of September in the year of our Lord one thousand eight hundred and thirty two personally appeared in open court before the Court of Common Pleas of the County of Montgomery now sitting Benjamin Sammons, a resident of the Town of Johnstown in the County of Montgomery and State of New York aged seventy three years on the fifth day of December last past, who being first duly sworn according to law, doth on his oath, made the following declarations in order to obtain the benefit of the Act of Congress passed June 7, 1832.

That he entered the service of the United States under the following named officers and served as herein stated: In the year 1776, in the month of November he went out to Albany Bush, in Tryon County under Captain John Davis belonging to Frederick Fisher's Regiment and was out three days.

He was out in the same month 2 days under the command of Major Giles Fonda.

In the year 1776 the 7th of January in the 7th of January he was ordered out by Captain John Davis, belonging to Fisher's Regiment and was out at this time 10 days.

In the month of May the day he cannot state, in the year 1777, year applicant served in a detachment of Albany Militia, who were ordered out by General Schuyler, to go to Lake George this detachment was commanded by Col. Cuyler, to the company to which your applicant belonged was commanded by Capt Nicholas Marselis.

We went to the place where they were ordered to go and was out one month and does not recollect the particular time when discharged.

In July of the same year he served under the above mentioned officers, at Fort George, one month longer. He again during the summer and fall of that year served five weeks under the same officers as above stated.

In November of the same year he again went out under Nicholas Marselis, Captain, and carried 104 British prisoners from Albany to Hartford and was out at this time 20 days.

In the month of March in the year 1777, he was drafted for nine months in the Company of Captain Stanten, Henry Pawling and Levi DeWitt, Lieutenants; belonging to Col Albert Pawlings Regiment, Elias Van BenScouten, 1st Major Channoult, 2nd Major. We went from Shawangunk, Ulster County, State of New York to Fort Shamdawn Ulster County.

He served then at that place two or three months from thence to a place called Aquago and from there again to Stoney Point ?? on the North River or Hudson below the highland whence they went by an order of General George Washington to rebuild the fort at that place that he served the full term of nine months but does not recollect the particular time he was discharged and was discharged at the latter place.

Your applicant says that in the month of May in the year 1780 he served 10 days in an expedition with the whole of the Albany Militia under Captain Marselis belonging to Col. Cuyler's Regiment, that he went from Albany to Fort Hunter on the Mohawk River, then Tryon County now Montgomery County and State of New York.

Your applicant says that in July of the same year he went out on an other expedition under the same officers last aforesaid and went from Albany to Fort Plain along the Mohawk River, this was at the time that the place was burned and destroyed by the enemy.

Given applicant says that he was out on the expedition under the same officers as above stated and went from Albany to a place called the German Flatts, Herkimer. They had at this time an engagement with the enemy at Col. Clock's at a place now called Oppenhiem (Battle of Klock's Field) Montgomery County. He was out at this time twenty days.

Your applicant says that during the ?? of the winter they had and kept a Continental Store House at the City of Albany, which our people was compelled to guard, that he was obliged as one of the Militia of that city to turn out every other night and keep guard of the stores kept in the Continental Store House, when he was out on those expeditions above stated, he was charged and served as such guard, during the first five years of the Revolution, except the times as above stated, at smallest calculations at least one month in each year, making in all five months.

That when he was out and did serve he was under the officer last above mentioned. He said he served in all 20 months and no longer. He has no documentary evidence of his service. He knows of no person of whom he is able to prove all this service.

He had no documentary evidence of his services.

He was born in Shawangunk, Ulster County, State of New York in the year 1758. He has no proof of his age.

He resided at Shawangunk and Albany and Johnstown, Montgomery, when called into service and he has lived since the Revolution in Johnstown, Montgomery County.

He is acquainted with the following persons residing in his neighborhood who can testify as to his character for which they verily and their belief of his services as a soldier of the Revolution.

(Rev. Abraham Van Horn, William Wallace)

He hereby relinquishes every claim whatever to a pension except the present and declares that his name is not in the pension roll of the agency of any state.

Sworn and subscribed to the day and year aforesaid.

(His Mark) Benjamin Sammons

Geo. D. Ferguson, Clerk.

November 1, 1935

Mrs. E. Middleton
2826 Prince Street
Conway, Arkansas

Dear Madam:

Reference is made to your letter in which you request the Revolutionary War records of James Davis, of North Carolina or Virginia, who married Miss Tyner and died prior to September 3, 1850; James Sammons and Benjamin Sammons of New York.

A search of the Revolutionary War records has been made and no record could be identified as that of the James Davis in which you are interested and there is no claim for pension or bounty land on file on account of the services of a James Sammons. Such claims are the source of the date furnished by this office.

It is suggested that as a possible means of obtaining information in regard to the military service of those soldiers, you apply to the Adjutant General, War Department, this city, who is custodian of military records.

The record of Benjamin Sammons has been found and is given herein, the data for which were obtained from the papers on file in Revolutionary War pension claim, S. 11345, based upon the military service in that war of said Benjamin Sammons.

Benjamin Sammons was born December 5, 1758, in Shawangunk, Ulster County, New York. The names of his parents are not shown.

While residing in said Shawangunk, Benjamin Sammons enlisted in 1775, served in that year and in 1776 and 1777, on short tours under Captains John Davis and Nicholas Marselius, Major Giles (Jellies) Fonda, Colonels Frederick Fisher and Abraham Cuyler in the New York Troops; he enlisted in March or April, 1779, served as a private in Captain Robert Hunter's Company, Colonel Albert Pawling's New York Regiment; length of this service, nine months: in 1780, he again served on short tours under Captain Marselius and Colonel Cuyler in the New York Troops and was in a small engagement at Colonel Klock's at a place which was latter called Oppenheim, in Montgomery County, New York.

He stated that during five years of the Revolution, when not out on regular tours, he acted as a guard for the Continental Store House at Albany, New York, which service amounted to at least one month in each year and that his entire service amounted to twenty months.

Benjamin Sammons was allowed pension of his application executed September 19, 1832, while residing in Johnstown, Montgomery County, New York.

It is not stated that soldier was ever married.

In 1832, Cornelius Sammons, then a resident of Springfield, Otsego County, New York, stated that he was a cousin of the soldier, Benjamin Sammons.

In order to obtain the date of last payment of pension, the name and address of person paid and possibility the date of death of the Revolutionary War pensioner, Benjamin Sammons (S.11345), you should address the Comptroller General,

General Accounting Office, Records
Division, this city.

Cite the following data:
Benjamin Sammons
Certificate No. 24094 issued October 30, 1833
Rate $43.44 per annum
Commenced March 4, 1831
Act of June 7, 1833, New York Agency.

Very truly yours,
AD Hiller
Executive Assistant to the Administrator.

Pension Application for Frederick Sammons

Frederick was left with grave injuries as a result of his imprisonment in Canada where he was kept in heavy chains. Gangrene had begun to destroy his leg, and he suffered the rest of his life for this abuse. This is an interesting pension to read.

State of New York
Montgomery County

Thomas Sammons of the Town of Johnston County of Montgomery, former being duly sworn says that his brother Frederick Sammons who is an applicant for a pension was to this deponents knowledge actively engaged as a partisan soldier a great number of times during the Revolutionary War that he was frequently sent out with the Militia on scouting parties which was a dangerous, laborious service that to his knowledge, he the said Frederick, frequently turned out and did duty under arms at various places and under various officers in the County of Tryon, now Montgomery County.

And this deponent further states that he this deponent and his brother the said Frederick Sammons were both taking prisoners on the 22 day of May 1780 that this deponent made his escape from the same day but his brother Frederick Sammons remained a prisoner and was taken a prisoner to Canada where he remained till the fall of the year 1782 when he made his escape from the enemy which this deponent well recollects he arrived at Schenectady and wrote to father. I went with a wagon and fetched him and a Mr. McMullen who made his escape with him to the place wherein I said.

THO. SAMMONS

Subscribed and sworn to this 28 day of May 1833 and I certify that the said Thomas Sammons is a person of the first respectability and a credible witness.
Before me, Aaron Harring Jus. Peace of Montgomery County NY State.

State of New York
Montgomery County

On this 24th day of December one thousand eight hundred and thirty six personally appeared before the Honorable Abraham Morrell Peace Justice of Montgomery County, Frederick Sammons, aged seventy six who being first duly sworn according to law doth on his oath make the following declarations in order to obtain the benefit of the act of Congress passed April 10th, 1806 and the several acts amounting the same. On the twenty second day of May one thousand seven hundred and eighty while in the services of the United States and in arms at Johnstown NY, he this claimant, was commanded by a superior force of the enemy to lay down his arms and surrender himself a prisoner of war and as such was marched from Johnstown aforesaid to Canada where he was detained as a prisoner two years and four months or thereabouts.

That during the period of his captivity aforesaid, he this claimant, was inhumanly treated by the enemy and received wounds and contusions that has rendered him and invalid from that time to this day and in all human probability he must so remain during the remainder of his life. Which wounds and disability were received and now are of the above so stated.

Now that when captured to Canada he was lodged in the said at Chamblee where being confined he found means to escape the 13th day and made his way through the wilderness to Otter Creek in the State of Vermont where he was taken sick, here he was discovered and taken by the enemy and being unable to travel was carried to the shore of the lake and precipitated down the slope on his feet perpendicular on rocks and stones whereby he received a wound to his body and a contusion on his right knee. The joint of which hinders him movement in being calcified and stiffened. From thence he was put on board and imprisoned back to Chamblee and there confined in irons for the space of fourteen months in which time he was not allowed to see the sun. The severity of the irons was such that the shackles wore the flesh to the bone of his legs and induced an extensive "bruising, inflammation and indolent ulcers" which has proved incurable and rendered him incapable of procuring his support by manual labor and the known wound and disabilities he now claims to be placed on the invalid pension roll of his country.

He further declares that he continued in service during the whole time that he was severally attacked on for which he engaged except the tour when he was made a prisoner, was absent from his company on leave of his officer and after his disability was incapaciting to near the close of the Revolutionary War.

That since he left the service his mode of life has been that of moderation and compromise endeavoring to live the life of a Christian and rendering to every man his best due.

That his employment having been that of a mechanic having carried on the burden of shop joiner, employing workmen laboring himself occasionally as far as his health would permit. That since leaving the service as aforesaid he has resided four years in Ulster County three years in Dutchess County and the reminder of the time here. He now resides in Johnstown, Montgomery and in the State of New York.

For the proof of which statements as set forth from this declaration he must defend in part to the affidavit of Forgeift Patchin to be found the declaration of this claimant for a pension under act of 7 June 1832 now in the files at the War Department (said Patchin now deceased)

And he further declares that the reasons why he has not made an application for a pension for service from the United States he has been unable to support himself to this time but his advanced age and sickeness in his family now induced him to make this application that he is not on the pension list of any state or territory. Subscribed and sworn to the day and year above written before me.

Signed Fred'k Sammons.

Abrm Monell, First Judge of Montgomery County NY

Doctor's certification for Frederick Sammons, Invalid Pension

Mr. Richard Davis and James W. Miller practicing physicians and surgeons, Johnstown, Montgomery County, State of New York, so certify that we are personally acquainted with Frederick Sammons. The person mentioned in the affidavit of ??? hereunto ??? and have this day examined the legs of the said Frederick and from such examination we are fully satisfied and believe that the cause mentioned in the annexed affidavit has produced the demise of the legs of the said Frederick and our examination of the inflammation and indolent ulcers under which he now labors, and that they are incurable and at his advanced age about seventy seven years, wholly disabled him for labor which requires much bodily exercise dated this twenty second day of December 1836.

James N. Miller MD

Richard Davis MD

The following is very difficult to read, so the transcription may not be accurate.

(Can't read where this deposition was taken.)

May 10, 1845

This may certify that I was taken a prisoner in the spring of the year eighty by Captain Joseph Brandt and a party of Indians and Tories commanded by Brandt and conveyed by them to Niagara and given up to the British from thence sent down to Montreal in Canada from thence sent to Chamblee where I was close confined for the space of about two years in which time I became acquainted with Frederick Sammons and his brother Jacob who was captured as they told me by a party of the enemy to the United Stated commanded as they told me by Sir John Johnston.

I understood the Sammons were captured in Montgomery County so Sammons was confined with me in the prison in Chambly for the space of about ten days until it came to their turn to carry out our necessary tub and bring our allowance of Spruce Beer ordered by the doctor of the Garrison in consequence of our having been serving by our close confinement and lying in irons when out of the Garrison said Sammonses set down the tub and made their escape from the guard across the plains to the woods.

In about five or six weeks afterwards Fred'k Sammons was brought back to the garrison in a most deplorable condition from this suffering as he told me in trying to make his escape from the enemy and as soon as he was scarcely able to walk he was again put into the prison with me and inhumanely ironed and in that condition kept under his irons was about covered with the rotten flesh occasioned by having the scurvy from thence he with myself and others was conveyed up the river to St. Lawrence about forty miles from Montreal and confined upon and island called fortimer or Table Island from which place Frederick Sammons made his escape by swimming the St. Lawrence, a distance of about four miles and further this deponent knows nothing of the sufferings only what Sammons told him that he suffered everything but death in getting home through wilderness and I for myself do believe that no man living has suffered more for the Independence of his country then said Frederick Sammons has. Given under my hand the date as within mentioned.

Subscribed and sworn before me. (Signed) Freefit Patchin.

State of New York
Montgomery County

On this 21st day of September 1837 personally appeared in open Court before Aaron Horning, Samuel A. Gilbert, John Hand, Henry Diefendorf and Abraham Morrel, Esquire, Judges of the County Court of Common Please in and for the County of Montgomery now sitting Frederick Sammons a resident of the Town of Johnstown in the County of Montgomery aged seventy seven years who being first duly sworn according to law doth on his oath make the following declaration in order to obtain the benefit of the Act of Congress dated June 7th 1832.

That he entered into the service of the United States under the following. Names of officers and service as herein stated.

A statement of the services done by Frederick Sammons in the Revolutionary War aged 77, years and three months.

The first was in guard ordered by Capt. ??? at his house in 1776 with others, three days.

Next at Sand Flatts head quarters as Timothy Leandersey Commanded by Captain John Davis, I think ten days.

Next was ordered by Capt John Davis to go with him in hunt some Tories who kept concealed to go off to Canada in this town we took Sheriff White and delivered him in Johnstown. I had two days.

Next I was ordered by Col. Fisher to go with some men to hunt some Tories whose names was given me Safer Sneeke? and Siser Simons and two more we got them all but one and delivered them to Johnstown goal, three days.

Next I was ordered in a detachment of our Militia Commanded by Major Calarons? Sent to pursue a trove of Tories and we went from Caughnawaga to Balstown and overtook them one way, joining with Balstown where they had killed a yoke of oxen and was preparing their knapsacks for their journey to Canada 66 of them were taken prisoners without firing a gun and made their escape William Wallace, myself and 10 more of our militia was ordered to pursue after them we overtook the 2d day where they was dispersed, five of them prisoners and lodged them in Johnstown, goal, 7 days.

In January 1777 there was a draft made of every man in the whole of our Militia in Gen'l Herkimer's Brigade. Col. Cox was appointed our commander, I served in Capt. Saml. Pettingils Company when organized we was marched to Ticonderoga where we did duty until the ice went out of the Lake. I think 90 days.

After I returned from Ticonderoga I was a scout with Solomon Woodworth near Johnstown, Woodworth herewith had the command, out 6 days.

About the first of May, I was ordered by Col. Fisher to run a scout with Henry H. Vrooman and John Frey. I had the charge out 5 days about the last of May I was employed by Lieut Col. Volkert Veeder in running scout with Henry H. Vrooman and Jonathan ???, I had the charge, out 7 days.

About the first of July the whole of Militia of Col. Fisher's Regiment was ordered to meet at the Village of Johnstown. I was employed the same time by the Col. To run a scout from there to Fort Miller? ??? Sacandaga. Lieut Cooslin? And John Van ??? and turned out voluntarily with them was out 8 days. Took some prisoners here. (Can't read this section, he gives the name of a Tory.) brought him to Johnstown goad and was continued in that service until the whole of the Militia was ordered out to meet Genl Herkimer at the German Flats. Except here five days on our march ??? was informed there was some Indians preparing themselves to ? upon the inhabitants when his men were gone, immediately ordered out company back Capt John Fisher to the Village of Johnstown and ordered out with men to scout that part north of the lake and return by way of Mayfield. I was out eleven days the Oriskany Battle was fought before I returned.

I was on duty until Gen'l. Arnold went up with his Brigade to relieve the garrison at Fort Stanwix. I with 30 more of our Militia ordered the army of whom McMaster was one who was appointed our Capt. and commander the same order with the regular troops when we came within 12 or 13 miles of the fort and our express sent by Gansvoort informing Arnold that the British had raised the siege and some of the volunteers was dismissed immediately afterwards there was a detachment of our Militia ordered to join our Army at Stilwater commanded by Lietut. Col. Volkert Veeder. I was employed two days to procure wagons and carry our baggage did duty in Capt. Abraham Veeder's Company and when we came to our army I was briefly employed as pilot to scouting parties of the regular troops. Our Militia was discharged about the ___ Oct 1773. Col. Fisher's Regiment was ordered to Sacandaga. I served in Captain Abraham Veeder's Company where we built a large blockhouse, out 10 days.

Next the whole of the Militia of Col. Fisher's Regt was ordered out, we were marched up to Canajoharie head quarters at Gosse Van Alstine's part of the Regt was discharged, to Fort Plain and I think 16 days.

Two companies ordered out of Col. Fisher's Regt to garrison the Block House at Sacandaga and keep and keep our daily scouting. I was under Capt Fisher, one month.

Next the whole of the Militia was ordered out of Fisher's Reg't and marched to Canajoharie head quarters of Martin Van Alstine's. I served in Captain Abraham Veeder's Company one week.

Next the whole of the Militia of Col. Fisher's Reg't was ordered out and marched to Cherry Valley. I served in Capt Abram Veeder's Company 3 or 6 days.

1779. Col. Fisher's Regt was ordered to Stone Arabia where I did duty in Captain Abraham Veeder's Company and (can't read this sentence) by order of Col. Fisher part of companies kept guard at the Caughnawaga Church commanded by Capt. John Fisher. I did duty 6 days some time in the fall Fishe's Regt was ordered to march to Bowman's Creek where I did duty in Veeder's Company until the Regt was dismissed.

1780. In April was ordered by Col. Fisher to do a scout with ? men. Out six days.

In May the whole of Fisher's Regiment was ordered to the Village of Johnstown where I did duty in Capt. Veeder's for one week.

At the same time Capt. Wemple with some more of our Militia Officers deserted to the enemy. I was sent out to search some Tory Houses with Abraham Davis and 2 more in searching Philip Cline's house and barn, I found John Coyne knapsack after he surrendered himself. I was out 1 day and night.

The 22nd day of May my father's house was surrounded by about 600 British and Tories at brake of day my older brother and myself was for making defense not knowing the number as I shoved my musket out the window to fire there was about 50 muskets presented at me. My brother took hold of me and asked for quarters. They answered they would give us quarters if we did not fire, we give up our arms and surrendered our selfs prisoners and we was tied together with a rope and traveled that way to Canada. I was prisoner for two years and four months.

Deponent gives answers to the questions proposed.

I was born the 4 July 1760 in the Town of Chainwinking, Ulster County in the State of New York.

I have a record of my age in my family Bible and in the church book when called into service. I lived at Johnstown, Tryon, now Montgomery County and has lived here almost ever since. I went into the service as a draft and volunteer. The regular officers under whom I served were Capt. Sool at Ticonderoga, Col. Fisher in the Militia. I am very lame and inform and unable to support myself and family, the reason is before mentioned. (Can't read a sentence.) Thomas ??? and ??? almost in the neighborhood.

He hereby relinquishes every claim to a pension or annuity from the United States except the present and declares that his name is not on the pension roll of the agency of any state only that of the State of New York as a bounty given to him by act of the legislature for his services and suffering during the Revolutionary War, April 20th 1823. (Can't read the sentence.) ....injury which he sustained while in service and as a prisoner during the said times.

Sworn to and subscribed the day and year aforesaid. (signed) Fred'k Sammons (signed)) Geor. D. Ferguson, Clerk)

A Statement of The Services Done by Frederick Sammons in the Revolutionary War. Aged 72 years ? months.

The first was on guard ordered by Capt. Wemple at his house in Januray 1776 with Wallace Folkers, I think 3 days.

Next, at Sand Flatts he had quarters at Timothy Leandursey Commanded by Capt John Davis, I think 10 days.

Next was ordered by Capt. John Davis to go with him to hunt some Tories who kept ?? to go off to Canada in this time we took Sheriff White and delivered him in Johnstown Goal, 2 days.

Next I was ordered by Col. Fisher to go with 4 men to hunt some Tories whose names was given to me (unsure of names) Traser, Smike, and Platoo from Warren's Bush Peter Bowen and 2 more we got them all but one and delivered them on to Johnstown Goal, 3 days.

Next I was ordered in a detachment of our Militia Commanded by Maj'r Blavens sent to pursue a trove of Tories we went from Caughnawaga to Balstown and overtook them one days journey north of Balstown where they had killed a yoke of oxen and was preparing their knapsacks for their journey to Canada, 66 of them was taken prisoners without firing a gun, 14 made their escape, William Wallace, myself and 10 more of our Militia was ordered to pursue after them we overtook the 2d day were they was disposed we took 5 of them prisoner and lodged them in Johnstown Goal, 7 days.

In Jan 1777 there was a draft made of every 4th men in the whole of our Militia in Gen'l Herkimer's Brigade, Col. Cox was appointed our Commander. I served in Capt. Sam'l Pattengal's Company and when organized we was marched to Ticonderoga were we did duty until Ice went out fo the Lake, I think 90 days.

After I returned from Ticonderoga I run a scout with Solomon Woodworth and John I. Kinderson. Woodworth had the command out 6 days.

About the 1st of May I was ordered by Col. Fisher to run a scout with Henry H. Vrooman and John Frey, I had the charge, out 5 days.

About the last of May I was employed by Lieut Col. Volkert Veeder to run a scout with Henry H. Vrooman and Jonathan Runyans. I had the charge, out 7 days.

About the first of July the whole of the Militia of Co. Fisher's Reg't was ordered to march at the Village of Johnstown and was employed the same time by the Col. to run a scout from thence to Fort Miller by way of Sacondaga Sam'l Coplen and John Van Antwerpen Jr. turned out voluntarily to go with me. We was out 4 days and took one prisoner, Mr. Borgains Camp, and brought him to Johnstown Goal and was continued in that service until the whole of the Militia was ordered out to meet Gen'l Herkimer at the German Flatts except 4 or 5 days when on our march the Col. was informed there was some Indians preparing themselves to fall upon the inhabitants when the men were immediately ordered, one company back, Capt. John Fisher, to the Village of Johnstown and ordered me with 2 men with me to run a scout West and North of the lake and return by the way of Mayfield. I was out 7 days the Oriskany Battle was fought before I returned, I was on duty until Gen'l Arnold went up with his Brigade to relieve the garrison at Fort Stanwix.

I with 30 more of our Militia entered the army as volunteers of whom David McMaster was one who was appointed our Capt. and came under the same order with the regular troops when we came within 12 or 18 miles of the fort sent an express out by Gansvoort informing Arnold that the British had raised the siege and gone off, the volunteers was dismissed immediately afterwards, there was a detachment of our Militia ordered to join our army at Stilwater Commanded by Lieut Col. Volkert Veeder.

I was employed two days to procure wagons to carry our baggage did duty in Capt. Abrahom Veeder's Company but when we came to our Army I was chiefly employed as Pilot to scouting, parties of the regular Troops our Militia was discharged about the ____ of October.

1778. Col. Fisher's Regiment was ordered to Sacandaga. I served in Captain Abraham Veeder's Company where we built a large blockhouse, out 10 days. The whole of the Militia of Col. Fisher's Regt was ordered up to Canajoharie head quarters at Gosse Van Alstine's part of the Regt was sent to Fort Plain and I think 16 days.

Two companies was ordered out of Col. Fisher's Reg't to garrison the Block House at Sacondaga and keep out and ??? I served under Capt. John Fisher one month.

Next the whole of the Militia was ordered out of Fisher's Reg't and marched to Canajoharie Head Quarters at Martin VanAlstin's. Scouted in Capt. Abraham Veeder's Company one week.

Next the whole of the Militia of Col. Fisher's Reg't was ordered out and marched to Cherry Valley. I served Capt. Abraham Veeder's Company 5 or 6 days.

1779. Col. Fisher's Reg't was ordered to Stone Arabia where I did duty in Capt. Abraham Vceeder's Company and Head Quarters at Col. Brown's. By order of Col. Fisher part of 2 companies kept guard at the Caughnawaga Church Commanded by Capt John Fisher. I did duty 6 days. Sometime in the fall Fisher's Reg't was ordered to march to Bowman's Creek where I did duty in Veeder's Company until the Reg't was dismissed.

1780. In April I was ordered by Col. Fisher to scout with 2 men out six days.

In May the whole of Fisher's Reg't was ordered to the Village of Johnstown where I did duty in Capt. Veeder's for one week. At the same time Capt. Wemple with some more of our

Militia officers and Tories deserted to the enemy, I was sent out to search some Tory Houses with Abraham Davis and 2 more in searching Phillip H. Clines house and barn, I found John Conyore's knapsack after he surrendered himself, I (was) out 1 day and night.

The 22d day of May my Father's house was surrounded by about 500 British and Torys at break of day my elder brother and myself was for making defense not knowing the number as I shoved my musket out the window to fire there was about 50 muskets presented at once my brother took hold of me and asked for quarters. They answered they would give us quarters if we did not fire. We give up our Arms and surrendered ourself prisoners we was tied together with a rope and traveled that way to Canada I was a prisoner two years and 4 months.

Answers to questions proposed.

I was born on the 4th July 1760 in the Town of Chainwinking Ulster County in the State of New York.

I have a record of my age in my family Bible and in the church books.

When called into service I lived at Johnstown Tryon (now Montgomery) County and lived there almost ever since. I went to the service as a draft and volunteer. The regular officers under whom I served were Col. Peat??? At Ticonderoga. Col. Fisher of the Militia.

I am lame and infirm and unable to support myself and family. I am known to the judges before mentioned and my Bother Thomas Sammons, and David Cady, and John W. Cady,??? members of Congress to Nathan Sourls? The present members, and to every one almost in the neighborhood.

Pension Application for Thomas Sammons

Thomas is the youngest brother; first Jacob, Frederick and then Thomas, sons of Sampson Sammons. The birth date is given as 1762, so he was thirteen years old in 1775 when he enlisted in the Militia.

District of Columbia
City of Washington

Thomas Sammons of the County of Montgomery in the State of New York being duly sworn doth depose and saith that he is aged seventy two years and was a soldier in the Militia and State Troops during the Revolutionary War and is now on the pension Roll of the United States that is brother Frederick Sammons of the same county was in the years 1780 on the 22 day of May taken a prisoner of war along with this deponent while in arms against the common enemy and while actually engaged in a military capacity having been ordered out by Col. Fisher commandant of the regiment to which he belonged as a sergeant in Capt Abraham Veeder's Company.

The week previous to his capture and this deponent further says that the said Frederick was permitted occasionally to return to his father's house but without having been discharged from the service as this deponent believes and this deponent further says that he was informed and then believed and still does believe that the said Regiment as commanded by Col. Fisher was ordered into service pursuant to and according to the laws of the State of New York and this deponent further says that when the said Frederick Sammons was on the 22 day of May in the year 1780 made prisoner along with this deponent and this deponent had not then to his knowledge been discharged from the service but on the same day made his escape from the enemy and returned to the picket fort.

The said Frederick was taken to Chamblee in lower Canada from there soon afterwards made his escape, was retaken by the enemy and remained a prisoner there and at prison island more than two years afterwards the most part of the time in irons, from prison island he and another prisoner by the name of McMullen by jumping or throwing themselves into the river and swam off, released themselves from the enemy and arrived at Schenectady after traveling through the wilderness about two weeks.

Sworn to before me, J. Broeck, (Justice of the Peace) February 24, 1834.

State of New York
County of Montgomery

On this 20th day of September one thousand eight hundred and thirty-two, personally appeared in open court before the judges of the court of Common Pleas in and for said County now sitting Thomas Sammons a resident of the Town of Johnstown in said county and state aged nearly seventy years, who being first duly sworn according to law, doth on his oath make the following declaration in order to obtain the benefit of the Act of Congress passed June 7th 1832.

That he was born in the town of Shawgunk in the County of Ulster in said State on the 29th October 1762. he has no record of his age except that contained in his family Bible.

When called into the service of the United States in the War of the Revolution he resided in the said Town of Johnstown, and has lived there ever since except for about three years to wit from the latter part of the year 1780, to the end of the war when his father's family removed to the Town of Marbletown in said County of Ulster, they being obliged to abandon their residence in said Town of Johnstown in consequence of the enemy who destroyed their dwelling house and other property.

He entered the service of the United States under the following named officers and served as herein stated.

In the month of June 1775 he entered the company of Militia under the command of Captain Abraham Veeder in the Regiment of Colonel Frederick Fisher at the Town of Johnstown aforesaid as a volunteer; and discharged the duty of a sentinel at the Village of Caughnawaga in said Town for the turn of one week. In the year 1778 in the month of October he was enrolled in the company aforesaid. The other company field officers whom he recollects were Nicholas Dockstader, Lieutenant; Volkert Veeder, Lieutenant Colonel and Major John Newkirk. He continued to serve in said company whenever called upon until the year 1780 when he moved to Ulster County as aforesaid.

The several expeditions in which he engaged, were as near as he can recollect them as following:

To the Town of Palatine for the term of a week with the beginning of the month of November in the year 1778 aforesaid, to the Town of Stone Arabia about six days in the month of November aforesaid.

During the year 1779, he served for the term of one month in the month of July with the whole of said Regiment of Col. Fisher at the German Flatts from thence he volunteered with the consent of said Colonel Fisher in the Regiment of Colonel Gansevoort commanding United States troops to Lake Otsego and served in said Regiment last named nearly two weeks, at the sand flatts in said town of Johnstown guarding this frontier eight days in the beginning of the month of September in the year last named to Fort Plank at Canajoharie and other places in that quarter eleven days in the month of November in the year last named.

Sometime in the month of April 1780 he was ordered out to guard the frontiers at the residence of Adam Fonda in said town of Johnstown and elsewhere in that quarter for the term of eight days and more. In the month of May the next in the said Town of Johnstown at the village in said town named there a few days and from there went out with a scouting party under Lieutenant William Wallace and served in this tour about nine days.

On the 22d day of the month last named he was taken prisoner together with his father and his two brothers by a party of the enemy about 500 strong under Sir John Johnston, the same day he succeeded in effecting his escape and returned to the Village of Johnstown aforesaid and was there examined by Col. John Harper and Lt. Col. Veeder respecting the condition of the enemy, he there joined the Militia when in pursuit fo the enemy. He was in this town only three days when the Militia aforesaid were dismissed.

In the month of June then next was ordered out in search of Tories who rendezvoused in the vicinity of Johnstown aforesaid for about four days.

In the month of July he was ordered out again in the Militia on an alarm that the enemy were approaching which however did not prove to be the case.

In the latter part of the month of July last named he volunteered to join the Militia in pursuit of the enemy who were then engaged in destroying the settlements at and near Fort Plank and was out in this town about four days.

In the month of November in the year last named Sir John Johnson with the troops under his command having attacked Schoharie by surprise marched to Fort Hunter on the Mohawk River and from thence proceded up the Mohawk River burning and destroying everything within their reach on both sides of said river as far as Palatine.

The Militia on this occasion were ordered out under General Van Rensselaer to pursue the enemy, he the claimant joined with the volunteers under Captain McKean who had a party of Oneida Indians with him, and served under said Captain McKean in this expedition about fourteen days. He was in the battle fought on this occasion.

In the year 1781, he enlisted and served for the term of nine months in the company of State Troops commanded by Captain Henry Pauling in Colonel Albert Paulding's Regiment. He enlisted in said company at the Town of Marbletown aforesaid and served in said County of Ulster in guarding the frontiers in that quarter, and at the end of said term of nine months he was discharged at Marbeltown aforesaid, but received no written discharge of his service.

In the following year 1782, he served as a substitute for Thomas Broadhead in Colonel Wysenvelt's Regiment of State Troops under said Henry Paulding for the term of one month at Churchland in said County of Ulster in guarding the frontiers. During said year 1782 he served several times in the company of Militia in his ?? in said County of Ulster to wit, Captain Frederick Shoonmaker's company in John Cantine's Regiment, for how a period he served in the Militia aforesaid he cannot give an exact account, but knows that the whole period for which he served his country, as a soldier in the War of the Revolution exceeds thirtten months and eight days.

He knew Major Van Benschoten, Colonel Lewis Dubois, Colonel James Livingston, and Major Thomas DeWitt, Captain Andrew Finks, Captain Fincks.

He never received any written discharge. He has no documentary evidence, but can product the testimony of witnesses who can swear to his services.

The following are the names of persons to whom he is known in his present neighborhood, and who can testify as to his character for veracity and their belief of his services as a soldier of the Revolution. Viz.

He hereby relinquishes every claim whatever to a pension or annuity except the present and declared that his name is not on the pension roll of the agency of any state.

Signed Tho. Sammons

Subscribed and swore the day and year aforesaid. (can't read that name)

We, Isaac S. Ketcham a clergyman residing in the Town of Palatine in the County aforesaid and Simon Veeder of the Town of Johnstown in said county do hereby certify that we are well acquainted within Thomas Sammons who has subscribed and sworn to the foregoing declaration: that we believe him to be nearly seventy years of age, that hid is reputed and believed in the neighborhood where he resides to have been a soldier of the Revolution and that we concur in that opinion.

Subscribed and sworn the day and year aforesaid.

Signed, Simon Veeder

Isaac S. Ketcham

And the said court do hereby declare their opinion after the investigation of the matter and after putting the interrogatories prescribed by the War Department.

State of New York

County of Montgomery

On this twenty fifth day of January in the year one thousand eight hundred forty three personally appeared before me, Jacob Graff, a Judge of the County Courts of Montgomery County (the same being a Court of Record) Mary Sammons, a resident of the Town of Mohawk in said County, aged sixty nine years, who being first duly sworn, according to law, doth on her oath, make the following declaration in order to obtain the benefit of the provision made by the Act of Congress, passed July 7th 1838 entitled "An Act granting half pay and pensions to certain widows." That she is the widow of Thomas Sammons who was a soldier in the Revolutionary Army and was a pensioner under the Act of Congress passed June 7th 1832. She further declares that she was married to the said Thomas Sammons on the sixteenth day of December in the year seventeen hundred and ninety two, that her husband the aforesaid Thomas Sammons died on the twentieth day of November in the year eighteen hundred and thirty eight.

That she was not married to him prior to his leaving the service, but the marriage took place previous to the first of January Seventeen Hundred and Ninety four, viz at the time above stated. She further declares that her surname previous to her marriage was Wood, and that she was married in the Town of Caughnawaga, County of Montgomery, and State of New York by the Rev'd Thomas Romeyn, a minister of the Dutch Reformed Church in that town and that owing to infirmity she cannot write.

Sworn and subscribed on the day and year above written before me. Her Mark, Mary Sammons.

Jacob Graff, a Judge of Montgomery County.

Jacob Shew, In the Ranger Service

Anecdotal Attending the Ranger Service in the Mohawk Valley in 1780, Related by Jacob Shew, one of their number.-- In the spring of 1780, Jacob Shew went for one of a class as then termed, in Capt. Garret Putman's company for the term of nine months, a part of which time he was on duty at Fort Plank. The ranger service often called the troops from one frontier fort to another. Shew was one of a guard of perhaps a dozen men once sent with a drove of cattle to Fort Stanwix. While encamped for the night near Shoemaker's place, near the now village of Mohawk, they were fired upon after dark by concealed foes, who had doubtless kept an eye of vigilance on their movements. The fire was a random one, and none of the Americans were injured; but it was promptly returned in the direction of the enemy, and they were not again disturbed that night. On resuming their march in the morning, the guard found blood on the ground, and supposed they had killed or wounded one or more of the "night watch."

At another time, Shew was one of a guard sent up the Mohawk with several boats laden with provisions and military stores, also for Fort Stanwix. The boats were usually laden and started from Schenectada, a military escort receiving them in charge at Fort Plain. The troops went along the shore, and at rapids had to aid in getting the boats along; which were laid up nights, the boatmen encamping on shore with the guard.

When moving up the Mohawk from Fort Plain to take charge of Fort House, a little stockade on the north side of the river enclosing the dwelling of George House--situated nearly opposite Fort Windecker, a party of Putman's men, of which number was my friend Shew, halted over night at a similar stockade at George Klock's, a mile or two below. On their arrival, the citizens clustered within the little post were much gratified at having their security increased, and gave to the men in war's panoply a cordial welcome. Moses Van Camp, on of the latter and a fine soldier, was not a little annoyed by the warm reception he met from a buxom wench who chanced to know him. "Oh Moses!" she exclaimed, "how glad I am to see you; now we are safe!" and running up she grasped his muscular hand and held on as though she had a life lease of it. She did not give him a hug and a kiss, though his companions told him afterwards that she wanted to. The ardor of this artless, dark eyed and darker skinned maiden, put the blush on young Van Camp, who subsequently had often to hear of the joyous tears his presence had caused to flow down cheeks, whose rosy flashes refused at the surface to answer to his own. His is not the last we shall have to say of this daring young man.

Some time in the summer of this year (1780) several Indians appeared down the river from Fort Herkimer, and attempted, as supposed, to draw a scout from the fort. They burnt a train of powder on a log, and thus raised a smoke to attract notice. By a maneuver, Capt. Putman, then on duty at this post, attempted to surprise them. At the head of his company, with martial music, he made quite a circuit in the woods and returned to the fort, leaving, concealed by the way, his Lieut., Solomon Woodworth, Shew and several other soldiers. But the ruse did not succeed. The Indians, from some position, no doubt counted their numbers and were aware that all had not gone back to the fort.

In the fall of 1780, a girl in her teens went from Fort Herkimer to pick apples, not far distant; and while thus engaged at a favorite tree, just out of sight of the fort, she was surprised by an Indian; was tomahawked and scalped. She left the fort early in the day, and not returning at the proper time, her friends became alarmed for her safety and sought her at her favorite tree, which stood in a retired part of the orchard; beneath which she lay, weltering in her own blood. She was borne to the fort, her wounds dressed, and she recovered and lived after the war.

Source Material:

The Frontiersmen of New York
by Jeptha R. Simms
Albany, NY 1883
Vol II, Page 346-7

Henry Smith Application for Pension

State of New York
Montgomery County

This 20th day of September 1832 personally appeared in open court before the judges of the court of Common Pleas in and for said County now sitting Henry Smith a resident of the Town of Johnstown in said county and state aged nearly seventy years, who being first duly sworn according to law, doth on his oath make the following declaration in order to obtain the benefit of the Act of Congress passed June 7th 1832.

That he entered the service of the United States under the following named officers and served as herein stated:--

In the year 1778 this applicant then fourteen years of age enrolled himself as a volunteer in the militia company of Capt. Nicholas Richtor. This company was located in the north part of what was then the town of Palatine. And the inhabitants were in continual alarm from the mauradering parties of Indians and Tories that were then in Tryon County. Captain Richtor and his company had frequent skirmishes with those parties in one of which a number of his men were killed and he himself was wounded and remained a number of years to the time of his death a pensioner to the United States.

That this applicant served in this company two years during which time he knows of no officer in command than his captain. That once while in this company they were ordered and marched from the fort at Stone Arabia to assist in raising an alarm at Fort Stanwix but their principal duty was to guard the inhabitants in there own immediate vicinity until the latter part of his service in this company when being overpowered by the enemy the company and the inhabitants were obliged to seek refuge in the block house at the fort at Stone Arabia.

That about the 1st part of April 1782 he enlisted into the company of rangers under Captain John Casselman and served in said company nine months the period of his enlistment and was discharged about the 1st January 1781.

The service in this company was ranging the country in small parties (called scouting parties) where duty was to give an alarm in care of danger and was of much service to such of the inhabitants as were obliged leave the forts to attend to agriculture and other pursuits.

That about the 1st of April of the latter year viz 1781 he enlisted into the company of nine months men under Captain Lawrence Gross in Col. Marinus Willett's regiment that his service while in this company was also guarding the frontiers from Fort Hunter in the Mohawk River to Fort Stanwix and the interior of Tryon County.

That he fought at the Battle at Johnstown on the 22nd of October 1781 he was at this time in Captain Gross's Company in the immediate command of Col. Willett.

That in the day preceding the battle he was sent express by Col. Willettt to the Commander of the fort at Stone Arabia ordering him to advance what force he could spare toward Johnstown.

That after the battle he returned with his company to Fort Plain and continued in the service until the first of Jan'y 1783 when he was discharged and was again enrolled in the Militia Company now under the command of Captain Henry Miller and continues to do duty in said company a the fort at Stone Arabia until the close of the war.

That he knows of no more or other testimony than the affidavits hereunto annexed. That he hereby relinquishes every claim whatsoever to a pension or annuity except the present and declares that his name is not on the roll of any agency of any state.

To the questions directed to be responded he answered:

He was born in the town of Cattskill in the county of Green State of New York on the 31st day of March 1764. He has at present no record of his age, that he formerly had one recorded by his father in his Bible it was burnt several years since at his mother's house in Ephratah. He lived at Stone Arabia when he entered the service after the Revolutionary War he has ever lived where he now lives in Ephratah, Montgomery County. He entered the service as a volunteer under Captain Nicholas Richtor and afterward enlisted into the companies of Captain Casselman and Gross as stated above. He served along with Col. Willett, Col. Brown, Col. Klock, Major Fink and the officers in the stations along the Mohawk River and in Tryon County.

Sworn and subscribed this 20th day of September 1832
Signed with his mark, Henry Smith.
In open court, Geo D. Ferguson, C. Clerk

After Henry's death May 3, 1840, his widow Nancy Smith applied for his pension.

Pension Application for William Smith, Private

State of New York
Montgomery County

On this 20th day of September 1832, personally appeared in aforesaid court before Aaron Haring, Abraham Morell, Henry I Dievendorf, John Hand and Samuel A Gilbath, Judges of the Court of Common Please now sitting William Smith a resident of Ephratah in the County of Montgomery and State of New York aged sixty nine year and four months who being first duly sworn according to law doth on his oath make the following declaration in order to obtain the benefit of the Act of Congress passed June 7th 1832. That he entered the service of the United States under the following named officers and served as herein stated, viz.

That in the month of May in the year 1779 he was enrolled in the company of Capt. Nicholas Richter in Col. Jacob Klock's Regiment of Militia in the Town of Palatine County and state aforesaid where he then resided.

That he entered the service immediately after being enrolled by order of Captain Richter and marched with the company to repel the invasions of the Indians and Tories who were at that time continually invading the then new settlements in this county.

That he served in this company as a private from the time above mentioned until the first day of April 1780, when he enlisted into a company of Rangers Commanded by Captain John Casseleman attached to Col. Klock's Regiment.

That he served in this company until the first day of January 1781. That the service performed in this company was principally in guarding the Fort at Stone Arabia (Whither the inhabitants principally been obliged to flee for refuge and ranging the country by small parties called scouting parties that while in this company the applicant was at the Battle at Johnstown and followed the enemy on their retreat towards the East Canada Creek but was taken lame before they (the enemy) were overtaken and went to Fort Herkimer and marched to Fort Stanwix as a guard for boats going to that fort.

That in the summer of 1781 he enlisted into the company of Capt. Skinner for three months but was attached to the company of Captain Lawrence Gross in Col. Marinus Willet's Regiment and served until his tour had nearly expired when he returned to Captain Skinner's company and served out his time which was in the month of November.

That he then served one month in Capt Smith's Company as a substitute for one Miller, this was also in Willett's Regiment. That on the first day of April 1781 he enlisted into Capt. French's Company Col. Willett's Regiment for nine months was stationed at Fort House and Fort Herkimer doing garrison duty at the forts and ranging the county in scouting parties until his term of service expired which was on the 1st day of January 1783 when he received a discharge at Fort Herkimer. He knows of no more or other testimony than the affidavits hereunto annexed. He hereby relinquishes every claim whatever to a pension or annuity except the present and declares that his name is not on the roll of any agency of any state.

To the questions directed to be provided he answered:

He was born at Canajoharie on the 19th day of May 1783. He has a record of his age made by his father it now is in his possession. He lived in Palatine when he entered the service. After the Revolutionary War he has always lived in Ephratah taken from Palatine where he now resides. He entered the service in the first instance by being ordered by his Captain and at the other times under enlistment and as a substitute as stated above. He served with Conrad Van Rinsclai?r, Col. Klock, Col. Williet, Major Finck and Regiments on the stations on the Mohawk River and in our county.

Sworn and subscribed to this 20th day of September.

William Smith (his mark)

Geo. D. Ferguson, Clerk.

State of New York
Montgomery County

Lodowick Kring of Ephratah in said county being duly sworn doth depose and say that he has been well acquainted with William Smith of Ephratah since the commencement of the Revolutionary War that is well knowing to his service in that war in the Militia Company of Captain Nicholas Richter, Col. Klock's Regiment in 1779 and of his service in Capt Casselman's

Company, Col. Klock's Regiment in 1780 that of the end of that year he removed to Fort Plain and as this depon;ent understood enlised into the company of Capt. Lawrence Gross in Col. Willett's Regiment and further this deponent says not.

Subscribed and sworn June 25th 1832 before Henry M Livingston J. Peace.

Lowwick Kring (Signed)

State of New York
Montgomery County

Peter Getman and George Youker being duly sworn do depose and say that they were each well acquainted with William Smith of Ephratah and have known him since the year 1779 at which time he was in the service of the United States in the Militia Company of Capt. Nicholas Rightor, Col. Klock's Regiment and afterwards they knew and served with him in the company of Capt. French, Col. Willetts, Regt. nine months in the year 1782. That they this deponents and the said William Smith were discharged from said sompany in the 1st day of Jan 1783 and returned home in company.

Subscribed ans sworn June 24th 1832 before Henry M. Livingston J. Peace

Peter Getman (signed)

Geroge Youker (his mark)

Pension Application for John Spankable (now written Sponable)

On this 11th day of October 1836, personally appeared before me Mr. David Gania a Judge of the Court of Common Pleas of said County, being a court of record, Elisabeth Spanknable a resident of the Town of Ephratah in the County of Montgomery and State of New York aged eighty four years who being first duly sworn according to law doth on her oath make the following declaration in order to obtain the benefit of the provision made by the act of Congress passed July 4th 1832. That she is the widow of John Spanknable who was a private soldier in Captain Nicholas Richtor's Company of Militia in Colonel Jacob Klock's Regiment and General Nicholas Herkimer's Brigade that he was ordered and marched with the company for Fort Stanwix about the first of August 1777, and that on the march and in duty in the service of his company he captured and taken prisoner by the enemy and conveyed to Canada where he was such prisoner rand emained for upwards of four years.

Elisabeth Spanknable (her mark)

Pension Application for Cornelius Van Camp, Sergeant

This pension is the first where I have seen a soldier guarding the Tories during their trials and then transporting them down the Hudson River.

State of New York
Montgomery County

On the 19th day of September in the year of our Lord on thousand eight hundred thirty two personally appeared in open court before the Judges of the Court of Common Pleas of said county now sitting Cornelius Van Camp a resident of the Town of Minden in the county and state aforesaid, aged seventy one years in November last, who being first duly sworn according to law doth on his oath make that following declaration in order to obtain the benefit of the act of Congress passed June 7th 1832. That he entered the service of the United States under the following named officers and served as herein after mentioned.

That about the middle of January in the year 1777, he volunteered in a company of drafted Militia then commanded by Capt. Henry Diefendorf which company with several other companies under Colonel Ebenezer Cox were then marched to Ticonderoga where they with some regular troops were commanded by General Hays where they remained on duty building fortifications and works for the better defense of the country until the forepart of April following when they were discharged and in about a week thereafter he served at Minden, his place of residence.

That about the first of June following he was again called upon and marched to Caughnawaga under his aforesaid officers that they returned in about ten days, that about the first of July they were again called upon and marched to Stone Arabia to Fort Keyser remained there a short time and then returned and the latter part of the same month they were again called upon and marched to Bowman's Creek or Frey's Bush in the Town of Canajoharie were out five days when they returned.

That about the first of September serving and gone after the Oriskany Battle he was called upon by the commandant of his company (Capt. Henry Diefendorf having been killed in the Oriskany Battle) and was ordered across the Mohawk River to wait upon and attend the War Committee where settlers detecting and trying the Tories, that he here remained on duty guarding the Tories during and after their trials until five or six were tried and convicted when he with a number of others under Sergeant Counrad Timmerman were directed to take the Tories so convicted to take the Tories so convicted to Esopus (Kingston) a place about sixty miles from Albany down the Hudson River and there to deliver them to Governor Clinton which they then did, then returned and he went home about the last of September and that the latter part of October he with a party of men by order of the War Committee to Turlock in the County of Schoharie in pursuit of Tories but found none there and returned.

That about the first of November following he was again called upon, ordered across the Mohawk River to attend on the War Committee as before that he did do attend and guard the Tories during and after their trials until four or five were convicted that he was then put in charge of six or seven men as a guard and was directed to convey the Tories as convicted to Albany which they did and delivered them to the jailor and then returned home where he arrived about the middle of the month. That soon thereafter he with a company of men under Lieut. Countryman, Ensign Bort were ordered to march to Johnstown and insure rescue a Commissioner of Forfeitures (who had been convicted as he understood by force, person for taking forlisted property) which they did, broke down the door rescued the said commissioner, and then returned when they were discharged about the last of November or first of December following and that during that year he did as he believed six months and half actual duty in the service of his country and that during the time before the committee and trials foresaid he was a sergeant and discharged his duty as such until his service closed for that season.

That in the month of April 1778 he was again called into service under Capt. Jacob Diefendorf, Lieut. Countryman, Ensign Bort, Major Coopmain in Col. Clyde's Regiment that they were left on duty and at building Fort Plank and out Scouting at different times and directions to the Geisenburgh settlements and at different times to Cherry Valley with about the (Can't read it but he says something about forming a company of Rangers and then I can make out Helmer and Fort Herkimer, scouting to the south and Andrustown ----- lake of the Unidilla River – first of January discharged and returned home) He believes he served eight months duty in service of his country. He was discharged as sergeant until he ---?

That in the month of June 1779 he was again called out into service under Capt Diefendorf, Lieut Countryman, Ensign Bort and Colonel Clyde's Regiment and stationed at Fort Plank was there left on duty and out in scouting parties to the Indian Castle west and south to Bowman's Creek and Cherry Valley at different times and pursing Tories and drawing timber for the work at Fort Plain and also in taking beef cattle for residents to supply the Tories that went the first of July they were called out by Colo. Klock to go south against the Tories marched to Frey's Bush where they were informed that they were not needed and were again returned that they were again called upon by Major Coopman and sent south to meet a part of Tories and Indians, found in the south part of Minden a number of persons, the family of the Sunouths? There killed and their force pursued. They buried the dead and returned.

That sometime in the month of September there was an alarm sounded and they were marched against a party of Tories and Indians said ot have been near the fort they found thy had taken Reuben Davy prisoner and fled that a party of our men pursued them and they returned that some time in the month of October they marched to Bowman's Creek by there a five ? and again returned that sometime after the forepart of November hostilities being ended they were allowed to return home and during that season he did he believes full three and a half months actual duty and that during that season he was Sergeant and discharged his duty as such.

That in the month of April 1780 he was again called into service under his last foresaid officers that they were sent out scouting as aforesaid sent various directions and on duty at Fort Plank and building a picket fort about two miles from Fort Plank wherein they called Fort Walrath until sometime in May when he and part of their company were sent to Cherry Valley to check the Indians and Tories and guard the inhabitants, were stationed at the fort there several times during that season.

That some time in August following they were called and marched under General Van Rensselaer at Fort Stanwix to guard the boats with Continental provisions that they returned in about ten days that some time the next month they marched under command of Colo. Marinus

Willet and Major Coopman in pursuit of a party of Indians and Tories who were burning and committing other depredations up the north side the Mohawk River. They pursued them to the Royal Grant in Herkimer County when finding they could not overtake them they returned.

That about the twelfth of October they were marched across the Mohawk River several miles above Fort Plain there found a body of Militia under Command of Gen. Van Rensselaer and pursued the enemy under Sir John Johnson up the north side the river towards the East Canada Creek. Overtook them about ? commenced an engagement fought some time when the enemy retired and that night crossed the river and marched westward, the next morning they pursued them several miles, finding they could not overtake them they returned, that they were kept on duty and out scouting and guarding the inhabitants as before mentioned when required until the last of November when they were discharged. That he did and he believes that season four months actual duty and that he was sergeant and discharged his duty as such during that season.

That in the month of March 1781 March he was again called into service under Lieut. Countryman, Ensign Bork in Col. Clyde's Regiment that they were kept on duty at Fort Plank? and out in scouting parties at different times and directions as required until about the month of July when he marched to Fort Herkimer under Colo. Willet to bring down a piece of cannon wherein he obtained and returned again in about three days.

They were then kept on duty at Fort Willet and scouting as heretofore stated until about the first of August when he with a party of men under Ensign Bort marched to Fort Dayton where they remained about two weeks when they were relieved and again returned to Fort Willet when they received about two weeks on duty as before stated when they were again marched to Fort Dayton where they were stationed as before about two weeks when they again returned and remained at the fort and out in scouts as required until the twenty fourth of October.

They were marched to Johnstown under command of Lieut. Countryman, Ensign Bort and Major Coopman where the next day he was engaged in a battle against a party of British troops, Indians and Tories under command of Colo. Butler and Major Ross which lasted until night.

The next morning they returned again to Fort Willet where they remained on duty and out in scouting parties as before mentioned and required until sometime in November when they were discharged and returned home and that he did as he verily believed that season at least three and a half months actual duty and that he was that season a sergeant and discharged his duty as such and that he has no documentary evidence of his service and that he knows of no person whose testimony he can procure who can testify to all his service.

That he was born in the Town of Marsing in the County of Ulster and state aforesaid in the year 1751.

That he was living in the Town County and State aforesaid when called into service and since returned where he has continued to live since the Revolution and since lived.

That he was called into service at the different times and in the manner above stated.

That he cannot state the names of officers of Regular Troops Continental or which Regiments or the general circumstances of his service other than as the same as above stated, and that he never received any written discharge from the service.

That Jacob Waggoner and Jacob H. Diefendorf are the names of persons to whom his is known in his present circumstances who can testify as to his character for veracity and their belief of his services as a soldier of the Revolution and that no clergyman resides therein.

Here hereby relinquishes every claim whatsoever to a pension or annuity benefit except the present and declares that his name is not on any other pension roll of the agency of any state.

Sworn and subscribed the day and year aforesaid. Cornl. Van Camp (signed)
Geo. D. Ferguson, Clerk

He died November 21, 1839.

Pension Application for Isaac Van Camp, Orderly Sergeant

State of New York
Orleans County

On this 23rd day of August 1832, personally appeared in open court before the Judges of the Court of Open and ?? now sitting at the Court House in the Town of Banim in and for the County of Orleans. Isaac Van Camp a resident of the Town of Banim in the County of Orleans and State of New York aged Seventy Three years who being first duly sworn according to law doth on his oath make the following declaration in order to obtain the benefit of the act of Congress passed June 7th, 1832. That he entered the service of the United States under the following named officers and served as herein stated.

That he was born at a place called Warasing in the County of Ulster in the State of New York in the year seventeen hundred and Fifty nine. That he has a record of his age in his Bible at home which is transcribed from an old Bible that became worn out and is destroyed.

That he was living in the Town of Canajoharie in the County of Montgomery in the State of New York. When he entered the service that he has served since the Revolutionary War in the said Town of Canajoharie that he moved to the Town of Sullivan in the County of Madison a few years before the Commencement of the late war, that he removed to the Town of Watertown in the County of Jefferson and about six years since he came to the place where he now resides.

That he has always lived in the State of New York and now lives in the Town of Barim in the County of Orleans aforesaid. That he entered the service as a volunteer. That he contacted in the month of March or the first of April seventeen hundred and seventy six, under Captain E. Van Knaps for nine months as a boatman.

That he served under the said VanKnaps about six months where his Captain the said Evert VanEps was broke for some misconduct. That at that time he was in Schenectady. That on the same day he enlisted into Captain Garret Lansing Company and served until the first of January 1777.

That his service consisted in boating on the Mohawk River in transporting troops around, Militia and provisions for the army. That he was subject to strict military discipline during the whole time. That he frequently had to march on duty and that the company in which he served and their captain were under the command of the officers of the regular Continental Troops.

That they drew their daily rations and monthly pay and were subject to the same penalties for desertion as the Regular troops. That on the said first of January 1777, he was discharged, but that he received a written discharge. That the captain called his company together and thanked them for their faithful service and told them they were discharged.

That in the month of February or March 1777, he enlisted a second time under Captain Reuben Simons for nine months as a boatman that the company in which he was went first to Saratoga from there to Ford Edwards and were employed on the Hudson River in conveying the many provisions and arms between Fort Edwards and Albany until about the Time that Burgoyne surrendered when the company in which he was were ordered to Schenectady and from there to Fort Stanwix that they were commanded by Colonel Hale but most of the time by Colonel Schuyler.

That he was discharged at Schenectady on the first of January 1778 in the same month as he was from the first term of service. That the company in which he served were regularly enlisted were subject to the commands of the Regular or Untied States Officers and were subject to the same discipline and served their daily rations and received their pay in the same manner as the soldiers employed on the land.

That whenever they were not transporting soldiers, who could defend their boats that the company in which he served were furnished with arms and had their sentinels on watch and that he was not hired or employed on a civil contract but Regularly enlisted and served under such enlistment during both of the terms of such enlistment as aforesaid.

That he enlisted again in March 1779 under Capt. John Breadbake for nine months. The company was raised as a company of Rangers and were under the Command of Colonel Van Rensselear, that part of the company and he among them were first stationed at Cherry Valley but were soon relieved and joined the rest of their company at German Flatts. That for the first four months he was chosen by the company and acted as second Sergeant and was then appointed Orderly Sergeant and served five months as such. That he was discharged on the first of January 1780.

That when the term of enlistment had expired the company were called out and thanked by their commander and discharged. But no written discharges were given, that he had a Sergeants warrant signed by Captain John Breadbake which he kept a number of years but that the same is now lost.

That he understood that at the time the said company of Rangers under Captain John Breadbake were called. That several other companies were also needed and that one of them were stationed at Schoharie one at Cherry Valley and one at Stone Robby (Arabia) and one at Johnstown. That he never was under this last term of service any officer higher in command than the said Captain, John Breadbake. But that he understood the companies raised at that time were under the command of Colonel Van Renssalear as above stated.

That while the company in which he was were at the German Flatts, he thinks in the month of September he was sent with twelve? men who were placed under his command to a place about forty miles south called the Carr Place or Farm to see if they could obtain any information of the enemy that they went to the said Carr Place and were there surprised by the enemy and that some of the men that were with him were killed.

That he and five of the men escaped and got back to the German Flatts. That he got into the fort the same day. That they were surprised at the Carr Place but that the other two men did not get in until a day or two after that on the day following his return to the German Flatts the enemy came and discharged the property around the fort and drove off the cattle. But did not attack the Fort. That they were enforced from below and pursued the enemy and retook some of the cattle. That he has no documentary evidence and that he knows of no person whatsoever whose testimony he can procure who can testify to his service. That he is acquainted with Abraham H. Cob and Gideon Hand Esq. Who reside in this neighborhood and can testify to his character for veracity and their belief of his service as a Soldier of The Revolution.

Isaac Van Camp (signed)

We, Abraham H. Cob and Gideon Hand, residents of the Town of Barse in the County of Orleans hereby certify that we are well acquainted with Isaac VanCamp who has signed and sworn the above declaration that we believe him to be seventy three years of age that he is reputed in the neighborhood where he resides to have been a Soldier of The Revolution and that we concur in that opinion.

He died April 20, 1843 in Hanover, Chautauqua County NY. Leaving five surviving children and no widow.

Pension Application for David VanDerheyden or VanDerHyden

Make sure and read the second deposition, it is full of marvelous details about his service and very different from the first one.

State of New York
County of Schenectady

On this seventeenth day of October in the year of our Lord one thousand eight hundred and thirty two, personally appeared in open court before the Judges of the Court of Common Pleas in and for said county now sitting David Van Derheyden or Van Derhyden a resident of the City of Schenectady in said county and state aged upwards of seventy-four years who being first duly sworn according to law, doth on his oath make the following declaration in order to obtain the benefit of the Act of Congress passed June 7th, 1832.

He was born in the City of Albany in the County of Albany in the then Colony of New York on the 26th day of February 1753. He has no record of his age other than that contained in the Record of Baptisms of the Reformed Protestant Dutch Church in said City of Albany.

When he was called into the service of the United States in the Army of the Revolution he was living in said city of Albany and since the Revolutionary War he has lived in the then town ship in City of Schenectady and he now lives in the City of Schenectady aforesaid.

He entered the service of the United States under the following named officers and served as herein stated.

In the spring of the year 1776 he enlisted for the term of six months in Captain Henry Moorsclus's Company in Colonel Van Schaick's regiment. He believes one Van Antwerp was Lieutenant of said company. He served out said six months at Skenesborough, Fort George and Fort Ann.

In the month of March 1777, he enlisted and served for the term of nine months in Captain Lewis Fischer's company of State Troops under command of Lt. Colonel Christopher C. Yates.

In this service he aided in the transportation of public stores and did military duty with the Continental Army for the most part of the time at Fort George. He also was on duty at Crown Point and at Ticonderoga and at the landing a few miles distant from the last named fortress. During the evacuation in June 1777 he was on duty with said army and proceeded with it to Skenesborough and from thence with General Schuyler to Saratoga and served with the troops under General Schuyler during the whole of his retreat and until the final surrender of Burgoyne and his army.

In the beginning of the year 1778, he enlisted and served for the term of nine months in Captain William Peters' company of state trips employed in the transportation of military stores for the use of the army and performed only in said company on the Mohawk River from Schenectady to Fort Stanwix.

In the year 1779 he enlisted and served for this term of nine months and was in the company of officers the name of his captain not recollected and served at Saratoga under the Superintendence of Col. Christopher C. Yates for the term of four months in said engagement and he marched with General Sullivan's army on his expedition against the Indians in the summer and fall of 1779. In this expedition he marched to Wyoming, Lake Otsego, Tioga, etc.

In the year 1781 he enlisted and served for the term of four month in Captain Aaron Hale's Company of State troops in Colonel Marinus Willett's regiment. His other company officers were George Cossage 1st Lieutenant and Jacob Van Ingen 2nd Lieutenant or Ensign. He served in this engagement at the middle fort in Schoharie, Captain Dubois commandant. A party of about forty Indians of the Mohawk Tribe lead on by a Tory named Adam Chrisler made an attack upon the upper fort in Schoharie. The claimant volunteered his services and joined the detachment which had an engagement with Chrisler's party.

In the year 1780 his family being removed to Schenectady, he was enrolled in the Militia Company viz, the company commanded by Captain Thomas B. Banner and served in said company when not under the enlistment aforesaid and until the end of the war.

He marched with a detachment of militia under command of said Captain Banner or Bauster in Ballston in the fall of the year 1780 and joined in pursuit of the enemy who had then laid waste to the country in that quarter. In this expedition he was about out one month.

In the spring of the year last named he marched with a detachment of militia from Schenectady against the enemy who at that time destroyed the Mohawk Settlements.

He has performed garrison duty at Fort Plain more than one month under the immediate command of Captain Philip Van Vorst. He thinks in the fall of the year.

He has served with a great many scouting and reconnoitering parties in pursuit of Tories and their savage associates to Beaverdam, Clifton Park, and other places where they rendezvoused. In short the country in the quarter where the services of the militia were in constant acquisition and the claimant declares that the period in his actual service in the garrison and field during service exceeds four years.

He never received any written discharge from the service.

He has no documentary evidence but can produce the testimony of several persons who can testify to his services as aforesaid.

(Then he lists some people who can testify to his character and veracity. He relinquishes claim to any other pension or annuity, etc.)
Signed David Van Derheyden (his mark)

State of New York
County of Schenectady

David Van Derheyden of the City of Schenectady in said county and state, being duly sworn and examined in relation to a certain portion of his services in the War of the Revolution not particularly set forth in the papers mow on file in the War Department in the matter of his application for a pension under the act of Congress of 7th June 1832, doth depose and says.

That in the spring of the year 1779 this deponent enlisted for the term of nine months, if this deponent's memory serves his right as an artificer (he being a cooper by trade) at Schenectady aforesaid by the procuration and under the direction of Col. Yates aforesaid this deponent believes in the Company's Department. Some time after his enlistment as aforesaid a regiment from the state of Pennsylvania one from Massachusetts and two if not more regiments from the State of New York under command of Colonels Dubois and Gansevoort and Lieutenant

Colonel Marinus Willett passed through said city the town of Schenectady on their way to join the forces under General Sullivan in his contemplated expedition against the Indians.

This deponent was then attached to one of the New York Regiments he thinks the one under command of Colonel Gansevoort and in the company commanded by Captain Aaron Austin though this deponent was occasionally commanded by other officers than said Captain Austin. This deponent thereupon marched with said Regiments to Canajoharie where the said Regiments encamped and there this deponent part of the time performed garrison duty and apart of the time as his services were required attended by virtue of his enlistment in the company's department to the preparation of preservation of the military stores. From thence he marched with said regiments, he thinks in the latter part of the month of June 1779 to Otsego Lake where they again encamped while here the deponent was detailed with parties of soldiers and erected a dam across the outlet of said lake, to enable the troops to proceed into the Indian country. This deponent after said dam had been built proceeded with said troops (or a part of them for some part by land) to Tioga point aforesaid. Here this deponent mounted guard about a fortnight and as was then ordered with a party detailed for that purpose to Wyoming there to procure and to bring from thence stores for the army.

This deponent accordingly engaged in this expedition and on his return to Tioga Point he remained there pursuant to the commands of his superior officers which the main army proceeded into the Indian country. While there he was employed in ministering to the sick of the army who were left at said Tioga Point to be taken care of, this deponent also performed his quota of duty in mounting guard and was also employed in the different duties connected with the company's department.

On the return of the troops from the Indians country as aforesaid, eh proceeded with them to Wyoming aforesaid where they then camped for some time. From thence this deponent in company with Colonel Dubois aforesaid, two commissaries? by the name of Pratt and a party of soldiers proceeded through the woods to New Windsor and from thence this deponent, being now dismissed from this expedition proceeded to Albany and from thence to Schenectady.

This deponent upon reflection thinks the time of his enlistment was in the month of March in the year 1779 and previous to the arrival of the army at Schenectady as aforesaid her thinks he was employed under Henry Glen a ccommissary? Residing at Schenectady and under his directions assisted in preparing the stores to have them in readiness against the arrival of the army.

As to the services of this deponent in the companies of Captains Fisher and Peters in the years 1777 and 1778 this deponent can only state in addition to what is set forth in his said declaration, that in the spring of the year 1777 this deponent enlisted in said company of Captain Fisher at the City of Albany aforesaid for the term of one year or nine months, he does not remember which and marched with his said company to Lake George from thence to Ticonderoga Landing. The character of his services in said company was the transportation of Military stores from said Lake to Ticonderoga aforesaid and he was then employed until the investment of Ticonderoga by General Burgoyne, on leaving this fortress this deponent remembers to have aided in setting on fire for sinking such batteaux as they could not in the hurry of the retreat take with them.

Deponent retreated with the American troops to Fort George and remained there and at Skeenesborough and Fort Ann and Edward discharging duty as aforesaid and after the surrender of Burgoyne this deponent served out his enlistment till some time in the winter of the year 1777 under direction and by order of General Schuyler and other Continental officers in the cutting of timber and other fortified duty of that description.

This deponent enlisted in the spring of the year 1778 in said company of Captain Peters he thinks for the term of nine months. The character of this service in this company was the same as in that of Captain Fisher's aforesaid. He served in this company in the transportation of stores for the army up the Mohawk River from Schenectady to Fort Stanwix.
Signed David Van Derheyden (his mark)

October 1857 he states he receives an income of thirty-six dollars and seventy-five cents for a pension and is reapplying because some of his services were not allowed. This part of the application is not legible.

Pension Application for Joseph Van Ingen, Surgeon's Mate (Lieutenant)

(This pension application is in very bad shape!)
State of New York
Lewis County
(1832, Court of Common Pleas, the usual opening phrases. This pension application because of the quality of writing will be paraphrased.)

That in the year 1778 he entered service of the United States as a Surgeon's Mate under Dirck Van Ingen, Physician and Surgeon of the Eastern Continental Department at Schenectady, New York with the rank of First Lieutenant and served until May 1, 1779.

That in the month of June 1779 he again entered the service of the United States as Surgeon's Mate under the command of Doct. Stephen McCree who was Physician and Surgeon General in the Regiment of General Sullivan with the rank and pay of First Lieutenant on his Indian expedition and was in the Battle of Newtown. He marched from Albany to Canajoharie then to Otsego Lake, to Susquehanna River to Tioga, to Chemung and Newtown. That he remained in this department until the month of November 1779 when the army returned and he had been transferred to the hospital department in the City of Schenectady in the same capacity and remained there until the following spring as Clerk and Surgeon's Mate under Dirck Van Ingen Physician and Surgeon, at which time he was attached to the Quarter Master's Genera Department in the capacity of Clerk under Teunis Van Waggoner, Quarter Master General of the Brigade of Troops of the New York Line commanded by General James Clinton. That he served in this capacity until he arrived at West Point in the Spring of 1780 when he was transferred to the Commissary Generals Department under the Commissar General _____ Marshall under whom he acted as Clerk of that department for about two months after the arrival of the brigade.

That he received his appointment from General James Clinton as Commissioner? of Ordinance and Military Stores with the rank and pay of Lieutenant and acted in this capacity for more then nine months. That he remained at West Point until marched to Tappan and then to Schenectady to winter quarters.

April 28, 1781, he was appointed Ensign to Lieutenant Colonel Marinus Willett's New York Regiment and on November 7, 1781, he was appointed Lieutenant of Captain Aaron Hale's Company in said regiment where he served until late in 1781.

He was allowed his pension applied for on September 20, 1832, he was seventy years of age.

He died in Diana, Lewis County November 5, 1842. He was married March 13, 1784 to Eleanor Van Alstyne. She was allowed pension on her application dated July 21, 1848 at which time she was eighty-one years of age and was a resident of Diana, New York. She died January 5, 1845, leaving the following children: Richard, Margaret who was the widow of Henry Plant and Nancy who was the wife of Malachi Van Duzon.

Pension Application for Ruliff Voorhis

State of New York
Delaware County

Of this seventeenth day of August 1839, personally appeared in open court before the Court of Common Pleas now sitting Delhi in and for the County of Delaware Ruliff Voorhis a resident of Stamford, County of Delaware and State of New York aged eighty years last January who being first duly sworn according to law doth on his oath make the following declaration in order to obtain the benefit of the Act of Congress passed June 7, 1832.

That he entered as a private soldier in the Revolutionary War in the Militia of the State of New York in the years 1777, 1778, 1779, and 1780. That he was a single man and made it his home at his father's who resided about a mile from Johnstown.

In the year 1777 he was out serving in the fall at Canajoharie which lay twelve or fifteen miles up the Mohawk River from Johnstown, one time he was gone a fortnight and the other time a week. The latter time he went from Johnstown and Canajoharie under command of Lieutenant Quackenby's where the company lay about a week over their dismissed. Camp was captain of the regiment which was commanded by Colonel Fisher (Visscher).

In the three following years he was out here often and in the two last years in the summer season was out most of the time during the time aforesaid. The said Ruliff was called out to the Blockhouse six times. The last time was under Captain Vader, sometimes under Captain Fisher who was brother of the colonel and who was killed by the Indians. The Blockhouse was at Sacandaga about twelve miles north of Johnstown. Colonel Fisher was scalped 22 May 1780 but not killed and then Lieutenant Colonel Vader took the command. Sometime was under Capt. Wood now and most of the time was under Capt. Camp till the last year when we with most of his company went to Canada. The six times called and sent to the Blockhouse was a week each time.

The said Ruliff Voorhis was called out to Johnstown ten times where he lay a week each time, sometimes under Camp and sometimes under Capt. Voorhis and thinks was once under Capt. Maybee Who belonged to same regiment ??? the one commanded by Col. Fisher.

Twice went up to German Flatts with the whole regiment when was out a week or more each time. One time went with Regiment to Fort Stanwix to guard prisoners up and was gone ten days at least and the Oneida Indians came back with them and went down to Schenectady.

Before going to Fort Stanwix the said Ruliff went to Cherry Valley with the regiment the next day after Cherry Valley was burnt, arrived there in evening of second day. It rained and snowed that night. Saw one woman and four children lying on the ground. Officers as well as privates had to lie out, the fort was so full.

In March 1779 or 1780 went on account on snowshoes after Indians. There were six of us after seven Indians.

That one of the Indians was wounded by Wood and one of our party and one of the Indians had to carry him. We followed them fifty miles. They had three days the start and we got five out of seven and the other two we reckoned had gone to Canada. We came upon them as they et (ate) around the fire busy roasting meat having killed an Elk the day before. Their snowshoes were off. Wood now clenched one ??? him down and tomahawked him and tomahawked another, the rest were shot by us.

There were a great many alarms where we were called out, but a day at a time. At one time went to Canajoharie when he lay at the Fort a fortnight, during the time went to Cherry Valley upon a scout. Once the Tories was out in the time and lost all and was glad to get off so, second time were sent out when a scouting party, the said Ruliff once lay a week at Col. Vader's in the Mohawk a little ways across Caughnawaga there were fifteen or twenty men in company. The ??? what they went for, recollects Capt Vader killing a snake for the men. At another time lay a week at Chester Van Eps or Vaneyps somewhere, about twenty men were there, can't tell why we were there. Was a week he thinks at Henry Hans, there were perhaps thirty or forty of us and if we had lain two or three days longer might have lost some life for the Indians came soon after we had left and burnt his house and barn, murdered Hans, took off two of his horses and his two sons prisoners, though one of them was a married man but lived in the house with his father. The said Ruliff was drafted to go to the Blockhouse and to Johnstown as before stated. Sometimes the said Ruliff volunteered with others on the occasions afore mentioned. The said Ruliff is very confident he served on the whole as much as ten months and using the times before aforesaid the said Ruliff was not employed in any civil pursuit.

He knows of no person whose testimony he can procure excepting his brother Garret who lives in Sullivan County. In the several times called out on little alarms were usually gone two or three days and sometimes not so long. Had to carry provisions along. The said Ruliff hereby relinquishes every claim whatever to an annuity or pension except the present and he further says he has no documentary evidence of his services aforesaid and declares that his name is not on the pension roll of the agency of any state, they he has not received any written discharge from the service and the said Ruliff further says that in April 1781 he went to New Jersey about two miles from; New Brunswick when he lived about three years when he returned to Schohaire ?? about two miles he ??? towards Gilboa where he lived three years and them moved on the hill and went a mile from Gilboa in Blenheim Schohaire County where he lived fifteen years, then moved to the town of Harpersfield about three miles from his present residence where he resided about thirty years. Others moved to the village of Harperstown Of Stamford where he now resided six years. The said Ruliff says he was born near New Brunswick in New Jersey on the 20th of January 1759. He father's family moved to the Mohawk Country about the time the war began and lived near Johnstown five years and then moved to the Mohawk River on the place of old Major Feenday or Fonda where we lived one year. Others went to New Jersey as afore mentioned.

The time of said Ruliff's birth was entered in his father's Bible which was burnt up the Indians when he the said Ruliff lived on the Mohawk River and the said Ruliff would further state that he is well known to William Trotten Justice of the Peace, John Griffin Postmaster and Servinus Morris, attorney of law residing in Hobart aforesaid who with others as he mentions can testify to his the said Ruliff's character for veracity and their belief of his services as a soldier of the Revolution and he further says that the only clergyman who resides in the village remained there only some two or three months since from the state of Massachusetts and he is not much acquainted with him.

       Sworn and subscribed the day …………..etc.

       Signed Ruliff Voorhis

Pension Application for Isaac Jacob Vroman

State of New York
County of Albany

       On this twenty-second day of September in the year one thousand eight hundred and thirty four, personally appeared before the Justices of the Justice Court of the City of Albany, the same being the court of record. Isaac J. Vrooman, now a resident of the Town of Guilderland, in the County of Albany and State of New York, aged seventy-three years and about six months who being first duly sworn according to law doth on his oath make the following declaration in order to obtain the benefit of the provision made by the Act of Congress passed June 7th 1832.

       That he served in the Army of the United States in the year 1776 in the Regiment in the New York Line commanded by Col. Wynkoop and of which Courtland Schuyler? Of Albany was Lieutenant Colonel.

       That this deponent served in the company in said regiment commanded by Capt. John F. Wendell late of the City of Albany, deceased. John Ten Broeck, now of the City of New York, First Lieutenant of said company, and the said John Ten Broeck now being a pensioner of the United State and John Welch, Second Lieutenant and John Ostrander Ensign of said company.

       That this deponent enlisted with the said John Welch Second Lieutenant in Schenectady on or about the month of May 1776. That he went from Schenectady to Albany and from thence to Ticonderoga when he joined the said company.

       That the said company with this deponent remained about three months at Ticonderoga according to the recollection of the deponent and from thence was ordered to Skeensborough. That the said regiment was discharged at Skeensborough in January succeeding from a belief founded on his best recollection that it was after the holy days, and his return home from Albany he came part of the way and crossed Wood Creek on the ice.

       That this deponent enlisted in said company for sic months but that he remained in the service of the said army eight months. After the said time of service this deponent returned to Norman's Kill now the Town of Bethlehem in the County of Albany which was the native place of this deponent and when he resided until he enlisted with the said John Welch.

       And this deponent further says that after the said term of service as aforesaid he served in the militia in active duty when he was drafted for scout purposes.

       That his first tour of service in the militia was in the Regiment of New Yorker Militia commanded by Col. Peter Vroman who was a second cousin of this deponent, Capt John Groot was captain of the company in which the deponent served, Bartal Myndert First Lieutenant, Levi Van Auken 2nd Lieutenant and Adrian Vroman Ensign who was a brother of this deponent.

       This deponent was an Orderly Sergeant in said company. He was drafted for the defense of the forts at Schoharie; the militia at said forts were relieved every fortnight. This deponent served for said time, this way near as he can recollect in 1778.

       And this deponent further says that he afterward served in two successive years in the same service in guarding the forts in Schoharie during two weeks of each year for which period the militia was drafted for the above service and this deponent was ordered and served in each of said drafts.

       The names of the officers of this company in which the deponent served in the first of the two last years aforesaid were Capt. Hager—Peter Hager, 1st Lieutenant, and Ebenezer Olen Ensign.

       On the last tour of service Capt Walter Vroman, the oldest brother of this deponent was the Captain of the company and Jellis Fonda late of Schenectady, deceased was First Lieutenant. Col. Peter Vroman was also the Col. Of the regiment to which said Companies belonged and Commanded the forces ??? at Schoharie Forts of the time the deponent served at said Forts. This deponent was stationed at the Middle Fort so called at Schoharie when our Expedition of the British and Indians under the command of Sir John Johnson was directed against it. This fort was partially invested by him that was soon driven off though there was not a great deal of fighting. This deponent was stationed at different times at all of the three posts at Schohaire.

       And this deponent further says for more than forty years past he has been without any family and during said time has had no permanent place of abode. He went into the Western Country (Ohio) about twenty-five years ago. He was engaged in collecting furs from the Indians

– after having returned to the State of New York he again when to Ohio and from thence to Michigan. That the deponent left Michigan in May last for this part of the country for the purpose of getting evidence ??? on this deponent supporting to obtain this pension.

That he went to the City of New York to see Lieut John C. Ten Broeck the First Lieutenant of this deponents company, saw him there, that his mind was said to be too much broken by age and distance to admit of his making any deposition in favor of this deponent.

That said Ten Broeck did not recollect the deponent, but seemed to recollect some incidents that were mentioned by this deponent to him.

And deponent further says that his Christian name is Isaac Jacob that he used to use his middle name in making his signature. There was an Isaac Vroman and an Isaac A. Vroman and this deponent signed his name Isaac Ja'b Vroman to distinguish between them and him. This deponent has seen a receipt now forwarded him dated 2nd April 1776 at Skeensborough for 5 pounds six shillings as received of Capt Wendell. This receipt was signed by this deponent at the time it was dated and the same period mentioned in the said receipt.

And this deponent hereby relinquishes every claim whatever to a pension or annuity except the present. And declares that his name is not on the Pension Roll of the Agency of any State. And is unable to write his name.

Sworn this 22nd day of September 1834 in open court.

Isaac J. Vrooman (his mark)

John G. Watson, clerk

The following letter is part of the pension folder.

December 29, 1937

Mrs. Eula R. Spencer
The American Red Cross
125 ½ South Ohio Street
Bedalia, Missouri

Isaac Jacob Vroman-S.11612

Dear Madam:

Reference is made to your letter in which you request the record of Jacob Vrooman, a soldier of the Revolutionary War.

You are furnished herein the record of Isaac Jacob Vrooman or Vroman, the data for which were obtained from the papers on file in Revolutionary War pension claim, S.11612, based upon his military service in that war.

Isaac Jacob Vrooman was born at Norman's Kill, Albany County, New York. The date of his birth and names of his parents are not shown.

While residing in said Norman's Kill, Isaac Jacob Vrooman enlisted in May, 1776, served as a private in Captain John W. Wendell's Company, Colonel Wynkoop's New York Regiment, marched to Ticonderoga, where he served three months, thence to Skeensborough, where he was discharged in January following: he enlisted in 1778, for the defense of the forts at Schoharie and served as orderly sergeant in Captain John Groot's Company, Colonel Peter Vroman's (soldier's second cousin) New York Regiment: his brother Adam was ensign of said company: Afterward, he served on short tours of two weeks each, over a period of two years as part of the garrison at Schohaire under Captains Hager and Walter Vroman (soldier's oldest brother) in the New York troops, on one occasion, while at the middle fort in said Schoharie, they were attacked by a party of British and Indians under command of Sir John Johnson and succeeded in driving the enemy away.

Isaac Jacob Vroman stated that for more than forty years after the Revolution, he had no family; that about 1809, he went to the western part of Ohio and collected furs from the Indians, that he made several trips between his old home and Ohio, and finally went to Michigan in the vicinity of Detroit from which place he returned to New York State in May 1834.

Isaac Jacob Vroman was allowed pension on his application executed September 22, 1834 while residing in Guilderland, Albany County, New York, aged seventy-three years and ten months. He was named on the pension rolls as Isaac J. Vroman.

It is not stated that soldier was ever married.

In 1836, one Adam Vroman was aged seventy-five years and made affidavit in Schenectady County, New York in support of the pension claim of Isaac Jacob Vroman, but did not state his relationship.

In order to obtain the date of last payment of pension, the name and address of person paid and possibly the date of death of the Revolutionary War pensioner, Isaac J. Vroman S.11612, you should address the Comptroller General, General Accounting Office, Records Division, this city and cite the following data:

Isaac J. Vroman
Certificate No. 30112
Issued August 5, 1835
Rate, $26.66 per annum
Commenced March 4, 1831
Act of June 7, 1832
New York (Albany) Agency

Very truly yours
A.D. Hiller
Executive Assistant
To the Administrator

Pension Application for Jacob H. Walrath, Corporal

(Very difficult to read, make sure and read the next one, it tells a clearer story.) Walrath was wounded in the shoulder in the Battle of Oriskany. Due to his lack of supporting affidavits, he never received a pension.

State of New York
Montgomery County

On this eighth day of November A.D. 1842 personally appeared before Hon. Stephen Yates a Judge of Montgomery County Courts of ? in the supreme court Jacob H. Walrath, a resident of the Town of St. Johnsville County of Montgomery and state aforesaid aged eighty four years on the 17th day of November first being duly sworn according to law doth on; his behalf make the following declaration in order to obtain the benefit of the act of Congress passed June 7th 1832.

That he entered the service of the United States in the spring of 1776 and served first under Captain John Haddock in Col. Jacob Klock's Regiment and General Herkimer's brigade two months and a half at Stone Arabia and Oswagatchie.

That in the next campaign 1777 he served under the same officers as above as a corporal in the militia in the said Capt Bradbecks company and was stationed in Fall Hill and German Flatts until the month of August of said year when he was ordered to march to the relief of Fort Stanwix that the marching by the way of the Mohawk River and Herkimer to Oriskany at which latter place a battle was fought between the militia under General Herkimer and a large party of British and Indians and that he was wounded in the right shoulder in said Battle of Oriskany by a musket ball which was not extracted and that he served during this campaign three months.

That the next service rendered by him as corporal in the militia under Capt Bradbeck was at Palatine and Johnstown the length of time he served during this campaign of 1778 was one month and a half. That in the next campaign he served he thinks under Capt Van Slyke about one month at Stone Arabia and that he has no documentary evidence and that he knows of but one living person at this time whose testimony he can prove and who was in the same battle in which he was wounded and who can testify to some of his services and whose affidavit is hereunto annexed.

Her hereby relinquishes every claim whatever to a pension or annuity except the present one, declares that his name is not on the pension roll of the agency of any state and he further testifies that the first interrogations mentioned in the ? that he was born in Palatine district then Tryon county now Montgomery county New York on the 17th day of November 1758 to the said he testifies that he had a record of his age until recently but that it is now lost or destroyed.

When called into service he was living at the place where he was born as above stated and that he has since the Revolutionary War lived in the same county Montgomery and lives now in the Town of St. Johnsville in the county aforesaid. That he was called into service as a volunteer or went when ordered by his officers to the 5th ? ? in the beginning as to the names of the officers to the 8th he testifies that he never received a discharge from service to the 7th the names of some persons to whom I am known in my present neighborhood and who can testify as to my character for ? and namely and he believes of any services as a soldier of the Revolution are named in the following certificate.

Signed, Jacob H. Walrath

United States of America
Territory of Wisconsin
Racine County

On this twenty-first day of June A.D. 1847, personally appeared before the undersigned one of the Justices of the Peace in and for said county. Jacob H. Walrath a resident of the Town of Raymond in said county and territory aged ninety-one years being first duly sworn according to law doth on his oath make the following declaration in order to obtain the benefit of the act of Congress passed June 27, 2832.

That he entered the service of the United States under the following named officers and served as herein stated. That on or about the fifteenth day of June in the year of our Lord Seventeen hundred and seventy seven he entered the service of the state of New York as a corporal in the company of Captain John Breadbake, which said company was attached to Colonel Jacob Klock Regiment. This declarant further states, that he was in the Battle of Oriskany on the sixth day of August A.D. 1777. And that he was wounded in said engagement by a musket ball which entered his right shoulder.

Which wound disabled this declarant from the service during the war and that he was disabled even since in consequence of said wound. This declarant further states that when he entered the service he resided in the town of Palatine in the County of Montgomery and State of new York and that he was drafted and that which he was in the service he marched through to Fort Stanwix and Oriskany and that he remained in the service from the term of his draft until the time of said Battle of Oriskany was fought and that he then left the service for the reasons above disclosed.

This declarant further states, that he now applies for a pension for the sole purpose of obtaining the necessary means of support and that he should have made application before now if had not heretofore had the means of maintaining himself that he has lost his property and by reason of age is unable to support himself that he has no documentary evidence and that he knows of no person whose testimony he can procure who can testify to his service. He hereby relinquishes every claim whatsoever to a pension or annuity except the present and declares that his name is not on the pension roll of any agency of any state or territory.

This declarant further states that by reason of old age and consequent loss of memory he cannot state the term of his service any more definitely than he has herein stated and that by reason of infirmity his is unable to go before the district judge of this district for the purpose of making this declaration sworn and subscribed fore here the day and year aforesaid.

Signed Jacob H. Walrath.

This letter was included in the Pension Application.

Marion Brown Gruening
119 N. 34th Street
Omaha, Nebraska

February 20, 1929

Madam:

I advise you from the papers in the Revolutionary War pension claim R.11093, it appears that Jacob W. Walrath was born in 1756 or November 17, 1758 in Palatine District (then Tryon County later Montgomery County), New York.

He applied for pension November 8, 1842, at which time he was a resident of St. Johnsville, Montgomery County, New York, and alleged that he enlisted in the spring of 1776 and served two and one-half months as a private in Captain John Bradbick's or Breadbake's Company, Colonel Jacob Klock's New York Regiment; and that he enlisted in 1777 served three months as a corporal under the same officers and was in the battle of Oriskany where he was wounded in his right shoulder by a musket ball; and that in 1778 he enlisted and served one and one-half months as a corporal in Captain John Bradbick's Company, Colonel Jacob Klock's New York Regiment and that he alter served one month under Captain Van Slyke, no dates or details of service given.

His claim was not allowed as he failed to furnish proof of service as required by the pension laws.

He remained in Palatine, New York, until 1845, then moved to the State of Illinois. In 1847 he was living in Raymond, Racine County, Wisconsin.

There are no data concerning his family.

The Revolutionary war records of this bureau fail to afford any information in regard to Nicholas Walrath, all spelling searched.

Respectfully,
Winfield Scott
Commissioner.

Pension Application for John Woolaver (Woolover, Wolever, Wolover, Woleber)

State of New York
Madison County
On this twelfth day of March 1840 personally appeared before Horatio Gates Warner, Judge for the Court of Common Pleas in and for the County of Madison in said state, Catherine Woolaver, a resident of the town of Lenox in said County aged nearly seventy nine years who being first duly sworn according to law, doth on her oath make the following declaration in order to obtain the benefit of the provision made by the Act of Congress passed on July 11, 1836.

That she is the widow of John Woolaver who was a soldier during the War of the Revolution, declarant owing to old age and consequence loss of memory cannot now relate if she ever knew all the particulars of her said husband's revolutionary services. She well remembers hearing him relate particulars of the service which he performed previous to her entering marriage with him which took place in the month of January 1781, to wit, his service with a company of boatmen under Captain Peter Peterson the Mohawk River this service in various expeditions with the Militia.

And declarant further testifies that after the said marriage with the said John Woolaver, he the said John was taken prisoner by the Indians, conveyed to Canada, and confined for a period of Eighteen months (or at least that period elapsed before his return to his home after his said capture.)

That he was there taken prisoner in the summer of the same year when which her said marriage occurred about five or six months after said marriage. She further declared that she was married to the said John Woolaver on the 11th day of January 1781 in the church at Palatine in said state by the Rev'd Mr. Gross then pastor of said church.

Declarant does not know of any person now living who was present at her said marriage except Peter Woolaver, her husband's brother. That her husband the said John Woolaver died on the 13th day of August 1838 (while he was engaged in applying for a pension) and that she has remained a widow ever since that period as will more fully appear by references to the proof hereto annexed.

Subscribed, etc……..
Catharine Woolaver (her mark)

Montgomery County
Lawrence Gros of Canajoharie in the county aforesaid being sworn says that he was personally acquainted with the Rev. Johan Daniel Gros during part of the Revolutionary Was and served up to the time of the death of Rev. Johan Daniel Gros which took place the 25th day of May 1812. That Rev. Johan Daniel Gross had charge of the Dutch Reformed Church at Fort Plain in the Town of Minden during said Revolutionary War. That to the knowledge of deponent said church was destroyed by fire in the latter part of said Revolutionary War and the deponent thinks in the year 1781 or 1782 and that all the records of marriages kept by said Johan Daniel were destroyed at the burning of said church by the enemy (was informed by said Gross and believes to be true) that this deponent has been informed by Johan Daniel frequently since said Revolution and by others that all the records of marriages kept by said Gros during said Revolutionary War were destroyed as aforesaid and which this deponent believes to be true.

That this deponent has in his possession all the papers of said John Daniel Gros (this deponent being one of the heirs of said Johan) and that no records of marriages during said war appear amongst said papers and that this deponent is now upwards of sixty three years old and further says not.

Subscribed and sworn, etc.....

2nd day of April 1840

Signed, Lawrence Gros

Herkimer County

On the fourth day of April 1841 personally came before me, John P. Snell a Justice of the Peace in said county, Peter Woolever who resides in the Town of Manheim in said county, being duly sworn testified and said that he is seventy five years old and upwards that he was born at a place called Stone Arabia now the Town of Palatine in the County of Montgomery and State of New York and that John Woolever late of the Town of Lenox in the County of Madison, aforesaid was his brother and that on or about the fourteenth day of January 1781 he this deponent was present at the house of Col. Jacob Klock in the then Town of Palatine in said County of Montgomery when and at that time his said brother John Woolever was duly married to Catharine McNaughton to me then personally known and that I have since that time been acquainted with the said Catharine and that the same person is now the widow of the said John Woolever deceased and that the Rev'd Daniel Gros then officiating clergyman with whom I was then personally acquainted married and performed the marriage ceremony between the said John Woolever and Catherine McNaughton and that they ever since then to the day of his brother's death resided together as man and wife.

The said Peter Woolever says and testifies that according to the records kept by his father that his brother John Woolever deceased was born the 13th day of September 1760 and that his said brother John Woolever died the 13th day of August 1838.

Sworn and subscribed before .....

Signed Peter Woolever

State of New York

Montgomery County

On the 29th day of June 1838 personally appeared before me, John Everson, a Commissioner for the county aforesaid. John Woolever a resident of the Town of Lenox, County of Madison, and the state aforesaid aged seventy seven years doth first having been duly sworn according to law deposeth and saith under oath that he has been a Revolutionary Soldier and that he hath applied and had had a M'Koon employed as he agent to assist and to present his petition in order to obtain his pension (Can't read the rest of this paragraph nor the rest of the next two pages. Apparently he was employed in the boating services along the Mohawk River between Schenectady and Fort Stanwix.)

Claimant states that he considers himself honorably enlisted for his imprisonment taken by the Indians and kept in captivity for the length of one year and when released returned to his place of residence. Claimant believes he was actually engaged in the service of the United States whether he was unmindful in being on his guard, and declaration to ??? heretofore by Mr. Snell.

Claimant states, that believes the Pension commissioners will be satisfied that claimant was engaged under the command of Gen'l Herkimer at Oriskany Battle 6th Aug 1777.

Claimant further declares that he was engaged in Battle generally called Col. Brown's Battle on the 19th Oct 1780 in Palatine Stone Arabia when Col. Brown was killed in battle besides forty-four killed and several wounded.

The applicant further beg leave to solicit the attention of his Honor the Commissioner of Pensions to the Testimony of Capt. Frederick Sammons and Mr. Henry Shults, who both have testified that he the said claimant with themselves had been kept in prison vizt on ??? Island and there kept in captivity from October 1782 during winter 1783 until sometimes forepart ??? when the said Frederick Sammons absconded him and a Mr. McMullen swam away from the Island, and with great difficulties made a safe return home. When the said claimant and Henry Shults and two others, brothers of Shults was on the said Island and continued in Captivity until sometime in fall 1783. When sent to Montreal and exchanged and not returned until between Christmas and New Year and who is credible, Capt. Sammons aged about eighty, and honored previous to the last presidential election, service and elected one of the electors and Mr. Shults aged eighty eight years and always considered truthful and veracity.

(Rest of record very hard to read.)

Declaration
> In order to obtain the benefits of the Act of Congress of the 7th of June 1838

State of New York

County of Madison SS on this day of October in the year of our Lord one thousand eight hundred and thirty four personally appeared before the house of Common Please it being a court of record held in and for the County of Madison John Wolever, a resident of the Town of ??? in the County of Madison and state of New York aged seventy four years who being first duly sown according to law doth on his oath make the following declaration.

> That he was drafted into the service of the Revolution in the spring of 1777 for the term of three months in Capt. Joseph Dygert's Company in Col. Cox's Regiment and served during the whole of that period of time he lived at and entered the service at Canajoharie in the County of Montgomery and state of New York and was marched to Fort Stanwix and was stationed there and at Fort Bull.

> On Wood Creek and was engaged in watching the movement of the enemy and in blocking Wood Creek by falling trees into the ??? to stop the enemy from coming up said creek and was discharged the latter part of July as he believes and returned home where he stayed but a short time before he was pressed into the service of the Revolution and marched forthwith to Fort Dayton and from there to the Oriskany and was there engaged in the well known battle called the Oriskany Battle in which Gen'l Herkimer was mortally wounded when he served in the same company and regiment and under the same Capt and led as in the ??? and was ??? at Fort Dayton and actual service on scouting parties and ??? for four more times and was discharged about the first of November 1777.

> That in the spring of 1778 he enlisted at the house of his residence aforesaid for the space of nine months under Capt Peter Peterson in Col. Willett's Regiment and was stationed at Fort Stanwix and was engaged in watching the movement of the enemy and some part of the time in carrying provisions from Schenectady to Fort Stanwix for the army and was discharged late in the fall of that year at first of winter after having served the whole term of nine months for which he enlisted.

> That he was drafted in the spring of 1779 for three months and served with the same Captain as the first service in Col. Cox's Regiment at the same place and was stationed at Fort Dayton aforesaid, name the town and county of Herkimer and was a part of the time engaged in carrying dispatches from that place to Fort Plain and that he served the whole of that term and was discharged verbally as on all other occasions.

> That in the spring of 1780 he was again drafted for three months at that place aforesaid in Capt. Tygert's (Dygert's) Company and Col. Cox's regiment aforesaid and served under Gen'l Browen and was stationed at Stone Arabia on the Mohawk River and was in the Battle called Bowen's Battle in which the gen'l was killed and that he was frequently called out on alarms for that served at one time under and order of Col. Willett he entered the service as a volunteer nor for any length of time and while on an excursion for provisions was captured and was taken prisoner by the enemy in the month of July 1781 from his best recollection and was carried north into Canada and there left for the space of eighteen months and until he was exchanged for prisoner on the other side.

> He hereby relinquishes every claim whatsoever to a pension or annuity except the present and declares that his name is not on the pension roll of the agency of any state. Sworn to and subscribed this day and year aforesaid in open court.

> John Wolever (his mark)

Pension Application for Peter Wolever
(Also spelled Wolleber, Woolever, Wooleben, Woleber, Wohleben, Wooliver)

This pension is very difficult to read and lots of the papers included in the folder are not legible.

State of New York

Herkimer County

> On this 11th day of February in the year one thousand eight hundred thirty three personally appeared in open court before the Judges of the county of Common Pleas in the County of Herkimer now sitting Peter Woolever, resident of the town of Manheim in the said county of Herkimer, state aforesaid, aged sixty eight years who being first duly sworn according to law doth depose to make the following declarations in order to obtain the benefit of the act of Congress passed June 7, 1832.

That he was born in the year 1764 in Stone Arabia in the now county of Montgomery then county of Tryon on the 27th day of November and that there was a record of his age but he has not seen it for many years and cannot recall where it may be.

That he entered into the service of the United States in the New York line of Militia in the spring of the year 1779 at the Mohawk Castle in the now county of Herkimer. The Captain of his company was Joseph Dygert the Lieutenant was John Windecker and the company belonged to a regiment commanded by Colonel Peter Bellinger.

He (Woolaver) was a Corporal in his company. The company marched to Fort Dayton, near the village of Herkimer now stands and served there for some time as a guard and they were marched to the fort at the Mohawk Castle to repair the fort and stand guard and Woolaver and his company were ordered to stand in readiness to march at a moment's warning to the different forts and stations on the Mohawk River in the county of Herkimer by the Committee of Safety of that section and they did keep themselves in readiness and were employed in different forts in the ??? and on scouts to different directions of the county and they spent much of this year at the house of General Nicholas Herkimer on the Mohawk and which was guarded and used in some respects as a fort at that time in the year 1780 he in the same company and with the same officers marched to Stone Arabia in now Montgomery County, then Tryon County and there was a fort there, and after they had been there as guard for some time but he cannot say the length of time. The Indians, Tories and British attacked that place he believes it must have been in the month of October in the year 1780 and a sever battle was fought in which Colonel Brown, an American died about forty-two privates were killed. Colonel Brown commanded at this fort and his force was something more than one hundred men, the Americans were compelled to retreat because General Van Rensselaer who was expected to come on with more militia from Schenectady did not arrive and some people suspected that he intentionally kept back.

The enemy were led by Sir John Johnson and Joseph Brant was there and received a wound in his heel and after this battle the enemy proceeded up the Mohawk towards Fort Plain and Gen. Van Rensselaer came after the battle proceeded to attack said enemy. That he (Woolaven) and his company remained at Stone Arabia most of the year 1780 and both before and after the battle he was sent out in scouting parties every few days, and as a spy to bring intelligence of the operations of the incendiaries and he was frequently out with the other from one fort to anther on the Mohawk for intelligence and as often as alarms were raised of the approaching of Indians and Tories during the whole year of 1780 he was on duty as a soldier either as a guard, spy, and with a scouting party.

During the year 1781 he belonged to the same company and was commanded by the same officers and was under orders to march at a moment's warning and did keep himself in readiness and was on duty at the different forts in the county of Herkimer.

There was during this year, a skirmish at the house of Gen. Herkimer in which Woolaven took part between some Indians and Tories and the garrison at that place.

During this year he with others was ordered to drive some ??? cattle from Mohawk Castle to Fort Plain by Col. Willett who was there. This order he performed but on his return, a party of Indians waylaid them and his oldest brother and his brother-in-law were killed and another brother in the same company was made a prisoner but he (the applicant) scalped with a severe wound in his thigh and shoulder, which disabled him doing duty about one year.

During the year, 1782 and until the enemy and Indians called to be hostile and to commit depredations which was in the last part of that year, 1782, in this section of the county, Woolaven belonged to the same company and same officers and was under orders to march from fort to fort in the county of Herkimer as a guard and spy and to go on scouts, but not battles or skirmishes ever and this year in which he took any part, he was dismissed in the fall at Fort Plain.

He never received any written discharge from the army nor did any of his company. That he has continued to reside in the county of Herkimer ever since he left the service in the Revolution and that according to his recollection he served three years of active service in said War. That he was born in Stone Arabia in the now county of Montgomery in the year 1764.

That there was record of his age but it is lost and he now has none. That he lived at Mohawk Castle in Herkimer County when he entered the service and that ever since the Revolutionary War and after (Can't read about two dozen lines here.)

The following letter is included in the pension application papers.

May 18, 1937
Mr. Roger F. Williams
Thurmont, New York

Dear Sir:

Reference is made to your letter in which you request the Revolutionary War record of Peter Wooliver, a pensioner of Manheim, Herkimer County, New York.

The data given herein were found in pension claim, W. 19659, based upon service of Peter Wolever in that war.

Peter Wolever (as he signed his name), a son of Henry, was born November 27, 1764 at Stone Arabia, Tryon (later Montgomery) County, New York, the name of his mother is not shown. He lived with his parents at "Mohawk Castle", called later Danube, at the time he entered service in the Revolutionary War.

Peter Wolever enlisted in May 1779 and served at various times until the summer of 1781, amounting in all to at least ten months and twenty-four days, as corporal in Captain Joseph Dygart's company, Colonel Peter Bellinger's regiment of New York Militia; during his service, he was stationed near Fort Mohawk, Fort Dayton and Fort Schuyler, was in the battle of Stone Arabia, was fired upon by the Indians and received a wound in his shoulder, and July 18, 1781 was shot in his right thigh when attacked by the Indians. Peter's oldest brother and brother-in-law were killed at the same time, and his younger brother, John Wolever, was taken prisoner and was carried to Montreal. The names of the other brother and of the brother-in-law are not shown.

Peter Wolever applied February 11, 1833 for pension on account of his service in the Revolutionary War, at which time he resided in Manheim, Herkimer County, New York. His claim was allowed. His name was born Peter Woolever on the pension roll. The soldier died September 13, 1943 in Manheim, New York.

Peter Wolever married July 10, 1785, Catherine, daughter of Jacob Snell; they were married by the Pastor of the Reformed Protestant Dutch Church of German Flats, New York. The names of her parents are not shown.

Catharine Wolever, the soldier's widow, was allowed pension on her application executed December 23, 1843; she was aged then seventy-nine years, and resided in Manheim, New York, where she was living in 1848. Her name was borne on the pension roll as Catharine Wooliver.

The soldier and his wife, Catharine, had six children: Margaret, the oldest, born in the year 1786, was a resident of Manheim, New York in 1845, her name then Margaret, Lepper; Nicholas Wolever, the fifth child, resided in said Manheim in 1847, at which time he gave his age as forty-seven years. No other names of soldier's children were designated.

In 1823, John Woliever, Peter's brother, was a resident of Lenox, Madison County, New York; John's wife, Catharine, also of Lenox, stated then that when Peter was wounded in the Revolutionary War he was brought to her house.

John P. Snell was a resident of Manheim Centre, Herkimer County, New York in 1839; no relationship to the soldier's wife was stated.

In order to obtain the date of last payment of pension, name of person paid, and possibly the date of death of Catharine Wolever, you should address The Comptroller General, General Accounting Office, Records Division, this city and cite the following:

Catharine Wooliver, widow of Peter Woolever.
Certificate #2726
Issued December 30, 1848
Rate $39.59 per annum
Commenced March 4, 1848
Act of February 2, 1848
New York Agency.

Very truly yours,
A. D. Hiller,
Executive Assistant
To the Administrator.

Pension Application, Peter Wormwood (Wormuth)

July 9, 1821. State of New York Montgomery County, town of Johnstown, county and state aforesaid being duly sworn says that he served in the Revolutionary War as a private soldier in Captain Moody's Company Colonel Lambs Regiment of New York, Artillery that he enlisted in said company of the artillery about the month of March in the year 1782 and three years more and that he served faithfully to the end of said term of three years, when he was honorably discharged at Fort Plain in the State of New York which discharge ? and this deponent further says that by m? of his distressed circumstances he needs the assistance of his country for support and that he receives no pension and present from the United States.

Sworn and etc.
Peter Wormwood (his mark)

State of New York, Montgomery County
Mathias Wormwood being duly sworn says that Peter Wormwood, a soldier of the revolution, his brother, that he well remembers that Peter his brother enlisted in the Continental Army (in the revolutionary war), at Palatine near the Mohawk River, sometime after Cornwallace was taken as he believes, that his brother Peter went away to serve the army at West Point as he understood and believes that some considerable time after the said Peter Wormwood came from ? still as a soldier, soldiers at Fort Plain Black House.

Mathias Wormwood (his mark)

I, Peter Wormwood the aforesaid named applicant do in addition to my former declaration say that I was in the engagement against the British forces on about the 22nd day of October 1781 at Johnstown in the County and State aforesaid the American forces were commanded by Colonel Marinus Willet and the British forces were commanded by officers whose names the deponent cannot now state, that in said engagement this deponent received a severe wound in the side when opened to cleanse and cure it exposed to view two of the cracked ribs party the flesh torn.

Peter Wormwood (his mark)

State of New York,
Northern district, Montgomery County
Be it remembered that on the 13th day of June in the term of June in the year of our Lord one thousand eight hundred and twenty three personally appeared in open court in the Court of Common Please at the Court House in Johnstown in the County aforesaid (the said court being a court of record for the county aforesaid having the power of fine and imprisonment proceeding according to the courts of the common law with a jurisdiction unlimited in front of a?t keeping a record of their proceedings Peter Wormwood aged sixty five years resident in the Town of Johstown in the County aforesaid who being first duly sown according to law doth on this oath declare that he served in the Revolutionary War as follows to wit in Captain Moody's company, Colonel Lambs Regiment. New York line that the date of his pension certificate is the first day of May 1809 and is numbered ?? and I do solemnly swear that I was a resident citizen of the named state on the eighteenth day of March in the year of our Lord on thousand eight hundred and eighteen and that I have not since that time by gifts, sale or in any manner disposed of my property or any part thereof with which so be dismissed it as to being myself ----   privilege and act entitled "and act to ….for certain persons engaged -----and service of the United State in the ----Revolutionary War ---on the eighteenth of March 1818 that I have not nor has any person in --- for me any property or services contacts or debt due to me nor have I any income other than what is considered in the schedule here --- consigned and by me subscribed to with real estate --

(Then he lists his assets: one spinning wheel one saw, one kettle one corn saw?, another kettle, etc. The writing is so bad here I can't read it. Farm animals are listed too. Then he said "My family consists of myself and my wife May being about sixty seven years, infirm in health that I am very infirm and wholly unable to support myself and family without the aid of government.)

Peter Wormwood (his mark)

A similar document dated October 14, 1820 states pretty much the same thing and lists the assets.

This letter was included in the Pension Papers.

Anna P. Smith
47 Standart Avenue
Auburn, New York

Dear Madam:
Reference is made to your letter in which you request the Revolutionary War records of Peter and William Wormouth or Warmoot of Stone Arabia, New York.

Revolutionary War data furnished by this office are obtained from claims for pension and bounty land, which have been made to the Untied States, based upon service in that war. A search of the records fails to show such claims on file on account of the Revolutionary War service of William Warmouth, under any spelling of that surname.

The records of Peter Wormwood (Wormuth) which follows was obtained from pension claim W. 22680, based upon his service in the Revolutionary War.

The date and place of birth of this soldier are not given, nor are the names of his parents stated.

Peter Wormwood (Wormuth) enlisted in Stone Arabia (later Palatine) on the Mohawk River, New York, March 5, 1782, served as a private and matross in Captain Noodlie's company, Colonel John Lamb's Regiment of Artillery, until "Peace of 1782". He also served in the militia at various times in Colonels Klock's and Marinus Willett's New York regiments, was in the Battle of Johnstown, there severely wounded in the side.

He was allowed pension on his application executed April 9, 1818, at which time he was living in Johnstown, Montgomery County, New York, and gave his age fifty-seven years, in 1820 he stated that he was sixty-two or sixty-three years of age.

The soldier, Peter Wormwood (Wormuth) married April 19, 1786 in Caughnawaga, New York, Sarah Putman. The date and place of her birth not given, nor names of her parents stated.

The soldier died July 23, 1836. His widow, Sarah, was allowed pension on her application executed January 17, 1843, at which time she was living in Glen, Montgomery County, New York, Aged about eighty-six years. The widow was at one time referred to as Mary, no explanation given as to the use of both names.

Reference was made in 1820 to their daughter, Eva aged seventeen years. There is no further reference to children.

The soldier's brother, Matthias Wormwood, was of Montgomery County, New York in 1818.

John Putman was residing in 1843 in Glen, New York; he stated that he was well acquainted with the widow, but did not give any relationship.
Very truly yours,
A.D. Hliler
Executive assistant
To the Administrator

Pension Application for Thomas Zielley

State of New York
Montgomery County

On the 21st day of September in the year of our Lord One Thousand Eight Hundred and thirty two, personally appeared in open court before the court of Common Pleas in and for the County of Montgomery and State of New York now sitting.

Thomas Zielley a resident of the Town of Ephratah same county and state aforesaid aged sixty eight years five months and fourteen days.

That this applicant declares that he did perform Militia duty as a volunteer in watching and guarding some of the inhabitants at Fort Keyser during the summer season for at least two months in the year 1779 when yet under the age of sixteen and that this applicant further declares that the foregoing, services as mentioned were performed under the command of a Sergeant generally and that "Emmediatly" (Immediately) after he arrived to the age of sixteen he was enrolled in the company of his father who had the Command of the Company of Militia previously and until the memorable battle at Oriskany on the 6th day of August 1777 when Capt John Breadbag had the Command over the same Company who in the same battle received a serious wound after which time 1st Lieut John Zielly the father of this soldier afterwards succeeded to the Command of the said Company belonging to the Regiment Commanded by Col. Jacob Clock's 2nd Battalion.

That this applicant declares that he hath been ordered by his Commd't of the Company to watch and to assist in guarding the families those which had moved into the fort, occasionally alternating his services and duties performed in guarding against the incursions of the incendiaries until Spring 1780 at an average of 2 month service annually.

That this applicant further declares that in the month of May vigt 22d, in the year 1780 when Sir John Johnson at a distance from and at around about Caughnawaga terrorizing the inhabitants with his incendiary crew, merciless tomahawk, scalping, and combustibles to set fire almost to every building, with murdering and taking prisoners, both men and women and children at which time this claimants marching along under the command of Lieut Zielley with his company to Caughnawaga then in pursuit of the enemy in running, Col. Harper when then under the Emmediant Command of Col. John Harper marching to Johnstown Village when they see the enemy marching away from the Hall and across the hall farm into the woods, and afterwards were released by the incendiaries so women and children could return those respective homes but alas but for who found shelter after their arrival at their former places of residence but suffice it to say that the raiding commenced before he arrived to the age of sixteen and continued to the close of the war that from the commencement of his services he has always kept himself in constant readiness well armed and alert in compliance with the orders and directions given by his superior officers or also in conformity to the resolution passed on the 27th day of May 1773.

Whereas it was resolved that the Militia of New York by armed and trained and in constant readiness to act at a moments warning and this claiment declares that he was born at Schoharie on the 7th April in the year 1764.

That emmediently previous to the Revolutionary War his father with the family removed from Schohary to the Town of Palatine, then County of Tryon now County of Montgomery when this claiment resided Emmediately previous, during and since the Revolutionary War with the exception that since last spring this claimant residing in the Town of Ephrath and same county aforesaid and further this applicant saith not----

Sworn to and subscribed this day and year aforesaid, George D. Ferguson, Clerk Signed Thomas Zielley.

American Prisoners of War

Not all the Prisoners of War were taken to Canada, here are those who were kept in part of our state.

From
New York In The Revolution as Colony and State
by James A. Roberts, Comptroller
Compiled by Frederic G. Mather
Second Edition 1898, Two Volumes

Previous to the battle of Long Island, Aug. 27, 1776, very few of the Americans had become Prisoners to the Enemy. One thousand were taken after that Battle; and 700 at Fort Washington, when the British came in full possession of the City of New York and its immediate vicinity. The Presbyterian and Dutch Reformed Churches of that City were the first Prisons for the captive Americans. Then other Churches, the Provoost (later the Hall of RecordsColumbia College and the sugar houses in Liberty and Duane Streets were used for the same purpose. The accommodations being crowded, transport ships were used in Wallaboul Bay on the Brooklyn shore. The worst of the Prison Ships was the "Jersey". Others were:--the "Scorpion", the "Falmouth", the "Good Hope", the "Chatham" and the "Prince of Wales". While the deaths in the Prisons on shore were frequent, the mortality on the Prison Ships was far worse-as many as 15,000 in the latter case. In 1808, the bones of many of the Prisoners were given public burial in

Brooklyn, by the Tammany Society of New York; and, in 1826, a monument was erected to their memory at the Wallabout.

John Beaty, Elias Boudinot, Thomas Franklin, Lewis Pintard and Abraham Skinner were Commissaries of Prisoners; and Thomas Franklin and Garret H. Van Wagenen were Deupty Commissaries. Thomas Linn was director of the Hospital, in Canada. Henry Dodge Commissary of Prisoners' Pay.

American Prisoners were also kept in New Utrecht, Flatbush (the Bergen Homestead), Gravesend, Flatlands and New Lots - all on Long Island. These Prisoners were taken, for the most part, at Fort Washington, Fort Montgomery and Germantown. Col. Samuel B. Webb, of the Connecticut Line, himself a Prisoner, was active in making exchanges. He corresponded, at great length, with Gen. Washington and the Continental Congress on this subjject. Little was done, however, because the British and American authorities could not tgree upon a ratio of exchange. (See Sparks' Life of Washington; and the several volumes of The Public Papers of George Clinton.) Col. John Ely, also of the Connecticut Line, as a Prisoner, ministered to the wants of the Prisoners on Long Island. He was a physician, especially skilled in the treatment of small-pox. His son led a sortie, captured a British officer of equal rank and made all the arrangements for the exchange of Col. Ely. But the latter refused to leave the Prisoners; and he remained with them almost to the end of the War.

Governor Clinton was an active agent in bettering the condition of the Prisoners. He expended as follows:-Dec. 15, 1777, a certain amount to Miss Clopper for three barrels of flour to be delivered to the Prisoners in the General Hospital, in New York City; Nov. 15, 1782, £84 to Captains Ward and Drake for the use of the Prisoners in Canada; Nov. 21,1782, £3.4. to Capt. Harper for the use of the Prisoners returning from their captivity in Canada; Mar. 26, 1783, £3.14.6 for the same purpose; July, 1783, £175 to Nicholas Covenhoven for money advanced by him to the Prisoners on Long Island; September, 1783, £300 to Colonels Allison and McClaughry, and £2000 to Col. Allison, for the same purpose; Apr. 20, 1784, £30 to Thomas Tillotson for the use of the Prisoners; and, November, 1784, £34. to Alexander Harper for the same purpose.

The Governor, Jan. 21, 1783, had raised £25566.17.6 on the credit of the State in this manner:

Any Person upon Long Island who will advance to Colo. William Allison for the Use of himself and the other Officers of this State Prisoners of War the Sum of Five hundred Pounds in specie shall be repaid as soon as conveniently may be; for which the Faith of the State is hereby pledged-Given under my Hand at Kingston this 20th June 1780 Geo. Clinton.

Received 1 September 1780 of Mr. Rem Cowenhoven the Sum of Three Hundred and Eleven Pounds in Gold and Silver, in part of the Within draft.
Wm. Allison Col.
N. Y. Militia.

[Indorsed] Reed. April l3th 1785. from Gerard Bancker Treasr. three hundred and eighty two pounds nineteen Shillings in full for the principal and Interest of this Note. £382 19.
Jno. R Cowenhoven
Son and Heir to Rem Cowenhoven

We the Subscribers, received of Col. William Allison the Sum fixed opposite our respective Names for Money Sent in by his Excellency Genl George Clinton for the Use of the Officers taken up the North River at Forts Montgomery and Clinton. New Utright Long Island.

Novr. 27th. 1777.
Long Island October 23d. 1779.

We the Subscribers do acknowledge to have received of his Excellency George Clinton Esquire Governor of the State of New York the Sums affixed to our several names annexed as witness our hands the day and year above written, recd. by the hands of Col. James Mc Claughry.

We the Subscribers do hereby Severally acknowledge to have received of his Excellency George Clinton Esqr. by the hands of Colonel William Allison the respective Sums annexed to our names it being Money advanced for our uses while Prisoners on Long Island, and paid to us on or about the following dates Viz Augst 8th and Octr. 30th. 1780.

The Prisoners were paid in Depreciation Notes for the time they were in captivity. In July, 1782, Nicholas Covenhoven paid £798,14.9 for the use oi the Officers who were Prisoners on Long Island. Philip Bevier was paid £42.7 for negotiating an exchange of the Prisoners in Canada. Samuel Fraunces was paid £200 " as a gratuity for his kindness in feeding our Prisoners in N. York & for secret services. This was done indiscriminately to the Continental Troops & Militia".

Although the rules for exchanging Prisoners were very strict, yet each side seemed to allow very free access to the other to help its Prisoners. This is seen not only in the sending of money, noted above, but also in the frequent arrival of supplies of flour, clothing &c. Egbert Benson and Col. John Frear sent large quantities of flour into New York City. The paroles, also, were quite liberal:-

I Caleb Laurence an inhabitant of Rye in the County of Westchester in Province of New York and a Capt of Militia in the Province aforesaid do acknowledge myself a Prisoner of War to the King of Great Britain and being permitted to go to the American Lines on parole do pledge my faith and word of honor that I will not do or say anything prejudicial to his Majesty or his subjects and that I will Return and deliver myself up to the commanding officer of his Majesty's out-post, at or near Kings Bridge, or to the Commissary of Prisoners for his Majesty whenever summoned, in witness whereof I have hereunto Set my hand & Seal this 27 May 80.

Witness Caleb Laurence

Thos Devanport

Access to the American Prisoners was made easy and systematic through the Commissary of Prisoners, Lewis Pintard, and his Deputies. His Accounts were kept in a most thorough manner. In one item, alone. Col. Brinton Paine acknowledges the receipt of £81.15.4.

Lieut Jacob Van Tassell to State of New York Dr

To a Short Credit in Settlement of his Accot 17th Septr 1784 of Cash rece'd from Lewis Pintard Comy of Prisoners .... £ 8.10.10

To Cash rece'd of Abraham Skinner Corny of Prisoners & omitted crediting in former Accot 83.17. 9

1786

Cr. £92. 8. 7

Feby 21. By an Omission of One Ration pr day in selling his former Accot 17th Septr 1784 is 866 Rations at 10d........................ 36. I. 8

Due the State of N York................................... £56. 6.11

New York 21st Febry 1786 I have examin'd the above Account & find the Sum of Fifty Six Pounds Six Shillings & Eleven Pence Currency to be due to the State of New York from Lieut Jacob Van Tassell which Sum he is to pay into the Treasury of this State in certificates dated November 1781 which was the date of the certificate which he received out of the Treasure for his pay. Gerard Bancker Esqr., Treasurer.

Peter I. Cortenius, State Audr

For further information as to the splendid services of Lewis Pintard, consult James Grant Wilson's Memorial History of the City of New York, Vol. IV. p. 293.

Pay Office Philad. 23 Nov. 1784.

Sir; Agreeable to your Request of the 13 Inst. to Mr. Pierce, I have enclosed you the Account of Monies etc advanced to the Officers of your State while in Captivity by the several Commissaries of Prisoners: the Returns made to this Office does not in many instances Specify the State to which the Officers belong, by which I apprehend you will receive application from Numbers not included in this List, in this Case you will send me the Names of those applicants and the several charges against them shall be forwarded.

Several Officers have made a Settlement with Mr. Pierce, the Books not being posted I cannot inform you who they are excepting a few which are marked in the outer Column of the Return. In Order to avoid Errors it may be necessary to ask the Officer if his Accounts as Prisoner were ever liquidated by the late Auditors of the Army, by Mr. Pierce or Mr. Milligan the Comptroller of the Treasury, as any Settlements made by them must be final.

It is usual in Settling the Accounts of the Continental Officers to charge them with the Monies and supplies Received in Specie and oppose their Rations to those Monies, and the Old Emissions reed. is opposed to their pay from the time of Captivity to the 1 Aug. 80 & if any balance is due from them in 0. E. (which is generally the case) it is reduced to Specie at the Rate of 75 for 1 and carried to their Debit in the Specie a/c.

It will be necessary for me to know what Officers you settle with and if time will admit you, should be glad of a duplicate of the Account that I may govern myself by it.

I make no doubt thro the course of your business, that a Communication between your Office and this will be found necessary if so you will please to direct your Letters to Jno. Pierce P. M. G.

to my Care, this will avoid Postage. Mr. Pierce is now on his Circuit to the Southward, the business of this Office now rests with Sir Peter T. Curtenius, Esq. Your very Hble Servt. Joseph Howell Junr

Ass. Comm. Accts

The American Prisoners of War, mentioned in the documents, are the following--all of them from the State of New York, unless otherwise designated:--

Aarhart George
Abarr Peter
Abbot James, Ens. (Conn)
Acker Abraham
Acker Jacob
Allen Ethan, Col.
Allison Richard
Allison William, Col.
Andrews Rich., Lt., (N.C.)
Andrews Wm., Lt. (Mass.)
Angavine Gilbert
Antil Edward, Col.
Archart George
Ashfield John
Ashton Joseph, Serjt.
Bancker Nicolas
Banks Jonathan
Banks Samuel, Ens.
Banter Christian
Banter Henry
Barkem William
Barnum Joshua, Capt.
Barnum, Thomas
Bashford William, Serjt.
Baxter John
Baxter Thomas
Beard Robert
Bellinger Christian
Bellinger Fred., Lt. Col.
Bellinger Philip
Belt J. Sprigg, Capt. (Md.)
Benedict Caleb, Ens.
Benedict Elias
Benedict Elisha
Benedict Felix
Bennett Mat., Capt. (Penn.)
Benninger Isaac
Berwick Robert
Bice James
Bingham John
Birdsall Benjamin, Lt. Col.
Black Isaac
Blakeney Gabriel (Conn)
Bleecker John James
Blewer George, Lt. (Penn)
Bliss Theodore, Capt.
BluenJohn, Major
Bogert Gilbert
Bon Joseph
Bost Christian
Bourguin Jean Josei
Bouton Daniel

Bowen Timothy
Bower William, Capt.
Bowne Benjamin, Major
Boyce Thomas, Ensign
Boyd Samuel
Boyer Valentine
Brannon Abraham
Brewer Deliverance
Brewster Henry, Lt.
Brewster Henry, Lt (Penn)
Brier T.
Brinsmade Zach. (Conn)
Brocket Moses
Brooks John
Brown Annanias
Brown Joseph
Bruce, Robert, Serjt.
Bruyn James Lt. Col.
Bryson Samuel, Lt. (Penn)
Buckbee Russel
Buice Abraham
Bulkley Ed., Capt. (Conn)
Bunker W.
Burgess Archer
Burlingham Pardon, Capt.
Burst Jacob I.
Buyker Silas
Buyse William
Caien Barrent
Calder Rudaff
Cannan Matthew
Cantine Moses, Serjt.
Carpenter George
Carpenter Nehemiah, Q.M.
Carpenter Rufus
Carpenter Thomas
Carptenter Wright, Lt.
Carter Daniel
Case J., Capt.
Casselman Peter
Chanpenois Thomas
Charlick Henry
Charpanard Simon
Charpanat Simon
Clapp Henry
Clark Charles, Lt. (Penn)
Clark Daniel
Clark John, jr., Lieut. (Va.)
Clark Martin
Claughry John, Ens.
Clock Conrad
Collins Tyrans

Comb George, Capt.
Concklin Samuel
Cooper Robert
Covenhoven Edward
Coventins Moses
Cox John Luke
Cos, Joseph, Lt. (Penn)
Cozens John, Capt. (Penn.)
Craft William
Craig John, Capt (N.J.)
Craig John, Lt. (Penn.)
Crane Isaac, Adjt.
Crane John, Adjt.
Crane Joseph, Capt.
Crawford Wm., Lt. (Penn.)
Crowley Jeremiah
Croxell Charles, Lt. (Penn)
Cudner John, Lt.
Cudney John, Lt.
Cunningham Henry
Curtis Joel
Davis John
Day Thomas
Dean Joseph
Dearkis John, Serjt.
Delamater Isaac
Deline Benjamin
DeLong John
Denton Isaac
Denton Preston (Conn)
De Utricht (Baron)
Devoe David
Dinus Jacob
Dodge Samuel, Lt,
Donaldson Joseph
Douglass Ephram, Q. M. (Penn)
Drinkwater Wm. (Conn)
Dubois Matthew
Dubois Zachariah, MaJ.
Duguid John, Lt. (Penn)
Dunscomb Edward
Dusenberg Richard
Dutcher Abraham
Dygart Sevrinus
Eastwood John
Eckerson Cornelius, Lt.
Eckler Leonard
Ely John, Col. (Conn.)
Everit Abner, Lt. (Penn)
Faling Jacob
Feeks Robert

Feeling Jacob
Feeling John D.
Feeling John I.
Fenno Ephraim, Capt.
Ferdon Abr., Serjt. Maj.
Ferguson William, Capt.
(Penn)
Ferris Daniel
Field Reuben, Lt (Va)
Finch Einathan
Finley John, Lt. (Penn)
Finley Samuel, Lt. (Penn)
Fisher Bartholomew
Fisher Elijah
Fisher Sam'l, Capt. (Penn)
Floisar Ethnel
Forbush John
Forbush Nicholas
Forre Adam
Foster Jacob, Lt.
Foster Robert, Ens. (Va.)
Franke Lawrence
Franklin James
Fry John, Brig. Maj.
Furman Alexander, Ens.
Furman John, Lt.
Furro Rudolph
Gardinier Harmanus, Lt.
George William, Lt. (Va)
Gerlach Adam
German David
Gettman Frederick, Capt.
Gifford William B., Capt.
(N.J)
Gilchrist Adam, Asst.
Com. Gen.
Gilchrist Geo., Capt. (Va.)
Gilchrist Samuel
Gilcrease Samuel
Giles Aquila, Maj. (Penn)
Gill Erasmus, Lt. 4th Lt.
Dragoons
Gilleylon William, Lt.
Gillikins James, Director
of Ordnance
Gilliland William. Lt.
Glean Oliver, Dy. Q.M. G
Gloss David
Godwin Henry, Capt.
Graham Robert
Grant Jesse, Lt. (Conn)
Gray John (Conn)
Gray Richard, Capt.
Gray William (Conn)
Green Amos, Serjt.
(Conn)
Green John, Ens. (Penn)
Greenman Jeremiah, Ens
(R. I.)
Hains David

Hall Edward, Lt. (Md)
Halstead Benjamin, Lt.
Hambright Henry, Capt.
(Penn.)
Hamman James, Lt. Col.
Harmil Daniel, Maj.
Harning Lienert
Harper Alexander, Capt.
Harris Moses
Harris William
Hartford Ephraim
Hatch William
Hatfield Moses, Maj.
Haviland John, Lt. (N. J)
Hawkins Stephen
Hawkins Z.
Hegens Ebenezer
Helker John
Hellegas Peter
Hellmer John
Hendry Robert
Henry Hugh
Herter Lawrence
Hetfield Moses/ Maj.
Hews James
Higby John
Higby Lewis
Hillegas Peter
Hiller John
Hobby David
Hobby Jonathan
Hogeboom Peter
Hogel Peter
Holland Shelly
Hollister Josiah
Holmer David
Holms Nathaniel
Honeywell Israel, Capt.
Hoogland Jeronimus, Adjt
Hopkins Elisha, Adjt.
(Conn.)
Horton Thomas, Capt.
House George
House Jacob
House Nicholas
Huchens Absolom
Huchings Absolom
Humphrey George
Humphrey James, Capt.
Humphrey William
Humphreys Wm., Serjt.
Humphry James
Humphry William, Serjt.
Hunt Philip
Hunter John, Lt.
Hunter John
Hyle James
Hynard Michael
Irvin James
Irvine James, Brig, Gen

(Penn.)
Israel John
Itig Christian, Serjt.
Jackson Patten, Lt.
Jacobs Abraham
Jamison Daniel, Lt. (Penn)
Jenney Thos., Lt. (Penn.)
Johnson Jno., Adjt.
(Penn.)
Johnson John
Jones James, Lt.
Jump William
Keeler Isaac, Lt.
Keeler Isaac, Ens.
Keeler Isaiah
Kelly John
Kelsey Ebenezer
Kennedy Thomas
Kerby Stephen
Kip Garret, Lt.
Klock Jacob Conrad, Lt.
Knap Joel
Knapp Joseph, Jr.
Knox Abraham
Kring John
Kronkhite James, Capt.
Kronkright John, Capt.
Lamb William
Lamareaux John
Lamberdson Lambert
Lambert Jonathan
Lang Robert, Q. M. Serjt,
Langler James
Lattimore Francis
Lavish John, Ens. (Md)
Laucks George
Laurence Caleb, Capt.
Lawrence Nathaniel, Lt.
(N. C.)
Lawler Conrad
Lawler John
Lay Asa, Lt. (Conn.)
Lay Lee, Capt. (Conn.)
Leggett Abraham, Ens.
Lent Isaac
Lewis John, Serjt.
Lewis Samuel (Conn.)
Lingau James McCubbin,
Lt. (Va.)
Livingston William S., Lt.
Col. Cont'l Army
Lobdell Joseph
Logan Samuel, Maj.
Cont'l Army
Lonas John
Loucks Peter
Lucas William Budd
Luke James
Lumis Adam
Lush Stephen, Maj.

Lyman Geo., Capt. (Conn)
Lyon Gilbert, Capt
Lyon John
Lyon Samuel
McArthur Alexander, Lt.
McChain John
McClaghry James, Lt. Col.
McClaghry James, Capt.
McClaughry John, Ens.
McClellen William
McClue William
McDonald John, Capt, (Penn)
McMullen John
Malloy Thomas
Marbury Luke, Col (Md)
Marlin Daniel. Capt.
Marrener William
Martin Daniel, Capt.
Martin John
Martin Joseph, Lt (Penn)
Martin William, Lt.
Martling Daniel, Capt.
Martling David
Marvin Ephraim, Adjt
Matthews Geo., Col. (Va)
Mayer Jacob, jr.
Maynard Elija B.
Mayo Jonathan (Conn)
Meales Matthew
Menbeth James
Mercer John, Lt (N. J.)
Miller Samuel
Mitchel James
Monross Jesse
Moore Joseph
Moore Roger (Conn)
Morfit Henry, Lt. (Penn)
Morrell Abraham
Morrison Thomas
Moseman Marcus, Capt.
Mosher John
Moss Simeon
Mott Ebenezer, Lt
Mullin William
Munro Joseph
Munson Levi (Conn.)
Murfits Henry, Lt. (Penn)
Murray Peter
Musk Ebenezer
Muxum Adonijah (Conn.)
Myer Henry, Ens.
Neelson Eli
Nelles George
Newcomb James
Newman Joseph
Nichols Guisham
Niles Sands, Ens., (Conn)
Noble Peter (Conn.)
Northrup Abijah

Oakley Isaac
Oakley John
Oakly John, Ens.
Oline Benjamin, Lt.
Oliver Thomas
Olman John
Orendorff Christian, Lt. (Md)
Organ Cornelius
Orsor Jonas, Capt.
Osmand Benajah, Lt. (N. J.)
Oustrander Henry
Owne Joseph, jr.
Pain Brinton, Maj.
Pain Joseph
Palmetier Isaac
Parmerton Abijah
Parsons Abr., Lt. (N. J.)
Patchen Freegift
Patchin Isaac
Patchin Jabez
Patchin Samuel
Paulding John.jr.
Paulding William
Pawling Henry, Lt.
Peifer Joh.
Pellanger B.
Pellinger Frederick
Pendleton Nathaniel, Lt. (Va.)
Pendleton Solomon, Lt.
Pennear William
Penoyer William
Peterson John
Petry Jacob, Ens.
Pettie Abel
Pickard Bartholomew
Piper Andrew
Polk John
Poor David, Lt. (Mass.)
Porter Jonathan, Lt.
Potten James
Poultson John, Capt. (Va)
Pownal Thomas, Lt.
Poyton James
Preston Wm., Lt. (Penn.)
Purdy Solomon, jr., serjt.
Putnam David
Putnam David, Corp.
Quick John
Ramsay Nathaniel Lt. Col. (Md.)
Rankins James, Jr,
Raqua Isaac, Adjt.
Raqua Isaac, Lt.
Raymond Sands, Serjt.
Read Thomas, Ens.
Reder T.
Reed Thos., Ens. (Penn.)

Renex Andrew
Requa Isaac, Adjt.
Requa Isaac, Lt.
Requaw Daniel
Requaw Gabriel, Capt.
Requaw Isaac, Adjt.
Requaw James, Jr.
Resequie John
Retong William
Revenshon John Peter
Revere Cornelius
Reverston John Peter
Reynold William
Reynolds Nathaniel, Lt.
Rickard Jacob
Rigel Frederick
Riggs Daniel
Riley John, Lt. (Conn.)
Riverson John Peter
Robertson John, or Wm., Adjt. (Va.)
Rogerts William, Lt. (Va.)
Roosa Cornelius
Roose James
Rose James
Rouse Thomas, Ens. (Md.)
Ruamay John
Rumsey Asa, Fifer
Rumsey David
Rumsnider Henry
Rundell Richard
Runnels William
Rutherford Samuel, Ens. (Penn.)
Sackett Richard, Capt.
Sackett Thomas H., Lt. (Md.)
Sammons Fred'k, Serjt.
Sample Robert, Capt. (Penn.)
Savage Joseph
Shefer Adam
Schomaker John
Shomaker Thomas
Shoomaker Henry
Schot Joseph
Schulds Hendrick
Schults Johannis
Schulds William
Schumaker John
Schuyler David
Schuyler Jacob
Schuyler Nicholas
Scott Joseph
Scott William
Sears Elnatham, Corp.
See David
See James
Seeley Isaac, Capt. (Penn.)

Sharender Richard
Sharp Peter
Sharp Thomas
Sherer James
Sheridan Richard
Sherman Peter
Sherwood Job
Sherwood Newcom
Sherwood Seth, Capt.
Sherwood Stephen, Ens.
Shew Godfrey
Shew Jacob
Shew John
Shew Stephen
Shireman George, Corp.
Sifer Jacob
Siffer John, Sr.
Siffer John
Sitz Peter, Ens.
Skiget Richard, Serjt.
Slott Cornelius, Serjt.
Slutt William
Smith Isaac
Smith James, Lt. (Penn.)
Smith Johannes
Smith John, Qr. Mr. Serjt.
Smith John, Lt.
Smith Josiah, Lt. (Conn.)
Smith Richard
Snead Charles, Lt. (Va.)
Snead, Smith, Capt. (Va.)
Sniffen James
Sniffen Reuben
Spankneble John
Sparks Pearl
Staring George
Staring Henrich
Staring Henry
Staring Jacob
Stark Nathan
Starring Jacob
Stayner Roger, Capt.
(Penn.)
Stenson William
Steward Stephen
Steyments Casper

Sticklen John
Stinson William
Storm Abraham
Stotesbury John. Capt.
(Penn.)
Stuart Charles (Conn.)
Swartwout Cornelius,
Capt. Lt.
Swartwout Henry, Ens.
Swope Michael, Col
(Penn.)
Tanner Jacob, Serjt.
Taylor Elijah
Taylor Henry
Taylor Samuel
Teller James, Capt.
Terbush Isaac
Terwilliger Harmanus,
Serjt.
Thomas Edward, Adjt.
Thomas Thomas, Col.
Thompson Andrew, Ens.
Thompson James
Thwait Thos., Capt. (Va.)
Van Brunt Leonard, Dy.
Qr. Mr. Gen.
Van Buren Leonard
Van dercok Benjamin
Van Dyke Abraham, Capt.
Van Eps Evert
Van Nosdall John, Corp.
Van Osterand William
Van Slyke Garret
Van Slyke Jacobus
Van Tassel Abraham
Van Tassel Cornelius, Lt.
Van Tassel John
Van Tessel David
Van Tellse Isaac, Serjt.
Van Tellel Jacob, Lt.
Van Tessel Peter
Van Wagenen G. Surg.
Van Wagenen Garret H.,
Lt.
Vermelya Jacob M.
Virgil Abijah

Vols Conrad
Vorhas Samuel
Vroman Ephraim, Lt.
Vrooman Walter, Capt.
Walker Robt. Lt. (Mass.)
Wardell Eliakim
Warman Thos., Lut. (Va.)
Watrous Edward A.
Webb Sysumet
Weeks James
Wells Levi, Col. (Conn.)
Wells Michael, Serjt.
Wentworth James, Lt.
(Penn.)
Wescot Annanias
West Ebenezer, Adjt.
(Conn.)
White Epenetus
Whiting Samuel, Lt.
Whitney James
Williams Daniel, Capt.
Williams Gilbert
Willis John, Capt. (Va.)
Willson Andrew
Wilson Andrew
Wilson Isaac
Winne Kelian
Winter Thomas
Witherall William
Woleben Nicholas
Wood Enoch
Wood James
Wood John, Capt.
Woodson Robert, Lt (Va.)
Wool Ellis
Wood Robert
Woolver John
Worden George
Worden Voluntine
Wright William, Lt.
Young Joseph
Youngs Joseph
Zaling John
Zeely John, Lt.
Zimmer Peter

Notes on the pension applications from James Morrison:

The men who served nine months or enlisted for a year or two were with the New York Line or New York Levies. The Militia were called only as needed and were to be ready at a moment's notice with three days provisions, a musket and ammunition. This is why so many in their pension application make a point of saying they held themselves ready at a moment's notice, or minutes notice, and they were called minute men.

Colored men you see reference to were the men who were in charge of the regiment's colors.

Those who were "degranged" were officers who were put down in rank because at times there was an over abundance of officers, indeed at one point there were more officers than soldiers. In this case, deranged doesn't mean mentally ill.

Key to pension numbers. The starting letters mean:

Number code: S means it is the pension of a survivor.

Number code: W means it is an application from a widow.

Number code: R means the pension was rejected.

**Life in The Valley
after The War**

After The War

After the war, real peace was slow in coming to New York State and life did not resume a normal stance for many years. There were tremendous issues from the war to settle; the devastation repayments, the huge public debt the war created, the dissolution of the army and the consequent payments due the soldiers, the rights of the states versus the federal government and establishing a stronger federal government, the border of New York State and Vermont, the protection of our borders as the British withdrew, the Indians and their claims, the Loyalists claims and the naval protection of our waters. To help stabilize the financial situation, France loaned the United States the sum of $1,200,000.

Part of the problem was the weak Confederation; laws were passed easily enough, but the government was unable to finance the laws they passed. For instance, they offered half pay to officers who would serve to the end of the war. Compensation was owed for payment of rations and, clothing and back pay in addition. Understandably the men were upset at the lack of payments.

The worry about invasion or raids from Canada remained very much on everyone's minds. The Indians wanted their lands returned to them and so did the Loyalists. It seemed the new country was besieged with some overwhelming problems. Before long a strong federal government was in place and one by one the problems were resolved. It just took some time to work them out.

Washington's Mohawk Valley Tour

In the spring of 1783, an order for the cessation of hostilities between Great Britain and the United States officially ended the war, but an army organization was kept up until fall. Because of the part the area played in the war, General Washington as Commander In Chief wanted to view the field where such a determining factor was played.

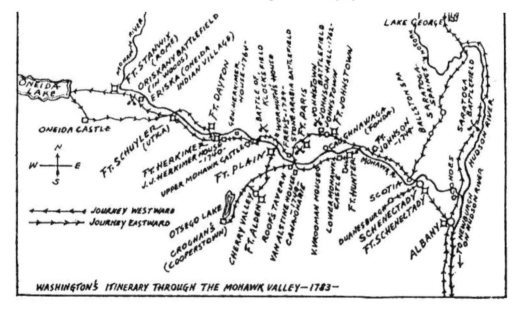

WASHINGTON'S ITINERARY THROUGH THE MOHAWK VALLEY – 1783 –

In contemplation of his tour of observation in central New York, Gen. Washington wrote to Gen. Philip Schuyler, from his Newburgh headquarters, July 15, 1783, as follows: "Dear Sir:-I have always entertained a great desire to see the northern part of this State, before I returned Southward. The present irksome interval, while we are waiting for the definite treaty, affords an opportunity of gratifying this inclination. I have therefore concerted with Geo. Clinton to make a tour to reconnoiter those places, where the most remarkable posts were established, and the ground which became famous by being the theatre of action in 1777. On our return from thence, we propose to pass across the Mohawk River, in order to have a view of that tract of country, which is so much celebrated for the fertility of its soil and the beauty of its situation. We shall set out by water on Friday the 18th, if nothing shall intervene to prevent our journey. "Mr. Dimler, assistant quartermaster-general, who will have the honor of delivering this letter, precedes us to make arrangements, and particularly to have some light boats provided and transported to Lake George, that we may not be delayed upon our arrival there.

"I pray you, my dear sir, to be so good as to advise Mr. Dimler in what manner to proceed in this business, to excuse the trouble I am about to give you, and to be persuaded that your kind information and discretion to the bearer will greatly increase the obligations with which I have the honor to be, etc." Sparks Life, 8, 425.

On July 16, Washington wrote the President of Congress as to his intended trip. He returned to his headquarters at Newburgh, August 5, 1783, and on the following day, August 6, wrote to the Congressional President a brief record of his journey. After speaking of his return, which was by water from Albany to Newburgh, he says:

"My tour, having been extended as far northward as Crown Point, and westward to Fort Schuyler [Stanwix] and its district, and my movements having been pretty rapid, my horses, which are not yet arrived, will be so much fatigued that they will need some days to recover, etc."

In another letter, of the same date, he refers further to his tour in these words: *"I was the more particularly induced by two considerations to make the tour, which in my letter of the 16th ultimo, I informed Congress I had in contemplation, and from which I returned last evening. The one was the inclination to see the northern and western posts of the State, with those places which have been the theatre of important military transactions; the other a desire to facilitate, as far as in my power, the operations which will be necessary for occupying the posts which are ceded by the treaty of peace, as soon as they shall be evacuated by the British troops."*

He had his eye upon Detroit as a point to be looked after and wanted some of the well off citizens of that place to preserve the fortifications and buildings there "until such time as a garrison could be sent with provisions and stores sufficient to take and hold possession of them. The propriety of this measure has appeared in a more favorable point of light, since I have been up the Mohawk river, and taken a view of the situation of things in that quarter.

"I engaged at Fort Rensselaer [Fort Plain] a gentleman whose name is Cassaty, formerly a resident of Detroit and who is well recommended, to proceed without loss of time, find out the disposition of the inhabitants and make every previous inquiry which might be necessary for the information of the Baron on his arrival, that he should be able to make such final arrangements, as the circumstances might appear to justify."

"This seemed to be the best alternative on failure of furnishing a garrison of our troops, which, for many reasons, would be infinitely the most eligible mode, if the season and your means would possibly admit. I have at the same time endeavored to take the best preparatory steps in my power for supplying the garrisons on the western waters by the provision contract. I can only form my magazine at Fort Herkimer on the German Flats, which is 32 miles by land and almost 50 by water from the carrying place between the Mohawk river and Wood creek. The route by the former is impracticable, in its present state, for carriages and the other extremely difficult for bateaux, as the river is much obstructed with fallen and floating trees, from the long disuse of the navigation. That nothing, however, which depends upon me might be left undone, I have directed 10 months provisions for 500 men to be laid up at Fort Herkimer, and have ordered Col. Willett, an active officer commanding the troops of the state [evidently meaning state troops in this locality], *to repair the roads, remove the obstructions in the river, and, as far as can be effected by the labors of the soldiers, build houses for the reception of the provisions and stores at the carrying place [Fort Schuyler] in order that the whole may be in perfect readiness to move forward, so soon as the arrangement shall be made with Gen. Haldemand [Governor General of Canada.]"*

October 12, 1783, Washington wrote to the Chevalier Chastelleux, as follows: *"I have lately made a tour through the Lakes George and Champlain as far as Crown Point. Thence returning to Schenectady, I proceeded up the Mohawk River to Fort Schuyler and crossed over to Wood creek, which empties into the Oneida lake, and affords the water communication with Ontario."*

"I then traversed the country to the eastern branch of the Susquehanna, and viewed the Lake Otsego, and the portage between that lake and the Mohawk River at Canajoharie. Prompted by these actual observations, I could not help taking a more extensive view of the vast inland navigation of these United States, from maps and the information of others, and could not but be struck by the immense extent and importance of it, and with the goodness of Providence, which

has dealt its favors to us with so profuse a hand. Would to God we may have wisdom enough to improve them."

"I shall not rest contented till I have explored the western country, and traversed those lines or a great portion of them, which have given bounds to a new empire. But when it may, if it ever shall happen, I dare not say, as my first attention must be given to the deranged situation of my private concerns, which are not a little injured by almost nine years absence and a total disregard of them, etc., etc."

He is supposed to have spent a night in the Volkert Vrooman house at Randall, near Currytown, and also at Canajoharie. "There is, however, no real proof of these or other visits at Mohawk Valley homes," Devereux pointed out.

Here is a brief description of Col. Clyde's life and service.

Col. Samuel Clyde, then in command at Fort Plain, was born in Windham, Rockingham County. New Hampshire, April 11, 1732, his mother's name being Esther Rankin. He worked on his father's farm until 20, when he went to Cape Breton and labored as a ship carpenter, from whence he went to Halifax and worked on a dock for the English navy. In 1757 he came to New Hampshire and raised a company of batteaux men and rangers, of which he was appointed captain, by Gen. James Abercromby, said company being under Lieut. Col. John Bradstreet. This commission was dated at Albany, May 25, 1768. He marched his company to Albany and to Lake George where he fought in the battle of Ticonderoga and the British were defeated. Clyde was afterward at the capture of Fort Frontenac, and returning from the campaign to Schenectady in 1761, he married Catherine Wasson, a niece of Matthew Thornton, a signer of the Declaration of Independence. Judge Hammond, who knew Mrs. Clyde, wrote of her in 1852 as follows: *"Mrs. Clyde was a woman of uncommon talents, both natural and acquired, and of great fortitude. She read much and kept up with the literature of the day. Her style in conversing was peculiarly elegant, and at the same time easy and unaffecting. Her manner was dignified and attractive. Her conversation with young men during the Revolutionary War, tended greatly to raise their drooping- spirits, and confirm their resolution to stand by their country to the last."* Not a few noble women of the frontiers thus made their influence felt in the hour of need.

In 1762 Clyde settled at Cherry Valley and while there he was employed by Sir William Johnson to build the church for the use of the Indians at the upper Mohawk castle in the present town of Danube. At the beginning of the country's trouble with England, a company of volunteers was raised in Cherry Valley and New Town Martin for home protection, of which Samuel Clyde was commissioned its captain by the 40 men he was to command. John Campbell, jr., was chosen lieutenant and James Cannon ensign. Among the names of the volunteers voting for these officers appears that of James Campbell, afterwards colonel. Capt. Clyde's commission was dated July 13, 1775. On Oct. 28, 1775 the state provincial congress commissioned him as a captain and adjutant of the first (Canajoharie) regiment of Tryon County Militia. Sept. 5, 1776, he was commissioned second major of the first (Canajoharie) regiment commanded by Col. Cox.

After the Battle of Oriskany and death of Gen. Herkimer, many of the officers of the brigade wanted Major Clyde to consent to accept the office of Brigadier-General, whose appointment they would solicit. This he would not do, as other officers in the brigade outranked him and he would not countenance an act that would originate jealousies, however well merited the honors might be. It has surprised the student of the Revolutionary War that Gen. Herkimer's position remained unfilled during the war. That the eye of the army was fixed upon Major Clyde for this honorable promotion is not surprising when we come to know that of all men in that bloody ravine, no one better knew his duty or acquitted himself more valiantly than he. He was in the thickest of the fight, and in a hand to hand encounter was knocked down by an enemy with the breech of a gun, while in another he shot an officer whose musket he brought from the field to become an heirloom in his family. Besides Gen. Herkimer slain, and Brigade Inspector Major John Frey a prisoner, he is believed to have been the only man at Oriskany who ranked as high as a captain in the French war, which doubtless had something to do with the confidence reposed in him.

After Cherry Valley was destroyed in 1778, Col. Clyde moved with his family to the neighborhood of the Mohawk where he lived six or seven years, at least part of the time in the Van Alstine house in the present village of Canajoharie.

June 25, 1778, Major Clyde was appointed Lieutenant-Colonel of the Canajoharie Regiment, James Campbell then being colonel. His commission as such passed the secretary's office with the signature of Gov. George Clinton, March 17, 1781. That Clyde was acting colonel of this regiment long before the date of his commission as lieutenant-colonel, there is positive evidence. The acting colonels of the Tryon County Militia in May, 1780, so recognized by the government at Albany, were Cols. Klock, Visscher, Clyde and Bellinger. Col. Clyde seems to have been on duty every summer in the bounds of his regiment until the close of the war. As colonel of the Canajoharie district regiment, he was naturally on duty at its principal fortification of Fort Plain, during Washington's visit in 1783. On the organization of the state government in 1777, he was a member of the legislature. March 8, 1785, true to Washington's pertinent suggestion at Fort Plain, he was commissioned as Sheriff of Montgomery County by Gov. Clinton, which office he discharged with conscientious fidelity. It is said he frequently swam his horse across the Mohawk at flood tide at Canajoharie in order to attend court at Johnstown.

Simms says: *"After the destruction, In 1778, of Cherry Valley, Col. Campbell made his home at Niskayuna and is not remembered to have taken any part in military affairs [in this vicinity] after that date."* It is doubtless true that, although he held a lieutenant-colonel's commission, Samuel Clyde was recognized by the Albany military authorities and the Tryon County Militia as Colonel of the Canajoharie Regiment, which Clyde says was "the best regiment of militia in the county." Col. Clyde was the leading figure in militia affairs in the district of Canajoharie during the years 1779, 1780, 1781, 1782 and 1783. He died in Cooperstown Nov. 30, 1790, aged 68 years.

On reaching Canajoharie, August 1, 1783, Washington and his company were received by Col. Clyde, who had ridden down from Fort Plain in the morning to receive the commander's party on its return from Otsego Lake. It is said, Washington and his party were the guests of Col. and Mrs. Clyde at dinner on August 1, 1783 at the Van Alstine House. Part or all of the distinguished party probably returned to spend the night at Fort Plain, where there were accommodations.

Undoubtedly crowds of valley people gathered at points where Washington stopped on his trip. A considerable assemblage of patriots must have been present at Fort Plain on this eventful long ago midsummer day. There had been no severe raids in the Canajoharie and Palatine districts in two years. The much tried people were rebuilding their homes, those who had removed to safer localities were returning to their abandoned farms, and, with the assurance of peace, new settlers were already coming in. Mr. S. L. Frey gives the following list of names of persons who probably accompanied General Washington into the Mohawk Valley in 1783: Gov. George Clinton, Gen. Hand, Mr. Dimler (Assistant Quartermaster), Col. David Humphries, Hodijah Baylies, Wm. S. Smith, Jonathan Trumbull jr., Tench Tilghman, Richard Varick (recording secretary), Benjamin Walker, Richard K. Mead, David Cobb, and many officers of the New York line.

Jeptha Simms in Frontiersman of New York 1883, published the following account of Washington's visit to Fort Plain, during his trip through this section:

"The reader will observe by Washington's correspondence that he made the northern trip by water to Crown Point, but from Schenectady to Fort Stanwix [Schuyler], or rather its site, on horseback. The tour of inspection, as shadowed in his letters, is devoid of all incident, and whether or not he halted at Fort Plain on his way up is uncertain; but as he speaks last of going to Otsego lake, it is presumed he made no halt at the river forts going up, nor is there any account of his visiting Johnstown in his tour, but it is reasonable to conclude that he did. He did not mention Fort Plain, but it is well known that he was there, giving it another name [Fort Rensselaer]. Arriving in this vicinity [on July 30, 1783], said the late Cornelius Mabie, who was thus informed by his mother, he tarried over night with Peter Wormuth, in Palatine on the late Reuben Lipe farm, the former having had an only son killed, as elsewhere shown, near Cherry Valley. It was no doubt known to many that he had passed up the valley, who were on the quivive to see him on his return, and good tradition says that, in the morning, many people had assembled at Wormuth's to see world's model man, and to satisfy their curiosity, he walked back and forth in front of the house, which fronted toward the river. This old stone dwelling in ruins, was totally demolished about the year 1865."

"We have seen that Washington found Col. Willett in command at Fort Herkimer [then together with Fort Dayton, the most advanced frontier posts in the state], at which time Col. Clyde was in command of Fort Plain. Just how many attended his Excellency through the Mohawk valley, is not satisfactorily known. His correspondence only names Gov. George Clinton. Campbell in his Annals of Tryon County 1831, says he was accompanied by Gov. Clinton, Gen. Hand and many other officers of the New York line. The officers making the escort were no doubt attended by their aids and servants. Whether any other officer remained with Washington at Wormuth's over night is unknown. It is presumed, however, the house being small and the fort only a mile off, that his attendants all went thither, crossing at Walrath's Ferry, opposite the fort, some of whom returned in the morning to escort the Commander-in-Chief over the river. [July 31, 1783]

A pretty incident awaited the arrival on his eminence near the fort. Beside the road Rev. Mrs. Gros had paraded a bevy of small boys to make their obeisance (her nephew, Lawrence Gros, from whom this fact was derived, being one of the number). At a signal, they took off and swung their hats, huzzaed a welcome and made their best bow to Washington, when the illustrious guest gracefully lifted his chapeau and returned their respectful salutation with a cheerful 'Good morning, boys!' Immediately after, he rode up to the fort where he received a military salute from the garrison.

"I suppose Washington to have been welcomed within the large blockhouse, and on introducing the guest to its commandant, Gov. Clinton took occasion to say to him; 'Gen. Washington, this is Col. Clyde, a true Whig and a brave officer who has made great sacrifices for his country.' The General answered warmly, 'Then, sir, you should remember him in your appointments.' From this hint, Gov. Clinton afterward appointed him Sheriff of Montgomery County. Gen. Washington dined with Col. Clyde, after which, escorted by Maj. Thornton, they proceeded to Cherry Valley, where they became the guests over night, of Col. Campbell, who had returned not long before and erected a log house. Burnt out as the Campbells had been, their accommodations were limited for so many people, but they were all soldiers and had often been on short allowance of 'bed and board' and could rough it if necessary. Besides, it is possible other families had returned to discover their hospitality for the night. They found themselves very agreeably entertained, however. Mrs. Campbell and her children had been prisoners in Canada. In the morning, Gov. Clinton, seeing several of her boys, told Mrs. Campbell, 'They would make good soldiers in time.' She replied she 'hoped their services would never be thus needed.' Said Washington, 'I hope so too, madam, for I have seen enough of war.' One of those boys, the late Judge James S. Campbell, was captured so young and kept so long among the Indians that he could only speak their language when exchanged. After breakfast the party were early in the saddle to visit the outlet of Otsego lake, and see where Gen. James Clinton dammed the lake, just above its outlet, to float his boats down the Susquehanna, to join in Sullivan's expedition. The party returned the same evening to Fort Plain, via. the portage road opened by Clinton to Springfield from Canajoharie, and the next day, as believed, they dropped down the valley."

"Washington," according to historian Leslie W. Devereux in a presentation dated March 1, 1932, *"appears to have had in mind the purchase of land in the Mohawk Valley."* In a personal letter to Gov. George Clinton, Washington stated: *"'I am sorry we have been disappointed in our expectancy of buying the mineral spring at Saratoga, and the purchase of that part of the Oeriskeney (Oriskany) Tract on which Fort Schuyler stands.'"*

"General Philip Schuyler seems to have had similar views regarding the beauty and fertility of the Mohawk Valley when he purchased the site of Old Fort Schuyler in 1772," according to Devereux.

On July 18, 1783, Washington left his Newburg headquarters and traveled northward by sloop to begin his 750 mile journey by land and water to visit the frontier of New York State.

There is little descriptive material available regarding Washington's 19 day trip through New York State to inspect the fortifications and battle scenes of the Revolution. It would be interesting to know the exact route he followed and where he stopped on the way.

The Cassaty whom Washington "engaged at Fort Rensselaer" as his emissary to Detroit was Colonel Thomas Cassaty. He married Nancy, a daughter of Peter Wormuth and a sister of Lieut. Matthew Wormuth, who was shot by Brant near Cherry Valley in 1778. Cassaty was living near or at his father-in-law's when Washington stopped there (in Palatine near Fort Plain) during his valley tour of 1783. This probably readily led to his engagement in the service mentioned. Colonel Cassaty as a boy and young man was stationed at the British post of Detroit, where his father, James Cassaty, was a captain in the English service. At the outbreak of the Revolution the two Cassatys, both American born, sided with the colonists. The commandant of Detroit denounced Capt. James Cassaty and in the altercation young Thomas Cassaty, then a youth of seventeen, shot down the British officer. He then fled into the Michigan woods and escaped. He lived with the Indians and there is one report, which says he was the father of the noted chief, Tecumseh. Toward the end of the war he appeared in the Mohawk valley. Colonel Cassaty died at Oriskany Falls, Oneida county, 1831, aged about 80 years, leaving two sons and five daughters. After the Detroit affray, Capt. James Cassaty was confined in a Canadian dungeon for three years.

It will be noted that Washington speaks of Fort Plain as "Fort Rensselaer." This is the name it bore in the last four years of the Revolution, being named for the Gen. Van Rensselaer, whose conduct was so dubious when there at the operations of 1780, ending at Klock's Field. As previously shown, at the court martial of Gen. Van Rensselaer in Albany for dereliction in the campaign of 1780, witnesses referred constantly to "Fort Rensselaer or Fort Plain" or vice versa.

On General Washington's journey, he made a stop at Fort Plain, on the south side of the river. Some accounts say that on that occasion, he empowered Col. Marinus Willett to organize Fort Herkimer as the western base of supplies for the American posts as far west as Detroit. He also appointed Col. Thomas Cassaty to go to Detroit and take command of that important point. Cassaty set out but, at the British post of Fort Oswego, he was arrested and kept in jail for several years. During the Revolution, Cassaty had shot the British commandant at Detroit, in a fight between the redcoat and Cassaty's father, and it was probably for this offense that the English commandant at Oswego held Cassaty. Col. Cassaty had married a daughter of Peter Wormuth and he was probably living at the Wormuth house at the time of Gen. Washington's visit.

General Washington, stopped at the home of Peter Wormuth on July 30, 1783. News that he would be there must have spread through the middle Mohawk Valley as a large crowd of the neighborhood people gathered there to see the general of the American Army. After his arrival, Washington left the house and strolled about it to satisfy the curiosity of the crowd. He also stopped and chatted with several people after which he had supper and spent the night there. The women of the Wormuth house served the General a large and satisfactory supper according to the late Mrs. William Wagner, Fort Plain, born a Wormuth and conversant with family history. On the following day, July 31, 1783, after breakfast at the Wormuth house, General Washington visited Fort Plain, where Simms says he was probably received with full military honors.

The General and his party had dinner there as guests of Colonel Samuel Clyde, commandant, Colonel Willett, who Commanded all New York State troops north of the Highlands, made his headquarters at Fort Plain but he was then on duty at Fort Herkimer, as previously stated. An incident occurred as Washington rode up the hill to the fort. Mrs. Gros, the wife of the Dominie, Johan Daniel Gros, paraded a group of small schoolboys along the road. As the General approached, they swung their hats and gave a loud hurrah and then made their best bow. Washington raised his hat and returned their salutation with a cheerful *"Good morning, boys."* Lawrence Gros, who built the original section of the Dunn residence on Willett Street, Fort Plain, was one of the schoolboys and he told of the incident to Jeptha R. Simms, the historian.

Peter Wormuth was a Palatiner. There is no known date of the erection of the house but it is of the type of the earliest construction of the small stone houses built by the Palatines after they came into our Middle Mohawk Valley about 1722 and it probably dated from about 1725 or 1730. Other stone houses like Fort Ehle, Fort Frey and Fort Klock were all built close to the King's Highway as was the Wormuth house. One reason the Wormuth house was finally destroyed was probably because of this location, as it was some distance from the Mohawk Turnpike, now Route 5, which was built on or before 1800. The railroad tracks generally follow the path the Mohawk Turnpike took. The location of the Wormuth house was south of the present day Longhorn Trucking location. Fort Frey, Fort Ehle and Fort Klock were close enough to Route five to have an easy outlet.

Besides Washington's stay at this local home, the Wormuth house has other historical significance. In May 1778, Chief Joseph Brant, at the head of a raiding party of the Indians, attacked and burned the little settlement of Springfield at the head of Otsego Lake. Brant then moved on to the little village of Cherry Valley with the idea of destroying it. It is reported that from a distant hill, he saw a large group of boys drilling in front of Fort Alden. Thinking it too heavily garrisoned for an attack, he moved his war party to the deep glen beyond Judd's Falls, thinking he might capture some "rebels" passing by.

On the morning of that day, Lieut. Matthew Wormuth, with a companion named Sitts, had ridden from Fort Plain to Cherry Valley with the message that valley militia would come up next day to aid the Cherry Valley post, as Brant was known to be in the neighborhood. Wormuth and Sitts were riding back in the evening over the Fort Plain road in the glen, where Brant had deployed his war party in an ambush in the dense forest growth. The Indians fired on the horsemen, mortally wounding Wormuth and wounding and capturing Sitts. Wormuth was an officer in Col. Klock's Palatine regiment. Klock and some troops came up from Fort Plain the next day but all they could do was to take Wormuth's body back to Fort Plain and from there across the river to his father's home in the Palatine district. Lieut. Wormuth was a strapping and handsome young soldier, who was universally popular among the valley folks and there was general sorrow over his death. It was indeed a sad day in the Wormuth house, when the body of Peter Wormuth's only son was brought back to the doorstep of his home. One of the most stricken was the Lieutenant's young wife, Gertrude Herkimer. Brant drew off his Indians but returned with Walter Butler in November and perpetrated the Cherry valley massacre.

Dr. Hough published an account of the Klock's Field campaign and the subsequent court martial of Gen. Van Rensselaer, showing that the latter officer writing from Fort Plain, a name which had been established for years, dated his papers at "Fort Rensselaer;" anxious, as it would seem, to have this principal fort take his own name.

It is believed that never before that time had it ever been called by any other name than Fort Plain. About three years later General Washington was here and dated his correspondence from "Fort Rensselaer," and others probably did so, unaware that the name of the fort had been changed.

The following document, from the papers of the late William H. Seeber, shows how the vanity of the inefficient soldier had temporarily affected the name Fort Plain:

By virtue of the appointment of his Excellency, George Clinton, Esq., Governor of the State of New York, etc., etc.

We do hereby, In pursuance of an act entitled an act to amend an act, entitled an act to accommodate the inhabitants of the frontier, with habitations and other purposes therein mentioned, passed the 22d of March, 1781, Grant unto William Seeber, Peter Adams, George Garlock and Henry Smith, license and liberty to cut and remove wood or timber from the lands of John Laile (or Lail), George Kraus, John Fatterle, John Plaikert, Wellem (William) Fenck, George Ekar, John Walrath and Henry Walrath, lying contiguous to Fort Plain, being a place of defense, for fuel, fencing and timber for the use of the first above mentioned persons.
Given under our hands at Canajoharie, this 8th day of November, 1782.
Christian Nellis,
M. Willett,
Commissioners.

This instrument was drawn up in the handwriting of Squire Nellis and taken to Col. Willett to sign. In the handwriting of the latter and with the ink of his signature, Willett crossed off the word "Plain" and interlined the name "Rensselaer." Simms says: *"It seems surprising that Col. Willett, who so disapproved of changing the name of Fort Stanwix, should have connived at changing the name of Fort Plain; and it can only be accounted for by presuming that he was thereby courting the influence of wealth and position."*

The foregoing quotation does not coincide with Willett's sturdy character, and it seems entirely probable that Van Rensselaer had succeeded in having his name adopted, at least for the time, as the official designation of Fort Plain.

The foregoing chapter is taken entirely from Simms's "Frontiersmen of New York," with some few additions.

S. L. Frey says, in his interesting
paper on "Fort Rensselaer," (published
in the Mohawk Valley Register, March
6, 1912):

In 1786, Capt. B. Hudson was in command of the place, taking care of the stores and other government property. As this is the last time that 'Fort Rensselaer' is mentioned as far as I can find, I give a copy of an old receipt:

Fort Rancelair, Aug. 22d, 1786.
State of New York, Dr.
To John Lipe, Senior.

For Timber Building the Blockhouse, for fire wood, Fancing & Possession of the Place by the Troops of the United States Under the Command of Colonel Willet one hundred & fifty Pounds, being the amount of my Damage.
(His Mark) John Lipe.

Witness Present
B. Hudson.

From this it will be seen that Johannes Lipe had not been paid for his timber, used in the blockhouse six years before. Following is a note by Rufus Grider, of Canajoharie: Copy of a paper found and obtained on the Lipe Farm, where Fort Plain and Fort Rensselear was located. The present owners are the descendants of the Lipe who owned it during and after the Revolution; the ownership has not gone out of the family.

R. A. Grider.

June 17, 1894,

Mr. Frey continues: *"We thus have a continuous mention of 'Fort Renssalear,' as another name for Fort Plain, from Sept. 4, 1780, to Aug. 22, 1786. It would be well if the old Revolutionary families in the vicinity would examine any paper they may have relating to that period; possibly we might find that 'Fort Renssalear' is mentioned after 1786."*

Thus we are able to trace the history of the Fort Plain fortifications through a period of ten years of important service. Although the fort and blockhouse probably stood for some years after 1786, reference to Fort Plain, after that date, implies the Sand Hill settlement (which took its name from the fort) and the later village which thus became known during the construction of the Erie canal. The name has thus been in existence for a period of almost 140 years. How long Fort Plain or Fort Rensselaer continued to exist as an army post after 1786 is not now known. During the war time, Fort Plain generally housed from 300 to 400 American troops.

The accounts to follow deal with western Montgomery County and with the settlement adjacent to Fort Plain, known as Sand Hill and Fort Plain and a continuation of the record of life and events, in the old Canajoharie and Palatine districts, until about 1825, when the old settlement ceased to be important and the new canal town which sprang up adopted the honored name of Fort Plain. For convenience the end of the second series of sketches is put at 1838, the date of the severance of Montgomery and Fulton counties. Washington's visit to Fort Plain properly marks the end of the first series of chapters of the story of old Fort Plain.

The last victims of savage marauders near Fort Plain were Frederick Young and a man named House, of the town of Minden. They were in a field when a small party of Indians shot them both down. Young was not killed and when an Indian stooped over to scalp him, the victim seized the knife, the blade nearly severing his fingers. Both were scalped but Young was found alive and taken to Fort Plank, where he died before night. The two Minden men were shot within sight of the fort but the Indians got away before the patriot militia could assemble to engage them. This event happened in 1783, eight days after the inhabitants had news that peace had been ratified, and it is probable that the savages had not heard of this.

One of the first murder trials in the Johnstown jail after the war was that of John Adam Hartmann, a Revolutionary veteran, for killing an Indian In 1783. They met at a tavern in the present town of Herkimer, and the savage excited Hartmann's abhorrence by boasting of murders and scalpings performed by him during the war, and particularly by showing him a tobacco pouch made from the skin of the hand and part of the arm of a white child with the finger nails remaining attached. Hartmann said nothing at the time and the two left the tavern on their journey together, traveling a road, which led through a dense forest. Here the savage's body was found a year later. Hartmann was acquitted for lack of evidence. He had been a ranger at Fort Dayton. On a foray, in which he killed an Indian, at almost the same instant, he was shot and wounded by a Tory. Hartmann was a famous frontiersman and had many adventures. He was a fine type of the intrepid soldiers in the tried and true militia of Tryon County.

Following are the principal events of 1783 summarized: The treaty of peace with Great Britain, acknowledging the independence of the United States of America was signed in Paris, Sept. 3, 1783; 1783, Nov. 25, "Evacuation Day," British left New York and an American force under Gen. Washington and Gov. Clinton entered New York city, shortly after which Washington bade farewell to his officers at Fraunce's Tavern in that city and left for Mount Vernon, Md., his journey through New Jersey, Pennsylvania, and Maryland being a triumphal tour; 1783, Dec. 23, Washington resigned his command of the American army to Congress at Annapolis, MD.

On his celebrated tour of the Mohawk Valley, Washington was accompanied by a party of about 40 officers and officials including Governor George Clinton and General Philip Schuyler. Members of the party on the Mohawk Valley Tour: Henry Glen, of Schenectady, Deputy American Army Quartermaster for that district, accompanied Washington on his tour of the valley in 1783. His papers show some of the notables who were with the Commander at Fort Plain: Governor George Clinton, General Philip Schuyler, General Ten Broeck, Stephen Van Rensselaer and an Italian Count.

General Washington fully appreciated the importance of Fort Plain, and a main defensive post and military headquarters on the worthier frontier during the Revolution as indicated by the letter in possession of the Fort Rensselaer Club of Canajoharie. A copy of the letter hangs on the walls of the clubhouse.

Headquarters, Newburgh,
July 2, 1783.
Sir—
    Colonel Reid has informed me of the ill condition of Fort Plain and of the magazine at that place. As it is of the greatest importance that they should be repaired, I might request you to make every possible exertion to supply the necessary materials.
I am Sir,
Your very humble servant,
G. Washington.
Mr. Quackenboss, Q. Master.

    A month later, after his tour of the Mohawk Valley and his visit to Fort Plain, General Washington referred to the post as "Fort Rensselaer," which shows the great historical confusion caused by the use of the names, "Fort Plain" and "Fort Rensselaer," from 1780 through 1786.

    In the afternoon of July 31, 1783, General Washington and his party rode to Cherry Valley where they spent the night. On August 1, they visited Otsego Lake and the site of Cooperstown. They returned to Canajoharie over the Clinton road. Other member of the party of 40 put up at Roof's tavern in Canajoharie or returned to Fort Plain for the overnight.

    Col. Willett, the valley commandant, met Washington at the Fort Herkimer Church and in this church Washington ordered Fort Herkimer to be made the western depot of supplies for all the western British posts soon to be taken over by the Americans.

←Colonel Marinus Willett. A brave soldier and competent Commander of New York State Troops (militia and levies) from 1781 to 1784, with headquarters at Fort Plain, where he was greatly admired and respected by soldiers and civilian alike. Willett Street, in Fort Plain, was named in his honor. He was later elected Mayor of New York City.

    Supplies came to Fort Herkimer via the Mohawk River and then shipped westward over the water routes to Fort Niagara, and then via portage to La Salle on the Niagara River. Col. Willet was given command of the supply depot.

    Washington stopped and ate dinner under a tree in the yard of the Shoemaker place (West Main St., Mohawk). At the time this was one of the few houses left standing in this section of the Mohawk Valley after the Revolutionary raids.

    The Shoemaker House was destroyed by fire some years ago, thus removing a famous landmark. The house was built before the Revolution. It was a Revolutionary Tory secret meeting place and here Walter Butler was captured after the Battle of Oriskany in 1777. He later escaped from the Albany jail. Like a number of other Tory valley houses it was spared by the enemy during the war.

    It was the last pre-Revolutionary house on a tour westward toward Buffalo, and the first if you were traveling easterly.

    "It was in the Mohawk Valley that Washington first saw the vision of the great civilized republic stretching from coast to coast that the United States were later to become," Devereux noted. "As surveyor for Lord Fairfax in the Shenandoah Valley, and with the armies of Braddock and Forbes in the Ohio region, Washington had learned something of the country's interior - "which was more than almost any of the contemporaries could boast." Devereux pointed out.

    "The vast inland navigation of these United States!" This utterance was made at a time when only a small fringe of the Eastern Seaboard was populated and the interior was a vast, uncharted wilderness, shows the profound wisdom and forethought of Washington.

    After his return to his Newburg headquarters on March 5, he wrote the president of Congress: "My tour northward and westward to Fort Schuyler and my movement have been pretty rapid, my horses which had not yet arrived would be so much fatigued that they will need several days rest."

    After his tour of the Mohawk Valley, where he saw the importance of river traffic, he began to consider how the country might grow and turned his attention first to the possible use of the waterways. For his vision of the future, fully as much as for his great deeds, does he deserve the title of "Father of His Country." It is also significant that he first glimpsed the vision in the Mohawk Valley, which was soon to become the pathway of pioneers into the interior and also the great commercial route from the seaboard to the West. This route to the West was the Erie Canal, the railroad, and the modern motor car route, all to come later. Washington foresaw western growth, and how important the Mohawk Valley was destined to play a major role. He truly was a man of vision.

Almost 150 years later, in July of 1932, the Mohawk Valley celebrated the anniversary of the famous visit. A group representing the General and his staff made their way up the valley, with local celebrations in each town and village. Nelliston was reached on July 20, 1932. Following a Canajoharie parade, the Fort Plain-Nelliston reception committee met Washington and his staff in Nelliston with a welcome and speeches. Then the group was escorted to Fort Plain. In the evening there was a two mile parade with 15 bands and drum corps, and 55 floats. More than 60 windows had historical displays with artifacts and heirlooms on display.

Source Material:
The Story of Old Fort Plain and the Middle Mohawk Valley
by Nelson Greene
O'Connor Brothers Publishers, Fort Plain, NY 1915 CHAPTER XXIV.

From an old crumbling newspaper:

Annals of Tryon County;
or, the Border Warfare of New York,
During the Revolution.
By William W. Campbell
New York; Printed and Published by J. & J. Harper 1831

Cochran Farm

The house was built in 1790 by Major James C. Cochran for his father Doctor John Cochran, on land given him in partial payment for his services as Director General of hospitals through the Revolutionary War. Located a little east of Fort Klock on Route 5.

General Cochran was a close friend of General Washington. After the war, he was appointed by Washington as Commissioner of Loans. A stroke disabled the doctor, and he moved to his home at St. Johnsville, where he died in 1803. He was buried in Utica. Two sons, James and Walter were Army officers. In the early 1800's the Cochrans moved out of the area.

Much of the furniture in this house was from General Washington to his friend. Some of it came from Washington's Headquarters at Newburgh. Local tradition says that the historic site in Newburgh purchased some of the historical furniture back for display at the headquarters.

Source: Forts and Firesides of the Mohawk Country by John J. Vrooman, Published by Baronet Litho Co., Inc., Johnstown, NY 1951

A VIEW OF THE SITUATION IN THE VALLEY AFTER THE WAR.
From The Public Papers of George Clinton
Volume VIII
Preface by Hugh Hastings, State Historian, December 22, 1904

To all intents and purposes, the Revolutionary War had become a memory. The terrors of strife and bloodshed had ceased to exist in the thickly populated districts; along the frontier of New York, however, latent sparks continued to glow and burn and glisten, disturbing the peace of the inhabitants who were kept in a condition of nervousness by frequent alarms and unexpected raids of the incorrigible red skins and blood-thirsty Tories who refused to surrender to the inevitable and who were dying hard. Statesmen in American regarded the war as over in spite of the obduracy of the King and the machinations of sordid English contractors who manipulated Parliament and the Court. Against the interests of America, English politicians resorted to practices that would have been repudiated by English generals who had had experience here. The public mind of Great Britain was poisoned by misleading and malignant rumors affecting the situation in the United States, supplemented by the unjust charge that the Americans were incompetent to govern themselves.

The contempt with which the Articles of Confederation were held and the impotency exhibited in every effort that was exerted by progressive and representative men in the different states to strengthen and fortify them and to whip them into practical and popular shape, justified the criticisms of the enemies of America and created a feeling of discouragement among her friends. The army was dissatisfied and with every reason. The threatened uprising at Newburgh was the natural culmination of a concatenation of cankered grievances that had been festering far months, that had been irritated and inflamed by the indifference of the States and the studied neglect of Congress which stupidly failed to apply efficacious remedies. Jealousy between the states, was the over-shadowing menace to fraternal consolidation. The question of State rights had begun to blossom and was fostered by the sympathetic touch of leaders of the George Clinton school.

The army was, to all intents and purposes, disbanded in June 1783, only after a threatened mutiny which the wise mediation of Washington countervailed. The official dissolution of the Continental Army occurred November 3d when Washington promulgated the extraordinary military document known as his farewell orders. From the last week in March when intelligence was received that the Articles of Peace had been signed at Paris on the 30th day of November 1782, the evacuation of New York was the paramount subject of discussion in this State. But the British moved with exasperating deliberation, and Sir Guy Carleton, who had succeeded to the command of the English forces in America in place of Sir Henry Clinton, who had requested to be recalled, was charged by Americans with acting with too much indulgence and consideration towards the loyalists. The first week in April, it is estimated that nine thousand Loyalists sailed from New York for Nova Scotia. Many important and original propositions arose consequent upon the transfer of New York from British to American rule. There was no end of complications over real estate and the rights of Americans who had abandoned their property seven years before. The British manufactured excuse upon excuse for the delays, and Sir Guy Carleton was exposed at times very unjustly to severe criticism. November 6, Washington pointedly asked the British commander, and was informed that the troops would be withdrawn before the end of the month. After a few more delays the British evacuated New York November 25.

THE FIRST MAIL CARRIER WEST OF ALBANY

Eighty years ago there was not a post office west of Schenectady, and no regular postal route even as far as that. What little mail business there was transacted at that point was carried between Albany and Schenectady as chance occurred.

In 1797, Col. William Feeter, who was then living three miles north of the village of Little Falls, Herkimer County, established the first mail facilities through the Mohawk Valley, as a private enterprise. The entire mail that then went west of Albany was carried on horseback. Perhaps it will not be amiss here to state that Col. William Feeter was born at Stone Arabia, in this county, February 2d, 1756. His father, Lucas Feeter, who was a native of Wuertemberg, Germany, stood high in the confidence of Sir William Johnson. At the commencement of the Revolution, and after the death of Sir William, the Feeter family were so much under the influence of the Johnsons that all of them, excepting William, followed the fortunes of Sir John Johnson, and went with him to Canada. William Feeter remained and took an active part in the Revolutionary War. He was frequently entrusted with hazardous and important duties, which he never failed to discharge with promptness. After the war he settled upon his farm in Herkimer County, and cultivated the same for upwards of fifty years. He reared a highly respected family of twelve children, and died at Little Falls, May 5th, 1844, at the ripe age of eighty-eight years, lamented by a large concourse of friends. During his life he was an active member of the Fairfield Lodge of F. & A. M.

Mr. Feeter being a man of marked intelligence and feeling the disadvantage that the people were laboring under through being deprived of facilities of getting letters, and more particularly newspapers, of which there was none printed west of Albany of that early day, conceived the idea of establishing a mail route on private account. Thus, as stated above, in 1797 he fitted out his sons, Adam, who was then a lad of sixteen years, with a good horse, well equipped with saddle and bridle, and large saddle bags, and sent him forth upon his mission. Young Adam's duty was to procure subscribers for newspapers and carry all the letters entrusted to him between Albany and Little Falls on both sides of the river, and at Johnstown and vicinity, through the Royal Grant north of Little Falls, and at German Flatts, and nearly to Utica, which was then the border of civilization, or nearly so. Adam met with signal success in procuring a large number of subscribers which he had to supply at their doors, and also was entrusted with all the letters sent and received by private individuals along his route, and also had the business of what few merchants then were trading in the valley. At that time there was only one store at Little Falls, kept by John Porteous, who did a thriving business, both with the white settlers and Indians, there being at this time a considerable number of the latter in this vicinity. The only other store of any importance west of Schenectady was kept by one Kane just east of the village of Canajoharie, on the bank of the Mohawk River. The stone dwelling occupied by him, with its antiquated roof, is still standing as an ancient landmark, but is in dilapidated condition. These two merchants were his best patrons, and Adam in his older days remarked to us, the merchants, Porteous and Kane, frequently gave me much encouragement when I was "desperately tired and sore of riding and cold and wet."

The writer has listened more than once to accounts of Adam's hardships and narrow escapes in various ways during the three years of his mail service. His customers being on both sides of the river it was necessary to effect a crossing quite frequently. This generally had to be done by fording, for at that day there were no bridges and very few ferries. Frequently the stream was much swollen, which would compel him to swim his horse to the great danger of losing his life. In such instances he would get completely wet, in which condition he would be compelled to ride the remainder of the day. The trip would generally occupy from four to five days, and was performed by him during three years without interruption. The writer has frequently conversed with him in his old age about Mohawk Valley matters in his younger days and gained much valuable information from him. At the time he was occupied in the mail service there was not a white family in the valley which he did not know, and I have frequently heard him refer to many of them as among the most prominent, such as the Yates, Clutes, Barhyghts, Schermerhorns, Tolls, Mabies, Van Antwerps, Myers, Swarts, Truaxes, DeGraffs, Marcelluses, VanSlykes, Putmans, Vosburghs, Conynes, Fishers, Fondas, Dockstaders, Veeders, Sprakers, Wagoners, Klocks and an host of others. During his visits to Albany he became acquainted with the Governor and all the State officials, who entrusted him with the transmission of State papers for Schenectady and points in the valley, and occasionally they presented him with an extra fee for promptness of delivery and close attention to duty. It was his pride to mention that in three years he had never missed a trip, lost single letter or paper, and had always delivered all monies and valuable securities to the perfect satisfaction of every one.

In 1800 a government mail route was established, which was offered to him, but he declined, choosing to pursue a more domestic life. Shortly after this he married, and commenced the milling business at a place now called Ingham's Mills, in Herkimer County,which business he followed for a few years, but not finding it to agree with his health he disposed of it and purchased a farm in Manheim, where he spent the remainder of his days. He died in 1865, at the advanced age of eighty-three years. His memory will long be cherished by a large number of relatives and admiring friends. He lived to see the valley changed from a sparsely settled country to beautiful and well-cultivated farms, with numerous thriving villages, large and extensive manufacturing, turnpike, plank and railroads, and telegraph lines; verily, wonderful improvements and inventions. And this was the man that carried the first mail in the Mohawk Valley! This was the pioneer in the mail service west of Albany, which now stretches to the Pacific coast, with its thousands of branches.

We have been informed lately that the weight of mail matter now carried and distributed west of Albany will not come much short of one hundred tons per day. All this has been accomplished within the space of eighty years. And now as we are chronicling the above the New York papers come to hand with the astonishing news that arrangements are about completed between the Postmaster-General and the H. R. & N. Y. C., Lake Shore and Northern Indiana Railroads to establish a daily mail line between New York and Chicago, (*) which will consist of four cars, each sixty feet long, and will not occupy more than twenty-four hours in running from one of the last named places to the other. It is calculated that the weight of mail matter by this daily line will not be less than forty or fifty tons a day. We are a progressive people, and no one dares to venture a prediction as to what advance will be made in the eighty years to come. We can only say in regard to mail matters, that the small beginning commended by the sixteen year old land, Adam Feeter, now employs thousands of men, many horses and wagons, and a large amount of steam transportation to accomplish the needed service. --*Fonda Democrat.*
*This article was written probably in 1870.

Source Material: <u>This History of William Feeter, A Soldier in the War of American Independence and of His Father, Lucas Vetter,</u> *the ancestor of the Feeter-Feder-Feader-Fader families*
IN THE UNITED STATES AND CANADA, with genealogy of the family compiled at the request of JAMES D. FEETER, by John B. Koetteritz, MEMBER HERKIMER COUNTY HISTORICAL SOCIETY.
Little Falls, N.Y. Press of Stebbins & Burney, 1901
Copyright by James D. Feeter, 1901

Claims for Damages by the Enemy

<u>New York In The Revolution as Colony and State</u>
by James A. Roberts, Comptroller
Compiled by Frederic G. Mather
Second Edition 1898
Two Volumes

No Claims, against the State are more pathetic than those for Damages by the Raids of the Enemy. Some of the comments were as follows:-"The Robbers has taken out of my House "; "His wife after being taken prisoner and a child of 18 mos. murthered"; "To one son Kild"; " Two brothers murthered and his father taken"; " by the wanton destruction of the Enemy"; " Widow ot ------- who was Killed by the Enemy and all his effects burned'; " by the Enemys to Americ"; " Killet and Daken of this Fammely My Father and Mother My Brothers wife with 8 Children and one sarvan maith one Brother Daken Brasnor [Prisoner] lost"; "by the Enemy, the Indians & worse as they, the British and Torrys";"His father killed by the Enemy"; "I loose more than Double the sum above, besides my son of Seventeen years of age who was killed same time "

A bill of Dammage of Isaac Davis May 22nd yr. 1780.
Bildings housses barens and barks valued att...£250-0-0
Wheren Close of all my famaly valued att...34-14-0

Waggon an plow gers all Complete valued att...20-10-0
three beds garnished wed all valued att...20-0-0
horsses and Ship and bids valued att...12-0-0
Chist and Sugger and money valued att...19-3-0
Houssel furnish all valued att...15-0-0
fences gren and apeltrees valued att...12-10-0
horn Cuttels to they valued att...7-16-0
Arms and Cutterments Sords and pistils...7-18-0
Hoksseds pots an Cartels att... 4-0-0
taner and Currermen tolls att...7-10-0
Sleys and gers wed all att... 6-10-0
Sadals bridles Sets and Sids att... 6-10-0
Carpentters tuls wed all Complete att... 4-10-0
Sumekers tuls and lader att...3-0-0
Total £465-11-0

Dated 12 Feby. Isaac Davis.

The Claims are more accurately localized than is the case with any other class of Claims. In Albany County the sufferers lived in the Districts of East Rensselaerwyck, Hoosack, Saratoga, Schenectady and Schoharie, the latter District having been raided in 1778, 1780 and 1781. The great majority of the Claims from this County, however, arose from the Invasion of Gen. Burgoyne, in 1777. Some of them began in May, when he was at Ticonderoga. Others follow on his track Southward to his defeat at Saratoga; and still others refer to damages by his troops "on their way to Boston."

An Estimation of Damages Dun by The Enemy at the time When General Borguyn Was Douon with his army in this quarter in year 1777.
To Cornelius Van Veghten at Saratoga.
His Dwelling house Computed ... £ 250-0-0
A Large new barn with Exetant Buildings of 3 Berrags and Sheep pan and Cornhouses... 250-0-0
1 Store house ... 140
I Grist mill ...320-0-0
I Dwelling hous of my miller ... 90 0 0
The army Laing at this place not apennal of fence left on this farm which I Supose I cannot have Egin for ... 160-0-0
one wind mill ... 7-0-0
5 Eyron Shad Slays .. 28-0-0
3 plows ... 14-0-0
2 Harres 8-0-0
6 Horn Cattle 24-0-0
7 Hors lind.... 70-0-0
45 Hogs lind..... 40-0-0
a quantety of Grean Left in the Stoorhouse and in the mill which I cannot account for,
31 Jany. Cornelius Van Veghten.

The County of Tryon was the worst sufferer. Bills for Damages were sent from the following localities: Andreastown, Beaver Dam, Butler's Borough, Canajoharie District, Caughnawaga District, Cherry Valley, Coenradt's Town, Curry's Town, Durlach, German Flats District, Herkimer's Town, Kingsland District, Jerseyfield, Little Falls, Mohawk District, Old England District, Palatine District, Remasniders Bush, Saggenigo, Sand Flats, Springfield, Stone Arabia, Warrensborough, Warren's Bush.

The second Raid of Sir John Johnson, in October, 1780, was the cause of nearly all the claims in Tryon County. Full descriptions will be found in the Public Papers of George Clinton in The Northern Invasion, by Franklin B. Hough, 1866; in Schoharie County and Border Wars of New York, by J. R. Simms, 1845; and in The Old New York Frontier, by Francis Whiting Halsey, 1900. Briefly stated, the object of the raid was to cut off the supplies upon which General Washington depended; and to destroy the resources of all in the valleys of the Mohawk and the Schoharie who were friendly to the American Cause. Johnson's Army, organized in Canada, made a detour to the westward and began by attacking the three forts on the Schoharie, none of which were taken. The enemy devastated the Schoharie valley, and continued the work in the Mohawk valley. They defeated Col. John Brown at Fort Paris (between Stone Arabia and Palatine Bridge); but, in the end, they were defeated by the men who fought under Gen. Robert Van Rensselaer and fled. The documents give the dates when the following places were raided: Caughnawaga, Oct 18; Durlach, Stone Arabia and Mohawk District, Oct. 19; Warrensborough, Oct. 25.

The documents also record a raid, by John Dockstader, July 9, 1781. On Oct. 24, of that year, about 700 British and Indians, under Maj. Ross and Maj. Walter Butler, entered Curry-town, among the Mohawk River settlements. They continued on the south bank of the River, burning buildings and taking Prisoners. From Auriesville, they proceed to Fort Hunter, crossed the Schoharie River and went as far as Yankee Hill in the present town of Florida. Thence they turned directly back to Johnstown. The next day Col. Willett overtook then near Johnson Hall, and the enemy retreated to the East and West Canada Creeks.

Earlier raids had been made on Cherry Valley, Nov. 11, 1778; and on Caughnawaga, May 22, 1780; and still other Raids were made in 1782. Several claims are made for "Damages to the Oneidas and Tuscaroras, the Allies of the Confederated States", Herkimer's Town and the German Flats were raided at the time of the Battle of Oriskany, Aug. 6, 1777. The latter was also raided in Sept., 1778.

A List of the Real and Personal Effects of Frederick Fisher Wantonly taken and destroyed by the Enemy in the Year 1780.
A Dwelling House-Burnt.... £ l00-0-0
Beds and Bedding.... 20-16
Mens and Womens Ware ...23-4
A Tea Kittle....4
A Brass Kittle...0-9
Plates...19-19
Earthen Ware...1-11
2 Brass Ladles....0-9
A Silver Mounted Sword....7
2 Guns....1-10
Holstors and Pistols...2-16
A Saddle Bridle and Saddle Bags....3-4
A pair Boots...1-12
2 Negroes and a wench - carryed off ...240
A Barn and 2 Barracks Burnt 35
12 Load Hay do 15
50 Scipples Indian Corn do 3/....7-10
2 Horses-carryed off......30
A Set Horse Harness.... 22-10

£ 494 7 0

Definition of wench

Pronunciation: (wench)
—*n.*
1. a country lass or working girl: *The milkmaid was a healthy wench.*
2. *Usually facetious.*a girl or young woman.
3. *Archaic.* a strumpet.

State of New York SS. Frederick Fisher being duly sworn deposith and saith that the above Account contains the Articles belonging to him which were burnt or destroyed or carryed off by the Enemy and that the prices affixed opposite to the same are reasonable. Sworn before me this day of Jany. 1782. Fredk. Fisher [Col.] Robt. Yates.

State of New York Tryon County. An Account of the Damages which Samuel Campbell of Cherry Valley have Sustained by the Enemy on the Eleventh of November 1778.

£ S D
To one Dwelling house burnt... 150
To Two barns burnt.... 150
To two horses taken away.....30
To two mears and one Coalt do...20
To one Cow taken away....5
To one beet burnt...5
To four fat hogs killed....12
To one Negro boy carried off...50
To one Waggon burnt.....7
To one Slay and Harness burnt....6
To thirty Loads of hay do.... 30
To wheat and peas and oats burnt in the Straw....50
To Corn and Potatoes and flax burnt....10
To one watch taken away...6
To two Sadls and bridles carryed off....5 10
To Cloathing and house all furniture burt or carryed off...200
To Cash taken away.....60

Jany. 25, 1782. £795 10 0

Saml. Campbell [Col.]

After some of the worst efforts of the Enemy had been made, the Legislature, Nov. 22, 1781, passed this concurrent resolution:

Resolved that the honorable the Chief Justice and puisne justic of the Supreme Court of Judicature of this State for the time being, be, and they are hereby respectively authorized and requested to collect returns and evidence in the manner described in the letter from the Honorable Robert R. Livingston Esqr of the 12th instant to his Excellency the Governor of this state attendant on his Excellency's Message of this Day of the Damage done by the Enemy within this state, by the wanton destruction of property, and that the Legislature will make provision tor defraying the Expense attendant on this business and for compensating the Chief Justice and puisne justices for their services herein.

Judge Robert Yates acted under this Resolution. He gave two separate Reports to the Legislature; one of them in 1781, and the other without a date. His charge was 2/- pr each deposition.

State of New York to Robert Yates Dr.
To taking a Number of Depositions respecting Losses sustain'd by the Depredation of the Enemy in the Northern Parts of this State Vizt 227 a 2/ £ 22. .14..
[This Account was audited and paid in 1790]

The following were claimants for damages by the enemy:

Albany County

Abeel James	Becker John Albertus	Davis Catherina
Ball Johannis	Becker Peter	Deitz William
Bauck Johannis	Becker Storm	Eckeson Thomas
Bauck John William	Becker Storm, jr.	Eckeson Tiunes
Bauck Thomas	Belknap Abel	Enters Peter
Bauck William	Bellinger Johannis	Enters Jacob
Beck Martinus	Bellinger Marcus	Forster Anna
Becker Abraham	Bergh Philip	Forster George
Becker Albertus	Borll Johannis	Freymier Johannes
Becker Harmanus	Borst Baltus	Graham John
Becker Isaac	Borst Hendrick	Hills George
Becker Johannes Jos.	Brown Christian, Capt.	Honak Henry
Becker John	Cramer Charles	Kercher Philip

Kest Richard
Kniskern Johannes
Kniskern William
Koeningh Michael
Lansing Garret J.
Lansing Isaac N.
Lawyer Jacob
Lawyer Johannis
Lawyer Lorence
Luke Jacob
McCrea John
Mann Peter
Mattise Johannis
Merkel John
Merkle Hendricik
Meyer Christian
Nukel Gerrit C.
Nukerk John
Porks Daniel
Rechtmeyer George
Reinhardt George Fr.
Rickart Eva

Rickart George
Rickert Johannes
Robinson Charles
Schaefer Jacob
Schaffer Martinis
Scheffer Jost
Schell Jost
Schelman George
Schneider Peter
Shafer Hendrick
Sidnich Wiiliam
Sillenick Harmanus
Snyder William
Sternberg Abraham
Sternberger Nicklas
Sternbergh David
Stubrach Hendrick
Swart Peter
Swart Tuenis
Taylor Jeremiah
Van den bergh Evert
Van den bergh John

Van Slick Marteynis
Vroman Adam
Vroman Peter I.
Vrooman Barent
Vrooman Barent, Jr.
Vrooman Johan
Vrooman Peter
Vrooman Simon
Vrooman Tunis
Waite William
Warner George
Warner Nicholas
Wendell Abraham
Wendell Evert
Werth John Jacob
Winne Daniel
Winne John
Yates Peter
Zielie Martinis
Ziellie Peter, Jr.
Zimmer Jacob

Charlotte County (now part of Vermont)

Baker Albert
Belknap Abel
Bitler John
Bristoll Silas
Durkee James
Durkee Thomas

Gilliland William
Harris Elizabeth
Harris Moses
Moor James
Moor James, jr.
Parks David

Sanders Peter
Sherwood Seth
Vallance David
Watson John
Wilson Samuel
Winne Peter

Tryon County

Abeel John
Antus Coenrat
Armstrong Archibald
Badas Michael
Bader Michael
Baldsperger John
Banner Johannis
Barbelat Jacob
Barden Michael
Barth Margaret (Widow)
Baschou John
Batcheller Zephaniah
Baxter Thomas
Bell Dorothy (Widow)
Bellinger John
Bellinger Peter, jr.
Bellinger William
Bennett Amos
Bowman Eva
Boyay Catharine
Boyer John
Brookman Godfried
Campbell James
Campbell John
Campbell Samuel, Col.
Cannan Andrew
Cannon Matthew
Clyde Samuel, Col.
Coppernoll Nicholas
Coppernoll Richard

Crissman Gottfried
Cristman Frederick
Cristman Jacob
Cristman Nicholas, sr.
Cromwell Jacobus
Dachsteder John Nicholas
Davis Jacob
Davis James, jr.
Davis Patrick
Davis Thomas
Deline William
Dellinbagh John
Dickson James
Diefendorff Jacob, Jr.
Dietz Jacobus
Dietz John
Dietz William
Dockstader Frederick
Dorrs Matthias
Doxstadder George
Durmot Michael
Earnest Christian
Ecker George
Ecker Jacob
Eliot Andrew
Ellwood Peter
Finck Andrew
Fisher Frederick, Col.
Folmer Thomas
Foltz Peter

Fonda Adam
Fonda Jelles
Fonda John
Foror Rudolph
Fox Frederick
Fox George
Fox John
Frank Albart
Frank Frederick
Frank Johannis
Frank John
Frank Lawrence
Frank Timothy
Frantz Sebastian
Gardener Samuel
Gardenier Jacob
Gettman Frederick
Gibson William
Gordon Robert
Grim Henry
Guile John
Haag Frederick
Hall William
Hansen Hendrick
Hansen Nicholas
Hansen Peter
Harnes John
Haywisen Martin
Herder Lawrence
Harter Henry

Hess Augustinis, jr.
Hess Augustinus, sr
Hess Frederick
Hess Johannes
Hess John
Hessler John
Hews Catharine
Hews James
Heyser John
Hoff Richard
House Joseph
Hunt Timothy
Hyer Peter
Iseman John
Ittig Christian
Keller Henry
Keller Johannes
Keltz Conrath
Kennedy James
Kennedy Robert
Kentor John
Kesler John, jr.
Kessler John
Kinkead Crownidge
Klumph Thomas
Kortright Henry
Lambet Peter
Lampfor Peter
Lewis Adam
Lewis David
Lewis Frederick
Lewis Hendrick
Lively Simon
Loucks Henry
Loup William
Lythaal Niclas
Mabie Harmanus
McCollom Daniel
McDermid Michael
McGraw Daniel
McKillip John
McKillup Archibald
McKown James
Marlatt Mark
Marr James
Miller Henry

Miller Valentine
Mitchell Hugh
Moor James
Moore Jacob
Moore John
Notman Jacob
Nukerk George C.
Nukle John
Ohrendorff George
Ohrendorff Peter
Ohrendorph Frederick
Ohrendorph Frederic, jr.
Ohrendorph John
Oneidas & Tuscaroras
Oothout Abraham
Osterhout John
Park John
Petri Johannes M.
Petri Mars
Retry John Marks
Petry William
Philipse Volkert
Phillips William
Pifer Peter
Potman David
Potman David, Jr.
Potman Frederick
Quackenboss Abraham, jr,
Quackenboss Peter J.
Quackenbush Myndert W.
Raspoll Martes
Relley John
Remsnyder Hendrick
Rickey James
Rung Hendrick
Ryckart Lodowick
Sammons Samson
Schell Johannes
Schimmell Francis
Schmit Johannes
Schoemaker John
Schoemaker Thomas
Seroos Christian
Shaddack Thomas
Shallop Frederick
Shell John, sr.

Shew Godfrey
Shoemaker Frederick
Shultys Christopher
Slouwits (Widow)
Small Susanna (Widow)
Smith John
Snock William
Spornheyer William
Staring Adam
Starring Nicholas
Steen Conrad
Stine William
Throop George
Tillebagh John
Toror Rudolph
Van Alstine Gilbert
Van Brackelen Gysbert
Van Brackelen Nicholas
Van den berg Wynant
Van der merk John
Van der Wycke John
Van Eps Charles
Van Eps John E.
Veeder Abraham
Veeder Johannis
Veeder Volkert
Vrooman Henry
Warts Matise
Waset George
Weatherstraw Henry
Weaver Nicholas
Wempel Barent
Wempel Margareta
Wemple John B.
Wever Jacob
Wicks Samuel
Wiilson Andrew
Willson James
Wiilson Samuel
Wimer Andrew
Winkel John
Wohleben Abraham
Wolleben Peter
Woolhaver Jacob
Young Adam
Zieleis John

The following Claims for Damages cannot be identified, as to location. It is probable that most of them were caused by Johnson's Raids in the Valley of the Mohawk.

Bancker Evert
Banda Melchior
Carner Charles
Cunningham William
Davis Elizabeth
Davis Isaac
Docksteder John
Doty Isaac
Fisher Catharine
Hansen Barant
Hen Marka

Hesler Conradt
Ittig Michael
Kelly John
Kock Jurgen
Kock Soferines
Lansing Abraham
Lansing Gerret A.
Lansing Isaac H.
Lewis Peter
Mabee Petrus
McDavitt Charles

Marks (Mr.)
Newkirk Abraham
Patingill William
Potman Cornelius
Poyar John
Rechtmeyer George
Christian
Scott James
Snell Adam
Steens John
Sternberger Abraham

Tisese John	Van Schaick Jacob	Vroman Jonas
Van Alstine Jacob	Van Valkenburgh Abraham	Vrooman Peter C.
Van den bergh Cornelius	Van Valkenburgh Jacob	Weaver George
Van Everah Cornelius	Van Veghten Cornelius	Weaver Johan George
Van Everah John	Vroman Bartholomew	

Other pension papers of a different sort give another side of life after the war. Those who were gravely injured during battle applied for a pension from the state.

The Board to examine invalids consisted of Col. Peter Gansevoort, Richard Platt, Surgeon Nicholas Schuyler, General Philip Schuyler, General Abraham Ten Broeck and Richard Varick.

Pension Application for Frederick Fisher (Visscher)

Coll. Frederick Fisher Came before me Simon Veeder one of the Justices of the County of Montgomery in the State of New York and made Oath that he was examined by Abraham Ten Brook and Peter Gansevoort Junier Esquires, appointed by the said State for that purpose obtained a Certificate or had his Certificate Examined and Countersigned Setting forth that he had served as a Colonel of the Militia in the County of Montgomery that he was disabled by being wounded & Scalped at Caughnawaga on the 22 day of May 1780 by a Party of the Indians and that he now Lives in the District of Caughnawaga in the County of Montgomery.
Fredk Fisher (Col.) (See page 214 A Time of Terror for the story about the attack.)
Sworn Before me this 2d Day of May 1789
Simon Veeder Justice

Pension Application for Jacob Gardinier

Jacob Gardinier of Mohawk's District in the County of Montgomery Blacksmith & Farmer being duly sworn maketh Oath That during the late war he was Captain of a company in the Regiment of Montgomery (then Tryon County) Militia commanded by Colo. Frederick Fisher; That in August 1777 the same Regiment was ordered to march with others of Militia under the Command of B. Genl Harkimer to the relief of the Garrison of Fort Schuyler then invested by the Troops of the Enemy under the Command of B. Genl St. Leger; That upon the March of the same regiment to wit on the Sixth Day of the same Month they were attacked by a Party of the Enemy between Oriska & Fort Schuyler aforesaid and were defeated. That in the Action the Deponent received three Wounds one of them in his Left Groin, a Second in his right Thigh and a third in his right leg. That by Means of the several Wounds aforesaid he is in a great Measure rendered incapable of obtaining a Livelihood by his Trade or other hard Labor; That on the thirty first day of January last he was fifty seven Years of Age and that he now actually resides in Mohawk District in the County of Montgomery aforesd. (See page 114, A Time of Terror.)
Jacob Gerdenyir
Sworn this twelfth Day of April 1787
Before me Richd Varick, Recorder

1790 Town of Palatine Census
(In 1790, the area now called St. Johnsville was located in the Town of Palatine)
Look at the difference in the number of people in the town between 1790 and 1800. It took a long time for the valley to recover from the war.

Allback, John	Beck, John	Bome, Frederick
Ayle, Michael	Beekman, Henry	Boyer, Falatine
Ayle, Petres	Bees, William	Boyer, John
Ayle, William	Bellinger, Adam	Brame, John
Bader, Melchor	Bellinger, Adam A.	Breadback, John
Bador, Ulrich	Bellinger, Frederick	Brewer, Aaron
Baltsly, Andrew	Bellinger, Henry	Brewer, Herman
Baltsly, Peter	Bellinger, Henry	Broat, Henry
Barnes, Henry	Bellinger, John L.	Brown, Godlip
Barnes, Thomas	Bellinger, Peter	Brown, Phillip
Barsh, Adam	Belor, Jacob	Bush, George
Barsh, Rudolph	Bevee, Anthony	Buye, John
Bauder,Michael	Bishop, Charles	Cadle, George
Becker, Henry	Bliss, Ruben	Calhoun, Benjamin

Calun, Benjam
Calhoun, Joseph
Calhoun, Rennolds
Care, Thomas
Carmen, Charles
Carter, Henry
Caugh, Henrick
Caugh, Nicholas
Caugh, Bodus
Caugh, Gosper
Caugh, Peter
Caugh, Rudolph
Caugh, Severinius
Causselman, Bartly
Causselman, John
Causselman, John Jr.
Cesler, Nicholas
Chalkgo, Nicholas
Chivers, Ebenezer
Christman, John
Cisseller, Joseph
Claus, Peter
Conyngham, William Jr.
Coppernall, Adam
Coppernoll, John
Coppernoll, Nicholas
Coppernoll, Richard
Coppernoll, William
Cough, John
Coughman, Anthony
Cramer, Christian
Crane, Josiah
Crane, Josiah, Jr.
Cressy, Naughton
Cring, John
Cringe, John Ludwick
Crisman, Nicholas
Cross, Jacobus
Crouse, John
Crouse, Leonard
Culman, Henry
Culman, Henry
Curtis, Ebenezer
Curtis Nathaniel
Davis, Jacob
Desler, Jacob
Dockstader, John
Douglass, John
Ducky, John
Duncan, John Jr.
Dylleback, Baltus
Dylleback, Henry
Dyllenback, John
Dyllenback, Richard
Eadle, Honyost
Eaker, George
Eaker, Jacob
Eaker, Mary Elizabeth
Ecker, Nicholas
Empier, John

Empier, John Jr.
Engush, John
Erenbrodt, John
Ecgenbrodt, John
Ecgenbrodt, Peter
Fealing, Henry
FEaling, Jacob
Fealing, Jacob Jr.
Fealing, Richard
Feavel, John
Finck, Andrew
Find, Christian
Find, Honyost
Fink, William
Flander, John
Flander, Teunis
Foekus, Yohan Hendrick
Fonda, Jellis
Forbus, James
Forbus, Mabus
Fouks, Peter
Fox, Christopher
Fox, Daniel
Fox, George
Fox, Honyost
Fox, Philip
Fox, William
Fox, William W.
Fort, Abijah
Fort, Andrew
Frank, Susannah
Frear, Peter
Frebugh, Francis
Frey, Jacob
Frey, John
Fyckle, John
Fys, George
Garlock, Adam
Getman, Fredrick
Getman, Peter
Gillet, Sephus
Girtman, Christian
Girtman, George
Girtman, Thomas
Gray
Gray, Adam
Gray, John
Gray, Samuel
Grisman, Jacob
Grove, Christian
Haan, Johannes
Hamlen, Giles
Haring, Henry
Harris, William
Hart, Daniel
Hart, Conradt
Hart, John
Hatwick, Aaron
Haze, Henry
Haze, John

Headcock, Daniel
Hees, Frederick
Hellebolt, Teunis
Hellgas, Conrodt
Hellgas, Peter
Hellenburgh, Cornelius
Hellnuich, John
Hellnuich, John
Helmer, Honyost
Helmer, John G.
Helmer, John P.
Helmer, Leonard
Helmer, Philip
Helmer, Philip L.
Herman, John
Hess, Daniel
Hess, David
Hess, John
Hight, Elihu
Himing, George
Honk, Nicholas
Horduck, Andress
Horduck, John
Hose, Henry
House, Adam
House, Christian
House, Elias
Humfry, William
Hynes, Christopher
Inkerson, Jesse
Jennings, Samuel
Johnson, James
Johnston, Abraham
Kaskadon, Robert
Kearn, John
Keller, John
Kelly, George
Kenedy, Patrick
Kenter, Henry
Kettle, Daniel
Kettle, Jacob
Keyser, Barant
Keyser, Henry
Keyser, John
Keyser, Yost
Khull, Hendrick
Kill, Christopher
Kilts, Adam
Kilts, Peter
Kilts, Peter N.
Kisner, William
Kitts, Conradt
Kitts, Conradt
Kitts, Peter
Klock, Adam
Klock, George G.
Klock, Henry
Klock, Honyost
Klock, Jacob
Klock, Jacob C.

Klock, Jacob G.
Klock, Jacob I.
Klock, John
Klock, John J.
Kontz, Adam
Krams, John
Kramts, Peter
Kramtz, Henry
Krantz, John
Kretzer, Leonard
Krotz, Domini
Krous, Gertrude
Labdon, Daniel
Lamperson, Cornelius
Lasher, Garrit
Launtman, Peter
Layman, John
Leaper, Wyont
Lee, William
Lee, William Jr.
Lesher, Garrit Jr.
Lesher, John
Louks, Adam
Louks, George
Louks, Henry
Louks, Henry A.
Louks, Jacob
Louks, Joseph
Louks, Peter
Louks, Peter H.
Louks, Wendell
Low, Samuel
Lower, Conradt
Lyning, Jacob
Marsh, Stephen
Marsielus, Saunder
Matin, Peter
Martin, Veeder
McDougall, Eve
Merkle. David
Merkle, Henry
Merkle, Samuel
Miller, Henry
Mont, John
Moore, Jacob
Moyer
Moyer, David
Nellis, Adam
Nellis, Christian
Nellis, David
Nellis, Henry W.
Nellis, John
Nellis, John H.
Nellis, Ludwick
Nellis, Peter W.
Nellis, Philip
Nellis, William
Nellis, Yost
Nestle, Godlip
Nestle, Martin

Newman, John
Newman, Joseph
Nicholas, Hesekiah
Nicholas, Simeon
Oserhout, Frederick
Osman, Henry
Patrick, Robert
Pellendom, James
Petrie, Barbara
Pfyfer, Andrew
Phillips, Adam
Pickart, Bartholimew
Pickart, John
Pickart, Joseph
Pier, Ernest
Pierson, Pool
Plank, Henry
Plupper, Christian
Poss, Nicholas
Potter, Michael
Price, John
Prime, Elizabeth
Radtly, Jacobus
Reaver, Andrew
Rees, Jonas
Rees, Peter
Remesnider, John
Remsen, Jonathan
Rice, John
Richter, Nicholas
Rickart, Conradt
Rickart, Ludwick
Rider, George
Ried, John
Ritter, Frederick
Ritter, Henry
Rosback, Frederick
Rote, Charles
Runnils
Runyan, Benjamin
Russell, Daniel
Saltsman, George
Saltsman, Henry
Saltsman, John
Saltsman, William
Schuyler, Peter
Scott, David
Scott, Thomas
Seley, John
Selleback, John
Senof, Lucas
Serenias, Christopher
Shaffer, Henry
Shaffer, John
Sheldon, Asa
Shepperman, Christian
Shever, Partle
Shok, Zacariah
Sholl, Honyost
Sholl, John

Shoults, Henry
Shoults, John
Shoults, John Jacob
Sholtz, George
Shoultz, Henry I.
Shoultz, John I.
Shoutz, Jacob.
Simmons, Abraham
Skill, Jacob
Skulgraft, Richard
Smith, Baltus
Smith, George
Smith, Hendrick
Smith, Hendrick Jr.
Smith, Henry
Smith, Jeremiah
Smith, John
Smith, Nicholas
Snell, Eve
Snell, Jacob
Snell, John
Snell, John J.
Snell, John S.
Snell, Nicholas
Snell, Peter
Snell, Peter G.
Snell, Severinius
Squires, Ichabod
Soutch, George
Soutch, John
Soutch, John P.
Soutch, Peter
Soutch, Peter P.
Sponable, John
Spraker, George
Spraker, Joseph
Stam, Elizabeth
Stauring, Conradt
Stauring, George
Stauring, Jacob
Stempler
Steuart, Palatine
Stone, George
Straback, Frederick
Strader, Nicholas
Strayer, Jacob
Stroup, William
Stroup, William Jr
Sylleback, Garrit
Syphert, John
Taylor, Aaron
Tehurst, Abraham
Tehurst, Martin
Tehurst, Philip
Thorne, Samuel
Timmerman, George
Timmerman, Henry
Timmerman, Jacob
Timmerman, Lawrence
Timmerman, William

Tum, Adam & Conradt
Tunn, Nicholas
Tygart, Siverenius
Van Alstine, Cornelius I.
Van Ater, Samuel
Vander Worker, Thomas
Van Drusen, John
Van Elter, Peter
Van Ness, William
Van Slyke, Jacobus
Van Slyke, Nicholas
Van Slyke, Sylvanus
Van Vleet, Dury
Van Vee, Andrew
Van Vee, John
Vernor, Andress
Visger, John
Waffle, George
Waffle, Henry
Waffle, John
Waggoner, George
Waggoner, Honyost
Waggoner, John
Waggoner, Peter
Wallason, Christian
Walradt, Isaac
Walradt, Jacob H.
Walradt, Nicholas
Walradt, Peter H.
Walter, George
Wanger, Isaac
Weaver, David
Werner, Christian
White, Alleburt
Wick, John
Williams, George
Williamson, John
Windecker, Conradt
Windecker, Frederick
Witt, Moses
Wolrodt, Adam
Wolrodt, Adolph
Wolrodt, John
Wolrodt, John
Woolkinwood, John
Woolkinwood, John
Woolliber, Henry
Wormwood, Peter
Wormwood, Ryena
Wymer, Andrew
Youker, George
Youker, Jacob
Youker, John
Youker, Solomon
Young, Seth
Youran, Jacob

Town of Palatine Census Records for 1800.

Head of Household. St. Johnsville was located in the Town of Palatine at this time.

Aldenburgh, William
Amach, John
Ar*son, Robert
Antony, George
Averist, isaac
B****nger, Jost
B*****, Leonard
Bader, Leonard
Bader, Melchoir
Bader, Michael
Bader, Michael M.
Bader, Michael W.
Bader, Urich
Baldwin, Asa
Baldwin, Noah
Ballard, Alpheus
Ballard, Rufus
Ballard, Thomas
Banker, John
Barsh, Roudolph
Bartles, Christopher
Bass, Adam
Bass, George
Bass, Rudolph
Bates, Isreal
Bates, Jacob
Baum, Frederick
Beardsly, John
Beck, John S.
Beckman, Cornelius C.
Beckman, Henry
Beckman, John J.
Been, Wm.
Bellenger, Henry
Bellenger, Frederick
Bellenger, John Junr.
Bellenger, John L.
Bellinger, Frederick
Bellinger, John N.
Benedict, Nathan
Benneger, John
Bennett, Joseph
Bents, Francis
Berry, Benjamin
Best, Jacob
Bice, John
Bice, John
Bice, Peter
Billington, James
Billington, John
Blank, John
Boam, Frederick
Bortick, Esra
Brevoort, John
Brewer, Arent
Brewer, Hermances Junr
Brown, Cutlip
Brown, Philip
Bugdorf, Henry
Bureng, Conrad
Burlington, Benjamin
Burtis, William

C****, Thomas
Carley, Albert
Cater, Abraham
Chase, David
Cheedle, ***jamin
Cheedle, **zza
Churchile, Benjamin
Clause, Andrew
Clause, John
Clause, Peter
Clause, Peter Junr
Cline, Henry
Clock, Crestion
Clock, Jacob J.
Clock, Jacob J.
Clock, Jacob John Junr
Clock, Johanes
Clock, John
Clock, John Jr.
Clock, Joseph
Clock, Joseph G.
Clock, Joseph Junr.
Clyne, Peter
Cochran, John
Cole, John
Coney, Wm
Congton, Henry
Conney, William
Cook, Beadus
Cook, Casper
Cook, John B.
Cook, John
Cook, Simeon
Copely, William
Copernall, Adam
Crane, Caroling
Cross, Jacobus
Cross, James
Cule, Henry
Cule, Philip
Culeman, Henry
D***min, Jonathan
Dawson, Wm.
Dayton, Jessey
Deharsh, Abraham
Deharsh, Isaaeh
Deharsh, Martin
Deharsh, Philip
Dellenbach, Andrew J.
Dellenbach, John
Derry, Lundon
Dewandeller, John
Dewer, Edward
Dewey, William
Deygert, Peter S.
Deygert, Peter S. Junr
Deygert, Rudolph
Deygert, Severinus
Dicgson, Robert
Diefendorf, Jacob
Dillenbach, Hervey
Dillinbach, Richard

Donalds, James
Douglass, John
Doustr***, Jacob F.
Doxtrader, John F.
Du**, Wm.
Ducher, John
Dueslar, Elisabeth
Dueslar, Jacob Junr
Dueslar, John Jacob
Dueslar, Marcus
Dumb, Adam
Dumb, Conrod
Dumb, David
Dumb, Nicholas
Dumon, Jonathan
Eaker, George
Eaker, Jacob
Edwards, Samuel
Edwards, Samuel Junr
Ehle, William
Ehle, Petrus
Ehle, Peter Junr
Eigabroadt, George
Eigabrout, Peter
Eigerbroat, Christion
Eisenlord, Jogn
Empie, Frederick
Empie, Jacob
Empie, John F.
Empie, Philip
England, Benjamin
Fa**ing, John
Failing, John J.
Failing, John R.
Fancher, Benjamin
Faulknow, Caleb
Felt, Nathan
Fink, Andrew
Fink, Wm
Flander, John
Flander, Phillip
Flanders, Augustinus
Flanders, George
Flanders, George
Flander, Henry
Flanders, Henry
Flanders, Jacob
Fleiss, Nicholas Junr
Forbes, Jacob
Fox, Christopher
Fox, Christopher C.
Fox, Christopher W.
Fox, Christopher W.
Fox, Daniel
Fox, Daniel
Fox, Daniel C.
Fox, David
Fox, Jacob
Fox, John
Fox, Peter
Fox, Peter C.
Fox, Peter G.

Fox, Peter W
Fox, Wm
Fox, Wm
Frecker, John
Frederick, John C.
Freeman, Joseph
Freims, John F.
Frey, Abraham
Frey, James
Frey, John
Frey, John
Fry, Jacob
Fry, Jacob Senior
Fry, Phillip
Fygle, John
G***ble, John
Garter, Leonard
Gates, Freeman
Gender, Henry
Getman, Christian
Getman, Christian Junr
Getman, Frederick
Getman, Frederick Junr
Getman, George
Getman, Peter
Getman, Thomas
Gibson, John
Glen, John S.
Goodal, Stephen
Graff, Christian
Graff, Christian Junr
Graff, John
Gray, Andrew
Gray, Robert
Gray, Robert
Gray, Robert
Gray, Samuel Junr
Gary, Titus
Gray, Widow
Grembs, Henry
Grembs, Jacob
Grembs, John
Guile, Daniel
Guran, Jacob
H***ard, Rufas
Hansburgh, Anthony
Harding, Jacob
Hardy, James
Hart, Conrad
Hart, Henry
Harting, Jacob
Hele, Christopher
Hellebolt, Adolph
Hellicos, Conrod
Hellicos, Peter
Herring, John
Herring, Leonard
Herring, Lodewick
Herring, Philip
Hess, Daniel
Hess, John
Hewett, Randal
Hewitt, Josiah
Heyney, George

Heyney, Henry
Hicks, George
Hilts, Phillip
Hilts, Samuel
Hoak, Anthony
Horth, james
House, George
House, John C.
Huntly, Zadock
Hurding, John
Hyde, Elli
Hyde, Jelihu
Hyde, Joel
Ingersole, Daniel
Ingersole, John
Jefferst, Wm
Jenny, Bangs
Jennings, Samuel
Jewell, Joseph
Jingersole, Jessey
Johnson, James
Johnson, Moses
Jo*ns*n, Wm
Jon***, John
Kees, Henry
Keller, Michael
Kelly,George
Kennedy, Patrick
Kern, John
Kessler, Joseph
Kies, Peter
Kilts, Conrod
Kitts, Adam
Kitts, Peter L.
Klause, Jacob
Klause, John
Klause, Peter
Klo**, George
Klock, Christian
Klock, George G.
Klock, George J.
Klock, George Jo.
Klock, John J. Junr
Knap, James
Koch, Peter
Koons, Nocholas
Kram, John
Kretler, Leonard
Kring, Catharin
Kring, Jacob
Kring, Jacob
Kring, John
Kring, John
Kring, John Junr
Kring, John Ludwig
Krouse, John
Krouse, Widow
L**her, Henry
Ladaw, Jacob
Lampman, Peter Junr
Lansing, Sander
Lasher, Conrod J.
Lasher, Garrit
Lasher, George

Lasher, John
Lasher, John Junr
Lawrence, John
Layman, John
Lee, Abijah
Legeng, Jacob
Leip, **am
Leir, ***phus
Lepper, Conradt
Lick, David
Lighthall, Francis
Lockwood, James
Lodawich, Casper
Lodiwick, Abraham
Lodiwick, Peter
Longman, Peter
Lovelace, John
Loveless, Ezrom
Loveless, Joseph
Loux, Frederick
Loux, George
Loux, Jacob
Lyon, Banjamin
M*rtle, Jacob
March, Stephen
Marsielles, Gerrit
Marten, Alexander
McArthur, John
McNeil, Theodore
Merkle, Peter
Merkle, Dewalt
Merkell, Henry
Miller, Henry
Miller, Jellis
Miller, Phillip
Moher, Jacob
Moon, Jacob
Morfet, John
Moshur, Israel
Moshur, Peter
Moshur, Solomon
Moshur, Henry
Mott, Sears
Moyer, Jacob
Murphy, Francis
Near, Conradt
Near, Jacob
Near, Zachereas
Neehots, Wm
Nellis, Adam A.
Nellis, Henry W.
Nellis, John C.
Nellis, John L.
Nellis, John V.
Nellis, John W.
Nellis, Joseph
Nellis, Joseph Junr
Nellis, Ludwig
Nellis, Peter
Nellis, Peter, H.
Nellis, Peter M.
Nellis, Philip Junr
Nellis, Wm
Nellis, William Junr

Nestle, Gotlieb
Nestle, Henry
Newkirk, Charles
Nichols, Simon
Nillis, John D.
Nyhoff, John
Nyneman, Henry
Olney, Joseph
Oothout, Jonas
Par***, James
Parker, James
Patrick, Robert
Peckle, John
Petit, Jabes
Phillips, Abraham
Phrickey, John
Pier, John E.
Plank, Henry
Pleppe, Christian
Pool, James
Post, Henry
Putman, Arent
Putman, Gilbert
Quiema, Samuel
Rarick, John
Raum, Jacob
Reeber, Andrew
Richard, Ludwick
Richer, Nicholas
Richter, John
Ridley, James
Ries, Gideon
Ries, Jonas
Ries, Philip
Ross, Christian
Rouse, Andrew
Rouse, Andrew
Runnolds, Benjamin
Russell, John
Rutt, Charles
Saltsman, John
Saltsman, Henry Junr
Saltsman, William
Scott, Jacob
Scott, John
Scott, Samuel
Scott, Thomas
Scouton, Simon
Scram, Wm.
Selter, Henry
Shaver, Andrew
Shaver, Bartholomew
Shaver, Peter
Shaw, Comfort
Sheperman, Chrestion
Sherman, Gilbert
Shill, Jacob
Shitterly, John
Shole, Jost
Sholt, John
Sholt, John
Shoul, Joseph
Showl, Johanes
Shrum, Isaac

Shu***, Adam
Shutes, John P.
Shutes, John J.
Shults, Jacob
Shults, John
Shults, James
Shuts, Henry S.
Shuts, John Jo.
Sellinbach, Gerrit
Sillenbach, John
Slawson, Bowels
Slette, Peter
Smith, Balser
Smith, George Junr
Smith, Henry
Smith, Henry
Smith, Henry
Smith, Jeremiah
Smith, Nicholas Junr
Smith, Peter N.
Smith, Seth
Smith William
Sn*ll, Peter
Snell, Frederick J.
Snell, Frederick N.
Snell, George
Snell, John
Snell, John J.
Snell, John Jo.
Snell, Nicholas
Snell, Peter J.
Snell, Peter N.
Sobreskie, Andrew
Souls, Benjamin
Spankneble, John
Spankneble, John
Spankneble, Philip
Sprecker, Conrod
Sprecker, John
Sprecker, Joseph
Starr, George H.
Steenborough, Jeremiah
Stuward, Obediah
Stillwell, Samuel
Storms, David
Storms, Peter
Strader, Nicholas
Straher, John
Strayder, Nicholas
Strecker, Fredeick
Strecker, Philip
Stroup, Henry
Suits, Catharine
Suits, Peter
Suits, John P.
Suts, Nicholas
Suts, Peter J.
Suts, Peter R.
Suts, Richard
Swart, Lodewick
Swartwout, John
Sweetman, Henderson
Tench, Jost
Thum, Dewalt

Timmerman, Henry
Timmerman, Jacob
Trumbull, Jonethan
Trumbull, William
Trumbull, Wm Junr
Tuesler, John J.
Tusler, Marcus
Van*nbo*, Peter
Van ***, James
Van Beuren, Wm
Van Deusen, Chauncey
Van Dewelker, Albert S.
Van Dewerker, John
Van Driesen, Peter
Van Etton, Samuel
Van Skiver, Abraham
Van Sleick, Peter
Van Sleigh, Nicholas
Van Slyck, Adam H.
Van Valkenburgh, James
Van Vangenburgh, John
Van Wie, Andrew
Vender, Ephriam
Vedder, Harmanus
Vedder, John
Vedder, Widow
Veeder, Jacob
Vrooman, Simon J.
W***ner, Peter
Wagganer, George
Wagoner, John
Waldrat, Adolphus
Waldrot, Johanis
Wall, William
Wallett, Nathan
Walrat, Adam
Walrath, John A.
Walrath, Isaac
Walrath, Peter H.
Walrot, Adam J.
Walrot, John A.
Wanser, Isaac
Wanser, Thomas
Washburn, Miles
Waters, David
Waters, Samuel
Weaver, Daniel
Weaver, Jacob G.
Weaver, John Jo.
Weilds, George
Wemple, Cornelius
Wenworth, John
Wetherbee, Isaac
Whitmire, George
Wick, Severimus
Wilds, David
Williams, James
Williams, Lewis
Williamson, Henry
Wolf, Valantine
Wolgemuth, Widow
Wohlgemuth, Wm
Wormwood, Conradt
Wormwood, Regina

Yerrington, Wm.	***ler,John	*nell, Frederick
Yucker, George	**o*k, Joseph	***e, George
Yucker, Solomon	****tle, Leander	***nyans, Philip
Ziely,David	**or****, Jacob	***e, Henry
Ziely, John	*****st, John	*u*n, Conra*
Ziely, Thomas	****oll, Nicholas	

Check the website for a list showing how many in the household.etc. http://threerivershms.com

---

Assessment Roll, 1799

The record is difficult at best to read. In many cases, I had to guess at the names and some were omitted because they were blurred.

This assessment roll shows who was on the land in the year of 1799 and from the names on the roll you can tell which area of the town where they were located.   Look at the patent maps for the patentees, then you can figure out who were neighbors and where they lived.

Apparently this was the first year the assessments were done for the purpose of taxation. At any rate, this was the earliest record available. The records were found in the Albany Archives, for the County of Albany. No assessor's maps were available for helping in the assessment process until in the 1970s. It had to be difficult for the assessors to determine if all the land was accounted for on the assessment roll.

The Town of Palatine was much larger in 1799. It had to be a very time consuming process to ride around to all the various pieces of land and determine the value.

The people were assessed on land, buildings and personal property which probably included livestock and household goods. Some names appear to be children and they were assessed on personal property. Often the numbers are not clear and there are tears on some pages. I did my best.

The title at the top of the record reads:

"Assessment Roll of the Real and Personal Estates in the Town of Palatine in the County of Montgomery made this eighteenth day of October in the year of our Lord one thousand seven hundred and ninety nine, according to the directions of the statute entitled "An Act for the Assessment and collection of Taxes." By Peter Grames Junr. Hanjost Scholl, Coenradt Lepper and Peter Clank, Jr. Assessors of said Town."

In other words, the people paid taxes on their real property, land, houses, farms, etc. and also on personal property. You will note there are many instances of property listed as personal with no real property listed. My guess is the young son had a nice horse and he paid a tax on the horse.

Names of Persons	Description of Real Estate	Real Estate Value	Personal Estate Value	Taxes to be Paid
		Dollar	Dollar	Dollar
Adam Lipe Junr.	House and Farm	2170.00	251.00	2.42
Isaac Walradt	House and Farm	3460.00	470.00	3.93
Peter H Walradt	House and Farm	1090.00	205.00	2.90
Samuel Stedwell	House and Farm	220.00	23.00	0.24
Soverinus Cook	House and lot	120.00	30.00	0.15
John Nighoft	House and Farm	240.00	62.00	0.30
Eupraim Veeder	None		99.00	0.09
George G. Snell	House and Farm	2250.00	171.00	2.42
Caroline Cram	House and Farm	2500.00	112.00	2.61
Harminus Van Slyck	House and Farm	11020.00	231.00	4.25
Adam Van Slyck	House and Farm		72.00	0.07
Widow Starin	House and Farm	2940.00	120.00	3.60
Adam Starin	None		20.00	0.02
Soverinus Starin	None		60.00	0.06
George L. Starin	None		50.00	0.05

John Starin	None		35.00	0.03
Jacob Shill	House and Farm	1200.00	121.00	1.40
Sander Martin	House and Farm	1300.00	124.00	1.42
Peter Van Slyck	House and Farm	1305.00	44.00	1.34
Edward Oeser	None		44.00	1.34
Jacob Eaker	House and Farm	5310.00	575.00	5.75
Widow Eaker	House and Farm	2010.00	2.62	2.27
George Eaker	House and Farm	4970.00	424.00	5.35
Loverinus Dygert	House and Farm	2600.00	200.00	2.80
Peter Dygert	None		145.00	0.14
Several entries are not legible				
John Finck	House and Farm	3300.00	564.00	3.06
George Waggoner	House and Farm	4240.00	1110.00	4.35
William Nellis	House and Farm	4150.00	456.00	4.60
William Nellis Junr	None		456.00	4.60
Philip Nellis	House and Farm	20700.00	313.00	3.11
Philip Nellis Junr	None		160.00	1.60
Nicholas Coppernoll	House and Farm	2360.00	624.00	0.16
Harmeaus Brower	None		106.00	1.06
Cornelius Brower	House and Farm	2100.00	26.00	2.50
Nicholas R. Sutz	None		10.00	0.01
John Coppernoll	House and Lot	40.00	0.00	0.04
Hanjost Finck	House Farm and Mill	1600.00	139.00	1.73
Peter Homan	House and Lot	210.00	35.00	0.24
John Sitterly	House and Farm	2415.00	96.00	2.51
Christian Ruff	House and Farm	1760.00	103.00	1.06
John I Sutz	House and Farm	2360.00	309.00	2.66
Arent Brower	House and Farm	2634.00	151.00	2.70
John B. Cook	House and Farm	1003.00	160.00	2.40
Christian Finck	House and Farm	3700.00	3400.00	4.04
Baltus Dillenback	House and Farm	2000.00	166.00	2.16
Richard Dillenback	House and Farm	1250.00	201.00	1.45
Henry Lasher	None	"	1.00	0.00
Gerrit Lasher	House and Farm	2177.50	166.00	2.34
Adam Kilts	House and Farm	810.00	130.00	0.94
John L. Zielmann	House, Farm & Mills	630.00	30.00	0.66
Jeremiah Smith	House and Lot	80.00	70.00	0.15
John A. Cook	House and Lot	65.00	41.00	0.10
Coenradt Lasher	House and Farm	1900.00	127.00	2.20
Jacob Near	House and Lot	85.00	87.00	0.17
Widow Wolkamuth	House and Farm	2040.00	206.00	3.12
Elias Ruto	None	"	55.00	0.05
William Wolkamuth	House and Farm	4090.00	479.00	5.36

Thomas Ziely	House and Farm	2003.00	212.00	2.29
Conradt Spracker	House and Farm	3020.00	212.00	4.30
John Van Wie	House and Farm	6210.00	626.00	6.03
Lewis Williams Junr	None		129.00	0.12
Lowrance G Stam	House and Farm	800.00	111.00	0.91
Andrew VanWie	House and Farm	3030.00	660.00	4.49
Henry Keyser	House and Farm	4500.00	532.00	5.30
John Wavel	House, Farm & Mill	2064.00	194.00	2.25
John Cook	House and Farm	3650.00	337.00	3.90
Rudolph Dygert	House and Farm	1600.00	436.00	2.11
Adam Snell	House and Farm	2000.00	3135.00	5.93
Yost? A. Snell	None		77.00	0.07
Lodwick Young	House and Farm	2470.00	150.00	2.62
Henry Shults	House and Farm	3624.00	335.00	3.75
George Saltsman	House and Farm	3300.00	331.00	3.71
Daniel C. Fox	House and Farm	3060.00	339.00	3.39
Peter Sutz	House and Farm	1740.00	136.00	1.07
Henry Coolman	None		15.00	0.01
John L. Nellis	House and Farm	4160.00	345.00	4.50
John Spanknable Junr	House and lot	250.00	29.00	0.27
Lodwick Nellis	House and Lot	400.00	100.00	0.50
Richard Loucks	House and Farm	1770.00	265.00	2.03
Harmen Brower Junr	House and Farm	2100.00	153.00	2.25
Jacob Loucks	House and Farm	2150.00	300.00	2.53
Coenradt Kilts	House and Farm	2010.00	467.00	3.27
Peter A. Suitz	House and Farm	350.00	97.00	0.44
Jacob Snell	House and Farm	9904.00	725.00	10.70
Nicholas Eaker	House and Farm	4000.00	560.00	5.44
Adam Loucks	House and Farm	3400.00	200.00	3.69
Henry Cook	House and Farm	3060.00	262.00	3.32
Jacob Mohr	House and Farm	105.00	40.00	0.22
John Straher	House and Farm	5463.00	2054.00	7.51
George Shults	House and Farm	3050.00	640.00	5.69
Jacob Shults	House and Farm	530.00	60.00	0.59
George Loucks	House and Farm	3240.00	566.00	3.00
Andrew Gray	House and Farm	4200.00	508.00	4.70
Adam Gray	None		20.00	0.02
Andrew Coljadon	None		42.00	0.04
John P. Grames	House and Farm	2750.00	615.00	3.36
Henry Grames Junr	None		450.00	0.45
Henry Grames Junr	House and Farm	3200.00	36.00	3.23
Arnoudt Vedder	House and Farm	7230.00	600.00	7.03
Harmen Vedder	None		30.00	0.03
Peter Cook	House and Farm	500.00	220.00	0.72

Peter Grames Junr	House and Farm	3450.00	954.00	4.40
Christopher C. Fox	Farm or Lot	1005.00	146.00	2.03
Henry N. Smith	House and Farm	255.00	115.00	0.07
Charles Newkerck	House, Farm Mill?	9837.00	855.00	10.69
Peter G. Fox	House and Farm	4000.00	729.00	5.52
Peter Waggoner	House and Farm	9575.00	1173.00	10.74
Peter Waggoner, Junr	Farm or Lot	240.00	637.00	0.07
Jacob Bersh	None		35.00	0.03
George Birsh	House and Lot	1400.00	80.00	0.22
Peter Wormuth	House and Farm	7570.00	559.00	8.12
John Waggoner	House and Farm	4000.00	437.00	4.43
Benjamin Fermen	None		55.00	0.05
James Dun	None		5.00	0.00
Archibald Gibson	None		10.00	0.01
Joseph Waggoner	House, Farm and Mills	11200.00	1727.00	12.92
John G Klock	Farms	1100.00	330.00	1.43
George I Klock	House and Farm	1400.00	140.00	1.54
John Eisenlord	House and Farm	1860.00	233.00	2.09
Hilkert Bauder	House and Farm	3440.00	306.00	3.74
Philip Galor	House and Lot	250.00	50.00	0.30
John Walradt	House and Farm	4060.00	284.00	5.24
Gerrit I Walradt	None		402.00	0.40
John I Walradt			3030.00	3.03
John Tygel			443.00	0.44
Peter Ehl	House and Farm	6055.00	463.00	6.51
Peter Ehl Junr			165.00	0.16
Nicholas Van Slyck	House, Farm & Mill	9225.00	550.00	9.77
John Frey, Major	House and Farm	5306.00	4538.00	9.94
William Ehl	House and Farm	1460.00	184.00	1.64
Simon Nicholls	House and Farm	755.00	66.00	0.82
Geroge Starin	House and Farm	833.00	178.00	1.10
Genderson Sweetman	House and Farm	3170.00	135.00	3.30
Cloudy Van Deusen	House and Farm	2470.00	142.00	2.61
Isaac Weatherby	House and Lot	200.00	45.00	0.24
Joseph Bovee	House and Lot	55.00	15.00	0.07
Henry Herman			10.00	0.01
George Watser			54.00	0.05
John Van Slyck			9.00	0.00
? Spracker	House, Farm & Store	6060.00	660.00	7.52
George Spracker			32.00	0.03
John DeWarDelaer?	House and Farm	7933.00	1072.00	9.00
John Spracker	House and Farm	2363.00	2.41	2.60
Anthony Huyck	House and Farm	475.00	95.00	0.56
Abraham Geater			4.00	0.00

Gerrit Sillebach	House and Farm	2470.00	407.00	2.95
Philip Kils	House and Farm	1920.00	164.00	2.08
Widow Warmuth	House and Farm	890.00	75.00	0.96
Adam Coppernoll	House and Farm	160.00	32.00	0.19
Alexander Van Lies			40.00	0.04
Joseph Van Lies			30.00	0.03
George House			75.00	0.07
Coenradt Warmuth			7.00	0.00
Jacob Leavere	House and Farm	341.00	100.00	0.44
George Kelly	House and Farm	1570.00	234.00	1.80
Gutlip Nestle	House and Farm	2630.00	240.00	2.87
Christopher Harin			12.00	0.01
Peter Nestle			12.00	0.01
Henry Dillenback	House and Farm	1200.00	131.00	1.31
John Dillenback	House and Farm	4660.00	450.00	5.11
Coenradt Dillenback			40.00	0.04
John Dillenback Junr			40.00	0.01
John Ziely	House and Farm	3850.00	470.00	4.32
David Ziely	Farm or Lot	1000.00	112.00	1.00
John Martin			30.00	0.03
Jonas Rur	House and Lot	75.00	53.00	0.12
Peter Van Etten	House and Lot	45.00	8.00	0.05
John I Shuttes	House and Farm	2335.00	249.00	2.58
Theobato Merkell	House and Farm	3005.00	353.00	3.35
Peter Merkoll			71.00	0.07
Henry Merkell	House, Farm and Mills	6280.00	515.00	6.79
John Merkell	Farm	833.00	84.00	0.95
Casper Cook	House and Farm	2850.00	125.00	2.97
Rudolph Cook			55.00	0.05
John Lasher	House and Farm	3850.00	4.90	3.84
George Lasher			39.00	0.03
John Lasher Junr.			45.00	0.04
Zachariah Near	House and Lot	120.00	10.00	0.13
Michael M Bauder	House and Farm	1000.00	192.00	2.07
Peter G. Sutz	House and Farm	250.00	41.00	0.29
John Merril	House and Farm	130.00	41.00	0.17
Widow Saleman	House and Farm	700.00	99.00	0.79
John Pickle Junr	House and Farm	295.00	57.00	0.35
Benjamin England	House and Farm	1430.00	93.00	1.52
John F. Dockstader	House and Farm	1600.00	195.00	1.87
John Silleback	House and Farm	2260.00	225.00	2.40
Samuel Gray Junr			66.00	0.06
Michael Ehl	House and Farm	3665.00	298.00	3.96
William Ehl Junr	House and Lot	130.00	29.00	0.15

Josiah Rees	House and Farm	1450.00	0.84	1.53
Martin Nestle	House and Farm	2300.00	190.00	2.49
Martinus Nestle Junr			48.00	0.04
Henry Near	House and Farm	1150.00	80.00	1.23
George Starin Junr	House and Lot	650.00	210.00	0.86
Peter N. Kils	House and Farm	1410.00	199.00	1.60
Peter Rus	House and Farm	2730.00	126.00	2.86
Henry I Shultis	House and Farm	1864.00	193.00	2.05
Jacob Sutz	House and Farm	818.00	110.00	0.92
Martinus B Dillenback			35.00	0.03
Henry Sutz	House and Farm	3420.00	300.00	3.72
Andrew Dillenback	House and Farm	2500.00	135.00	2.71
William Garner			95.00	0.09
Peter Staller	House and Farm	5.95	0.55	0.65
Soverinus Wick	House and Farm	1750.00	209.00	1.95
John Pickel	House and Lot	340.00	2010.00	2.35
Andrew Finck	House and Farm	5390.00	8.94	6.28
John Hees	House and Farm	1950.00	434.00	2.38
Gorton Lathrop	House and Lot	650.00	40.00	0.39
John Winworth	House and Lot	350.00	40.00	0.39
James Finley			130.00	0.13
Jacob Raum			14.00	0.01
Nathanel Kimball			314.00	0.31
Widow Prium			6.00	0.00
John I Pruim Junr			5.00	0.00
John Nellis	House and Farm	5950.00	3737.00	9.68
John I Nellis			42.00	0.04
Isaac Schram			19.00	0.01
Andrew Rouse	House and Farm	1480.00	140.00	1.62
Henry Lodwick			105.00	0.10
Casper Lodwick	House and Farm	2160.00	220.00	2.30
Daniel Fox	House and Farm	2155.00	274.00	2.42
Daniel J. Fox			45.00	0.04
Rudolph Barre	House and Lot	169.00	54.00	0.22
Joseph Fox	House and Farm	316.00	99.00	0.41
Wiliam Fox			45.00	0.04
Peter Fox	House and Farm	1850.00	172.00	2.02
John Flander			102.00	0.10
William W. Fox	House, Farm and Mills	2700.00	219.00	2.91
Jacob G Fox	House and Farm	2480.00	548.00	3.02
Christopher W. Fox Junr	House and Farm	1590.00	171.00	1.76
Coenradt Thum	House and Farm	860.00	75.00	0.93
David Thum	House and Farm	500.00	87.00	0.58
Peter Clause	House and Farm	1550.00	35.00	1.58

John Clause			239.00	0.23
Jacob Clause			5.00	
James Radley	House and Farm	1000.00	114.00	1.11
Frances Lighthall			9.00	0.00
Benjamin Toler			75.00	0.07
William Welch			8.00	
John Leaman	House and Farm	770.00	82.00	0.85
Peter Lampman Junr.	House and Farm	4450.00	1847.55	6.24
Joseph Nellis	House and Farm	1978.00	689.00	2.66
Peter W. Nellis	House and Farm	1510.00	170.00	1.68
John C. Fox	House and Farm	1250.00	122.00	1.37
Widow Krouse	House and Farm	1160.00	204.00	1.35
Joseph Klock	House and Farm	1515.00	85.00	1.60
Henry W. Nellis	House and Farm	1000.00	135.00	1.13
George Weaver			35.00	0.03
William Schram			6.00	
John Kring Junr	Farm	800.00	34.00	0.83
John Kring	House and Farm	1100.00	218.00	1.31
Adam Nellis	House and Farm	3550.00	1858.00	5.40
Adam Nellis Junr			15.00	0.01
Jacob I Klock	House and Farm	5150.00	332.00	5.48
John J Klock			10.00	0.01
Adam Bearse	House and Farm	1000.00	126.00	1.72
Christian Shepperman	House and Farm	1100.00	74.00	1.17
Philip Helmer			5.00	0.00
John Rickert			7.00	0.00
Adam Thum Junr	House and Lot	80.00	364.00	0.44
George Anthony	House and Farm	2650.00	5620.00	8.27
George Flander			46.00	0.04
James Bool			10.00	0.01
John G Brown	House and Farm	30.00	147.00	0.17
Jacob Best, Juns			22.00	0.02
John Hefs	House, Farm and Mills	1790.00	792.00	2.58
Peter Eygebroat	House and Lot	200.00	0.81	0.28
John Van Valkenburgh	House and Lot	300.00	25.00	0.32
John Dingus			5.00	
Jesse Dayton	House and Lot	300.00	15.00	.35
Simon Dayton			42.00	0.04
Herny I Bellinger	House and Farm	3600.00	306.00	3.90
Jonas V. Oothout	House and Lot	1000.00	600.00	1.60
Benjamin Lyon			170.00	0.17
Caleb Faulkner	House and Lot	95.00	78.00	0.17
John Gibson	House, Lot and Farm	700.00	105.00	0.80
Christian Eygebroat			12.00	0.01

Name	Property	Value	Personal	Tax
Peter C. Fox			300.00	0.30
Christopher W Fox	House and Farm	4625.00	280.00	4.90
John I Bellinger	House and Farm	4625.00	280.00	4.90
John March	House and Farm	1791.00	167.00	1.95
John P. Sutz	House and Lot	35.00	20.00	0.05
Agus Fairchild	House and Farm	750.00	10.00	0.76
Joseph B Ames	House and Farm	1675.00	13.00	1.68
Adolph House	House and Farm	765.00	80.00	0.84
Moses Johnson	House and Farm	750.00	57.00	0.80
Solomon Youker			23.00	0.02
Adolph Hellebold			11.00	0.01
Peter Bellinger	House and Farm	605.00	54.00	0.65
Jacob G. Klock Junr	House and Farm	1420.00	75.00	1.49
Elihu Hyde	House and Farm	2150.00	147.00	2.29
Elle Hyde	House and Farm	200.00	17.00	0.26
Joel Hyde	House and Farm	500.00	17.00	0.51
John Girn	House and Lot	65.00	75.00	0.13
Samuel Ginnance	House and Lot	75.00	12.00	0.08
John Ingersoll			41.00	0.04
Frederick Osterhout	House and Farm	1700.00	191.00	1.89
Peter Storms	House and Farm	1100.00	136.00	1.23
Michael N Bauder	House and Farm	2350.00	171.00	2.07
David Storms	House and Farm	240.00	37.00	0.28
Benjamin Grittengton	House and Farm	165.00	31.00	0.19
Frederick Bellinger	House and Farm	2950.00	239.00	3.10
Joseph Bellinger	House and Farm	620.00	87.00	0.70
Sophy Bellinger			22.00	0.02
Henry Bellinger	House and Farm	2550.00	171.00	2.72
Henry Flander	House and Farm	1837.50	133.00	1.97
Deanus Flander	House and Farm	1275.00	127.00	1.40
Henry Hardt	House and Farm	750.00	86.00	0.83
John Salsbury	House and Farm	600.00	65.00	0.66
Michael Keller	House and Farm	250.00	1.00	0.25
Jacob Ladue	House and Farm	350.00	45.00	0.39
John Ladue	House and Farm	541.00	41.00	0.58
William Yandon	House and Farm	541.00	41.00	0.58
John Dutcher	House and Farm	270.00	35.00	0.30
Mahirm Benedict	House and Farm	290.00	20.00	0.35
Peter Moses	House and Farm	452.00	35.00	0.48
James Lockwood			1.00	.
William Been	House and Farm	300.00	35.00	0.33
Isreal Bates			35.00	0.03
Jacob Bates			21.00	0.02
Daniel Guildes	House and Farm	500.00	60.00	0.56

Randall Hewit	House and Farm	520.00	58.00	0.57
Richard Hewit	House and Farm	1049.00	63.00	1.11
Benjamin Cheedle	House and Farm	320.00	23.00	0.31
Serus Mott	House and Lot	10.00	1.00	0.08
Ezra Cheedle			32.00	3.00
Abjah Lee	House and Farm	532.00	36.00	0.56
John Moffet	House and Farm	532.00	20.00	0.56
James Sefert			31.00	3.00
Noah Baldwin			45.00	0.04
Simon Cook	House and Farm	520.00	2.00	0.52
Asa Baldwin			14.00	0.01
Asaram Lovelefs			20.00	0.02
David Leek			30.00	0.03
Henry Cline	House and Farm	880.00	452.00	1.33
Peter Cline	House and Farm	1305.00	140.00	1.52
Gilbert Shaman	Farm	200.00	13.00	0.21
John Swarworst	Farm	534.00	30.00	0.58
Samuel Edwards	House and Farm	545.00	42.00	0.58
Samuel Edwards Junr	House and Farm	525.00	27.00	0.55
William Burtes	Farm	962.00	1.00	0.96
Benjamin Barry	House and Farm	1020.00	82.00	1.10
Abraham Berfoe			2.00	0.00
John Lesit			53.00	0.05
John Berfoe	House and Farm	210.00	53.00	0.26
James Lovelefs	House and Farm	420.00	33.00	0.45
Alphus Ballard			40.00	0.04
Leonard Haring	House and Farm	750.00	54.00	0.80
Jacob Flander	House and Farm	1180.00	124.00	1.30
Philip Flander			31.00	0.03
Ludwick Haring			61.00	0.06
Peter A Nellis	House and Farm	625.00	68.00	0.69
Henry Hees	Farm	600.00	62.00	0.66
Coenradt Flander			220.00	0.22
Joseph J Klock	House and Farm	800.00	53.00	0.85
John C. House	House and Farm	760.00	65.00	1.06
Zadock Hundley	Farm	600.00	14.00	0.61
Hanyost Scholl	House, Farm & Mill	5690.00	883.00	6.57
Jacob Empey	House and Farm	1750.00	132.00	1.88
Adam Kils	House and Farm	1910.00	247.00	2.15
John Shultis	House and Farm	2960.00	357.00	3.35
Henry Saltsman Junr	House and Farm	3600.00	444.00	4.12
John Salsman	House and Farm	3250.00	373.00	3.62
Richard Suitz	House and Farm	450.00	70.00	0.52
Badus Cook	House and Farm	2440.00	186.00	2.63

John Kelsh			47.00	4.00
John Kirker	House and Lot	65.00	27.00	0.09
John Shultes Jr	House, Farm and Mill	4492.00	429.00	4.92
Michael Bauder	House, Farm and Mill	3260.00	227.00	3.40
William Salsman	House and Farm	2780.00	402.00	3.10
Frederick Getman	House and Farm	5000.00	1410.00	6.11
Henry Miller	House and Farm	3000.00	75.00	3.07
Richard Young	House and Farm	1441.00	111.00	1.55
George Getman	House and Farm	1070.00	123.00	1.19
John Gramer			7.00	0.00
Loversinus Caselsman	House and Farm	600.00	109.00	0.70
John Caselman	House and Farm	1460.00	202.00	1.66
Henry Bradt	House and Farm	848.00	69.00	0.95
Richard Coppernoll	House and Farm	1250.00	103.00	1.35
John Frey Jr	House and Farm	270.00	55.00	0.32
Adam Cosselman			8.00	0.00
Nicholas Christman	House and Farm	550.00	31.00	0.58
John Gray	House and Farm	2573.00	185.00	2.78
Thomas Getman	House and Farm	3760.00	288.00	4.04
John A Beck	House and Farm	930.00	110.00	1.04
Jacob Getman	House and Farm	500.00	30.00	0.53
Ludwick Rickert	House and Farm	1770.00	241.00	2.05
John Snell	House and Farm	2975.00	183.00	3.15
Christian Getman	House and Farm	2300.00	180.00	2.40
Frederick Snell Junr			14.00	1.00
John Snell Junr			30.00	3.00
William Owen			14.00	1.00
Baltus Smith	House and Farm	300.00	59.00	0.35
Henry A Smith	House and Farm	300.00	104.00	0.04
Jermiah N. Smith	House and Farm	300.00	90.00	0.39
Christian Getman Junr			110.00	0.11
John Osman			30.00	0.03
Jeremiah Steenburgh	House and Lot	50.00	5.00	0.05
Jacob Beeler			5.00	0.00
Frederick Getman Junr			96.00	0.09
Bartholomew Shaver	House and Farm	3100.00	530.00	3.53
Samuel Gray	House and Farm	3690.00	259.00	3.94
Jasper Lodweick Junr	House and Farm	2350.00	123.00	2.47
John Reed	House and Farm	950.00	147.00	1.09
Frederick Barris	House and Farm		36.00	0.03
John Braim	Farm	160.00	38.00	0.19
Frederick Snell Junr	House and Farm	1142.00	138.00	1.28
John Snell Jr	House and Farm	1142.00	142.00	1.28
Jacob Christman	House and Farm	3263.00	1723.00	3.98

Henry Williams				74.00	0.07
John T Empey	House and Farm		1590.00	225.00	1.81
Frederick Empey				54.00	0.05
John Graff	House and Farm		2250.00	381.00	2.63
Jabez Pettit	House and Farm		342.00	31.00	0.37
Ludwick Kring	House and Farm		534.00	120.00	0.65
Philip Miller	House and Farm		900.00	179.00	1.07
Jellis Miller				85.00	0.08
Charles Rutt	House and Farm		1559.00	124.00	1.60
Christopher Bartels	House and Farm		1000.00	126.00	1.12
John Hordig	House and Farm		330.00	74.00	0.40
Jacob I Snell	House and Farm		1030.00	135.00	1.16
John Scholl	House, Farm and Mill		805.00	196.00	1.00
Albert Vanderwerken				56.00	0.05
James Villington	House, Farm and Mill		740.00	105.00	0.85
Simon Scouton				25.00	0.02
John Lawrence	House and Farm		170.00	39.00	0.20
Samuel Van Etten	House and Farm		640.00	92.00	0.73
Peter Getman	House and Farm		635.00	110.00	0.74
Samuel Van Etten Junr	House and Farm		400.00	81.00	0.48
William Dowsen	House and Farm		510.00	62.00	0.57
Cornelius Wemp				16.00	0.01
William Cooplin	House and Farm		700.00	12.00	0.71
Nicholas Richter	House, Farm and Mill		1300.00	714.00	2.01
Abraham Philinse	House and Farm		250.00	20.00	0.53
Frederick Strobeck	House and Farm		505.00	32.00	0.53
John Storbeck				20.00	0.02
Frederick Strobeck Junr				30.00	0.03
Philip Strobeck				34.00	0.03
Christian Plapper	House and Farm		250.00	60.00	0.31
William Smith	House and Farm		620.00	122.00	0.71
John Haring	House, Farm and Mill		450.00	85.00	0.53
Henry Haring	House, Farm and Mill		300.00	86.00	0.30
William Wall				24.00	0.02
Isaac Dehorse				20.00	0.02
Phillip Dehouse	House and Farm		463.00	117.00	0.58
Abraham Dehouse	House and Farm		463.00	76.00	0.53
Philip Empey	House and Farm		1050.00	88.00	1.13
John Richter	House and Farm		1047.00	111.00	1.15
Martin Dehorse	House and Farm		463.00	90.00	0.56
Nicholas Snell	House and Farm		1350.00	199.00	1.54
Frederick N. Snell	Farm		200.00	10.00	0.21
Seth Smith	House and Farm		300.00	44.00	0.34
Robert Patrick				4.00	0.00

John Trumbull			70.00	0.07
Daniel Bennett	House and Farm	265.00	44.00	0.30
William Water			11.00	0.00
Isaac Everest	House, Farm and Mill	766.00	60.00	0.82
George Phye	House and Farm	600.00	1600.00	0.76
Henry Phye			12.00	0.01
Banks Binny	House and Farm	500.00	45.00	0.54
John Dunckels	House and Farm	500.00	102.00	0.60
Henry Smith	House and Farm	500.00	250.00	0.52
Samuel Waters	House and Farm	400.00	60.00	0.46
Josiah Hewitt	House and Farm	600.00	121.00	0.72
Philip Coole	House and Farm	950.00	120.00	1.07
John Spanknable	House and Farm	1500.00	720.00	2.22
Jacob Teresler Junr	House and Farm	820.00	126.00	0.94
Henry Coole	House and Farm	880.00	130.00	1.03
Elizabeth Teresler			97.00	0.09
Gilbert Putman			120.00	0.12
Peter N Smith	House and Farm	110.00	?	0.22
George Reyter			17.00	0.01
Jacob Hasting			70.00	0.07
William Van Dusen	House and Farm	690.00	74.00	0.76
John Fricken	House and Farm	500.00	64.00	0.64
Ernest Geer	House and Farm	300.00	63.00	0.36
Robert Gray	House and Farm	1200.00	45.00	1.24
Nicholas Straytor	House and Farm	1150.00	91.00	1.24
Henry Gynsing?			66.00	0.06
Leonard Kretzer	House and Farm	400.00	110.00	0.51
George Hyning?	House and Farm	555.00	112.00	0.66
George Smith	House and Farm	750.00	149.00	0.89
Nicholas Smith	House and Farm	1150.00	179.00	1.32
Christian Billington			45.00	0.04
John Billington			300.00	0.03
Petrus Billington			42.00	0.04
Christopher Shutes			27.00	0.02
Casparus B. Cook			5.00	0.00
George I Shults			15.00	0.01
George Getman Junr			15.00	0.01
Daniel Phye			5.00	0.00
Jacob Yoran	House and Lot	300.00	114.00	0.49
Samuel Tuesnover?	Farm	1500.00	25.00	1.52
Leonard Garence			5.00	0.00
Nicholas Shafer			37.00	0.03
Andrew Shafer			106.00	0.01
David Fancher	House and Farm	1060.00	106.00	1.16

Henry Reynols	House and Farm	1990.00	71.00	2.06
Jacob Failing	House and Farm	1230.00	77.00	1.30
Daniel Ingersol	House and Farm	800.00	100.00	0.90
Ephraim Fancher			45.00	0.04
Thomas Clark	Farm	250.00	12.00	0.26
Robert Anderson	House and Lot	150.00	15.00	0.16
John Tuesler Jr	House and Farm	775.00	70.00	0.84
Marcus Tuesler	House and Farm	330.00	60.00	0.39
Nicholas Thum Junr	House and Farm	770.00	65.00	0.83
Jacob Frey	House and Farm	320.00	21.00	0.34
William Dewy			3.00	0.00
Jacob Frey Junr	House and Farm	320.00	43.00	0.36
Harmanus Veeder	House and Farm	305.00	63.00	0.44
Jacob H. Failing	House and Farm	2550.00	116.00	2.66
John Genter			2.00	0.00
Frederick Klock	House and Farm	120.00	53.00	0.07
George Wiles	House and Farm	2150.00	175.00	2.32
Conradt Hilligas	House and Farm	1000.00	1100.00	2.37
John Banker	House and Farm	1000.00	130.00	1.33
David Nellis			21.00	0.02
John Failing Jr			107.00	0.10
Henry Failing Jr			265.00	0.26
Christian Klock	House and Farm	2930.00	251.00	3.10
Jacob Timmerman	House and Farm	5166.00	413.00	5.57
Joseph Keller			39.00	0.03
George Stout			15.00	0.01
Henry I Timmerman	House and Farm	3255.00	214.00	3.16
Peter Hilligas	House and Lot	210.00	25.00	0.23
Jacob Veeder	House and Farm	3150.00	111.00	3.26
John Veeder			55.00	0.05
Adolph H. Walradt	House and Farm	1200.00	65.00	.1.26
Jacob G Klock	House Farm and Mill	9000.00	250.00	10.13
George Klock Jr.			50.00	0.05
John A Walradt	House and Farm	3700.00	155.00	3.85
Adam I Walradt	House and Lot	92.00	92.00	0.10
William Walradt			5.00	0.00
George G. Klock	House Farm & Mills	11095.00	1166.00	13.06
James Barker			5.00	0.00
Francis Jacobs			5.00	0.00
Pater Van Alen			2.00	0.00
James Barker (The Weaver)			3.00	0.00
William VanDriesen	House and Farm	1000.00	1.00	1.00
George Eygebroat	House and Farm	1000.00	140.00	2.02
George Witmyer			66.00	0.06

Name	Property	Value	Amount	Tax
James Cochran	House and Farm	11722.00	1135.00	12.85
Charles Walton			15.00	0.01
Philip Spanknable			42.00	0.04
Peter Van Driesen	House and Farm	1500.00	127.00	1.62
Jacob Forbush	House and Farm	20.00	73.00	0.09
Jacob Hory	House and Farm	750.00	43.00	0.79
Thomas Ballard	House and Farm	520.00	40.00	0.56
Rufus Ballard			20.00	0.02
James Johnson	House and Farm	1117.00	135.00	1.25
Henry Post	House and Lot	70.00	12.00	0.08
Caleb Gardner			5.00	0.00
Freeman Gates	House and Farm	390.00	20.00	0.41
Nicholas Coons	House and Farm	731.00	40.00	0.77
Stephen Goodale			2.00	0.00
Christian Nellis	House and Farm	6485.00	1036.00	7.52
John C. Nellis	Farm	500.00	567.00	1.06
Peter N. Snell	Farm	600.00	38.00	0.63
Jacob Kring			74.00	0.07
Nicholas Post	House and Farm	1052.00	130.00	1.18
John R. Failing	House and Farm	4700.00	160.00	4.94
Cornelius C. Beeckman	House and Farm	1925.00	89.00	2.03
Henry Beeckman	House and Farm	1300.00	163.00	0.12
Anthony Frame	House and Lot	350.00	74.00	0.42
Leonard Bauder	House and Farm	750.00	91.00	0.84
William Johnson	House and Farm	85.00	12.00	0.09
Thomas Schoot	House and Farm	1630.00	56.00	1.68
Samuel Schoot	House and Farm	830.00	90.00	0.92
John Youker	House and Farm	450.00	37.00	0.40
Leonard Gerter			3.00	0.00
Henry Burendorf	House and Farm	365.00	37.00	0.40
George Youker	House and Farm	540.00	67.00	0.60
Henry Nestle	House and Farm	765.00	30.00	0.80
Christian Grove, Junr	House and Farm	1830.00	129.00	1.95
John K Klock Junr	House and Farm	290.00	85.00	0.35
Peter Buse	House and Farm	315.00	37.00	0.35
Lipe Slocum	House and Farm	315.00	3.00	0.35
John Coll	House and Farm	750.00	110.00	0.86
Gideon Rees	House and Farm	1500.00	59.00	1.55
Frederick I Bellinger	House and Farm	1300.00	85.00	1.46
Elisha Lovelefs	House and Farm	420.00	29.00	0.44
John Lovelefs	House and Farm	539.00	12.00	0.55
Mills Washburn			2.00	0.00
Anthony Flansburgh	House and Farm	390.00	37.00	0.42
Francis Beandz			12.00	0.01

William Attenburgh	House and Farm	1000.00	84.00	1.08
John Rasick	House and Farm	518.00	37.00	0.55
Lipe Ingersoll	House, Farm and Mill	1500.00	83.00	1.50
Jacob Youker	House and Farm	550.00	60.00	0.61
Joseph Freeman			20.00	0.02
Peter Clause Junr	House and Farm	1000.00	107.00	1.10
Andrew Clause	House and Farm	270.00	30.00	0.30
William Been Junr	House and Farm	285.00	`32	0.31
Henry Mosier	House and Farm	600.00	40.00	0.64
Elijah Westover			2.00	0.00
Thomas A. Barnes	House Farm and Mill	370.00	26.00	0.39
Lodewick Swart	House and Farm	1000.00	43.00	1.04
Solomon Mosier	House and Farm	465.00	51.00	0.51
John W. Markell			14.00	0.01
John Campble			5.00	0.00
Valentine Wolfe			80.00	0.08
William Coony			15.00	0.01
James Van Valkenburgh	House and Farm	700.00	22.00	0.72
George Praim	House and Farm	100.00		0.10
Jacob Tusler	House and Farm	730.00		0.73
Dolphus Lew	House and Farm	700.00	45.00	0.74
John Jacob Beeckman	Farm or Lot	132.00		0.13
Goldsbrow Banyer	Farm and Lots	30490.00		30.49
John R. Bleecker Junr	Farms and Lots	4032.00		4.03
Stephen N Bayard	Farm and Lots	1624.00		1.62
Barent Bleecker &				
John R. Bleecker Junr	Farm and Lots	2000.00		2.00
Catherine Bleecker	Farm and Lots	7052.00		7.05
John Brinkerhoff	Farm and Lots	1920.00		1.92
Barent Bleecker &	Farm and Lots	10257.00		10.25
Corlls Bloot	Farm and Lots	2560.00		2.56
Jacob Diefendorf	Farm or Lot	250.00		0.25
John Diefendorf	Farm or Lot	250.00		0.25
Richard Duncan	Farm or Lot	400.00		0.40
Nicholas Dunkell	Farm or Lot	200.00		0.20
Simeon DeWitt	Farm or Lot	2000.00		2.00
Isaac Denniston	Farm or Lot	960.00		0.96
John Darby	Farm or Lot	700.00		0.70
Benjamin Elwood	Farm or Lot	125.00		0.12
Alexander Ellis	Farm and Lotts	24240.00		24.24
Leonard Gansevoort	Farm and lots	13962.00		13.96
Cornelius Glen	Farm and Lot	902.00		0.90
Philip L. Hoffman	Farm and Lot	5830.00		5.83
William Haroby	Farm and Lots	1200.00		1.20

Daniel Hefs	Farm and Lot	1200.00		1.20
Caty Kring	Farm	84.00		0.08
Adam Keeling	Farm or Lot	320.00		0.32
Jacob G. Lansing	Farm or Lot	2000.00		2.00
Stephen Lusk	Farm or Lot	1600.00		1.60
Richard Lusk	Farm or Lot	150.00		0.15
Jacob Merkell	Farm or Lot	1500.00		1.50
Jacob Moyer	Farm or Lot	1500.00		1.50
John D Nellis	Farm or Lot	700.00		0.70
Andrew Nellis	Farm or Lot	200.00		0.20
Abraham Oothout	Farm or Lot	200.00		0.20
John Blank	Farm or Lot	400.00		0.40
George Parson	Farm or Lot	2000.00		2.00
Philip Runan	Farm or Lot	40.00		0.04
John Rice	Farm or Lot	125.00		0.12
John Shafer Junr	Farm or Lot	1050.00		1.05
John Shafer	House and Farm	2500.00		2.50
Lewis Williams Junr	House and Farm	1420.00		1.42
Henry Setten	Farm or Lot	700.00		0.70
John F. Tolly	Farm or Lot	2000.00		2.00
John E. Trusmors	Farm or Lot	230.00		0.23
Simon I Vrooman	Farm or Lot	200.00		0.20
Cornelius Van Schellerynic	Farm or Lot	4360.00		4.36
Teunis Van Vichten	Farm or Lot	1200.00		1.20
Abraham Van Vechten	Farm or Lot	2000.00		2.00
Isaac Wanser	Farm or Lot	310.00		0.31
John Weaver	House and Farm	890.00		0.89
Amor Witmore and Asher	Farm or Lot	888.00		0.88
Catharine Westerlo	Farm or Lot	9712.00		9.71
Charles Williamson	Farm or Lot	2000.00		2.00
Joseph C. Yates	Farm or Lot	3240.00		3.24
Adam Koons	House, Lots, and Mill	1000.00		1.00
Elias Gouse	House and Farm	1365.00		1.36
Mary Scott	House and Lot	20.00		0.02
Peter P. Skutt	House and Lot	25.00		0.02
Andrew Raber	House and Farm	3250.00		3.25
William Gunt	House and Lot	65.00		0.06
William Hart	House and Lot	60.00		0.06
John Harmans	House and Lot	275.00		0.27
Gerrit Lasher Junr	Lot	45.00		0.40
John McAndor	Lot	651.00		0.65
Abraham Norrus	House and Farm	160.00		0.16
Henry Plank	House and Lot	32.00		0.03
Catharine Sutz Widow	House and Lot	145.00		0.14

John Henry Dysling	Farm	1000.00		1.00
John Visher	House and Lot	90.00		0.09
John Van Dewerkin	House and Lot	185.00		0.18
Tomothy T. Kimball	House and Lot	65.00		0.06
Christopher Kell	House and Farm	215.00		0.21
William Been	House and Farm	300.00		0.30
George Roppole	House and Lot	300.00		0.30
James Williams	Farm or Lot	286.00		0.28
Jacob Bellinger	Farm or Lot	550.00		0.55
William Finck	Farm or Lot	1500.00		1.50
John C. Frederick	Farm or Lot	640.00		0.64
Andrew Reeber	House and Farm	3250.00		3.25
Isaac Osden	Farm or Lot	5830.00		5.83
Lander Lansing	Farm or Lot	6910.00		6.91
Johathan Turnbell	House and Farm	565.00		0.56
William Turmbull Junr	House and Farm	260.00		0.26
William Trumbell	House and Farm	130.00		0.13
John Aumock	House and Lot	55.00		0.05
Nicholas Pickert	House and Farm	980.00		0.98
Philip Rees	Farm	800.00		0.80
James Credtendon	House and Farm	165.00		0.16
Total		973037.00	124239.00	1092.00
Petor Cramos Junr				
Hanjost Scholl				
Peter Clank Junr				
Conrad Lepper				
ASSESSORS				

The Move West

The Mohawk Valley was the frontier before the war, but shortly after hostilities ceased, the soldiers from New England who served in our area began moving into New York State, into our valley and farther west. The Clinton/Sullivan campaign showed the men what beautiful and fertile lands existed in the western part of the state and these lands were settled soon after the war. Eventually the frontier was pushed west and more people began seeking the free land available in the far west.

Following you will find a representation of the westward movement, letters from Oregon. If you visit the website <www.threerivershms.com> you will find other Klock letters from other places the family settled.

Letters from Oregon

April 17th 1848 Dier parents we are all wel and are wel suted with the country we got into the valy in 4 months and 20 days from the time we left missourie river oposite St. Joseph where we left the first of May every thing went quite nise till we got in the mountains then we had to clime sum verry hy hills but hansum and smooth rode wen we got down to the columbia river next day after we got started the nois cum the Indians had robed a cumpany ahead of us and ther was another cumpany ahead of us wich sent us vord they wold wate for us about 22 miles ahead it was a heavy travling sandy rode they all commensed drive we must go that to day or be robed by the indians and maby killed our usual drives vare only 10 or 12 miles a day and I expected my cattle wold give out being I had the heviest load and about 4 or 5 o'clock sum of my cattle lay down so tired they I cold not get them along any more and wilst I was un yoking them the indians cum gathering aroun my wagon proty thick and that put me to a hel of a thinking at onst I dident no what then Katherine and the children comensed criing I dident no what the Devel to do the company out of site there we ware all alone amung the indians I had a revo'ving pistel laying in the wagon ready loded but it had ben loded ever sins ve cum therein the paune cuntry aboat 2 months or more and I was afrid it wodent go but I will try it any how so I got the pistel and told them begon or I wold kil every dam the one of then they left they run oph toward the river apeas and then comensed holloowin and beckoning to others down at the river on an island then they cam out their wigworms proty soon the river was fool of suox cuming as fast as they cold so I told katherine not to show any fear if they cum and tel them I was gon after help and if they tuck any thing we wold kill them all so I went as hard as I cold run and maby a little faster and wen I get in site of the wagons mis bellinger sea me swinging my hat and then they cum back only 8 men dair too cum out of 20 it was quite a trying time to sea so many indians cuming runing up towards us yoping their wor yops sum of our boys then hung back old bellinger drew his old long sowerd out he swong it round he nocked the wild sage bushes he made the piece fly godam yew cum up don't be afraid the indians made terible big eyes they never sea sitch an Indian killer before they sea fear in men then they wil be robed and so they left us wen ever they sea fear in men then they wil surtainly rob ther is war hear with the indians now but yew wil (?)have that newis before yew get this we apprehend no danger as for the indians hear we kin rais 10000 able bodied soldiers if it is required enough to whip all the indians in Americay.

Oregon is a good country I have no fault to find with it as yet last faul after we got hear our cattle ware very poor and now they are fit for beaf and nothing but gras our winters are about the same as your faul months the coldest weather only made ise an inch thick we have occasional frost from October til April the wether is not as hot in sumer as it is in NY year ago last winter there was an uncomon winter hear there was 9 or 10 inches of snow and it lay about 35 days the oldest indians never new it to be so before they think the whites fetch it with them as fetch bad signesses the hare died oupt hear by hundreds last winter they are fast diminishing oregon is a grate grain country and I was down to that (?) last fall and I sea 100 bushels of potatoes dug of 70 yards square and a red beat 28 inches in surcumphrens but corn will do about as wel hear as in York state peach treas bare here the third year its a grate fr cuntry the old setlers hear sais foase never dies hear the just drey up it is so veery healthy hear that is so for I neve sea foase so much exposed as they are hear and never sea sick ones un les they fetch it with then from the states there is men hear now over hundred years old 106 the oldest and as smart as they are in the states wen 70 foase actuelly duz live to grater age than tahey doin the states this is good grain cuntry wheat is worth one dollar per bushel butter 25 cts cheas 20 cts it costs more mone to winter chickens hear than it duz cattle u better all pack up and cum to oregon but you never wold listen to me and I dont know as u wil yet if u remember what u sed before I left it is veery favorable to consumption thisick and grate many other disease I havent had the headke nor tooth ake sinc I am hear it is so because a purson hardly ever takes cold hear we never hve ny hrd rains hear not so as to wash the land and never veery mody as it is for a few days rain and then hansam sun shine weather marchantdise is a getting to be quite reasonable as there is grate opposition in the Brittish and American merchants its about the same as in the western states Emergrants from NY state should cum by water as they gain about 8 munts time by going acrost the istmus the trip may be made in about 2 months we intende to make yew a visit in a few years it is ony about 4500 miles acrost the istmus send our letters by the way of New york and we wil get them the quickest Oregon is about one half timber and one haf prairy the timber is xer hansum in the thick woods treas no more than 4 feat thick frequently runs up to 300 feat in heith it almost brakes a mans neck to look to the top of them out in the open praries they grow verry thick and ful of limbs there is treas hear upwards of 300 feet hy I paised one ouph that broke down and it was 107 paces long this was in acove betweenn two large hills about 5 miles north of the columbia and 40 from the sea the reason timber grow so mich larger hear than in the states is because the wind dont strain them like it dus in the states turnups frequently gros so large that they cant be put into a half bushel it is really a sho to se this cuntry ther is 5 mountain peaks to the east about 70 miles oph and they don't appear to be more than 10 or 12 miles oph in cloudy weather we cant sea their tops as they are hyer than the clouds it looks curiors to se the clouds brake around them white peaks the other 3 is oph north of us and the one is a volcano or burning mountain, James Klock

March 6th, 1858
Dear Grandfather:--

It is with pleasure I take pen in hand to inform you how we are getting along. We are all well at present and hope these lines will find you all the same. We would like to see you all veyr mutch indeed. We have not heard from you for a long time till the other day we saw Mr. Bellinger he said he received a letter form his Brother-in-law by the name of John Crane he said that you was all well which we was very glad to here except your wife and she was dead we are sorry to here it Father died about three years after we came in Oregon he died with the consumption and Mother and us five children -- which was John Adam, Catherine, Casper, Henry and I was left among stranger and about two years after Father died Casper died with the same complaint that Father died with Henry is the youngest of us four aliving about a year after Fahter died, Mother married a man by the name of Chamnes which I suppose you have heard we are all living with Father and Mother we like our stepfather very mutch indeed he treats us as he would his own children he had three children before he was married to Mother two girls and one boy they are all married know and doing well mother has had three Children since she has been married the last time two boys and one girl the oldest one is a boy his name is Marion the next oldest ones name is Olover Howard Pettery the youngist one is a girl her name is Lucy we have been going to school last summer and this winter John Adam has been studying Reading, Spelling and Arithmatic and can write a little and Catherine has been studying Reading and spelling and can read tolerable well I have been studying Reading, writing Arithmetic and Grammar Mohter sya she would like to go back to see you all very mutch though she says sh like to live here a great deal better than there because she things it is healthier here than there and the winters are not near so Could here as there, we have had a very pretty winter here except a little snow about four weeks ago it did not lay on the ground but four of five days people are know making garden here no more at present write as soon as this comes to hand.

Adam I. Clock,
Sallyann Clock.
Marion County, O. T.

Yew must excuse me for writing sutch an auquid letter for I am not yous to writing leters we have another boy in the famly Mr. Bellinger ask Adam the other day ware is granpap was way ouph over biger hilly Adam said he youse to have to walk up the hy hils or mountains sumtimes a hot days travel up hil they wil never for get them hils as soon as he would sea a hil he wold cral back in the wagon and hide himself I was veery much disscou in the road to oregon I always was told a hansum smooth road and so it is but they dident tel about the monstrous hils and sand as ox has enough to do to travel let lone drawing any thing cattle is not the rite thing to cum with no how good horses and a lite wagon about 6 before one wagon and then take care the indians dont steal them Emergrants sholdent fetch anything else but what they want to eat and ware direct my letters to oregon sitty we have plenty fish and oisters hear the river are alive with trou and salmon tel Mr. Flint Buck and brite moad their own gras hear and moad it away too my claim is down to the Columbia 20 miles from its mouth it is up on a hy bank and we can look out to sea and sea the ships cumin my family was so situated we codent go on it this spring so I went to work on a plais 20 miles south of the sitty til faul.
On the reverse side:
Linden Mo.
July 7
TO: Adam J. Klock
Pallatin Church
Montgomery County
New York
FROM: Oregon

Marion County O. T.
February 16th, 1859
Dear Grandfather

I now take the preasent opportunity to inform you how we are all well at preasent and hope these few lines may find you enjoying the same blessings Mr. Bellinger toald us he received a letter from his Brotherinlaw by the name of Crain which said you wanted us children to write to you which I did immediately; it has been abought for or five months since and we have not received an anseere yet we would like to know the reason whether you received the letter I wrote you or not You cannot imagine how well pleased we would be if we could see you all once more or even if we could receive a letter from you since weve been in Oregon we receive a letter from uncle John King Dated January the 8, 1857 is the last letter we receive from the state of New York abought a year after father died Mother maried a man by the name of Israel Chamness which I suppose you have heard he had three children before Mother maried him they ae all maried now and are doing well I am rejoised to tell you that he treats as he does his one children he is very kind to us there are four children alive I and Adam and Catharine and henry; Casper is dead he died with the same complaint that father died with we have not had school here for several months untill about three weeks ago they hired a school teacher a bout six months and we are all agoing I am studying Grammar and Arithmetic Reading and writing Adam is studying Reading writing spelling and Arithmetic, Catharine is a studying Reading writing spelling and arithmetic Catharine is almost as large as me she weighs almost ninty eight pounds and I weigh abought a hundred and six pounds and Adam weighs abought a hundred and eight and henry weighs about forty five; Henry can read and spell tolorable well Mother says she like to live here a great deal better than there on the count of the coald weather there and she thinks the climent is a great deal healthaer here than there for my part I donot know how I would like it there for I was quite small when we left there which I presume you know we have had a very pleasant winter except the three last weeks we have had considerable rain and a little snow about two inches deep on the ground which laid on the ground one day and one night that is about all the snow we have had this winter and they fed our horses and cattle but very little this winter and they are in pretty good order, a good american horse is worth from two hundred and fifty to three hundred dollars in this Country and a good cow is worth from forty to fifty dollars here and sheep is worth from five to ten dollars each. Dear Grandfather we want to see you very much indeed though I am afraid we never will unless you come to this country when father died he said he wanted to see you but it was to late he died in a few minutes it makes my heart ake within me to think we had to give up our dear father and see him laid under the sod and leave us poor wander to fight our way through the world though I hope we may live a hapy life with our Mother and step Father yet we are all living at home and are getting along very well. Dear Grnfather when this letter comes to hand writ me an ansere for we want to hear from you very much. Direct your letters to Santian City Marion County O.T.

　　　　We live about five miles from Santiam City.
Sally Ann Clock

Dear Granfather
　　　　I make effort to write a few lines to inform you that I am well and hope that these few lines may find you enjoying the same blessing I am going to school and am studying reading writing and arithmetic (?) to go to school about six months this summer I want to see you very mutch I want you to write to us and let us know how you are getting along and let us know whether you are ever coming to this country write as soon as this comes to hand no more at present.
John Adam Clock.

Jackson Co. Ogn., July 29, 1877
Mr. Amos Klock sir
　　　　I have given ample time since my last letter written to you for an answer and have got none so I again send you a few lines letting you know that I am well at present and hope these few lines will reach you the same I have written to you two or three letters and got but one from you I begin to think it a very doubtful business letter writing letter, your received apr 20th gave me great satisfaction to hear from you and I had good hopes of hearing from you all through other letters thugh it appears very hard to get any letter from your part of the world if you did not get my answer to your letter please write to me all about my Mothers folks and where they are living and tell them to write to me as I would like very much to get a few letters from them. You asked me about my Fathers Family in your letter of which I wrote you all about and will state some of it again as I suppose my other letter is doubtful my Mother died in 1859 I think and my step Father died 8 months after ward then Perry and Marion and Loocy went to live with his children and Catharine Adam and myself to live with Sarah Ann Thorp our oldest sist and her man catharine soon married off and died just 10 years after sarah ann died in 1865 in the summer J.R. Throp her man who sent to you for our Grand Fathers estate Drank and gambled it all away but $700.00 of Adams part and near $300 of mine and then was drowned in the river I have one of his children the eldest boy with me now he is 15 years old I was born in 1859, 5 of october and all I command now is by hard earnings I have some several head of cattle a good many hoyvs and sold one of my horses a while back so I could get a smaller one I have a good tract of land the best outlet for range I ever seen any where and I am trying to get it started with stock as fast as I can trade and work it out I am not married but would like to find I wok at the carpenters trade some and at the wagon business some I hire but little such as chopping and sawing and grabbing or clearing land I have got stock to sell but prices dont soot and I am helping on a brick yard now for a few dollars to fill all demands as clehk in school district I yoused a few dollars 10 or 12 and must have it when call upon now I coud write ten times as much tho will wait till next time please send me the price of good Buskin Gloves and buskin well dressed as I could furnish a good supply in a short time If call upon from your country send what style of gloves what kind of fur for suffs and if any market Ill send you a sample to try for me. Such is quite plenty here and prices are very low if any of my people think of emigrating from that old country just send them to southern regon or Jackson C. Oregon they can buy or take up good wranches that I know of yet in the best rang Ive ever ben on and can raise most any kind of grain ever growed any where and vegetables of all kinds allmost will grow and they nead knot fight hoppers or crickets or wear their coats one quarter of the winter stock des well that is not fed any thing at all In fact I think living is very easy earned though a man must work and keep things up well now enough wright without fail direct to JacksonVille Jackson Co. Ogn.
Henry Klock
To Amos Klock yur Nephew

LOYALISTS

The Loyalists

Biographical Skletches of Loyalists of The American Revolution
Volume I ONLY, there are two volumes in the set, By Lorenzo Sabine, Published 1864
This book was written by an American and was recommended by a Loyalist friend.

THE AUTHOR: Sabine, Lorenzo (1803-1877)— of Eastport, Washington County, Maine; Framingham, Middlesex County, Mass.; Roxbury, Boston, Suffolk County, Mass. Born in New Concord (now Lisbon) Grafton County, N. H., February 28, 1803.   Member of Maine State House of Representatives, 1833-34; U.S. Representative from Massachusetts 9th District, 1852-53.   Died in Roxbury, Boston, Suffolk County, Mass. April 14, 1877.

Benedict Arnold. Of Connecticut. Major-General in the Continental Army.   A man whose life and infamy are so universally known, forever associated with being the worst type of traitor. He was descended from the Arnolds of Rhode Island, an honorable family, who for a long period figured in the public affairs of that Colony. He was bred to be an apothecary, and from 1763 to 1767 was settled at New Haven, as a druggist and bookseller. I am inclined to believe that he was a finished scoundrel from early manhood to his grave. Nor do I believe that he had any real and true hearted attachment to the Whig cause. He fought as a mere adventurer, and took sides from a calculation of personal gain, and chances of plunder and advancement.

No honorable man would have formed a copartnership with others for purchasing goods within the enemy's lines as he did, and to the enormous amount of one hundred and forty thousand dollars. And no honest man would have lived, could have lived as he did, while at Philadelphia. His play, his balls, his concerts, his banquets, were enough to impaired the fortune of a European noble. His house was the best in the city, and had been the mansion of Penn, the last royal governor of Pennsylvania, and the descendant of the illustrious founder of the Colony. This dwelling he furnished magnificently, kept his coach-and-four, and a numerous retinue of servants, and indulged in every kind of luxury, and ostentatious and fain profusion and display.

He was made a brigadier-general in the British service, and received a large amount of gold to cover his alleged losses in deserting the standard of his country. After he went to England, Mr. Van Schaack, a New York Loyalist, who was also there, paid a visit to Westminster Abbey. "His musings were interrupted by the entrance of a gentleman accompanied by a lady. It was General Arnold, and the lady was doubtless Mrs. Arnold. They passed to the cenotaph of Major Andre where they stood and conversed together. What a spectacle! The traitor Arnold in Westminster Abbey, at the tomb of Andre, deliberately perusing the monumental inscription which will transmit to future ages the tale of his own infamy.   The scene, with the associations which naturally crowded upon the mind, was calculated to excite various emotions in an American bosom; and Mr. Van Schaack turned from it with disgust."

From the conclusion of the war till he death, Arnold resided chiefly in England; but for a while he was engaged in trade and navigation at St. John, New Brunswick. He was disliked, was unpopular, and even hated at St. John. Persons of that city still relate instances of his perfidy and meanness. George Gilbert, Esquire, (a sons of Bradford Gilbert, who was a Massachusetts Loyalist,) has now (August, 1846,) twelve chairs which are called the "Traitor's Chairs," and which were carried from England to St. John by Arnold. When he removed from New Brunswick he sold them to the first Judge Chipman, who, after keeping them some years, sold them to their present possessor. They are of a French pattern, are large, and covered with a blue-figured damask; the wood-work is white, highly polished or enameled, and striped with gold.

The *Lord Sheffield,* the first ship built in New Brunswick, came over the falls of the River St. John, in June 1786. The current story in that Province is, that the builder was unable to purchase the necessary sails and rigging, and that Arnold became the owner—by fraud.

He died in London, June 14, 1801. The following brief notice appeared in the "Gentleman's Magazine:"—"Deceased at his house in Gloucester Place, Brigadier-General Arnold. His remains were interred on the 21st, at Brompton.   Seven mourning-coaches and four state-coaches formed the cavalcade.

His first wife bore him,--Benedict, who was an officer of artillery in the British Army, who, it is believed, was compelled to quit the service, and who died young in the West Indies; and Richard and Henry of whom are alive presently. The names of five other children appear in the preceding notice.

"We" (the English nation), said the 'London Times,' in 1850, "are actually this moment supporting, out of the public funds, the descendants of Arnold the American traitor."

It may be added that General Arnold's mother had six children, of whom he and his sister Hannah alone lived to the years of maturity. This sister adhered to her brother Benedict throughout his eventful and guilty career, and was true to him in the darkest periods of his history. She died at

Montague in Upper Canada in 1803, and was, as is uniformly stated, a lady of excellent character. She was accomplished, pleasing in person, witty and affable. She loved, but at the bidding of her brother, broke off the engagement. She never married.

In 1852 the newspapers announced the decease at Norwich, Connecticut, of Elizabeth Arnold cousin of the traitor, and the last of his kindred in that vicinity. Her age was ninety-two. She was carried to the poor-house at her own request, and died there.

Becraft, _____ A Tory leader, cruel, and noted for deeds of blood. He boasted to his associates of having assisted in the massacre the family of a Mr. Vrooman, in Schoharie, New York. The family, he said were soon dispatched, except a boy of fourteen, who ran from the house, when he started in pursuit, overtook him, and cut his throat, took his scalp, and hung his body across the fence. After the peace, he had the hardihood to return to Schoharie. He was seized, stripped naked and bound to a tree, and whipped nearly to death by then men, some of whom had been his prisoners, and had heard him recount this exploit. Thus beaten, he was dismissed with a charge never to show himself in that country again; an injunction which he carefully kept.

Captain Bull. Of New York. He was in the service of the Crown, and his name appears in the interview between the celebrated Mohawk, Brant, and the Whig General Herkimer, at Unadilla, New York, in 1777. When the Indian chief met the Whig, he was accompanied by Bull, a son of Sir William Johnson by Brandt's sister, Mary or Molly, and about forty warriors. During the meeting, Herkimer demanded the surrender of several Tories, which Brant peremptorily refused. This was the last conference held with the hostile Mohawks.

John Butler. Of Tryon, now Montgomery County, New York. Before the war, Colonel Butler was in close official connection; with Sir William, Sir John, and Colonel Guy Johnson, and followed their political fortunes. At the breaking out of hostilities, he commanded a regiment of New York militia, and entered at once into the military service of the Crown. During the war his wife was taken prisoner, and exchanged for the wife of the Whig Colonel Campbell. The deeds of rapine, or murder, of hellish hue, which were perpetrated by Butler's corps, cannot be related here. It is sufficient, for the purpose of these Notes, to say, that he commanded the sixteen hundred incarnate fiends who desolated Wyoming. I feel quite willing to allow, that history has recorded barbarities which were not committed. But though Butler did not permit or directly authorize women to be driven into the forest, where they became mothers, and where their infants were eaten by wild beasts, and though captive officers may not have been held upon fires with pitchforks until they were burned to death, sufficient remains undoubted, to clamp his conduct with the deepest, darkest, and most damning guilt. The human mind can hardly frame an argument which shall clear the fame of Butler from obloquy and reproach. To admit even as a solved question, that the Loyalists were in the right, and that they were bound by the clearest rules of duty to bear arms in defense of lawful and existing institutions, and to put down the rebellion, will do Butler no good. For, whatever the force of such a plea in the minds of those who urge it, _he was still bound to observe the laws of civilized warfare._

That he, and he alone, will be regarded by posterity as the real and responsible actor in the business and slaughter at Wyoming, may be considered, perhaps, as certain. The chieftain Brant was, for a time, held accountable, but the better information of later years transfers the guilt from the savage to the man of Saxon blood. There was nothing for Saxon blood. There was nothing for which the Mohawk's family labored more earnestly than to show that their renowned head was not implicated in this bloody tragedy, and that the accounts of historians, and the enormities recounted in Campbell's verse, as far as they relate to him, are untrue. It has been said very commonly, that the Colonel Butler who was of the Whig force at Wyoming, and Colonel John, were kinsman; but this too, has been contradicted. The late Edward D. Griffin,--a youth, a write, and a poet of rare promise,-- and a grandson of the former, denied the relationship.

Colonel John Butler was richly rewarded for his services. Succeeding, in part, to the agency of Indian Affairs—long held by the Johnson—he enjoyed, about the year 1796, a salary of 500 pounds sterling per annum, and a pension as a military officer of 200 pounds more. Previously, he had received a grant of five hundred acres of land, and a similar provision for his children. His home, after the war, was in Upper Canada. He was attainted during the contest, by the Act of New York, and his property confiscated. He lived before the Revolution in the present town of Mohawk. (North side of the Mohawk River, just east of Fonda.) His dwelling was of one story, with two windows in front, and a door in the center. It was standing in 1842, and was then owned and occupied by Mr. Wilson. The site is pleasant and commanding, and overlooks the valley of the Mohawk.

(Colonel Butler's son, Captain Walter N. was noted for his vindictive nature and was killed after the Battle of Johnstown by a pursuit in October 1781.)

John Doxstader. A Tory leader. On an incursion to Currietown, he and his Indian associates took nine prisoners, who, in an affair at a place called Ourlaugh, (Turlough?) New York, the day succeeding their capture, were bound to standing trees, tomahawked, and scalped. The bodies of these unfortunate men were hastily buried by friends. But one of them, Jacob Diefendorff, was alive, and was afterwards found on the outside of his own grave; he recovered and lived to relate the story. In 1780, on one of his incursions in New York, Doxstader carried away a horse belonging to a Whig; but coming to the same region, from Canada, after the war, he was arrested by the owner, and compelled to pay the value of the animal.

Hendrick Frey. Of New York. He served the crown during the war and was a major. After the peace he returned to his native state. In 1797 he and Brant met at Canajoharie, where, at a tavern, "they had a merry time of it during the livelong night. Many of their adventures were recounted, among which was a duel that had been fought by Frey, to whom Brant acted a as second." The meeting of the Chief and the Major is described as "like that of two brothers."

Philip R. Frey. Of Tryon (now Montgomery) County, New York. He entered the military service of the King, and was an ensign in the Eighth Regiment. He was engaged in the battle of Wyoming. He died at Palatine, Montgomery (formerly Tryon) County, in 1823. His son, Samuel C. Frey, settled in Upper Canada, and communicated particulars of the sanguinary scenes at Wyoming, for Colonel Stone's use in writing his "Life of Brant." The testimony of the Freys is, that Brant was not present with Butler at Wyoming, and this, according to the son, the father steadily maintained through his life.

Helmer_____. Of Tryon (now Montgomery) County, New York. He accompanied Sir John Johnson to Canada, when the Baronet violated his parole and fled; and was one of the party who, in 1778, returned to Johnstown for the purpose of securing some of Sir John's valuable effects. While bearing off the iron-chest, he injured his ankle, and was compelled to go to his father's house, where he remained concealed. But in the spring of 1779 he was arrested as a spy, tried, and sentenced to death, chiefly on his own admissions to the Court.

Colonel Hanjost (John Joost) Herkimer. Of New York. He was a son of Johan Jost Herkimer, one of the Palatines of the German Flats, New York; and a brother of the Whig General, Nicholas Herkimer. He served in various county offices until the Revolution. His property was confiscated. He went to Canada, and died there before 1787.

New York In The Revolution as Colony and State
by James A. Roberts, Comptroller
Compiled by Frederic G. Mather
Second Edition 1898
Two Volumes

Estates Forfeited
The Military and Civil Titles, given in this list, had been granted under the Colony, before the War.

Ackerson Garret	Becker Bastian	Carpenter Archelaus
Ackerson John	Bedford Jonathan	Carpenter Henry
Ackerson Matthias	Billop Christopher	Carpenter Latting
Alyea Isaac	Blauvelt David	Carrigan Patrick
Anderson John	Blauw Waldron	Chase Reuben
Anderson Jonathan	Bobbett Daniel	Chew Joseph
Armstrong John	Bogart Guysbert	Claus Daniel, Col.
Avery Thomas	Bogart Jacobus	Clement Lewis
Axtell William, Council	Bond Richard	Clinton Henry, Sir
Barclay Thomas	Bowen William R.	Cloos Abm.
Barclay Thomas H.	Bower Casper	Cloos Benj.
Barker Thomas	Bowne James	Clows Peter
Bartlefalk Johannis	Brown Johannes	Cock Zoar
Bates John	Brush Shubal	Colden Cadwallader, Lt.
Bauck Frederick	Butler John, Col.	Gov.
Bayard Robert	Butler Walter, Ens.	Colden David
Bayard William, Col.	Butler William, Lt. Col.	Cole Simon
Beach Theophilaet	Cameron Duncan	Constable Abraham
Beach Theophilus	Campbell Allen	Corey Griffin
Beaty David	Campbell Duncan	Cornwell George

Cotter James
Covel Simeon
Crannell Bartholomew
Crawford James
Crawford John
Crookshank Alexander
Cruger John Harris, Council
Cummings Patrick
Cuyler Abraham C.
Davenport Gabriel
Dean Nicholas
De Lancey James, Lt. Gov. & Council
De Lancey Oliver, Adjt. Gen.
De Lancey Stephen
De Lancey & Jauncey
Des Brosses Elias
Desbrosses Elizabeth
Desbrosses Magdalen
Devoe Frederick
Dickenson Gilbert
Dickinson James
Dickinson Samuel
Dickinson Tertullus
Dobbs Walter
Dockstader John
Dodge Stephen
Dowers Joseph
Drake Peter
Duncan Richard
Eckerson Garrit Jacob
Emmons Eli
Emmons John
Empie Johannis W.
Empie John P.
Empie Philip
Ennis John
Fisher Daniel
Fisher Donald
Flewelling Abel
Flewelling Thomas
Floyd Richard
Folliott George
Ford Joseph
Fowler Jonathan, jr.
Fowler Solomon
Fowler Stephen
Fowler William
Frazier Hugh
Frazier Thomas
Frazier William
Freehoudt Isaac
French Benjamin
French Charity
Frost Caleb
Frost Jacob
Fuller Lemuel
Furnival James
Getman John
Gibbons Dennis
Gibson John, Sr.
Gidney John

Gidney Joseph
Gidney Joshua
Green James
Green Joseph
Gregg Abraham
Gregg John
Griggs Abraham
Griggs Johannes
Griggs John
Hare James
Harring Peter T.
Harris Samuel
Hatfield Barnes
Hawley Ezekiel Jr.
Herkimer Johan Jost
Heustice David
Hoaksley Robert
Hoffnagle John
Hoffnagle Michael
Hogel John
Holmes James
Holmes Lewis
Holmes Stephen
Holt Moses
Howard John
Huggeford Peter
Hulet James
Huls James
Hultse James
Hunt Benjamin
Inglis Charles, Rev.
Ireland John
Jansen Simon
Jauncey James, Council
Jauncey & De Lancey
Jessup Ebenezer
Jessup Edward
Jessup Joseph
Johnson Abraham
Johnson Elizabeth
Johnson Guy, Col.
Johnson John, Sir
Johnson John
Johnson Magdalen
Johnson Margaret
Johnson William, Sir
Jone Daniel
Jone David
Jone John
Jones Jonathan
Jones Philip
Jones Thomas, Justice
Kane John
Kempe John Tabor, Atty, & Advocate Gen.
Kip Benjamin
Kissam Daniel
Kool Johannis
Laight Edward
Laight William
Lamb James
Lawrence Effingham, Capt.
Lawrence John

Leake John
Leake Robert
Leake Thomas
Leight Edward Capt.
Leight W.
Lent Abraham
Lent Adolph
Lent Peter
Leonard George
Leonard James
Leonard John
Lewis Benjamin
Lloyd Henry
Long David
Lounsbury William
Low Isaac
Low John
Ludlow Gabriel G.
Ludlow George D.
Mabbett Joseph S., Admr,
Mabbett Samuel
Mabie Cornelius
Mabie Cornelius P,
Mabie Lewis
McAdams William
McAlpin Daniel
McAlpin John
McClannen Peter
McComb John
McDonald James
McDonald John
McDonnell John
McGinnis George
McGinnis Robert
McKenzie Roderick
McLarin Peter
McLeod Norman, Capt.
McNiff Patrick
McNish Joseph
Macomb John
Matthews David
Matthias Hannicol
Matthias Hendrick
Mattice Hendrick
Mattice John
Mattice John Nicholas
Medlar John
Menzes Alexander
Menzes Thomas
Menzies Alexander
Menzines Alexander
Merikle Jacob
Merkle Christopher
Merkle Jacob
Merrit Joseph
Merritt John
Merritt Thomas
Miller Anthony
Miller Gilbert
Mitchell John
Moffatt William
Moore William
Moorhouse Jonathan
Morris Richard E.

Morris Roger, Maj. & Col.& Council
Morrison John
Morrison Malcom
Mosher Hugh
Mott Jacob
Munro Daniel
Munro Hugh
Munro John
Murison George
Nellis Henry W.
Nellis Robert
Nellis Robert Wm.
Noxon Bartholomew
Oakley Miles
Ogden Benjamin
Oliver Frederick
Osborn Nathan
Outwater Daniel
Outwater Thomas
Palmer Edmund
Palmer Edward
Palmer Lewis
Partelow Amos
Pearsall Thomas
Peck Caleb
Peemart Francis
Pell John
Pell John, jr.
Pell Joshua
Pell Joshua, jr.
Peters Valentine H.
Petrie Johan Jost, jr.
Phillipse Frederick, Col.
Pine Stephen
Polhemus Johannes
Quackenboss Adrian
Quackenboss Gosen
Rapalje Abraham
Rapalje Dina
Rapalje John
Reed William
Rider Ebenezer
Riemer John
Robinson Beverley
Robinson Thomas
Rodgers William
Roosa Guisbert
Roosa Jacobus
Row John Peter

Rowland Smith
Ruble John
Ruble Thomas
Russell Jacob
Ruyter Henry
St. Croix Joshua Temple De
Sammons Thomas
Schell Johannis
Schut Alexander
Scutt Alexander
Seaman Adam
Seaman Benjamin
Seaman Israel
Service Christian
Service Christophe
Service Clara
Sharpe Guysbert
Sheets Jacob
Shell Johannes
Sisson James
Skene Andrew Philip, Lt.
Skene Philip, Maj.
Skene Philip & Andrew
Smith Austin
Smith John
Smith John Johnson
Smith William
Smith William, Jr.
Snedeker Theodorus
Sneden Teunis
Sniffin Shubal
Soles Howland
Sprage Thomas
Springer William
Sprong Volkert
Summers Peter
Ten Brook Peter
Theal Charles
Thompson Edward
Thompson John
Tice Gilbert
Titus Isaac
Tobias Christian
Tobias Joseph
Townsend Uriah
Travis Charles
Travis Jeremiah
Travis William
Tryon William (Sir) Gov.

Turner John
Tuttle Stephen
Underhill Benjamin
Van Alstyne Peter Sander
Van Cortland Augustus
Vanderpool Isaac
Van Dyne Dow
Van Home Augustus
Van Home David
Van Petten Arent
Van Waggenen James
Vedder Cornelis A.
Ver Planck Gullian
Waite Benjamin
Wallace Alexander
Wallace Hugh, Council
Ward Edmond
Ward Edmund
Ward Israel
Watson Jacob
Watts John
Weatherhead John
Weeks John
Welling John
Welling Peter
Welling William
Wemple Andrew
Wheaton John
White Alexander
White Eve
White Henry, Council
White Thomas
Whitney Nathan
Wickham Parker
Wilcox Hazard
Williams Isaac
Williamson Garrit
Wood John
Woods James
Wragg Richard
Wright Jonathan
Wright William
Yoemans George
Youmans John
Young Adam
Young Frederick
Youngs Isaac
Zielie Adam
Zielly Adam

Loyalist Estates Confiscated (Entire State)

Abbot Joseph
Acker Garret
Acker Joseph
Acker Jost
Acker Tice
Ackerley Joshua
Ackerman William
Ackerson John I.
Adams Nathaniel
Addams John
Adolphin
Albertson John

Albrant Henry
Alexander
Algyer M.
Allen
Alyea Isaac
Ames Jonas
Ames Nicholas
Amory John
Andersen James
Anderson John
Anderson Joseph
Anderson Joshua

Anjouvine John
Anjouvine Peter
Anker Caleb
Anthony Joseph
Antis Peter
Apthorpe
Archer Caleb
Ardencock J.
Arkenburgh William
Armstrong John
Arskine John
Backer Abraham

Backes Peter, Jr.
Bailey
Bailey Abraham
Bailey Levy
Bailey William
Baisley John
Baizley Abraham
Baker Jonathan
Baker Samuel
Baker William
Ball George
Ball Jacob
Banyar Gouldsbury
Banck Frederick
Barclay (Mrs)
Barclay Thomas
Barclay Thomas H.
Barker John
Barker Thomas
Barnard Conrad
Barnet Ochabed
Barnett Ichabod B.
Barnhart D.
Barnhart Herman
Barnhart Joseph
Barns John
Barns Joshua
Bartlefalk Johanms
Bartley Esions
Basely John
Basely Thomas
Basler
Bates Gilbert
Bates John
Baxter Samuel
Baxter Thomas
Bayard Samuel
Bayard William, Col.
Beardsley John
Beaty Thomas
Bedford Jonathan
Belding Samuel, Dr.
Bell George
Bell John
Bend Grove
Bennet Thomas
Benton
Bergh Christian, Jr.
Berkley E,
Berkley J.
Best
Bevens William
Beyea James
Bird Henry
Birdsalls John
Black John
Black Nation
Blakely James
Blauvelt David
Bloomendall John
Bloomer Robert
Bobbett Daniel
Boen Luykert
Bogart Abraham

Bogait Guysbert
Bogart Jacobus
Bogart James
Bolt Moses
Bonett Peter
Booth William
Bort Peter
Bortick
Bory
Boslar Frederick
Bowen William
Bower Capt.
Bowser John
Bradshaw Stephen
Brady Thomas
Brevort Elias
Brewer Jeremiah
Briggs Elkanah
Briggs William
Brill Jacob
Brill Johannis
Brink Samuel
Brinkley Thomas
Brisbe John
Broadhower Nicholas
Brower Jeremiah
Brown Abraham
Brown Betle
Brown Caleb
Brown Casper
Brown Ebenezer
Brown Edward
Brown Everit
Brown Hendrick
Brown James
Brown Nathaniel
Brownson Samuel
Brundige Joshua
Brush Hendrick
Brush Joseph
Brush Shubal
Brust M.
Buckhout
Buckhout John
Buckhout Peter
Buckley Evert
Buckley Jochim
Buckstone
Buel Timothy
Buise John
Bullock
Burch
Burch John
Burges
Burnet Matthew
Burnet Thomas
Burnet William
Burnett Ichabeed B.
Burns William
Burtis
Burtis Barent
Bush Christian
Bush Hendrick
Bush Martin

Butler John, Col.
Butler Walter, Ens.
Butson George
Buyce Peter, sr.
Buyce Peter, jr.
Buyck Christopher
Buyse William
Byre Michael
Calkins Capt.
Cambron John
Cambron William
Cameron Duncan
Cameron John
Cameron William
Campbell
Campbell Archibald
Campbell Duncan
Campbell James
Campbell Jno
Campbell Neal
Campbell William
Carehart Daniel
Carithers Thomas
Carle Thomas
Carle William
Carleton Dennis
Carpenter Archelaus
Carpenter Daniel
Carpenter Henry
Carpenter Israel
Carpenter Jonathan
Carpenter Latting
Carpenter William
Carpenter Zeno
Carrigan Patrick
Carrigan Peter
Casimer John
Castleman
Chace Daniel, jr.
Champenvois John
Chatterdon Michael
Cherry John
Cherrytree Jacob
Chew Josiah
Chisholm George
Christian
Christler Philip
Clapp Jesse
Clark Hugh
Clark John
Clark Robert
Clark Samuel
Clark Simon
Clarwater Abraham
Clarwater Daniel
Clarwater Frederick
Clarwater Isaac
Clarwater Jacob
Claus Daniel, Col.
Clement Jennet
Clement Joshua
Clement Lewis
Clement Peter
Cline Michael

Clopper Cornelius
Close Abraham
Close Benjamin, jr
Cock Jorden
Coevert Adolphus
Cole Daniel
Cole Jacob
Cole John
Cole John I.
Cole Simon
Coles Daniel
Concklin Joseph
Conckling
Conckling Abraham
Cones John
Conner Peter
Conner Thomas
Constable Abraham
Cook George
Cook Ichabod
Cooke Matthias
Coone Jacob
Coone John
Cooper Jacob
Cooper Thomas
Corey Griffin
Corney Peter
Cough Philip
Covel Simeon
Covert George
Cowan M.
Cox Samuel
Craft David
Craft John, Jr.
Crafts William
Crannell Bartholomew
Craney Capt.
Crathers Thomas
Crawford David
Crawford James
Creighton John
Criestar William
Crissy Simon
Cronk John
Cronkhyte Isaac
Crookshank Alexander
Crossfield Stephen
Crow Joseph
Crows John
Crum William
Crysler Adam
Cummings Patrick
Cummins John
Cummins William
Currien David
Curry Joseph
Curry Joshua
Curry Peter
Curry Stephen
Curwin
Cutler Roger
Cutwater
Cutwater Dr.
Cutwater Daniel

Cuyler Abraham C.
Cuyler Nicholas
Dan David
Danford Richard
Danford Stephen
Danielson Thomas
Dann Abraham
Darrot James
Davis Charles
Day John
Dayfoot Daniel
Dean Nicholas
Deas James
DeBleanas John
DeFries Abraham
DeGraugh Abraham
DeLancey James, Lt. Gov
& Council
DeLancey Stephen
Demarest Peter
Demilts John
Demott Isaac
Dennis
Derby William
DesBrosses Elias
DeVoe Frederick
DeWitt Jacob
Dick
Dickinson Gilbert
Dickinson James
Dickinson Samuel
Dickinson Tertuilus
Dingey Solomon
Dingwill James
Dixon John
Dobbs Michael
Dobbs Walter
Dockstader George A.
Dodge Ithamer
Dodge Stephen
Dop John
Doty Abraham
Doty Philip
Doughty Edward
Dow Joseph
Downs James
Drake Cornelius
Drake Jeremiah
Drake Peter
Drumming Patrick
DuBois Cornelius
DuBois Peter
Dumond & Oothout
Duncan James
Dusenbury Woolsey
Ebbets Daniel
Edwards Manuel
Elder William
Elleback Emanuel
Ellis William
Ellison Richard
Ellistone Abraham
Elswrath
Emmons Eli

Emmons John
Empie Christopher
Empie Philip
Ennist John
Esselstyne Peter
Everit Richard
Every John
Every Thomas
Fairchild
Falconham
Faulk Isaac
Faulkner John
Feather John
Fellinger (the Drummer)
Ferdon
Ferdon Jacob
Ferguson
Ferguson A.
Ferguson John
Ferres Jacob
Festor Francis P.
Feterly Peter
Fetter Lucas
Fetter Philemon
Field Benjamin
Fiks Peter
Finckle George
Fisher
Fisher Alexander
Fisher Daniel
Fisher John
Fisher Thomas
Flagler Simon
Flandreau John
Flewelling Abel
Flewelling John
Flewelling Lemuel, jr
Flewelling Morris
Flewelling Samuel Jr
Flewelling Thomas
Flock Harmanes
Folliott George
Ford Joseph
Forman James
Forman Zebulon
Foster
Foster P.
Fowler Andrew
Fowler Benjamin
Fowler David
Fowler George
Fowler Jeremiah
Fowler Jonathan Jr.
Fowler Newbury
Fowler Reuben
Fowler Samuel
Fowler Sarah
Fowler Solomon
Fowler William
Fox Frederick
Fradrick Barant
Frail John
Frazier Hugh
Frazier John

Frazier John Due
Frazier Simon
Frazier William
Freehoudt Isaac
Freel Jonathan
Freligh Jacob
French Benjamin
French Chanty
French Gershom
French Jeremiah
French John
Frost Caleb
Frost Jacob
Fuller Lemuel
Furman
Furman James
Futer Lewis
Gale Griffin
Galpin Joseph
Gardiner Jacob
Gardner
Gardner Charles
Gardner Covel
Gardner Thomas
Garlough Peter
Gee John
Gentill George
Germond Silas
Getman John
Ghons Hans Jury
Gibson Andrew
Gibson John
Gidney Caleb
Gidney David
Gidney Isaac
Gidney Jacob
Gidney James
Gidney John
Gidney Jonathan
Gidney Joshua
Gidney Solomon
Gifford Benjamin
Gisner John
Gleason John
Golden Joseph
Golding Benjamin
Golding John
Gonong Isaac
Gourmand Arthur
Graham John
Graham John I.
Graims (Mrs).
Grains
Grant Col.
Grant Alexander
Grant James
Grass Michael
Gray
Gray Capt
Gray William
Graypoll Peter
Green Abraham
Green Absolom
Green James

Green Joseph
Green Samuel
Grey William
Grifeth (Squire)
Griffin Josiah
Griffith Dr.
Griffith John
Griggs
Griggs (Mrs)
Grigson Thomas
Groat Henry
Groat R.
Guile John
Guion Jonathan
Hadden John
Hadler Adam
Haff Paul
Hageman John
Haight James
Haight Joseph
Hains Alexander
Hains Daniel
Hains Elijah
Hains James
Hains John
Hains Peter
Haire Alexander
Hait David
Hait James
Hait William
Halenbeck John
Ham Frederick, Jr.
Hambleton John, Dr.
Hamman James
Hammell Briant
Hamond Isaac
Haner Frederick
Hannabell John
Hanse Harmanse
Hansicker Andries
Hardin Magdalen
Hare Alexander
Hare James
Harris
Harris Brewer
Harris Francis
Harris Samuel
Hars Uriah
Hart James, jr.
Hasbrouck Jacob
Haslop James
Hatfield Barnes
Havens John
Haviland Charles
Haviland John
Hawkins John
Hawkshurst Jesse
Hawley Ezekiel
Hawley Ezekiel, jr.
Hawley John
Hayes John
Heliker Augustus
Heliker Jacob
Heliker Jeremiah

Heliker John
Helium Peter
Helmer Adam
Hemstead Nathaniel
Henderson Thomas
Henderson William
Henning Philip
Henry
Herkimer Johan Jost,
Capt.
Herkimer John
Herron Isaac
Higgins John
Hill Zacheus
Hilliback Baltus
Hitchcock Joseph
Hoag Nathan
Hoaksley Robert
Hober Adam
Hock John
Hodges E.
Hodges T.
Hoff Hendrick
Hoffman Ludlow
Hoffnagel
Hoffnagle John
Hoffnagle Melcher
Hoffnagle Michael
Hofle Hendrick
Hogel A.
Hogel John
Hoit David
Hoit Joshua
Holden James
Holland John
Hollenback
Hollenback D.
Holmes Col.
Holmes David
Holmes James
Holmes Samuel
Hoogtaling Jacob
Hooper John, jr.
Hooper Stephen
Hoover Adam
Hople Henderick
Horton Elisha
Horton Gilbert Bud
Horton James
Horton Samuel
Hough John
Hough Stephen
Houser Frederick
Howard John
Howard Matthew
Hoxie
Hoy Richard
Hoyt David
Huested Jonathan
Huestis Lewis
Huff Henry
Huff Paul
Huff Stephen
Huggeford Dr.

Huggeford Peter
Hughsted Bishop
Hull Robert
Hunt Benjamin
Hunt Frederick
Hunt Joshua
Hunt Levi
Huntley Bethuel
Husted Jabes
Hustice Jonathan
Hustice Solomon
Hyatt John
Hyatt Thomas
Ingram Abijah
Ingram Benjamin
Ireland John
Isenhert Christopher
Jackson James
Jackson Samuel
Jacobs Richard
Jacocks William W.
Jager Lemuel
Jaidencock
James Paul
James William
Jaycock William
Jenkes Thomas
Jenkins Samuel
Jessup
Jessup Ebenezer
Jessup Edward
Jessup Joseph
Jewell Isaac A.
Johnson
Johnson (Lady)
Johnson Abraham
Johnson Guy, Col.
Johnson James
Johnson John (Sir)
Johnson John
Johnson Jonathan
Johnson Peter, Capt.
Johnson William (Sir)
Johnston Capt.
Johnston John
Johnston Jonathan
Jones Edward
Jones John
Jones Jonathan
Jones Jotham
Jones Philip
Kane John
Kater Hana
Keeler Job
Kempe John Tabor Atty
& Advocate Gen.
Kennedy Robert
Ketchum Abijah
Kettle Andrew
Kimball Stephen
King Gideon
King John
Kipp Jacobus
Knapp Moses

Kniffen
Kniffen Daniel
Kniffen John
Kniffen Jonathan
Kober Adam
Kouck Philip
Kresler Hanse
Kresler Philip
Kronkhyte Abraham
Laight Edward
Lake Abraham
Lake I.
Lake N., jr.
Lamb James
Lane Peter
Lang John
Langdon Thomas
Lantman Henderick
Lards William
Lashle Alexander
Lassing Isaac
Lassing Isaac I.
Lassing Isaac P.
Lassing Johannes A.
Lassing Johannes E.
Lassing Johannes L.
Lassing Johannis Det.
Lassing Johannis P.
Lassing Johannis Wm.
Lassing John P.
Lassing John Peter Wm.
Lassing Laurence L.
Lassing Peter Johannis
Lassing Peter John
Lassing Peter P.
Lawrence John
Lawrence Stephen
Lawrence William, Dr.
Lawson Jotham
Leake Robert
Leake Thomas
Lee Misper
Lent Abraham
Lent Adolph
Lent Hercules
Lent Isaac
Lent John
Lent Peter
Lentman John
Leonard James
LeRoy Francis
Leslie Alexander
Lester Cornelius
Lester John
Lester Mordccai
Lewis Benjamin
Lewis J.
Lewis John
Lewis Thomas
Litchart John, jr.
Livingston John
Lockwood Peter
Lockwood Solomon
Logan David.

Loines Henry
Long David
Lorway J., Dr.
Losee George
Lossee Abraham
Lott John
Lotterage Robert
Loucks George
Lounsberry Henry
Lounsbury William
Low Jacob
Low John
Ludlow James
Luke (Mrs)
Lyng John B.
Lyon Gilbert
Lyon Henry
Lyon Joseph
Lyon Shubal
Mabbett Joseph S.
Mabbett Samuel
Mabie
Mabie Cornelius
Mabie Jacob
Mabie Jeremiah
Mabie Lewis
Mabie Peter
Mabie Silas
Mabie Simon
Madders
Manhart Philip
Mann I.
Mapes Joseph
Marker Hugh
Markle Joseph
Markwart Johannis
Marsellas H.
Martin Agrippa
Martin John
Martin Walter
Matheson James
Matrass Isaac
Mattes James
Matthews Fletcher
Matthews William
Mattice Hendrick
Mattice Johannis Nicholas
May William
McAdams William
McAlpin Capt.
McAlpin Daniel
McAlpin Walter
McAuley Donald
McCarsan
McCarty John
McCollom John
McComb John
McCormick James
McCray William
McCree James
McDarne Randall
McDole John
McDonald Alexander
McDonald Allen

McDonald John
McDonald Rorey
McDonald T.
McDougal Allen
McDougall
McDowl Hugh
McGreger Peter
McGregor Jno
McGrewer John
McGruir Hugh
McHerrin Richard
McKenzie Laudot
McKiel William
McKinney John
McLean Peter
McLeod Daniel
McLeod Don'd
McLeod Norman, Capt.
McLeod William
McMartin John
McMaster James
McMullin Dougal
McMullin Hugh
McNeal John
McNeal Thomas
McNight Malcom
McNutt David
McTaggert James
Mead Ezekiel
Menzies Alexander
Menzincs Alexander
Merkle Jacob
Merritt Cornberry
Merritt Daniel
Merritt Gilbert
Merritt Hackaliah
Merritt Nathaniel
Merritt Robert
Merritt Samuel
Merritt Thomas
Merritt Underbill
Merritt William
Merselus Hanse
Middagh Jacob
Miller Anthony
Miller Jacob
Miller John
Miller John A.
Miller Joseph
Miller Lyon
Miller N.
Miller Obadiah
Miller Peter
Miller William
Minthorne
Minthorne Mangel
Mitchell John
Mitchell Thomas
Mock Johannes
Monford David
Montross Peter
Moore Lambert
Moore Thomas
Moore William

Moorney Pat
Mordon Joseph
Morduff George
Morehouse Ezra
Morey Jonathan
Morgan Caleb
Morgan Caleb, jr.
Morison Alexander
Morrel John
Morrell Thomas
Morrill Benjamin
Morris Duncan
Morris Roger Maj. & Col,
Council
Morrison John
Morrison Malcom
Mosher Hugh
Mosher Jonathan
Motrass Peter
Mott John
Mozer Christopher
Mulford
Mulford David
Mullen Dott
Mullen Peter
Munro Daniel
Munson George
Munson Nathaniel
Murphy Francis
Murry John
Murry Robert
Murry T.
Mutch Johannes
Myer William
Nallour Michael
Nation Black
Near Christian
Near Jacob
Nellis Henry
Nelson Riche
Nichollson David
Nichols Thomas
Nickerson Joseph
Noble Capt.
Noble Reubin
Nodine A.
Nodine B.
Nodine Peter
Oackley Peter
Oakley Benjamin
Oakley Timothy
Odell Daniel
Odell Joshua
Ogden Benjamin
Ogden Jehu
Ogden John
Ogden William
Olinus John
O'Neil James
Ore William
Orser Evert
Orser Isaac
Osborn Capt.
Osborn Nathan

Ostrander Peter
Ostrom Andries
Owens Moses
Palmatier Peter
Palmatier Peter I.
Palmer David
Palmer Edmund
Palmer Edward
Palmer Lewis
Palmer William
Panter G.
Panter Philip
Panton Francis
Parent Jacob
Park Ryner
Parks James
Parret J.
Parrot I.
Partelow Amos
Pasent Jacob
Pasent John
Pasent Levy
Passing Lawrence L.
Patrick Adam
Patten
Pearce Richard
Pearce William
Peck Caleb
Peck James
Peemart Francis
Peers Alexander
Peers Samuel
Pemart
Penmart Teunis
Perry Samuel
Persons James
Peters Richard
Peters Thomas
Peterson Conradt
Peterson James
Phillips Adolphus
Phillipse Frederick, Col.
Philo Samuel
Phister I.
Pickel John
Pickins Robert
Pinckney Samuel
Pine Amos
Pitcher James
Planton John
Plats John
Proctor
Poser Levy
Prosser Dr.
Post
Post Frederick
Post Jacob
Post Teunis
Powel Jesse
Powell James
Powell John
Powell Solomon
Poucher Jacob
Prouner John

Purchas Thomas
Purchas William
Purdy Enoch
Purdy Gilbert
Purdy Hackaliah
Purdy Henry
Purdy Isiah
Purdy JaWinn Still
Purdy James
Purdy Jesse
Purdy Joseph
Purdy Joshua
Purdy Josiah
Purdy Jotham
Purdy Stephen
Purdy Still John
Purdy Timothy
Quackenboss Adrian
Queen Michael
Randall John
Ransier G.
Rapelyea Jacob
Rapelyea Thomas
Ray Robert
Reed Charles
Reed Leonard
Reid John
Reynolds Samuel
Rhinelander Frederick
Rhodes John
Rice John
Richardson John
Richardson Thomas
Rider Ebenezer
Rider Zadoc
Riley Dennis
Roberts Peter
Robertson Robert
Robins I.
Robinson Beverley
Robinson Beverley, jr.
Robinson Thomas
Robinson & Price
Roche William
Roebuck James
Rogers William
Roome John L. C.
Roosa Egbert
Roosa Guisbert
Roosa Jacobus
Rose Matthias
Rosenberger
Ross Daniel
Ross Philip
Ross William
Ross Zebulon
Row John Peter
Runnels Robert
Ruscraff Henry
Rush John
Russel John
Ruyter John
Rykert Barent
Rykerts Philip

Ryley Charles
Sabin Jeremiah, jr.
Salomon John
Salsberger James
Sammons Thomas
Sanford Ephraim
Saris George
Savage Reuben
Savage Richard
Saxton William
Sayre James, Rev.
Schurman William
Scotsman
Scrivener Samuel
Scriver Peter
Seaman Adam
Seaman Benjamin
Seaman Israel
Seaman Silvanus
Secore Benjamin
See Abraham
See Jacobus
Seelye Ebenezer
Seelye Jacob
Segas John
Sepcrly Peter
Server Peter
Service Philip
Seymore Henry
Shatter John
Shannon Simeon
Sharp John
Sharp Peter
Sharp Richard
Sharpe Guysbert
Shaver Hanse
Shaver Philip
Shaw George
Shaw John
Shaw Moses
Sheek Christian
Sheldon Joseph
Shell John
Sherbrooke Miles
Sherman William
Sherwood Dyer
Sherwood Stephen
Sherwood William
Shipton William
Shirid Thomas
Shulop Henry
Shultes John
Siefer Lodovick
Simmons James
Simmons Maurice
Simson Alexander
Simson Isabel
Skeans Governeur
Skeans M.
Skene Philip, Maj.
Skinner Sam'l Spencer
Slingerlant Teunis
Slocum William
Slutts John

Slutts Michael
Sluyter James
Smith Austin
Smith Benjamin
Smith Christopher
Smith Daniel
Smith Isaac
Smith J.
Smith Jacob
Smith John
Smith Joseph
Smith Joshua M.
Smith Reuben
Smith Samuel
Smith Stephen
Smith Thomas
Smith William
Snedeker Richard
Snedeker Theodorus
Sneden Robert
Sneden Stephen
Snell Robert
Snider
Snider John
Snider Peter
Snider Simon
Snider William
Sniffen Jonathan
Sniffer Caleb
Sniffin Shubal
Soles Rowland
Soils Benjamin
Spencer Hedley
Spoolman Henry
Sprage Thomas
Springer William
Springstaed John
Square B.
Stalker Stephen
Staples J.
Staples Jacob
Staples John
Steenbergh William
Steenburgh Fleming
Steenburgh Simeon
Steenrod Cornelius
Stener Caspar
Stevens Eliphalet
Stevens Josiah
Stewart Walter
Stimes Jasper
Stipper Peter
Stocker Stephen
Storm
Storm Gilbert
Storm Henry
Story Zachariah
Stout Benjamin
Stover Martinus
Straught John
Street Timothy
Sturd Dr.
Stuyvesant Peter
Summers Peter

Sunderland Jacob
Sutton Caleb
Sutton William
Sutts John
Swart Joshuah
Swart Josiah
Swart Peter
Sybles Robert
Talmage
Teakle John
Ten Brook Peter
Terborney P.
Terbush Jacob
Terril Anthony
Terrill Daniel
Terwilleger Moses
Theal Charles
Theal Ebenezer
Therston John
These Jacob
Thompson John
Thorne Robert
Thousand M.
Tibbie John
Tice Gilbert
Tidd Benjamin
Tidd Samuel
Tiehout William
Tilleback Christian
Tilman John
Tissell James
Tissot Gideon
Titchort Gideon
Tobias Christian
Tobias Joseph
Tomkins Israel
Tong Joshua
Totten James
Totten Jonas
Totten Joseph
Townsend Epenetus
(Parson)
Townsend John
Townsend Uriah
Traver
Travis Jeremiah
Travis William
Tredwell Capt
Tredwell Samuel
Tucker Daniel
Turnbull Robert
Turner John
Underbill Frederick
Underbill John
Underbill Nathaniel
Underbill Nathaniel, jr.
Underbill William
Ustick Henry
Ustick William
Vail John
Vail Moses

Van Allen John
Van Alstyne Peter
Van Cleaf John
Van de Car James
Van de Voort John
Van de Warken Elbert
Van den Bergh Henry
Van den Bergh Peter
Van den Bergh Richard
Van der Heyden Dirck
Van der Voort John
Van deusen Conradt, Col.
Van Dreson James
Van Dyke Francis
Van Kleeck Barent
Van Noostrant George
Van Noostrant John
Van Nourst John
Van Valkenburgh John
Van Valkenburgh William
Van Vourst John
Van Wagenen Hans
Van Wagenen James
Van Wart Jacob
Van Wiers Henry
Van Woort John
Vartman
Velthuysen John
Venkell G.
Vermilers John
Vermillier Benjamin
Vincent Charles
Vinson John
Visscher
vredenbergh John W.
Wacken John
Wacker James
Waddle William
Wager Frederick
Wagner John
Wagstaff William
Waight Jonathan
Wallace Jonathan
Wallace William
Walldorph Martin
Walsworth
Walter Martin
Walter Philip
Wanaker Conradus
Wanamaker Dirick
Wansor Thomas
Ward
Ward Edmond
Ward Edmund
Ward Israel
Ward John
Warner Michael
Warner Thomas
Warning F.
Washborn Isaac
Washborn Jonathan

Waterburry Sylvanus
Waters John
Watson James
Weatherhead John
Weaver
Weaver Johannes
Weaver John
Weed Solomon
Weeks Stephen
Weeks William
Wemple Andrew
Westbrook Anthony
Wexton John
Wheaton Daniel
Wheeler George
White Alexander
White Sybert
White Sylvanus
Whitmore
Whitney Nathan
Wickwire Jonathan
Wiggins Stephen
Wilcox
Wilcox Hazard
Williams Abraham
Williams Benjamin
Williams Frederick
Williams Isaac
Williams John
Williams William
Wilmot Lemuel
Wilson G.
Wilson I.
Wilson James
Wilson Jonathan
Wilson Joseph
Wilson Jotham
Wilton James
Wing David
Winn Joseph
Winne Jacob
Winterton William
Wood Frederick
Wood Solomon
Wood Stephen
Woods Thomas
Woolcomb Joseph
Worden John
Wright Jacob
Wright Jonathan
Wright Uriah
Yates
Yates Richard
Yerukes Isaac
Yourmans Arthur
Yourmans John
Yourmans Thomas
Young Adam
Young Frederick
Young John

Source Material:

New York In The Revolution as Colony and State
by James A. Roberts, Comptroller
Compiled by Frederic G. Mather
Second Edition 1898

APPENDIX

Montgomery County

A FEW FACTS ABOUT OUR COUNTY'S PAST AND PRESENT
From a very old and brittle newspaper, origin unknown

In 1772, three years before the outbreak of the Revolution, the legislature of New York divided the original county of Albany, creating two additional counties, one of which was called Tryon, in honor of William Tryon, the British governor of the province. What an immense county it was, embracing all the territory of the state which lay west of the Delaware river and a line extends north through Schoharie County and along the west line of Montgomery, Fulton and Hamilton counties and continues to Canada.

Governor Tryon became so offensive to the victorious Americans in the Mohawk Valley, that in 1784, the name was changed to Montgomery in honor of the patriotic General Richard Montgomery who fell in the attempt to capture Quebec. In 1778 the boundaries of the then existing counties of the state were accurately defined, and Montgomery County was made to include all the territory of the state west of Ulster, Albany, Washington, and Clinton counties.

The first territorial reduction of old Montgomery was made in 1789, when Ontario County was created, including within its boundaries all that part of the state west of Seneca Lake and amounting in the aggregate to more than two million acres. In 1791 Montgomery was again reduced in area by the creation of Hamilton, Herkimer, Otsego and Tioga counties, leaving only the territory, which it now includes with that of Fulton County. Hamilton, however was restored to the mother county in 1797, but it was again set off in 1816.

In 1838 Fulton County was created leaving Montgomery County as it is today. In this manner old Montgomery has been reduced from an original area of about eight million acres (roughly estimated) to its present 289040 acres, or 436 square miles.

Soon after the creation of Tryon County (March 24, 1772) its inhabited territory was divided into five provisional districts, namely; Mohawk, Canajoharie, Palatine, German Flats and Kingsland. The sixth district of the county --- old England--- including lands west of the Susquehanna River, was formed April 3, 1775. On March 9, 1780, that part of the Mohawk district lying north of the river was set off under the name of Caughnawaga.

In 1788 this district was formed into a township and included all the county lying north of the Mohawk and east of a line extending from the Nose of Canada. Five years later (1793) this town was divided and Amsterdam, Mayfield, Broadalbin, and Johnstown were organized from its territory. When that division took place, the old name (Caughnawaga) was limited to the ancient village, which forms part of Fonda.

Canajoharie, both as a district and a town, has been preserved in name since its original formation in 1772. In 1788 this district became a town, but its territory has since been in part taken in the creation of other towns – Minden in 1798 and an addition in 1749, and a part of Root in 1823.

Palatine was at first a district called Stone Arabia. This was in 1772, but in 1775 the name was changed to Palatine. It embraced all the territory between Little Falls and the Noses, and extended from the Mohawk to Canada. The towns of Salisbury, Stratford, Oppenheim, and Ephratah have been formed, in whole or in part, from the original Palatine district.

Mohawk District originally included all the territory between the eastern boundary of Tryon County and a north and south line crossing the river at Anthony's Nose, and extending north and south between these lines as far as the limits of the county.

Caughnawaga, north of the river was taken from this vast tract in 1788 and sub-divided, as has been stated, in 1793. The present town of Mohawk was formed from Johnstown in 1837, while Johnstown itself was originally a part of Caughnawaga, the latter was a part of the still older district of Mohawk.

Charleston and Florida were both formed from lands of the old Mohawk district by an act passed March 12, 1793.

Glen was formed from Charleston, April 10, 1823: Minden was taken from Canajoharie, March 22, 1798; Danube, Herkimer county, was taken from Minden in 1817; Root was formed from Canajoharie and Charleston. January 17, 1823 and St. Johnsville from Oppenheim, April 18, 1838, but it is part of the old Palatine district.

Having thus briefly mentioned the gradual method by which Montgomery county (as at present constituted) and its several towns were brought into existence, we now appropriately give a general topographical and geographical description: Montgomery is bounded on the north by Fulton county, east by Schenectady and Saratoga, south by Schenectady, Schoharie and Otsego, and west by Herkimer. It lies on both sides of the Mohawk, centrally distant from Albany less than 40 miles and contains 436 square miles. The general range of highlands, which forms the connecting links between the northern spurs of the Allegheny Mountains on the south and the Adirondacks on the north, extends through the county in a northeast and southwest direction.

The Mohawk cuts through the upland and forms a valley one or two miles in width, and skirted by hills from one hundred to five hundred feet in height. The valleys of the several tributaries of the Mohawk extend several miles into the highland districts at nearly right angles with the river. The hills bordering upon the latter generally rise gradual slopes and from their summits the county spreads out into an undulating upland, with a general inclination toward the river, into which every part of the county is drained.

The principal tributaries of the Mohawk are the East Canada, Garoga, Cayadutta, Chuctanunda creeks, and Eva's Kill, on the north and Chuctanunda, Cowillega, Schoharie, Auries, Flat, Canajoharie and Otsquago creeks on the south. The highest point of land in the county is said to be Bean Hill, in Florida, and is estimated at 700 feet above tide. The lowest point is in the bed of the Mohawk, on the east line of the county about 200 feet above tide.

Gneiss, the only primary rock in the county, is found in patches, its principal locality being near the Nose on the river. Resting directly upon this are heavy masses of calciferous sandstone, appearing most frequently on the North side of the Mohawk and trending northward into Fulton county. This rock is occasionally found to contain in its cavities quartz and modules of anthracite coal, which have led to vain expenditures in mining for coal. Near Sprakers, traces of lead have been found.

Above the sandstone and next to it are the Black River and Trenton limestone, not important as surface rocks, but furnishing valuable quarries of building stone. The slates and shales of the Hudson river group extend along the south border of the county, and are found a few places north of the river.

The Naming of The Village of St. Johnsville
The Town of St. Johnsville too!

St. Johnsville was named after the surveyor Alexander St. John.
St. Johnsville was named after the church, St. John's.
Which statement is correct?

You might call this one of HISTORY'S MYSTERYS. Some of the things were probably not recorded in the past because it was common knowledge at the time and not worth mentioning. Through the passage of time the explanation for some things has been lost, like how the town and village got its name.

The controversy about the naming of St. Johnsville has swirled about for many years. It was one of those historical mysteries that never seemed to clear up. At last, there seems to be a definitive answer. With most historical puzzles, the answer was out there, but in pieces and needed to be put together. My conclusion is that both of these statements are correct -- to a point.

In 1804, Klock's Church (which was located just outside the eastern end of the now village of St. Johnsville), moved into Zimmerman's (where St. Johnsville is now located) and changed its name to St. John's Reformed Church. The full name of the church was The Reformed Calvinist Church of The Upper Part of Palatine In The County of Montgomery. The local populace began referring to the settlement as St. John's Church.

More than 14 years later, the name St. Johnsville first appeared. Alexander St. John came into the area to lay out the New Turnpike to Johnstown in 1811. When the new post office in what we now know as W. St. Johnsville along the present Mill Road, was begun in 1818, it was named after Mr. St. John. The larger population at the time, was located in the then village of St. Johnsville (W. St. Johnsville), St. John's Church had very few people. One factor in locating the Post Office in W. St. Johnsville at Mill Road was Sander's ferry crossing which was available in (West) St. Johnsville. Another factor was originally the road before 1800, (Mohawk Turnpike, now Route 5) did not go along the north side of the river to Little Falls; it crossed the river and went along the south shore of the Mohawk River. In 1800 the bridge over the East Canada Creek was completed and the road to Little Falls went on the north side of the river.

The area around the church was known for many decades as "St. John's Church". There are records of men or their widows applying for war pensions stating they lived or were born at St. John's or St. John's Church, which was puzzling until more references were found to fill in the pieces. So, for many years this area had a place named St. Johnsville by Mill Road and a settlement to the east called by the local people, St. John's Church. What we now call St. Johnsville did not attract a lot of residents until the Erie Canal was completed in 1825. The shift in population began towards the area called St. John's Church.

Here are the first three postmasters for St. Johnsville:
Henry I. Lloyd . . . . .February 27, 1818
Jabez Lewis . . . . December 21, 1824
Horatio Averell . . . . January 16, 1826

The name Averell is a familiar one even today, we have a street named after Mr. Averell. On East Main Street, which was then known as the Mohawk Turnpike, the "Old Stone Store," was built by the Averells in 1831.

The St. Johnsville Post Office, somewhere between 1826 and 1831, was moved to the larger center of population, and since the Post Office was named St. Johnsville, the name of the village became St. Johnsville. So in a way the village was named after the surveyor, sort of by default. In 1838, the Town of St. Johnsville was formed and the Village of St. Johnsville (once known as St. John's Church) was incorporated in 1857.

Supporting Documents

St. John's Reformed Church 150th Anniversary (1920) booklet has a reference to land donated for a church at East Creek, to be built by Rev. Peter VanDriesen.

Inter-Centenary Celebration of Saint John's Reformed Church (1920) *"In 1722 we find Petrius VanDriessin, who served the first church at Albany for nearly a quarter of a century, applying to the crown to establish a mission among the Mohawks. This was granted to him and in 1732, the three tribes of the Mohawks, Bear, Wolf and Turtle, because of their love and in appreciation of the labors of Petrius VanDriessen and Johannes Ehl, gave a considerable grant of land on the North Bank of the Mohawk. Ehl was co-missionary with VanDriessen, and the Ehl family are yet residents of Palatine district."*

Rev. VanDriessen served Albany's First Reformed Church from 1712 to 1738. Apparently, the reverend was nearing the end of his life, and died before he could carry out his plans. There is no evidence a church was ever built at East Creek, it is not on old maps, nor are there any references to a church in any other writings. Here is an excerpt from Sir William Johnson's Indian Journal, dated January 26, 1762.

"We formerly gave a piece of land to a minister, on condition he should build a church for us, which was never done. This minister whose name was VanDriessen deceived us. We are now without any persons to instruct us in the Christian Religion, excepting three or four visits in each year from the Rev. Mr. Ehle; and we are informed that VanDriessen being dead, his heirs have sold the land, which we intended for so good a purpose. If the clergy are thus to deceive us, who can we rely on? If he performed his promise we should now have been better people and our children would become good Christians, but as it hath fallen our otherwise, we beg you will take this likewise into your consideration, and procure us justice therein."

From: The History of Montgomery Classis, R.C.A. by W.N.P. Dailey, Recorder Press, Amsterdam, NY 1916.

"St Johnsville Church: The Francis Harrison patent of 12,000 acres was obtained of the Indians in 1722, and a year later the entire tract was partitioned off, the first church having been built on Lot No. 13, owned by George C. and Jacob Klock (cf Bk. Deeds 48, 213)."

Klock's Church was located, to the east of the present Village of St. Johnsville. The Frontiersmen of New York by Jeptha R. Simms, Albany, NY 1883; Volume I, Page 285.

"The first church at St. Johnsville.-- In this connection I should mention the fact that a German Reformed church was erected at St. Johnsville, then known as "Zimmerman's," in 1770. This structure was built of wood, was of good size, and stood not far from its burying ground, yet to be seen about a mile eastward of the village. It was finished with a sounding board, as were nearly all churches at that period. When erected it was intended also to benefit the Indians in the neighborhood, having seats for them and the slaves of the white citizens. This edifice was demolished about the year 1818, near which time a church was erected to serve its purposes within the present village. Who first labored in this church I am unable to state. Rev. John Henry Dyslin, a man of good repute, was its pastor from 1790 to 1815, (wrong date, he died in 1812) when he died. The Rev. David Devoe was its pastor from 1816 to 1830, during which time the old church was demolished, and the one in the village erected. The second edifice gave place to a new one constructed of brick in 1881."

From A History of St. John's Reformed Church Formerly The Reformed Calvinist Church of The Upper Part of Palatine In The County of Montgomery, by Norman Edwin Thomas, Minister.

"The congregation continued to worship at Klock's Church, however, for some years before action was taken. About 1802 John L. Bellinger was elected treasurer and he took the lead

in promoting the enterprise. Work was started and after the expenditure of $1861.05 1/2, a great sum for those days, the new building was ready by January 2nd, 1804, for its first Congregational Meeting, at which Conrad Hellicoss, Andrew Zabriskie, John L. Bellinger, Jacob Zimmerman, Adam A. Walrath, and Henry Beekman were elected trustees; and the eventful step of adopting a new name for the new church was taken. Its official title now became the "Dutch Reformed Congregation of St. John's Church in Palatine Town, Montgomery County."

In the Department of History and Archives in Fonda the final piece of the puzzle was found. In the archives..."in the Highway/Road records that the area was referred to as Zimmermans' Mills in the late 1790s. One particular road running from Zimmermans north was referred to as 'The road starting at Zimmermans or Failing will run north to Denis Flander's being seven gates between.' The same road was to be widened in 1832 and was described as 'starting at St. Johns Church and running north to Denis Flander'......"

From the Pension papers of Denis Flander, 1832.

"He was in the battle under Gen. Van Rensselaer against the British and Tories and the Indians near the Mohawk River at fording place that the Indians and Tories were under the command of Sir John Johnson, said battle was fought at now town of Oppenheim near the house of Richard Failing about three or four yards from the now village of St. John in said town that the British force after a slow start on the day of the battle crossed the Mohawk River from the north to the south side that during that time he served Hess Co. that he was drafted out of said Co. into Christian Houses Co. and went to the Royal Grant for a few days and after a time for 14 days as before stated.

Further states that he had no documentary evidence to any claim whatsoever to a Pension or Annuity except this present and declared that his service is not on the Pension Roll of the agency of any state, that he was born 15 October 1757 at the now town of German Flats in Herkimer County has no evidence of his age seventy four, resided in St. Johns of Palatine in the now County of Montgomery that he served as before mentioned and has lived since the revolution in the same place where he now resides that he enlisted twice as a boatman as before mentioned each time for nine months, but served one time three months."

The St. Johnsville Post Office was established on February 27, 1818, according to records of the Post Office Department. The following is a bit of history leading up to this event.

Excerpts from <u>Town of St. Johnsville, Sesquicentennial History, 1838-1988</u> by Anita Smith:

"On March 4, 1811, the Legislature named three commissioners "to lay out a new turnpike road from the house of Henry Gross, in Johnstown, to the house of John C. Nellis, in the Town of Oppenheim." This road terminated in the Mohawk Turnpike, and is what is known as the "New Turnpike," just east of our village. Johnstown was then the county seat of Montgomery County and this new road provided a shorter route from this section of what was the Town of Oppenheim to the county seat. It also furnished a highway for the convenience of the farmers in a rich agricultural section then being developed.

One of the three commissioners named in the act of the Legislature was Alexander St. John of the Town of Northampton (now in Fulton County). Mr. St. John was a surveyor by occupation and surveyed the new road and acting as one of the commissioners charged with its construction, was actively engaged in building the thoroughfare. In this way, Mr. St. John became acquainted with the leading citizens of this locality, then a hamlet known as "Zimmerman's" named for the original settler, Jacob Zimmerman.

Mr. Zimmerman built the first pioneer home within the limits of St. Johnsville and soon after built the first gristmill along the creek, which bears his name.

Mr. Shaffer believed that Mr. St. John made so favorable an impression on the residents of this locality, that when a post office was established, the name of St. Johnsville was chosen as a token of esteem for the surveyor and commissioner who had so much to do with building the new road. However, later facts indicate that it was named after the St. John's Reformed Church that was the pioneer church in this area.

Location of Post Office

The highway records of the township show that Henry I. Lloyd, our first postmaster, was a resident in the township in 1838, and was assessed four days of labor on the highways that year. His name, appears on the records, each year, to include 1842. He was assigned to Road District No. 7 which was described as "commencing at the Mohawk River at Sanders' Ferry, running thence, northerly, across the Mohawk Turnpike, between Daniel Leonard's and George Lake's, thence northerly, to the head line road, near James Wilson's." The road described is what is known as "Mill Road" in west St. Johnsville, so named from the fact that it led to Leonard and Curran's grist mill, later, "Beekman's Mill." The fact that 42 taxpayers were, assigned to this particular road, indicates that there was a large population at the 4 corners of the Upper Village and naturally that particular locality would appeal as a good location for a general store.

With the known facts, and with no tradition to the contrary, it is not unreasonable to conclude that our first post office building was located at the Upper Village in the store operated by Henry I. Lloyd. This assumes that Mr. Lloyd conducted the store at that point in 1818, in the Town of Oppenheim, twenty years before his name appears on the records of the new Town of St. Johnsville. In locating post offices, the Post Office Department requires a reasonably central location for the convenience of the patrons to be served. In 1818, the Upper Village my have been that logical location. At that time the hamlet at "Zimmerman's" was small in size and there was a thriving little community at East Creek, far outnumbering the future village of St. Johnsville in population. Locating the post office at Upper St. Johnsville in Lloyd's store would be for the convenience of a greater number than at "Zimmerman's," when the hamlet at East Creek was considered.

Henry I. Lloyd was appointed in 1816 under the administration of James Monroe, our fifth President.
Post Office, St. Johnsville
Established February 27, 1818"

Quit Rents

This is another of history's mysteries. Sure England tried the tea tax and the stamp tax, but there had to be some way England made money in the previous 100 years. They didn't just colonize out of the goodness of their hearts. I couldn't figure out why they would bother, there had to be something I was overlooking. Then I found out about the Quit Rents.

And what was a quit rent? Many of the old documents use the term, quit rent, and it seemed to be something the older writers understood, but I did not. Here is what I found out about Quit Rents.

The definition of QUIT RENT:
--Quit rent was a medieval term used to designate the portion of the agricultural product planted, raised, and harvested by the sharecropping tenant-peasant serf that was withheld by the feudal landlord. Both taxes AND profit are the present-day expressions of quit rent.
--According to Black's Law Dictionary "A rent paid by the tenant of a freehold, by which he goes quit or free, that is, discharged from any other rent." The "quit rent" paid in colonial times went to the Governor of a colony [as the representative of the Crown, or the Crown's Designee] for the use of the land.
Before launching into the subject of quit rents, it is important to note the Mohawk Valley was for the most part, settled peacefully. White and red men lived side by side and there were very few instances of violence, with the exception of a few raids until the Revolutionary War. Land was always the big issue, red men had it and white men wanted it.
In the early view, simply put, the English crown viewed all land as theirs, and the occupants paid rent on it, Quit Rent.
Our system of taxation grew out of the quit rents of the early days of the colony. Even after independence, the term quit-rent was used for many years and the nation used the English pounds.
There has been a lot of disagreement as to the exact nature of the title held by the American Indians for the soil on which they lived. European governments, upon the discovery of America, branded the American Indians as nomads. They laid down the proposition of international law that the European Government had an absolute right to the land on the American continents, which either they or their representative citizens should discover. Proprietorship by right of discovery was asserted, with utter disregard to the true rights of the American Indians.
Often in the history books you read, "I discover this land in the name of the King of England....." Usually the person discovering the land had no idea how much his discovery encompassed, he simply declared it as being owned by the crown.
The American Indians had a very loose arrangement for land usage; they hunted and fished and then when necessary, moved to a new place. The white man saw it differently, he wanted absolute possession of land, as much of it as possible, to cultivate, fence in and to build houses and barns on the land.
Under the colonial government it was customary that the Indian title, should be surrendered before land grants were issued to the parties wishing to purchase. A deed from the Indians was usually procured by holding a council with them, and this being accomplished, the Surveyor General was directed to make the survey and in his report furnish a map and field notes of the premises.

The draft of a patent was then prepared by the Attorney General, and, if approved by the Governor of the colony and his council it was granted and recorded. Under an established ordinance, only one thousand acres could be granted to one person, but this regulation was frequently overlooked by associating, as patentees, a large number of persons who were only nominally parties to the purchase. Land speculators were plentiful in those early times and there was corruption among the officials.

In addition, the officials who charged the remunerative fees obtained by the performance of their duty, were often participants in the purchase. In a few instances land grants were issued from the Crown of England instead of through the colonial government. In some of the grants for patents under the colonial government, the conditions required the payment of the annual quit-rent, which at that time constituted an important source of revenue, and which subsequently became due to the State. The payments for quit-rent were sometimes specified to be made in money, but more often in grain or other produce such as furs.

In a word, TAXATION.

In an effort to contain foreign interference, the Federal Government prohibited the Indian tribes in the United States from making or entering into treaties with political powers other than the Federal Government.

I was surprised to discover some very early assessment records in the Albany County Archives.

The early state Assessment Roll of real and personal Estates in the Town of Palatine in the County of Montgomery made this eighteenth Day of October in the Year of our Lord One Thousand seven hundred and ninety nine, according to the Directions of the Statute entitled "An Act for the Assessments and Collection of Taxes."

These 1799 records are included in the Appendix and show the value of the real property (land), buildings and personal property such as animals. How they managed to keep it all straight without maps and not have blank land, which was not assessed, I can't imagine. New York State didn't have assessment maps until into the 1970s.

"Necessity is paramount to law."

Source Material:

English Crown Grants by S. L. Mershon, p 90
1918
A History of Herkimer County
DY NATHANIEL S. BENTON.
ALBANY: J. MUNSELL, 78 STATE STREET, 1856

New York In The Revolution as Colony and State
by James A. Roberts, Comptroller
Compiled by Frederic G. Mather
Second Edition 1898
Two Volumes

Tryon County Militia--First Regiment

Colonel Samuel Campbell; Colonel Ebenezer Cox; Lieutenant Colonel Samuel Clyde; Major Abraham Copeman; Major Peter S. Deygert; Adjutant Jacob Seeber; Quarter Master John Pickard; Surgeon Adam Frank; Surgeon David Younglove

Capt. John Bowman	Lieut. Abraham Arnt	Lieut. Henry Shrumbling
Capt. Matthew Brown	Leiut. Nicholas Barth	Lieut. John Van Everen
Capt. Jost Deygert	Lieut. Henry Brate	Lieut. Hanes Windecker
Capt. Jacob Diffendorff	Lieut. Conrad Braun	Ensign John L. Bellinger
Capt. Joseph House	Lieut. George Conderman	Ensign John Cunderman
Capt. Adam Leyp	Lieut. Nicholas Deygert	Ensign Richard Ellwood
Capt. John Roof	Lieut. Dedrick Horning	Ensign Adam Flind
Capt. John Russ	Lieut. Jacob Matthews	Ensign Jacob Hanes
Capt. Ryner Van Everen	Lieut. Charles Powell	Ensign Henry Myer
Capt. Nicholas Weyser	Lieut. Jacob Schneyder	Ensign Cornelius Van Every
Capt. Japes Wilson	Lieut. John Seeber	Ensign Henry Walwrath
Lieut. Peter Adamy	Lieut. William Seeber	

Additional Names on State Treasurer's Pay Books

Lieut. Englehardt Wagener; Ensign John Pickert; Ensign Jeremiah Young

Enlisted Men

Adamy Peter
Ale Christian
Ale Peter
Apel Henry
Batenauer Jacob
Batenaur George
Bearmour Henry
Becker Henry
Becker Peter
Beellinger Adam
Bell Fredrick
Belleanger Fredrick
Belliner Henrick
Bellinger Adam
Bellinger Philip
Bellinger William
Bendeman Peter
Benteman Simmon
Besner Jacob
Bettinger Martin
Bickerd Henry
Bickerd Isaac
Billing William
Billinger William
Bitelman Peter
Blats George
Bleats George
Bohall Adam
Bolier Frederick
Bolt Fillip
Boom Fredrick K.
Boss Christian
Bost Christian V.
Botman Adam
Brate James
Brisenbecker Balser
Broukman Godfret
Bruckeman John
Bruckman Godfrid
Brunner Christian
Bush George
Butcluter John
Buterfield James
Cannan Matthew
Castler Thomas
Christman John
Clapsattle William
Clapsedel George
Clebsater William
Clock Joseph
Cockton Thomas
Cohat Adam
Cohert Adam
Conterman John
Contryman John
Contryman John M.

Coon John
Crais George
Cramer Godfred
Cramer Joast
Creamer John
Creamer Joseph
Crimm Jacob
Crisman John
Crosmen Frederick
Crouse Friederick
Crows George
Crum Adam
Crum Jacob
Cuff (colored)
Cunderman Cunrath
Cunderman Frederick
Cunderman John J.
Cunderman Marius
Cuntrman Adam
Cuntryman Cunrad
Curtner Peter
Cypher John
Damuth Richard
Darwind Bindier
Dasler John
Deck Henry
Defendorf Jacob, H. R.
Demult Richard
Demuth Dederick
Devery Arent
Devy Adam
Deygert Nichlas
Didenbeck Baltus
Diefendorff H. Jacob
Diefendorff Johannes
Diefendorff John J.
Diefendurff John
Diefendurff John, Jr.
Dietrich Dewald
Dilenbeck Baltus
Dilenbeck Martin
Dinstman Antony
Dinstman Denis
Docksteader John
Dreisselmann Christian
Dunckel Frank
Dunckel Nicholas
Dunckel Peter
Dunckell Garrett
Dunkle George
Dunlap John
Dunlap William
Dusler Jacob
Dusler John
Dusler Marx
Dycfcert Thaboft

Dygart Sevnnus
Dygert Henry
Dykert Henery
Eatkens William
Eckler Christ Sogel
Eckler Christstofel
Eckler Ernest
Eckler Hanos
Eckler Henry
Eckler Henry, Jr.
Eckler Johannes
Eckler Lenet
Eckler Pitter
Ehl Christian
Ehl Peter
Ehle Anthony
Ehle Harmanus
Ehle Johnerick
Ehts Adam
Ehts Christopher
Ehts John Christ.
Ehts William
Elfendorf Debois
Ell John
Ellwood Benjamin
Ellwood Isaac
Elvendorf Tobias
Elwood Peter
Embody Henry
Estter John C.
Farbus Nichlas
Faubele Johnas
Feeble John
Fehling Andreas
Feling Henry
Felling Jacob
Felling Nicholas
Felling Peter
Fetterly John
Fetterly John T.
Fouston John
Flack Peter
Flind Alexander
Flint Alexander
Flint Cornelles
Flint John
Flint Robert
Folkert John
Folyg Peter
Forbush Johnes
Fork Isaac
Forre Adam
Foster John
Foster Moses
Fox Peter
Fox William

Frantz Stoffel
Fretcher Conraed
Fuks Peter
Fun Adam
Furro Rudolph
Furry Adam
Ganger Isaac
Garlock Adam
Garlock George F.
Garlock Jacob
Garlock Philip
Gelly Thadeus
Gerlach Henry
Gerlack George
Gerlack Han Christian
Gerlock George W.
Givet John J,
Givit Fridrick
Grim Jacob
Haber Jacob
Haberman Jacob
Hack Fredrick
Haffer Jacob
Hake Frederick
Hako Fradrick
Harning Lienert
Haus Adam
Haus Henrick
Haus Peter
Heerway Charles
Helmer John
Helmer John G.
Helmer Joseph
Helmer Jost
Henry Andrew
Hess George
Hess Henry
Heuth Joshua
Heyntz William
Hicky George
Hicky Michal
Himer William
Hines Andrew
Hootmaker Adam
Hoover Jacob
Horning Adam
Horning Dederick
Horning George
Horning John
Horning Lanert
Hous Harman
House George
House Jacob
House John
House Joseph
House Jost C.
House Nicholas
House Peter
Jacob Henry
Johns William
Jordan Adam
Jordan Casper
Jordan Casper L.
Jordan Gasper

Jordan George
Jordan John
Jordan John Peter
Jordan Nicholas
Jorden John P.
Jorden Peter
Jung Jacob
Jung Thommes
Jungijo Jacob
Kellar Jacob
Keller Andras
Keller Andres, Jr.
Keller Felix
Keller Gasper
Keller Jacob R.
Kelly Thomas
Kelmer John
Kerlach Henry
Kesles Thomas
Kessler Peter
Killy Thomas
Kling Ludwig
Knausz Johannes
Knautz John
Knieskern Fitter
Knouts George
Koemer Johannes
Korning Adam
Kretsinger Jacob
Lambert George
Lambert Peter
Lambert Peter, Sr.
Lambert Peter, Jr.
Lampert Peter
Lape John
Lappius Daniel
Leeve Phillip
Leipe John L.
Lentner George
Lepert Fredrick
Levey Michael
Leyli Simon
Lint Georg
Lints Gorg
Lipe John
Lipe John, Jr.
Loucks Peter
Loux Jost
Low Lawrence Gras
Lure Philip
Lurzdemann Simon
McCartey Dunkon
McCartey John
Mc Fie Alexander
McKillip John
McLonis Jurry
McVagulhen Peeter
Mai Henrich
Marten Robert
Mayby David
Mayby Joseph
Mayer H. Henry
Mayer Jacob
Mayer Jacob S.

Meier Matthew
Meyer Henrick
Meyer Henrick S.
Meyer Jacob
Meyer Jacob R.
Meyer Johan Henrick
Meyer Solomon
Mier John
Miler John C.
Miller Conraed
Miller Dionysius
Miller Garret
Miller John
Monck John, Jr.
Monke John
Moone James
Moos Pitner Rufus
Morfey Henry
Moyer David
Moyer John
Murphy Henry
Murphy Thomas
Myer Matthias
Myers Dewel
Myers John
Myre Henry
Myre John
Neles Cris John
Neles Rowerd
Neles Willem
Nelles Christian
Nelles George
Nelles Gerry
Nelles Henrick
Nelles Henry
Nelles Henry N.
Nelles John
Nelles William
Nellies Gerry
Nellis Henry
Nellis Jacob
Netherly John.
Netherly John H.
Netherly John I.
Nolgert John
Ohn Jacob
Outerman Jacob
Ovendurff Conrad
Paba Ernst
Parsheall James
Pauly Jacob
Phenes Michael
Pickard Cunrad
Pickerd Adolph
Pickerd Nicholas
Pickert Conradt
Pickert George
Pigner Tise
Plets George
Plough Nichlas
Plunes John
Price George
Qollinger Henry
Quackenbos Honter Soct

Quackenboss Isaac
Quakenbush David
Quakenbush Jeremiah
Quakenbush Peter
Quollenger Gosper
Quollinger Andrew
Radenaer Jacob
Radimour Jacob
Ransier George
Ratnower George
Ratnower Jacob
Reasnor James
Reinhartd Willem
Remer Jacob
Remer John
Remer Martin
Revenshon John Peter
Ribsomer William
Rice John
Riebsomer Matteys
Riverson John Peter
Rodgers Samuel
Roneons Jonathan
Ronnin John, Jr.
Roof John
Roseel John
Roth John
Ruff John
Runnins John, Sr.
Runnins John, Jr.
Sacknar John
Sander Henrick
Scheat Andony
Schefer Adam
Schiely Martin
Schimmel Francis
Schneck George
Schneider Michael
Schreiber Steffan
Schuyler David
Schuyler Jacob
Schuyler John Jost
Schuyler Nicolas
Schuyler Peter P.
Schyler David, Jr.
Scoulen Essias
Scoulen Tosseos
Seaber John W.
Seeber Jacob
Seeber John
Seyber John
Shall Henry
Sheafer Adam
Sheafer Henry
Shelly John
Shimel Dieterich
Shireman George
Shmit Hendrick
Shnyder Gottlieb
Simmerman Conratce
Simmerman Henery
Sits Hendrick
Sits John
Sits Nichlos

Sitts Peter
Sitz Baldes
Smidt Philip
Smith Johannes
Smith John
Smith Philip
Snake George
Snyder John
Sober Jacobus
Spalsbeck John
Sparback Martinus
Sparks Pearl
Stansell Nicolas
Steinmetz Philip
Stensell George
Stensell Nicoles
Stensell William
Stephen John
Strawbeck Adam
Stroback Fradrick
Strobeck Jacob
Sullenger Gosper
Suller Andrew
Suiter Gosper
Tailor Nathan
Tetterly John H.
Thompson Aaron
Thompson John
Thompson Thomas
Thompson William
Tillenback Martin
Tom (colored)
Tucks Peter
Tulling Henry
Tygert Henry
Ullendorff Daniel
Ulsever Stephen
Ulzhaven Bastian
Uthermark John B.
Uttermark John J.
Van Johannes
Van Allstine Abraham
Vanallstine Abraham C.
Van Allstine Peter
Van Alsten Cornelius C.
Van Alstin Harmans
Vanalstine Cornelius
Vanalstine Cornelius J.
Vanalstine John
Vanalstine John G.
Vanalstine John M.
Vanalstine Martin
Vanalstine Martin A.
Vanalstine Martin G.
Vanalstine Philip
Vanalstyn Peter
Van Camp Isaac
Van Campen Cornelius
Van Derwarken Harms
Vanderwarker Joshua
Van Derwartin Joshua
Van Eaverak John
Van Everen John
Van Slike George

Van Slyke Garret
Van Slyke John
Wagener Engelhard
Waggoner Isaac
Waggoner Jacob
Wagner George
Wagner Jacob
Wagoner George
Wallart Hannes
Wallrad George
Wallrate Adolph
Wallrate Frederick
Wallrate Jacobs
Wallse Conraed
Wallse Conraed, Jr.
Wallse Jacob
Walrad Jacob
Walrate Henrick
Walrath George
Walrath Henry
Walrath Jacob
Walrath William
Wals Cunrath
Wals Cunrath, Sr.
Wals Cunrath, Jr.
Warmood Pete
Warmorte Petter
Warmuth John
Wath Jacob
Westerman Peter
Wiele Henry
Wiele Joss Henry
Wilson James
Windecker Fredrick
Windker Nicolas
Winn John
Wohlgemuth John
Wohlgemuth William
Woldorf Johannes
Wolkemood John
Wollever John
Wollever Nicholas
Woolf Jacob
Wormut John
Wright Jacob
Yates Chris P.
Young Adam
Young Andreas
Young Andrew
Young Christian
Young Christian A.
Young Crist, Jr.
Young Frietrick
Young Godfred
Young Henry
Young Henry P.
Young John
Young Joseph
Young Jost
Young Lodwick
Young Peter
Young Robert
Young Thomas
Zola Casper

Tryon County Militia -- Second Regiment
The list of this regiment is in the first book, A Time of Terror.

New York In The Revolution as Colony and State

Tryon County Militia -- Third Regiment
by James A. Roberts, Comptroller
Compiled by Frederic G. Mather
Second Edition 1898
Two Volumes
Colonel Frederick Fisher; Lieut. Col. Volkert Veeder; Major John Bluen; Major John Nukerk;
Adjutant Peter Conyn; Adjutant John G. Lansingh, Jr.; Adjutant Gideon Marlatt; Q'R Master
Theodorus F. Romine; Quarter Master Abraham Van Horn; Quarter Master Simon Veeder;
Surgeon John George Folke; Surgeon William Petry

Capt. Amunneiel Degrauf	Lieut. Benjamin Deline	Lieut. Garett S. Van Bracklen
Capt. John Fisher	Lieut. Nicklis Dockstetter	Lieut Thomas Van Horn
Capt. Jellis Fonda	Lieut. Christ Ernest	Lieut. Peter Van Olynde
Capt. Jacob Gaerdenyer	Lieut. William Hall	Lieut. Derick Van Veghten
Capt. Dirik Hogoboom	Lieut. William Lard	Lieut. Henry H. Vroman
Capt. John Littel	Lieut. Gerritt Newkirk	Lieut Peter Yates
Capt. Harmanus Mabie	Lieut. Benjamin Oline	Lieut. Peter Yong
Capt. David McMaster	Lieut. Josop Printup	Ensign Henry Lewis
Capt. Isaac Marselis	Lieut. Francis F. Pruyn	Ensign Gideon Marlatt
Capt. Gerrit Putnam	Lieut. Abrahand Quacenbosh	Ensign Rechrt Potman
Capt. Samuel Rees	Lieut. Mc W. Quackenbush	Ensign Francies Potman
Capt. William Snook	Lieut. Vincent Quackenbush	Ensign Conrad Stone
Capt. Abraham Veeder	Lieut. Lorentz Schuler	Ensign Gorg Stone
Capt. Andrew Wemple	Lieut. John Snook	Ensign Garrett G. Van Bracklen
Capt. John Wemple	Lieut. Isias J. Swart	Ensign Peter Vroman
Capt. Robert Yates		
Capt. Joseph Yeomans		
Lieut. Amos Bennet		

Additional Names on State Treasurer's Pay Books

Lieut. David Beverly	Lieut. Francis Reyner
Lieut. Jacob Dinghardt	Lieut. Jeremiah Swart
Lieut. Charles Hubbs	Lieut. William Swart
Lieut. James McMaster	Lieut. Solomon Woodworth
Lieut. Joseph Prentiss	Ensign Thomas Harrison
Lieut. Victor Putnam	Ensign Ephraim Pierce
Lieut. Myndert W. Quackenbush	Ensign Teunis Van Vaughn

Enlisted Men

Acker John	Barbat John	Bell John
Aker Gorge	Barely Isaas	Bell Matthew
Albrant Hendrick	Barhydt Thunis	Bellinger Christian
Albrant Henry	Barkilt Lowis	Bellinger Philip
Algire John	Barnes Jacob	Berkley Isaes
Allen William	Barnes John	Berlett John
Anderson William	Barnhart Charls	Berrey Nicholas
Antus Coenrad	Barnhart John	Berry William
Antus John	Barns Aron	Beverly David
Any Jacob	Bayer John, Jr.	Beverly Thomas
Archer Ananias	Beakemen Eshemeal	Billings James
Baker Adam	Beddle Benijah	Bodin John

Bogards Henry
Bogert Henry
Booldman John
Boshart John
Bove Nicholas
Bowman John
Breem John
Brewster John
Brothers John
Bun Jacob
Bun John
Burch Jeremiah
Butler Thomas
Cachey Andrew
Cady Nathalen
Cagal John
Caimon Andrew
Caine John
Caine Peter
Caine Thomas
Calyar Isaac
Campbell John
Campbell Nathaniel
Campel Samul
Cane Samuel
Cannan Andrew
Canner John
Carey William
Carrall John
Cas Peter
Caiman William
Chrasse Francis
Chrisse Simon
Clark William
Clemant John
Clement Lambert
Cline Adam
Cloes Reuben
Cobon William
Cochran Andrew
Cock Fetter
Cogmer Jacob
Cohenut Jacob
Colun William
Colyar Jacob
Colyer John
Colyer William
Comrie James
Connelly Hugh
Conner James
Conradt Joseph
Conyne John
Corsaart David
Cossaart Tracis
Cossote James
Coughvenhover Isaac
Coughvenhover John
Counrad Nicholes
Covenhove Abraham
Covenhoven Isaac
Covenhoven Peter
Cownovan Jacob
Crackenberch Adam
Crackenberch George

Crannell Thomas
Crans Henry
Croll John
Cromert Aaron
Cronkhite Abraham
Crook Christopher
Crossett Benjamin
Crossett John
Crowley Jeremiah
Crummel Herman
Dachsteter John F.
Dachstetter Frederick F.
Dachstetter Markus
Daline Benjamin
Dallimthis James
Dannel John M.
Darrow John
Dasinham John
Daukstetor Fredrick H.
Davis Isaac
Davis James, Jr.
Davis John
Davis Thomas
De Eifix Max
Deline Benjamin
Deline Isick
Deline Ryer
Diefendorff Jacob
Diline Willim
Dingman Gerrit
Dingman Jacob
Dingman Peter
Dingman Samuel
Divis Abraham
Dockstader George A.
Dockstader John H.
Dockstater Henry H.
Dockstator George
Docksteder Adam
Docksteder Haniskel
Docksteder Nicholas H.
Docksteter Leonhart
Dockstetter Henrich
Dockstetter Nicolas
Dopber Robert
Doranberagh John
Doren Alicksander
Dorn David
Dorn John
Doron Jacob
Dorp Mattias
Doucksteter John
Doughstedar Jacob
Doyle Stephen
Dum Richard
Dunham Ebenezer
Dunham John
Dunn James
Dunn John
Eargesengar John
Earnest Jacob
Eaten Elezar
Eaton Ephraim
Eel Nichel

Eliot Andrew
Eliot Jacob
Elliot Joseph
Ellis John
Eman Jacob
Ener Peter
Eney John
England Benjamin
Eny George
Eny Godfret
Ernest Jacob
Eten Efrim
Eten Elezer
Eten James
Eten Tomes
Eversay Adam
Eversen John, Jr.
Farguson Willimi
Fars Christian
Ferrel Charles
Fie George, Jr.
Files John
Fine Andrew
Fine Frances
Fishar Harmams
Fishback Henry
Fisher John
Fithpatrick Peter
Fonda Adam
Fonda John
Forgason Darnel
Forrest Matthew
Fowler James
Frakk Henry
Frank Adam
Frank Albart
Frank Andrew
Frank Henry
Frederick Francis
Frederick Peter
Fredreck Jacob
Fredrick Phillip
French Ebenezer
French Josuf
Frenk Henry
Fuller Abraham
Fuller Isaac
Fuller Michel
Gallenger Henry
Gardenar William
Gardener Martin
Gardenir Abraham
Gardinier Martyn J.
Gardinier Matthew
Gardinier Nicholas
Gardinier Nicholas T
Garsling Peter
Gerdanell John
Gibson William
Giles John
Goihnet John
Grace Owan M.
Graft Jacob
Grass Philtith

Hagal John
Hagal Magal
Hains John
Hall Jacob
Hall John
Hall Peter
Hall William
Han Jacob
Han Peter
Hanna James
Hanna William
Hansen Ficktor
Hansen Nicholas
Hanson John
Hanson Richard
Hare James
Harpper Archiball
Harrison Harmanis
Harrison Peter
Harrison Tomis
Havinser Tore
Helmer John
Henn Marks
Herring John, Sr.
Hird Leonard
Hoch Georg
Hodges Abraham
Hoff Richard
Hoff Richard, Jr.
Hogoboom Christion
Hogoboom John
Hogoboom Peter
Holdenbergh Abraham
Horn Jams
Horn Mattis
House Jacob
Hubbs Alexander
Hubbs Charles
Hulsbarker Addem
Hunt Timothy
Hutchson Edward
Inxale Joseph
Johnson Andrew
Johnson John
Johnson Robert
Johnson Ruliph
Johnston Witter
Jones James
Jones Harmanus
Jones Richard
Juman David
Jurry John
Kartright Hanry
Keech James
Keech Jorge
Keelman Jacob
Keith Jacob
Kell Nicolas
Keller Jacob
Kelly Peter
Kenneday Robert
Kennedy James
Ketcham Ephraim
Kiley Henry

Kitts John
Kitts John, Jr.
Kline John
Kline Martin
Lacess Samul
Lane Daniel
Lane Jacob
Lannen Rechert
Lapper John
Lawis David
Leets David
Lenardson James
Lenardson John
Lenardson Timothy
Lennes William
Lever John
Lewis Adam
Lewis David, Jr.
Lewis Frederick
Lewis John
Lewis William
Leyd Richard
Leypert Jacob
Liddel John
Lincompetter Mighael
Link John
Linox John
Loyde Daniel
Mabee Peter
McArthur Daniel
McArthur Donaldi
McArthur Duncan
McCallum John
McClumpha Thomas
McCollam Findlay
McCredy William
McDonald James
McDonald Nicholas
McGraw Christopher
McGraw Danel
McGraw Dennis
McGraw John
McGraw William
McKenney Dainnel
McMaster Hugh
McMaster James
McMaster Robert
McMaster Thomas
McNaughton Petar
McRadey William
McTaggert James
Mambt Willem
Manness Hugh M.
Mariat Michael
Mariatt Abraham
Mariatt Gideon
Mariatt John
Mariatt Thomas
Martin John W.
Martin Peter M.
Martin Philip
Mashel John
Mason Jacob
Mason John

Mayer Jacob
Mayer Jacob, Jr.
Hears Thomas
Melone John
Mets Henry
Meurinus William
Miller Adam
Miller Fredrick
Miller Gorge
Miller James
Miller Jillis
Miller Johan
Milloy Alexander
Montek Willam
Montgomry Peter
Moon Jacob
More Conrad
More John
Mount Joseph
Mount Samuel
Mower Barrant
Mower George
Mower Henry
Murdorph Gorge
Murray David
Musner John
Myers George
Myers Peter
Nave John
Nelley John
Newkerk Garrit C.
Newkirk Abraham
Newkkerk Garret
Nukerck Jacob
Ogden Daniel, Sr.
Ogden David
Panter Ulrich
Pater Francis
Patteson Adam
Percy Ephraim
Peters Joseph
Peters Joseph, Jr.
Pettengell John
Pettingell Henry
Pettingell Jacob
Pettingell Joseph
Pettingell Samuel
Pettingell William
Phileps Abraham
Philes Henry
Philips Henry
Philips Phillip
Philipse James
Philipse Volkert
Phillips Jacob
Phillips John
Phillips Lewis
Phillips William
Phillipsa Harmanis
Phillipsa John
Pickes John
Plank Adam
Plank John
Potmanter Thomas

Polmateer John
Polmateer Willem
Potman Aaren
Potman Adam
Potman George
Potmon Hendrik
Prentes Daniel
Prett John
Prime David
Prime Henry
Prime Petter
Prine Luis
Printup William
Pruime John
Pruyn John
Pruyne Henry
Putman Cornelys, Jr.
Putman David
Putman Factor
Putman Fredrick
Putman Hanry
Putman Jacobus
Putman John
Putman Lewis
Putman Lodiwik
Putman Victor
Putman William
Pyrune Daniel
Quack John
Quack Petar
Quack Willem
Quackenbush Abraham, Jr.
Quackenbush David
Quackenbush Isaac
Quackenbuss John G.
Quackinboss Nicholas
Redy Charles
Reed Conrad
Renins Samul
Richardson Jonathan
Riker Henry
Rinyens Samuel
Roberson Robert
Robeson George
Robison Joseph
Roelofson Abraham
Rogers John
Rogers Samul
Roges Samuel
Rombough Ausmus
Romeyn Theodorus F.
Romien Abraham
Romien Nicholas
Runyans John
Runyens Henry
Rury Henry
Rury William
Ruse Jacob
Salsbury John
Sammons Frederick
Sammons Thomas
Sammore Frederick
Saron Philip

Sarvis Frederick
Sarvis Richart
Scarbury William
Schaffer John
Schoonmaker Thomas
Schot Joseph
Schrambling Dewald
Schramling Henry
Schuler Lorentz
Schuts Joseph
Scoot Joseph
Scott James
Scott Joseph
Semple Hugh
Semple Samuel
Serves Christian
Servies Philip
Serviss George
Servos Christian
Servos John
Shaddack Tomis
Shaddock Jams
Shaffer James
Sharpenstine Jacob
Shasha Abraham
Shasha William
Sheham Butler
Shelp Fredrick
Shew Godfrey
Shew Henry
Shew Jacob
Shew John
Shew Stephen
Shilip Christian
Shilp Frederick
Stunner Tomes
Ship George F.
Shoemaker Rudolph
Shoemaker Thomas
Shoemaker Tomis
Sitlebach Christayane
Sillibig John
Sillibogh Hincrist
Simpson Henry
Simpson Nicholas
Sixbarry Adam
Sixbary Comelus
Sixberry Bangnen
Sixberry Cornelius, Jr.
Skinner John
Slack Martinis
Smith Harmanus
Snook Henry
Snyder Adam
Southwoth Willam
Spencer Aaron
Spencer Jonathan
Spencer Nathan
Spoor Nicolas
Spore John
Stabits Micheal
Stale Gorg
Staley Henry
Stall Joseph

Stalye Roulof
Starin Frederick
Starin John
Staring Joseph
Starn Adam
Starn Philp
Stephens Amasa
Sterman Christiana
Stern Neckliss
Sternberg Christian
Sternbergh Jacob
Sternbergh Joseph
Stine William
Storme Jacob
Strail John
Stuart William
Stung Peter
Swart Benjamin
Swart John
Swart Tunes
Swart Walter
Sylmur Marsster
Tanner Jacob
Terwilliger Hermanus
Terwilliger James
Thelm John
Thompson James
Timmerman Christian
Tims Michael
Tontill Joseph
Tyms Michael
Ulman Burnt
Ulman Johanes
Ulman Leonard
Vadder Isack
Vaghte John
Van Allen Jacob
Van alstine Jacob
Van Alstin Gilbert
Van Alstine Abraham
Van Alstine Cornelius
Vanalstine Isaac
Van antwerpen John, Sr.
Van Antwerpen John, Jr.
Van Bracklen Alexander
Van Bracklin Garret G.
Vanbrakel Malkert
Van Bralan Gisbert
Van Darwark Willim
Vandelinder Benjamin
Vanderwerken Albert
Van Derwerkin Gasper
Van Deusen Harpert
Vandeuson Abraham
Van Dewarck Thomis
Van Dewerkin John
Van Duzen Gilbert
Van Duzen Mathu
Van Eps John
Van Geyseling Peter
Van Horn Cornelius
Van Horn Henry
Vanhorn John
Van Husen Albert

Vannolinde Benjamin
Van Olinden Benjamin
Vanolynde Jacob
Van Sice Cornelius
Vansickler Ryneer
Vanslick Nechless
Van Vorst Jelles
Van Wurst Jelles
Vedder Albert
Veeder Abraham
Veeder John J.
Veeder Cornelius
Veeder John
Ven Husen Albert
Venolinde Benjam
Vinter William
Vroman Henry H.
Vroman Simon
Vrooman Henry B.
Vrooman Isaac
Vrooman John J.
Vrooman Peter

Walrath Adolphus
Wampal Cornelius
Wampel Handrick
Wample John
Wample William
Wart Andrew
Wart Matise
Weart John
Weaver Nicholas
Weener Peter
Weks Sammul
Wemple Barent
Wemple John T.
Wemple Myndert
Weser Nicholas
Wile Christian
Wiley Nicholas
Williams Daniel
Willson Almer
Willson John
Wilson Abner
Wilson Andrew

Wilson Samuel
Wiser John
Witbeke Leonard
Wheeler Isaac
Whiler Henry
White Edward
Wood William
Woodcock Abraham
Woodcock John
Woodcock Peter
Woodworth
Woodworth Selah
Wright David
Yanney Christian
Yanney Henry
Yoran Jacob
Yost Peter
Young George
Young Lodowick
Young William

New York In The Revolution as Colony and State
by James A. Roberts, Comptroller
Compiled by Frederic G. Mather
Second Edition 1898
Two Volumes

Tryon County Milita--Fourth Regiment
Colonel Peter Bellinger; Adjutant George Demuth; Quarter Master Peter Bellinger, Jr.

Capt. Hans Mark Demuth
Capt. Frederick Frank
Capt. Frederick Gettman
Capt. Henrig Herder
Capt. Henry Huber
Capt. Michael Ittig
Capt. Jacob Small

Capt. Henrich Starring
Lieut. Patrick Campbell
Lieut. Hannes Demuth
Lieut. Timothy Frank
Lieut. George Helmer
Lieut. Jacob Myer
Lieut. John Smith

Lieut. Gorg A. Weber
Lieut. Peter Weber
Ensign Hannes Bellinger
Ensign John Mayer
Ensign Jacob Petry
Ensign Adam A. Starring

Enlisted Men

Ahrendorff Frieterich
Ahrendorff Piter
Ahrentarff Peter
Ahrentorff Gory
Armstrong Archibald
Armstrong John
Badcock John
Balthaser Breih
Bany Ichabod
Bauman Adam
Bauman Frederick
Bauman Georg A.
Bauman Jacob
Bauman Johannes
Bauman Nicolas
Bauman Stophet
Becker Henrich
Beffer Jacob

Bell G. Henry
Bell Jacob
Bell Nicolaus
Bell Thomas
Bellinger Frederick
Bellinger John
Bellinger Peter
Bellinger Peter B.
Bellinger Peter P.
Bellinger Stoffel
Bendel Catren
Bender Jacob
Benrich Frans
Bercki Jacob
Berckie Peter
Berdrick Frantz
Bersh Lutwig
Bersh Rudolph

Beshar Jacob
Betrer Jacob
Bonny Ichabod
Bouman Adam
Bouman Frederick
Bouman Nicholas
Breidenbucher Balthass
Breidenbue Baldes
Brothack Jacob
Brothak Bartholomay
Brothock John
Burcky Peter, Sr.
Burti Jacob
Byrky Jacob
Byrky Peter
Campbell John
Campbell Ludwig
Camples Patrick

Casler Conrad
Casler Jacob, Jr.
Casler Jacob H.
Casler Jacob J.
Casler Jolin
Casler John T.
Casler Nicholas
Casler Peter
Caslor Malger
Chiller John
Chokin Thomas
Christman Frederick
Christman Fretrich
Christman Jacob
Christman John
Christman Nicolaus
Clapsattel Andrew
Clapsattle William
Clements Jacob
Clements Philip
Clenicum John
Cline William
Cochen Tliomas
Coken Dome
Colsh John, Sr.
Colsh John. Jr.
Conneghem Willem
Corrol George
Cox Fauct
Cox Fesser
Cram Jacob
Crantz Hanry
Cremm Jacob
Cristman Jacob
Cunicum Wiliem
Cunningham John
Dabush Jacob
Dachsteter Georg
Dachsteter John
Dachsteter Piter
Davis
Davis George
Davis John
Davis Peter
Dawie John
Daygert William A.
Deisellman Chrisdian
Demote Marx
Demuth Diterich
Demuth John
Demuth Marx
Dinges Hannes
Dinus Jacob
Dom Melger
Dunuss Jacob
Edie Frederick
Eiseman Stephen
Etig Gorge
Etigle Morse
Eyseman Johannes
Eyseman Steffe
Feelis Jacob
Finster John
Flack Fitter

Flock Peter
Follick Thomas
Folmer Christian
Folmer Conrad
Folmer Thomas
Folmer William
Fols Conrath C.
Fols Georg
Fols Jacob
Fols Melger
Fols Peter
Folts Conrad
Folts Jost
Foltz John Jost
Fox Friederich
Fox John
Frank Henry
Frank John
French Henrich
Fux Hannes
Getman Conrad
Getman Frederick
Gettman Frederik, Jr.
Gettman Potter
Gortuer Peter
Harlam Adam
Hartch Adam
Hartman Adam
Hatz Peter
Hayer Georg
Hebrissen Martin
Heller John
Helmer Frederick
Helmer Frederick A.
Helmer Philip
Hendert John
Herchmer Jost
Herckmer Abraham
Herkemer John
Herkimer George
Herkimer Nicholas
Herder John
Herder Lorens
Herder Niklas
Herter Frederick, Jr.
Herter Lawrence
Herter Lorens
Herter Lorens F.
Herter Lorens N.
Herter Lorens P.
Herter Nicolas
Herter Nicolas F.
Herter Philip
Herter Philip F.
Hes Conrat
Hesler Morten
Hess Augustinus
Hess Christian
Hess Conrad
Hess Fridrik
Hess George
Hess John
Heyer George
Heyer George Frederick

Heyer Peter
Hils Georg
Hils Hannes
Hilt George N
Hilts John
Hiltz Georg
Hiltz George, Jr.
Hiltz George G.
Hiltz George N.
Hiltz Gotfrid
Hiltz Hannes
Hiltz Laurence
Hiltz Nicolas
Hochstrasser Christian
Hoffstader Christian
Hoyer George
Hoyer Gorg Friederich
Hoyer Peter
Huber John
Hyser Martin
Itig Georg
Itig Marck
Ittig Christian
Ittig Conrath
Ittig Frieterich
Ittig Jacob
Ittig Jacob J.
Karle George
Kast Frederick
Keller Nicolaus
Kelsch John, Sr.
Kelsch John, Jr,
Kesler Hannes
Kesler Nicholas
Kesslar Conrat
Kesslar Jacob John
Kesslar John
Kessler Jacob
Kessler Jacob J.
Kessler John P.
Kessler Johney
Kessler Joseph
Kessler Melger
Kiltz Georg
Kiltz Laurants
Koch Jost
Krans Michel
Krantz Henrich
Kreim Jacob
Kuran Michael
Kyler Nichlas
Lantz
Leithal Abraham
Lentz Jacob
Lentz John
Lentz John, Jr.
Lentz Peter
Lighthal Nicholas
Lighthall George
Lithall Abraham
Macnod Jeams
McNutt James
Manderback John
Mauyer Nicklas

Mayel Matthias
Mayer Frederick
Mayer Henry
Mayer John
Mayer Joseph
Mayer Mates
Mayer Michel
Mayer Nicolas
Mayer Piter
Meller John
Miller Fette
Miller Henrich
Miller Johannis
Miller John, Sr.
Miller John, Jr.
Miller Niculaus
Miller Valentine
Millor Hanry
Molter Jacob
Molter Peter
Moyer Frederick
Moyer Hanry
Moyer Joseph
Moyer Margeris
Moyer Peter
Muller John
Multer Jacob
Multer Piter
Munterba Hannes
Myer Josaph
Myer Michel
Myndnbach Johannes
Nahs James
Nesch Schims
Newkerk Benjamin
Ogt Georg
Ohrendorph Frederick, Sr.
Ohrendorph Frederick, Jr.
Ohrendorph George
Ohrendorph Peter
Osterhout John
Osteroth Johannes
Osterttout John
Pedery Marx
Pedri Ditrich
Peifer Jacob
Pesausie John
Petrey John Marx
Petri Daniel
Petri Jacob
Petri Johannes
Petri Joseph
Petrie Marx
Petry Diterich
Petry John
Petry John M.
Petry Jost

Phyfer Andrew
Phyfer Jacob
Piper Antoore
Piper Jost
Rabold Georg
Rasbach John
Regel Godfray
Remah George
Rickel Christian
Riema Georg
Riema John
Riema John, Sr.
Rigel Frederick
Rima Johannis, Jr.
Rima John, Sr.
Rimer Hannes
Rosckrantz Nicolaus
Ryan John
Schell Christian
Schell Johannes
Schenck Georg
Schieff Georg
Schmid Friedrich
Schmit Adam
Schmit Frederick
Schmit George
Schmit John
Schmit Jost
Schmit Peter
Schumacher John
Schumacher Stoffel
Schut Wiliem
Seimer Isack
Shall Fredrick
Shell John
Shoemaker Christopher
Shoemaker Frederick
Shoemaker Hanjost
Shoemaker John
Shoemaker Jost
Shoemaker Thomas
Shute Frederick
Shute William
Simer Gesom
Smith John
Smith Nicholas
Smith William
Sneck George
Spon Nicklas
Spoon Werner
Stahring Attam, Sr.
Stahring George
Stale Gorge
Staring Adam
Staring Adam J.
Staring Conrat
Staring Henrich

Staring Margred
Staring Nicklas
Staring Peter
Starring Nicholas, Sr.
Starring Nicholas N.
State George
Steal Ditrick
Steale Adam
Stehl Ditterich
Stering Adam
Straubel Stoffel
Strobel Christoph
Tinis Jacob
Tinis John
Usner Peter Gorg
Van Slyck Jacobus
Weaver George
Weaver Nicholas, Jr.
Weaver Nicholas H.
Web Nicolas G.
Weber Frederick
Weber Frederick, Jr.
Weber Frederick G.
Weber George
Weber George, Jr.
Weber George F.
Weber George M.
Weber Jacob
Weber Jacob, Sr.
Weber Jacob G.
Weber Jacob J.
Weber Jacob N.
Weber Johannes
Weber Michel
Weber Nicolas
Weber Nicolas G.
Weber Nicolas H.
Weber Peter
Wederstine Henry
Wents George
Widerstein Henry
Widrig Jacob
Widrig Michael
Witerig Georg
Witrig Conrat
Witterstein Henrich
Wohleben Abraham
Wohleber Abraham
Wohleber Jacob
Wohleber Fitter
Woleben Jacob
Wolff Johannes
Wolleben Peter
Wollerver Abraham
Won Niclas

Tryon County Militia--Fifth Regiment
Colonel John Harper; Major Joseph Harper
(No enlisted men found)

Tryon County Militia--Battalion of Minute Men

New York In The Revolution as Colony and State
by James A. Roberts, Comptroller
Compiled by Frederic G. Mather
Second Edition 1898
Two Volumes

Colonel Samuel Campbell
Capt. Francis Utt; Lieut. Adam Lipe; Lieut. Jacob Matthais; Ensign William Suber

Ayle Christian	Hickey George	Schall John
Ayle Peter	Jones William	Schall Matthyas
Ayles William	Jordan Adam	Scrembling Henry
Bellinger William	Jordan Casper	Scremling David
Bohall Adam	Jorand George	Seeber Jacob
Bydaman Simon	Jordan John	Stansel Nicholas
Countreyman Counradt	Keller Andrew	Steffan John
Countreyman John	Kerlack Adam	Truax John
Cramer John	Kerlack George	Ulshaver Bastian
Crows George	Kesler Thomas	Wahadt George
Dedrick David	Kessler John	Walradt William
Duncle Nicholas	Korey Benjamin	Westerman Peter
Duncle Peter	Lapp Daniel	While Henry
Dunkle Gerrit	Lipe John	While Youst Henry
Endler Michal	Miller Deonycenons	Woulkermough John
Felling Henry John	Netherly John	Wourmuth John
Felling Henry Nicholas	Netherly John, Jr.	Wourmuth Peter
Felling Peter	Othermark John B.	Young Jacob
Flock John	Plats George	Young John
Harld Henrey	Schall Hendrick	Young Peter

New York In The Revolution as Colony and State
by James A. Roberts, Comptroller
Compiled by Frederic G. Mather
Second Edition 1898
Two Volumes

Tryon County Militia--Associated Excempts

Capt. Jessis Fonda; Lieut. Zepheniah Batcheller; Lieut. Abraham Garrason; Ensign Samson Sammon;
Ensign Lawrance

Enlisted Men

Algyre John
Allin Thomas
Alt Johannis
Anderson Duncan
Ansley Samuel
Antes Jacob
Barmore William
Barry Guilbert R.
Bashan Jacob
Benson Jonathan
Bickle John
Boshart Jacob
Boss Heinrich
Bridelburgh Baltus
Brook Robert
Cameron Angus
Cochnet Jacob
Collins Richard
Conner Edward
Cratchenberger Conrate
Creesy John
Cromel Jacobes
Cromnel James
Crossett Benjamin
Crossett James
Crotchinbrge Conrad
Crowley Jeremiah
Dachstetter Marx
Dachstetter Nicolaus
Dochstader Frederick
Dockstader John H.
Dop David
Dunn Richard
Ecker John
Ensign Lawrance
Eversas Adam
Everson Adam
Everson John
Fey Jacob
Finck Mattgred
Fonda Adam
Fonda John
Frederick Barent
Frichert Henry
Froman Henry
Fyes George
Fyles George
Graft Jacob
Hall John
Hall William
Hanson Barent
Hanson Richard
Hardle Johannes

Herring John
Hover Johannes
Hower Nicholas
Johnson Andrew
Kelder Henry
Kelder John
Kilts Johannes
Kinkead Crownidge
Kitts Jacob
Krose Moses
Ladde Johannes
Lenardson Timothy
McCollum John
McDonald John
McDonnel John
McGlashen Robert
McGrigor Duncan
McIntire John
McKenny John
McKerque Duncan
McKinney John
McManus Hugh
McMarlinger Duncan
McMarten Duncan
McVain Daniel
Marlatt Mark
Marseles John
Mason Jeremiah
Michard Henry
Mickle John
Miller Philip
Momtrute Steven
Morgan John
Merger John
Myers Michael
Nanes Joseph
Nest Johannes
Perine Daniel
Perine David
Phile George
Philips Abraham
Philips William
Plants John
Platto James
Poter France
Putman Cornelius
Quackenbush David
Remise John
Reyer John
Rickle John
Rightmyer Johannes
Roase James
Robertson John

Ruport Adam
Ruport D.
Rykert Hendrick
Ryer Henry
Sammons Jacob
Schieb Georg Friderick
Schwob Michel
Seeber Henry
Shanck George
Shaver Nicholas
Sheep Georg Friderick
Shew George
Shew Steven
Shewmaker Hanjost
Shoeman William
Sixberry Cornelius
Smith Arent
Smith Conradt
Smith Cornelius
Smith Daniel
Smith John
Snell Robert
Staly Jacob
Staring John
Stealy Jacob
Stoner Nicholas
Terwillegen Harmanis
Vactor John
Van Alstine Cornelius A.
Van Alstyne C. V.
Van Antwerp John
Van Bracklen Gysbert
Van Bracklen Nicholas
Vanderwerke Johannis
Vanderwerkin Albert
Vandesen Melgert
Van Deusen Jacobus
Van Deusen Matthew
VanDewarkin Class
Van Dewerken Jacob
VanDewerker Henry
Van Eps Charles
Van Eps Evert
Van Zeien John
Vorhis John
Wallace William
Wallrad Johannes
Walters John
Well John
Wemple Barent
Wemple Hendrick
Whitekar Thomas
Wilton John

New York In The Revolution as Colony and State
by James A. Roberts, Comptroller
Compiled by Frederic G. Mather
Second Edition 1898
Two Volumes

Tryon County Militia--Rangers

Capt. John Winn; Lieut. Lawrence Gross; Lieut. Peter Schremling

Enlisted Men

Adamy Peter
Andrews Lewis
Anthony John
Atkins William
Bellinger Adam
Bratt James
Bush George
Bush William
Christman Nicholas
Cogdon John
Countryman Johannes
Dingman John
Embody Henry
Franck Adam
Freeman Joseph
Fritsher Conradt
Gueenall James
Hamilton James
Hayes Thomas
Heath Josiah
Hellegass Peter
Helmer Godfried
Hornung Burent

House Elias
House George
House Johanjost
House John
Jackson Joseph
Johnston Richard
Kaach John
Kennedy Samuel
Kesslaer Johannes
Kook William
Kremer Johanjost
Kronckhite Abraham
Lampford Peter, Sr.
Lampford Peter, Jr.
Leathers Ezekiel
Lepper Fredrick
Liewry Jacob
Llump Thomas
McCollum John
McDonnald John
Mackly Felix
Maybee John
Nellis Christian

Nellis William
Ogden Daniel
Pickerd John
Price Adam
Reebsamen Francis
Reebsumen Johannes
Reader Jacob
Roorey William
Scotten Josiah
Seger Fredrick
Shillip Christian
Snyder Gonlieb
Snyder Johannes
Stensell Nicholas
Stensell William
Stevens Samuel
Styne Conradt
Timmerman Jacob
Van Der Warke Geranom
Vander Warke James
VanSlyck George
Weaver Jacob
Young Richard

Tryon County Militia -- Rangers

Capt. Christian Getman; Lieut. James Billington; Lieut. Jacob Sammans

Agin Joshua
Biller Michel
Box John
Brame John
Canton John
Coplin Samuel
Coppernol Adam
Coppernol Richard
Cratzer Leonhart
Crum John
Dop John
Earl William
Empie Jacob
Fishbock Jacob
Flander Hendrick
Flune John
Fralick Felter
Freman Richard
Fry Jacob
Fuller Isaac
Fuller Michel
Getman Thomas

Hails John
Hart Conrad
Hart Daniel
Hawk George
Hodges Abraham
Hoyney Fredrick
Hoyney George
Hulser John
Jenne Christian
Karin William
Kind William
Kring Ludwick
Kufe Jolianes
Leather Christian
Leather Johanes
Loux George
Miller Johanes
Mills Cornelius
Phillips Philip
Rickard Jacob
Saltsman George
Saltsman George, Jr.

Shafer Hendrick
Shuell John
Shuell Peter
Smith Bolzer
Smith John
Spankrable Johanes
Storing Jacob
Strader Nicholas
Sutes Johanes
Tusler Jacob
Vananwarp John
Vanderworkin Hendrick
Vanderworkin John
Vanderworkin Martin
Vrooman Hendrick
Vrooman Minehart
Walliser Christian
Williams Nehemiah
Wormwood Christian
Wormwood Johanes

Tryon County Militia -- Rangers

Capt. John Kasselman; Lieut. John Empie; Ensign George Gittman

Backer John	Haynes George	Smith William
Bickerd Adolph	Hortigh Andrew	Strater Nicholas
Dusler Jacob	House Peter	Tillenbach Christian
Empie John	Kasselman John	Vander Werke John
Ettigh Coenr'd	Kretzer Leonard	Walter Adam
Fry Jacob	Kulman Henry	Walter Chruti
Gittman Peter	Shuell John	
Harth Daniel	Smith Henry	

List of Patentees, Burnetsfield

From Benton's <u>History of Herkimer County</u>

name	Lot no.	acres	side of the river	remarks
1. Beerman, Mary	11	100	N	at the Little Falls
2. Beerman, Johannes*	26	100	N	
3. Same,	26	100	N	
4. Bowman, Jacob	27	100	S	
5. Bowman, Johan Adam	14	30	N	All the 30 acre lots were set on wat were called the Great Flats, in and near the present village of Herkimer. The 70 acre lots are described in the patent as wood land.
same	14	70	N	
6. Dacksteder, Anna, wife of Jurgh Dacksteder	28	100	S	
7. Dacksteder, Jurgh	18	30	N	
same	18	70	N	
8. Edich, Elizabeth	5	100	N	
9. Edigh, Johan Michael	33	100	S	
10. Edich, Jacob	21	100	S	
11. Editch, Michael	20	100	S	Mohawk Village
12. Erghemar, Jurgh	44	100	S	
13. Erghemar, Johan Jost	36	100	S	
14. Erghemar, Madalana	24	70	S	And large island in river
15. Erghemar, Catharina	5	100	S	
16. Feller, Nicholas	7	30	N	
17. Feller, Mary, wife of Nicholas Feller	16	100	S	
18. Felmore, Coenradt	19	100	S	Mohawk Village
19. Felmore, Christiana	18	100	S	
20. Fols, Jacob	3	100	S	
21. Fols, Melgert	2	30	N	
same	2	70	N	
22. Fox Christopher	26	100	S	
23. Heger, Henry	8	100	N	
24. Helmer, Elizabeth, wife of Lendert Helmer	14	100	N	
25. Helmer, Philip	25	100	N	E. side of West Canada Creek

26. Helmer, Johan Adam	6	30	N	
27. Helmer, Lendert	21	30	N	
28. Helmer, Frederick	1	100	N	
29. Helmer, Anna Margaret, wife of John Adam Helmer	12	100	S	
30. Herter, Apolone	7	100	S	
31. Herter, Lowrens	37	100	S	
32. Hess, Augustines	10	100	N	At the Little Falls
33. Hoss, Johannes	31	100	S	
34. Keslaer, Johannes	45	100	S	
35. Keslaer, Nicholas	25	100	S	Near Rankin's Lock
36. Kast, Johan Jurgh, Jr.	5	30	N	
same	5	70	N	
37. Kast, Johan Jurgh	22	30	N	
same	22	70	N	
38. Koons, Mary Catharine, widow	1	30	N	
same	11	70	N	
39. Korsing, Rudolph	29	100	S	
40. Korsing, Belia, wife or Rudolph Korsing	13	100	S	
41. Koues, Lodowick	2	100	S	
42. Lant, Anna Catherine, widow	13	30	N	
same	13	70	N	
43. Mayor, Hendrik	11	30	N	
same	11	70	N	
44. Mayor, Anna	29	100	S	Opposite Great Flats
45. Miller, Johannes	43	100	S	
46. Orendros, Conradt	10	100	S	
47. Orendorf, Hendrik	39	100	S	
48. Pears, Catharaine	23	100		Opposite Great Flats.
49. Pears, Lodowick	27	90	N	And 1/4 of an island
50. Pell, Frederick	15	100	N	On east side of West Canada Creek
51. Pell, Anna Mary	16	100	N	Same
52. Pellinger, Johannes	20	30	N	
same	20	70	N	
53. Pellinger, Peter	23	30	N	
same	23	70	N	
54. Pellinger, Margaret, wife of Peter Pellinger	4	100	N	
55. Pellinger, Frederick	34	100	N	
56. Pellinger, Margeret, wife of Johannes Pellinger	22	100	S	Near Mohawk Village
57. Petri, Johan Joost	8	30	N	
same	8	70	N	
58. Petri, Gurtruydt, wife of Johan Joost Petri	17	86	N	Stone Ridge, Herkimer Village
59. Petri, Mark	15	100	S	
60. Poenradt, Johannes	46	100	N	Capt. Peter Klock
61. Poenradt, Gurtruydt, wife of Johannes Poenradt	9	100	N	

62. Reelle, Godfrey	15	30	N	
same	15	70	N	
63. Reele, Godfrey, Jr. *	10	100	S	
64. Reele, Godfrey	10	100	S	Ilion Village
65. Rickert, Lodowick	19	30	N	
same	19	70	S	
66. Rickert, Catharine	3	100	N	
67. Rickert, Conradt	34	100	S	
68. Rickert, Mark	6	100	S	
69. Shoemaker, Rudolph	17	100	S	
70. Shoemaker, Thomas	12	30	N	
same	12	70	N	
71. Smith, Adam Michael	4	30	N	
same	4	70	N	
72. Smith Johan Jurgh	9	30	N	
same	9	70	N	
73. Smith Ephraim	9	100	S	Ilion Village
74. Smith, Marte	4	100	S	
75. Speis, Peter	38	100	S	
76. Speis, Elizabeth wife of Peter Speis	8	100	S	
77. Spoon, Hendrik	32	100	S	
78. Spoon, Hendrik, Jr.	7	100	N	
79. Staring, Mary Eva, wife of John Adam Staring	13	100	N	At the Little Falls
80. Staring John Adam	28	94	N	And 1/4 of an island
81. Staring, Frederick	24	30	N	
same	24	70	N	
82. Staring, Johannes Velden	6	100	N	
83. Staring, Nicholas	42	100	S	
84. Staring, Joseph	41	100	S	
85. Staring, John Velde, Jr.	1	100	S	
86. Temouth, John Jost	12	100	N	At Little Falls
87. Temouth, Fredrigh	17	30	N	
same	17	70	N	
88. Veldelent, John	3	30	N	
same	3	70	N	
89. Veldelent, Anna	2	100	N	
90. Wever, Jacob	10	30	N	
same	10	70	N	
91. Wever, Nicholas	16	30	N	
same	16	70	N	
92. Wever, Andries	11	100	S	
93. Wever, Jacob Jr.	15	100	S	
94. Wellevern, Nicholas	30	100	S	Ft. Herkimer, Stone Church

*Same lot to Godfrey Reele and Godfrey Relle, Jr.

Index of Mostly Names
"T" indicates A Time of Terror
"S" indicates So It Was Written

Index
The index is for A Time or Terror and for So It Was Written,
hence the T and the S to differentiate between the two books.
Book one was reformatted, and you might have to search a bit for the occurrence of the name

Bany, Ichabod S 353
Banyar, Gouldsbury S 331
Banyard, Stephen N . S 319
Banyer, Goldsbrow S 319
Baptist, Johan S 97
Barbara, Anna S 93, S 97
Barbara, Maria S 87
Barbat, John S 349
Barbelat, Jacob S 296
Barber, Timothy T 340
Barber, Silas T 340
Barcley (Mrs.) S 331
Barclay, Thomas S 328, S 331
Barclay, Thomas H S 328, S 331
Barden, Michael S 296
Barder, Nicholas T 170, 255
Bardof, Martin S 121
Bardorst, Catharina Elisabetha S 121
Bardt, Christian T 340
Bardt, Nicholas T 340
Barely, Isaas S 349
Barhudt, Thunis S 349
Barkem, William S 274
Barker, James S 317
Barker, James (The Weaver) S 317
Barker, John S 331
Barker, Thomas S 328, S 331
Barker, William T 340
Barkilt, Lowis S 349
Barkman, Izaac S 93
Barkman, Joost S 87
Barmore,William S 357
Barnes, Jacob S 349
Barnes, John S 349
Barnum, Joshua, (Captain) S 274
Barnum, Thomas S 274
Barnard, Conrad S 331
Barnard, Anna Eulalia S 122
Barnard, Johannes S 122
Barnard, Maria Margaret S 122
Barnes, Calvin T 305
Barnes, Henry S 298
Barnes, Thomas S 298, S 319
Barnet, Ochabed S 331
Barnett, Ichabod B. S 331
Barhart, ChAris S 349
Barnhart, D. S 331
Barnhart, Herman S 331
Barhart, John S 349
Barnhart, Joseph S 331
Barns, Aron S 349
Barns, John S 331, S 349
Barns, Joshua S 331
Barnum, Joshua (Capt) T 340
Barrabam, Andries S 87
Barre, Rudolph S 310
Barre, Roudolph S 302
Barringer, Coenraed S 112
Barris, Frederick S 314
Barry, Benjamin S 313
Barry, Guilbert R. S 357
Barsh, Adam T 170, S 298
Barsh, Ludolph T 170
Barsh, Rudolph T 254, S 298
Bart, Henrik S 93
Bartel, Andries S 111
Bartel, Henrik S 93
Bartel, Philip S 111
Barth, Margaret (widow) S 296
Barth, Nicholas (Lieutenant) S 345

Barthel, Andreas S 121
Barthel, Elisabatha S 121
Barthel, Henrich S 121, S 142
Barthel, Johan Andreas S 122
Barthel, Maria Margretha S 122
Barthel, Philip Balthasar S 122
Barthelin, Anna Dorothea S 142
Barthin, Anna S 142
Bartlefalk, Johanms S 328, S 331
Bartles, Christopher S 302, S 315
Bartlett, John T 340
Bartley, Esions S 331
Basbach, Frederic T 254
Baschin, Frances S 116
Baschin, Margaretha S 116
Baschou, John S 296
Basely, John S 331
Basely, Thomas S 331
Bashan, Jacob S 357
Bashford, William (Sergeant) S 274
Basler, S 331
Bason, Niclaus S 122, S 142
Bass, Adam S 302
Bass, George S 302
Bass, Rudolph S 302
Basseler, Frants S 93
Bast, Anna Dorothea S 122
Bast, Anna Maria S 122
Bast, Jacob S 120, S 142
Bast, Georg S 142
Bast, Johann Henrich S 122, S 142
Bast, Joost Hendrig S 103
Bast, Michel S 87
Bastiaen, Andries S 83
Batcheller, Zephaniah S 296
Batcheller, Zepheniah (Lieut) S 357
Batelman, Mattias S 97
Batenauer, Jacob S 346
Batenaur, George S 346
Bates, Gilbert S 331
Bates, Isreal S 302, S 312
Bates, Jacob S 302, S 312
Bates, John S 328, S 331
Bates, Michael T 170, 255
Battle of Bemis Heights T 208
Battle of Bennington T 36
Battle of Brandywine Creek T 38
Battle of Camden SC T 52
Battle in the Caribbean T 40
Battle st Chamblee S 185
Battle of Cowpens SC T 55
Battle of Eutaw Springs SC T 58
Battle of the Flockey T 35
Battle of Fox's Mills T 149
Battle of Germantown T 38
Battle of Guilford Courthouse NC T 56
Battle of Hubbarton T 32
Battle of Johnstown T 59, 153, 183, 187, 196, 201, 207, 229, 238, S 178, S 182, S 183, S 202, S 237, S 250
Battle of King's Mountain SC T 53
Battle of Klock's Field T 54, 149, 212, 229, 238, 250, S 175, S 178, S 183, S 238

Battle of Lampman's or Landman's T 57, 226, 238, S 175, S 178, S 183
Battle of Lexington T 313, S 229
Battle of Monmouth T 43, S 193, S 194
Battle of New Dorlach T 57, 229
Battle of Newtown T 49
Battle of Oriskany T 34, 187, 191, 201, 206, 223, 224, 228, 229, 238, 288, S 175, S 178, S 183, S 198, S 214, S 216, S 226, S 232, S 234, S 265
Battle of Princeton T 29
Battle of Saratoga T 38, 39
Battle of Stone Arabia (Brown's Battle) T 54, 146, 182, 201, 207, 228, 250, 253, S 175, S 178, S 180, S 183, S 198, S 229, S 237, S 254
Battle of Stony Point T 47
Battle of Trenton T 29
Battle of Turlough (Turlock) T 193, 196, 202, 207, 212, S 158, S 205, S 205, S 233, S 234, S 236
Battle of Waxhaws SC T 51
Battle of White Plains S 162
Battle at Yorktown T 196
Battorfin, Anna S 142
Batyn, Nocholaas S 83
Batz, Anna Catharina S 122
Batz, Fridrich S 122
Batzin, Anna Cath. S 116
Batzin, Anna Catherin S 142
Batzin, John Ludwig S 116
Bauch, Anna Dorothea S 122
Bauch, Anna Margretha S 122
Bauch, Christian S 44, S 122, S 142
Bauck, Frederick S 328
Bauck, Johannis S 295
Bauck, John William S 295
Bauck, Thomas S 295
Bauck, William S 295
Bauder, Hilkert S 308
Bauder, Leonard S 318
Bauder, Michael S 298, S 314
Bauder, Michael M. S 309, S 312
Baue, Kristoffel S 93
Bauer, Anna Margreet S 87
Bauerin, Anna Maria S 103
Baug, Fredrig S 93
Baug, Johan S 93
Baul, Simeon T 170
Baul, Samuel T 170, 255
Baum, Abram S 93
Baum, Frederick T 170, 255
Baum, Christian S 142
Baum, Friedrich (Colonel) T 36
Baum, Frederick S 302
Baum, Johan Jost S 142
Baum, John George T 170
Baum, Mathias S 142
Baum, Philip T 170, 255
Bauman, Adam S 142, S 353
Bauman, Frederick S 353
Bauman, Georg A. S 353
Bauman, Jacob S 353
Bauman, Johannes S 353
Bauman, Nicolas S 353
Bauman, Stophet S 353
Baumann, Adam S 122

Baumann, Anna Maria S 122
Baumann, Anna Margretha S 122
Baumann, Henrich S 122
Baumann, Johann Adam S 122
Baumann, Margretha S 122
Baumann, Maria Catharina S 122
Baumannin Anna Margaretha S 142
Baumarsin, Anna Maria S 142
Baume, Frants Heller S 103
Baumin, Johan Niclaus S 116
Baumin, Magdalena S 116
Baun, John Geo. T 170, 340
Baunert, Johann Georg S 122
Baur, Elias S 83
Baur, Johan Mikel S 93
Baur, Kasper S 97
Bauwer, Peeter S 97
Bay, John T 329, 334
Bayard, John (Corporal) T 170
Bayard, Nicholas S 41, 48, 49
Bayard, Robert S 328
Bayard, Valentine (Corporal) T 170
Bayard, William (Colonel) S 328
Bayer, John, Jr. S 349
Bayerin, Anna Margretha S 142
Baylies, Hodijah S 283
Baxter, John T 340, S 274
Baxter, Roger T 327
Baxter, Samuel S 331
Baxter, Thomas T 327, S 274, S 296, S 331
Bayard, John T 255
Bayard, Samuel S 331
Bayard, Valentine T 255
Bayard, William (Colonel) S 331
Bayer, Jacob S 112
Bayer, John T 170, 255
Bohyt, Anthony S 111
Beacher, Henry T 170
Beacraft T 50
Beach, Theophilaet S 328
Beach, Theophilus S 328
Beard, Robert S 274
Beacker, Henry T 255
Beacraft S 327
Beakermen, Eshemeal S 349
Bealer, John T 170, 255
Bealer, Joseph T 170
Bealor, Joseph T 170, 255
Beandz, Francis S 319
Beardsley, John S 331
Beardsly, John S 302
Bearles, Rutulph T 254
Bearmour, Henry S 346
Bearse, Adam S 311
Beaty, David S 328
Beaty, John S 272
Beaty, Thomas S 331
Beaum, Philip T 170, 255
Bechtel, Jacob S 93
Beck, Adreas Friderich S 142
Beck, Johanna Maria S 122
Beck, Johannes S 83
Beck, John A. S 314
Beck, John S. S 298, S 302
Beck, Lodewick S 205
Beck, Martinus S 295
Beck, Nancy S 205
Beck, Simon S 103
Beck, Thobias S 83
Becker, Abraham S 295

Becker, Albert S 103
Becker, Albertus S 295
Becker, Anna Catharina S 122
Becker, Anna Juliana S 122
Becker, Barent S 152
Becker, Bastian S 328
Becker, Catharina S 122
Becker, Conrad S 122
Becker, Cornelia T 144
Becker, Elisabetha S 122
Becker, Hans Henrig S 103
Becker, Harmanus S 295
Becker, Hermann S 122
Becker, Henrich S 353
Becker, Henry T 170, 255, S 103, S 116, S 298, S 346
Becker, Isaac S 295
Becker, Jacob S 115
Becker, Johann S 122
Becker, Johann Christian S 122
Becker, Johan Friderick S 142
Becker, Johann Henrich S 122
Becker, Johann Jacob S 122
Becker, Johann Michael S 122
Becker, Johann Peter S 122
Becker, Johannes T 34, S 122
Becker, Johannes Jos. S 295
Becker, John S 295
Becker, John Albertus S 295
Becker, Peter T 170, 204, S 122, S 142, S 295, S 346
Becker, Philip T 170, 255
Becker, Sebastian S 122
Becker, Storm S 295
Becker, Storm, Jr. S 295
Becker, Zoden S 97
Beckerin, Anna Catharina S 142
Beckerin, Anna Dorothea S 142
Beckerin, Elisabetha Sr. S 142
Beckerin, Elisabetha Jr. S 142
Beckerin, Maria S 142
Beckerin, Magdalena S 142
Beckman, Cornelius C. S 302
Beckman, Henry S 302
Beckman, John J. S 302
Beckman, Michel S 87
Becraft, Francis S 154
Beddle, Benijah S 349
Bedheg, John T 170
Bedford, Jonathan S 328, S 331
Beeber, (Capt.) S 185
Beeckman, Cornelius C. S 318
Beeckman, Henry S 318
Beeckman, John Jacob 319
Beehr, Nicholaas S 94
Beekman (Captain) S 225
Beekman, Henry T 297, S 298, S 343
Beekman, Theophs T 170
Beeler, Jacob S 314
Beeker, Peter T 255
Beeler, Jacob T 170, 255
Beelinger, Adam S 346
Beely, Jacob T 170, 255
Been, William S 302, S 312, S 321
Been, William Jr S 319
Beenner, Jurry S 111
Beer, Johann S 122
Beerman, Johannis S 111, S 359
Beerman, Mary S 359

Beers, F. W. & Co. History of Montgomery and Fulton Counties. Book used as reference
Bees, William S 298
Beesch, Ludwig S 97
Beffer, Rudolph S 353
Behr, Hermanus S 122
Behringer, Conrad S 122
Behringer, Johann Henrich S 122
Beisch, Johan S 87
Bek, Johannes S 87
Bekker, Antony S 87
Bekker, Johan Peter S 87
Bekker, Michel S 87
Bekker, Mighel S 87
Bekker, Simon S 87
Beijerin, Susanna S 116
Belding, Samuel Doctor S 331
Bele, Johan Jacob S 103
Belger, Johan S 103
Belknap, Abel S 295, S 296
Bell, Anna Maria S 122
Bell, Betsey T 276
Bell, Christina (Catherine?) T 276
Bell, Dorothy S 296
Bell, Fredrich T 341
Bell, Frederick T 276, S 120, S 346
Bell, George S 331
Bell, George H. T 341
Bell, G. Henry S 353
Bell, Henry S 114
Bell, Jacob T 341, S 353
Bell, Johan Frederick S 111, S 122
Bell, Johann Jacob S 122
Bell, John S 331, S 349
Bell, Matthew S 349
Bell, Nicolaus S 353
Bell, O.W. (Captain) T 199
Bell, Thomas T 276, S 353
Bellanger, Philip S 116
Belleanger, Frederick S 346
Bellenger, Fred S 119
Bellenger, Frederick T 341, S 302
Bellenger, Henry S 302
Bellenger, John Jr S 302
Bellenger, John L. S 302
Bellenger, Marcus S 120
Beller, Hans Jacob S 94
Bellin, Elizabetha S 142
Belliner, Hendrick S 346
Bellinger, Adam T 170, 234, 255, S 155, S 298, S 346, S 358
Bellinger, Adam A. S 298
Bellinger, Adam (Lieut) T 170, 255, 325
Bellinger, Adam S 155
Bellinger, Ann S 155
Bellinger, Christian S 274, S 349
Bellinger, Christopher T 121
Bellinger, Elizabeth T 168, 234
Bellinger, Elizabetha S 142
Bellinger, Fred., (Lieut. Colonel) S 274
Bellinger, Frederick T 168, S 44, S 111, S 298, S 302, S 312, S 353
Bellinger, Frederick I. S 318
Bellinger, Friedrich T 170, 255
Bellinger, Friederich Jr T 308
Bellinger, Fredrik T 121, 321

Bellinger, Hannes (Ensign) S 353
Bellinger, Henrich T 170, 255, S 142
Bellinger, Henry T 254, S 120, S 298, S 312
Bellinger, Henry I. S 311
Bellinger, "Hoffrich" S 110
Bellinger, Jacob S 321
Bellinger, Johann Henrich S 122
Bellinger, Johannes T 64, S 142, S 295
Bellinger, Johannes F. T 341
Bellinger, John T 170, 336, S 296, S 353
Bellinger, John (Lieut) T 170, 341, S 183, S 212
Bellinger, John Fredk T 341
Bellinger, John C. T 234
Bellinger, John I. T 296, S 312
Bellinger, John L. (Ensign) S 345
Bellinger, John L. S 298, S 342
Bellinger, John N. S 302
Bellinger, Joseph S 312
Bellinger, Jost   T 255
Bellinger, Lena S 155
Bellinger, L. F. S 110
Bellinger, Marcus S 122, S 142, S 295
Bellinger, Mark (Lieut)
Bellinger, Nancy S 182
Bellinger, Niclaus S 142
Bellinger, Peggy T 65
Bellinger, Peter T 170, 198, 255, 341, S 110, S 113, S 122, S 268, S 298, S 312, S 353
Bellinger Peter (Colonel) T 46, 109, 124, 168, 209, 240, 326, S 110, S 217, S 283, S 353
Bellinger, Peter Jr. S 296, S 353
Bellinger, Peter B. S 353
Bellinger, Peter P. S 353
Bellinger, Philip S 274, S 346, S 349
Bellinger, Sophy S 312
Bellinger, Stoffel S 353
Bellinger, William T 170, S 296, S 346, S 356
Bellington, Jas. T 170, 341
Bellross, Christoph S 122
Belor, Jacob S 298
Belt J. Sprigg, (Capt.) (Md.) S 274
Belts, Johan S 103
Belts, Leenart S 87
Belvin Major T 112
Bend, Grove S 331
Bendel, Catren S 353
Bendeman, Peter S 346
Bender, George S 120 S 142
Bender, Henrig S 87, S 97
Bender, Jacob S 353
Bender, Johan Bernhart S 97
Bender, Koenraet S 97
Bender, Peter S 142
Bender, Philips S 113
Bender, Valentin S 142
Benderin, Anna Maria S 116, S 142
Benderin, Eve Catharina S 116
Benderin, John Matheus S 116
Bendysh, Henry S 41
Benedik, Peter S 97
Benedict, Caleb, (Ensign) S 274

Benedict, Elias S 274
Benedict, Elisha S 274
Benedict, Felix S 274
Benedict, Mahim S 312
Benedict, Nathan S 302
Benedict, Thomas R
Benteman, Peter S 346
Benetin, David T 341
Benjamin, John T 71
Benjamin, Sarah Osborn T 67
Bennenger, John S 302
Bennet, Amos (Lieut) S 349
Bennet, John T 341
Bennet, Thomas S 331
Bennett, Amos S 296
Bennett, Daniel S 316
Bennett, Joseph S 302
Bennett, Mat., (Capt.) (Penn.) S 274
Bennett's Corners T 158
Benninger, Isaac S 274
Bennington T 209
Benrich, Frans S 353
Bensch, Jacob S 94
Benschoten Major
Benson, Jonathan S 357
Benteman, Simmon S 346
Benter, Baltes S 97
Benton S 331
Benton, Nathaniel S. A History of Herkimer County is a resource book.
Bentram, Geerlof S 97
Bents, Francis S 302
Ber, Andries S 97
Ber, Hans Peter S 97
Berck, Christian S 113, S 142
Bercki, Jacob S 353
Berckie, Peter S 353
Berderum, Phillips S 97
Berdolff, Jacob S 94
Berdram, Johan S 103
Berdrick, Frantz S 353
Berenhard, Anna Maria S 122
Berenhard, Elisabetha S 122
Berenhard, Johann S 122
Berfoe, Abraham S 313
Berfoe, John S 313
Berg, Abraham S 142
Berg, Johan S 122
Berg, Johan Henrig S 103
Berg, Johann Christian S 122
Berg, Johannes S 142
Berg, Kasper S 97
Bergen, Hans S 94
Berger, Kornelis Reusner S 87
Bergh, Christian, Jr. S 331
Bergh, Philip S 295
Bergman, Andreas S 87, S 119, S 142
Bergs, Hans S 83
Beringer, Anna Elisabeth S 122
Beringer, Conrad S 112, S 142
Beringer, Maria Elisabetha S 112
Berk, Abraham S 112
Berkley, E. S 331
Berkley, Isaes S 349
Berkley, J. S 331
Berkman, Anna Elisabet Betha S 83
Berkman, Anna Margreta S 83
Berkman, Anna Barbera S 83
Berkman, Johannes S 83

Berks, Martin S 103
Berlag, Koenraet S 97
Berlee, Frans S 103
Berleman, Johannes S 142
Berlett, John S 349
Berman, Jacob S 122
Berman, Johan S 97
Berman, Johan Christian S 122
Berner, Georg Ludwig S 142
Berner, Johan S 103
Berner, Mattys S 97
Bernhard, Anna S 122
Bernhard, Anna Elisazetha S 122
Bernhard, Johannes S 120, S 122
Bernhard, Johan S 122
Bernhard, Johann Ulrich S 122
Bernhard, Johannes S 142
Bernhard, Ulrich S 142
Bernhart, Johan S 104
Bernhard, Josep S 103
Bernhard, Jost S 122
Bernhart, Johann Jost S 142
Bernhart, Johann Just S 142
Bernhart, Peeter S 97
Berrey, Nicholas S 349
Berringer, Michael S 115
Berry, Benjamin S 302
Berry, William S 349
Bers, Adam T 254
Bersh, Jacob S 308
Bersh, Lutwig S 353
Bersh, Rudolph S 353
Bert, Johan S 97
Bert, Willem S 98
Bertin, Anna S 142
Bertin, Gerhard Berter S 142
Berthrma S 83
Bertold, Adam S 122
Bertold, Anna Margretha S 122
Bertram, Martha S 122
Bertram, Jacob S 142
Bertsch, Jan. S 122
Berwick, Robert S 274
Beruer, Johann S 122
Beryer, Johan Jacob S 142
Beyerin, Susanna S 142
Bes, Johan S 87
Bescher, Henrig S 104
Beschop, Berhard S 87
Beschop Henrig S 87
Beshar, Jacob S 353
Besharn, Johan Jacob S 113
Besme, Henrig S 104
Besner, Jacob S 346
Besser, Jurg S 94
Besser, Kasper S 94
Besser, Nicklaas S 98
Best S 331
Best, Christina S 122
Best, Jacob S 112, S 122, S 302
Best, Jacob Jr S 311
Best, Johann S 122
Best, Johann Hermann S 122
Best, Johan Hirg S 104
Bestuh, Daniel S 122
Betrer, Jacob S 353
Betser, Harma S 112
Betser, Peter S 112
Better, Johan Peter S 83
Bettinger, Anna Christina S 80
Bettinger, Caty T 94
Bettinger, Martin T 94, S 346
Bettinger, Susannah T 94

Betzer, Herman S 142
Beuer, Catharine S 116
Beus, Ferdinant S 98
Bevee, Anthony S 298
Bevens, William S 331
Beverly, David (Lieut) S 349
Beverly, David S 349
Beverly, Thomas S 349
Bevier, Philip S 272
Bevit, Johan S 98
Beyea, James S 331
Beyer, Hans Peter S 98
Beyer, Henrig S 98
Beyer, Mikel S 104
Beyer, Sagond S 104
Beyer, Tomas S 94
Beyscher, Johan S 87
Bice, James S 274
Bice, John S 302
Bice, Peter S 302
Bickel, Hans Michel S 98
Bicker, Corse T 170, 255
Bickerd, Adolph S 359
Bickerd, Henry S 346
Bickerd, Isaac S 346
Bickle, John S 357
Bickman, Abraham S 83
Bickman, Andries Vredrig S 83
Bickman, Jacob S 83
Bickman, Justina Madeleena S 83
Bickman, Anna Christina S 83
Bickman, Maria Dorta S 83
Bieferin, Susanna S 116
Bieler, Henrig S 87
Bien, John S 80
Beinlein, Hans S 98
Bierman, Johannes S 142
Biettel, Willem S 98
Biettleman, Hans Michel S 87
Bigbread, (Breudbuke) Juhn (Captain) S 168, S 188
Bigbratt (Captain) T 229
Bilar, Johan S 83
Biller, Michel S 358
Billing, William S 346
Billinger,Willaim S 346
Billings, James S 349
Billington, Christian S 316
Billington, James (Lieut.) T 192, S 186, S 216, S 358
Billington, James S 302
Billington, John S 302, S 316
Billington, Petrus S 316
Billington, Samuel T 112, 170
Billip, Christopher S 328
Bilobrowka, Elizabeth (donated material on   Nellis Tavern for use in the book.)
Biltstein, Hans Jacob S 98
Binder, Johannes S 83
Binder, Valentyn S 83
Bingham, John S 274
Binney, Banks S 316
Bintslin, Anna Kornelia S 98
Birber, Sacharias S 87
Birck, Johan S 98
Bird, Henry S 331
Birdsalls, John S 331
Birck, Henrig S 94
Birdsall, Benjamin, (Lieut. Colonel) S 274
Birk, Lys S 94
Birk, Mattys S 94

Birsh, George S 308
Bischop, Lodewyk S 83
Bishelt, Charles T 170, 255
Bishet, Charles T 170, 255
Bishop, Charles T 170, 255, S 298
Bishop, Joshua T 341
Bitelman, Peter S 346
Bitler, John S 296
Bitz, Hans Gorg S 98
Bitzer, Herman S 120
Bitzer, Maria Catharina S 122
Bitzer, Peter S 122
Bitzwig, Anna Maria S 122
Black, Isaac S 274
Black, John S 331
Black, Nation S 331
Blakely, James S 331
Blakeney, Gabriel (Conn.) S 274
Blanick, Maria Catharina S 122
Blank, John S 302, S 320
Blank, Niklaas S 98
Blasch, Johan S 104
Blasch, Koenraet S 87
Blass, Johannes S 120, S 142
Blast, Adam S 122
Blast, Anna Maria S 122
Blats, George S 346
Blaum, Anna Cartel S 83
Blaum, Gerrard S 83
Blaum, Herman S 83
Blauveld, Abraham
Blauvelt, David S 328, S 331
Blauw, Waldron S 328
Bleats, George S 346
Bleecker Barent S 319
Bleecker, Catherine S 319
Bleecker, Jan. Janse S 111
Bleecker, John James S 274
Bleecker, John R. Jr S 319
Bleezen, Kristiaan S 94
Bles, Penetek S 87
Blesinger, Danue S 80
Blessen, Lorance T 170, 255
Blessus, Lorents T 170, 255
Blettel, Johan Jacob S 122
Blewer, George (Lieut.) (Penn) S 274
Blie, Christian T 341
Bliss, Enrich S 112
Bliss, Ruben S 298
Bliss, Theodore (Capt.) S 274
Blittersdorf, Koenraet S 98
Bliven, John (Major) T 319, 322, 326, 333, S 244
Blomreeder, Willem S 98
Bloms, Kristiaen S 87
Bloomendall, John S 331
Bloomer, Robert S 331
Bloot, Corlis S 319
Blosch, Jacob S 87
Bluen, John (Major) S 274, S 349
Boam, Frederick S 302
Bobbett, Daniel S 328, S 331
Bodin, John S 349
Boemer, Elisabetha S 122
Boemer, Hans Jorg S 122
Boemer, Johann Adam S 122
Boen, Luykert S 331
Boeshaar, Anna Catharina S 122
Boeshaar, Jacob S 122
Boeshaar, Johann S 122
Boey, Wendel S 87

Boff, Johann Georg S 143
Bogait, Guysbert S 328, S 331
Bogards, Henry S 349
Bogart, Abraham S 331
Bogart, Jacobus S 328, S 331
Bogart, James S 331
Bogert, Gilbert S 274
Bogert, Henry S 349
Bohall, Adam S 346, S 356
Bohenstihl, Anna Margretha S 122
Bohenstihl, Nichlaus S 122
Bohenstihl, Susanna Margretha S 122
Bohl, Anna Sophia S 122
Bohl, Lastar S 122
Bohler, Johan Henrich S 142
Bohm, Henrich S 142
Bohm, Johannes S 80
Bohr, Mattys S 94
Bois, Henrich S 122
Bois, Pieter S 122
Bois, Wilhelmina S 122
Bok, Joseph S 98
Bol, Gerards S 87
Bol, Gerland S 98
Bolier, Frederick S 346
Bolker, Charles S 80
Bolla, Jacob S 83
Bollin, Sophia S 142
Bolloer, Philips S 98
Bollon, Christoff S 80
Bols, Johan S 83
Bols, Jorig S 83
Bols, Jurig Bols S 83
Bolt, Fillip S 346
Bolt, Moses S 331
Bolton, (Lieut-Col) T 164
Bom, Frans S 87
Bon, Joseph S 274
Bond, Jannike S 122
Bond, Johan S 122
Bond, Mattheus S 122
Bond, Rachel S 122
Bond, Richard S 328
Bonderskel, Johan S 87
Bonenstiel, Niclaus S 142
Bonett, Peter S 331
Bonn, Frans S 87
Bonn, Sophia S 142
Bonner, Frederick T 94
Bonner, Jacob T 94
Bonnesteel, Niecolas S 112
Bonny, Ichabod S 353
Bonroth, Phonnes S 142
Bool, James S 311
Booldman, John S 349
Boom, Fredrick K. S 346
Boonsteel, Henry (Sergeant) S 210
Boos, John Henry S 80
Booth, William S 331
Border, Maria S 122
Boril, Johannis S 295
Borits, Johannes S 87
Born, Gorg S 98
Born, Hans S 98
Borne, Jacob S 14 2
Borner, Johann Georg S 122
Borniger, Kasper S 87, S 98
Bornman, Hans Peter S 83
Bonroth, Johannes S 120
Bort, (Ensign) S 252

Bort, Peter S 331
Bornwaserin, Maria Cath. S 116
Bornwaster, Herman S 94
Borsch, Elizabeth S 143
Borsch, Ludwig S 142
Borsig, Rudolph S 87
Borst, Baltus S 295
Borst, Christina S 156
Borst, Hendrick S 295
Borst, Henry S 157
Borst, Jacob S 143
Brost, Johannis S 157
Borst, John S 155
Borst, Mariah S 157
Bort, Peter
Bortran, Pieter S 83
Bortick, S 331
Bortick, Esra S 302
Bory, S 331
Bos, Hans S 83
Boshaar, Jacob S 143
Boshaar, Johann Jacob S 143
Boshart, Jacob S 357
Boshart, John S 349
Boss, Christian S 346
Boss, Heinrich S 357
Bost, Christian S 274
Bost, Christian V. S 346
Botman, Adam S 346
Botser, Anna Maria S 104
Botser, Johan Herman S 104
Box, Hans Janz S 87
Bos, Kasper S 83
Bos, Mighiel S 83
Bos, Philip S 83
Boslar, Frederick S 331
Bost, Andres T 170, 255
Bost, Johannes T 341
Botermer, Joseph S 87
Bots, Fredrig S 94
Bouche, Daniel S 143
Bouck William T 204
Boudinot, Elias S 272
Bouman, Adam S 353
Bouman, Frederick S 353
Bouman, Jacob S 98
Bouman, Joost S 98
Bouman, Nicholas S 353
Bourguin, Jean Joseph S 274
Bousche, Daniel S 143
Boush, George T 170, 255
Bouton, Daniel S 274
Bouwer, Elias S 83
Bouwer, Elisa Margreta S 83
Bouwer, Kritiaan S 83
Bouwer, Johan S 87
Bouwer, Tomas S 87
Bouwerman, Miggel S 98
Boumain, Anna Maria S 94
Bove, Nicholas S 349
Bovee, Joseph S 308
Bovie, Nicholas T 341
Bovlentzer, Johan S 94
Bowen, Frederick T 170
Bowen, Peter T 327
Bowen, Timothy T 341
Bowen, William S 331
Bowen, William R. S 328
Bower, Casper S 328
Bower, George S 116
Bower, William (Captain) S 274,
S 331
Bowman (Captain) T 112

Bowman, Abraham S 115
Bowman, Eva S 296
Bowman, Golliep S 115
Bowman's Creek T 201, 250, S
192
Bowman, Jacob S 359
Bowman, Johan Adam S 359
Bowman, John (Captain) S 345
Bowman, John S 349
Bowmann, John T 341
Bowne, Benjamin (Major) S 274
Bowne, James S 328
Bowser, John S 331
Box, John S 358
Boyay, Catharine S 296
Boyce, Thomas (Ens.) T 341, S
274
Boyd, Ebenezer, (Capt) T 341
Boyd, Samuel S 274
Boyd, Thomas (Lieut) T 141,
144, 203
Boyer, Esther S 158
Boyer, John S 158, S 296, S 298
Boyer, Valentine S 158, S 274, S
298
Brackin, Anna Catharina S 143
Braem, Bastiaen S 87
Brack, Johan Michael S 143
Bradaw, Wilhelm S 143
Bradpick, John (Capt.) T 341
Bradford, William S 42
Bradorff, Jost S 143
Bradpick, John (Capt)
Bradshaw, Stephen S 331
Bradstreet, John (Lieut. Colonel)
S 282
Bradstreet, (General) T 180
Bradt, Henry S 314
Bradt, James T 341
Bradt, Lieut T 195
Bradt, Peter T 195
Brady, Thomas S 331
Brack, Anna Maria S 122
Brack Hans Michall S 111
Brack, Johann Michel S 122
Brack, Maria Catharina S 122
Brack, Michel S 122
Braedvis, Godvried S 98
Braim, John S 314
Brame, John S 298, S 358
Branck, Emanuel S 98
Brand, Koenraet S 87
Brandau, Anna Christina
Elisabeth S 123
Brandau, Elisabetha S 123
Brandau, Elisabeth Catharina S
123
Brandau, Hannes S 123
Brandau, Jonannes S 123
Brandau, Johann Fridrich S 123
Brandau, Johann Wilhelm S 123
Brandau, Liesbeth S 123
Brandau, Maria Elisabetha
Catharina S 123
Brandau, Nicklas S 123
Brandau, Wilhelm S 123
Brandeau, Johan Weyant S 94
Brandenburg, Blathus T 341
Brandeurf, Joost S 98
Brandlyn, Kasper S 87
Brando, John Willem S 94
Brannon, Abraham S 274
Bransan, Johann Wilhelm S 123

Brant, Catherine T 275
Brant, Christina T 275
Brant, Elizabeth T 275
Brant, Isaac T 275
Brant, Jacob T 275
Brant, John T 275
Brant, Joseph (Captain) T 9, 25,
30, 32, 34, 52, 104, 127, 149,
196, 240, 249, 267, 271, 285,
292, S 175, S 178, S 208, S
217S 241
Brant, Joseph T 275
Brant, Margaret T 275
Brant, Mary T 275
Brant, Molly (Mary) T 37, 135,
198, 271, 293
Brant, Nichus T 271
Brate, James S 346
Bratt, Henry T 170, 255
Bratt, Jacobus T 170, 255
Bratt, James S 358
Brauchler, Anna Magdalena S 123
Brauchler, Johann Jacob S 123
Brauchler, Johann Henrich S 123
Brauchler, Magdalena S 123
Braum, Andries S 87
Braun, Bastiaan S 98
Braun, Christian T 170, 255
Braun, Johann Jost S 143
Braun, Johan Jurg S 94
Braun, Johan Niklaas S 94
Braun, Johann Paul S 143
Braun, Johann Philip S 123
Braun, Ulrig S 98
Breadbake, (Bedhig, Bradbig,
Bradbuck, Breadback, Bradpick,
Breadbag, Bigbratt, Bradpick,
Bradbig, Bigbread) John, Captain
T 182, 229, 237, 254, 255, S
204, S 205, S 212, S 214, S 254,
S 262, S 298
Brate, Henry (Lieutenant) S 345
Braun, Conrad (Lieutenant) S
345
Bredfort, H. S 123
Breem, John S 349
Breidenbacker, Baltus T 341
Bregel, Georg S 143
Brehjis, Christoph S 123
Brehjis, Margretha S 123
Breidenbucher, Balthass S 353
Breidenbue, Baldes S 353
Brendel, Caspar S 143
Bressler, Valentin S 143
Breigle, Geo. S 119
Brein, Elisabetha S 123
Brein, Johann S 123
Briein, Maria S 123
Breis, John T 254
Breitenbger, Baltus S 116
Brekedir, Barent S 87
Brekhamer, Throk S 87
Bremer, Jacob S 104
Brendel, Anna Agatha S 123
Brendel Anna Margretha S 123
Brendel, Caspar S 123
Brensard, Johan Jurrey S 83
Bresch, Klaas S 94
Bresly Johan S 83
Bressler, Andreas S 116
Bressler, Anna Eliz. S 116
Bressler, Anna Gertrude S 116
Bressler, Anthony S 116

Bressler, Maria Agnes S 116
Bressler, Cristina S 116
Bressler, Valtin S 116
Bretsch, Anna Maria S 123
Bretsch, Catharina S 123
Bretsch, Johann, Ludwig S 123
Bretsch, Ludwig S 123
Bretschi, Lorentz S 80
Bretta, Mary S 98
Bretter, Antoni S 143
Brevoort, John S 302
Brevort, Elias S 331
Brewer, Aaron S 298
Brewer, Arent T 254, S 302
Brewer, David (Colonel) S 161, S 163
Brewer, Deliverance S 274
Brewer, Herman (Lieut) T 170, 255
Brewer, Herman S 298
Brewer, Hermances Jr S 302
Brewer, Jeremiah S 331
Brewer, John, 255
Brewer, William T 170, 255
Brewster, Henry Jr (Lieut) T 341, S 274
Brewster, Henry (Lieut) (Penn) S 274
Brewster, John S 349
Brewster, Oliver (Dr.) T 14, 1787
Breyn, Johan Belzar S 98
Brick, Anna Maria S 123
Brick, Johann S 123
Brick, Maria Barbara S 123
Brick, Maria Elizabeth S 98
Bridelburgh, Baltus S 357
Bridger, John S 40, 44
Brier, T. S 274
Brigel, Johan George S 123
Briggs, Elkanah S 331
Briggs, William S 331
Brill, Jacob S 331
Brill, Johannes S 87
Brill, Johannis S 331
Brillenmannin, Helena S 143
Brillin, Anna Margretha S 143
Brilmannin, Helena S 116
Brinck, Matteus S 123
Brink, Samuel T 257, S 331
Brinkerhoff, John T 351, S 319
Brinkley, Thomas S 331
Brinsmade, Zach. (Conn)
Brisbe (Captain) S 185
Brisbe, John S 331
Brisenbecker, Balser S 346
Bristoll, Silas S 296
Briti, Jacob S 94
Broadhead, Thomas S 247
Broadhower, Nicholas S 331
Broat, Henry S 298
Brocket, Moses S 274
Brodbeck, John (Capt) T 169
Brohen, Nicolas S 94
Brom, Johannes Joost S 87
Bron-ka-horse T 114
Bron, Mattys S 104
Bronck, Anna Christian S 116
Bronck, John Hendrick S 116
Bronck, Matheis S 116
Brong, Mattheus S 143
Bronner, Jacob T 94

Bronnwasser, Anna Gertrude S 143
Brookman, Godfried S 296
Brook, Robert S 357
Brooks, John (Lieut Col) T 117, 341
Brooks, John S 274
Brooks, Michael T 341
Brosch, Frederig S 98
Brothack, Jacob S 353
Brothak, Bartholomay S 353
Brotheder, Joost S 94
Brothock, John S 353
Brouer, Wm. T 308
Broukman, Godfret S 346
Brounet, Hans Philips S 98
Brouve, hans Jacob S 98
Brouwer, Diderick S 87
Brower, Arent S 177, S 306
Brower, Cornelius S 306
Brower, Harmeaus S 306
Brower, Harmen Jr S 307
Brower, Helmer T 170
Brower, Jeremiah S 331
Brower, William T 170, 255
Brown, Abraham S 331
Brown, Annanias S 274
Brown, Betle S 331
Brown, Caleb S 331
Brown, Casper S 331
Brown, Christian (Capt.) T 42 , S 295
Brown, Cutlip S 302
Brown, Daniel T 176
Brown, David (Lieut) T 341
Brown, Ebenezer S 331
Brown, Edward S 331
Brown, Everit S 331
Brown, Hendrick S 331
Brown, George T 341
Brown, Godlip S 298
Brown, Jacob T 177
Brown, James S 331
Brown, Johannes S 328
Brown, John (Colonel) T 54, 146, 176, 189, 196, 201, 230, 238, 241, 291, S 168, S 179, S 182, S 198, S 229, S 230, S 237, S 248, S 267, S 294
Brown, John G. S 311
Brown, Johan S 98
Brown, John T 170, 341
Brown, Joseph S 274
Brown, Matthew (Captain) S 345
Brown, Nathaniel S 331
Brown, Nicholas T 341
Brown, Philip S 298, S 302
Brown, William (Colonel) S 173
Brown's Battle T 182, S 175
Brownson, Samuel S 331
Bruce, Robert (Sergeant) S 274
Bruch, Hans Georg S 98
Bruch, Hans Henrig S 104
Brucher, Ulrich S 143
Bruchle, Henrich S 143
Bruchly, John Henry S 80
Bruckeman, John S 346
Bruckman, Godfrid S 346
Brucker, Margretha S 123
Bruckhard, Ulrich S 123
Bruckhart, Ulrich S 120
Bruckin, Katrina S 98
Bruen, Christian S 123

Bruen, Johan S 123
Bruen, Margretha S 123
Brug, Carla S 98
Brug, Johannes S 83
Bruiere, Jeane S 116
Bruiere, Jacque S 116
Bruiere, Susannah S 116
Brull, Joost S 94
Brummer, Johannes S 87
Brumsilly, Charles S 162
Brunck, Anna S 123
Brunck, Christian S 123
Brunck, Mattheus S 123
Brunck, Niclaus S 123
Brundige, Joshua S 331
Brunk, Johan Michel S 87
Brunner, Christian S 346
Brunner, Jacob T 170, T 255
Brusel, Johan Mikel S 104
Brush, Hendrick S 331
Brush, Joseph S 331
Brush, Shubal S 328, S 331
Bruschi, Elsgen S 123
Bruschi, Margretha S 123
Bruschi, Weinsan S 123
Brust, M. S 331
Brustel, Johan Gorg S 104
Brustel, Johan Melgior S 104
Brutzman, Adam S 170
Brutzman, Nicholas S 170
Bruyere, Jeanne S 143
Bruyere, Susanne S 143
Bruyn, James, Lieut. Colonel) S 274
Bryce, George T 151
Bryson, Samuel (Lieut) (Penn) S 274
Bsheere, Jacob S 111
Buch, Daniel S 112
Buch, Fredrig S 98
Buch, Johan Hend. S 112
Buchanan, John (Capt) T 341
Buchler, Michel S 94
Buck, Maria Gerdaut S 123
Buck, Martin S 143
Buckbee, Russel S 274
Buckhout S 331
Buckhout, John S 331
Buckhout, Peter S 331
Buckjo, Abraham S 83
Buckjo, Izaak S 83
Buckjo, Jacob S 83
Buckjo, Johan Jorge S 83
Buckley, Andrew S 210
Buckley, Jochim T 193, S 331
Buckstone S 331
Buderman, Johan S 94
Buehler, John S 80
Buel, Timothy S 331
Buenner, Jeurg Baltazev S 94
Buers, Ludwig S 116
Buers, Maria Cath. S 116
Buff, George S 80
Buford, Abraham (Colonel) T 51
Bug, Henrig S 94
Buger, Kasper S 94
Bugdorf, Henry S 302
Bugspul, Augustyn S 94
Buice, Abraham T 341, S 274
Buisch, Johan Rain S 87
Buise, John S 331
Buk, Dunges S 98
Buks, Johan Bernhart S 87

Carleton, Sir Guy (General) T 16, 18, 27, 29, 30, 43, 45, 53, 266, 286, S 290
Carlton Island T 209
Caribbean Naval Battle
Carmen, Charles S 299
Carner, Charles S 297
Carpenter, Archelaus S 328, S 331
Carpenter, Daniel S 331
Carpenter, George S 274
Carpenter, Henry S 328, S 331
Carpenter, Israel S 331
Carpenter, Jonathan S 331
Carpenter, Latting S 328, S 331
Carpenter, Nehemiah (Q.M.) S 274
Carpenter, Prospect S 210
Carpenter, Rufus S 274
Carpenter, Thomas (Lieut) T 341, S 274
Carpenter, William S 331
Carpenter, Wright (Lieut) S 274
Carpenter, Zeno S 331
Carrall, John S 350
Carrigain, Gilbert T 341
Carrigan, Patrick S 328, S 331
Carrigan, Peter S 331
Carr, Parcifer T 128
Carter, Daniel S 274
Carter, Henry S 299
Cartuir, Peter S 83
Cartuir, Johannes S 83
Cas, Peter S 350
Case, John T 341
Case, J. (Captain) S 274
Caselmen, John S 314
Caselsman, Loversinus S 314
Caselman Sefrenus (Capt) T 209
Casimer, John S 331
Casler, (or Kasler) Abram T 91
Casler, Adam S 163, S 165
Casler, Conrad S 354
Casler, Henry S 210
Casler, Jacob, Jr. S 354
Casler, Jacob H. S 354
Casler, John T 91, S 165, S 210
Casler, Jolin S 354
Casler, John T. S 354
Casler, Joseph T 306
Casler, Maria S 164
Casler, Nicholas S 165, S 354
Casler, Peter T 341, S 354
Casler, Thomas T 91
Caslor, Malger S 354
Caspasus, Johannes Valentine S 114
Cass, Peter T 213
Cassaty, James (Captain) S 284
Cassaty, Nancy S 284
Cassaty, Thomas (Colonel S 284 S 281
Casselman, And. Lod'k S 112
Casselman, John T 170, 255, S 205
Cassellman, John (Capt.) T 169, 189, S 176,   S 177, S 186
Casselman, Corporal T 170
Casselman, Bartel 217
Casselman, Barth'w T 170
Casselman, Barthe T 170
Caselman, Betsey S 205
Casselman, Jon T 170

Casselman, John F. S 205
Casselman, Jonas S 205
Casselman, Peter T 94, 171, 255, S 274
Cast, Johannes S 143
Cast, Johann S 123
Castler, Thomas S 346
Castleman S 331
Castleman, Anna Judeth S 117
Castleman, Eve Maria Cath. S 117
Castleman, Christian S 117
Castlemann, Anna (Kasselman, Kessel, Kissel) S 123
Castlemann, Anna Elizabeth S 123
Castlemann, Anna Maria Judith S 123
Castelmann, Anna Maria S 123
Castelmann, Christian S 123
Castelmann, Christian S 123
Castelmann, Dietrich S 123
Castelmann, Eva Cathatina S 123
Castelmann, Johann Dietrich S 123
Castelmann, Johann Ludwig S 123
Castelmann, Johann Ludwig S 123
Castelmann, Johann Peter S 123
Castelmann, Maria Justina S 123
Castelmann, Sophia Magdalena S 123
Castelmann, Wilhelm S 123
Castin, Anna S 123
Castner, Johann Conrad S 143
Castner, Johann Peter S 143
Cater, Abraham S 302
Cauer, Jacob Mittell S 83
Caugh, Bodus S 299
Caugh, Gosper S 299
Caugh, Henrick S 299
Caugh, Nicholas S 299
Caugh, Peter S 299
Caugh, Rudolph S 299
Caugh, Severinius S 299
Caughnawaga T 146, 182, 202, 216, 238, S 209
Caujun, Belicka S 123
Caujun, Fransa S 123
Causselman, Bartly S 299
Causselman, John S 299
Causselman, John Jr. S 299
Cayser, Bayard (Sergeant) T 170
Cayser, John T 170, 255
Cebi, Kristiaan S 98
Cerman, Jacob S 113
Certain, James T 341
Cesler, Nicholas S 299
Ceubel, Hans Dienes S 88
Chace, Daniel Jr S 331
Chainwinking T 223, S 243
Chalkgo, Nicholas S 299
Chambers, Henry S 210
Chambers, Jacob T 171
Chamblee T 217
Chamborary, Johann S 123
Chamborary Barbara Elisabetha S 123
Champanois, Daniel S 143
Champenvois, John S 331
Chance, John T 341
Channoult (Major) S 238

Chanpenois, Thomas S 274
Chapin, (Capt) T 208
Charleston, SC T 51
Charlick, Henry S 274
Charpanard, Simon S 274
Charpanat, Simon S 274
Chase, David S 302
Chase, Reuben S 328
Chatterdon, Michael S 331
Chawgo, Jacob T 171
Cheedle, Benjamin S 302, S 313
Cheedle, Ezra S 313
Cheedle, **zza S 302
Chiller, John S 354
Chemung T 138
Chennessee T 140
Chenussio T 144
Cherry, John S 331
Cherrytree, Jacob S 331
Cherry Valley T 127, 225, 246, S 175, S 183, S 208, S 216, S 234
Chevenius, Bernhard S 143
Chew, Josiah S 331
Chiernte, Mischael S 88
Chisem, Anna S 123
Chisem, Annike S 123
Chisem, Christina S 123
Chisem, Henrich S 123
Chisem, Jan S 123
Chisem, Margretha S 123
Chisem, Robert S 123
Chisholm, George S 331
Chivers, Ebenezer S 299
Chreiter, Kristoffel S 88
Chierts, David S 111
Chokin, Thomas S 354
Chrasse, Francis S 350
Chrisfilips, Domink S 88
Chrisfilips, Hans Wilhem S 88
Chrisfilips, Jerg S 88
Chrisler, (Crysler) Adam S 256
Chrisse, Simon S 350
Christian S 331
Christian, Andreas Christian S 123
Christian Elisabeth S 123
Christian, Pieter S 123
Christler, Philip S 331
Christman, Frederick S 354
Christman, Fretrich S 354
Christman, Hanns S 143
Christman, Jacob, (Corporal) T 170
Christman, Jacob T 255, S 315, S 354
Christman, Johann S 123
Christman, John S 354
Christman Gertraut S 123
Christman, Johans S 112
Christman, John T 255, S 299, S 346
Christman, Nicholas S 314. S 354, S 358
Christmannin, Elizabeth S 143
Churchile, Benjamin S 302
Cioch, Nancy Timmerman T 243, 252
Cirbb, Philippus Jacob S 88
Cisseller, Joseph S 299
Citider, Martin S 88
Cl----[blotted], Johan S 88
Clake, Joseph T 171
Clank, Peter Jr. S 305

Conterman, John T 171, 255, S 346
Contryman, John S 346
Contryman, John M. S 346
Connoly, Hugh S 224
Conyne, John S 350
Conyn, Peter (Adjutant) S 349
Conyngham, William Jr. S 299
Conyore, John S 245
Cook, Badus S 314
Cook, Beadus S 302
Cook, (Kock) Casper T 171, 308, S 302, S 309
Cook, Casparus B. S 316
Cook, George S 332
Cook, Henry S 307
Cook, Ichabod S 332
Cook, John T 171, 341, S 302, S 307
Cook, John A. S 306
Cook, John B. S 302, S 306
Cook, Peter S 308
Cook, Philip T 213
Cook, Rudolph S 309
Cook, Samuel 184
Cook, Severines (Suffrenus) (Capt.) T 169, 195, 255, S 160, S 172, S 179, S 180
Cook, Simeon S 302
Cook, Simon S 313
Cook, Soverinus S 305
Cook, Suffernus T 233
Cooke, Matthias S 332
Cool, John T 121
Coole, Henry S 316
Coole, Philip S 316
Coolman, Henry S 307
Coon, John S 346
Coone, Jacob S 332
Coone, John S 332
Coonrad, Mr. T 137
Coons, Nicholas S 318
Coony, William S 319
Cooper, Jacob S 332
Cooper, John T 341
Cooper, Robert S 274
Cooper, Thomas S 332
Cooplin, William S 315
Coopmain (Major) S 252
Copal, Barhart (minister) S 88
Copely, William S 302
Copeman, Abraham (Major) S 345
Copernail, Adam
Copiak, Mattys S 98
Coplin, Samuel S 358
Coppernall, Adam S 299, S 302
Coppernol, Adam S 358
Coppernol, Richard S 358
Coppernoll, Adam T 341, S 309
Coppernoll, John T 171, 255, S 299, S 306
Coppernoll, Nicholas Lieut (later Captain) T 170, 194
Coppernoll, Nicholas S 296, S 299, S 306
Coppernoll Richard (Lieut) T 170, 194, 255
Coppernoll, Richard S 296, S 299, S 314
Coppernoll, William T 171, 255, 307, 308, S 299
Corey, Griffin S 329, S 332

Corhof, Maria Catharina S 124
Corkins, Joseph T 334
Corney, Peter S 332
Corning, Johan Lodoph S 112
Cornwallis Charles (General) T 29, 52, 57, 58, 274
Cornwell, George S 329
Corrol, George S 354
Corsasart, David S 350
Cossaart, Tracis S 350
Cossote, James S 350
Corwin, Gershom T 341
Cos, Joseph (Lieut) (Penn) S 274
Cosa, Elizabeth T 252
Cosat, David T 341
Cosby's Manor
Coselman, Bartley S 210
Cosselman, Adam S 314
Cotter, James S 329
Couch, Stephen T 173
Cough, John S 299
Cough, Philip S 332
Coughman, Anthony S 299
Coughvenhover, Isaac S 350
Coughvenhover, John S 350
Couls, Magdeleena S 83
Couls, Maria S 83
Counrad, Nicholes S 350
Counterman, Anna Eva S 124
Counterman, Elisabetha S 124
Counterman, Johan Fridrich S 124
Counterman, Jacob S 124
Counterman, Maria Barbara S 124
Counterman, Sibylia S 124
Courtland (Colonel) S 162
Countreyman, Counradt S 356
Countreyman, John S 356
Countryman, Adam S 217
Countryman, Frederick T 341, S 217
Countryman, George T 161
Countryman, Johannes S 358
Countryman, John T 161
Countryman, John Jr. S 217
Countryman, (Lieut., Captain) T 202, S 252
Courtney, Francis T 341
Cous, Hans S 83
Cous, Johannes S 83
Covel, Simeon S 329, S 332
Covenhove, Abraham S 350
Covenhoven, Edward S 274
Covenhoven, Isaac S 350
Covenhoven, Nicholas S 272
Covenhoven, Peter T 341, S 350
Coventins, Moses S 274
Covert, George S 332
Cowan, M. S 332
Cowenhoven, Rem S 272
Cownovan, Jacob S 350
Cox, Charles S 210
Cox, David T 318, 319, 327
Cox, Ebenezer (Lt Colonel) T 105, 109, 168, 169, 192, 209, 229, 243, 246, 319, 325, 326, 333, 341, S 159, S 161, S 166, S 199, S 208, S 209, S 216, S 232, S 266, S 345
Cox, Fact S 354
Cox, Fesser S 354
Cox, John Luke S 274

Cox, Samuel S 332
Cox, William T 115
Cozens, John (Captain) (Penn) S 274
Crackenberch, Adam S 350
Crackenberch, George S 350
Craft, David S 332
Craft, John Jr S 332
Craft, William S 274
Crafts, William S 332
Craig, Andrew S 169
Craig, John (Captain) (NJ) S 274
Craig, John (Lieut) (Penn) S 274
Crais, George S 346
Cram, Caroline S 305
Cram, Jacob S 354
Crama, Jacob T 171, 255
Cramer, Charles S 295
Cramer, Christian S 299
Cramer, John S 356
Cramerin, Anna Catarina S 116
Cramerin, Anna Maria, Widow S 116
Camerin, her eldest son S 116
Cramerin, Juliana Maria S 116
Cramerin, John Hendrich S 116
Cramerin, Maria Eliz. S 116
Cramer, Andreas T 171, 255
Cramer, Godfred S 346
Cramer, Joast S 346
Crane, Caroling S 302
Crane, Isaac (Adjt) S 274
Crane, John (Adjt) S 274
Crane, Joseph (Captain) S 274
Crane, Josiah S 299
Crane, Josiah Jr S 299
Crane, Thaddeus, (Major) T 341
Crannell, Bartholomew S 329, S 332
Crannell, Thomas S 350
Cranney (Captain) S 332
Crans, Henry S 350
Crans, Jacobus T 341
Cranse, Jacob T 171, 255
Crantz, Hanry S 354
Cratchenberger, Conrate S 357
Cratser (Kretser) Leonhart S 115
Crathers, Thomas S 332
Cratzer, Leonard T 171
Cratzer, Leonhart S 358
Craus, Jost T 255
Crause, Leonard T 171
Crause, Jacob T 255
Crawford, David S 332
Crawford, George T 333
Crawford, James S 329, S 332
Crawford, John S 329
Crawford, Thomas T 341
Crawford, William (Lieut) (Penn) S 274
Creamer, John S 346
Creamer, Joseph S 346
Credtendon, James S 321
Creighton, John S 332
Creitzin, Elizabeth S 94
Cremm, Jacob S 354
Cressy, John S 357
Cressy, Naughton S 299
Crew, Joseph S 328
Crieg, Johan Just S 88
Criestar, William S 332
Crim, Hendrick T 171, 255
Crimm, Jacob S 346

Cring, John S 299
Cringe, John Ludwick S 299
Crisler, George T 171
Crisman, John S 346
Crisman, Nicholas S 299
Crisser, Hans Musil S 83
Crisser, Katrina S 83
Crissman, Gottfried S 296
Cristman, Frederick S 296
Crissy, Simon S 332
Cristman, Jacob S 296, S 354
Cristman, Nicholas, Sr. S 296
Croghan, Catherine T 275
Croghan, (Col.) T 275
Croll, John S 350
Cromel, Jacobes S 357
Cromert, Aaron S 350
Cromnel, James S 357
Cromwell, Jacobus S 296
Cronk, John S 332
Cronkhite, Abraham S 350
Crook, Christopher S 350
Crookshank, Alexander S 329
Crosmen, Frederick S 346
Cross, Jacobus S 299, S 302
Cross, James S 302
Crossett, Benjamin S 350, S 357
Crossett, James S 357
Crossett, John S 350
Cronkhyte, Isaac S 332
Cronkhyte, (Kronkhuit) John
Jacob S 183
Crookshank, Alexander S 332
Crossfield, Stephen S 332
Crosset T 157
Crotchinbrge, Conrad S 357
Crouse, Friederick S 346
Crouse, John T 171, S 299
Crouse, Joseph T 171
Crouse, Leonard S 299
Crouse, Robert (Captain) T 112,
116, S 166
Crounhart, George S 332 T 171,
255
Crow, Joseph S 332
Crowley, Jeremiah S 350
Crows, George S 346, S 356
Crowhart, Georg T 255
Crowley, Jeremiah S 274, S 357
Crown Point T 51, 149, 178
Crows, John S 332
Croxell, Charles (Lieut) (Penn) S
274
Cruduck, William T 341
Cruger, John Harris S 329
Crum, Adam S 346
Crum, Jacob S 346
Crum, John S 358
Crum, William S 332
Crumb, John T 341
Crummel, Herman S 350
Crump. Johann S 124
Crysler, Adam T 60, S 332
Crysler, John T 84
Crysler, Margaret T 86, 204
Crysler, Philip T 84, 87
Cruyler, George T 171
Cruysler, George T 255
Cuddeback Abram (Capt) T 171
Cuddeback, Peter T 171
Cudner, John (Lieut) S 274
Cudney, John (Lieut) S 274
Cuff, (colored) S 346

Cuits, Johan Kristoffel S 83
Cule, Henry S 302
Cule, Philip S 302
Culeman, Henry S 302
Culman, Henry T 255, S 299
Culver, David S 210
Cummings, Patrick S 329, S 332
Cummins, John S 332
Cummins, William S 332
Cun, Anna Catharina S 124
Cun, Veltin S 124
Cunderman, Cunrath S 346
Cunderman, John J. S 346
Cunderman, Marius S 346
Cunderman, John (Ensign) S 345
Cunicum, Willem S 354
Cunningham, Andrew T 341
Cunningham, Henry S 274
Cunningham, John S 354
Cunningham, Johannis T 171,
255
Cunningham, William T 171, 255,
322, S 297
Cuntrman, Adam S 346
Cuntryman, Conrad S 346
Cuntz, Anna Margretha S 124
Cuntz, Johann Jacob S 124
Cuntz, Johan David S 124
Cuntz, Johann S 124
Cuntz, Ludwig S 124
Cuntz, Maria Catharina S 124
Cuntz, Matheus S 124
Cuntz, Philip S 124
Cuntz, Philipp Henrich S 124
Cup, Jacob S 120
Curdendolph, Solomon T 171
Currien, David S 332
Curring, Johann Ludolph S 124
Curring, Anna Catharina S 124
Curring, Catharina S 124
Curring, Lodolst S 124
Curring, Ottillia S 124
Curring, Rololph S 124
Curry, Joseph S 332
Curry, Joshua S 332
Curry, Peter S 332
Curry, Stephen S 332
Currytown T 57, S 209
Curtenius, Peter T. S 273
Curtis, Ebenezer S 299
Curtis, Joel S 274
Curtis, Nathaniel S 299
Curtner, Peter S 346
Curwin S 332
Curwin, Theophilus T 341
Curwin, Timothey T 341
Cutler, Joseph (Ensign) T 341
Cutler, Roger S 299
Cutwater S 332
Cutwater Dr. S 332
Cutwater Daniel S 332
Cuykindolph, Peter T 171
Cuyler, (Colonel) T 150, S 238
Cuyler, Abraham C. T 322, S
329, S 332
Cuyler, Nicholas S 332
Cworhart, Georg T 171
Cypher, John S 346
Dabush, Jacob S 354
Dachastatter, Georg S 143
Dachsteter, John S 354
Dachsteter, John Nicholas S 296
Dachsteter, Piter S 354

Dachsetter, Anna Elizabeth S 124
Dachstader, George S 44, S 119,
S 354
Dachsteter, Hannes T 121
Dachsteter, John F. S 350
Dachstetter, Frederick F. S 350
Dachstetter, Georg S 124
Dachstetter, Johann Fridrich S
124
Dachstetter, Markus S 350
Dachstetter, Marx S 357
Dachstetter, Nicolaus S 357
Dacksteder, Anna S 359
Dacksteder, Jurgh S 359
Dackson, John T 171, 255
Dacy, Samual (Rev.) S 169
Daet, Hans Bernhardt S 113
Daet, Johannis S 113
Dagstatter, Barbara Elizabeth T
235
Dahles, Johan Wilhelm S 143
Dailey, W.N.P. (History of
Montgomery Classis RCA, History
of The Old Fort Herkimer Church
German Flatts Reformed Church
1723. Used as references
through the books)
Dal, Andreas S 98
Dales, John Wm. S 120
Daline, Benjamin S 350
Dalis, Johan Willem S 112
Dallimthis, James S 350
Dalton, Thomas T 341
Dames, Mattys S 94
Daman, Esther S. S 152
Damuth, Richard S S 346
Dan, David S 332
Danck, Johan Jurg S 94
Dandler, Uldrich S 113
Danemark, Anna Hargt. Widow S
117
Danford, Richard S 332
Danford, Stephen S 332
Daniel, Antony S 94
Danielson, Thomas S 332
Daninger, Jacob S 80
Danke, Elezar S 162
Danler, Ulrich S 143
Dann, Abraham S 332
Dannel, John M. S 350
Dannemarcker, Christoph S 143
Danner, Urban S 88
Dansweber, Melchoir S 143
Darby, John S 319
Darrot, James S 332
Darrow, George S 167
Darrow, John S 166, S 350
Darrow, Martha S 167
Darsel, Philip S 83
Dars, Abram S 83
Dars, Maria Susanna S 83
Darwind, Bindier S 346
Dasinham, John S 350
Dasler, John S 346
Daslum, Lampare S 83
Daslum, Maria Lysa S 83
Dather, Lorentz S 143
Datt, Johann Bernhard S 143
Daub, Michel S 98
Daukstetor, Fredrick, H. S 350
Daull, Mattys S 88
Daumer, Johan S 88
Daun, George S 80

Dings, Jacob S 143
Dinus, Jacob S 354
Diril, Bernhard S 83
Diril, Anna Elisa S 83
Diril, Magdaleena S 83
Diril, Maria Croda S 83
Diril, Hans Fildin S 83
Diril, Jorg Henry S 83
Dippel, Anna Barbara S 124
Dippel, Anna Catharina S 124
Dippel, Anna Eva S 124
Dippel, Anna Maria S 124
Dippel, Johann Peter S 124
Dippel, Peter S 124
Dippel, Philipp S 124
Dision, David S 81
Distenbach, Dorothea S 124
Ditir, Hans Bernhart S 88
Dittendorf, Henry (Capt) T 341
Divin, Annda S 83
Divis, Abraham S 350
Dixon, John S 332
Dobbs, Michael S 332
Dobbs, Walter S 329, S 332
Dobus, Abraham, S 124
Dobus, Jann S 124
Dobys, Jorig S 83
Dochstader, Frederick S 357
Dockstader, John H. S 357
Dockey, Gertrude T 253
Dockey, Henry T 253, 306
Dockey, John Alexander T 252, S 214
Dockstader, Darcus
Dockstader, Frederick S 296
Dockstader, John T 231, S 294, S 299
Dockstader, John F. S 309
Dockstater, (Dagstetter), Barbara Elizabeth T 303
Dockstader, George A. S 332, S 350
Dockstader, Nicholas (Lieutenant) S 246
Dockstader, John S 329
Dockstader, John H. S 350
Dockstater, Henry H. S 350
Dockstater, John F. S 205
Dockstater, John Nicholas T 181
Dockstater, Maria S 205
Dockstater, Nicholas T 171, 256
Dockstator, George S 350
Docksteder, Adam S 350
Docksteder, Haniskel S 350
Docksteter, Leonhart S 350
Docksteader, John S 346
Docksteder, John S 297
Dockstetter, Henrich S 350
Dockstetter, Nicklis (Lieut) S 349
Dockstetter, Nicolas S 350
Dodge, Henry S 272
Dodge, Ithamer S 332
Dodge, Samuel (Lieut) S 274
Dodge, Stephen S 329, S 332
Doerner, Anna Margretha S 124
Dog, Frans Henrig S 88
Doit, Joseph T 341
Dole, James T 341
Dole, Willaim T 341
Doll, Hans Adam S 104
Dolmet, Johan S 88
Dom, Melger S 354
Domels, Barber S 104

Domnis Mattys S 88
Dompsback, Franz S 112
Dompsback, Jost Hend. S 112
Donalds, James S 302
Donaldson, Joseph S 274
Done, Thomas T 341
Donely, James T 341
Doni, Johan Martin S 94
Dontizbach, Franz S 143
Dontzbachin, Anna Elisabetha S 143
Dop, David S 357
Dop, John S 332, S 358
Dopber, Robert S 350
Dopf, Anna Maria S 124
Dopf, Johann S 124
Dopf, Margretha S 125
Dopf, Peter S 125
Dopff, Jno. Peter S 119, S 143
Dopp, Johann Peter S 125
Dopper, Leborges S 83
Dopper, Johan Peter S 83
Dopper, Angeniet S 83
Dor, Peter S 83
Doranberagh, John S 350
Doren, Alicksander S 350
Dorff, Reys S 88
Dorman, Johannes S 104
Dorn, Anna Margreth S 125
Dorn, David S 350
Dorn, Johann Peter S 125
Dorn, John S 350
Dorn, Lazarus S 125, S 143
Dorn, Maria Barbara S 125
Dorn, Michael S 125
Dorner, Jacob S 143
Dorner, Johannes S 117, S 143
Dornheiser, Jacob S 143
Doron, Jacob S 350
Dorp, Mattias S 350
Dorreman, Geertruy S 104
Dorrs, Matthias S 296
Dorst, Robbert S 98
Doty, Abraham S 332
Doty, Isaac S 297
Doty, Philip S 332
Doub-dysul, Peter S 83
Doucksteter, John S 350
Dougharty, John T 341
Doughtery, (Captain) S 195, S 196
Dougherty, William T 341
Doughstedar, Jacob S 350
Doughty, Edward S 332
Douglass, Amos S 187
Douglass, Ephram (Q.M.) (Penn) S 274
Douglass, John S 299, S 302
Douglass, William T 341
Doup, Diderig S 98
Douw, Volkert P. T 25
Dow, Joseph S 332
Dowers, Joseph S 329
Downs, James S 332
Dowsen, William S 315
Doxstadder, George S 296
Doxtrader, John F. S 230, S 327
Doyle, Stephen S 350
Drake, Cornelius S 332
Drake, Jeremiah S 332
Drake, John R. S 162
Drake, Peter S 329, S 332
Drake, Samuel T 341

Draks, Johan Jacob S 104
Draurch, Ludwig S 143
Drechsler, John Peter S 81
Drechsler, Peter S 143
Dreisselmann, Christian S 346
Dunuss, Jacob S 354
Drerenbach, Anna S 143
Drerenbach, Conrad S 143
Dreschel, Johan Jurg S 104
Dreschler, Anna Catharina S 125
Dreschler, Catharina S 125
Dreschler, Peter S 125
Dreshauser, Willem S 104
Dreuthin, Catharina S 143
Dreuthin, Elisabetha S 143
Drew, William T 341
Driesen, P. V. S 125
Drinkwater, Wm. (Conn) S 274
Drisel, John S 94
Drissell, Willem S 94
Drom, Andries S 98
Drom, Johan Andries S 111
Drous, Kirstiaan S 98
Drum, Maria Catharina S 125
Drumbaur, Niclaus S 143
Drumm, Andreas S 143
Drumming, Patrick S 332
DuBois, Abraham S 81
DuBois, Cornelius S 332
DuBois, (Captain) S 156
DuBois, Lewis (Colonel) T 146, 149, 178, 250, S 156, S 168, S 179, S 183, S 247, S 256
DuBois, Matthew S 274
DuBois, Peter S 332
DuBois, Zachariah (Major) S 274
Dubous, Michel S 98
Ducher, John S 302
Ducky, John S 299
Dueslar, Elisabeth S 302
Dueslar, Jacob Jr S 302
Dueslar, John Jacob S 302
Dueslar, Marcus S 302
Duesler, Jacob T 121
Duesler, John S 200
Duffing, Willen S 98
Dugaart, John (Captain) T 341
Duguid, John (Lieut) (Penn) S 274
Duister, Johannes S 83
Duits, Pieter S 83
Dulies, Koenraet S 88
Dum, Conradt T 171, 256
Dum, Mergert T 171, 256
Dum, Nicholas T 171, 256
Dum, Richard S 350
Dumb, Adam S 302
Dumb, Conrod S 302
Dumb, David S 302
Dumb, Nicholas S 302
Dumm, Adam (Thumb or Thume) S 116
Dumm, Nelicher (Melchoir or Matthew S 116
Dumm, Nicholas S 116
Dummer, Nicholas T 171
Dumond & Oothout S 332
Dumon, Jonathan S 302
Dun, James S 308
Duncan, James S 332
Duncan, John (Captain) T 341
Duncan, John Jr. S 299
Duncan, Richard S 319, S 329

Ehl, Peter Jr S 308
Ehl, William T 187, 256, S 308
Ehl, William Jr S 310
Ehle, Anthony S 346
Ehle, Boyd Dominie John Jacob Ehle and His Descendants, used as a reference in the books
Ehle, Delia S 182
Ehle, George T 186
Ehle, Harmanus S 346
Ehle, Jacob T 186
Ehle, John (Sergeant) T 230
Ehle, John C T 65
Ehle, John (or Johannes) Jacob (Reverend or Dominie) T 297, 298, 305, 308, S 110, S 113
Ehle, John W. T 188
Ehle, Johnerick S 346
Ehle, Michael
Ehle, (Ale) Peter H. (Captain) T 183, S 165, S 166
Ehle, Petrus T 299, S 302
Ehle, Peter Jr S 302
Ehle, William S 302
Ehlig, Andreas S 143
Ehmann, Thomas S 125
Ehts (Etz) Adam S 346
Ehts, Christopher S 346
Ehts, John Christian S 346
Ehts, William S 346
Eichler, Andreas S 125
Elfendorf, Debois S 346
Eighler, John T 341
Eigabroadt, George S 302
Eigabrout, Peter S 302
Eigebrode, Peter S 116
Eigenbrook, Hannes S 114
Eigenbroot, John (Lieut) T 255
Eigenbrade, George   T 171, 256
Eigenbrod, Johannes T 254
Eigenbrod, Peter I.   T 171
Eigenbrodt, Elisabeth S 143
Eigenbrok, Peter I., Jr T 171
Eigenbrook, Johannes S 114
Eigenbroot, John Lieut
Eigerbroat, Christion S 302
Eigler, Christian S 143
Eiglig, Andreas S 143
Eigman, Henrig S 94
Eigner, Peter S 125
Eikler T 156
Eiller, Johan Henrig S 94
Einbag, Hans Jurig S 84
Einel, Stoffel S 94
Eiseman, Stephen S 354
Eisenlord, John (Captain then Major) T 112, 169, 182, 321, 325, 341, S 115, S 172
Eisenlord, John S 116, S 302, S 308
Ekar, George T 171, 256, S 286
Ekder, George (Ensign) T 170
Eker, Jacob S 88
Eker, Nicholas T 171, 256
Ekl, Michael T 171
Ekman, Daniel S 104
Elasser, Paul S 143
Elbertson, William T 341
Elder, William S 332
Elenberger, Jurig S 84
Elenore, (Major) S 230
Elgenbrook Johannes S 114
Elgerbroat, Christion

Elhart, Johan S 98
Elkener, Hans Adam S 98
Elleback, Emanuel S 332
Elich, Andreas S 117
Elich, Anna Rosina S 117
Elich, John George S 117
Elig, Andreas S 125
Elig, Anna Rosina S 125
Elig, Christian S 117
Elig, Hans Jurge S 125
Eliot, Andrew S 296, S 350
Eliot, Jacob S 350
Elizabeth, Anna S 98
Ell, John S 346
Ellich, Andreas S 125
Ellich, Anna S 125
Ellich, Anna Sophia S 125
Ellich, Johann Wilhelm S 125
Ellich Sophia S 125
Ellich, Souphia S 125
Elliot, Joseph S 350
Ellis, John S 350
Ellis, Alexander S 319
Ellis, William S 332
Ellison, Richard S 332
Ellistone, Abraham S 332
Ellwood, Benjamin S 346
Ellwood, Isaac T 171, 256, 341, S 346
Ellwood, Peter S 296
Ellwood, Richard (Ensign) S 345
Elmer, Johannes Peter S 125
Elmore, Lieut Col T 30, 334, S 185
Elroot, Johan Dider S 98
Elsaesser, Paul S 125
Elsaesser, Gertrauda S 125
Elswa, Benjamin S 125, S 319
Elswa, Faenige S 125
Elswa, William S 125
Elswrath S 332
Elvendorf, Tobias S 346
Elwood, Benjamin
Elwood, Jonas T 306
Elwood, Peter S 346
Ely, John (Colonel) S 272
Ely, John (Colonel) (Conn.) S 274
Ely, Levi (Captain) S 229
Eman, Jacob S 350
Emaus, Bonefacius S 104
Embie, Philip T 171, 256
Embody, Henry S 346, S 358
Emerich, Anna S 125
Emerich, Anna Catharina S 125
Emerich, Anna Elisabetha S 125
Emerich, Anna Margretha S 125
Emerich, Catharina S 125
Emerich, Elisabetha S 125
Emerich, Hannes S 125
Emerich, Johann Michael S 125
Emerich, Johann S 125
Emerich Johannes S 125
Emerich, Johanna Catharina S 125
Emerich, Johann Peter S 125
Emerich, Maria Martha S 125
Emerich, Margreth S 125
Emge, Fredrich T 254
Emge, John T 254
Emge, Johnnes T 171, 256
Emge, Johannes, Jr. T 171, 256
Emge, Phillip T 171, 256
Emich, Johan Niclaus S 143

Emichen, Ernst S 81
Emichen, Johan Ernst S 143
Emmell, Johannes S 88
Emmell, Johan S 98
Emmerich, Johannes S 143
Emmerich, JohanMichael S 143
Emmons, Eli S 329, S 332
Emmons, John S 329, S 332
Empey, Frederick S 315
Empey, Jacob S 313
Empey, John T. S 315
Empey, Philip S 315
Emphe, John T 171, 256
Empie, Adam T 171, 189, 256
Empie, Adam (Lieut) S 176
Empie, Andrew T 171, 256
Empie, Christopher S 332
Empie, Frederick T 171, 256, S 302
Empie, Jacob T 171, 341, S 302, S 358
Empie, Johannis W. S 329
Empie, John T 171, 256, S 359, S 359
Empie, John F. T 171, 188, S 217, S 302
Empie, John Jr. T 171, 256
Empie, John P. S 329
Empie, Philip T 171, 256, S 176, S 302, S 329, S 332
Empier, John S 299
Empier, John Jr. S 299
Emrichin, Anna Maria S 143
Emrig, Peter S 88
Ende, John Philip S 81
Endler, Michal S 356
Endters, Bertram S 125
Endters, Johann Wilhelm S 125
Endters, Maria Christina S 125
Ener, Peter S 350
Eney, John S 350
Engel and wife S 98
Engel, Adam S 88
Engel, Johan S 98
Engel, Johannes S 125, S 143
Engel, Martin S 88
Engel, Robbt S 88
Engelbert, Johan Peter S 143
Engeler, Peter S 94
Engelin, Maria Elizabetha S 143
Engelle, Anna Christina S 117
Engelle, Anna Eliz. S 117
Engelle, Anna Maria S 117
Engelle, Johannes S 117
Engelsbrurger, Tilleman S 143
Engelsman, Jurg S 104
Engesbrucher, Niclaus S 143
England, Benjamin S 302. S 309, S 350
Engle, Jacob S 94
Engle, Johan S 94
Engle, Johan Willem S 94
Engle, Margreta S 98
Engle, Philip S 98
Ends, Matthew S 81
Engelsbruecher, Nichol S 81
Engus, John T 171
Engush, John T 256 , S 299
Enners, Bertram S 143
Ennis, John S 329
Ennist, John S 332
Enters, Peter S 295
Enters, Jacob S 295

Eny, George S 350
Eny, Godfret S 350
Eperhart, Johan Mighel S 88
Ephratah T 41, 121
Epply, (Epy) Jacob T 202, 224
Eralter, Hans Jacob S 88
Erberg, Ary Mag Ronolt S 94
Erbin, Anna Catharina S 117
Erbin, Catharina S 143
Erbin, Eliz. Catha. S 117
Erbs, Hans Henrig S 88, S 98
Erckel, Bernhard S 143
Erenbrodt, John S 299
Erhard, Anna Margretha S 125
Erhard, Simeon S 125
Erhard, Maria Catharina S 125
Erhard, Simon S 143
Erichman, Gottfried T 171, 256
Erghemar or Herkimer Family T 197
Erghemar, Catharina S 360
Erghemar, Johan Jost S 360
Erghemar, Jurgh S 360
Erghemar, Madalana S 360
Erkel, Anna Maria S 117
Erkel, Bernard S 81
Erkel, Bernhard S 117
Erksen, John T 171, 256
Erlang, Johan S 104
Ermitter, Frants S 94
Ernest, Christ (Lieut) S 349
Ernest, Jacob S 350
Eschelmanns, Anna S 81
Eschenreuter, Anna Margretha S 125
Eschenreuter, Henrich S 143
Escher, Jacob S 98
Escherich, John S 81
Eschideins, Thomas S 143
Eschoffin, Catharina S 143
Eschwiler, Jacob S 94
Eschweiler, Tomas S 94
Ess, Jacob S 120, S 143
Esselstyne, Peter S 332
Esswein, Anna Elisabetha S 125
Esswein, Elisabetha S 125
Esswein, Jacob S 125, S 143
Esswein, Johann Wendell S 125
Esswein, Margretha S 125
Esswein, Veronica S 125
Esswein, Thomas S 125
Ester, John C. S 346
Eswine, Jacob S 113
Eten, Efrim S 350
Eten, Elezer S 350
Eten, James S 350
Eten, Tomes S 350
Etig, Gorge S 354
Etigle, Mose S 354
Ettigh, Coenr'd S 359
Etz, (Ehts) Adam T 230
Eulembag, Hans Jurg S 94
Eva, Anna S 98
Evans, (Captain) S 41, 42
Evans, Jacobus T 341
Evathi, Barbara S 88
Everest, Isaac S 316
Everit, Abner (Lieut) (Penn) S 274
Everit, Richard S 332
Eversas, Adam S 357
Eversay, Adam S 350
Eversen, John Jr. S 350

Everson, Adam S 357
Everson, John S 265
Every, John S 332, S 357
Every, Thomas S 332
Eweling, Johan S 88
Ewold, Koenraet S 84
Eyech, John Valentine S 81
Eyesler (Captain) S 188
Eygebroat, Christian S 312
Eygebroat, George S 317
Eygebroat, Peter S 311
Eygner, Peter S 143
Eygerin, Jeremia S 143
Eysaman, Abram T 234
Eyseman, Johannes S 354
Eyseman, Steffe S 354
Eysler, (Major) T 209
Faech, Johan S 98
Faeg, Johannes S 143
Faeg, Peter S 143
Fahling, Henrich S 143
Failing, Adam S 171
Failing, Catherine T 248, S 171
Failing, Daniel S 171
Failing, Henry Jr S 317
Failing, Jacob T 171, 248, S 170, S 213, S 274, S 317
Failing, Jacob H. S 317
Failing, Jacob K. T 191
Failing, John S 302
Failing, John D. T 190
Failing, John Jr S 317
Failing, John Richard T 162
Failing, John J. T 190, S 302
Failing, John R. S 302, S 318
Failing, Magdalena T 245
Failing, Margaret S 171
Failing, Nicholas T 245
Failing, Philip T 171, S 168, S 170
Failing, Richard T 192, S 343
Fairchild S 332
Fairchild, Agus S 312
Fairfield T 40
Fairlie, (Colonel) S 166
Falck, Anna Eliz. S 117, S 125
Falck, Arnold S 117, S 125, S 143
Falck, Gertraut S 125
Falck, Johannes S 117
Falck, Johann Peter S 125
Falckenburg, Agnes S 125
Falckenburg, Anna Gertraut S 125
Falckenburg, Elisabetha Maria S 125
Falckenburg, Gertrud S 125
Falckenburg, Hans Veltin S 125
Falckenburg, Johann Hieronymus S 125
Falckenburg, Johann Falentin S 125
Flackenburg, Johann Wilhelm S 143
Falckenburg, Veltin S 125
Flackner, Justus Rev. S 125
Falconham S 332
Faling, (Paling) Jacob T 256, S 168, S 169
Faling, (Paling) Philip T 256, S 168
Falee, Hans S 84
Falig, Arholt S 88
Fall Hill T 205

Fall Hill Patent T 197
Falls, Samuel T 341
Falthum, Henrig S 84
Falthum, Peter S 84
Fancher, Benjamin S 302
Fancher, David S 317
Fancher, Ephraim S 317
Fansher, Squire T 341
Fansher, William T 341
Farbus, Nichlas S 346
Farbush, John T 171
Farguson, Willimi S 350
Fars, Christian S 350
Farster, Martinus T 341
Fasius, Johannes S 143
Fasius, Valentin S 143
Fatterle, John S 286
Faubele, Johnas S 346
Faubell, John S 81
Faulk, Isaac S 332
Faulkner, Caleb S 311
Faulkner, John S 332
Faulkner, William (Capt) T 341
Faulknow, Caleb S 302
Faver, Adam S 94
Favill, John S 217
Feader T 232
Feagan, William T 341
Fealing, Henry S 299
Fealing, Jacob S 299
Fealing, Jacob Jr S 299
Fealing, Richard S 299
Feanes, Michael T 171, 256
Feather, John S 299, S 332
Feather, William T 171, 256
Feavel, John S 299
Feber, Abraham S 56
Feber, Isaac S 56
Feberin, Chatarina S 56
Feeble, John S 346
Feeck, Cornelius T 205
Feeck, Johannis S 111
Feeck, Margaret T 203
Feeg, Anna Margaretha S 125
Feeg, Johann S 125
Feeg, Johann Peter S 125
Feeg, Johannis S 119, S 125
Feeg, Leonard S 125
Feeg, Maria Margretha S 125
Feegen, Elisabetha Barbara S 125
Feegan, Johann S 125
Feeks, Robert T 341, S 274
Feel, Jacob S 98
Feeling, Jacob S 275
Feeling, John D. T 171, 254, S 275
Feeling, John I. T 254, S 275
Feeling, John J. T 171
Feelis, Jacob S 354
Fees, Christina S 125
Fees, Henrich S 125
Feeter, Adam A. T 305, 306, S 291
Feeter, Lucas S 291
Feeter, Johannes (John) T 234
Feeter, Peter T 234
Feeter, William (Colonel) T 234, S 291
Feg, Catharina S 125
Fehling, Andreas S 346
Fehling, Henrich T 308, S 125
Fehling, Henry S 44, S 346
Fehling, Jacob T 171, 255, S 346

Fehling, Johannes T 308
Fehling, John T 171, 256
Fehling, Maria Kunigunda S 126
Fehling, Miclaus S 126
Fehling, Nicholas S 346
Fehlinger, Anna Junigunda S 126
Fehlinger, Johann Jacob S 126
Feling, George T 171
Fehling, Henrich S 120
Feigsfint, Mattys S 104
Feiseler, Andreas S 104
Feller, Catharina Elisabeth S 126
Feller, Johann Niclaus S 126
Feller, Johann Philipp S 126
Feller, Maria Elisabetha S 126
Feller, Mary S 360
Feller, Niclaus S 119, S 126, S 143
Feller, Nicholas S 360
Feller, Valentin S 143
Felling, Dirck T 254
Felling, Henry John S 356
Felling, Henry Nicholas S 356
Felling, Peter S 346, S 356
Fellinger, (the Drummer) S 332
Felmore, Coenradt S 360
Felmore, Christiana S 360
Felt, Gerhart S 94
Felt, Nathan S 302
Fenck, Wellem (William) S 286
Fenk, John T 254
Fenno, Ephraim (Captain) S 275
Fenny, Daniel 184
Ferdener, Hans Jurg S 104
Ferdon, Jacob S 332
Ferelon, Abr., (Sergeant, Major) S 275
Ferguson S 332
Ferguson, A. S 332
Ferguson, George D S 150, S 164, S 175, S 226, S 238
Ferguson, John S 332
Ferguson, William (Captain) (Penn) S 275
Fermen, Benjamin S 308
Ferrel, Charles S 350
Ferres, Jacob S 332
Ferris, Daniel S 275
Ferris, Isaac (Reverend) T 306
Ferris, John T 341
Ferris, Silvanus T 341
Fert, Jacob T 171, 256
Feschler, Johan Wendel S 104
Feske, Daniel S 84
Feske, Jacob S 84
Festor, Francis P. S 332
Feterly, Peter S 332
Fetter, Lucas S 332
Fetter, Philemon S 332
Fetterly, John S 346
Fetterly, John T. S 346
Feuhert, Emig S 94
Feversback, Deitrich S 117
Fevinegea, John T 171
Fewersbach, Dietrich S 143
Fey, George (Ensign) T 171, 255
Fey, George, Jr T 171, 256
Fey, Jacob S 357
Feysters, Herman S 104
ffelton, Anna Clara S 117
ffelton, Antoni S 117
ffelton, Christina S 117
ffelton, John Wm. S 117

ffucks, frau, Johanna Eliz. S 117
ffucks, John Christopher S 120
ffucks, John Peter S 117
Fidler, Elisabeth S 126
Fidler, Johann Gottfrid S 126
Fiddler, Gottfriend S 143
Fie, Geoirge Jr. S 350
Fiedel, Fredrik S 104
Field, Benjamin S 332
Field, Reuben (Lieut) (Va) S 275
Fiere, Andreas S 56
Fiere, Anna Maria S 56
Fiere, Daniel S 56
Fiere, Johannes S 56
Fiks, Peter S 332
Files, John S 350
Filips, Paulus S 88
Filling, John T 171, 256
Fills, Philip S 144
Fills, Wilhelm Philip S 143
Finch, Christian T 157, 171, 256
Finch, Einathan S 275
Finch, Hanyost T 171
Finch, John T 171
Finch, Jonathan T 341
Finch, Nathaneal T 341
Finch, William T 171
Finchley, George   T 341
Finck (Fink), (Andreas) Andrew (Captain, Major) T 157, 171, 228, S 126, S 144, S 176, S 177, S 185, S 199, S 201, S 205, S 209, S 247, S 248, S 250
Finck, Andrew T 24, 171, 256, 305, S 296, S 299, S 310
Finck, Andrew Jr. T 317
Finck, Christian T 256, 341, S 172, S 306
Finck, Frantz S 44, S 119, S 126, S 144
Finck, Hanyost T 171, 256, S 306
Finck, Harrison S 171
Finck, Jacob S 126
Finck, Johann Adam S 126
Finck, Johann Wilhelm S 144
Finck, John (Captain) T 254
Finck, John T 171, 256, S 306
Finck, John (Lieut) T 161, 255
Finck, Jno. Wm. S 44
Finck, Maria S 126
Finck, Maria Magdalena
Finck, Mattgred S 357
Finck, Myndert T 157
Finck, Wilhelm
Finck, William Jr. T 171, 256
Finck, William T 254, S 321
Finckel, Anna Catharina S 126
Finckel, Johann Philipp S 126, S 144
Finckin, Magdalena S 144
Finckle, George S 332
Find, Andreas T 308
Find, Andrew T 307
Find, Christian S 299
Find, Honyost S 299
Fine, Mrs. Adam T 155
Fine, Andrew S 350
Fine, Frances S 350
Fink, Andrew S 302
Fink, Kasper S 98
Fink Johan Willem S 98

Fink, William T 171, S 299, S 302
Finley, James S 310
Finley, John (Lieut) (Penn)
Finley, Samuel (Lieut) (Penn) S 275
Finkin, (Wede.) S 98
Finsinger, Philips S 98
Finster, John S 354
Fischbac, Johannes S 84
Fischbag, Diderig S 104
Fischbag, Johan Bast S 104
Fischbag, Joost S 104
Fischer, Andreas S 56, S 126
Fischer, Johann S 126
Fischer, Johannes S 56, S 126
Fischer, Lewis (Captain) S 256
Fischer, Margretha S 126
Fischer, Maria S 126
Fischer, Peter S 144
Fischer, Sebastian S 120, S 144
Fischerin, Maria Barbara S 56
Fischering, Maria Barbara S 126
Fishback, Henry T 171, S 350
Fisel, Ada S 98
Fish, Howland S 234
Fishbock, Jacob S 358
Fisher S 332
Fisher, Alexander S 332
Fisher, Bartholomew S 275
Fisher, Catharine S 297
Fisher, Daniel S 329, S 332
Fisher, Donald S 329
Fisher, Elijah S 275
Fisher, (see also Visscher)
Frederick (Colonel) T 168, 341, S 207, S 209, S 219, S 221, S 222, S 224, S 232, S 237, S 245, S 259, S 294, S 296, S 298, S 349
Fisher, Harmams S 350
Fisher, John S 116, S 332, S 350
Fisher, John (Captain) S 349
Fisher, Maria S 126
Fisher, Sam'l (Capt.) (Penn) S 275
Fisher, Thomas S 332
Fisser, Andries S 104
Fitcher, Coenrad T 171, 256
Fithpatrick, Peter S 350
Flack, Fitter S 354
Flack, Peter S 346
Flagler, Simon S 332
Flander, Coenradt S 313
Flander, Deanus S 312
Flander, Dennis Augustus T 191, S 343
Flander, Daniel T 171
Flander, Hendrick S 358
Flander, Henry T 171, 191, 192, 256, S 217, S 302, S 312
Flander, Jacob T 171, 256, S 115, S 116, S 313
Flander, John T 171, 256, S 299, S 302, S 310
Flander, Phillip S 302, S 313
Flander, Tenus T 171, 256
Flander, Augustinus
Flander, George S 311
Flander, Teunis S 299
Flanders, Augustinus S 302
Flanders, George S 302
Flanders, Henry S 302

Garret, Samuel T 341
Garrinot, Peter S 81
Garrison, John T 172, 256
Garrison, Richard Qr. Mr. T 341
Garsling, Peter S 350
Garter, Anna Eve S 155
Garter, Leonard S 303
Gates, (Captain) S 185, S 186
Gates, Freeman S 303, S 318
Gates, Horatio (General) T 37, S 167, S 225,
Gathman, Friederic T 254
Gavlin, Anna Maria S 117
Gearne, Charles T 172
Geater, Abraham S 309
Gebelin, Anna Margretha S 144
Gedman, Gorg T 254
Gee, John S 333
Geer, Benajah T 341
Geer, Ernest S 316
Geerlach, Johan Koenraet S 94
Geerlof and wife S 98
Geerlof, Johan S 98
Geerlof, Peeter S 98
Geertrug, Anna S 98
Gees, Jurg S 98
Geis, Jurg S 98
Geis, Niklass S 98
Geisch, Johan S 94
Geisell, George S 81
Geisenberg T 233
Geiser, Johan Paltzer S 88
Gelly, Thadeus S 347
Gender, Henry S 303
Genedig, Johan S 88
Genir, Jacob S 88
Georg, Johann Anthoni S 144
Georg, Johann Wilhelm S 144
Georgin, Anna Elizabetha S 144
Gesel, Johan Philippus S 94
Genter, John S 317
Genter, John Henry T 194
Gentill, George S 333
George, Wm., Lieut. (Va) S 119, S 275
Gerard, Hans Peter S 88
Gerber, Jacob S 98
Gerdanell, John S 350
Gerder, Henrich T 172, 256
Gerder, Robert T 308
Geres, Jurg S 99
Gerhard, John George S 81
Gerhart, Johan S 99
Gerhart, Valenteyn S 88, S 99
Gerheim, Johan S 99
Gerlanch, Adam S 275
Gerlach, Henry S 347
Gerlach, John Christian S 144
Gerlach, Peterr S 144
Gerlach, William S 114
Gerlachin, Otilla S 144
Gerlack George T 256, S 347
Gerlack, Han Christian S 347
Gerlock, George W. S 347
Gerlag, Adam T 172, 256
Gerlag, Philip T 256
Gerlin, Johan S 99
Gerlock, Christian (Ensign) T 170, 256
Gerlock, Hiram T 306
Gerlock, John T 306
Gerlock, Philip T 172
Gerlock, William G. T 172, 256

Gerlough, William T 201
German, Anna Catharina S 126
German, David S 275
German Flatts T 44, 125, 152, S 225
German, Jacob S 126, S 144
Germond, Silas S 333
Gerter, Leonard S 318
Gertner, Jacob S 99
Gerystler, Catharina S 126
Gesinger, Henrich S 144
Gesteler, Anna Louisa S 126
Gessienger, Henry S 81
Gessner, Koenraet S 94
Get, Peter S 88
Getel, Daniel S 144
Getman, Ann Elizabeth (nee Frank)
Getman, Catharina S 177
Getman, (Gettman) Christian (Captain) T 147, 163, 169, 178, 192, 194, S 175, S 186, S 216, S 358
Getman, Christian T 172, 256, S 303, S 314
Getman, Christian Jr. S 303, S 314
Getman, Conrad S 354
Getman, Daniel T 306
Getman, (Kitman) Elisabeth S 177
Getman, Frederick S 296, S 299, S 303, S 314, S 354
Getman, Frederick (Captain) T 169, S 275
Getman, Frederick Jr S 303, S 314
Getman, George T 172, 256, S 303, S 314
Getman, George (Ensign) T 147, 189, 202, S 176
Getman, George Jr S 316
Getman, Jacob S 314
Getman, John S 329, S 333
Getman, John, Jr. T 172
Getman, Johannes T 172, 256
Getman, Peter T 172, 256, S 176, S 217, S 251, S 299, S 303, S 315
Getman, Thomas T 172, 256, S 303, S 314, S 358
Getmannin, Barbara S 144
Getmannin, Maria Barbara S 144
Gettenson, William (Captain) S 180
Getter, Henrig S 104
Gettman, Frederick T 256, 308, 309, S 353
Gettman, Frederick Jr. S 354
Gettman, George S 174
Gettman, Potter S 354
Gevell, Henrig S 94
Gevell, Johan Andries S 94
Gewte[blotted], Jacob S 84
Ghons, Hans Jury S 333
Gib, Michel S 94
Gibbons, Dennis S 329
Gibbs, Samuel (Lieut) T 341
Gibson, Andrew S 333
Gibson, Archibald S 308
Gibson, John S 303, S 311, S 329, S 333

Gibson, John Sr. S 329
Gibson, William S 296, S 350
Gidney, Caleb S 333
Gidney, David S 333
Gidney, Isaac S 333
Gidney, Jacob S 333
Gidney, James S 329, S 333
Gidney, John S 333
Gidney, Jonathan S 333
Gidney, Joseph S 329
Gidney, Joshua S 329, S 333
Gidney, Solomon S 333
Gieserin, Sibilla S 144
Giesler, Peter S 144
Gifford, Benjamin S 333
Gifford, William B. (Captain) (NJ) S 275
Gilbath, Samuel A. S 250
Gilbert, Judson
Gilbert, Samuel A. S 215, S 242
Gilchrist, Adam (Asst. Com. Gen.) S 275
Gilchrist, Geo., (Captain) (Va) S 275
Gilchrist, Samuel S 275
Gilcrease, Samuel S 275
Gildersleeve, Daniel T 341
Giles, Aquila (Major) (Penn) S 275
Giles, John S 350
Gilig, Andreas S 88
Gill, Erasmus (Lieut. 4th Lt. Dragoons) S 275
Giller, Barbara S 126
Giller, Franz S 126
Giller, Joseph S 126
Gillet, Sephus S 299
Gilleylon, William (Lieut) S 275
Gillikins, James (Director of Ordinance) S 275
Gilliland, William S 296
Gilliland, Mr. T 334
Gilliland, William (Lieut) S 275
Ginder, Henry T 172, 256
Ginnance, Samuel S 312
Ginter, Kristiaan S 94
Girn, John S 312
Girtman, Christian S 299
Girtman, George S 299
Girtman, Thomas S 299
Giseler, Johan Henrig S 104
Giseling, Johan Hendrig S 99
Gisler, Anna Lucia S 126
Gisler, Johann Hermann S 126
Gisler, Peter S 126
Gisner, John S 333
Gittman, George (Ensign) S 359
Gittman, Peter S 359
Gitz, Frederigh S 88
Givet, John J. S 347
Givit, Fridrick S 347
Glaents, John S 81
Glantz, John T 172, 256
Glaser, Hans Jurg S 88
Glean, Oliver (Dy. Q.M.G.) S 275
Gleason, John S 333
Gleich, Sovia S 104
Glen, Cornelius S 319
Glen, Henry (Quartermaster) T 185
Glen, John S S 303
Glock, (see Clock, Klock), Henrich S 126, S 144

Grems, Peter (Ensign) T 170, 255
Gresserin, Maria Elizabetha S 144
Grey, Andrew T 256
Grey, William S 333
Greysler, Johannes S 127
Greyloff, Urby S 88
Grider, Rufus A. T 298, 302, S 286
Grieschman, Johan Heinrig S 88
Griet, Hans Jurig S 84
Griet, Maria, Bern S 84
Griet, Hans Lenart S 84
Griet, Johan Jurig S 84
Griet, Hans Miggel S 84
Griet, Hans Peter S 84
Grifeth (Squire) S 333
Griffin, John S 259
Griffin, Josiah S 333
Griffith Dr. S 333
Griffith, John S 333
Griffiths, Barney T 342
Griffon, Marie S 144
Griggs S 333
Griggs, (Mrs) S 333
Griggs, Abraham S 329
Griggs, Johannes S 329
Griggs, John S 329
Grigson, Thomas S 333
Grim, Henry S 296
Grim, Jacob S 347
Gring, Jacob S 81
Gring, John T 172
Griot, Jean S 144
Grisman, Jacob S 299
Griswold, (Capt) T 334
Gritnig Hans S 94
Grittengton, Benjamin S 312
Groat, Henry S 333
Groat R. S 333
Groet, Petrur T 342
Grof, Daniel (Rev. Doctor) T 226
Grof, Lawrence (Lieutenant) T 246
Gronce (Grantz or Crontz) Peter S 115
Groos, Anna Madeleena S 84
Groos, Geertruy S 84
Groos, Philippus S 84
Groot, John (Captain) S 260
Groots, Philipps S 84Gros T 121
Gros, Johan Daniel (Reverend) T 114, 248, 309, S 182, S 285
Gros, Johan Daniel S 116
Gros, Lawrence S 165, S 169
Gros, Philip, (Reverend Doctor) T 309
Grosch, Diderig S 94
Grosch, Falenteyn S 88
Grosch, Joggen S 88
Grosch, Johannes S 104
Grosch, Philips L;einhart S 88
Grosch, Wilhem S 88, S 94
Groschman, Johan S 88
Gross, (?) Bendrick S 88
Gross, Daniel (Reverend) S 264
Gross, Henry T 172
Gross, Johan S 88
Gross, Johan Jorg S 88
Gross, John T 342
Gross, Laurence (Captain) T 154, 172, 193, 212, 276, S 170, S 200, S 202, S 205, S 236,

S 248, S 250, S 358
Gross, Lawrence (Lieutenant) S 197
Gross, Lawrence T 256
Groster, Anna Catharina S 127
Groteclass, Gilbert T 342
Grousch, Han Miggel S 88
Grove, Christian S 299, S 318
Grucko, Arnold S 144
Gruco, Johann Peter S 144
Gruendner, Matthew S 81
Grug, Hans Gorg S 99
Grunnig, Bendik S 99
Gruwer, Hans S 104
Grybel, Johan Bernhart S 94
Grysman, Henrig S 88
Guchin, Heinrich S 127
Guchin, Magdalena S 127
Gudtud, Peter S 99
Gueenall, James S 358
Guenall, James (Lieut) T 342
Guildes, Daniel S 313
Guile, Daniel S 303
Guile, John S 296, S 333
Guint, Anders S 88
Guion, Jonathan S 333
Guitte, John, (Orderly Sergeant) S 185
Gulch, Ana Catharine S 127
Gulch, Melchoir S 56, S 127
Gulchin, Ana Catharina S 56
Gulchin, Henrich S 56
Gulchin, Magdalena S 56
Gulk, Johannes S 88
Guloch, Christian T 172
Gulon, Jonathan
Gunt, William S 320
Gunterman, (see Countryman, Konderman), Andreas S 127
Gunterman, Anna Barbara S 127
Guran, Jacob S 303
Guss, Mattheus S 127
Guth, Henry S 81
Guth, Johan S 104
Gutir, Johan Philip S 94
Guywit, Fred'k T 172
Guywitz, Frederick T 172, 256
Gynsing, Henry S 316
Gysbert, Johan Joost S 94
Haag, Frederick S 296
Haan, Johan Jurg S 104
Haan, Johannes S 299
Haas, Hend S 99
Haas, Anna Barbara S 127
Haas, Anna Elisabeth S 127
Haas, Anna Sabina S 127
Haas, Catharina S 127
Haas, Jannike S 127
Haas, Johann Niclaus S 127
Haas, John S 81, S 127
Haas, Maria Sabina S 127
Haas, Michel S 94
Haas, Niclaus S 127, S 144
Haas, Paulus S 99
Haas, Rosina S 127
Haas, Sabina S 127
Haas, Simon S 127, S 144
Haas, Zacharia S 127
Haber, Barthel S 84
Haber, Christian S 119, S 127, S 144
Haber, Ditmut S 99
Haber, Jacob S 347

Haber, Susanna S 84
Haberman, Jacob T 172, S 347
Habner, Andrew T 172, 256
Haberstig, Henrig S 104
Habuch, Jno. Wm. S 120
Hack, Fredrick S 347
Hack, Johan Koenraed S 88
Hacker, Pat T 181
Hadden, John S 333
Haddock, John (Captain) S 2;62
Haddock, Samuel T 121
Hadeach, Daniel T 172
Hadler, Adam S 333
Hager, Johann Fridrich S 127
Haeger, John Frederick (Reverend) T 308, S 41, 52, S 127
Haemen, Peter T 172, 256
Haen, Marthin S 84
Haff, Paul S 333
Haffer, Jacob S 347
Hag, Johan Henrik S 94
Hag, Mattys S 99
Hagal, John S 351
Hagal, Magal S 351
Hagan, Joseph T 342
Hagder, John S 81
Hagedoren, Peter S 94
Hagedorn, Christophel S 111
Hagedorn, Cristo S 119
Hagedorn, Johann Peter S 127, S 144
Hagedorn, John
Hagedorn, Maria Gartraut S 127
Hagedorn, Peter S 119, S 127, S 144
Hagedorn, Willem S 113
Hageman, John S 333
Hagenback, Frederick S 81
Hager, (Captain) S 260
Hager, Johann Friderick S 144
Hager, Peter (Lieut) S 260
Hagerty, Enos T 342
Hagerty, Morter T 342
Hagerin, Maria S 144
Hahn, Conrad T 342
Hahn, Johann Georg S 144
Hahrlaender, Conrad S 81
Haight, James S 333
Haight, Joseph S 333
Hails, John S 358
Hainer, Hendrick T 172, 256
Hains, Alexander S 333
Hains, David S 275
Hains, Daniel S 333
Hains, Elijah S 333
Hains, James S 333
Hains, John S 333, S 351
Hains, Peter S 333
Haines, Henry T 85
Haintz, Urbanus S 144
Haire, Alexander S 333
Hairtinam, Koenraet S 88
Haiser, Johannes S 84
Haister, Martin S 88
Hait, David S 333
Hait, James S 333
Hait, William S 333
Hake, Frederick S 347
Hakl, John George S 81
Hako, Fradrick S 347
Haldeman, Hans Henrig S 84
Haldeman, Ulrigh S 84

Hassman, Dietrich S 144
Hassmann, Elisabeth S 127
Hassmann, Elisabetha S 127
Hassmer, John S 81
Hasting, Jacob S 316
Hastings, Hugh T 251
Hatch (Sergeant) S 225
Hatch, William S 275
Hatenkrowst, Philip S 99
Hatfield, Barnes S 329, S 333
Hatfield, Moses (Major) S 275
Hathers, Thomas T 342
Hattler, Ulrig S 99
Hatz, Peter S 354
Haub, Leikert S 94
Haubt, Kristoffel S 88
Haug, Lucas S 127
Haug, Magdalena S 127
Hauch, Anna Magda S 117
Hauch, Johannes S 117
Hauch, John Jacob S 117
Hauch, John George S 117
Hauch, Lucas S 117
Hauch, Maria Cathar. S 117
Hauch, Maria Eliz. S 117
Hauch, Maria Margt. S 117
Hauck, Anna Elisabeth S 127
Hauck, Anna Margretha S 127
Hauck, Georg S 127
Haug, Plaichard S 144
Haugh, Lucas S 144
Haum, Andrew S 81
Haupt, Anna Catharina S 127
Haupt, Cathrina S 127
Haupt, Gertraut S 127
Haupt, Philipp S 127, S 144
Haus, Adam S 347
Haus, Etias T 254
Haus, Henrick S 347
Haus, Johan S (wede.) S 104
Haus, Johann Christian S 144
Haus, Johan Adam S 88
Haus, Peter S 347
Hause, Adam T 172, 256
Hausman, Ludwig S 99
Hauss, Christian S 127
Hauss, George T 172, 256
Hausz, Johannes S 113
Havart, John T 342
Havens, John S 333
Haver, Christiaen S 112
Haviland, Charles S 333
Haviland, Ebenezer T 342
Haviland, John S 333
Haviland, John (Lieut) (NJ) S 275
Havinser, Tore S 351
Hawer, John W. S 182
Hawerman, Jacob T 172, 256
Hawk, George S 358
Hawkey, Richard P. T 342
Hawkins, John S 333
Hawkins, Stephen S 275
Hawkins, Z. S 275
Hawkshurst, Jesse S 333
Hawley, Ezekiel S 333
Hawley, Ezekiel Jr S 329, S 333
Hawley, John S 333
Hawley, Joseph T 25
Hawley, Zadock S 210
Hayd, Niclaus S 120, S 144
Hayd, Peter S 120, S 144
Hayder, Henrich S 144

Haydin, Maria Cunigunda S 144
Hayer, Georg S 354
Hayner, Johannes S 127
Hayes, (Hays) (General) S 159, S 251
Hayes, John S 333
Hayes, Thomas S 358
Haynes, George S 359
Hayney, Henry T 172, 256
Haywisen, Martin S 296
Haze, Henry S 299
Haze, John S 299
Hazen, Moses Major T 17
Heaber, John T 172, 256
Headcock, Daniel S 299
Headeach, Daniel T 256
Heath, Josiah S 358
Heathcote, Caleb S 41
Hebenstreit, John Jas. S 81
Hebmann, Michael S 144
Hebmannin, Anna Engle S 117
Hebmannin, Anna Magdalena S 117
Hebmannin, Gertrude S 117
Hebmannin, Maria Cath. Widow S 117
Hebrissen, Martin S 354
Hebus, Johan S 88
Heck, Henrig S 104
Heck, Sebastiaen S 88
Heckman, Maria Gertraut S 127
Heds, Hen'd T 172
Heel, Jacob S 144
Heemer, Juryh Herck S 110
Heer, Casper T 172, 256
Heer, Johan S 94
Heerway, Charles S 347
Hees, Frederick S 299
Hees, Henrick T 254
Hees, Henry S 313
Hees, John S 310
Hees, Johannes T 172, 256
Heffen, Bartin S 81
Hefferink, Johannes S 144
Heffick, Johannes Conrad S 144
Hefs, Daniel S 320
Hefs, John S 311
Hegens, Ebenezer S 275
Heger, Hendrick S 114
Heger, Henry S 359
Heger, Johan Fredrik S 104
Hegt, Kasper S 88
Heidelberger, Hirchel S 104
Heiden, Anna Maria S 117
Heidman, Peter S 81
Heidorn, Henrich S 127
Heil, Anna Catharina S 127
Heil, Hans Jacob S 104
Heimsein, Paul S 89
Heipt, Philippus S 99
Heiner, Johannis S 111
Heiney, George T 172
Heintz, (Heints) Henry T 319, 333
Heintz, Andreas T 172, 256
Heister, Johan Jacob S 89
Heisterbach, Christina Cath. S 117
Heisterbach, Johan Jacob S 117
Heistrebach, Nicolaes S 89, S 117
Heitwig, Frants S 94
Hekiker, Conrad S 168
Held, Henrig S 104

Hele, Christopher S 303
Helffert, Peter S 81
Helfrig, Henrig S 94
Heliker, Augustus S 333
Heliker, Jacob S 333
Heliker, Jeremiah S 333
Heliker, John S 333
Heliker, Peter S 333
Helker, John S 275
Hell, Johan S 104
Hellebold, Adolph S 312
Hellebolt, Andrew T 256
Hellebolt, Dennis T 256
Hellebolt, Adolph S 303
Hellegas, Conrad T 172, 256, S 170, S 171, S 299
Hellegas, Peter T 172, 246, 256, S 275, S 299, S 358
Hellenbolt, Dennis T 172, 227
Hellebolt, Teunis S 299
Hellenbould, Tunis T 172, 256
Hellenburgh, Cornelius S 299
Heller, Hans Atam S 84
Heller, Jacob S 84
Heller, Johann Philipp S 127
Heller, Johannes S 84
Heller, John S 354
Heller, Leenhart S 84
Heller, Simon S 84
Heller, Wolff S 94
Hellich, Anna Marie S 117
Hellich, Conrad S 117
Hellich, Johannes S 117
Hellicos, Conrod S 303, S 343
Hellicos, Peter S 303
Hellicoss, Conrad T 296
Helm, Johann Peter S 127
Helm, Leenhart S 84
Helm Simon S 84
Helman, Adam S 104
Helmer, S 328
Helmer, Adam S 333
Helmer, (John) Adam T 44, 124, 172, 256, S 110
Helmer, Anna Catharina S 127
Helmer, Anna Margaret S 360
Helmer, Antonius S 127
Helmer, Captain T 112
Helmer, Elizabeth S 360
Helmer, Fredrick T 319, 329, 342, S 354, S 360
Helmer, Frederick A. S 354
Helmer, George (Lieut) T 342, S 212, S 353
Helmer, Gottfried T 308, S 358
Helmer, Honyost S 299
Helmer, Johan Adam S 360
Helmer, John T 254, 342, S 347, S 351
Helmer, John G. S 299, S 347
Helmer, John P. S 299
Helmer, Joseph S 347
Helmer, Jost S 347
Helmer, Leendert S 111
Helmer, Lenerd T 172, 256, S 360
Helmer, Lenerd L. T 172
Helmer, Leonard T 65, S 299
Helmer, Leonhardt T 308
Helmer, Peter S 144
Helmer, Philip T 64, 154, 254, S 299, S 311,

Hess, John T 256, S 29, S 297, S 303, S 354
Hess, John Frederick T 172, 200
Hess, John (Lieut, Capt) T 169, 192, 199, 205, 206, 238, 239, 255, S 170, S 190, S 205
Hess, Johannes T 199, 298, 342
Hess, Johannes II T 199
Hess, Joseph S 189
Hess, Niclaus S 128, S 144
Hesse, John S 81
Hessians T 252
Hessler, John S 297
Het, Koenraet S 99
Hetfield, Moses (Major) S 275
Hertiss, Andreas
Hetin, Anna Maria S 89
Hetirm, Koenraet S 95
Hettich, Anna Maria S 128
Hettich, Conrad S 128
Hettich, Johannes S 128
Hettman, Gartraut S 128
Heuth, Joshua S 347
Heve, Johannes S 84
Hewett, Randal S 303
Hewitt, Josiah S 303, S 316
Hews, Catharine S 297
Hews, James S 275, S 297
Heu, Litcken S 128
Heustice, David S 329
Heyde, Peter S 81
Heydee, Peeter S 104
Heydelbert, George Jacob S 144
Heydin, Anna Maria S 144
Heydorn, Hendrick S 112
Heydorn, Henrich S 128, S 144
Heydorn, Maria Barbara S 128
Heyer, George S 354
Heyer, George Frederick S 354
Heyer, Johan Jurg S 104
Heyer, Peter S 354
Heyg, Alexander S 89
Heyl, Catharina S 128
Heyl, Johann Wilhelm S 128
Heyll, Balser S 89
Heyll, Mattheys S 89
Heym, Johs S 89
Heymerley, Johan Jacob S 89
Heyn, Johannis Jury S 111
Heyner, Johannes S 144
Heyney, Frederick T 172, 256
Heyney, George S 303
Heyney, Henry S 303
Heyntie, Michiel S 112
Heyntz, William S 347
Heypert, Anna Elisabetha S 128
Heypt, Phillips S 112
Heyser, Hans Pieter S 111
Heyser, John S 297
Heyster, Herman S 89
Heytersbach, Niclaus S 144
Heu, Fredrig S 99
Heu, Kasper S 99
Heud, Jacob S 95
Heul, Mattys Gorg S 99
Heus, Johan Mikel & Katrina S 95
Heusen, Johan Peter S 144
Hewitt, Randall S 313
Hewitt, Richard S 313
Heyt, Joost S 99
Hibbard, George S 231
Hicks, George S 303, S 356
Hicky, George S 347

Hicky, Michal S 347
Hildebrand Anna Catharina S 144
Hiebesch, Johan S 99
Hiebis, Henrig S 89
Hiel, Ruldolf S 89
Hielman, Johan S 89
Higby, John S 275
Higby, Lewis S 275
Higgins, John S 333
Higgins, Jonathan T 342
Hight, Elihu S 299
Hill, Asa T 342
Hill, Carolus S 128
Hill, Maria S 128
Hill, Nicholas S 226
Hill, Zacheus S 333
Hillecas, Frederick S 115
Hillegas, John Peter S 114
Hillegas, Peter S 275
Hiller, Jacob (Ensign) T 342
Hiller, John S 275
Hillback, Baltus S 333
Hilligas, Conradt S 317
Hilligas, Peter S 317
Hills, Christ. S 120
Hills, George S 295
Hils, Georg S 354
Hils, Hannes S 354
Hilsch, Kristoffel S 99
Hilt, George N. S 354
Hilton, John T 342
Hilts, John T 172, 256, S 354
Hilts, Phillip S 303
Hilts, Samuel S 303
Hiltz, Georg S 354
Hiltz, George Jr. S 354
Hiltz, George G. S 354
Hiltz, George N. S 354
Hiltz, Gotfrid S 354
Hiltz, Hannes S 354
Hiltz, Laurence
Hiltz, Nicolas S 354
Hiltz, Peter T 172
Himer, William S 347
Himing, George S 299
Hinderschit, Michel S 104
Hines, Andrew S 347
Hines, Thomas T 234, 342
Hink, John T 342
Hinman, (Col.) T 334
Hirchemer, Georg S 144
Hird, Leonard S 351
Hirt, Stoffel S 89
Hirtzbach, Anton S 81
Hirzeach, Martin S 81
Hisirber, Johannes S 89
Hitchcock, (Ensign) S 229
Hitchcock, Joseph S 333
Hitserin, Kristiaan S 104
Hivang, Henrig S 84
Hoag, Nathan S 333
Hoak, Anthony S 303
Hoaksley, Robert S 329, S 333
Hobbersin, John Jurig S 84
Hobby, David S 275
Hobby, Jonathan S 275
Hober, Adam S 333
Hober, Krist S 99
Hobler, Abraham S 81
Hobst, Tomas S 89
Hoch, Michel S 99
Hochdihl S 128
Hoch, Georg S 351

Hochstrasser, Christian S 354
Hock, Hans Hendrick S 112
Hock, Johan S 104
Hock, John S 333
Hocky, Andrew S 81
Hocky, Peter S 81
Hodel, Izaak S 95
Hodge, Israel T 172
Hodges, Abraham S 351, S 358
Hodges, E. S 333
Hodges T. S 333
Hodrigzedel, Laurents S 95
Hoefler, David S 111
Hoeman, Peter T 172, 256
Hoener, Catharina S 128
Hoener, Johann S 128
Hoentz, Nicolaes S 89
Hoeper, Jacob S 89
Hoepert, Hans S 99
Hoerner, Margretha S 128
Hoenig, Anna Elisabeth S 128
Hoenig, Magdalena S 128
Hoenig, Michael S 128
Hoest, Jacob S 84
Hoest, Johannes S 84
Hoest, Michel S 84
Hof, Adam S 128
Hof, Anna Catharina S 128
Hof, Johann Philipp S 128
Hofen, Wilhem S 89
Hofer, Simon S 84
Hoff, Andreas S 144
Hoff, Hendrick S 333
Hoff, Johan Adam S 144
Hoff, Johan Melgior S 104
Hoff, Richard S 297, S 351
Hoff, Richard Jr. S 351
Hoffart, John Adam S 81
Hoffenbraut, Johan C 99
Hofferlin, Anna Maria S 144
Hoffin, Margaretha S 144
Hoffman, Albert S 99
Hoffman, Anna Gertrude S 117
Hoffman, Carl S 114
Hoffman, Ester S 128
Hoffman, Henry S 44, S 119
Hoffman, Henrig S 99, S 104
Hoffman, Herman S 144
Hoffman, Hermanus S 117
Hoffman, Johan Philippus S 95
Hoffman, Jury S 114
Hoffman, Koenraet S 95
Hoffman, Jacob S 95
Hoffman, Ludlow S 333
Hoffman, Mattys S 99
Hoffman, Michael S 114
Hoffman, Michel S 99
Hoffman, Philip L. S 319
Hoffman, Rennalt S 128
Hoffman, Sofia S 95
Hoffman, ZachArias S 128
Hoffmann, Conrad S 145
Hoffmann, Gabrial S 144
Hoffmann, Heinrich S 145
Hoffmann, Jacob S 145
Hoffmannin, Anna Catharina S 145
Hoffmannin, Anna Eva S 145
Hoffnagel S 333
Hoffnagel, Christian T 172
Hoffnagle, John S 329, S 333
Hoffnagle, Melcher S 333
Hoffnagle, Michael S 329, S 333

Howell, Zephaniah T 342
Hower, Nicholas S 357
Hoxie S 333
Hoy, Richard S 333
Hoyer, George S 354
Hoyer, Gorg Friederich S 354
Hoyer, Maria T 124
Hoyer, Peter T 124 , S 354
Hoyner, Fredrick S 358
Hoyney, George S 358
Hoyt, David S 333
Hubbs, Alexander S 351
Hubbs, Charles (Lieut) S 349, S 351
Huber, Henry (Captain) S 353
Huber, Jacob T 172
Huber, John T 172, S 354
Huberin, Margreta S 89
Hubig, Lisa Margreta S 95
Hubscher, Andrew S 81
Hubmacher, Niclas S 81
Huchens, Absolom S 275
Huckin, Barbara S 145
Hudson, B. (Captain) S 286
Huebner, Anton S 81
Huen, Anna Gertrauda S 128
Huen, Dietrich S 128
Huenschick, Michael S 128
Huerig, Joost S 95
Huested, Jonathan S 333
Huestis, Lewis S 333
Huff, Henry S 334
Huff, Paul S 334
Huff, Stephen S 334
Huffnagel, Christian   T 256, 342
Huggeford, Dr. S 334
Huggeford, Peter S 329, S 334
Hughsted, Bishop S 334
Hulet, James S 329
Hull, Robert S 334
Huls, Christoph S 145
Huls, James S 329
Hulsbarker, Addem S 351
Hulser,John S 358
Hultse, James S 329
Humbel, Elisabetha S 128
Humbel, Jerg S 128
Humel, Anna Margretha S 128
Humel, Hermann S 128
Humel, Peter S 128
Humfry, William S 299
Hummel, Georg S 145
Hummel, Herman S 104, S 128, S 145
Hummel, Johann Georg S 128
Hummel, Margretha S 128
Humphries, David (Colonel) S 283
Humphrey, George S 275
Humphrey, James (Captain) S 275
Humphrey, William S 275
Humphreys, William (Sergeant) S 275
Humphry, James S 275
Humphry, William (Sergeant) S 275
Hun, Mattys S 89
Hundley, Zadock S 313
Huner, Benedict S 145
Huniaben, Willem S 99
Huns, Koenraet S 89
Husman, Johannes S 89

Hunt, Benjamin S 329, S 334
Hunt, Colonel T 112
Hunt, Eden (Qr. Mr.) T 342
Hunt, Frederick S 334
Hunt, Joshua S 334
Hunt, Levi S 334
Hunt, Philip S 275
Hunt, Timothy S 297, S 351
Hunter, John S 210, S 275
Hunter, John (Lieut) S 275
Hunter, Robert (Governor) T 301, S 40, S 41
Hunter, Robert (Captain) S 239
Hunter, William S 170
Huntley, Bethuel S 334
Huntly, Zadock S 303
Huppers, Henrig S 104
Huppert, David S 120, S 145
Hupter, David S 95
Hurd, Daniel T 254
Hurding, John S 303
Hureuter, Willem S 84
Hurlbutt, Stephen T 342
Hurtz, John T 121
Hussman, Herman S 145
Hussmann, Johann Adam S 145
Husted, Jabes S 334
Hustice, Jonathan S 334
Hustice, Solomon S 334
Hutchson, Edward S 351
Hutmacher, Adam T 172, 256
Hutton, (Lieutenant) S 202
Huyck, Anthony S 308
Huyck, John T 172
Hyatt, John S 334
Hyatt, Thomas S 334
Hyer, Peter S 297
Hynce, Henry T 121
Hyde, Alva (Rev.) T 173
Hyde, Elli S 303
Hyde, Elle S 312
Hyde, Elihu S 312
Hyde, Jelihu S 303
Hyde, Joel S 303, S 312
Hyle, James S 275
Hynard, Michael S 275
Hyner, George T 172, 256
Hynes, Christopher S 299
Hyning, George S 316
Hyser, Martin S 354
Ifland, Anna Maria S 128
Ifland, Johann David S 128, S 145
Illes, Roypert T 301, S 99
Imig, Paulus S 84
Indian Castle Church T 292
Ingersole, Daniel S 303, S 317
Ingersole, John S 303
Ingersoll, John S 312
Ingersoll, Lipe S 319
Inglis, Charles (Reverend) S 329
Ingold, Hans S 104
Ingold, John, S 155
Ingold, Ulrich S 145
Ingram, Abijah S 334
Ingram, Benjamin S 334
Inkerson, Jesse S 299
Inxale, Joseph S 351
Ireland, John S 329, S 334
Irvin, Andrew (Adj) T 169, 255
Irvin, James S 275
Irvine, James (Brig. Gen. (Penn) S 275

Irving, Catherine T 210
Irving, Washington T 210
Iseman, John S 297
Isenhert, Christopher S 334
Isler, Nicolaes S 89
Israel, John S 275
Itig, Christian (Sergeant) S 275
Itig, Georg S 354
Itig, Marck S 354
Ittich, Johann S 128
Ittich, Johann Michael S 145
Ittich, Mich. S 120
Ittick, Michael S 44
Ittig, Christian S 297, S 354
Ittig, Conrath S 354
Ittig, Frieterich S 354
Ittig, Jacob S 354
Ittig, Jacob J. S 354
Ittig, Marcus T 322
Ittig, Michael S 297, S 353
Ittig, (Edick) Michael, 319, 333
Iver, Frederick T 342
Ivery, James T 342
Isenhert, Christopher
Jacker, George T 172
Jackson, Benjamin S 40
Jackson, James S 334
Jackson, Jehiel T 334
Jackson, Joseph T 342, S 358
Jackson, Patten (Lieut) S 275
Jackson, Samual S 334
Jacob, Hans S 89
Jacob, Henry S 347
Jacob, Johan S 99, S 104
Jacobi, Johan Adam S 89
Jacobi, John Thomas S 81
Jacobi, Philip S 104
Jacobi, Ulrich S 112, S 145
Jacobs, Abraham S 275
Jacobs, Barth S 95
Jacobs, Francis S 317
Jacobs, Richard S 334
Jacobs, William T 342
Jacobsz, Roel S 104
Jacocks, William W. S 334
Jadencock S 334
Jaefer, Christina Elisabetha S 128
Jaefer, Johann S 128
Jaefer, Wendell S 128
Jaeger, Anna S 84
Jaeger, Daniel S 84
Jaeger, Hans S 84
Jaeger, Jacob S 84
Jaeger, Kristiaan S 84
Jaeger, Lemuel S 334
Jacocks, William W
Jager, Beltes S 99
Jager, Christian S 145
Jager, Lemuel
Jager, Wendel S 145
Jalathe, John William S 81
James, Paul S 334
James, William S 334
Jamin, Peter S 145
Jamison, Daniel (Lieut) (Penn) S 275
Jan, a Negro S 128
Janea, Christian T 172, 256
Jansen, Mattherw Jr (Captain) T 342
Jansen, Simon S 329
Janze, Daniel S 112
Janze, Evert S 111

Jauncey, James S
Jauncey, De Lancey S 329
Jaycock, William S 334
Janson, Maria S 128
Janson, Peter S 128
Jefback, Johan Coenraet S 112
Jefferson, Thomas T 96
Jefferst, William S 303
Jeger, Kristiaan S 99
Jehoaikim T 144
Jemal (Wede.) S 99
Jenkes, Thomas S 334
Jenkins, Samuel S 334
Jenne, Christian S 358
Jenney, Thomas (Lieut) (Penn) S 275
Jennings, Samuel S 299, S 303
Jennison, Alexander
Jenny, Bangs S 303
Jerog, Hans S 95
Jerger, Karolus S 95
Jeurg, Johan Mikel S 95
Jessessee T 129
Jessup S 334
Jessup, Ebenezer S 329, S 334
Jessup, Edward S 329, S 334
Jessup, Joseph S 329, S 334
Jewell, Joseph S 303
Jewell, Isaac A S 334
Jingersole, Jessey S 303
Joggem, Johan S 99
Joggem, Mattys S 104
John, Johan Elia S 95
John, Johan Philips S 95
Jones, John Paul T 41, 49, 50
Jones, William S 356
Jong, Elisabeth S 84
Jong, Hendr. Pieter S 84
Jong, Katrina S 84
Jong, Maria Katharina S 84
Jong, Pieter S 84
Jonge, Jacob S 84
Johan, Henrig S 89
Johns, William S 347
Johnson, (Reverend) T 204
Johnson, (Lady) S 334
Johnson, Abraham S 329, S 334
Johnson, Adam Gordon T 266
Johnson, Andrew S 351, S 357
Johnson, Archibald Kennedy T 266
Johnson, Charles Christopher T 266
Johnson, Elizabeth S 329
Johnson, Guy (Colonel) T 25, 74, 101, 222, 284, 319, 322, 327, 333, S 329, S 334
Johnson, James T 266, S 299, S 303, S 318, S 334
Johnson, John Sir (Colonel) T 1, 27, 51, 54, 101, 103, 111, 118, 146, 149, 177, 182, 196, 202, 212, 214, 225, 265, 317, 328, 330, S 53, S 193, S 209, S 216, S 221, S 223, S 225, S 234, S 246, S 267, S 293, S 329, S 334, S 343
Johnson, John T 266, 342, S 178, S 179, S 275, S 329, S 351
Johnson, Jno. (Adjt) (Penn) S 275
Johnson, Jonathan S 334

Johnson, Magdalen S 329
Johnson, Margaret S 329
Johnson, Mary "Polly" (Lady) T 214, 269
Johnson, Moses S 303, S 312
Johnson, Peter, (Captain) S 334
Johnson, Robert T 266, S 351
Johnson, Ruliph S 351
Johnson, Susan Griffith Colpoys T 269
Johnson, Stephen T 266
Johnson, Warren T 266
Johnson, William Jr. T 26, 114
Johnson, William T 266, 327, 332, S 318
Johnson, William Sir (Bart) T 9, 73, 168, 232, 265, 272, 293, 305, S 291, S 329, S 334
Johnson, William George Sir T 268
Johnson, William Gordon T 269
Johnston, Abraham S 299
Johnston, (Captain) T 136, S 334
Johnston, John S 334
Johnston, Jonathan S 334
Johnston, Richard S 358
Johnston, William T 172, 256
Johnston, Witter S 208, S 351
Johnstown S 209
Joice, James T 342
Jone, Daniel S 329
Jone, John S 329
Jones, (Captain) T 247
Jones, Edward S 334
Jones, Harmanus S 351
Jones, James S 275, S 351
Jones, John S 334
Jones, John Paul T 41
Jones, Jonathan S 329
Jones, Jotham S 334
Jones, Philip S 329, S 334
Jones, Richard S 351
Jones, Samuel T 342
Jones, Thomas S 329
Joosten Johan S 99
Joost, Johan S 84
Joost, Kristoffel S 104
Joran, Joacob (Yerdon) S 116
Jorand, George S 356
Jordan, Adam S 347, S 356
Jordan, Casper T 172, 256, S 347, S 356
Jordan, Casper, Jun'r S 114
Jordan, Casper L. S 347
Jordan, Gasper S 347
Jordan, George T 172, 257, S 347
Jordan, Hannes Jun'r S 114
Jordan, John T 342, S 347, S 356
Jordan, John Peter S 347, S 347
Jordan, Koenraed S 84
Jordan, Nicholas T 342, S 347
Jordan, Peter S 347
Jordan, Stephen S 115
Jorg, Antony S 105
Jorg, Hans S 99
Jorg, Johann Niclaus S 128
Jorg, Maria S 128
Jorg, Wilhelm S 128
Jorgen, Hans S 84
Jorter, Andries S 84

Joseph, Jurig S 84
Josep, Anna S 99
Josten, Margreta S 105
Jourg, Hans S 84
Joy, Samuel S 210
Jsbraut, Hans Wolf S 89
Judik, Maria S 84
Juger, John T 172, 257
Julig, Johan Henrig S 95
Juman, David S 351
Jump, William T 342, S 275
Jung, (Young) Anna S 117
Jung, Anna Elisabeth S 128
Jung, Anna Margreth S 128
Jung, Anna Veronica S 128
Jung, Catharina Elisabetha S 128
Jung, Elisabetha S 128
Jung, Hendrick S 112
Jung, Eva Maria S 128
Jung, Gertrudt S 128
Jung, Henrich S 119, S 128, S 145
Jung, Jacob S 128, S 347
Jung, Jacob, Jr. T 172, 257
Jung, Jan Matthias S 128
Jung, Jerg Hans S 128
Jung, Johan S 99
Jung, Johann Adam S 128
Jung, Johan Eberhard S 105, S 128, S 145
Jung, Johan Henrich S 128
Jung, Johann Mattheus S 128
Jung, Johan Peter S 99
Jung, Johann Quirinius S 128
Jung, Johannes S 117, S 128, S 145
Jung, John S 84
Jung, Klaus S 99
Jung, Lutwig T 172, 257
Jung, Magdalena S 128
Jung, Maria Catharina S 128
Jung, Niclaus S 128
Jung, Peter S 145
Jung, Theobald S 128, S 145
Jung, Thommes S 347
Junge, Johannes' (Wede.) S 105
Jungens, Anna Magdalena S 117
Jungens, Nichlaus S 117, S 145
Jungijo, Jacob S 347
Jungin, Anna Elizabeth S 145
Jungin, Juliana S 145
Jungin, Maria S 145
Jungst, Johan Henrig S 99
Junik, Hans Art S 89
Junik, Johan S 89
Jurg, Hans S 89
Jurg, Johan S 89, S 99, S 105
Jurig, Abraham S 84
Jurig, Johan S 89
Jurry, John S 351
Kaach, John S 358
Kabsin, Anna Sibilla S 145
Kack, Casper T 172
Kaehl, Jorg Wilhelm S 128
Kaelman and wife S 84
Kaff, Bazar S 81
Kahl, Johann Wilhelm S 145
Kaisser, Johs S 89
Kak, Peter S 89
Kalbour, Johan Kasper S 95
Kaldauer, Valentine S 81
Kallenvolt, Andreas T 172
Kalley, George T 172, 257

Kamd, (Kame?) Gorg S 99
Kamer, Johann Wilhelm S 145
Kammer, Johan Wm. S 120
Kamp, Koenraet S 99
Kanadaseago T 129, 140
Kanakals T 129
Kane, John S 329, S 334
Kane's Store S 291
Kang, Johan Peter S 145
Kanhorner, Margreeta S 99
Kanikill, Emicke S 128
Kanikill, Johannes S 128
Kanikill, Peter Samuel S 128
Kanikill, Samuel S 129
Kaputzgi, Anna Dorothea S 129
Kaputzgi, Anna Magdalena S 129
Kaputzgi, Anna Margretha S 129
Kaputzgi, Jacob S 129
Kaputzgi, Johann Jacob S 129
Karb, Johan Philip S 89
Kargard, Peter S 95
Karin, William S 358
Karle, George S 354
Karty, Johan S 84
Karn, Michel S 99
Karol, Jacob S 99
Kartneer, Johan S 105
Kartrioght, Hanry S 351
Kas, Andries Laurens S 99
Kaschelin, Anna Margretha S 145
Kasin, Eva Catharina S 145
Kasner, Andreas S 99
Kass, George S 114
Kassellmann, John (Capt.) T 169
Kaselman, Bertel T 172, 257
Kaselman, John (Capt) T 147, S 248, S 250
Kasselman, John S. S 204
Kaskadon, Robert S 299
Kasselman, Johannes T 172, 254, 257
Kasselman, John (Captain) S 359
Kasselman, John S 359
Kasselmann, Christian S 145
Kasselmann, Dietrich S 145
Kast, Anna Mary S 84
Kast, Balter S 84
Kast, Frederick S 354
Kast, George S 354
Kast, Hans Jury S 111
Kast, Johann Georg S 145
Kast, Johan Jurgh Jr. S 360
Kast, Johan Jurgh S 360
Kast, Katrina S 84
Kast, Marita S 84
Kastner, Johan S 105
Kastelmen, Johannes
Kater, Hana S 334
Katrina, Anna S 99
Katrina, Maria S 99
Katrina (Wede.) S 99
Kaufaber, Johan Adam S 95
Kaulil, Frederig S 89
Kauts, Andreas S 95
Kayg, Anna Katrina S 99
Kayser, Henry T 195
Kayser, (Keyser) Johanes (Capt) T 170, 255
Kayser, Johann Matheus S 145
Kayser, Johann Wilhelm S 145
Kayserin, Maria S 145
Keaber, John T 172, 257
Keadman, John T 172

Kearn, John T 257, S 299
Kearny, Thomas T 342
Keasselman, John Jr. T 172, 257
Keasselman, Peardle T 172, 257
Kebels, Andries S 99
Kecs, Henrich T 257
Keech, James S 351
Keech, Jorge S 351
Keeler, Job S 334
Keeler, Isaac (Lieut) T 342, S 275
Keeler, Isaac, (Ensign) S 275
Keeler, Isaiah S 275
Keeling, Adam S320
Keelman, Jacob S 351
Keelman, Michel S 99
Kees, Henry S 303
Kees, Henrich T 172
Kees, Johan Peter S 99
Keffulm, Jacob S 100
Kefler, Henrich S 145
Kehl, Anna Sibylla Catharina S 129
Kehl, Gerdraut S 129
Kehl, Jorg Wilhelm S 129
Kehl, Jerg Wilhelm S 129
Kehl, Sibylla Catharina S 129
Keichel, Johan S 89
Keil, Johan S 105
Kel, Peeter S 99
Kell Christopher S 321Kell, Niklaas S 99
Kers, Adam S 95
Kieger, Johan S 89
Keil, Henrig S 89
Keiltz, Peter T 172, 257
Keiming, Johan Markus S 105
Keiseham, Johan Joost's (Wede.) S 105
Keiser, John Mattheus S 117
Keith, Jacob S 351
Keith, Sir William (Governor of PA) S 50
Keizer, Anna Elisabet S 84
Keizer, Mattheus S 84
Kelder, Henry S 357
Kelder, John S 357
Keldereich, Abram S 105
Keler, Peter S 89
Kelger, Peter S 84
Kelil, Johan S 89
Kell, Jurg Andries S 105
Kell, Nicolas S 351
Kellen, Raspur T 172
Keller, Andreas T 172, 257, S 114, S 347
Keller, Andrew S 356
Keller, Andrew Jr. S 347
Keller, Andrew, Jr. T 172
Keller, Barbara S 129
Keller, Christian S 145
Keller, Conrad S 120
Keller, Felix T 172, 257, S 114, S 347
Keller, Frantz S 129, S 145
Keller, Gasper S 347
Keller, Henry S 114, S 297
Keller, Jacob T 172, S 89, S 114, S 347, S 351
Keller, Jacob R. S 347
Keller, Johann Wilhelm S 129
Keller, Johannes S 297
Keller, John Junior S 116

Keller, John S 84, S 299
Keller, Joseph S 317
Keller, Kasher T 172, 257
Keller, Michael S 303, S 312
Keller, Nicolaas S 84, S 116, S 354
Keller, Piter T 172, 257
Keller, Rudolph T 155, S 114
Keller, Solomon T 172, 206, 342
Kelley, George T 172
Kelley, Thomas T 172, 257
Kellum, (Captain) T 173
Kelly, George, T 257, S 299, S 303, S 309
Kelly, John S 275, S 297
Kelly, Peter S 351
Kelly, Thomas S 347
Kelmer, Hend'k T 172
Kelmer, John S 347
Kelmer, Jurich S 112
Kelmer, Leonard T 172
Kelsch, John Sr. S 354
Kelsch, John Jr. S 354
Kelsey, Ebenezer S 275
Kelsh, John S 314
Keltz, Conrath S 297
Kemp, (Attorney General) T 73
Kempe, John Tabor (Atty & Advocate General) S 329, S 334
Keneman, Jurg Karel S 99
Kenmer, Hans Nikel S 99
Kenneday, Robert S 351
Kennedy, James S 297, S 351
Kenedy, Patrick S 299, S 303
Kennedy, Robert S 297, S 334
Kennedy, Thomas S 275
Kenny, Thomas T 342
Kenter, Henry S 299
Kenton, Richard S 210
Kentor, John S 297
Kentor, Robert S 297
Kerbel, Kasper S 99
Kerbel, Peter S 99
Kerby, Stephen S 275
Kercher, Philip S 295
Kercherin, Anna Maria S 145
Kerchmer, Grol. S 120
Kerger, Johan S 89, S 99
Kerlach, Henry S 347
Kerlack, Adam S 356
Kerlack, George S 356
Kern, John S 303
Kerm, Michael
Kermerroot, Johan S 99
Kern, Beads (Sergeant) T 170
Kern, Beads T 172, 257
Kern, Earl T 172
Kern, John T 172, 257, S 212
Kern, Michael T 172, 257
Kernar, Wolf S 84
Kernerin, Anna Maria S 84
Kernick, James S 129
Kernreiter, Johannes S 84
Kerry, Falentyn S 84
Kersner, Philip S 89
Kerver, Niklaas S 99
Keslaer, Johannes S 360
Keslaer, Nicholas S 360
Kesler, Hannes S 354
Keler, Nicholas S 354
Kesler, John Jr. S 297
Kesles, Thomas S 347, S 356
Kesselaer, David S 112

Kesselerin, Anna Maria S 145
Kesslar, Conrat S 354
Kesslar, Jacob John S 354
Kesslar, Jacob S 354
Kesslar, John S 354
Kessler, Jacob S 354
Kessler, Jacob J. S 354
Kessler, John S 356
Kessler, John P. S 354
Kessler, Johannis S 111
Kessler, Johney S 354
Kessler, Joseph S 303, S 354
Kessler, Melger S 354
Kesseler, Kasper S 95
Kessen, Houpvig S 99
Kess, Christian T 172
Kesslar, John A. S 165
Kesslaer, Johannes S 358
Kessler, Conrath T 172, 257
Kessler, Frans Niklaas S 95
Kessler, Johannes S 145
Kessler, John S 297
Kessler, Joseph T 172, 257
Kessler, Peter S 347
Kest, Richard S 296
Kessler, Anna Catharina S 129
Kessler, Mergert T 172, 257
Kestler, Anna Margretha S 129
Kestler, Johann S 129
Ketcham, Ephraim S 351
Ketcham, John T 342
Ketchum, Abijah S 334
Ketchum, Isaac (Reverend) T 306, S 247
Kettle, Andrew S 334
Kettle, Daniel S 299
Kettle, Jacob S 299
Keulen, Koenraet S 84
Keuler, Hans Peter S 89
Keusel, Hans Jacob S 95
Kever, Hans Philip S 99
Kever, Philip S 99
Keys, Johan Philip S 105
Keyser, Anna Margretha S 129
Keyser, Barent T 172, 257, S 299
Keyser, George Frederick S 81
Keyser, Hanjost T 172, 257
Keyser, Henry T 172, 257, S 299, S 307
Keyser, Johann S 129
Keyser, Johannis S 111
Keyser, John T 172, 305, 324, S 299
Keyser, John (Lieut., Captain) T 202, 209, 325, S 158, S 172
Keyser, John Jr
Keyser, Joost T 172
Keyser, Michael T 172, 257, 305
Keyser, Yost S 299
Keyserin, Anna Maria S 89
Keyzer, Henrig S 84
Khull, Hendrick S 299
Kieffler, Johan William S 145
Kies, Peter S 303
Kiesler, David S 145
Kieselbag, Johan S 99
Kien, Hendrig S 89
Kietman, Frederick S 111
Kiever, Balthasar S 129
Kiever, Catharina S 129
Kiever, Christina S 129
Kiever, Henrich S 129

Kigel, Henrig S 99
Kilberin, Barbera S 84
Kiles, Conrath T 172, 257
Kiley, Henry S 351
Kill, Christopher S 299
Killer, Andrew T 172
Killes, Peter T 173
Killey, Andrew T 172
Killey, Henrich T 172, 257
Killy, Thomas S 347
Kilmer, Eva Margretha S 129
Kilmer, Georg S 129
Kilmer, Johann Wilhelm S 129
Kils, Adam S 313
Kils, Anna Maria T 201
Kils, Conrath T 257
Kils, Peter T 257
Kils, Peter N. S 310
Kils, Pieter T 201, 257
Kils, Philip S 309
Kilts, Adam T 173, 257, S 299, S 306
Kilts, Coenradt T 257, S 307
Kilts, Conrath T 173
Kilts, Conrad T 101, 201, S 303
Kilts, Johannes S 115, S 357
Kilts, Nichelas T 173, 257
Kilts, Peter T 173, 257, S 299
Kilts, Peter N. T 173, 257, S 299
Kilts, Philip T 173, 257
Kilts, Philip T 257
Kiltz, Adam S 115
Kiltz, Johan Nekel S 115
Kiltz, Georg S 354
Kiltz, Laurants S 354
Kiltz, Peter S 115
Kimball, Nathaniel S 310
Kimball, Stephen S 334
Kimball, Tonothy T. S 321
Kimm, George T 173
Kind, William S 358
Kinderson, John I S 244
Kindr, Bendik S 99
Kinfeller, Frederick S 81
King, Gideon S 334
King, John T 173, 257
King, John S 334
King, Leonard T 342
King, Reuben T 342
King, Walter T 342
King's Ferry S 193
Kinkead, Crownidge T 329, S 297, S 357
Kinton, John T 325
Kip, Benjamin S 329
Kip, Garret (Lieut) S 275
Kipp, Jacobus S 334
Kirch, Johan Deisch S 105
Kirches, Paulus S 89
Kirchofen, Francis Ludwig S 81
Kirker, John S 314
Kirkland, Samuel T 26, 101, 272
Kirn, Beadus T 254
Kirn, George T 257
Kirtzenberg, Elizabetha S 145
Kiselback, Johan S 89
Kisner, William T 228, S 299
Kissam, Daniel S 329
Kister, Fredrig S 89
Kister, Palters S 89
Kistler, David S 129
Kistler, Eleanora Catharina S 129
Kittert, Mattys S 99

Kitts, Adam T 154, 306, S 303
Kitts, Conradt S 299
Kitts, Jacob S 357
Kitts, John S 220, S 222, S 351
Kitts, John, Jr. S 351
Kitts, Peter S 299
Kitts, Peter L. S 303
Klaar, Anna S 99
Klaas, Bartel S 99
Klaas, Johan S 95
Klaas, Peter S 89
Klaemer, Ludwig S 81
Klam, Daniel S 99
Klapp, Peter S 145
Klapper, Johan Willem S 99
Klapperin, Anna Agatha S 145
Klapsattle Major T 112
Klaser, Kitter S 89
Klaus, Bernhart S 99
Klause, Jacob S 303
Klause, John S 303
Klause, Peter S 303
Klobsatel, Andreas S 114
Klegs, Johan Gorg S 105
Klegs, Johan Henrig S 105
Klein, Adam S 129, S 145
Klein, Amalia S 117
Klein, Anna Catharina S 129
Klein, Anna Eva S 117
Klein, Anna Eliz. S 117
Klein, Anna Maria S 129
Klein, Anna Maria Clara S 129
Klein, Elisabeth S 129
Klein, Henrich S 145
Klein, Hinronimus S 117, S 129
Klein, Hyeronimus S 145
Klein, Jeronimus S 100
Klein, Johan S 105
Klein, Johan Willem S 95
Klein, Johann S 129
Klein, Johannes S 145
Klein, Johan Herman S 145
Klein, Johann Jacob S 145
Klein, John Jacob S 81
Klein, John S 81
Klein, Maria S 117, S 129
Klein, Maria Margretha S 129
Klein, Mattys S 100
Klein, Michael S 81
Klein, Michael S 81
Klein, Peeter S 100
Klein, Peter S 81, S 100
Klein, Philip S 95
Kleinin, Helena S 145
Kleinkor, Korn S 100
Kleins, Peter S 145
Kleisch, Kristoffel S 105
Klengs, Johan S 105
Kletters, Johan S 89, S 100
Kleus, Harler S 84
Kleus, Johannes S 84
Kleus, Margriet S 84
Kleyn, Adam S 113
Kleyn, Hans Willem S 89
Kleyn, Koenraet S 89
Kleyn, Lodewyk S 89
Kleyn, Ludwig S 89
Kleyn, Michael S 89
Kleyter, Hans Jurg S 89
Kleman, Pieter S 95
Klepper, Koenraet S 95
Kline, John S 351
Kline, Martin S 351

Kling, Ludwig S 347
Klinger, Nicolaes S 84
Klippingen, Johan Peter S 89
Kliuwe, Johs S 84
Klock's Church T 295, S 341
Klock, Abram T 305
Klock, Adam T 173, 257, 275, 276, 335, 336,
S 299
Klock, Adam (Lieut) T 342
Klock, Amos S 324
Klock, Barvalis T 168
Klock, Christian T 98, 335, S 303, S 317
Klock, Coenrad   T 173
Klock, Conrad T 305
Klock, Eva T 98, 335
Klock, Frederick S 317
Klock, George T 9, 73, 254, 335, S 303
Klock, George G. T 173, 257, 304, S 299,
S 303, S 317
Klock, George H. T 173
Klock, George I. S 308
Klock, George J. S 303
Klock, George Jo. S 303
Klock, George Jr S 317
Klock, Hendrick   T 168, 170, 257, 295, S 111
Klock, Hendrick I T 173
Klock, Hendrick J T 173, 257
Klock, Hendrick T 173, 302
Klock, Henery T 254
Klock, Henry S 299, S 324
Klock, Henry Sr T 173, 257
Klock, Honyost S 299
Klock, (Clock, Glock) Jacob (Colonel) T 9, 73, 98, 101, 109, 124, 154, 161, 160, 102, 100, 190, 191, 195, 201, 205, 213, 225, 228, 233, 236, 237, 245, 248, 254, 255, 295, 302, 317, 319, 321, 322, 325, 326, 332, 333, S 168, S 170, S 172, S 174, S 175, S 176, S 178, S 181, S 182, S 183, S 185, S 186, S 191, S 205, S 206, S 208, S 212, S 213, S 216, S 236, S 237, S 250, S 252, S 262, S 265, S 271, S 283
Klock, Jacob (Colonel) Will and last testament T 335, S 248
Klock, Jacob Conrad (Lieut) T 170, 233, 254, 265, 275, S 180, S 182, S 190, S 275
Klock, Jacob T 305, S 299
Klock, Jacob C. S 299
Klock, Jacob G. T 336, S 300, S 317
Klock, Jacob G. Jr S 312
Klock, Jacob I. S 300
Klock, Jacob H T 173, 257
Klock, Jacob I. S 311
Klock, Jacob Jas. T 327, 333
Klock, James S 322
Klock, Johann Henrich T 308
Klock, Johannes I (or Clock, Glock) T 294
Klock, John T 173, 257, 325, S 300
Klock, John G. S 308
Klock, John J. S 300 S 311

Klock, John J., Jr S 303
Klock, John K. Jr. S 318
Klock, Joseph T 257, 305, S 311
Klock, Joseph G. T 336
Klock, Joseph J. S 313
Klock, Jost T 173, 257
Klock, Levinus (Capt.) T 169
Klock, Rudolph (Capt)
Klock, Severinus (Capt) T 170, 255, S 160, S 161
Klock, William   T 235
Kloe, Barlin S 100
Kloosch, Simon S 95
Klop, Johan Nikel S 100
Klopper, Johan Willem S 100
Klos, Willem S 89
Kloter, Johan Paul S 89
Kloter, Paulus S 89
Klotter, Henrich S 145
Klotterin, Caspar S 145
Klotterin, Susanna S 145
Kloutt, Henrig S 84
Klug, George S 81
Klug, George S 81
Klug, Johann Georg S 129
Klug, Johannes S 129
Klug, Susanna S 129
Klumm, Anna Margretha S 129
Klumm, Johann Georg S 129, S 145
Klumm, Veronica S 129
Klumph, Thomas S 297
Klun, Jacob S 89
Klyn, Johan Palser S 89
Knab, Ludwig S 145
Knap, Aaron J. T 342
Knap, Abal T 342
Knap, Hans Nikel S 100
Knap, James T 342, S 303
Knap, Joel S 275
Knap, William T 173, 257
Knapp, Joseph T 342
Knapp, Joseph, Jr. S 275
Knapp, Moses S 334
Knauer, Sacharias S 95
Knaus, Hans Kristoffel S 89
Knausz, Johannes S 347
Knautz, John S 347
Knegt, Miggel S 89
Kneibin, Helene Sophia S 145
Kneskern, Hans Peter S 145
Kneskern, Johan Peter S 100, S 120
Knevel, Andries S 100
Knever, Paulua S 100
Knieskern, Fitter S 347
Knieskern, Peter S 111
Knieskern (Reverend) T 293
Kniestberg, Anna Maria S 129
Kniestberg, Elisabetha S 129
Kniestberg, Elisabetha Barbara S 129
Kniestberg, Johann Godtfrid S 129
Kniestberg, Johann Peter S 129
Kniffen S 334
Kniffen, Daniel S 334
Kniffen, John S 334
Kniffen, Jonathan S 334
Kniskern, Johannes S 296
Kniskern, William S 296
Knittle, Walter (Early Eighteenth Century Palatine Emigrations A

British Government Redemptioner Project to Manufacture Naval Stores. Book used as a reference)
Knouts Family & Henry T 95
Knouts, George S 347
Knox, Abraham S 275
Knox, George T 342
Knox, Henry General T 26
Knyker, Johan S 89
Knuppelberg, Paul S 105
Kobel, Anna Maria S 129
Kobel, Jacob S 120, S 129, S 145
Kobel, Johann Henrich S 129
Kober, Adam S 334
Koch, Anna Maria S 129
Koch, Beadus T 173, 257
Koch, Casparrus Jr. T 173, 257
Koch, Geo. Lud. S 120, S 145
Koch, Jan Joost S 114
Koch, Jost S 354
Koch, Peter S 303
Koch, Johannes T 308, 342
Koch, Johan S 105
Koch, John, 257
Koch, John (Lieut) T 170, 255
Koch, Jorg Ludwig S 129
Koch, (Kock), Rudolph Jr. (Capt.) T 169, 170, 255, 257
Kock, Jurgen S 297
Kock, Soferines S 297
Kock, Martin S 89
Kockerthal, Benigna S 56
Kockerthal, Benigna Sibilia S 129
Kockerthal, Susana Sibylia S 56
Kocherthal, Joshua (Reverend) T 308, S 35, 40, 54, 55, S 56, S 129, S 145
Kocherthal, Joshua S 129
Kocherthal, Susanna Sibylia S 129
Kockerthal, Sibylia S 56
Kocherthal, Sibylia Charlotte S 129
Kock (Cook), Casper T 308
Koeman, Bastiaen S 89
Koemer, Johannes S 347
Koen, Dinges S 100
Koeningh, Michael S 296
Koenraet, Hans S 100
Koenraet, Johan S 95
Koert, Michel S 100
Koen, Hans Veldekoen S 85
Koen, Hans Deterkoen S 85
Koen, Hans Jurgekeon S 85
Koen, Koenrate S 85
Koen, Mattheus S 85
Koening, Johannes S 157
Koenraed, Johan Anders S 105
Koenraed, Salmon S 105
Koenraet and wife S 89
Koenraet, Anna Katrina S 85
Koenraet, John Joris S 85
Koenraet, Kristoffel S 89
Koenraet, Mattys S 89
Koenraet, Martyn S 85
Koenraet, Nicolaes S 89
Koening, John Adam S 81
Koerner, Anna Magdalena S 129
Koerner, Catharina Elisabetha S 129
Koerner, Johann Adam S 129
Koerner, Johann Niclaus S 129

Kruitsch, Johan S 95
Krum, Johan Herman S 100
Krymaiser, Jacob S 90
Krys, Mattys S 100
Kueffer, John S 81
Kuester, Anna Maria S 129
Kuester, Johann Wilhelm S 129
Kuester, Johann Balthasar S 129
Kuester, Susanna S 129
Kuester, Wilhelm S 129
Kufe, Jolianes S 358
Kugel, Anna Margretha S 129
Kugel, Johann S 129
Kugel, Johannes S 145
Kuhl, Philip T 173, 257
Kuhlman, Catharina S 130
Kuhlman, Johann S 130
Kuhlmann, Georg S 145
Kuhlmer, Johannes S 145
Kuhlwein, Philip S 81
Kuhn, Anna Catharina S 130
Kuhn, Conrad S 120, S 145
Kuhn, Jacob S 119
Kuhn, Johanna Elisabeth S 130
Kuhm, Johann Jacob S 145
Kuhn, Margretha S 130
Kuhn, Samuel S 120, S 145
Kuhn, Valentine S 145
Kuhn, Valtin S 120, S 130, S 145
Kuhner, Anna Felice S 117
Kuhner, Benedictus S 117
Kuhner, Eva Barbara S 117
Kuhner, Jacob A. S 117
Kuhner, Jacob S 81, S 117
Kuiber, Daniel S 85
Kulen, Peter S 95
Kulk, Johan Peter S 90
Kulman, Henry S 359
Kurn, Carl T 173
Kum, Hans Jacob S 105
Kum, Philippus S 100
Kurne, Charley T 173, 257
Kumel, Peter S 90
Kumenstein, Johan Nikel S 100
Kuminer Hans Peter S 90
Kummer, Hans Peter S 90
Kumpff, Johan Peeter S 105
Kun, Elisabetha S 130
Kun, Herman S 95
Kum, Philippus S 100
Kunen, Nicolaes S 90
Kunteman, Kasper S 90
Kuntz, Jacob 1st S 145
Kuntz, Jacob 2nd S 145
Kuntz, Johannes S 145
Kuntz, Koenraet S 100
Kuntz, Margretha S 130
Kuntz, Mathias S 145
Kuntz, Mattheus S 119, S 145
Kunz, Johann Wilhelm S 130
Kuran, Michael S 354
Kurby, Michel S 85
Kurger, Henrig S 90
Kurts, Hans Jurg S 95
Kurts, Johan Kristoffel S 105
Kurtz, Johan Christop S 145
Kurtz, Lorentz Henrich S 130
Kurtz, Maria Margretha S 130
Kurtz, Margretha S 130
Kuseteler, Hendrig S 90
Kuster, Catharina Susanna 129
Kyler, Nichlas S 354

Kyser, (Capt) T 183
Kyser, Hanyost T 173, 257
Kyser, Hendrick T 173, 257
Kyser, Johan S 120
Kyser, Michael T 173, 257
Laam, Frans S 90
Lab, Georg S 100
Labach, Johannes S 145
Labag, Adam S 100
Labdon, Daniel T 173, 257, S 300
Lacess, Samul S 351
Ladaw, Jacob S 303
Ladde, Johannes S 357
Ladue, Jacob S 312
Ladue, John S 312
Lafayette (General) T 69, 127, 284
LaForge, John Wm. S 81
LaFransche, Entike S 130
LaFransche, Johann S 130
Lahmeyer, Johannes S 145
Laib, Johann Caspar S 145
Laight, Edward S 329, S 334
Laight, William S 329
Lake, Abraham S 334
Lake Champlain T 149
Lake, I. S 334
Lake, N. Jr. S 334
Laile, John S 286
Lamain, Frants S 105
Lamareaux, John S 275
Lamb, (Colonel) S 195, S 196, S 228, S 269
Lamb, James S 329, S 334
Lamb, William S 275
Lamber, Anna Elisabetha S 130
Lamberdson, Lambert S 275
Lambert, George T 65, S 347
Lambert, Johannes S 130
Lambert, Jonathan S 275
Lambert, Peter T 173, S 347
Lambert, Peter Jr. S 347
Lambert, Peter, Sr. S 347
Lambertin, Elizabetha S 145
Lambet, Peter S 297
Lambreg, Hans Jurg S 90
Lamert, Johann S 130
Lamet, Johannes S 145
Lamoth, Johan Daniel S 90
Lamperson, Cornelius S 300
Lampert, Peter S 347
Lampertin, Elizabeth S 118
Lampertin, Frantz Adam S 118
Lampfor, Peter S 297
Lampford, Peter T 173, 257
Lampford, Peter, Sr. S 358
Lampford, Peter, Jr. S 358
Lampman, Henry T 173, 342
Lampman, Peter T 173, 257, 342
Lampman, Peter (Corporal) T 170
Lampman, Peter Jr S 303, S 311
Lampmann, Peter S 145
Lancker, Johannes S 145
Land, Andanig S 90
Land, Anna Margretha 130
Landes, Peter T 254
Landgraff, Georg S 145
Landgrast Jerg S 130
Landgrast, Jerg S 130
Landman's Battle S 175
Landmann, Peter S 130

Landolt, Samuel S 95
Lane, Daniel T 319, S 351
Lane, Jacob S 351
Lane, Peter S 334
Lang, Abrm. S 100, S 130
Lang, Barbera S 85
Lang, Catharina S 85
Lang, Christaen S 112
Lang, Eles S 90
Lang, Hans Wolf S 95
Lang, Jacob S 85
Lang, Johan S 81, S 100
Lang, John S 334
Lang, Johannes S 85
Lang, Kristiaen, S 90
Lang, Mortis S 95
Lang, Peter S 85, S 90
Lang, Philip S 81
Lang, Robert (Qr. Mr.) T 342, S 275
Langbrin, Kristoffel S 85
Langdon, Thomas S 334
Langen, Abraham S 120
Langer, Abraham S 112
Langer, Abraham S 145
Langevelt, Hend. S 100
Langler, James S 275
Langry, Abraham S 130
Langry, Maria Catharina S 130
Langin, Magdalena S 145
Laning, Jacob T 254
Lank, Peter S 100
Lank, Hans Philip S 90
Lankr (?) Felten S 100
Lanks, Henry A. T 173
Lanks, Henry A., Jr. T 173
Lannen, Rechert S 351
Lansing, Abraham S 297
Lansing, Garret (Captain)
Lansing, Garret J. S 296
Lansing, Gerret A. S 297
Lansing, Isaac H. S 297
Lansing, Isaac N. S 296
Lansing, Jacob G. S 320
Lansing, Lander S 321
Lansing, Sander S 303
Lansingh, Jan S 110
Lansingh, John G. Jr. (Adjutant) S 349
Lant, Anna Catherine S 360
Lant, Philippus S 90
Lantin, Anna Catharina S 145
Lantman, Henderick S 334
Lantman, Peter T 254
Lantman, Peter Jr. T 254
Lantz S 354
Lape, Adam, (Captain) T 201
Lape, John S 347
Laper, Yari S 168
Lapius, Daniel T 173
Lapp, Daniel S 356
Lapper, Jacob T 342
Lapper, John S 351
Lappin, Agnes S 145
Lappius, Daniel S 347
Lard, William (Lieut) S 349
Lards, William S 334
Lasher, Coenradt S 306
Lasher, Conrod J. S 303
Lasher, Garrit T 173, 257, S 300, S 303
Lasher, Gavoet T 173, 257
Lasher, George S 303, S 309

Lasher, Gerrit S 306
Lasher, Gerrit Jr S 320
Lasher, Henry S 306
Lasher, John T 173, 257, S 303, S 309
Lasher, John Jr S 303, S 309
Lashle, Alexander S 334
Lassing, Isaac S 334
Lassing, Isaac I. S 334
Lassing, Isaac P. S 334
Lassing, Johannes A. S 334
Lassing, Johannes E. S 334
Lassing, Johannes L. S 334
Lassing, Johannis Det. S 334
Lassing, Johannis Wm S 334
Lassing, John P. S 334
Lassing, John Peter Wm. S 334
Lassing, Laurence L. S 334
Lassing Peter Johannis S 334
Lassing, Peter John S 334
Lassing, Peter P. S 334
Last, Anna S 130
Last, Anna Dorothea S 130
Last, Johann Georg S 130
Last, Johann Just S 130
Lastner, Johann Peter S 130
Lastner, Juliana Elisabetha S 130
Lastner, Magdalena S 130
Lathrop, Gorton S 310
Lattimore, Francis S 275
Lauber, Jacob S 81
Lauche, Dietrich T 308
Lauchs, Adam T 308
Lauchs, Henrich T 308
Lauchs, Wilhelm T 308
Lauck, Abraham S 130, S 145
Lauck, Anna Christina S 130
Lauck, Catharina S 130
Lauck, Elisabetha S 130
Lauck, Jacob S 130
Lauck, Johan Jacob S 145
Lauck, Maria Catharina S 130
Laucks, Adam T 173, 257
Laucks, Adam A T 173, 257
Laucks, George T 173, 257, S 275
Laucks, Henry W. T 173, 257
Laucks, Jacob T 173, 257
Laucks, Johann Niclaus S 146
Laucks, John T 173, 257
Laucks, Peter T 254, 257
Laucks, Piter T 173
Laucks, William T 173, 257
Laue, Johan Peter S 105
Lauer, Johann Mettheus S 130
Lauking, Anna Elizabeth S 118
Laurman, Eva S 90
Launert, Anna Catharina S 130
Launert, Anna Margretha S 130
Launert, Jerg S 130
Launert, HohannGeorg S 130
Launert, Philipp S 130
Launtman, Peter S 300
Laur, Arnold S 130
Laur, Maria Agnes S 130
Laurence, Caleb S 273
Laurens, Anna Margreta S 85
Laurens, Anna Rosina S 85
Laurens, Diderig S 95
Laurens, Maria Margreta S 85
Laurens, Mattys S 90
Laurens, Peter S 85
Laus, Philip S 120

Lautman, Peter S 112
Lauv, Johan S 95
Laux, Anna Elisabetha S 130
Laux, Conrad T 173, 257
Laux, Dietrick T 173, 257, S 130, S 146
Laux, Georg S 146
Laux, Hendrick T 173, 257
Laux, Jacob T 173, 257
Laux, Johann Adam S 130
Laux, Johann Dietrich S 130, S 146
Laux, Johann Just S 130
Laux, Johann Peter S 130
Laux, Philipp S 146
Laux, Johan Jost S 146
Laux, Johann Philipp S 146
Laux, Johann Wilhelm S 130
Laux, Johannes S 146
Laux, Maria Elisabetha S 130
Laux, Maria Margretha S 130
Laux, Niclaus S 130
Laux, Niclaus S 120
Laux, Peter T 173, 257
Laver, Conrad T 173
Laver, Conrath T 257
Lavish, John (Ensign) (Md) S 275
LaVore, Johan S 95
Lawer, Conrath T 257
Lawer, Peter S 146
Lawis, David S 351
Lawler, Conrad S 275
Lawler, John S 275
Lawrence (Engisn) S 357
Lawrence, Caleb (Captain) S 275
Lawrence, Effingham, (Captain) S 329
Lawrence, John S 303, S 315, S 329, S 334
Lawrence, Nathaniel (Lieut) (N.C.) S 275
Lawrence, Peter S 210
Lawrence, Stephen S 334
Lawrence, William (Dr) S 334
Lawson, Jotham S 334
Lawyer, Conrad T 173
Lawyer, Joacob S 296
Lawyer, Johannis S 296
Lawyer Lorence S 296
Lay, Asa (Lieut) (Conn) S 275
Lay, Lee, (Captain) (Conn) S 275
Layman, John S 300, S 303
Layper, Johan S 90
Leake, John S 329
Leake, Robert S 329, S 334
Leake, Thomas S 329, S 334
Leaman, John S 311
Leampetin, Erhard S 118
Leaning, Jacob T 173, 257
Leaper, Wyont S 300
Leasher, Garnet T 173, 257
Leather, Christian S 218, S 358
Leather, Christian L. T 173, 257
Leather, Johanes S 358
Leather, John T 173, 257
Leathers, Ezekiel S 358
Leavere, Jacob S 309
Leber, Willem S 100
Lecobs, (or Lecolis), Peter S 90
Ledder, Christian T 173, 257
Ledder, John T 173
Le Dee, John S 81
Lederer, Christian T 254

Lederer, John T 254, 257
Lederer, John Jr T 254
Lee, Abijah S 303, S 313
Lee, Harry Lighthorse (General) T 55
Lee, John T 342
Lee, Marvil T 342
Lee, Misper S 334
Lee, William S 300
Lee, William Jr. S 300
Leeber, Sylvanus T 186
Leek, David S 313
Leek, Johannis S 112
Leenhart, Hans Peter S 90
Leenhart, Johan S 95
Leets, David S 351
Leer, Anna Margretha S 130
Leer, Frederick Willem S 113
Leer, Johann S 130
Leer, Johannes S 130
Leer, Ottilia Helena S 130
Leer, Sibylia Catharina S 130
Leeve, Philip S 347
LeFevre, Abram S 81
Leffler, John (Capt) T 182, 185, 192, 193, S 198
Legeng, Jacob S 303
Leggett, Abraham (Ensign) S 275
Lehemann, Wilhelm S 146
Lehman, Maria S 130
Lehman, Wilhelm S 130
Lehmann, Anna Elisabeth S 130
Lehmann, Anna Margretha S 130
Lehmann, Clemens S 130
Lehmann, Johann Wilhelm S 130
Lehr, Johannes S 146
Lei, Hans Henrig S 100
Leib, Johan S 95
Leibrngut, John Wendell S 81
Leicht, Anna Eliz. S 118
Leicht, Anna Margatta S 118
Leicht, George Ludwig S 118
Leicht, Johan Henrich S 118, S 130
Leich, Elisabeth S 130
Leich, Georg Ludwig S 130
Leicht, Henrich S 146
Leich, Johann Eberhard S 130
Leich, Ludwig S 130, S 146
Leich, Maria Martha S 118
Leich, Philip S 130
Leick, Anna Catharina S 130
Leick, Johann S 130
Leick, Johannes S 146
Leick, Maria Barbara S 130
Leidecker, Henderick S 100
Leig, Simon S 95
Leight, Edward (Captain) S 329
Leight, W. S 329
Lein, Abraham S 118
Lein, Anna Maria S 118
Lein, Conrad S 118, S 130, S 146
Lein, Johann Peter S 130
Lein, Juliana S 118
Lein, Margretha S 118, S 130
Lein, Maria Marga S 118
Leinweber, Johan S 90
Leip, **am S 303
Leipe, John L. S 347
Leir, ***phus S 303
Leiser, Anna Castiaens S 85
Leiser, Anna Lys S 85
Leiser, Anna Margraet S 85

Leiser, Castiaen S 85
Leiser, Hans Jurig S 85
Leiser, Johan Jacob S 85
Leithal, Abraham S 354
Leitner, Johan Adam S 100
Leitz, Johannes S 130
Leitz, Maria Barbara S 130
Lelly, Toyn T 173, 257
Leman, Anna Maria S 130
Leman, Gertrud S 130
Leman, Maria Eva S 130
Leman, Willem S 130
Lemptinck, John T 342
Lenardson, James S 351
Lenardson, John S 351
Lenardson,Timothy S 351, S 357
Lenarker, Peter S 95
Lenckin, Maria Catharina S 146
Lenenbaig, Stoffel S 95
Lenhard, Eva Catharina S 118
Lenhard, Johan S 118
Lenhart, Hans S 85
Lenken Jan Willem S 100
Lennes, William S 351
Lent, Abraham S 334
Lent, Adolph S 334
Lent, Hercules S 334
Lent, Isaac S 275, S 334
Lent, John S 334
Lent, Peter S 334
Lenter, Jacob T 173
Lentz, Jacob T 173, 257
Lepper, Philipp Hermann S 146
Lepus, Mattys S 90
Lent, Abraham S 329
Lent, Adolph S 329
Lent, Hendrick T 342
Lent, Peter S 329
Lentman, John S 334
Lentner, George S 347
Lents, Henrig S 105
Lents, Willem S 105
Lentz, Jacob S 354
Lentz, John S 354
Lentz, John Jr. S 354
Lentz, Peter S 354
Leonard, James 329, S 334
Leonard, George S
Leonard, James S 329
Leonard, John S 329
Lepert, Fredrick S 347
Lephard, John T 173, 257
Lepper, Conradt S 303, S 305
Lepper, Frederick T 173, 257, S 358
Lepper, Jacob T 173
Lepper, Wiand T 173, T 257
Lerck, Henrich S 130
Lepper, Philippus Herman S 100
Lepper (Lebern) Savina S 237
Leppter, Maria Sophia T 253
Lerck, Wilhelm S 130
Lergerseiler, Johan Willem S 100
Lerhry, Johann Casper T 342
Lerner, Mattys S 95
LeRoy, Francis S 334
Lersas, Hans Philips S 90
Lesch, Balthasar S 146
Lesch, Burchent S 95
Lesch, Johann Adam S 130
Lesch, Johan Henrig S 90
Lescher Bastian S 130
Leschemis, Jeremias S 90

Lescherin, Magdalena S 146
Leschner, Michel S 95
Leschr, Gerred T 173, 257
Lesering, Antony S 100
Lesher, Garrit Jr S 300
Lesher, John T 173, 257, S 300
Lesit, John S 313
Leslie, Alexander S 334
Lesorin, Magdalena S 90
Lesser, Kristoffel S 90
Lessinger, Nichs T 173
Lester, Cornelius S 334
Lester, John S 334
Lester, Mordiccai S 334
Leuben, Peter S 105
Leucht, Lewis S 81
Leutken, Daniel S 131
Leuven, Mary Katryn S 100
Level, Johan Koenraet S 100
Lever, John S 351
Levey, Michael S 347
Levy, Michael T 342
Lew, Dolphus S 319
Lewis, Adam S 297, S 351
Lewis, Benjamin S 329, S 334
Lewis, David S 297
Lewis, David, Jr. S 351
Lewis, Frederick S 297, S 351
Lewis, Hendrick S 297
Lewis, Henry S 210
Lewis, Henry (Ensign) S 349
Lewis, Jabez S 342
Lewis, John (Sergeant) S 275, S 351
Lewis, J. S 334
Lewis, John T 155, S 334
Lewis, Morgan (Colonel) T 150, 159, 184
Lewis, Peter S 297
Lewis, Samuel (Conn) S 275
Lewis, Thornas S 334
Lewis, William S 351
Lewizell, Nicholas T 342
Leyd, Richard S 351
Leyer, Johan S 119
Leyer, Johannes S 146
Leyger, Koenraet S 105
Leyli, Simon S 347
Leyp, Adam (Captain) S 345
Leypert, Jacob S 351
Leyn, Eberhart Hieronimus S 105
Libern, Ludwig S 90
Liberty Pole T 100, 222
Liboscha, Maria Johana S 55, S 130
Liboscha Susanna S 130
Lichtnegger, Gottlob August S 81
Lick, David S 303
Lickard, Bernhard S 118, S 146
Lickard, Justina S 118
Licks, Willem Bernhart S 100
Liddle, (Captain) T 234
Liddel, John S 351
Lieb, Johan Casper T 236
Lieger, Johan Adam S 100
Liepe, Hans Casper S 113
Liesen, Anna Eva S 95
Liespel, Maria S 90
Liewry, Jacob S 358
Lighthouse, Harry Lee (General)
Lightfoot T 103
Lighthal, Nicholas S 354
Lighthall, Frences

Lighthall, Francis S 303, S 311
Lighthall, George T 173, S 354
Lighthall _____ T 173
Lilly, John T 173
Linch, Jno. Wm. S 120
Linck, Anna Eva S 130
Linck, Anna Gerdraut S 130
Linck, Wilhelm S 130
Linck, Martin S 95
Linck, Willem S 113
Lincken, Johan Wilhelm S 146
Lincoln, Benjamin (General) T 51
Lincompetter, Mighael S 351
Lind, Gerhard S 105
Linenbaug, Peter S 95
Lines, Michael T 342
Lingau, James McCubbin (Lieut) (Va) S 275
Lingelbach, Baltes S 100
Lingoret, Bernhart S 100
Link, John S 351
Linn, Thomas S 272
Linox, John S 351
Linsin, Apolonia S 146
Lint, Georg S 347
Lintner, George T 94
Lints, Gorg S 347
Lintz, John T 342
Lintzin, Anna Catha. S 118
Lintzin, Anna Eva S 118
Lintzin, Anna Margt. S 118
Lintzin, Apollonia S 118
Lipe, Adam (Captain) S 159, S 161, S 166
Lipe, Adam (Lieut) S 356
Lipe, Adam Jr. S 305
Lipe, Abram T 243
Lipe, Johannes S 286
Lipe, John S 286, S 347, S 356
Lipe, John Jr. S 347
Lipe, Reuben S 283
Lippert, Johan Walter S 90
Lisemus, Anna Maria S 130
Lispenaer, Abigail S 130
Listaboris, Lucas S 85
Listenius, Anna Maria S 130
Listenius, Bernhard S 130
Listenius Christianus S 130
Listenus, Anna Barbara S 130
Litchart, John Jr S 334
Lithall, Abraham S 354
Litig, Hand Jagol S 85
Litig, Hans Koenraet S 85
Litig, Jacob S 85
Litig, Kristoffel S 85
Littel, John (Captain) T 156, 342, S 349
Little, Francis T 173
Lively, Simon S 297
Livingston, (Levingston) James (Colonel) S 218, S 237
Livingston, John S 334
Livingston, Robert S 42
Livingston, William T 73
Livingston, William S. (Lieut Col. Cont'l Army) S 275
Lloyd, Henry S 329, S 342
Lloyd, William (Sergeant) T 204
Llump, Thomas S 358
Lobdell, Daniel T 173
Lobdell, Isaac T 173
Lobdell, Joseph T 254, S 275

Locharty, John T 342
Lochrugs, Ulrig S 100
Locks, Hans Nikel S 100
Lockwood, James S 303, S 312
Lockwood, Peter S 334
Lockwood, Moses T 342
Lockwood, Solomon S 334
Lodawich, Casper S 303
Lodawick, Peter S 303
Lodewyk, Antony S 95
Lodewyk, Henrik S 100
Lodiwich, Abraham S 303
Lodweick, Jasper Jr S 314
Lodwick, Casper S 310
Lodwick, Hendrick S 112
Lodwick, Henry S 310
Lodwick, Johan Pieter S 113
Lodwig, Antony S 85
Loedolf, Johannes S 85
Loedolf, Koenrad S 85
Loehn, Anna Margretha S 130
Loehn, Johann S 130
Loeshaar, Jacob S 130
Loeshaar, Maria Elisabetha S 130
Loeshaar, Sebastian S 130
Loscher, Sebastian S 146
Loet, Balthazer S 85
Loet, Hans Peter S 85
Logan, David S 334
Logan, Samuel (Major Cont'l
Army) S 275
Logrugs, Mattys S 100
Lohin, Anna Catharina S 146
Lohrentz, Alexander S 118
Lohrentz, Anna Barbara S 118
Lohrentz, Anna Margaretta S 118
Lohrentz, Johannes S 118
Lohrentz, Magdalena S 118
Loiner, Abigail S 130
Loiner, Robert S 131
Loiner, William S 131
Loines, Henry S 334
Loltkill, (Lieutenant) S 202
Lonas, John S 275
Long, David S 329, S 334
Long, Hendrick T 173, 257
Longman, Peter S 303
Loockstad, Elisabetha S 131
Loockstad, Georg S 131
Loockstad, Georgius S 131
Loomis, Ashabel S 212
Loost, Andries S 105
Lorentz, Alexander S 131
Lorentz, Anna Margretha S 131
Lorentz, Henrich S 131
Lorentz, Johannes S 131
Lorway, J., Dr. S 334
Los, Johan Adam S 90
Losch, Elisabetha S 131
Losch, Mattys S 100
Loscher, Conrad S 131
Loscher, Johann Bastian S 131
Loscher, Johann Georg S 131
Losee, George S 334
Lossee, Abraham S 334
Lossing, Benson J The Pictorial
Field-Book of The Revolution is
one of the references used in
both books.
Losting, Andreas S 131
Losting, Cornelia S 131
Losting, Peter S 131
Lots, Johan S 90

Lott, Johs S 85, S 334
Lotterage, Robert S 334
Lou, Johan Michel S 90
Louck, Abraham S 131
Louck, Hans Michel S 100
Louck, Johan S 100
Loucks, George S 184, S 334
Loucks, Johan Hendrick S 111
Loucks, Mary S 184
Loucks, Peter S 275
Loucks, Philip S 112
Loundert, Jurich S 113
Lotterage, Robert
Lou, William T 257
Loucks, Abraham S 112
Loucks, Adam T 210, 308, S 307
Loucks, Adam Justice
Loucks, Anna Margaret
Loucks, Catherine Elizabeth
Loucks, Diedrich S 113
Loucks, Elisabeth T 227
Loucks, Henry T 173, 257, S 297
Loucks, Jacob S 307
Loucks, Mary S 184
Loucks, John S 155
Loucks, Peter S 347
Loucks, Peter (Lieut) T 170, 188,
201
Loucks, Richard S 307
Loucks, William T 173, 257, S
184
Lough, John T 243
Louis, (Colonel) 150
Louks, Adam S 300
Louks, George S 300
Loucks, Henry S 300
Louks, Henry A. S 300
Louks, Jacob S 300
Louks, Joseph S 300
Louks, Peter S 300
Louks, Peter H. S 300
Louks, Wendell S 300
Louks, William T 227, 342
Lounsberry, Henry S 334
Lounsberry, William S 329, S 334
Loup, William S 297
Lourens and wife S 90
Lourens, Anna Lys S 85
Lourens, Anna Margriet S 85
Lourens, Johannes S 85
Lourens, Msgadelena S 85
Lout, Henrig S 90
Loux, Adam T 173, 257
Loux, Frederick S 303
Loux, George T 254, S 303, S
358
Loux, Hendrick T 308
Loux, Jacob T 173, 257, S 303
Lous, Jost S 347
Loux, Kirk T 307
Lous, Niclaus S 44
Loux, William T 173
Louz, Derick T 173
Lovelace, John S 303
Lovelefs, Asaram S 313
Lovelefs, Elisha S 318
Lovelefs, James S 313
Lovelefs, John S 318
Loveless, Ezrom S 303
Loveless, Joseph S 303
Low, Isaac S 329
Low, Jacob S 334
Low, John S 329, S 334

Low, Lawrence Gras S 347
Low, Samuel S 300
Lowen, Counread T 173
Lower, Conradt T 173, S 300
Lower, John T 173
Loyde, Daniel S 351
Luber, Gabriel S 100
Ludt, Castman S 95
Lucas, Francis S 81
Lucas, William T 342
Luce, Marvil T 342
Luck, Anonius S 105
Lucka, Maria Elisabetha S 131
Luckhard, Bernhard S 131
Lucas, Anna Catharina S 118
Lucas, Anna Maria S 118
Lucas, Anne S 118
Lucas, Frantz S 118
Lucas, Francois S 146
Lucas, Georg S 146
Lucas, William Budd S 275
Lucis, Maria Eliz. S 118
Ludlow, James S 334
Ludlow, Gabrial G. S 329
Ludlow, George D. S 329
Ludwig, Andreas S 100
Ludwig, Johan S 100
Ludwig, Johan Henrig S 95, S
146
Ludwig, Mattys S 100
Ludwig, Susanna Catharina S 131
Lueckhard, Bernhard S 131
Lueckhard, Johann Bernhard S
131
Lueckhard, Johann Daniel S 131
Lueckhard, Johann Peter S 131
Lueckhard, Johann Wilhelm S 131
Lueckhard, Johannes S 131
Lueckhard, Justina S 131
Lued, Johan Leonard S 131
Lukas, Hans Gorg S 100
Luke, Jacob S 296
Luke, James S 275
Luke, (Mrs.) S 334
Lumberton Sergeant T 69
Lumis, Adam S 275
Lun, Elisabetha S 131
Lun, Marcus S 131
Lun, Samuel S 131
Lup, Henry S 81
Lupo, Ruth V. Waymarks in
Nelliston NY used as a reference.
Lure, Philip S 347
Lurzdemann, Simon S 347
Lusa, Maria S 85
Lush, (Lusk) Richard T 184,
186, S 320
Lush, (Lusk) Stephen (Major) S
275, S 320
Luth, Hans Jacob S 90
Lutig, Johan S 85
Luts, Hans Adam S 85
Luts, Jan Jurig S 85
Luts, Johan S 95
Lutt, Anna Catharina S 131
Lutt, Barthas S 131
Lutt, Johann Balthas S 131
Luttig, Kristiaan S 85
Lutz, Anna Magdalena S 131
Lutz, Johann Christoph S 131
Lutz, George T 173, 257
Lutz, Hans S 95
Lutz, Jerog S 90

Lutz, Peter T 308, S 90, S 100
Lutzin, Anna Barbara S 146
Lutzin, Magdalena S 146
Luur, Kornelus S 85
Luur, Johan S 85
Luwy, Hans Nickel S 95
Luys, Mattys S 95
Lybok, Reinhart S 90
Lydyus, Geertry Isabella S 113
Lydyus, Maria Adrianata S 113
Lygert, William H T 173
Lyke, John, Sr. T 173, 257
Lyng John B. S 334
Lyning, Jacob S 300
Lyon, Banjamin S 303, S 311
Lyon, Gilbert (Captain) S 276
Lyon, Gilbert S 334
Lyon, Henry S 334
Lyon, John S 276
Lyon, Joseph S 334
Lyon, Samuel S 276
Lyon, Shubal S 334
Lyon, Thomas (Lieut) T 342
Lyons, Michael T 342
Lyman, George,(Captain) (Conn) S 276
Lys, Katryn S 100
Lysbet, Anna S 100
Lythaal, Niclas S 297
Maartsen, Anna Katrina S 85
Maartsen, Hans Jurig S 85
Maartsen, Mary S 85
Maartsen, Magdeleena S 85
Mabbett, Joseph S. S 329, S 334
Mabbett, Samuel S 329, S 334
Mabee, Cobus T 305
Mabee, Harmanus (Captain) S 220, S 222
Mabee, Peter S 351
Mabee, Petrus S 297
Mabie S 334
Mabie, Cornelius S 283, S 329, S 334
Mabie, Cornelius P. S 329
Mabie, Harmanus S 297
Mabie, Harmanus (Captain) S 349
Mabie, Jacob S 334
Mabie, Jeremiah S 334
Mabie, Lewis S 329, S 334
Mabie, Peter S 334
Mabie, Silas S 334
Mabie, Simon S 334
Machtig, Jacob S 81
Macknod, James   T 173
Macnod, Jeams S 354
Macomb, John S 329
MacWethy, Lou D. T 148
Madders S 334
Madebachin, Elnora S 146
Madelaer, Michel S 90
Madison, Corporal
Madison, James T 179
Maemig, Ferdinand S 131
Maemig, Maria Eliosabetha S 131
Maes, Johan Philip S 90
Maester, Paulus S 100
Maerten, Barbera S 85
Maerten, Johann Conrad S 131
Maerten, Johann Fridrich S 131
Maerten, Johann Henrich S 131
Maerten, Katharina S 85
Maerten, Maria S 131

Maerten, Maria Elisabeth S 131
Maerten, Matthys S 85
Maeyer, Just Tomas S 90
Mag, Johan Jurg S 95
Magdleena (Wede.) S 100
Mager, Nicolaes S 90
Mai, Henrich S 347
Maier, Andries S 90
Maier, Hans Adam S 95
Maisinger, Conrad S 120, S 146
Maisinger, Niclaus S 146
Maisinger, Sebastian S 146
Mackly, Felix S 358
Maller, Bastiaen S 90
Malloy, Thomas S 276
Maltsberger, Philippus S 90
Mambt,Willem S 351
Man, Herman S 100
Manck, Anna Veronica S 131
Manck, Eva Catharina S 131
Manck, Jacob S 146
Manck, Maria Elisabeth S 131
Mancken, Anna Veronica S 131
Mancken, Jacob S 131
Mandenagt, Willem S 100
Manderback, John S 354
Mangel, Johan Jurg S 100
Manges, Johann S 131
Mangreet, Anna S 100
Manhart, Philip S 334
Manheim T 41, 305
Manley, John (Reverend) T 306
Mann, Henrich S 131, S 146
Mann, I. S 334
Mann, Johann Henrich S 131
Mann, Johann Peter S 131
Mann, Maria Elisabetha S 131
Mann, Peter S 296
Manness, Hugh M. S 351
Mannich, Maria Elisabetha S 131
Mansbell, Kasper S 95
Mapes, Joseph S 334
Marbeltown T 221
Marbury, Luke (Colonel) (Md) S 276
March, John T 336, S 312
March, Peter T 336
March, Henry T 336
March, Stephen T 173, 257, S 303
Marea Eve S 90
Margreet, Anna S 105
Margriet, Anna S 90
Maria, Anna S 90, S 100
Maria, Anna (Wede.) S 100
Mariat, MichAel S 351
Mariatt, Abraham S 351
Mariatte, Gideon S 351
Mariatte, John S 351
Mariatte, Thomas S 351
Marines and wife S 85
Maring T 226
Marinus, Abraham T 173, 257
Marinus, William T 342
Marks, (Mr.) S 297
Marks, George T 161
Markel, John T 305
Markell, Jacob T 305
Markell, John and Anna Eva Zimmerman T 163
Markell, John W. S 319
Markell, John T 306
Marker, Hugh S 334

Markie, Dirk T 173
Markill, William T 342
Markle, Joseph S 334
Marlatt, Mark S 297, S 357
Marlin, Daniel (Captain) S 276
Marks, Joseph S 90
Markwart, Johannis S 334
Marlatt, Gideon (Adjutant) S 349
Marlett, Gideon (Ensign) S 349
Marlatt, John T 317, 333
Marlon, Francis T 55
Marman, Hans Joost S 90
Marr, James S 297
Marrener,William S 276
Marseles, John S 357
Marsellas, H S 334
Marselis, Isaac (Captain) S 349
Marselis, Nicholas (Captain) T 223, S 238
Marsh, (Captain) T 173
Marsh, Stephen S 300
Marshall, (Commissar General) S 258
Marshall, Elihu (Captain)
Marshall, Mead T 342
Marsielles, Gerrit S 303
Marsielus, Saunder S 300
Marstall, Kristoffel S 90
Marsteller, Henrig S 90
Marten, Robert S 347
Martenstock, Albrecht S 131, S 146
Martenstock, Albrecht Dietrich S 131
Martenstock, Daniel S 131
Martenstock, Elisabetha S 131
Martenstock, Johanna Maria Sophia S 131
Martenstock, Maria Christina S 131
Marstil, Kirstoffel S 90
Marten, Adam S 90
Marten, Alexander T 257, S 303
Marten, Stoffel S 90
Martheys, Hendrig S 90
Martian, Philip T 342
Martin, Agrippa S 334
Martin, Alexander T 173
Martin, Conrad S 131
Martin, Daniel (Captain) S 276
Martin Maria S 131
Martin, John S 276, S 309, S 334
Martin, John W. S 351
Martin, Joseph (Lieut) (Penn) S 276
Martin, Nicholas S 90
Martin, Peter S 95
Martin, Peter M. S 351
Martin, Philip T 173, 257, 342, S 351
Martin, Sander S 306
Martin, William (Lieut) S 276
Martin, Walter S 334
Martin, Veeder S 300
Martine, William T 342
Martins, Gertrud S 81
Martling, Daniel (Captain) S 276
Martling, David S 276
Martling, Isaac T 342
Martman, Ludwig S 100
Martyn, Thoms S 85
Marvin, Ephraim (Adjt) S 276
Marvin, Maria Magdalena S 146

Mary, Anna S 100
Masge, Niklaas S 100
Mashel, John S 351
Mason, Jacob S 351
Mason, Jeremiah S 218, S 357
Mason, John S 351
Mason, Niclas S 81
Mason, Thomas T 342
Maston, Eperim T 342
Mathais, Geo. S 119
Matheese, Johan Niclaas T 252
Mathell, Willem S 85
Mathesin, Ann S 146
Matheson, James S 334
Mathers, James T 342
Matheus, Henrich S 146
Mathous, Henr. S 119
Mathys, Jury S 113
Matin, Peter S 300
Matlock, Daniel T 342
Matrass, Isaac S 334
Matser, Johan S 100
Matterm, Abram S 95
Mattern, Marcus S 105
Mattes, James S 334
Matteus, Andreas S 146
Matteus, George S 146
Matteus, Henrich S 131
Matteus, Sabina S 131
Matthais, Jacob (Lieut) S 356
Mattheus, Johann Martin S 146
Mattheus, Martin S 95
Matthes, Anna Maria S 131
Matthes, Maria Appolonia S 131
Matthes, Peter S 131
Mattheus, Conrad S 131
Mattheus, Georg S 131
Mattheus, Jerg S 131
Mattheus Johan Jacob S 131
Mattheus, Maria Catharina S 131
Mattheus, Maria Sibylia S 131
Matthews, Algernon (Reverend) T 306
Matthews, David S 329
Matthews, Fletcher S 334
Matthews, Gertrude T 252
Matthews, George (Colonel (Va) S 276
Matthews, Jacob (Lieut) S 345
Matthews, William S 334
Matthias, Hannocol S 329
Matthias, Hendrick T 342, S 329
Mattise, Johannis S 296
Matthys, Hans S 105
Mattice, Hendrick S 329, S 334
Mattice Johnannis Nicholas S 334
Mattice, John S 329
Mattice, John Nicholas S 329
Mattys S 100
Mattys, Johannes S 90
Mattys, Laurents S 95
Mattys, Peter S 90, S 100
Mattyskolk, Johan S 90
Mauck, Jacob S 131
Mauer, Anna Catharine S 131
Mauer, Anna Catharina S 131
Mauer, Anna Margreth S 131
Mauer, Dorothea S 131
Mauer, Georg S 146
Mauer, Johann Georg S 131, S 146
Mauer, Johannes S 131
Mauer, Johann Peter S 131

Mauer, Jorg S 131
Mauer, Peter S 131, S 146
Maul, Anna Catharina S 131
Maul, Anna Elisabetha S 131
Maul, Anna Julian S 131
Maul, Anna Maria S 131
Maul, Anna Ursula S 118, S 131
Maul, Christoph S 131, S 146
Maul, Frederick S 118
Maul, Fredrig S 105
Maul, Fridrich S 131
Maul, Hendk S 105
Maul, Johan S 105, S 146
Maul, Johann Fridrich S 131
Maul, Johann Joacob S 131
Maul, Johannes S 131, S 146
Maul, J. Fridrich S 131
Maul, John Jacob S 118
Maul, John Paul S 118
Maul, Ursula S 131
Maulin, Anna Catharina S 118
Maulin, Anna Maria S 118
Maulin, Anna Ursela S 118
Maulin, Anna Eliz. S 118
Maur, Johan S 95
Maus, Michel S 95
Mauser, Johan Georg S 146
Mausin, Eva S 146
Mauyer, Nicklas S 354
May, Christoph S 146
May, Johan Peter S 100
May, Peter S 90, S 146
May, William S 334
Maybag, Dirk S 95
Maybee, John S 358
Mayby, David S 347
Mayby, Joseph S 347
Mayel, Matthias S 355
Mayer, Anna Gertraut S 131
Mayer, Dewalt T 257
Mayer, Catharina S 131
Mayer, Christian S 131
Mayer, Felix S 114
Mayer, Frederick S 355
Mayer, Gewalt T 173
Mayer, H. Henry S 347
Mayer, Hans Geerlag Jr. S 114
Mayer, Henry S 120, S 355
Mayer, Hendrick S 114
Mayer, Jacob S 114, S 347, S 351
Mayer, Jacob S. S 347
Mayer, Jacob Jr. S 276, S 351
Mayer, John S 355
Mayer, John Mayer S 353
Mayer, Johan Geerlag S 114
Mayer, Joseph S 114, S 355
Mayer, Krisstoffel S 90
Mayer, Mates S 355
Mayer, Michel S 355
Mayer, Nicolas S 355
Mayer, Piter S 355
Mayer, Solomon S 114
Mayin, Otilla S 146
Maynard, Elija B. S 276
Mayo, Jonathan (Conn) S 276
Mayor, Anna S 360
Mayor, Hendrik S 360
McAdams, William S 329, S 334
McAlpin (Captain) S 334
McAlpin, Daniel S 329, S 334
McAlpin, John S 329
McAlpin, Walter S 334

McAndor, John T 173, S 320
McArder, Duncan T 173, 257
McArder, John, 257
McArthur, Alexander (Lieut) S 276
McArthur, John S 303
McArthur, Daniel S 351
McArthur, Donaldi S 351
McArthur, Duncan S 351
McAuley, Donald S 334
McBride, Francis T 342
McCallum, John S 351
McCarsan S 334
McCartey, Dunkon S 347
McCartey, John S 347
McCarthy, John S 196, S 334
McCauly, Mary Hays
McCay, Alexander T 342
McChain, John S 276
McClannen, Peter S 329
McClaughry, James (Lieut. Colonel) S 272, S 276
McClaghry, James (Captain) S 276
McClaughry, John (Ensign) S 276
McClellen, William S 276
McClue, William S 276
McClumpha,Thomas S 351
McCollom, Daniel S 297
McCollam, Findlay S 351
McCollom, John S 334
McCollum, John S 358
McComb, John S 329, S 334
McCormick, James S 334
McCoy, John S 210
McCracken Joseph (Major) T 342
McCray, William S 334
McCrea, John S 296
McCredy, Willaim S 351
McCree, James S 334
McCree, Stephen S 258
McDarne, Randall S 335
McDavitt, Charles S 297
McDermid, Michael S 297
McDole, John S 335
McDonald, Alexander S 335
McDonald, Allen S 335
McDonald, Captain T 112
McDonald, Daniel T 342
McDonald, Donald T 342
McDonald, James S 329, S 351
McDonald, John (Captain) (Penn) S 276
McDonald, John S 329, S 335, S 357, S 358
McDonald, Nicholas S 351
McDonald, Rorey S 335
McDonald, T. S 335
McDonell, John T 35, S 357
McDougal, Allen S 335
McDougal, Daniel T 254, 317, 318
McDougal, Duncan T 318, 319, 331, 333
McDougall S 335
McDougall, Eve S 300
McDowl, Hugh S 335
McFall, Paul T 342
McFie, Alexander S 347
McGee, Robert (Captain) S 194
McGinnis, George S 329
McGinnis, Robert S 329
McGlashen, Robert S 357

McGrady, Robert S 225
McGraw, Christopher S 351
McGraw, Daniel S 219, S 226, S 297, S 351
McGraw, Dennis S 351
McGraw, James T 342
McGraw, John S 222, S 224, S 351
McGraw, Samuel S 223
McGraw, Willaim S 351
McGregor, Duncan T 157
McGreger, Peter S 335
McGregor, Jno S 335
McGrewer, John S 335
McGrigor, Duncan S 357
McGruir, High S 335
McHerrin, Richard S 335
McIntire, John S 357
McIntosh, Ralph S 158
McKean (M'Kean, McKeen) Robert (Capt, Major) T 128, 132, 150 , 154, 187, 193, 231, 342, S 168, S 169, S 193, S 215, S 233, S 246
McKean, Samuel T 231, 342
McKenney, Dainnel S 351
McKenny, John S 357
McKenzie, Laudot S 335
McKenzie, Roderick S 329
McKerque, Duncan S 357
McKillip, John S 347
McKinney, John S 357
McKesson, John T 342
McKiel, William S 335
McKillip, Archibald S 297
McKillip, John S 297
McKiney, Charles T 342
McKinney, John S 335
McKinstrie, (Major)
McKinstry (Colonel) C 167
McKinstry, John (Captain) T 342
McKown, James S 297
McLarin, Peter S 329
McLean, Peter S 335
McLeod, Daniel S 335
McLeod, Don'd S 335
McLeod, Norman (Captain) S 329, S 335
McLeod, William S 335
McLonis, Jurry S 347
McManus, Hugh S 357
McMarlinger, Duncan S 357
McMarten, Duncan S 357
McMartin, John S 335
McMaster, David (Captain) T 223, S 209, S 225, S 226, S 349
McMaster, Hugh T 342, S 351
McMaster, James T 319, 332, 333, S 335, S 351
McMaster, James (Lieut) S 349
McMaster, Robert S 351
McMaster, Thomas S 351
McMasters, James (Lieut.) S 220
McMullen, John S 276
McMullin, Dougal S 335
McMullin, Hugh S 335
McMullen see M'Mullen
McNaughton, Catharine S 265
McNaughton, Petar S 351
McNeal, John S 335
McNeal, Thomas S 335
McNeil, Theodore S 303
McNiff, Patrick S 329

McNight, Malcom S 335
McNish, Alexander T 342
McNish, Joseph S 329
McNutt, David S 335
McNutt, James S 354
M'Colley, (Lieut) T 139
McRadey, William S 351
McTaggert, James S 335, S 351
McVagulhen, Peeter S 347
McVain, Daniel S 357
Mead, Ezekiel S 335
Mead, Libbeus T 342
Mead, Richard K. S 283
Meales, Matthew S 276
Mears, Thomas S 351
Meby, Joseph T 324
Meder, Johan S 85
Medlar, John S 329
Meeis, Matys S 85
Meersterin, Margreeta S 100
Megel, Hans Wendel S 95
Mehs, Henrich S 131
Meier, Anna Devoda S 85
Meier, Johannes S 85
Meier, Johan Koenraad S 85
Meier, Johannes S 85
Meier, Koenraet S 100
Meier, Maria S 85
Meier, Matthew S 347
Meier, Paulus S 90
Meinhard, Burckhard S 131
Meinhober, Phillippus S 90, S 100
Meinsinger, Koenraet S 100
Meis, Henrig S 90
Meisser, Johan Jurg S 105
Meister, Koenraet S 95
Melbreg, Adam S 100
Melbreg, Johan S 100
Melchin, Anna Eliz. S 118
Melchin, Anna Maria S 118
Melchin, Sittonia S 118
Melck, Mighel S 85
Meliger, Frans S 90
Meller, John S 355
Melly (Captain) T 183
Melone, John S 351
Melries, Johannes S 85
Melsch, Johan S 105
Melsers, Stoffel S 100
Meltsberger, Phillips S 100
M'Mullen T 220, S 245, S 265
Menbeth, James S 276
Mendes, Maria Christina S 131
Mendon, Jacob S 81
Mengel, Hans Jorg S 100
Mengelsin, Anna Maria S 118
Mengelsin, John Carolus S 118
Mengelsin, Juliana S 118
Menges, Anna Elisabetha S 132
Menges, Anna Eva S 132
Menges, Gerdraut S 132
Menges, Hans S 90
Menges, Johannes S 132, S 146
Mengilin, Anna Maria S 146
Mengis, Johann S 132
Mengje, Fredrig S 100
Menias, Johan S 90
Menimeier, Frants S 95
Menin, Johan S 100
Meningen, John S 81
Mensch, Antony S 90
Mensch, Johan Jurg S 90
Menst, Peter S 100

Mentegen, Ferdo S 120
Menti, Firdinard S 112
Mentizeberges, Diderig S 90
Menzes, Alexander S 329
Menzes, Thomas S 329
Menzies, Alexander S 329, S 335
Menzines, Alexander S 329, S 335
Mercer, John (Lieut) S 276
Merchell, Henry (Major) T 169
Merckel, Dewalt T 173, 257
Merckel, Anna Barbara S 132
Merckel, Elisabetha S 132
Merckel, Eva S 132
Merckel, Fridrich S 132
Merckel, Johann Adam S 132
Merckel, Johann Fridrich S 132
Merckel, Johann Jacob S 132
Merckel, Maria Elisabetha S 132
Merckel, Peter T 173, 257
Merkle, Jacob S 335
Merckley, Catharine T 85
Merckley, Christopher T 85
Merckley, Frederick T 85
Merckley, Martin T 87
Merckley, Michael T 85
Merckley, William T 116, 173
Merckel, Frederick S 146
Merger, John S 357
Merikle, Jacob S 329
Merkell, Devel T 254
Merkle, Christopher S 329
Merkle, David S 300
Merkle, Dewalt S 303
Merkle, Hendrick S 296
Merkle, Henry S 300
Merkle, Jacob S 329
Merkle, Peter S 303
Merkle, Samuel S 300
Merkel, John S 296
Merkell, Henry S 303, S 309
Merkell, Jacob S 320
Merkell, John S 309
Merkell, Peter S 309
Merkell, Theobato T 304, S 309
Merkill, Jacob T 173, 257
Merkill, Richard T 173, 257
Merkle, Jacob S 335
Merks, Peter S 90
Merlee, Willem S 105
Merril, John S 309
Merrit, Joseph S 329
Merritt, Cornberry S 335
Merritt, Daniel S 335
Merritt, Gilbert S 335
Merritt, Hackaliah S 335
Merritt, John S 329
Merritt, Nathaniel S 335
Merritt, Robert S 335
Merritt, Samuel S 335
Merritt, Thomas S 329, S 335
Merritt, Underbill S 335
Merritt, William S 335
Merschel, Peter S 90
Mersellts, John J. T 342
Merselus, Hanse S 335
Mertin, Margaretha S 132
Mertz, Anna Catharina S 132
Mertz, Elisabetha S 132
Mertz, Johann S 132
Mertz, Sophis Elisabeth S 132
Mertzin, Anna Catharina S 146
Merrtz, Margaretha S 132

Mescherling, Benedik S 105
Mese, David S 90
Mese, Mattys S 100
Meserin, Johannes S 118
Meserin, Margaret S 118
Meserin, Susan Cath. S 118
Mess, Henrich S 146
Messer, Jacobus S 85
Messer, Koenraet S 90
Messer, Pieter S 85
Messer, Sylvester S 81
Messerin, Anna Margretha S 146
Mest, Abram S 95
Metgen, Ferdinand S 146
Metor, Dangel S 90
Mets, Andreas S 90, S 100
Mets, Henry S 351
Mets, Johan S 105
Mets, Simon S 95
Metsch, Maria Tys S 105
Metsgennen, Doretta S 100
Metseger, Johan S 95
Metsler, Philippus S 90
Meurin, Margreta S 95
Meurinus, William S 351
Mey, David S 81
Mey, Johan Dinges (Wede.) S 100
Meyars, Jacob S 115
Meyer, Arent S 95
Meyer, Anna Christina S 132
Meyer, Antony S 105
Meyer, Barbara S 132
Meyer, Bartel S 95
Meyer, Christian S 132, S 146, S 296
Meyer, Deobald T 173, 257
Meyer, Deowald T 173, 257
Meyer, Felix S 114
Meyer, Friderick S 146
Meyer, Gerdraut S 132
Meyer, Gerlach S 114
Meyer, Hans Jacob S 90
Meyer, Hartman S 81
Meyer, Hendrick S 113
Meyer, Henrich S 146,
Meyer, Henrick S 347
Meyer, Henrick S. S 347
Meyer, Henrig S 90, S 95
Meyer, Henry S 81
Meyer, Henry S 81
Meyer, Jacob (Lieut) T 342
Meyer, Jacob S 347
Meyer, Jacob R. S 347
Meyer, Johan S 90, S 132
Meyer, Johann Fridrich S 132
Meyer, Johan Henrick S 347
Meyer, Johan Jacob S 105
Meyer, Johann Peter S 132
Meyer, Johannes T 173. 257, S 90
Meyer, John T 173, 257
Meyer, John J. T 342
Meyer, Kristiaan S 105
Meyer, Leendert S 105
Meyer, Maria Barbara S 132
Meyer, Paulus S 95
Meyer, Simon S 105
Meyer, Solomon S 347
Meyer, Theobald T 173, 257
Meyer, Weyand S 105
Meyerin, Elizabeth S 146
Meyin, Amnma Eliz. S 118

Meyin, Barbara S 146
Meyin, Maria S 118
Meyin, Meylin S 146
Meynderton, Johannes S 47
Meyrer, Anna Gertraut S 132
Meyrer, Anna Kungunda S 132
Meyrer, Johann Henrich S 132
Meyrer, Johann Wilhelm S 132
Meyrer, Maria Elisabetha S 132
Meysenheim Anna Gertrud S 146
Meyser, Johann Michel S 132
Michael, Georg Andreas S 132
Michael, Hans Henrich S 146
Michael, Johan Georg S 146
Michael, Maria Barbara S 132
Michael, Niclaus S 132, S 146
Michard, Henry S 357
Michel, Anna Barbara S 132
Michel, Elisabetha Margretha S 132
Michel, Henrich S 132
Michel, Henrig S 95
Michel, Johan S 85, S 105
Michel, Johann Henrich S 132
Michel, Johann Niclaus S 132
Michel, Kasper S 105
Michel, Niklas S 95
Michel, Otto Henrig S 90
Michel, Susanna S 132
Michel, Susanna Gerdraut S 132
Michiel, Anthony S 112
Michiel, Hendrick S 112
Michiel, Hendrick Jun'r. S 112
Mickle, John S 357
Mickler, Anna Margretha S 132
Mickler, Jacob S 132
Mickler, Killiam S 132
Middagh, Jacob S 335
Middle Fort T 146, 204
Mier, John S 347
Miler, John C. S 347
Miesick, Fiet S 112
Miesch, Paul S 90
Migel, Hans S 90
Migel, Otto Henrig S 90
Migrigri, Letischa S 132
Migrigri, Peter S 132
Mikkeler, Johan S 100
Mikle, Henrig S 100
Milbert, John Martin S 85
Milch, Johan Eberhard S 146
Miler, Hans Jurig S 90
Milges, Johan Wilhelm S 146
Miller, Adam S 351
Miller, Anthony S 95, S 329, S 335
Miller, Christoffel S 115
Miller, Conrad T 173, 257
Miller, Conraed S 347
Miller, Cornelius S 114
Miller, Dionysius S 347, S 356
Miller, Mrs. Dyoniscius T 90
Miller, Falentyn S 85
Miller, Faltin (Valentine) S 116
Miller, Fredrick S 351
Miller, Garret T 173, 257, S 347
Miller, Gilbert S 329
Miller, Gorge S 351
Miller, Hans Gorg S 105
Miller, Hans Jacob S 85
Miller, Henrich S 355

Miller, Henry T 173, 188, 254, S 297, S 300,
S 303, S 314
Miller, Henry (Captain) T 170, 201, 225, 255,
S 174, S 176, S 182, S 183, S 190, S 236,
S 237, S 248
Miller, Jacob S 85, S 95, S 114, S 335
Miller, James T 342, S 351
Miller, James W. S 241
Miller, Jellis S 303, S 315
Miller, Jillis S 351
Miller, Johan S 100, S 351
Miller, Johan Christ. S 112
Miller, Johan Jacob S 95
Miller, Johan Willem S 95
Miller, Johanes S 358
Miller, Johanis T 254, S 111
Miller, Johannes S 85, S 360
Miller, Johannis S 355
Miller, John T 17, 257, 342, S 335, S 347
Miller, John Sr. S 355
Miller, John Jr. S 355
Miller, John A. S 335
Miller, John Andiel S 114
Miller, John Godfrey S 114
Miller, John Thomas S 114
Miller, Joseph S 335
Miller, Justus T 342
Miller, Katrina S 85
Miller, Lyon S 335
Miller, (Lieutenant) S 202
Miller, N. S 335
Miller, Nickel S 85
Miller, Niculaus S 355
Miller, Obadiah S 335
Miller, Peter S 85, S 95, S 335
Miller, Philip S 85, S 115, S 303, S 315, S 357
Miller, Samuel T 173, 257
Miller, Samuel S 95, S 276
Miller, Smich S 85
Miller, Steve S 85
Miller, Valentine S 297, S 355
Miller, Willem S 85
Miller, William S 335
Millerin, Susanna S 90
Milligan, Nathaniel (Lieut) T 342
Milliken, James (Captain) T 342
Millor, Peter S 355
Milloy, Alexander S 351
Mills, Alexander T 342
Mills, Cornelius S 358
Millur, Samuel S 116
Minckler, Killiam S 146
Ming, Kristoffel S 90
Mink, Hans Hendrig S 90
Mink, Hendrig S 90
Minisink T 47
Minkeler, Anna Margreta S 85
Minkeler, Kelioen S 85
Minthorne, Mangel
Milspaugh, John T 342
Mincklaer, Josias S 112
Mineklaer, Killean S 112
Minor, John (Reverend) T 306
Minsinger, Bastiaan S 100
Minthorne S 335
Minthorne, Mangel S 335
Misselman, Daniel S 85

Nelles, DeWalt T 254
Nelles, Gerry S 347
Nelles, Gorg T 173, 257
Nelles, Henrick S 347
Nelles, Henry T 173, 257, S 347
Nelles, Henry N. S 347
Nelles, George T 173, S 276, S 347
Nelles, Gerry S 347
Nelles, Johan Gerog S 146
Nelles, Johan Wilhelm S 146
Nelles, Johannes T 254
Nelles, Johannes Laurentius T 301
Nelles, Johannes Henricus T 301
Nelles, John T 173, 257, S 347
Nelles, Joseph T 173, 257
Nelles, Lodowick T 173, 257
Nelles, Peter T 173, 257
Nelles, Philles T 254
Nelles, Philiba T 173, 257
Nelles, Rupert T 301
Nelles, Wilhelm T 301
Nelles, William T 173, 257, S 113, S 119, S 347
Nellesin, Maria Elizabeth S 146
Nelley, John S 351
Nellice, Peter, Jr. T 173
Nellice, Robert T 173
Nellies, Gerry S 347
Nellis Tavern T 301
Nellis, Adam S 300, S 311
Nellis, Adam Jr. S 311
Nellis Adam A. S 303
Nellis, Andrew T 200, 302, S 320
Nellis, Catharina T 168
Nellis, Catherine T 200
Nellis, Catharina Elisabetha T 301
Nellis, Christian T 65, 162, 160, 173, 297, 302, 325, S 286, S 300, S 318
Nellis, Christian Jr T 162, 302
Nellis, Christian III T 302
Nellis, Deobolt T 173
Nellis, David T 206, 297, S 300, S 317
Nellis, George 218
Nellis, Hend'k T 173
Nellis, Henry T 90, 297, 302, S 335, S 347
Nellis, Henry W. T 302, S 300, S 303, S 311, S 330
Nellis, Jacob T 162, 342, S 347
Nellis, Jacob C. T 302
Nellis, Johannes T 297, 302
Nellis, John T 162, S 300, S 310
Nellis, John C. T 302, S 303, S 318
Nellis, John D. T 205, S 320
Nellis, John H. T 173, S 300
Nellis, John I. S 310
Nellis, John L. S 303, S 307
Nellis, John V. S 303
Nellis, John W. S 303
Nellis, Joseph T 173, 206, 257, S 303, S 311
Nellis, Joseph Jr. S 303
Nellis, Kevin T 97
Nellis, Lipe T 173
Nellis, Lodwick T 170, 255, S 307
Nellis, Ludwick S 300

Nellis, Ludwig T 302, S 303
Nellis, Margretha T 302
Nellis, Mary T 207
Nellis, Milo T 97
Nellis, Peter S 303
Nellis, Peter A. S 313
Nellis, Peter F. T 199, 298
Nellis, Peter, H. T 173, S 303
Nellis, Peter M. S 303
Nellis, Peter W. T 173, S 300, S 311
Nellis, Philip S 300, S 306
Nellis, Philip Jr. S 303, S 306
Nellis, Robert T 302, S 330
Nellis, Robert William S 330
Nellis Tavern T 301
Nellis, William T 207, 236, 301, 335, S 44, S 300, S 303, S 306, S 358
Nellis, William Jr T 297, 302, S 303, S 306
Nellis, Yost S 300
Nells, George T 173, 257
Nelson, Riche S 335
Nelson, Thomas (Governor) T 68
Neoman, Peter T 173
Nepeler, Johan S 91
Nerbel, Johan Georg S 146
New York City T 47
Nesch, Schims S 355
Ness, Georg Wilhelm S 146
Nest, Johannes S 357
Nestel, Andrew T 173, 257
Nestel, George T 173, 257
Nestel, Gottiel T 173, 257
Nestel, Gottlib T 257
Nestel, Henry T 257
Nestel, Peter T 173
Nestel, Martin T 257
Nestel, Mearly, Jr. T 173, 257
Nestle, George S 342
Nestle, Gottlib T 173, 254, S 300, S 304
Nestle, Gutlip S 309
Nestle, Henry T 173, S 304. S 318
Nestle, Martin T 173, S 228, S 300, S 310
Nestle, Martinus Jr S 310
Nestle, Peter T 173
Net, Jurg Fredrig S 105
Nethaway, Peter S 155
Netherly, John S 347, S 356
Netherly, John Jr. S 356
Netherly, John H. S 347
Netherly, John I. S 347
Netthaber, Quirness S 146
Netzbach, Jno. Mart S 120
Netzbacher, Anna Margaretha S 133
Netzbacher, Barbara Elisabetha S 133
Netzbacher, Johann Henrich S 133
Netzbacher, Johann Martin S 133
Netzbacher, Martin S 133
Netzbackes, Johan Martin S 146
Netzbaecher, Anna Barbara S 133
Netzbaecher, Anna Maria S 133
Neukrich, Anna Benigma S 133
Neukirch, Anna Maria S 133
Neukirch, Maria Catharina S 133
Neurich, Anna Maria S 133

Neus, Abraham S 133
Neus, Annd Elisabetha S 133
Newkerk, Benjamin S 355
Newkerk, Garrit C. S 351
Newkirch, Johann S 133
Newkirch, Johann Henrich S 133
Newkirk, (Major) S 221
Newkirk, Abraham S 351
Newkirk, Charles S 304
Newkkerk, Garret S 351
Neuman, Lodewyk S 91
Neumeiyer, Frans S 91
Neusch, Andreas S 91
Newberry, Gilbert (Sergeant) T 144
Newcomb, James S 276
Newkerck, Charles T 304, S 308
Newkirch, Johan Henrich S 146
Newkirk, Abraham S 297
Newkirk, Anna Maria S 118
Newkirk, Benjamin S 220, S 222
Newkirk, Cornelius S 234
Newkirk, Garnet S 226
Newkirk, Gerritt (Lieut) S 349
Newkirk, Johan Henrich S 118
Newkirk, Johannes S 118
Newkirk, John Henrich S 118
Newman, John (Major) S 246, S 300
Newman, Joseph T 173, 208, 257, S 276, S 300
Neymeyer, Arts S 91
Niagara T 209
Nichol, Mariah S 157
Nicholas, Hesekiah S 300
Nicholas, Simeon T 173, S 300
Nicholls, Simon S 308
Nichollson, David S 335
Nicholls, Simon T 254, S 304
Nichols, Guisham S 276
Nichols, Thomas S 335
Nicholson (Governor) T 301
Nicholson (Colonel) S 44
Nickerson, Joseph S 335
Nidermeyer, Andries S 91
Nier, Johan Gofvried S 105
Niesch, Anna S 105
Niesch, Anna Margreta S 105
Niesch, Gorg Willem S 101
Niesch, Hans Henrig S 105
Niesch, Jacob S 105
Niesch, Thomas S 105
Niesin, Maria S 118
Niesin, Maria Magdalena S 118
Nighoft, John S 305
Niklaas, Juties S 101
Niklaas, Peeter S 101
Niles, Hendrick S 111
Niles, Sands (Ensign) (Conn) S 276
Nillis, John D. S 304
Nisbet, Charles T 173
Nobel, Jacob S 96, S 229, S 229
Noble, James (Captain) S 229
Noble, Peter (Conn) S 276
Noble, (Captain) S 335
Noble, Reubin S 335
Noecher, Anna Constinia S 133
Noecher, Anna Maria S 133
Noecher, Carl S 133
Nodine, A. S 335
Nodine B. S 335
Nodine, Peter S 335

Noigt, Johan Philip S 105
Nol, Herbert S 101
Nolgert, John S 347
Noll, Bernhard S 133, S 146
Noll, Johan Danyell S 91
Nollin, Anna Margaretha S 146
Nollin, Elizabeth S 118
Nols, Bernhart S 91
Nonius, Johan Peter S 101
Northrup, Abijah S 276
Norris, Abraham S 320
Norton, Henry T 342
Notzel, Rudolf S 82
Nou, Wendel S 96
Noxon, Bartholomew S 330
Nreb, (Captain) T 241
Nudig, Hans S 96
Nuess, Johann Henrich S 133
Nukel, Gerrit C. S 296
Nukerck, Jacob S 351
Nukerk, George C. S 297
Nukerk, John S 296
Nukerk, John (Major) S 349
Nukle, John S 297
Nummenthal, Jacob S 96
Nusch, Lodwyk S 96
Nutzberger, Mattys S 96
Nyhoff, John S 304
Nyneman, Henry S 304
Nyney, George T 173
Oackley, Peter S 335
Oakley, Benjamin S 335
Oakley, Isaac S 276
Oakley, John S 276
Oakley, John (Ensign) S 276
Oakley, Miles S 330
Oakley, Timothy S 335
Oar, Jacob S 210
Obber, Valentyn S 105
Obel, Johan S 101
Obender, Samuel S 82
Oberbach, Anna Maria S 133
Oberbach, Christina S 133
Oberbach, Elisabetha S 133
Oberbach, Elisabetha Magdalena S 133
Oberbach, Georg S 146
Oberbach, Jerg S 133
Oberbach, Johann Christian S 133
Oberbach, Johann Georg S 133
Oberbach, Johann Peter S 133, S 146
Oberbach, Maria Christina S 133
Oberbach, Peter S 133, S 146
Oberer, Johan Jacob S 146
Oberholtzer, Mark S 82
Oberhubel, Jacob S 96
Oberin, Anna S 147
Obers, Peter S 105
Obreschur (?) Johan Hendrig S 101
Octer, Kristoffel S 101
Odilja (Wede.) S 101
Ode, Johannes S 85
Odell, Daniel 261, S 335
Odell, Joshua S 335
Odilioswal S 96
O'Connor (Captain) S 209
Oeknygm, Higab S 85
Oemich, Anna Catharina S 133
Oemich, Jerg Adam S 133
Oemich, Johann Adam S 133

Oemich, Lorentz S 133
Oemich, Niclaus S 133
Off, Jacob S 147
Offin, Anna Barbara S 118
Offin, Johan Jacob S 118
Offin, Magdalena S 118
Ogden, Benjamin S 330, S 335
Ogden, Daniel Sr. S 351
Ogden, Daniel S 358
Ogden, David S 351
Ogden, Jehu S 335
Ogden, John S 335
Ogden, William S 335
Ogs, Hans Mikel S 101
Ogt, Georg S 355
O'Hara, General
Ohrendorph, Frederick Sr. S 355
Ohrendorph, Frederick Jr. S 355
Ohrendorph, George S 355
Ohrendorph, Peter S 355
Ohll, Peter S 96
Ohmich, Anna Catharina S 133
Ohmich, Anna Maria S 133
Ohmich, Niclaus S 133
Ohn, Jacob S 347
Ohrendorff, George S 297
Ohrendorff, Peter S 297
Ohrendorf, Henrich S 133, S 147
Ohrendorf, Anna Margretha S 133
Ohrendorf, Maria Elisabetha S 133
Ohrendorph, Frederick S 297
Ohrendorph, Frederic, Jr. S 297
Ohrendorph, John S 297
Olendorf, Daniel T 94, 159
Olendorf, Henry T 92
Olinus, John S 335
Olen, Ebenezer (Ensign) S 260
Oline, Benjamin (Lieut) S 276, S 349
Oliver, Frederick S 330
Oliver, Thomas S 276
Olman, John S 276
Olney, Joseph S 304
Olthanier, Hans Jurg S 91
Omehie, John T 173
Omstad, Veldin S 85
Onatassa T 281
Onderling, Anna S 133
Oneidas S 85
O'Neil, James S 335
Onin, Maria Barbara S 118
Onondaga Village
Ooster, Arent S 85
Oosterman, Johan S 101
Oothout, Abraham S 297, S 320
Oothout, Jonas S 304, S 311
Openheizer, Philip S 101
Orendorff, Jno. Hen. S 120
Ordenier, Nicolaes S 91
Order (?) Johan Adam S 105
Ore, William S 335
Orendorff, Christian (Lieut) (Md) S 276
Orendorf, Hendrik S 360
Orendros, Conradt S 360
Ormen, Richard S 133
Organ, Cornelius S 276
Orser, Evert S 335
Orser, Isaac S 335
Orsor, Jonas (Captain) S 276
Ort, Hans Jacob S 105

Osborn, Aaron T 67
Osborn (Captain) S 335
Osborn, Danvers T 342
Osborn, Nathan S 330, S 335
Osborn, Sarah T 67
Osden, Isaac S 321
Oserhout, Frederick S 300
Osman, Henry S 300
Osman, John S 314
Osmand, Benjah (Lieut (NJ) S 276
Osterhout, Frederick S 312
Osterhout, John S 297, S 355
Osterroth, Frederick T 173, 257
Osterroth, Johannes S 355
Osterttout, John S 355
Ostrander, John, (Ensign) S 260
Ostrander, Peter S 335
Ostram, Andries S 335
Ostrom, John T 150
Ostwalt, Johan S 96
Oswegatchie T 217
Othermark, John B. S 356
Otsego T 139, 241
Ottman, Frederick T 155
Ott, Johan S 91
Otto I. S 32
Ouderkirk, John S 210
Ough (Och or Ox) George S 116
Ough, Robhold T 305
Oustrander, Henry S 276
Outerman, Jacob S 347
Outwater, Daniel S 330
Outwater, Thomas S 330
Ovendurff, Conrad S 347
Owandah T 271
Owen, William S 314
Owne, Joseph Jr. S 276
Owens, Eleasar T 342
Owens, Moses S 335
Paba, Ernest S 347
Pach, Daniel S 147
Pachman, Johan S 91
Pack, Jacob S 91
Paf, Johan Andries S 96
Pain, Brinton (Major) S 276
Paine, Joseph S 343, S 276
Paine, Thomas T 26
Palatine Church T 199, 297
Palerwaltman, Johan S 91
Palleueborg, Koenraed S 85
Palmatier, Peter S 335
Palmatier, Peter I. S 335
Palmer, David S 335
Palmer, Edmund S 330, S 335
Palmer, Edward S 330, S 335
Palmer, Lewis S 330, S 335
Palmer, William S 335
Palmetier, Isaac S 276
Palsberger, John T 173, 257
Paltzer, Henrig S 96
Panter, G. S 335
Panter, Phillip S 335
Panter, Ulrich S 351
Pantion, Francis S 335
Paoli Massacre T 38
Parent, Jacob S 335
Paris, Catherine T 210
Paris, Daniel T 210
Paris, Isaac (Lieut) T 24, 110, 112, 147, 170, 173, 178, 209. 254, 255, 317, 333, S 115
Paris, Isaac Jr. T 209, S 115

Post, Jacob S 335
Post, Johan Hend. S 112
Post, Nicholas S 318
Post, Teunis S 335
Poter, France S 357
Potman, Aaren S 352
Potman, Adam S 352
Potman, Arent T 174, 257
Potman, David S 297
Potman, Cornelius S 297
Potman, David, Jr. S 297
Potman, Francies (Ensign) S 349
Potman, Frederick S 297
Potman, George S 352
Potman, Rechrt (Ensign) S 349
Potmanter, Thomas S 351
Potmon, Hendrik S 352
Potten, James S 276
Potter, John S 165
Potter, Michael S 300
Poucher, Jacob S 336
Poucher, John S 336
Poultson, john (Capt) (Va) S 276
Powel, Jesse S 335
Powell, James S 335
Powell, John S 336
Powell, Solomon S 336
Pownal, Thomas (Lieut) S 276
Poyar, John S 297
Poyton, James S 276
Practer, Helena S 133
Practer, Joseph S 133
Prak, Hans Michel S 101
Praim, George S 319
Prang, Herman S 91
Prauw, Arnold S 91
Praux, Felten S 91
Preg, Michel S 91
Preker, Paulus S 91
Prentest, Daniel S 352
Prentiss, Joseph (Lieut) S 349
Presler, Valentine S 82, S 133
Preston, Jonathan T 343
Preston, William (Lieut) (Penn) S 276
Prett, John S 352
Prettert, Jeunes S 101
Pribl, Michel S 96
Price, Adam S 358
Price, George S 347
Price, John T 174, 257, S 300
Prime, Elizabeth S 300
Prime, David S 352
Prime, Henry S 352
Prime, Petter S 352
Prince George S 35
Prine, Luis S 133
Prints, Johan S 105
Printup, Joseph T 343
Printup, Joseph (Lieut) S 349
Printup, William I. T 155, S 352
Printz, Daniel S 101
Prium, John I. Jr S 310
Prium, Widow S 310
Proctor S 335
Propeet, Maria Barbara S 133
Proper, Johan Fred'k S 111
Proper, Johan Joseph S 111
Proper, Johan Pieter S 111
Propert, Anna Maria S 133
Propperty, Johann Jost S 147
Propper, Anna Elisabetha S 133
Propper, Johann Jost S 133

Propper, Johan Just S 96
Prouk, Peter S 101
Provo, Hans Peter S 105
Powell, Charles (Lieut) S 345
Pruime, John S 352
Prunck, Peter S 101
Prunet, Paul S 147
Prusie, Gabrial S 133
Prusie, Gertraut S 133
Prusti, Gabriel S 133
Prusti, Gertraut S 133
Pruyn, John S 352
Pruyne, Henry S 352
Pryl, Dewaeld S 111
Pseffer, Anna Maria S 118
Pseffer, Michael S 118
Pscheere S 91
Pudum, Lucus S 91
Pulfer, Anna Catharina S 133
Pull, Johan Peter S 96
Pulmer, William T 179
Pulver, Johann Wendel S 133
Pulver, Johan Wilhelm S 147
Pulver, Johannis Wm. S 112
Purchas, Thomas S 336
Purchas, William S 336
Purdy, Enoch S 336
Purdy, Gilbert S 336
Purdy, Hackaliah S 336
Purdy, Henry S 336
Purdy, Isiah S 336
Purdy, James S 336
Purdy, JaWinn Still S 336
Purdy, Jesse S 336
Purdy, Jonathan T 343
Purdy, Joseph S 336
Purdy, Joshua S 336
Purdy, Josiah S 336
Purdy, Jotham S 336
Purdy, Solomon Jr T 343, S 276
Purdy, Stephen S 336
Purdy, Still John S 336
Purdy, Timothy S 336
Puths, Wilhem S 91
Putman, Adam, S 218
Putman, Arent S 218, S 304
Putman, Clara T 266
Putman, Cornelius S 195, S 357
Putman, Cornelys, Jr. S 352
Putman, David T 174, 258, S 352
Putman, (Captain) Garrett S 158, S 202, T 230, S 224, S 226, S 234, S 249
Putman, Gilbert S 304, S 316
Putman, Factor S 352
Putman, Frederick T 155, S 352
Putman, Hanry S 352
Putman, Jacobus S 352
Putman, John S 270, S 352
Putman, Lewis S 352
Putman, Lodowick T 327 S 352
Putman, Victor S 218, S 352
Putman, William S 352
Putnam, David S 276
Putnam, David (Coporal) S 276
Putnam, Gerrit (Captain) S 349
Putname, Victor (Lieut) S 349
Putsch, Johannes S 91
Pyn, Marten S 86
Pyrune, Daniel S 352
Pruyn, Francis F. (Lieut) S 349
Qolinger, Henry S 347

Quacenbosh, Abrahand (Lieut) S 349
Quack, John S 352
Quack, Petar S 352
Quack Willem S 352
Quackenbos, Onter Soct. S 347
Quackenboss (Quarter Master) S 288
Quackenboss, Abraham, Jr. S 297
Quackenboss, Abram D T 114
Quackenboss, Adrian S 330, S 336
Quackenboss, Gosen S 330
Quackenboss, Isaac S 348
Quackenboss, Peter J. S 232, S 297
Quackenbush, Myndert W. S 297
Quackenbush, Myndert W. (Lieut) S 349
Quackendorph, Henry I. S 215
Quackinbush T 329
Quackenbush, Abraham Jr. S 352
Quackenbush, David S 348, S 352, S 357
Quackenbush, Isaac S 352
Quackenbush, Jeremiah S 348
Quackenbush, Mc W. (Lieut) S 349
Quackenbush, Peter S 348
Quackenbush, Vincent (Lieut) S 349
Quackenbuss, John G. S 352
Quackinboss, Nicholas S 352
Queen Anne S 35, 48
Queen Esther T 285
Queen, Michael S 336
Quick, John T 343, S 276
Quiema, Samuel S 304
Quit Rents S 344
Quollenger, Gosper S 348
Quollinger, Andrew S 348
Raads, Pieter S 96
Rab, Killiaen S 91
Rabel, Daniel S 147
Raber, Andrew S 320
Rabold, Georg S 355
Radenaer, Jacob T 343, S 348
Radimour, Jacob S 348
Radley, James S 311
Radtly, Jacobus S 300
Rageutzwey, Huybert S 101
Rainault, Peter S 147
Rainault, Pietter S 147
Raisner, Jacobus T 174, 258
Ram, Henrig S 91
Ram, Niklaas S 101
Raminger, Daniel S 105
Ramsay, Nathaniel (Lieut. Colonel) (Md) S 276
Randall, John S 336
Range, Martin S 101
Rankin, Esther S 282
Rankins, James Jr. S 276
Ransier, G. S 336
Ransier, George S 348
Ranson, Joseph T 343
Rapalje, Abraham S 330
Rapalje, Dina S 330
Rapalje, John S 330
Rapelyea, Jacob S 336
Rapelyea, Thomas S 336
Rapspel, Frederick T 174, 257

Romeyn, (Dominie) S 235
Romien, Abraham S 352
Romien, Nicholas S 352
Romine, Theodorus F. S 349, S 352
Romsch, Christian S 147
Roome, John L. C. S 336
Ronche, Thys S 105
Roneons, Jonathan S 348
Ronnin, John, Jr. S 348
Roof, John (Captain) S 345
Roof, John S 348
Roorback, John T 91
Roorey, William S 358
Roos, Andreas S 147
Roos, Catharina S 134
Roos, Ephraim S 134
Roos, Wilhelm S 134
Roosa, Cornelius S 276
Roosa, Egbert S 336
Roosa, Guisbert S 330, S 336
Roosa, Jacobus S 330, S 336
Roose, Kristoffel S 96
Roose, James S 276
Roost, Anna Maria S 86
Roost, Johan S 86
Root, Christian T 174, 258
Root, Oliver (Major) T 147, 178, S 230
Rop, Johannes S 86
Ropp, George T 174, 258
Roppole, George S 321
Rorbaalin, Anna Eliz. S 118
Rorballin, Anna Morga. S 118
Ros, Frederig S 91
Rosback, Frederick S 300
Roschkop, Martin S 101
Roschman, Anna Eliz. S 118
Roschman, Johannes S 118, S 120
Roschman, Maria Cath. S 118
Roschmann, Anna Elisabetha S 134
Roschmann, Johann S 134
Roschmann, Johannes S 134, S 147
Roschmann, Maria Catharina S 134
Rose, Andreas S 134
Rose, Peter S 134
Rose, Anna S 82
Rose, Catherine S 82
Rose, James S 276
Rose, Johanna S 56
Rose, Matthias S 336
Rose, Peter S 56
Rosebach, Peter S 96
Roseel, John S 348
Rosekrans, Abraham S 115
Rosekrans, Nicholas T 174, 258
Rosenbaum, Bernhard S 147
Rosenboom, Pieter S 96
Rosenberger S 336
Rosenberger, Johan Philip S 106
Rosencrantz, Abraham (Reverend) T 207, 227, 291, 309, S 155
Rosencrantz, George T 174, 258
Rosenkrantz, Nicolaus S 355
Rosenquest, Alexander S 134
Rosenweig, Agnes Gertrude S 147
Rosey, Justin S 225

Rosin, Umbert S 118
Rosor, Martinus Fredrik S 96
Ross, Charles (Captain) T 280
Ross, Christian S 304
Ross, Frances T 280
Ross, Jacobus (Captain) T 343
Ross, John (Major) T 59, 155, 156, 191, 196, 226, 231, 238, 250, S 164, S 170, S 175, S 182, S 217, S 218, S 221, S 294
Ross, Daniel S 336
Ross, Philip S 336
Ross, William S 336
Ross, Zebulon S 336
Rot, Peter S 96
Rot, Philyppus S 91
Rote, Charles S 300
Roth, Johann S 134
Roth, Hans Peter S 86
Roth, Johan Engelbert S 106
Roth, John S 348
Roth, John Joost S 91
Roth, Joost S 106
Roth, Peter 134
Rothin, Anna Catherin S 147
Rouch, Friderich S 147
Rouch, Johan Casper S 112
Roug, Kasper S 86
Rouse, Andrew S 304, S 310
Rouse, Elias T 174
Rouse,Thomas (Ensign) (Md) S 276
Rousman, Johannis S 111
Rover, Hans Jacob S 101
Row, Hans Jurch S 112
Row, John Peter S 330, S 336
Rowland, Smith S 330
Rowley, Aaron (Major)
Rowley, (Colonel) T 156
Royal Grant T 202, 250, 305
Ruamay, John S 276
Rubel, Johan S 96
Ruber, Andrew T 333
Rubert, Arnold S 101
Ruble, John S 330
Ruble, Thomas S 330
Ruch, Nicolas S 96, S 147
Ruchsal, Jacob S 91
Rudolff, John S 82
Ruebenich, Elisabetha S 134
Ruebenich, Mattaeus S 134
Rued, Johann Georg S 134
Rued, Johan Michael S 134
Rued, Johann Peter S 134
Rueger, Anna Margretha S 134
Rueger, Johann Philipp S 134
Rueger, Johannes S 134
Ruehl, Anna Catharina S 134
Ruehl, Anna Dorothea Margretha S 134
Ruehl, Gottfrid S 134
Ruehl, Gottfrid S 134
Ruehl, Gottfried S 134
Ruehl, Niclaus S 134
Rues, Ludwig S 147
Ruff, Christian S 306
Ruff, Johan S 101
Ruff, John T 174, S 348
Ruff, John (Captain)
Ruff, Michael T 174, 258
Ruffener, Thos. S 120
Ruffner, Thomas S 147
Ruger, Johann Philipp S 147

Ruhl, Fred. W. (Reverend) T 306
Ruhl, Niclaus S 120
Rumsey, Asa (Fifer) S 276
Rumsay, David S 276
Rumsnider, Henry T 174, 254, S 276
Runan, Philip S 320
Rundell, Richard S 276
Rung, Hendrick S 297
Runnels, Robert S 336
Runnels, William S 276
Runnils S 300
Runnins, John Jr. S 348
Runnins, John Sr. S 348
Runnolds, Benjamin S 304
Runyan, Benjamin S 300
Runyans, John S 352
Runyans, Jonathan S 244
Runyens, Henry S 352
Rupert, Rudolph S 91
Ruport, Adam S 357
Ruport, D. S 357
Rur, Jonas S 309
Rury, Henry S 352
Rury, William S 352
Rus, Peter S 310
Ruscraff, Henry S 336
Rusch, Anna Magdalena S 134
Ruse, Jacob S 352
Rush, John S 336
Rusin, Anna Catharina S 118
Rusin, Anna Congeunda S 118
Rusin, Anna Cmargaretta S 118
Rusin, Maria Catharina S 118
Rusmann, Elisabeth S 134
Rusmann, Johann S 134
Rusmann, Johannes S 134
Russer, John Peter S 91
Russ, Johannes (Capt) T 170, 255
Russ, John (Captain) S 345
Russel, John S 304, S 336
Russell, Daniel S 300
Russell, Jacob S 330
Russing, Mattys S 96
Rust, George T 174, 258
Rustiw, Andreis S 86
Ruth and wife S 86
Ruth, Kristiaan and wife S 86
Rutherford, Samuel (Ensign) (Penn) S 276
Ruto, Elias S 306
Rutsel, Kasper S 106
Rutt, Charles S 304, S 315
Rutz, Matteus S 101
Ruyter, Henry S 330
Ruyter, John S 336
Ryan, John S 355
Ryan, Thomas T 343
Ryckart, Lodowick S 297
Ryer, Henry S 357
Rykert, Barent S 336
Rykert, Hendrick S 357
Rykerts, Philip S 336
Ryley, Charles S 336
Rytchmeyer, Captain George S 153
Saalbach, Johann Smith S 134
Saalbach, Maria Margretha S 134
Sabin, Jeremiah Jr. S 336
Sabine, Lorenzo S 326
Sacia, David F. S 180
Sackett, Richard S 44

Schar, Peter S 91
Schart, Johan Daniel S 101
Scharts, Antony S 106
Schaster, Anna Sibylla S 135
Schaster, Margretha Elisabeth S 135
Schaster, Maria Margretha S 135
Schauer, Johann Michael S 135
Schauer, Magdalena S 135
Schauermann, Johan Emerich S 135
Schauermann, Maria Solomo S 135
Schauermann, Sibylia S 135
Schaull, Johannes S 114
Schauser, Michael S 135
Schawerin, Magdalena S 147
Schawerman, Conrad S 120, S 147
Schbut, Ellrug S 91
Scheat, Andony S 348
Schebber, Johannes T 174, 258
Schedp, Jacob S 135
Scheefer, Geerard S 101
Scheefer, Hans Jacob S 106
Scheefer, Johan Andries S 106
Scheefer, Niklaas S 101
Scheefer, Hendrig S 86
Scheenberger, Johan S 101
Scheever, Johan Hendrig S 101
Schef, Anna Maria S 135
Schefer, Adam S 348
Schefer, Johan Mikel S 106
Schefer, Lourens S 91
Scheff, Anna Margreta S 135
Scheff, Johan Willem S 106
Scheff, Lisabetha S 135
Scheff, William S 50
Scheffener, Reinart S 101
Scheffer, Andries S 96
Scheffer, Frederick S 111
Scheffer, Hans Adam S 91
Scheffer, Hans Peter S 91
Scheffer, Jacob T 174, 258, S 101
Scheffer, Johan Gorg S 106
Scheffer, Johannes S 135
Scheffer, Jost S 296
Scheffer, Philip S 111
Scheffer, Reynhaert S 111
Scheffier, Matteys S 91
Scheffing, Johanna S 106
Schehart, Michel S 101
Scheib, Anna Catharina S 135
Scheib, Anna Maria S 135
Scheib, Hieronymus S 135
Scheib, Maria Elisabeth S 135
Scheifer, Gerhardus S 106
Scheifer, Hans S 106
Schein, Michel Meing S 96
Scheit, Peter T 174, 258
Schel, Christian S 114, S 355
Schel, Jacob S 101
Schell, Christian S 115, S 147
Schell, Johannes S 115, S 147, S 297, S 330, S 355
Schell, Jost S 296
Schellengerger, Koenraet S 91
Schellenperge, Hans Jerog S 91
Scheller, Johan S 96
Schellin, Anna Margretha S 147
Schellin, Anna Gertrude S 147
Schelling, Johan S 96

Schelman, George S 296
Schelter, Kasper S 101
Schenck, Georg S 355
Schenckel, Jonas S 147
Schenckelberg, Christina S 147
Schenectady T 241, S 209
Schenk, Hans Koenraet S 101
Schenk, Hans Nikel S 101
Schenkelberger, Hans Jacob S 91
Schenkelberger, Herman S 106
Schepp, Antony S 106
Scherdel, Koenraet S 101
Scherer, Johann Theobald S 147
Scherer, Ulrich S 147
Scherhinger, Johs S 91
Scherin, Maria Margt S 119
Scherl, Jacob S 147
Scherman, Valentyn S 91
Schermig, Andries S 91
Schermann, Henrich S 147
Scherp, Anna Barbara S 135
Scherp, Jacob S 86, S 114, S 135
Scherp, Johan Jacob S 135
Scherp, (Sharp) John S 114
Scherp, Jurgen Henrigh S 135
Scherp, Jurich Emrig S 112
Scherp (Sharp) Michael S 114
Scherer, Justina S 135
Scherer, Theobald S 135
Schermerhorn, Mr. L. C. S 157
Scherts, Jurch S 113
Scherver, Joost S 91
Scherver, Philippus S 101
Schesbli, Joost Koenraet S 96
Schesdons, Kristoffel S 106
Scheser, (Schever?) Hans Hendrik S 101
Schesselmin, Henrig S 96
Schest, Johann Wilhelm S 135
Schester, Johann S 135
Schester, Johann Veltin S 135
Schester, Philip S 101
Schester, Serbus S 96
Schesting, Johannes S 91
Schet, Johan Henrig S 106
Schetmak, Johan S 91
Scheugh, Mattys S 101
Scheucher, Michel S 101
Scheue, Gilles S 101
Scheureder, Handerig S 91
Schever, (Schaffer) Harme S 114
Schey, Hans Peter S 101
Scheyt, Mander S 91
Schieb, Georg Friderick S 357
Schief, William S 111
Schieff, Georg S 355
Schieffer, Jacob S 111
Schieffer, Nicholas S 111
Schiely, Martin S 348
Schienck, Michael S 147
Schier, Hans Ulrig S 91
Schiets, Hans Adam S 111
Schiets, Johannis S 111
Schiffer, Peter T 174, 343
Schilderin, Margareet S 101
Schilfer, Ludwig S 106
Schilling S 102
Schiloser, Johan S 91
Schilt, Johan Henrig S 96
Schimell, Johan Nicolaes S 91
Schimberger, Henrig S 102
Schimmell, Francis S 297, S 348
Schimtin, Eva Maria S 91

Schinberger, Bartel S 102
Schinberger, Susan S 102
Schimell, Johan Nicolaes S 92
Schister, Philipp S 135
Schlicherin, Anna Margaretha S 147
Schieffeer, Philipp S 147
Schieumer, Mathias S 147
Schley, Johann Peter S 147
Schmit, Johannes S 297
Schmit, Michel S 102
Schmitz, Johan S 102
Schimtin, Eva Maria S 92
Schipper Jurig S 86
Schithel, Jacob S 96
Schits, Marten S 96
Schitsin, Anna S 106
Schlegt, Johan S 91, S 92
Schlepusch, Hans Peter S 92
Schletzer, Jeremy S 82
Schleyer, Johan S 92
Schleicher, Anna Catharina S 135
Schleicher, Anna Margretha S 135
Schleicher, Catharina Elisabeth S 135
Schleicher, Johann Adam S 135
Schleicher, Johann Georg S 135
Schlemer, Anna Eva S 135
Schlemer, Mattheus S 135
Schlemmer, Anna Elisabetha S 135
Schlemmer, Anna Veronica S 135
Schlemmer, Maria Catharina S 135
Schlemmer, Maria Gerdraut S 135
Schlemmer, Mattheus S 135
Schley, Anna Maria S 135
Schley, Johann Michel S 135
Schling, Henrik S 96
Schlingluff, John S 82
Schlitzler, Maria Elisabetha S 135
Schlug, Johan S 92
Schluk, Martin S 92
Schmick, Nicolaes S 92
Schmid, Adam S 135
Schmid, Adam Michael S 135
Schmid, Anna Elisabetha S 135
Schmid, Anna Maria S 135
Schmid, Bernhard S 135
Schmid, Christina S 135
Schmid, Conrad S 135
Schmid, Elisabeth S 135
Schmid, Elisabetha Margretha S 135
Schmid, Eva S 135
Schmid, Friedrich S 355
Schmid, Georg S 135
Schmid, Georg Adam S 135
Schmid, Henrich S 135
Schmid, Johann Adam S 135
Schmid, Johann Georg S 135
Schmid, Johann Henrich S 135
Schmid, Johann Peter S 136
Schmid, Johannes S 136
Schmid, Johannes Peter S 136
Schmid, Justus Adam S 136
Schmid, Ludwig S 136
Schmid, Margaretje S 136
Schmid, Maria Barbara S 136
Schmid, Maria Catharina S 136
Schmid, Nicklas S 136

Sheldon, Joseph S 336
Shell, Adam, Jr. T 174
Shell, Christian T 343
Shell, Johannes S 330
Shell, John T 174, S 336, S 355
Shell, John, Sr. S 297
Shelly, John S 348
Shelp, Fredrick S 352
Shen, Anna Gertraud S 137
Shen, Peter S 137
Sheperman, Chrestion S 304
Shepherd, Abraham (Lieut) T 343
Shepperman, Christian T 65, S 300, S 311
Sherbrooke, Miles S 336
Sherer, James S 277
Sheridan, Richard S 277
Sherman, Gilbert S 304
Sherman, Peter S 277
Sherman, William S 336
Sherwood, Dyer S 336
Sherwood, Job S 277
Sherwood, Newcom S 277
Sherwood, Seth, (Captain) S 277
Sherwood, Seth S 296
Sherwood, Stephen (Ensign) S 277, S 336
Sherwood, William S 336
Scheuer, John Adam S 82
Shever, Partle S 300
Shew, George S 357
Shew, Godfrey S 277, S 29, S 3527
Shew, Henry S 352
Shew, Jacob T 156, S 249, S 277, S 352
Shew, John S 277, S 352
Shew, Stephen S 277, S 352
Shew, Steven S 357
Shewmaker, Hanjost S 357
Shiely, Mantus T 258
Shiffen, George T 343
Shiffen T 343
Shiffer, Nicholas T 174
Shilip, Christian S 352
Shill, Jacob T 174, 258, S 304, S 306
Shillip, Christian S 358
Shilp, Frederick S 352
Shimel, Dieterich S 348
Shinkel, Jonas S 112
Shinkel, Johan Hendrick S 112
Ship, George F. S 352
Shipton, William S 336
Shireman, George (Corporal) S 277, S 348
Shirid, Thomas S 336
Shite, Peter T 174, 202
Shitterly, John
Shittser, Hendrick T 174, 258
Shmit, Johan Jurch S 112
Shoe, Johan Wm. S 112
Shoe, Johannis S 112
Shoe, Martinus S 112
Shoemaker, Christopher S 355
Shoemaker, Frederick S 297, S 355
Shoemaker, Hanyoost T 326, S 355
Shoemaker House T 124
Shoemaker, Hanjost S 355
Shoemaker, John S 355

Shoemaker, Jost S 355
Shoemaker, Rudolph T 125, 321, S 352, S 361
Shoemaker, Thomas S 352, S 355, S 361
Shoemaker, Tomis S 352
Shoeman, William S 357
Shoewaker, Godfried S 114
Shok, Zacariah S 300
Shol, Coenrad S 115
Shol, Johannes S 115
Shole, Jost S 304
Sholl, Hanyost T 174, S 300
Sholl, John T 121 , 17, S 3004
Sholl, John Jost T 174
Sholl, Joseph T 174
Sholt, John S 304
Sholtz, George S 300
Shonweiss, John S 82
Shoonmaker, Frederick (Captain) S 247
Shoul, Joseph T 174, S 304
Should, Geroge T 258
Shouldis, Hendrick T 258
Shoulds, John T 258
Shoults, Henry S 300
Shoults, John S 300
Shoults, John Jacob S 300
Shoultz, Henry I. S 300
Shoultz, John I. S 300
Shoultz, Jacob S 300
Showl, Johanes S 304
Showman, William S 115
Shrum, Isaac S 304
Shrumbling, Henry (Lieut) S 345
Shuell, John S 359
Shuell, Peter S 359
Shull, David S. S 174
Shull, Honyost (Ensign) S 216
Shull, Johannes (Lieut) T 188, S 216
Shullis, Jacob T 258
Shulop, Henry S 336
Shuls, Hemrich T 174
Shultes, John Jr. S 314
Shultes, (Lieut.) Mattice S 154
Shultis, Henry I. S 310
Shultis, John T 174, S 313
Shults, George T 116, 174, S 307
Shults, George I. S 316
Shults, Henry T 174, 258, S 265, S 307
Shults, Jacob S 304, S 307
Shults, James S 304
Shults, Johannes, Jr. T 174
Shults, John S 336
Shults, William T 174
Shultys, Christopher S 297
Shultys, Jacob T 254
Shultz, John T 258
Shultz, William T 258
Shurtliff, Robert
Shute, Frederick S 355
Shute, William S 355Shutes, Christopher S 316
Shutes, John P . S 304
Shutes, John J. S 304
Shuts, Henry S. S 304
Shuts, John Jo. S 304
Shutter, Henry T 174
Shutters, Georg T 258
Shuttes, John I. T 304, S 309

Shuttes, Philip S 114
Shutthers, George T 174
Shwab, Peter S 82
Shyke, Peter T 121, 174
Shwartz, Matthias S 82
Schwartze, John S 82
Sibel, Falenteyn S 96
Sibelin, Anna Getha S 148
Sibus, Hans S 92
Siefer, Lodovick S 336
Siegman, Hans Peter S 106
Siekerin, John Jacob S 119
Sieknerin, Anna Apolonia S 119
Sieknerin, Johannes S 119
Sien, Jno. Pet. S 120
Sidere, Johan S 92
Sidnich, William S 296
Siemon, Johan Wm. S 112
Sietz, George T 174, 258
Sies, Hans Peter S 102
Sifer, Jacob S 277
Siffer, John,Sr. S 277
Siffer, John S 277
Sigeler, Kristiaen S 92
Sigmund, Johannes S 86
Signer, Johannes S 148
Sikart, Mattys S 102
Sikert, Basser S 92
Siles, Mickel S 96
Silesy, Katrina S 96
Sillebach, Gerrit S 309
Silback, John T 174
Silleback, Christian T 174
Silleback, John T 174, S 309
Sillenick, Harmanus S 296
Siller, Johan S 96
Sillibogh, Hincrist S 352
Sillibig, John S 352Sillo, Klaud S 92
Simen, Johan Adam S 92
Simer, Gesom S 355
Simendinger, Anna Margaretta S 119
Simendinger, Ulrich S 119, S 148
Simmerman, Johan Jurg S 92
Simon, Anna Elisabetha S 137
Simon, Anna Maria S 137
Simon, Benedik S 102
Simon Johann Michael S 137
Simon, Johann Wilhelm S 137
Simon, Johann Ulrich S 137
Simon, Laurents S 102
Simon, Philippus S 92
Simon, Peter S 102
Simon, Wilhelm S 137
Simon, Sagarias S 102
Simmerman, Conratce S 348
Simmerman, Henery S 348
Simmons, Abraham S 300
Simmons, James S 336
Simmons, Maurice S 336
Simms, Jeptha The Frontiersmen of New York is referenced through out the books.
Simon, Philipp S 148
Simon, Whilhelm S 148
Simonin, Anna Margretha S 148
Simonin, Maria Magdalena S 148
Simpson, Andrew S 169
Simpson, (Captain) T 145
Simpson, Henry S 352
Simpson, Nicholas S 352
Simson, Alexander S 336

Simson, Isabel S 336
Sinder, Henrig S 92
Singraff, Henrig S 92
Simbluv, Johannes S 86
Sipler, Kristiaan S 96
Sisson, James S 330
Sitig, Krist S 102
Sitlebach, Christayane S 352
Sits, George T 174, 258
Sits, Hendrick T 174, 258, S 348
Sits, John S 348
Sits, Nichols S 348
Sittenich, Christian S 120, S 148
Sitterly, John S 304, S 306
Sittig, Christian S 137
Sittig, Herman S 96
Sitts, Baltus T 94
Sitts, Mary T 94
Sitts, Peter S 164, S 348
Sitz, Baldes S 348
Sitz, Peter (Ensign) T 127, 170, 255, S 277, S 285
Sixbarry, Adam S 352
Sixbary, Cornelius S 352
Sixberry, Bangnen S 352
Sixberry, Cornelius Jr. S 352, S 357
Sixt, Anna Elisabeth S 137
Sixt, Christian S 137
Sixt, Christina Elsabeth S 137
Sixt, Elsabeth S 137
Sixt, Gertraut S 137
Sixt, Henrch S 137
Skans, Johannis S 111
Skeans, Governeur S 336
Skeans, M. S 336
Skene, Andrew Philip (Lieut) S 330
Skene, Philip, (Major) S 330, S 336
Skiget, Richard (Sergeant) S 277
Skill, Jacob S 300
Skinner, Abraham S 272
Skinner, (Captain) S 250
Skinner, Isaac T 343
Skinner, John S 352
Skinner, Sam'l Spencer S 336
Skulgraft, Richard S 300
Skutt, Peter P. S 320
Slack, Martinis S 352
Slake, Susan S 86
Sleiger, Johan Jurg S 96
Slesser, Hendrik S 102
Sligt, Hans S 102
Slingerlant, Teunis S 336
Slaven, James T 343
Slawson, Bowels S 304
Slawter, Gilbert T 343
Sleeper (Quaker) T 128
Sleephaan, Johannes S 86
Slette, Peter S 304
Sloat, Polly T 70
Slocum, Lipe S 318
Slocum, William S 336
Slosher, Andreas S 102
Slott,Cornelius (Sergeant) S 277
Slouwits (Widow) S 297
Slutt, William S 277
Slutts, John S 336
Slutts, Michael S 336
Slutz, James T 174
Slutz, Jhanies T 258
Sluyber, Sacharias S 86

Sluyter, James S 336
Slycke, Wm. S. T 174
Small, Jacob T 234
Small, Jacob (Captain) S 353
Small, Susanna (Widow) S 297
Smeath, James T 258
Smeyer, Johannes S 92
Smidt, Philip S 348
Smies, Theodorus S 86
Smil, Paltcs T 258
Smit, Andries S 92
Smit, Bernhart S 106
Smit, Daniel S 92
Smit, George Volpert S 96
Smit, Hans Martin S 106
Smit, Hans Peter S 102
Smit, Hendrig S 92
Smit, Johan S 96, S 106
Smit, Johan Adam S 96
Smit, Johan Christ S 111
Smit, Johan Elias S 106
Smit, Johan Joost S 106
Smit, John Andreas S 102
Smit, Johannes S 92
Smit, Joost S 102
Smit, Karel S 96
Smit, Kasper S 92
Smit, Michel S 92
Smit, Niklaas S 102
Smit, Thomas S 102
Smith, Adam Michael S 361
Smith, Anita S 343
Smith, Arent S 357
Smith, Austin S 330, S 336
Smith, Balser S 304
Smith, Baltus S. T 258, S 314
Smith, Benjamin T 343, S 336
Smith, Bolzar T 174, 258, S 359
Smith, Charles A. (Reverend) S 193
Smith, Christopher S 336
Smith, Coenraed S 112, S 114, S 357
Smith, Conraat S 115
Smith, Cornelius S 357
Smith, Daniel S 336, S 357
Smith, Ephriam S 361
Smith, George T 121, 174, 258, S 300, S 316
Smith, George Jr S 304
Smith, Hans Miggel S 96
Smith, Harmanus S 352
Smith, Hendrick S 300
Smith, Hendrick Jr. S 300
Smith, Henry T 121, 174, 258, S 82, S 115, S 116, S 226, S 248, S 286, S 300, S 304, S 316, S 359
Smith, Henry A. S 314
Smith, Henry H.
Smith, Henry N. S 308
Smith, Isaac T 306, S 277, S 336
Smith, J S 336
Smith, Jacob S 82, S 336
Smith, James T 174, 258, 343
Smith, James (Lieut) (Penn) S 277
Smith, Jeremiah S 300, S 304, S 306
Smith, Jermiah N. S 314
Smith, John S 353, S 355
Smith, Johan Adam S 112

Smith, Johan Hendrick S 114
Smith, Johan Jurgh S 361
Smith, Johan Nicholas S 114
Smith, Johannes S 114. S 277, S 348
Smith, John T 121, 325, 343, S 82, S 115, S 116, S 297, S 300, S 330, S 336, S 348, S 357, S 359
Smith, John (Q.M. Sergeant) S 277
Smith, John (Orderly Sergeant) S 186
Smith, John (Lieut) S 277
Smith, John Conradt S 116
Smith, John Johnson S 330
Smith, John Willem S 86
Smith, Joseph S 336
Smith, Joshua M. S 336
Smith, Josiah (Lieut.) T 343, S 277
Smith, Kasper S 86, S 96
Smith, Magdeleena S 86
Smith, Maria Barbera S 86
Smith, Margreta S 86
Smith, Marte S 361
Smith, Martin S 114
Smith, Matthias T 174, 258
Smith, Nancy S 249
Smith, Nicolaus S 86, S 112
Smith, Nicholas T 174, 258, S 300, S 316, S 355
Smith, Nicholas, Jr. T 174, 258, S 304
Smith, Paltes T 174
Smith, Peter T 131, S 111, S 86, S 112
Smith, Peter N. S 304, S 316
Smith, Philip T 174, S 115, S 116, S 348
Smith, Reuben S 336
Smith, Richard S 277
Smith, Samuel S 336
Smith, Seth S 304, S 315
Smith, Signud S 86
Smith, Stephen S 336
Smith, Thomas S 336
Smith, Uriah S 165
Smith, Wilhelmus S 114
Smith, William T 73, 174, 179, 258, S 217, S 250, S 251, S 304, S 315, S 330, S 336, S 355, S 359
Smith, William, Jr. S 330
Smith, William S. S 283
Smitt, Johan S 111
Snake, George S 348
Snead, Charles (Lieut) (Va) S 277
Snead, Smith (Captain) (Va) S 277
Sneck, George T 174, 258, S 355
Snedeker, Richard S 336
Snedeker, Theodorus S 330, S 336
Sneden, Robert S 336
Sneden, Stephen S 336
Sneden, Teunis S 330
Sneek, George T 174

Timmerman, Peter A. T 305
Timmerman, Samuel T 306
Timmerman, Willem S 102
Timmerman, William T 175, 258, S 300
Timorman, William T 254
Tims, Michael S 352
Tinis, Jacob S 355
Tinis, John S 355
Tioga T 138
Tipenhove, Hans Jurg S 102
Tisese, John S 298
Tissell, James S 337
Tissot, Gideon S 337
Titchort, Gideon S 337
Titcomb, Major T 139
Titemer, Hans Martin S 92
Titus, Isaac S 330
Tobias, Christian S 330, S 337
Tobias, Joseph S 330, S 337
Tobich, Johann Peter S 138
Toler, Benjamin S 311
Tolly, John F. S 320
Tom (colored) S 348
Tomas, Hans Willem S 102
Tomas, Johan S 102
Tomas, Mattys S 102
Tomkins, Israel S 337
Tomson, William S 166
Tonese, Peter S 138
Tong, Joshua S 337
Tonius, Christina S 138
Tonnius, Anna Christina S 138
Tontill, Joseph S 352
Tonyea, John T 175
Toop T 193
Toos, Serris S 102
Torer, Hans S 92
Toror, Rudolph S 297
Totten, James S 337
Totten, Jonas S 337
Totten Joseph S 337
Toup, Michel S 86
Townsend, Daniel T 343
Townsend Epenetus (Parson) S 337
Townsend, John S 337
Townsend, Uriah S 330, S 337
Townshend, Roger T 343
Tozoll, Hans Jacob S 102
Traut, Elisabetha S 138
Traver S 337
Travis, Charles S 330
Travis, Ezekiel T 343
Travis, Jacob (Lieut) T 343
Travis, Jeremiah S 330, S 337
Travis, William S 330, S 337
Tread, Samuel T 175, 258
Treaty of Paris T 61
Treattermam, Martin S 92
Tredwell, Capt S 337
Tredwell, Samuel S 337
Triespeisser (?) Johan S 102
Trift, Matteus S 92
Trilhauser, Johannes S 119
Trilheuser, Johannes S 147
Trip, Mattys S 92
Trip, Katarina Margareet S 92
Tripes Hill S 222
Trombauer, Niclas S 82
Trombour, Dietrich S 138
Trombour, Johannes S 138
Trombour, Magdalana S 138

Trombour, Niclaus S 138
Trotten, William S 259
Truat, John S 82
Tryon, William (Governor) T 277, S 340
Truax, John S 356
Trumbull, John S 316
Trumbull, Jonethan S 304
Trumbull, Jonathan jr. S 283
Trumbull, William S 304
Trumbull, William Jr S 304
Trumph, John Michael S 82
Trusmors, John E. S 320
Tsmallenberger, Zill S 92
Tubenbeeker, Johan S 97
Tucker, Daniel S 337
Tucker, George T 175, 258
Tucker, Jacob T 175, 258
Tucker, Johannis T 175, 258
Tucks, Peter S 348
Tuesler, John J. S 304
Tuesler, John Jr S 317
Tuesler, Marcus S 317
Tulling, Henry S 348
Tusler, Marcus S 304
Turck, Isaac S 138
Turnbell, Jonathan S 321
Turnbell, William S 321
Turnbull, Robert S 337
Turnbull, William Jr S 321
Turner, John S 330
Tusler, Jacob S 359
Tuttle, Stephen T 343, S 330
Trumbull, John S 304
Trumbull, Jonethan S 283, S 304
Trumbull, William S 304
Trumbull, William Jr S 304
Turner, John S 337
Tryon, William (Governor) T 277, S 330
Tygart, Siverenius S 301
Tygel, John S 308
Tyger, Geroge T 175, 258
Tygert, Henry S 348
Tygert, Peter S. T 175, 258
Tygert, Peter T 182
Tygert, Warner T 318
Tygert, Sefrinus S 218
Tyler, Asa T 343
Tyler, Bezaleel T 343
Tyler, Ebenezer T 343
Tyms, Michael S 352
Tys, Mattys S 102
Tuesnover, Samual S 316
Turch, Caspar S 82
Turck, Isaac S 56
Tum, Adam S 301
Tum, Conradt S 301
Tunn, Nicholas S 301
Tuscaroras S 297
Tusler, Jacob S 319
Ubel, Kristiaen S 92
Uhl, Carl S 120
Uhl, Carol, S 147
Uhl, Christina S 138
Uhl, Henrich S 147
Uhl, Jno. Hen. S 120
Ulick, Johannes T 254
Ullendorff, Daniel T 175, 258, S 348
Ullerig, Hans Jeorog S 92
Ullersz, Henrig S 92
Ulman, Burnt S 352

Ulman, Johanes S 352
Ulman, Leonard S 352
Ulrich, Johannes Elias S 147
Ulrig, Albregt S 102
Ulrig, Daniel S 86
Ulrig, Elisabet S 86
Ulrig, Fredrig, Hartman S 106
Ulrig, Hans S 102
Ulrig, Johan S 106
Ulrig, Johan Elias S 97
Ulrig, Katharina S 86
Ulrig, Kristoffel S 86
Ulrigh, Anna Maria S 86
Ulsever, Stephen S 348
Ulsaver, Bastian S 356
Ulzhaven, Bastian S 348
Umducht, Jacob S 102
Umberto, Valentin S 147
Underbill, Frederick S 337
Underbill, John S 337
Underbill, Nathaniel S 337
Underbill, Nathaniel Jr. S 337
Underhill, Benjamin S 330
Undervill, William S 337
Union Church T 297
Unis, Johan S 92
Upper Fort, Schoharie T 149
Urban, Michel S 102
Urquhart, John (Rev.) T 282
Urzel, Hans Migel S 86
Usner, Peter Gorg S 355
Ustick, Henry S 337
Ustick, William S 337
Utt, Francis T 175, 258, S 356
Uttermark, John B. S 348
Uttermar, John J. S 348
Vaar, Daniel S 102
Vach (Fox) Johann George (Surgeon) T 169, 175, 213, 255
Vactor, John S 357
Vader, (Captain) S 258 (Veeder)
Vader, Elgin A. T 262
Vadder, Isack S 352
Vaghte, John S 352
Vail, Benjamin (Captain) T 343
Vail, Gilbert T 343
Vail, John S 337
Vail, Joseph T 343
Vail, Moses S 337
Valendin, Velden S 97
Vallance, David S 296
Valter, Christian T 175
Van, Johannes S 348
Van Aken, Daniel T 175
Van Alen, Peter S 317
Van Allen, Jacob S 352
Van Allen, John S 337
Vanallstine, Abraham C. S 348
Van Allstine, Peter S 348
Van Alsten, Cornelius C. S 348
Van Alstin, Gilbert S 352
Van Alstin, Harmans S 348
Van Alstine, Abraham S 348, S 352
Vanalstine, Cornelius S 348, S 352, S 357
Van Alstine, Cornelius I. S 301
Vanalstine, Cornelius J. S 348
Vanalstine, Isaac S 352
Van alstine, John S 348
Vanalstine, John G. S 348
Vanalstine, John M. S 348
Van Alstine, Gilbert S 297

Walter, Martin S 337
Walter, Philip S 337
Walters, John S 358
Walton, Charles S 318
Waltz, Conrad T 175, 259
Waltz, George T 175, 259
Walvel, Johann Gerg T 175, 259
Walwrath, Henry (Ensign) S 345
Wambach, Catharina S 139
Wambach, Wilhelm S 139
Wampal, Cornelius S 353
Wampal, Handrick S 353
Wample, John S 353
Wample, William S 353
Wanaker, Conradus S 337
Wanamaker, Dirick S 337
Wanbag, Hans Peter S 86
Wanbag, Nicolaes S 86
Wandle, Daniel T 344
Wanemacher, Anna S 139
Wanemacher, Anna Margretha S 139
Wanemacher, Dietrich S 139
Wanemacher, Johann Dietrich S 139
Wanemacher, Johann Michael S 139
Wanger, Isaac S 301
Wanmager, Koenraet S 106
Wannemacher, Dietrich S 147
Wannemacher, Peter S 147
Wannenmacher, Anna Kunigunda S 139
Wannenmacher, Elisabetha Ottilia S 139
Wannenmacher, John S 139
Wannemager, Peter S 103
Wanner, Agnes Barbara S 139
Wanner, Anna Barbara S 139
Wanner, Johann Ludwig S 139
Wanner, Johann Michael S 139
Wanner, Ludwig S 139, S 147
Wanner, Maria Dorothea S 139
Wanner, Lodwick S 113
Wannermacher, Johan Dietrick S 119
Wanninger, Johan S 106
Wanser, Isaac S 304, S 320
Wansor, Thomas S 304, S 337
Wapag, Herman S 106
Warambour, Mary S 82
Ward S 337
Ward, Edmond S 330, S 337
Ward, Edmund S 337
Ward, Israel S 330, S 337
Ward, John S 337
Ward, Joseph T 344
Ward, Thomas T 344
Wardell, Eliakim S 277
Warembourg, Maria S 148
Warman, Tho., (Lieut) (Va) S 277
Warmer, Aliken S 139
Warmer, Cornelius S 139
Warmer Jan S 139
Warmer, Johannes S 139
Warner, Michael S 337
Warner, Thomas S 337
Warning, F. S 337
Warmooth, Christian T 175, 259
Warmooth, William T 259
Warmorte, Petter S 348
Warmouth, Nathaniel T 175, 259
Warmooth, Peter T 175, 259

Warmouth, Peter J. T 175, 259
Warmouth, William T 175, 259
Warmud, Christian T 175, 254
Warmud, John, Jr. T 175, 259
Warmut, Christean T 175, 259
Warmuth, John S 348
Warmwood, Mathias T 259
Warmwood, Mathias (Lieut.) T 175
Warmwood, Peter T 175, 259, S 348
Warner, Andrews T 175
Warner, George S 296
Warner, Michael
Warner, Nicholas S 296
Warner, Seth Col. T 32
Warner, Thomas
Warmuth, Coenradt S 309
Warmuth, Widow S 309
Warner, Horatio Gates S 264
Warner, Michael S 116
Warno, Jacob S 120, S 148
Warno, Sibylla S 139
Warraven, Johan Adolph S 113
Warren, Gideon (Captain) T 344
Warren, William T 344
Warrensbush T 59
Wart, Andrew S 353
Wart, Matise S 353
Warts, Matise S 297
Warwarsing T 138
Waschpaelt, Johan S 93
Wasel, Adam T 175, 259
Wasel, George T 175, 259
Wasel, Henry T 175, 259
Wasel, John T 175, 259
Wasel, William T 175, 259
Waset, George S 297
Washborn, Isaac S 337
Washborn, Jonathan S 337
Washburn, Miles S 304, S 318
Washington, George (General) T 25, 69, 96, 129, 193, 208, S 196, S 198, S 201, S 209, S 238, S 272, S 280, S 288
Washington, William T 55
Wassel, Henry T 175, 259
Wasson, Catherine S 282
Wasser, Rudolf S 93
Water, George T 175, 259
Water, William T 175, S 316
Waters, Samuel S 316
Waterbury, Sylvanus S 337
Waters, David S 304
Waters, John S 337
Waters, Samuel S 217, S 304
Wath, Jacob S 348
Watrous, Edward A. S 277
Watser, George S 308
Watson, Jacob S 330
Waston, James S 337
Watson, John S 261, S 296
Watt, Gavin K. and James F. Morrison The British Campaign of 1777: The St. Leger Expedition used as a reference.
Watts, Anne S 269
Watts, John S 330
Watts, Mary "Polly" T 266
Watts, Steven (Major)
Wavel, John S 307
Wavill, George T 175
Wavill, Henry T 175

Wayner, Henry S 82
Waysal, Nicholas T 344
Weack, Sefrnus
Weak, John T 175, 259
Weart, John S 353
Weatherby, Isaac S 308
Weatherhead, John S 330, S 337
Weatherstraw, Henry S 297
Weaver S 337
Weaver, Daniel S 304
Weaver, David S 301
Weaver, Christian S 301
Weaver, George S 298, S 311, S 355
Weaver, Jacob T 175, 319, S 358
Weaver, Jacob G. S 304
Weaver, Jacob N. T 333
Weaver, Johannes S 115, S 337
Weaver, Johan George S 298
Weaver, John T 259, S 320, S 337
Weaver, John Jo. S 304
Weaver, Nichalas T 175, 259, S 297
Weaver, Nicholas S 353
Weaver, Nicholas Jr. S 355
Weaver, Nicholas, H. S 355
Web, Nicholas G. S 355
Weber, Frederick S 355
Weber, Frederick Jr. S 355
Weber, Frederick G. S 355
Weber, George S 355
Weber, George, Jr. S 355
Weber, George F. S 355
Weber, George M. S 355
Weber, Jacob S 355
Weber, Jacob Sr. S 355
Weber, Jacob G. S 355
Weber, Jacob J. S 355
Weber, Jacob N. S 355
Weber, Johannes S 355
Weber, Michel S 355
Webb, Samuel B. (Colonel) S 272
Webb, Sysumet S 277
Webber, Jacob S 44, S 120
Webel, Hans Jacob S 86
Webel, Orzel S 86
Weber, Anna Elisabetha S 139
Weber, Baltes S 103
Weber, Diderig S 97
Weber, Gorg A. S 353
Weber, Hans Jacob S 103
Weber, Henrich S 148
Weber, Jacob S 56, S 103, S 139, S 148
Weber, Johan Henrig S 103
Weber, John Jacob S 82
Weber, Johan Koenraet S 103
Weber, Johann Herman S 139
Weber, Johannes S 139
Weber, Martin S 93
Weber, Mattys S 103
Weber, Michel S 106
Weber, Mighiel S 93
Weber, Niclaus S 120, S 148
Weber, Niklaas S 103
Weber, Nicolaes S 93
Weber, Nicolas S 355, S 355
Weber, Nicolas G. S 355
Weber, Nicolass T 259
Weber, Nicholas H. S 355
Weber, Ottilia S 139

West Canada Creek T 241
Wester, Jacob T 259
Westerlo, Catharine S 320
Westerman, Peter S 348, S 356
Westfall, Abraham T 175
Westfall, Simon T 175
West, Ebenezer (Adjt) (Conn) S 277
West, Leonard T 344
Westheser, Johan Jacob S 93
Westover, Elijah S 319
West Point T 180, 215
Wetherbee, Isaac S 304
Wetmore, Seth T 187
Wettig, Barht S 93
Wever, Andries S 362
Wever, Christian S 155
Wever, Henrig S 93
Wever, Jacob S 297, S 362
Wever, Jacob Jr. S 362
Wever, Nicholas S 111, S 362
Wever, [blotted], Philip S 86
Weyant, Johan Martin S 97
Weydin, Gertrude S 149
Weydknecht, Andreas S 148
Weynants, Benediik S 106
Weyant's Swager S 97
Weyngert, Johan Melchier S 93
Weyniger, Hans Gerhard S 113
Weyniger, Uldrich S 113
Weysch, Matteus S 103
Weyser, Nicholas (Captain) S 345
Weyspaart, Jurg S 103
Weysgerber, Johan S 97
Weytman, Hans Marte S 113
Wexton, John S 337
Wezer, Nicholas T 259
Weuck, Sefrnus T 259
Wheaton, John S 330
Wheaton, Daniel S 337
Wheeler, George S 337
Wheeler, Isaac S 353
Wheelock, Eleazor, (Reverend Doctor) T 272
Whelan, Edward T 344
Whelps, (Captain) S 167
Whihs, Johann S 139
While, Henry S 356
While, Youst Henry S 356
Whiler, Henry S 353
White, (Adjutant) S 230
White, Alexander (Sheriff) T 102, 325, 326, 333, S 243, S 330, S 337
White, Alleburt S 301
White, Edward S 353
White, Elizabeth T 334
White, Epenetus S 277
White, Eve S 330
White, Henry S 330
White, John T 344
White, Joseph T 344
White, Stephen T 344, S 163
White, Stephen (Captain) S 187
White, Sybert S 337
White, Sylvanus S 337
White, Thomas S 330
White, William T 344
Whitekar, Thomas S 358
Whiting, Samuel (Lieut) S 277
Whiteworth, C. S 44
Whiting, Col. T 150
Whitmire, George S 304

Whitmore S 337
Whitney, James S 277
Whitney, Nathan S 330, S 337
Whittaker (Captain) S 208
Whitten, Archilaus T 334
Whoerner, Ludwig Ernst S 139
Wick, John T 175, 259
Wick, Michael T 175, 259
Wick, Severimus S 304
Wick, Soverinus S 310
Wickham, Parker S 330
Wickhaus, Eliz. Catharina S 119
Wickhaus, Elisabetha Maria S 139
Wichhaus, Maria Catha. S 119
Wickhausen, Peter S 149
Wickhous, Maria Magdalena S 139
Wickhaus, Peter S 119, S 139
Wick, John S 301
Wicks, Samuel S 297
Wickwire, Jonathan S 337
Widerstein, Henry S 115, S 355
Widerwachs, Andreas S 139
Widerwachs, Anna Barbara S 139
Widerwachs, Anna Cecelia S 139
Widerwachs, Hen. S 120
Widerwachs, Henrich S 149
Widerwachs, Johann Bastian S 139
Widerwachs, Johann Georg. S 139
Widerwachs, Johann Henrich S 139
Widerwachs, Henrich S 139
Widerwachs, Maria Catharina S 139
Widrig, Jacob S 355
Widrig, Michael S 355
Widt, Johan Joost S 106
Wiederwax, Hend. Ch'l S 111
Wiederwax, Johan And. S 111
Wiekel, Johan S 93
Wiele, Henry S 348
Wiele, Joss Henry S 348
Wier, James T 344
Wies, Melchoir S 149
Wiesner, Gorg S 106
Wiesener, Johan S 103
Wierstein, Hans S 106
Wiggert, Hans S 97
Wiggins, Stehen S 337
Wighalm, Mattys S 97
Wihler, Edwart S 139
Wihler, Robert S 139
Wilbert, Hans Marten S 93
Wilds, David S 304
Wilcox S 337
Wilcox, Hazard S 330, S 337
Wile, Christian S 353
Wiles, George T 254, S 317
Wiley, Nicholas S 353
Wilhart, Jacob S 87
Wilhart, John Hendrig S 87
Wilhellem, Andreas' (Wede.) S 106
Wilhellem, Henrig S 103
Wilhellem, Johan Joost S 106
Wilkley, Pother S 195
Willem, Anthony S 106, S 149
Wilhelm, Henrig S 93
Wilhelm, Jan S 97
Wilhelm, Johan S 87, S 106
Wilhelm, Johan Simon S 93

Wilhelm, Niclaus S 149
Wilhelm, Paul S 149
Willemse, Adriaan S 106
Wilkins, George T 344
Wilkinson, Levy T 334
Willard Elias (Quartermaster) T 147, 178
Willem, Hans S 87
Willem, Jorg S 103
Willett, Marinus (Colonel) T 57, 59, 107, 111, 112, 154, 183, 185, 189, 196, 199, 201, 207, 212, 222, 226, 230, 233, 239, 241, 242, 246, 286, 291, 304, S 152, S 155, S 158, S 161, S 162, S 164, S 165, S 167, S 169, S 170,
S 175, S 176, S 177, S 179, S 182, S 183, S 187, S 189, S 199, S 202, S 205, S 209, S 210, S 217, S 218, S 221, S 226, S 232,
S 237, S 248S 250, S 252, S 257, S 258, S 267, S 270, S 281, S 286, S 288, S 294
Willi, Johan Gristia S 87
Willi, Johan Hanrus S 87
William, Johanna S 97
William, Paul S 97
Williams, Abraham S 337
Williams, Benjamin S 337
Williams, Bartholomew T 228
Williams, Daniel (Captain) S 229, S 277
Williams, Daniel S 353
Williams, Eliser T 175
Williams, Ezekiel T 344
Williams, Frederick S 337
Williams, George S 301
Williams, Gilbert S 277
Williams, Henry S 315
Williams, Ichabod T 344
Williams, Isaac S 330, S 337
Williams, James S 304, S 321
Williams, John S 337
Williams, John T 121
Williams, John (Lieut) T 170
Williams, Lewis S 304
Williams, Lewis Jr S 307, S 320
Williams, Nehemiah S 359
Williams, Roswell S 230
Williams, William S 337
Williamson, Charles S 320
Williamson, Eliser T 175, 259
Williamson, Garrit S 330
Williamson, Henry S 304
Williamson, John S 301
Willich, Peter S 82
Willis, John (Captain) (Va) S 277
Willson, Almer S 353
Willson, Andrew S 277, S 297
Willson, James S 297
Willson, John S 353
Willson, Samuel S 297
Wilmer, Anton S 97
Wilmot, Lemuel S 337
Wilmy, Jacob S 103
Wilsing, Maria S 87
Wilson, Abner S 353
Wilson, Andrew S 277, S 353
Wilson, David T 344
Wilson, G. S 337
Wilson, I. S 337

Made in the USA
San Bernardino, CA
25 May 2017